Teaching to Change the World

Teaching to Change the World

THIRD EDITION

Jeannie Oakes
University of California, Los Angeles

Martin Lipton
University of California, Los Angeles

Boston   Burr Ridge, IL   Dubuque, IA   Madison, WI   New York
San Francisco   St. Louis   Bangkok   Bogotá   Caracas   Kuala Lumpur
Lisbon   London   Madrid   Mexico City   Milan   Montreal   New Delhi
Santiago   Seoul   Singapore   Sydney   Taipei   Toronto

Higher Education

TEACHING TO CHANGE THE WORLD

1 2 3 4 5 6 7 8 9 0 FGR/FGR 0 9 8 7 6

ISBN-13: 978-0-07-298200-8
ISBN-10: 0-07-298200-4

Vice President and Editor-in-Chief:
  Emily Barrosse
Publisher: *Beth Mejia*
Senior Sponsoring Editor: *Allison McNamara*
Freelance Developmental Editor:
  Beth Kaufman
Marketing Manager: *Melissa S. Caughlin*
Managing Editor: *Jean Dal Porto*
Project Manager: *Ruth Smith*
Art Editor: *Katherine McNab*

Designer: *Srdjan Savanovic*
Cover Designer: *Nery Orellana*
Cover Image: *Martin Lipton*
Photo Research Coordinator: *Natalia C. Peschiera*
Production Supervisor: *Jason I. Huls*
Composition: *10/12 ITC Century Light by Interactive Composition Corporation-India*
Printing: *45 # New Era Matte, Quebecor World*

Credits: The credits section for this book begins on page C-1 and is considered an extension of the copyright page.

Library of Congress Cataloging-in-Publication Data

Oakes, Jeannie.
    Teaching to change the world / Jeannie Oakes, Martin Lipton.—3rd ed.
        p. cm.
    Includes bibliographical references and index.
    ISBN-13: 978-0-07-298200-8 (softcover : alk. paper)
    ISBN-10: 0-07-298200-4 (softcover : alk. paper)
    1. Public schools—United States. 2. Education—Aims and objectives—United States.
3. Curriculum planning—United States. 4. Classroom management—United States.
5. Effective teaching—United States. 6. Educational change—United States. I. Lipton,
Martin, 1942– II. Title.
LA217.2.O25 2007
371.010973—dc22

                                                                    2006042009

About the Authors

JEANNIE OAKES holds UCLA's Presidential Chair in Educational Equity. A nationally recognized education researcher and social justice advocate, Oakes directs both UCLA's Institute for Democracy, Education, and Access, and the University of California's All-Campus Consortium on Research for Diversity. Jeannie Oakes was the founding director of Center X—the institutional home of the university's teacher education program—a program based on the research and principles included in *Teaching to Change the World*. Oakes is author of *Keeping Track: How Schools Structure Inequality* (1985/2005), which was honored by the Museum of Education at the University of South Carolina as one of the most significant books on education in the twentieth century. Her most recent book is *Learning Power: Organizing for Education and Justice* (with John Rogers). Oakes's awards and distinctions include the Distinguished Achievement Award from the Educational Press Association of America, the Ralph David Abernathy Award for public service, from the Southern Christian Leadership Conference, and the Jose Vasconcellos World Award in Education. The American Educational Research Association (AERA) has awarded Oakes its prestigious Early Career Achievement Award and the Palmer O. Johnson Award for the Outstanding Research Article. In 2004, she was elected to the National Academy of Education.

MARTIN LIPTON is an education writer and consultant and has taught in public schools for thirty-one years. He is coauthor with Oakes of *Making the Best of Schools* (1990). In 2001, Oakes and Lipton received AERA's Outstanding Book Award for their publication of *Becoming Good American Schools: The Struggle for Virtue in Education*. Lipton's photographs of teachers and their students in social justice classrooms appear on the cover and throughout the book's chapters.

Brief Contents

PART III
The Context of Teaching
to Change the World

PART IV
Teaching for the Long Haul

Contents

PART I
The Foundations of
American Schooling

PART II
The Practice of Teaching
to Change the World

PART III
The Context of Teaching
to Change the World

CHAPTER 11 Policy and Law: Rules to Make Schools Effective, Efficient, and Equitable   420

PART IV
Teaching for the Long Haul

CHAPTER 12 Teaching to Change the World: A Profession and a Hopeful Struggle   469

Introduction

*At the turn of the twenty-first century, nearly 3.5 million teachers worked in
public and private elementary and secondary schools across the country.
The U.S. Department of Education estimates that the nation's schools will
hire 2.2 million more by 2012.*

—U.S. Department of Education

In the fall of 1997, William was 5, and he was finishing his first week in kindergarten at Vallejo Mill Elementary School. First-year teacher Tracy Barnett was also finishing her first week as William's kindergarten teacher. When she announced that it was time for the class meeting, William asked, "Why do we have to do that again?" Mrs. Barnett answered obliquely with a question of her own, "Why, William, if we don't hear all the children's voices, how will we change the world?" William rolled his eyes upward, sighed with exasperation worthy of a teenager, and took his place in the circle. One week later, on a Monday morning, William walked into class and straight up to his teacher's desk. "Mrs. Barnett, what are we going to talk about today to change the world?"

In many ways, Tracy Barnett was a fortunate new teacher, and William was a fortunate 5-year-old. Their school illustrates what American public schools could be, but rarely are. Because our society is highly segregated by race and social class, the vast majority of American neighborhood elementary schools serve children who are culturally, linguistically, and economically similar. Most students in white and wealthier neighborhood schools achieve well; most in low-income communities and communities of color do not. In sharp contrast, Vallejo Mill Elementary School is extraordinarily diverse, and its students also achieve well.

Thirty-six percent of Vallejo Mill's students are white; 28 percent Latino; 6 percent African American; and 29 percent are Asian, Pacific Islander, and Filipino. Many of the Asians are South Asian immigrants—from India, Pakistan, and Afghanistan. Most of the South Asian children speak English, but many others do not. Of the 24 percent of the students still learning English, more than half speak Spanish as their primary language, the rest speak Farsi, Mandarin, Cantonese, and an assortment of other languages. At Vallejo Mill, not only are these students learning English, the entire student body is learning Spanish. Because most of the children come from middle-class families, Vallejo Mill doesn't qualify for the special funding for schools with large numbers of poor students. Nevertheless, about 20 percent of the students come from families whose incomes are low enough to qualify them for free or reduced-price lunches at school. All these diverse groups of students consistently show improvement on California's standardized achievement tests.

By Fall 2006 William had become a teenager and a high school student, and Tracy Barnett was still teaching at Vallejo Mill. Her career has been anything but stagnant. She went back to the university, where she earned certification as a special education resource teacher. She traded her job teaching 20 rambunctious 5-year-olds for a three-year stint working one-on-one with troubled learners. Then, she brought her expertise in learning disabilities back to the classroom where she now teaches a diverse group of 10-year-olds, including several with special learning needs. She's also the school's elected teachers' union representative.

As part of a team of highly qualified educators, Tracy has helped create an academically rigorous, multicultural environment at Vallejo Mill. She and her colleagues participated in extensive professional development in "Tribes"—an approach to developing learning communities characterized by caring and support, meaningful participation, and positive expectations for adults and children. Tracy's "special education" expertise allows her to make sure that students' cultural and linguistic differences aren't mistakenly seen as learning or behavioral disabilities, or that their learning disabilities aren't overlooked because of cultural and linguistic differences.

Knowing that they deserve applause in a world where schools often get little, Tracy recently led her colleagues in writing Vallejo Mill's application for a "distinguished school" award. As of this writing, they haven't yet heard. Most important, Tracy Barnett has remained true to the commitment she brought to teaching: All her students must know that they are amazing learners who can change the world; and all her colleagues are welcomed as allies.

By the year 2012, Tracy and others who have become teachers in the previous 15 years are likely to be about half of all the public school teachers in the nation. During the course of their careers, these teachers will touch the lives of millions of children and adolescents with their skills, their knowledge, their talents, and their passion. This could be a good time to change the world.

The Book's Perspective

This book provides a comprehensive introduction to teaching in twenty-first century American schools. Both foundational and practical, the chapters are organized around conventional topics—history, philosophy, curriculum, instruction, classroom management, school culture, policy, and so on. However, the book integrates these educational foundations into a coherent story that explains why schools are as they are, and how schools might change for tomorrow's teachers. That story is built around two themes: the first theme is that schooling is a social and cultural activity; the second theme is that the United States is a multicultural society. Together, these themes support a theory of education that positions new teachers to be highly competent in the classroom, lifelong education reformers, and education leaders and partners with students and families.

This book also has a point of view. It takes the position that a hopeful, democratic future depends on whether schools provide *all* students an education comprised of *social justice* and *rigorous, authentic learning experiences*. If we had to label this point of view, we would call it "social progressive." Its roots lie in John Dewey's turn-of-the-twentieth-century learning theories and political sentiments, and its current frames of reference are the sociocultural and democratic theorists who are Dewey's intellectual descendants at the start of the twenty-first century.

We define a *socially just* education as one that does three things: (1) It considers the values and politics that pervade education, as well as the more technical issues of teaching and organizing schools; (2) it asks critical questions about how conventional thinking and practice came to be, and who in society benefits from them; and (3) it pays particular attention to inequalities associated with race, social class, language, gender, and other social categories, and looks for alternatives to the inequalities.

We define *rigorous, authentic learning experiences* as curriculum, teaching, and assessment that allow students to construct and use knowledge in ways that (1) transform their thinking, (2) promote their intellectual development, and, over time, (3) prepare them to participate in and benefit from their society as knowledgeable citizens, capable workforce participants, and contributing members of families and communities. By knowledge, we mean culturally valued traditions, facts, and skills, as well as new and dynamic forms of intelligence, understanding, and problem-solving skills necessary to fill important roles in a diverse and democratic society.

The book takes the perspective that social justice and rigorous, authentic opportunities to learn are compatible and mutually reinforcing. Because so much of our nation's schooling tradition has been shaped by race and social class inequality, teachers need to augment their professional expertise with a commitment to the social justice perspective that we described above. Throughout this book, we emphasize research and historical analyses that show why the traditional conception of "good teaching" is not enough.

According to our analysis, academic excellence in a socially just world is not possible unless all students understand and experience both social justice and rigorous, authentic opportunities to learn. Thus, it is a mistake to view a social justice perspective as appropriate for low-income students and students of color, and more traditional teaching as just fine for students in more advantaged communities.

Because of this point of view, the book does not offer a smorgasbord of different educational theories and practices for readers to browse and then choose whatever suits their appetites. We believe it is neither honest nor objective to describe popular teaching practices in a neutral manner if they do not stand up to the standards of social justice or evidence that they lead to rigorous, authentic learning experiences. We do not believe that the world is a neutral place or that teaching is a neutral profession.

So, for example, when teachers are troubled by misbehaving students, the book does not offer a neutral choice between (a) struggling to build a caring classroom community or (b) working to perfect behavior modification routines. We consider (a) to be the correct option because theory and substantial research evidence reveal how caring classroom communities support high-achieving, socially just, intrinsically motivated teaching and learning and reduce unproductive student behavior. Behavior modification, on the other hand, provides teachers with techniques to control students' behavior. It does not meet our standards because it promotes a less community-like and less intellectually challenging classroom environment.

Making choices on behalf of social justice and rigorous, authentic learning requires personal qualities of integrity, decency, and the capacity to work very hard. We find these qualities in abundance in people who choose to be teachers. But making social justice choices also requires teachers to have a professional groundwork of social theory and educational research to make their efforts credible to others and sustainable for themselves.

Not having the tools to act on their commitments, many thousands of promising teachers quit the profession within their first few years. The tools required are the theory, practical knowledge, and experience that help teachers understand, critique, and replace "commonsense" views of schools and conventional practices with those that lead to social justice and rigorous, authentic learning. The goal of this book is to help teachers get started in that direction.

New to This Edition

We have made several changes to the third edition, most of which respond directly to readers' and reviewers' comments about what they liked about the book and what they thought would make it stronger. Below is an overview of the changes you'll find:

- **Changes in the way the text is organized.** We've divided the chapters into four major sections: the first on the *foundations;* the second on *practice;* the third on the larger *school, community, and policy contexts* of teaching; and the fourth on the teaching *profession.*
- **The elimination of two chapters from previous editions that focus on learning theories.** Our coverage of learning theory has not disappeared, however. Much of that material is now integrated throughout the text, particularly in Chapter 5 on instruction and Chapter 6 on assessment. This integration allows us to discuss theory in conjunction with the practices that bring those theories to life in classrooms and schools.
- **Two chapters devoted to instruction and assessment replace the combined chapter in previous editions.** As a result we've been able to elaborate on the increasing salience on testing and assessment in today's schools.
- **Two new chapters that link teaching today to the larger social context.** New Chapter 1 portrays the changing demographics and increasing inequality in U.S. schools and society that form the backdrop for today's teachers' work in classrooms. New Chapter 11 focuses on policy and law as it affects schools and teachers' work. Here, we outline the basics of education policy.

- **Treatment of *No Child Left Behind* throughout the book,** including an exploration of its origins, its goals, and the effects it's having on teaching and learning.
- **New pedagogical features in every chapter that make the material more user friendly.** These include chapter overviews, Focal Point boxes, educational timelines, concept tables, and so on.
- **New photographs of teachers and their students** that illustrate what *Teaching to Change the World* can look like in practice.

Overview of Chapters

The twelve chapters of this book are grouped into four parts:

I. The *foundations* of today's schooling
II. The *practices* of teaching, including subject matter, instructional practice assessment, classroom management, and grouping practices
III. The *context* for teaching, including schools, communities, and the local, state, and federal policy environment
IV. The *profession of teaching,* including strategies that sustain social justice teachers over their years of teaching and make it possible for their students to change the world

Because of the book's integrated, thematic approach, there are no separate chapters here on multicultural education, bilingual education, or special education. Rather, the book treats diversity among students and inclusive practices as an integral part of all elements of education—of curriculum and instruction, classroom management, assessment and testing, grouping, and the school culture. As a result, diversity and inclusion are a part of every chapter.

For example, in Chapter 1, we describe the U.S. student population in terms of students' disabilities and their status as "English learners," as well as their race, culture, and economic status. In Chapter 2, we review the historical context that led to policies requiring schools to serve students with special needs, and we discuss how deficit ideologies have constrained schools' responses to diversity. In Chapter 3, we explain how multicultural and sociocultural educational perspectives in the late twentieth century led to curricula that reject the deficit view of students' cultural and linguistic differences. In Chapters 5, 6, 7, 8, and 9, we discuss why some school responses to students with cultural, linguistic, or special education needs are respectful accommodations to diversity, and why others are not.

Similarly, throughout the book we emphasize the sociological, historical, and philosophical foundations of education. The first three chapters foreground these foundations. But because foundations make most sense when people can clearly see how they support actual practices and concerns, each chapter includes the history, philosophical positions, and social theories most relevant to that chapter's topic. Some chapters present entirely new foundational material; others offer a new view of material presented earlier.

Chapter 1, "The American Schooling Dilemma: Diversity, Inequality, and Democratic Values," surveys the unequal landscape on which American children go to school today. It looks at who are American students, what their lives are like outside of school, and what structural inequalities they experience in the educational system. We conclude this first chapter by introducing four teachers who recognize the diversity of their students, acknowledge the struggles they face, and apply their knowledge and skills as teachers to bring social justice and academic excellence to their classrooms. Mauro Bautista, Mark Hill, Kimberley Min, and Judy Smith are very different in their backgrounds, their reasons for teaching, their grade levels and subject matter emphasis. However, they all share the belief that schools and teaching can indeed change a world where lives are marked by poverty, discrimination, and injustice, and they work hard toward that goal.

Chapter 2, "History and Culture: Wrestling with the Traditions of American Education," explores our premise that today's schools are not the result of rational and neutral decisions to facilitate learning in the best possible ways. Rather, schooling is powerfully constrained by long established customs and beliefs, as well as by contemporary events. If we want to improve or reform schools, we must expose, understand, and challenge the expectations society has for schools and the beliefs that underlie those expectations. Specifically, we (1) provide a very brief outline of seminal events in the history of American schooling; (2) sketch how the expectations for schools have increased over the past 200 years; and (3) discuss two powerful and pervasive ideas—meritocracy and white superiority—that have shaped American schooling.

Chapter 3, "Philosophy and Politics: The Struggle for the American Curriculum," looks beyond the easy agreement that all children need reading and writing, mathematics, science, and whatever else it takes to be responsible citizens. Like everything else about schools, what schools teach, why they teach it, and to whom are rooted in philosophy, history, and politics, as well as in the intrinsic human eagerness to learn. This chapter looks first at how people in Western societies have thought about knowledge and the mind. We relate traditional and progressive educational philosophies that have emerged from these basic ideas, and we then show how Americans have historically mixed philosophy and politics in their struggles over the curriculum. We conclude with an overview of recent debates about what schools should teach, and the impact they have on teachers committed to social justice. Chapters 4, 5, 6, 7, and 8 show how these debates play out in specific academic subjects and in the practice of teaching.

Part II begins with Chapter 4, "The Subject Matters: Making School Knowledge Meaningful." This chapter helps teachers situate the mathematics, language arts, social studies, and science content they will teach in the current professional and political debates around these subjects. These intense disputes are often referred to as curriculum "wars," as they are fought by local school boards and state and national policymaking bodies. The chapter also describes how the current "standards movement" and the emphasis on testing-based "accountability" have shaped teaching and learning in each of the four major academic subjects.

Chapter 5, "Instruction: Classrooms as Learning Communities," begins with a bit of history of how teaching has changed—and how it hasn't changed—over the past 200 years. The chapter then discusses recent advances in our understanding of learning, including cognitive and sociocultural theories that present learning as something that each learner actively constructs in the context of social interactions. The remainder of the chapter focuses on three "authentic" instructional principles, each of which helps teachers structure active and interactive learning activities that make learning accessible to culturally and linguistically diverse groups of students.

Chapter 6, "Assessment: Measuring What Matters," describes the way educators measure student learning and explores the basic ideas that underlie these practices. The chapter begins by explaining a few basic assessment concepts and reviewing the history of testing, including the nineteenth and early twentieth century efforts to define and measure intelligence. We turn next to the modern descendants of early IQ tests, today's standardized achievement tests, and we describe their construction, meaning, and uses in twenty-first century education. Finally, we look at classrooms and suggest a set of principles to help teachers use assessment to foster learning and social justice.

Chapter 7, "Classroom Management: Caring, Respectful, and Democratic Relationships," surveys the legacy of management, discipline, and control that many contemporary teachers still rely on to organize classroom life. It also reviews a second tradition—caring and democratic classrooms—that, while less common, also has deep American roots. The chapter concludes by calling attention to the important contributions of critical theorists who address classroom issues of power and domination and how teachers may respond to these issues as they attempt to make their classrooms socially just.

Chapter 8, "Grouping, Tracking, and Categorical Programs: Can Schools Teach All Students Well?" deals with the often-controversial ways that schools respond to differences in students' abilities, achievements, and behaviors. We explain how the categories and labels schools assign to students are social and cultural constructions, rather than natural "facts," and we explain how labeling and sorting students became part of American schooling. We then review some of the evidence showing that these practices can do as much to *create* differences as they do to meet students' special needs. Finally, we describe the work of the many educators who attempt to give all students the attention and resources they need without isolating and alienating them from the mainstream.

Part III, "The Context of Teaching to Change the World," shows how teachers can contribute to their students' education well beyond the cliché of changing the world "one child at a time." The section explores the full (and often discouraging) weight of schooling contexts and juxtaposes these with the possibility of a "hopeful struggle"—that immensely rewarding, career-long dedication to creating opportunities for students to learn.

Chapter 9, "The School Culture: Where Good Teaching Makes Sense," identifies theory and research-based characteristics of schools that support excellent and democratic learning and teaching. The chapter describes several current, progressive reform projects based around *inquiry*—a mode of conversation that elicits from all members of the school community their understanding of the school's environment for socially just learning. These inquiry-based school reforms help individuals clarify others' and their own perceptions and help translate shared beliefs and values into democratic action.

In Chapter 10, "The Community: Engaging with Families and Neighborhoods," we first consider two dominant (and contradictory) complaints about parents—that they neglect their responsibilities to participate and support their children's schools; and that they are disruptive and overly involved in schools. We also examine four types of constructive engagement: (1) parents supporting the work of schools; (2) schools serving families' and communities' need for health and social services; (3) bridging the cultures of home and school through curriculum; and (4) engaging parents directly in schools through community empowerment. The chapter argues that however teachers engage with families, their efforts will be most constructive if they come together with parents of different racial groups and socioeconomic positions in order to act together as citizens on behalf of all children.

Chapter 11, "Policy and Law: Rules to Make Schools Effective, Efficient, and Equitable," provides an overview of the complex education policy system in the United States. We describe the roles and responsibilities of local, state, and federal government in moving public schools toward achieving their goals, and the various political ideologies that help explain predictable patterns in the laws that govern the kind of schools we have. We explain how these ideas and ideologies are reflected today in policies regulating large-scale testing, high school graduation, and grade retention, and the use of "scientifically based" curriculum—all elements of the federal *No Child Left Behind* Act. The chapter concludes with a brief discussion of the courts' role in protecting the rights of the nation's most vulnerable students.

Part IV consists of Chapter 12, "Teaching to Change the World: A Profession and a Hopeful Struggle." It begins with an overview of where the teaching profession stands today and describes some of the pressures that teachers face as they begin their careers. However, most of the chapter describes how new teachers can defy the odds by creating new odds. We offer strong evidence that the status quo is not a reason to give up on teaching, but the reason *for* teaching. We conclude the chapter, and the book, with five philosophical, practical, and personal strategies that teachers use to change the world. They include making a commitment to hope and struggle; building a learning community; becoming a social justice activist; expanding your professional influence; and finding satisfaction in the everyday.

Digging Deeper: Going Beyond the Text

Each chapter ends with a section called "Digging Deeper." Here we identify scholars who are studying or working on practical applications of the issues we raise, and we list a few of their books and articles that you might find interesting and useful. In some chapters, we also list professional organizations and activist groups working to make education policy or school practices more consistent with and supportive of socially just teaching. Wherever possible, we provide Internet sites that are good starting points for pursuing additional resources.

Perspectives of Those Engaged in Hopeful Struggle

Throughout the chapters, we include the observations of teachers—in their own words. The words of the teachers whom we cite come from the comprehensive portfolios they presented for their Master's Degree in Education at UCLA and other reflections on their teaching. Most, but not all of their observations were written during their first year of teaching. Four of these teachers are introduced in some detail in Chapter 1, since they and their students appear in photographs on the cover and scattered throughout the book.

We would expect these teachers to be struggling with lesson plans, discipline, paperwork, time management, school bureaucracy, and so on. And, of course, they are. But please listen carefully to their voices. What is crucial is not that they struggle, but the quality of the problems with which they struggle. Their reflections reveal the profound relevance of theory to their practice and to their mostly successful, often joyful, efforts to sustain their combined commitment to rigorous instruction and social justice.

These teachers belie one criticism of a social justice emphasis to a teacher's career—that these are soft "do-gooders" whose social agenda wipes out their obligation to teach. For readers who might need to ask, yes, these teachers have high expectations for their students; and the teachers are, indeed, very competent. They are among the most sought-after teachers in their communities because they expect their students to learn by thrusting themselves into a better, more humane, more equitable future.

We recommend that all potential teachers write about their experiences, thoughts, and observations, as the teachers quoted in this book have done. Whether a personal journal, or a portfolio that presents a full record of a teacher-candidate's intellectual and professional growth, a written record inevitably provides wonderful opportunities for reflection and learning.

Readers' "Tools for Critique"

Teaching to Change the World pulls no punches and invites lively discussion and debate. It challenges prospective teachers to think very differently about teaching K–12 students. Past readers have found it provocative and sometimes irritating, but engaging and interesting to read and learn from.

Learning with the book requires far more than simply repeating or summarizing the material. It requires that readers furnish what the book itself cannot provide— lots of discussion and elaboration that stretches readers to make sense of the material in light of their own experiences, observations, and prior knowledge.

To help readers get started with that discussion, we offer an online tool. "Tools for Critique"—located on the book's website at www.mhhe.com/oakes3e—provides a set of questions and prompts to provoke thinking about the topics and points of view in the book. Chapter-specific overviews, outlines, "generative" questions and activities, and additional Internet resources listed there can be a springboard for getting the most out of the text. "Tools for Critique" also offers generic prompts for critical thinking while reading the text. For example, What memories of your own schooling or other experiences does the book stir up? What connections can you make to your other knowledge? What makes you angry? What sounds reasonable, but you can't believe it is true? What have you always known, but you didn't know you knew it? What do you imagine your acquaintances would think about the material? And, of course, what are your questions?

Importantly, many of the prompts ask readers to read "against the text"—to challenge the text rather than to accept the data or views uncritically or be silenced while dismissing the book's perspectives.

The ultimate goal of this book and its "Tools for Critique" is to help new teachers take the first steps toward a fulfilling, lifelong commitment to social justice and rigorous, authentic learning. Judy Smith, one of the teachers quoted in this book, describes her experience taking these first steps. We wish just such beginnings for all the readers of this book.

Teaching challenges my every fiber—from lesson design to classroom management. My first year in the classroom showed me the tremendous joy of teaching and the work that must be done to be the best teacher I can be. Through constant self-reflection, student work assessment, and professional development, I am learning the craft to better bridge theory and practice and to better bridge students, parents, and the community. Through academically rigorous and culturally responsive curriculum, my students and I can begin to transform the school and the community. Indeed, the focus of my classroom is on all of our responsibility to make the community and the world a better place.

—JUDY SMITH
High school social studies

Acknowledgments

The most immediate inspiration for this book was the courage, passion, and hard work of the wonderful UCLA teacher education graduates whose words and photographs appear throughout the chapters. We are enormously appreciative of their commitment to students, their struggle to create democratic schools and classrooms, and for their hard questions about how to make a socially just education real. We are indebted to UCLA's teacher education faculty, notably Eloise Metcalfe, and Jody Priselac, and other Center X faculty advisers who've read and commented insightfully on the book, along with the novice and resident teachers at UCLA during the 1999 to 2005 academic years. Their reflections on their teaching provided illuminating direction. Teachers Mauro Bautista, Mark Hill, Kimberly Min, and Judy Smith, who are featured throughout the book, deserve special thanks for welcoming us into their classrooms and answering all our questions so generously and openly. McGraw-Hill editor Beth Kaufman remains a thoughtful and energetic champion; and Allison McNamara, Cara Harvey Labell, and Ruth Smith have ably marshaled the book through the complicated publication process. As with the first two editions, Laurie McGee fine-tuned our words.

Finally, we would like to thank the instructors who made helpful substantive suggestions:

Nancy Lauter
Montclair State University

Mary Sanford
Olympic College

Charles Jenks
Augusta State University

Mindy Adams
Amarillo College

Donna Bennett
CSU Fullerton

Richard McEwing
Youngstown State University

Richard Roames
Purdue University, Calumet

Colleen MacKinnon
University of Vermont, Burlington

Karina Otoya-Knapp
Bank Street College

Sherick Hughes
University of Toledo

Jan Connal
Cerritos College

Nancy Walker
University of La Verne

Suzanne Fondrie
University of Washington, Oshkosh

Judy Zalazar Drummond
University of San Francisco

Shari Saunders
University of Michigan

Jana Noel
*California State University,
    Sacramento*

Katrina Hunter
University of North Alabama

Deborah Hamm
*California State University,
    Long Beach*

Amy Barnhill
Central Missouri State University

We are also grateful to many scholars who, over the years, have contributed to the ideas and approach we take here. These colleagues' rich ideas and generous conversations have shaped our thinking in subtle and not-so-subtle ways. Among those, James Banks, Linda Darling-Hammond, Megan Franke, John Goodlad, Andy Hargreaves, Peter McLaren, Jennifer Obidah, Doug Pollock, John Rogers, Kenneth Sirotnik, Gladys Topkis, Amy Stuart Wells, and Anne Wheelock stand out as mentors and friends. We have also learned a great deal about schooling, multiple perspectives, and the struggle for social justice from former and current doctoral students and postdoctoral scholars whose academic work has enriched our own, most notably Arshad Ali, Lauren Anderson, Susan Auerbach, Anthony Collatos, Robert Cooper, Amanda Datnow, Diane Friedlaender, Laila Hasan, Diane Hirshberg, Rebecca Joseph, Makeba Jones, Michelle Knight, Ernest Morrell, Karina Otoya, Karen Hunter Quartz, Karen Ray, Michelle Rene, Myisha Wilcher Roberts, Steve Ryan, Irene Serna, Jamy Stillman, Linda Symcox, Elizabeth Vasquez, Kevin Welner, and Susan Yonezawa. Our appreciation to Jared Planas for his proofreading services. Thanks, too, are due the many generous funders who have sponsored Jeannie's research.

Our family provides a solid rock of support for which we are always grateful. Martin's parents, Irene and Nathan Lipton, were enthusiastic cheerleaders, and Jeannie's mom, Martha Nall, read carefully and made thoughtful comments along the way. Jeannie's dad, Ron Nall, had a sense of humor that still echoes, keeping us from taking ourselves too seriously. Our four children contributed to the substance of this book in amazing ways: Lisa Oakes brought her considerable expertise as a developmental psychologist and provided many helpful suggestions and examples of the learning theory that underlies teaching; Tracy Oakes Barnett, featured in our introduction, offered inspiring anecdotes and the constant reminder of how much fun teaching for social justice can be; Lowell Lipton, teacher of rhetoric and composition, contributed a fresh look at the postmodern struggle for meaning; and Ethan Lipton, a fellow writer, extended knowing encouragement and good dinner company throughout the writing process. Their spouses, Steve Luck, Ron Barnett, Rene Huey-Lipton, and Heather Phelps Lipton have been wonderful friends as well as spectacular parents to our grandchildren. Finally, Emily and Haley Barnett, Alison and Carter Luck, Max and Sophia Lipton, and others, as yet only dreamed of, remind us of why this matters so much. We thank them all.

PART I

The Foundations of American Schooling

CHAPTER 1

The American Schooling Dilemma

Diversity, Inequality, and Democratic Values

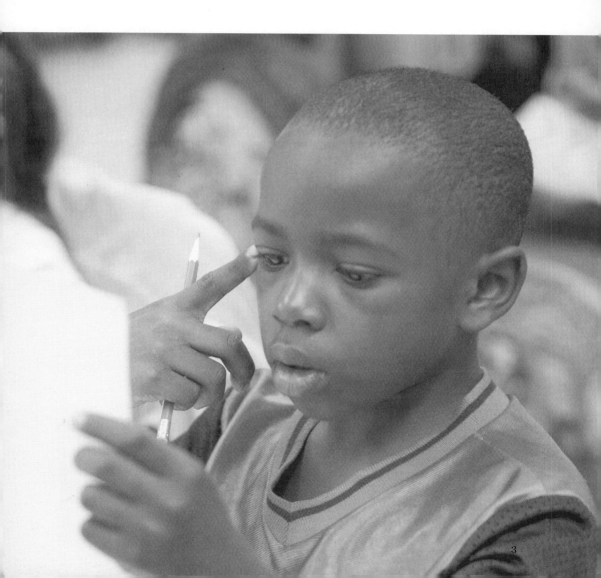

Students in most suburban schools have the resources, credentialed teachers, and cultural capital to be successful in postsecondary education. Students in many urban schools are underserved, unloved, and, to some degree, unaware of the gross inequities that exist between the two types of schools. How does a social justice teacher teach in an urban school where very large class sizes, minimal resources, low expectations, and low literacy affect both students and teachers? What does it mean to be a socially just teacher in a socially unjust world? What do all students deserve?

I grew up in a household that discussed these questions. My father, an accountant, and my mother, a professional educator, always led me to believe that education could solve just about any problem in the world. At mealtimes we often talked about the state of education, the gross inequities my mother observed between urban and suburban schools, and the reform efforts. I knew that someday I wanted to be a teacher.

My first year of teacher education was transformational. We discussed a variety of topics such as successful learning communities, critical pedagogy, standardized tests, and institutional racism. This exposure to theory, along with my inbred burning passion to provide equal access and opportunity to urban students, shapes my teaching philosophy.

Schooling in our society, though inherently democratic, needs to direct students toward critical consciousness—of their potential, of their freedom, of ongoing injustices, and of the obligation to ensure our democracy and improve upon it for future generations.

—JUDY SMITH
High school social studies

Teacher Judy Smith grapples every day with one of the most challenging teaching dilemmas of our time: making good on the promise of equal education in a society that is profoundly unequal. Teachers like Judy Smith and the others you'll meet in this book recognize the relationship between the nation's diversity and inequality, understand its history, and know why schooling inequalities persist. They have knowledge, skills, and a sense of possibility that arms them to be agents for education equity as they help their students become intellectually curious and competent. They teach to change the world.

Chapter Overview
—⚬—

Most Americans and certainly all teachers have heard about the nation's "achievement gap." However, many fewer have heard about the "opportunity gap." Yet persistent patterns of unequal conditions, resources, and opportunities in and outside of school that are related to students' race and social class underlie the disparities in students' achievement. Understanding the opportunity gap can help teachers combat our cultural tendency to blame students, their families, neighborhoods, or racial and other groups for their lower achievement—and to conclude that there is something fundamentally wrong with those who achieve less.

This chapter surveys the unequal landscape on which American children go to school today. It looks at who are American students, what their lives are like outside of school, and what structural inequalities they experience in the educational system. We conclude the chapter by introducing Judy Smith and three other teachers who recognize the diversity of their students, acknowledge the struggles they face, and are applying their knowledge and skills as teachers to bring social justice and academic excellence to their classrooms.

Who Are American Students?

By 2004, thanks in large part to the high number of baby boomers who themselves had babies between the 1970s and 2000—sometimes called the baby boom echo—school enrollments in the United States reached an estimated 48.3 million. And we're not finished growing. With increases of about 5 percent expected every year, projections are that schools will be teaching 50 million children by 2014.

Slightly more than 5 million, or 10 percent, of the school-aged children in the United States attend private schools. About half of them go to Catholic schools, but the percentage of private school students in conservative Christian schools and independent schools has grown considerably, and Catholic school enrollments have dropped steadily in the past 15 years. Despite all of the bad press that public schools have gotten in the past two decades, the proportion of students attending private schools has actually dropped slightly since 1989.

About 2 percent of students—a total of 1.1 million in 2003—were "homeschooled." These students received instruction under their parents' guidance at home and spent fewer than 25 hours a week at a public or private school.

Where Do Students Live and Go to School?

Much of the nation's population growth over the past 30 years has been in the South, and schools there now teach about 38 percent of the country's students. Schools in the West, where over a quarter of the nation's children go to school, have expanded as well. These are also the regions where future growth is expected. Increasingly smaller proportions of students live and go to school in the Northeast and the Midwest. This shift has consequences for the states' ability to provide education

because states in the South and West, except for California, have far less wealth
than the northeastern states where the fewest schoolchildren live.

How Racially and Ethnically Diverse Are Students?

Today, an extraordinarily diverse—racially, ethnically, culturally, and linguistically—
group of young people attend U.S. schools. This represents a dramatic change over
the past two generations. Long gone are the 1950s when American public school
students were overwhelmingly white, native born, and English speaking.[1]

Race   In 2003, white students made up 58 percent of the nation's student population. Hispanic/Latino students composed 19 percent; African Americans, 16 percent;
other racial groups, including Asians, made up 7 percent of the total. Since the 1970s,
Latinos have tripled their representation, and white students' proportion of the total
has fallen by 22 percent. Although still a relatively small proportion of the total, Asian
enrollment has also grown rapidly over the past 30 years. (See Figure 1.1.)

Racial groups are not distributed evenly across the country, although every region has experienced growth in students of color. In the West, white students are
now in the minority, at 46 percent in 2003, and decreasing slightly each year. Both
the South and West have higher proportions of nonwhite students than the Northeast or Midwest. In the South, Northeast, and Midwest, black students outnumber
Latinos.

Minority Enrollment: Percentage distribution of public school students in
kindergarten through 12th grade, by region and race/ethnicity
Fall 1972 and 2003

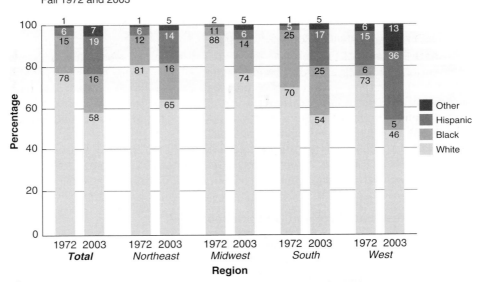

FIGURE 1.1 *Racial and Ethnic Diversity of K–12 Students in the United States.*

Source: U.S. Department of Education, *Condition of Education,* 2005.

Proportionately more students of color attend public than private schools. In 2002, private schools were 15 percent "whiter" than public schools. Homeschooled children are predominantly white as well, 77 percent in 2003.

Immigration   The United States has always been a nation of immigrants, with every generation seeking a new beginning—usually economic, often political. Three times as many immigrants entered the United States in the 1990s compared with the number that arrived in the 1960s,[2] and today 33 million immigrants live in the United States. However, the percentage of foreign-born residents is only slightly larger than in the 1950s—almost 9 percent then, compared with almost 12 percent in 2003.[3] The most recent surge in immigration has brought people from Latin America (53%) and Asia (25%), many of whom are escaping political turmoil or poverty. Some have come without legal documentation. Recent estimates put the undocumented immigrant population at over 10 million—about 30 percent of the total foreign born.[4]

Between 1970 and 1990, the share of students in K–12 schools who are children of immigrants tripled. One in five children in the United States today has an immigrant parent, and young children under 6 in immigrant families are the fastest-growing segment of the child population. Increasing numbers of immigrant children live in almost every region of the country. No longer do most immigrants head for California, New York, Texas, Florida, New Jersey, and Illinois; in the past few years, immigrants have increased their presence in states in the Southeast, Midwest, and Rocky Mountain region as well. Notably, children of immigrants are significantly more likely than those of natives to be limited English proficient, live in low-income families, and have parents with less than a high school degree.

Languages   Today's schools include approximately 10 million students who speak languages other than English at home.[5] In 2003 this group was 161 times larger than in 1979. (See Figure 1.2.) It now includes one of every five U.S. schoolchildren. Only 5 percent of both black and white students are included in this group, compared with 19 percent of American Indian, 65 percent of Asian, and 68 percent of Latino students. About 70 percent of these students speak Spanish as their first language. Almost a third of students who speak another language at home also have some difficulty speaking English themselves.

Nearly a third of students (31%) in the western states come from homes where languages other than English are spoken, compared with 19 percent in the Northeast, 16 percent in the Midwest, and 10 percent in the South. Eight states, including California, Florida, Illinois, New York, Texas, Massachusetts, New Jersey, and New Mexico, have large numbers of Latino students.

Disability   In 2000, about 8 percent (approximately 3.9 million) of American students in kindergarten through grade 12 in public schools were classified as having disabilities related to learning. Most (about 2.8 million) of these were identified as learning disabled. Of the remaining 1.1 million, about two-thirds were classified as mentally retarded and one-third as emotionally disturbed.

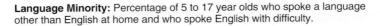

Language Minority: Percentage of 5 to 17 year olds who spoke a language other than English at home and who spoke English with difficulty.

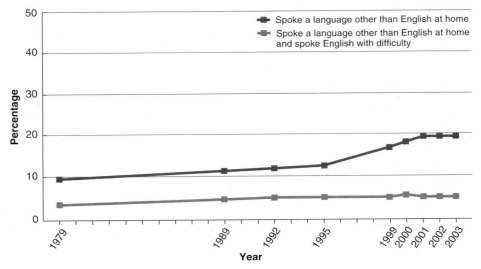

FIGURE 1.2 *K–12 Students Whose First Language Is Not English.*
Source: U.S. Department of Education, *Condition of Education*, 2005.

Multiculturalism Is a Demographic Fact, Not Political Ideology

—————————————————— ❈ ❈ ❈ ——————————————————

Most of my students either are recent immigrants from Latin America (most from Mexico) with limited prior academic experience or are low academic achievers for a variety of reasons. Out of twenty-nine students, one is vision impaired, three attend resource specialist classes daily, one attends speech therapy weekly, and two receive special math assistance two days a week. All of my students come from economically disadvantaged homes, every one receives either free or reduced price lunches at school, and 12 receive free breakfast. Twenty-eight are Mexican Americans and one is of Puerto Rican descent. Many of my students' parents have limited education; none attended schools in the United States. Two speak English.

What exactly is our obligation to prepare my students for the future? I hope that the everyday lessons of math, language arts, social studies, and science, which require the majority of my attention, are helping to prepare them for the world outside of our classroom. But I believe that becoming bicultural requires more than just readying the individual for the dominant society. It also requires preparing society for the minority members. I can

only guide my students in their quest to become individuals. I can help them
define valuable assets within their own culture, I can provide them with
assistance in achieving personal success, but eventually they will have to
face the rest of society without me or other educators at their sides.

—**MICHELLE CALVA**
First-year teacher, grades 4, 5, and 6

Today, classrooms like Michelle Calva's are common in cities like Los Angeles, New York, Chicago, and Miami. By the mid–twenty-first century, a majority of all American schoolchildren will be nonwhite. For teachers today, multiculturalism cannot be a lesson, a curriculum, a teaching style, or even a philosophy. Multiculturalism neither strengthens nor dilutes our society. Multiculturalism is simply a fact—a condition of culture. Nonwhite and immigrant voices and languages will be either heard or ignored, but they will not be silenced or assimilated out of existence. Some teachers will struggle, like Michelle Calva, to construct something whole and wonderful that connects these cultures; some won't. We hope most do, because we believe that this is the only way to provide a free and equal education to all. However, the inequalities of American society that most disadvantage children like those in Michelle Calva's classroom make the jobs of today's teachers especially challenging.

Inequalities Outside of School

"Generations of Americans have been told that they live in the world's richest nation. But the United States today might more accurately be described as the nation with the world's richest rich people," observed the authors of a recent report on inequality in the United States.[6] In fact, among the 20 rich, industrialized countries that belong to the Organization for Economic Cooperation and Development (OECD), the United States ranks highest in income per person.[7]

Despite its riches, however, the United States is one of the most economically unequal countries in the world, with poverty rates unmatched in other wealthy countries. Children, more than any other group of Americans, bear the burden of this inequality.

Economic Inequality

The gap between wealthy and poor Americans is enormous. As Figure 1.3 shows dramatically, the top 1 percent of Americans own a full third of the nation's wealth, and the top 5 percent own more than the remaining 95 percent put together. The bottom 60 percent of Americans together own less than 5 percent of the nation's wealth.

Moreover, the gap between rich and poor Americans is growing wider. Figure 1.4 shows how income inequality among families has accelerated over the second half of the twentieth century. In 2000, high-income households at the 95th percentile received 8.1 times the incomes of low-income households.

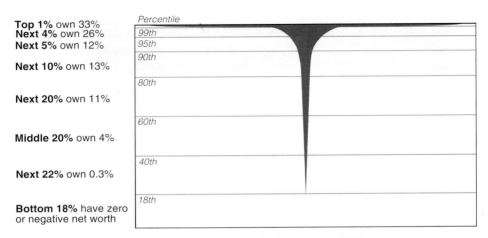

FIGURE 1.3 *Distribution of Wealth in the United States, 2001.*

Source: Edward N. Wolff, *Changes in Household Wealth in the 1980s and 1990s in the U.S.*, Jerome Levy Economics Institute, May 2004.

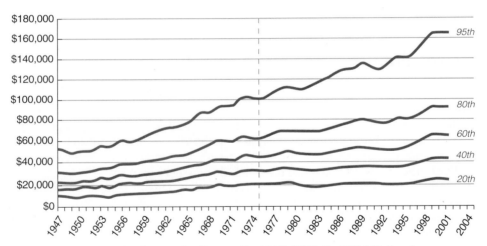

FIGURE 1.4 *Family Income by Percentile, 1947–2001 (in 2001 Dollars).*

Source: U.S. Census Bureau, Historical Income Tables, Table F-1.

As Figure 1.4 shows, most middle-to-low-income families have made only modest income gains over the past 25 years. Notably, these gains have resulted from families working longer hours, often by adding a second wage earner. In 2000, wives in the middle three income groups worked almost 12 weeks more a year, on average, than they did in 1979. In addition, it is more difficult for parents to afford time off to care for their children in the United States than most other OECD countries, because it is one of just three (the others are New Zealand and Australia) that do not mandate paid maternity or paternity leave.

U.S. poverty rates are higher and living standards are lower than for the poorest people in other industrialized countries. Poor people in the United States remain poor for a longer period of time, and the chances of moving out of poverty are lower. In fact, the rate of almost 10 percent of "permanent poverty" is twice as high in the United States as in any of these other nations.[8]

Increasingly, people who are fully employed do not earn enough to keep their families out of poverty (the "working poor"). It's not that U.S. workers earn less because they work less. In fact, workers in the United States, on average, work about 1,815 hours per year, far more than their counterparts in any of the other of the OECD countries except Australia and New Zealand.[9]

Perhaps most important for educators is that the child poverty rate, at 21 percent for children under 6, is the highest among industrialized countries. In the mid- and late 1990s, Clinton-era Democrats found common ground with conservative politicians and instituted significant welfare reforms, which reduced benefits and instituted more stringent eligibility requirements for Aid to Families with Dependent Children, food stamps, and other public assistance for poor children. These reforms have been hotly debated as to their effect on the overall economy, but they have done nothing to stem childhood poverty.

Inequality in the Basics of Life

On December 10, 1948, the General Assembly of the United Nations adopted and proclaimed the Universal Declaration of Human Rights. Following this historic act the Assembly called upon all member countries to publicize the text of the Declaration and "to cause it to be disseminated, displayed, read and expounded principally in schools and other educational institutions, without distinction based on the political status of countries or territories." Article 25 of the Declaration states:

> Everyone has the right to a standard of living adequate for the health and well-being of himself and of his family, including food, clothing, housing and medical care and necessary social services, and the right to security in the event of unemployment, sickness, disability, widowhood, old age or other lack of livelihood in circumstances beyond his control.

The United States was one of the original signers of the Declaration, but most Americans don't see the Declaration as necessary to ensure basic political, economic, and social rights for those living in our prosperous nation. Yet, because our government-supported social safety net is so weak, many Americans aren't guaranteed the basic rights of adequate food, health care, and housing. Access to the most basic social supports in the United States is profoundly dependent on wealth and income. As one report on inequality phrased it, "In the U.S., perhaps more than in any other prosperous society, inequality reaches into dimensions of life where most people would prefer to believe that money does not rule."[10]

Food   At the most basic level, many U.S. children are at risk of going hungry. About 13 million children in 2003 (18%) lived in households that reported they lacked access, at least some of the time, to enough food for an active, healthy life for all household members. Forty-five percent of families living below the official poverty line fell into this group, as did 34 percent of children living in families with children headed by a single mother. Although only a small proportion of these "food-insecure" households reported that their children go hungry, it is still significant when that many children grow up in a family where hunger exists at all. Hunger was more than twice as prevalent in poor families (13%) than in those living at or above the poverty line.[11]

Health   Children's health in the United States is highly related to their families' income status. In 1998, about 70 percent of children in families below the poverty line were in very good or excellent health, compared with 87 percent of children in families living at or above the poverty line.[12] Asthma and lead exposure are just two of the health problems that plague lower-income children at higher rates. As Figure 1.5 shows, children living below the poverty line are three times as likely as more advantaged children to have high levels of lead in their blood—a condition that relates to lower cognitive functioning and learning problems in schools.

Lower-income children are less likely to have access to health services. In 2003, 11 percent of all children (8.4 million) had no health insurance, and 5 percent had no regular source of health care.

Housing   Adequate and stable housing is also a serious problem for many American children. In 2003, 37 percent of U.S. households with children had a serious housing problem. These problems included physically inadequate housing, overcrowded housing, or housing that cost more than 30 percent of household income.[13] Half of the lowest-income households spend at least 50 percent of their incomes on housing,[14] leaving little for other basic necessities, such as food and health care.

The homeless population in the United States is made up increasingly of families with children. A survey of 25 U.S. cities found that families with children accounted for 36 percent of the homeless population in 2002. According to the National Coalition for the Homeless, 1.35 million U.S. children are homeless on any given night. School-age homeless children face barriers to enrolling and attending school, including transportation problems, residency requirements, inability to obtain previous school records, and lack of clothing and school supplies.[15]

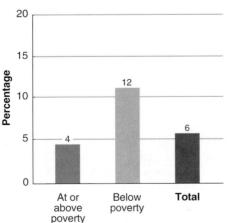

Percentage of children under age 6 with high lead levels, by poverty status
Average for 1988 and 1994

FIGURE 1.5 *Lead Exposure in U.S. Children.*

Source: America's Children: Key National Indicators of Well Being, 1998 (original data from Centers for Disease Control and Prevention, National Center for Health Statistics, Second and Third National Health and Nutrition Information in Surveys).

Racial Inequality

Children of color are far more likely than whites to grow up in persistent poverty. In 2003, 18 percent of all children ages 0–17 lived in poverty, up from 17 percent in 2002. Yet, the child poverty rate was far higher for black and Latino children than for whites. Ten percent of white children lived in poverty, compared with 34 percent of African American children and 30 percent of Latino children.[16]

Wealth, Jobs, and Income   Huge wealth disparities exist between white families and families of color. In 2003, for example, on average, white households headed by people between 51 and 55 years of age were about 4.5 times as wealthy as comparable African American and Hispanic households ($467,747 compared with $105,675). Similar differences occurred in families of all ages. Moreover, the worth of black and Hispanic college graduates was similar to the net worth of white high school graduates, and the net worth of African American and Hispanic high school graduates was similar to the net worth of white high school dropouts.[17]

Black and Latino children were less likely than whites to have a parent working year-round, full-time. Compared with 82 percent of white children, about 71 percent of Latino children and 61 percent of African American children had parents with secure employment in 2003. African American college graduates found jobs at about the same rates as whites with only a high school diploma.[18]

Persistent racial disparities in wages also contribute to the higher rates of poverty among children of color. In 2003, 30 percent of African American workers and 40 percent of Latino workers earned poverty-level wages. Women of color are even more likely to earn poverty-level wages—34 percent of African American women and 46 percent of Latino women in 2003.[19] Workers of color earn much less than whites even when they are of similar age and education. For example, in 2002, the average earnings of college-educated, full-time employed nonwhites aged 35 to 44 was at $46,000, $11,000 less than their white peers. Those with some college working full-time earned $7,000 less than whites in their same age group, and those with only a high school education earned $5,000 less.[20]

Food, Health, and Housing   These racial disparities in wealth and income create racial disparities in children's access to the basics of life—food, health care, and housing—as well as in access to high-quality schooling. The proportions of nonwhite children living in food-insecure households were substantially above the national average (18%) in 2003. Thirty-one percent of both African American and Latino children lived in households where they could not count on having enough food for an active, healthy life for everyone in their family.

African American and Latino families are also far more likely to experience housing problems than are white families, as are immigrant families.[21] In 2003, when nearly three-quarters of whites owned their homes, less than half of African Americans or Latinos were homeowners.[22] (See Figure 1.6.)

African Americans and Latinos are also far more likely to experience health problems and have less access to health care and health insurance. In 2003, 79 percent of Latinos children were covered by health insurance, compared with 93 percent of whites and 86 percent of African American children.[23]

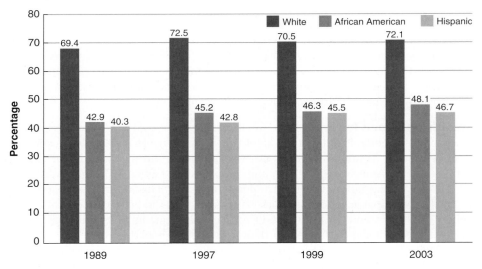

FIGURE 1.6 *Home Ownership Rates by Race, 1989–2003.*

Source: Lawrence Mishel, Jared Bernstein, and Sylvia Allegretto, *State of Working America, 2004–2005* (Washington, DC: Economic Policy Institute, 2005), www.epinet.org.

Finally, African American and American Indian children are more likely to be identified as having a specific learning disability, mental retardation, or an emotional disturbance than are whites, Latinos, and Asians. In 2000, although black students composed only 17 percent of the public school student population, they accounted for 33 percent of students identified as mentally retarded children, 27 percent as emotionally disturbed, and 18 percent as having a specific learning disability. Only about 3 percent of Asians are classified as having any of these three types of disabilities.

Racial, Geographic, and Economic Isolation

The racial disparities in children's access to basic life necessities are compounded by the segregation of low-income children and students of color in large urban centers.[24] One trend has been for middle-class families—minority and white—to move away from central cities, and for those remaining residents to face problems of unemployment, poverty, racial isolation, and crumbling schools. As city smokestack-industries continue to be "downsized," go overseas, or disappear entirely, jobs have also moved to the suburbs.

The jobs remaining in the city tend to be "new economy" jobs in information and high-tech industries that are more difficult to qualify for than jobs in the "old economy" factories. Few inner-city residents—especially the large number of newly arrived, hardworking immigrants—qualify for these jobs. Most settle for irregular, part-time work in "services" and lack security, benefits, or a "living wage" (this is an income, calculated for each community, that assures that a person working full-time will not fall below the poverty line).

FOCAL POINT 1.1

Student Bill of Rights

H.R.236
Student Bill of Rights

In the House of Representatives

To provide for adequate and equitable educational opportunities for students in
State public school systems, and for other purposes.

Be it enacted by the Senate and House of Representatives of the United States
of America in Congress assembled, SEC. 112. STATE EDUCATIONAL ADEQUACY
AND EQUITY REQUIREMENTS. (a) FUNDAMENTALS OF EDUCATIONAL
OPPORTUNITY- A State shall provide for all public schools in the State access, at
levels defined by the State under section 113 as ideal or adequate, to each of the
following fundamentals of educational opportunity: (1) high-quality classroom
teachers and school administrators (2) rigorous academic standards, curricula, and
methods of instruction (3) small class sizes (4) quality facilities, textbooks, and
instructional materials and supplies (5) up-to-date library resources (6) up-to-date
computer technology (7) quality guidance counseling

These limits on employment in inner cities, together with many housing policies and practices that exclude poor people and most people of color from middle-
class communities, mean that, despite our increased racial diversity, most young
people live in highly segregated neighborhoods. African American children, on
average, live in neighborhoods where more than half of other children are black;
Hispanic children typically also live in places where they are in the majority.[25]

Schooling Inequalities

In 2002, Senator Christopher Dodd and Congressman Chaka Fattah introduced
into Congress legislation that would ensure that basic educational opportunities
are available to all U.S. students. Their Student Bill of Rights Act would hold
states accountable for providing all students with the "fundamentals of educational opportunity," including highly qualified teachers and guidance counselors, challenging curricula, up-to-date textbooks and materials, and small
classes. These are resources known to have enormous positive impact on achievement, especially for disadvantaged students. See Focal Point 1.1 to read the text
of this legislation.

One might think that such a "Bill of Rights" would be unnecessary in the United
States, given its wealth and long history of public education, but many American
children do not routinely experience these basic elements of education in their

public schools. This declaration of student rights has yet to be passed, even though 200 members of the House and Senate supported it in 2004.

Segregated Schools

In the past 30 years, racial segregation and the division of the nation into poor cities and more affluent outer-urban and suburban communities have had profound effects on public schools. Many cities' public school systems are predominantly minority. Middle-class whites who live in urban centers—often older and more affluent than earlier generations of parents of school-aged children—increasingly choose private education. Some seek private schools for the resources, status, and privilege. Others worry that racial integration triggers a decline in school quality, and many others, swayed by dramatic—if exaggerated—accounts of school violence, fear for their children's safety. The withdrawal of vital middle-class support has left many urban public schools inadequate and decaying.

The level of school segregation for black and Latino students has been steadily increasing since the 1980s,[26] and with it have come increases in the schooling problems associated with poverty. In 1997, only 5 percent of segregated white schools faced conditions of concentrated poverty, compared with 80 percent of segregated black and Latino schools. This racial and economic segregation is paralleled by significant inequities in students' access to education resources and opportunities to achieve.

Unequal Spending

Most low-income children and children of color attend schools that spend less on their students than schools serving white students. The Education Trust (Ed Trust), a research and advocacy organization in Washington, D.C., recently found that most states in 2002 provided fewer dollars per student to their highest-poverty school districts than to their lowest-poverty districts. Most states also spend less on districts with the largest proportions of nonwhite students.[27]

Individual states vary greatly—some are much better, some are much worse. Illinois and New York have the largest funding gaps between wealthy and poor children—well over $2,000 per student. Alabama, Arizona, Louisiana, Michigan, Pennsylvania, Texas, and Virginia have gaps of over $900 per student.[28]

The Ed Trust also calculated the impact of the funding gap for individual schools. (See Concept Table 1.1.) In Illinois, it found that $61,625 a year less would be spent on a classroom of 25 students in a high-poverty district, and almost $1 million annually less would be spent at a high-poverty elementary school of 400 students. Ed Trust asks an obvious and important question: "Consider the daily struggle for progress that occurs in many of our poorest schools. What could those schools do with another $1 million per year—resources that their more wealthy peers already enjoy?"[29]

Funding gaps don't exist everywhere. States like Massachusetts, Minnesota, and New Jersey provide substantially more resources to their highest-poverty districts, even after taking into account the additional cost of educating poor children. States

CONCEPT TABLE 1.1 *Per-Student Funding Gaps*

Per-Student Funding Gaps Add Up		
For example, when you consider the cost-adjusted per-student funding gap for low-income students in . . .	**Between two typical classrooms of 25 students, that translates into a difference of. . . .**	**Between two typical elementary schools of 400 students, that translates into a difference of. . . .**
New York	$65,375	$1,046,000
Illinois	$61,625	$986,000
Virginia	$35,750	$572,000
Pennsylvania	$32,700	$523,200
Texas	$23,400	$374,400

Source: Education Trust, 2004.

that either have no gap or a gap of less than $100 per student include Georgia, Oregon, Utah, and a number of others.[30]

Similar funding gaps exist along racial lines. Thirty-five states spend less in high-minority districts, and the gap nationally averages $1,099 for each student.

Unequal Opportunities to Learn

―――――――――――――――――――――――――‰ ‰ ‰―――――――――――――――――――――――――

The fifth-grade class was relocated into portables in October. The portables are half the size of the regular classroom. There is barely enough room to walk around because all books and supplies are nestled around the perimeter of the room on the floor. There are no cabinets. There are no windows. The district is in such dire financial straits that the teachers can't make photo-copies; we don't have overhead projectors, nor do we have enough space for the children.

—**STEVEN BRANCH**
First-year teacher, grade 5

―――――――――――――――――――――――――‰ ‰ ‰―――――――――――――――――――――――――

My boys' and girls' bathrooms have been flooded for over two months. Finally, after winter break, I decided that the janitors did not intend to fix anything, so I put in a formal request for work to be done. Last week, after I complained numerous times to the principal and vice-principal, the bath-rooms were fixed. So, after two months of sickening smell and slimy scum (literally, the students were walking in slime), the bathrooms were fixed. But the way in which they were fixed was ridiculous. For two days straight, all day long, there was a jackhammer going off in the back of my room. Couldn't they have done this work after 2 P.M.? Or during recess and lunchtime? Or couldn't they at least have given me some advance notice that there was going to be a loud noise going off in my room for two straight days so that I could have made some outdoor plans? I lost two days. Learning can't take place in that sort of environment.

—JENNIFER HAYMORE
First-year teacher, grade 4

Steven Branch's and Jennifer Haymore's experiences in impoverished city school systems are not unique. Jonathan Kozol's wrenching account, *Savage Inequalities,* vividly portrays inequalities that other studies have documented. Kozol found black and Latino students in dilapidated Camden, New Jersey, schools learning keyboarding without computers, science without laboratories, and other subjects without enough textbooks to go around. Seven minutes away in white, affluent Cherry Hill, students enjoyed well-kept facilities, including a greenhouse for those interested in horticulture, abundant equipment, and supplies. Since its publication in the early 1990s Kozol's book has significantly increased the public's awareness of the enormous disparities in the conditions among schools in wealthy and poor communities, and activists in many states have pursued legal action to correct them.

In 1997 the *Los Angeles Times* published a humiliating story of textbook shortages in the city's schools. Fremont High School, with mostly Latino, all minority students, reported needing 7,200 textbooks simply to comply with the state law. For its 1,200 tenth graders, Fremont owned only 210 English textbooks. Within a few weeks of the exposé, the newspaper filled with reports of school district money, private donations, action at the state level, and large photos showing stacks of new books at Fremont.[31] The inescapable conclusion was that these stopgap measures solved the problem. Meanwhile, all of Los Angeles's schools faced serious problems. It is difficult to imagine that a school with mostly affluent white students, anywhere, would not have enough books. It is unthinkable that the nation would tolerate a lack of textbooks in an entire urban school district—one of the largest—if its children were white and not poor.

In 2000, some angry Californians joined together to ask courts to remedy such inequities. A group of young people and their parents filed suit in the name of Eliezer Williams, an African American student at a San Francisco middle school. Nearly all of the 48 student plaintiffs named in the case were black, Latino, or Asian Pacific Islander, and they all attended predominantly nonwhite and low-income schools. They sued California's governor, the state board of education, and the superintendent of public instruction.

The Williams plaintiffs claimed that they, and many other California students like them, attend "schools that shock the conscience."[32] They provided compelling evidence that schools across the state lacked "trained teachers, necessary educational supplies, classrooms, even seats in classrooms, and facilities that meet basic health and safety standards." They also showed that these schooling basics were systematically less available to low-income students of color, and that a school experiencing one of the problems was much more likely to experience more or all of them. The Williams students argued that, by permitting such schools, California's educational system failed to meet its constitutional obligation to educate all students and to educate them equally. In 2004, the governor of California agreed to settle the case, allocating one billion dollars and developing standards requiring that all students have qualified teachers, instructional materials, and decent and safe school buildings.

Such schooling inequalities are not confined to California. Across the nation, students at high-poverty and high-minority schools have fewer well-qualified teachers than their peers at affluent, white, suburban schools. Their schools suffer more teaching vacancies, and principals have a tougher time filling them. Figure 1.7 shows that middle-school and high school students who are in schools with large percentages of low-income students and students of color are considerably less likely to be trained by teachers with college degrees in the subjects they teach.

The lack of qualified teachers is particularly damaging because study after study shows that, of all the resources schools provide, teachers are the most important for student learning, and that not having a qualified teacher is particularly damaging for low-income children who have fewer learning resources outside of school.

Class size also matters, since the number of children in a class limits the amount of time that the teacher can spend with any one child. Nevertheless, teachers in high-minority and high-poverty schools are also more likely to have large classes to

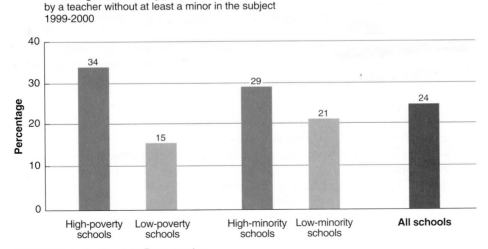

Percentage of secondary-level core academic courses taught by a teacher without at least a minor in the subject 1999-2000

FIGURE 1.7 *Teacher Preparation.*

Source: Paul E. Barton, *Parsing the Achievement Gap: Baselines for Tracking Progress* (Princeton, NJ: Educational Testing Service, 2003).

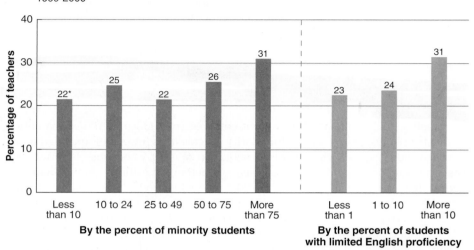

Percentage of teachers with classes of 25 or more students
1999-2000

*In classes with less than 10 percent minority students, 22 percent of the teachers have 25 or more students in their classes.
Source: National Center for Education Statistics, School and Staffing Survey (SASS), 1999-2000.

FIGURE 1.8 *Class Size.*

Source: Paul E. Barton, *Parsing the Achievement Gap: Baselines for Tracking Progress* (Princeton, NJ: Educational Testing Service, 2003).

teach. Again, national data show that teachers in schools where more than three-quarters of the students are of color tend to have the largest classes. A similar pattern holds with English learners. (See Figure 1.8.)

Perhaps because fewer teachers are well trained and more are saddled with larger classes, teachers at schools in low-income communities and communities of color tend to place less emphasis on having students develop inquiry and problem-solving skills, and they offer fewer opportunities for students to become actively engaged in learning.[33]

Further, schools attended by African Americans and Latinos often offer very few critical college "gatekeeping" courses such as advanced mathematics and science. Advanced Placement (AP) courses that enhance students' college-going opportunities are the most unevenly distributed. Figure 1.9 shows the dramatic under participation of African Americans and Latinos in AP exams, the capstone activity of these courses.

In 1999, Rasheda Daniel, a working-class African American teenager, sued her school district and the State of California for not offering the advanced classes at her high school that she needed to attend the state's university as a science major. Nobody thought she was wrong; and nobody thought she was an isolated case. Daniel's suit prompted the state legislature to provide new funding to schools like hers—mostly in low-income communities and communities of color—to begin offering advanced courses.

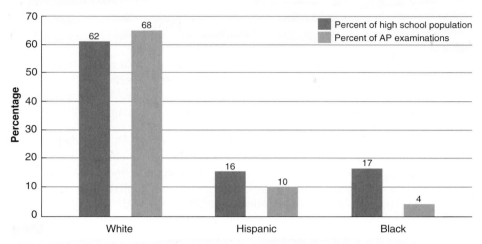

Distribution of advanced placement examinations compared with the distribution of the high school population, by race/ethnicity 1999 and 2002*

*AP examinations are for 2002; high school population data are for 1999.
Sources: AP data are from the College Board; high school population data are from *National Center for Education Statistics, Digest of Education Statistics 2001*, Table 42.

FIGURE 1.9 *Distribution of AP Exams Compared with Distribution of High School Population, by Race and Ethnicity, 1999/2002.*

Source: Paul E. Barton, *Parsing the Achievement Gap: Baselines for Tracking Progress* (Princeton, NJ: Educational Testing Service, 2003).

However, inequality is often a moving target. Even when schools in poor neighborhoods make some headway in providing new resources and college prep classes, the rate at which they improve their programs is typically outpaced by more advantaged schools.

Unequal Community and Peer Resources at School

Not all learning resources at schools are ones that the schools provide. In middle- and upper-middle-class communities students themselves bring both tangible and intangible resources from their homes and neighborhoods that benefit their lower-income classmates as well as themselves.[34] For example, orderly and safe school environments that allow students to focus on learning are taken for granted in most middle-class communities, unlike in many low-income communities where students are about twice as likely to report the presence of street gangs at school.

Students who attend school in stable, mostly middle-class communities benefit from the fact that students move less often and, therefore, add to the stability of the school environment that enhances learning. For example, in one study the percentage of students who transferred between schools in a 12-month period was 34 percent in high-poverty schools, compared with just 14 percent in affluent schools.[35]

Parents are more involved in traditional school activities at middle-class schools. For example, parents of children in middle-class schools are four times as likely to be members of the PTA and much more likely to participate in fund-raising. The schooling resources these parents generate—dollars, more adults to work with children, and so on—enrich the learning environment for all the students at the school.

Finally, peers in middle-class schools are more likely to do homework, less likely to watch television, less likely to cut class, and more likely to graduate—all of which have been found to influence the behavior of classmates. Other resources at middle-class schools include larger numbers of high-achieving peers who can share their knowledge with their classmates.

All these community and peer resources, combined with the more advantaged school resources in middle-class schools described earlier, help explain why low-income children do better in predominantly middle-class schools than in schools with large concentrations of low-income children. It also should be noted, however, that, even within the same school, students usually do not share equal experiences. Educators typically divide students into ability-grouped classes and track them into programs that prepare them for different post–high school opportunities. Those students who are not in "high ability," "college prep," or "gifted" programs typically have much less exposure to rigorous content, and teachers seldom ask them to grapple with critical thinking or problem solving. Seldom do they experience engaging, hands-on lessons; more often they read texts or fill out worksheets—inactive and alone.[36]

Gaps in Achievement, School Completion, and College Attendance

The differences in opportunity just described are followed by all too familiar differences in schooling outcomes. From at least the fourth grade on, African American, Latino, and low-income children lag behind their white and better-off peers. They more often take low-ability and remedial classes, and they drop out of school at higher rates. They consistently score lower on measures of student achievement that schools claim are crucial. Far fewer take college preparatory classes and go on to college; fewer still earn college degrees.

In a 2003 report from the Educational Testing Service, *Parsing the Achievement Gap*, analyst Paul Barton pulls together research evidence about inequalities in and out of school that relate to students' achievement (what he calls the "correlates" of achievement). There can be no doubt about the results. (See Concept Table 1.2.) In all 14 of the factors related to achievement, Barton shows gaps between white students and students of color, and gaps between low- and higher-income families in 11 of the 12 factors for which he found data. Clearly, these mirror inequalities in those aspects of schooling, early life, and home circumstances that research has linked to school achievement.

Three indicators of educational success—academic achievement, high school graduation, and college attendance—all reveal the impact of these persistent inequalities.

CONCEPT TABLE 1.2 *Correlates of Achievement and Gaps*

Correlates	Are there gaps between minority and majority student populations?	Are there gaps between students from low-income families and higher-income families?
School:		
Rigor of curriculum	Yes	Not available
Teacher preparation	Yes	Yes
Teacher experience and attendance	Yes	Yes
Class size	Yes	No*
Technology-assisted instruction	Yes	Yes
School safety	Yes	Yes
Before and beyond school:		
Parent participation	Yes	Yes
Student mobility	Yes	Yes
Birthweight	Yes	Not available
Lead poisoning	Yes	Yes
Hunger and nutrition	Yes	Yes
Reading to young children	Yes	Yes
Television watching	Yes	Yes
Parent availability	Yes	Yes

*The asterisk indicates that not all researchers agree that class size is a correlate with achievement for low-income students.

Source: Paul E. Barton, *Parsing the Achievement Gap: Baselines for Tracking Progress* (Princeton, NJ: Educational Testing Service, 2003).

Achievement   The academic achievement of the nation's schoolchildren is measured every few years by the National Assessment of Educational Progress (NAEP), a paper-and-pencil test in reading, writing, mathematics, science, U.S. history, civics, geography, and the arts. Often called "The Nation's Report Card," NAEP tests a sample of students in grades 4, 8, and 12 in every state. Unlike most standardized tests, NAEP doesn't produce scores for every child, but it does report the results for the nation's 9-, 13-, and 17-year-olds as a whole, and it compares the performance of males and females, racial groups, and poor and nonpoor students.

In every subject tested and at every grade level, low-income students perform at a lower level than more economically advantaged students, and Latino and African American students do worse than white and Asian students. Students with limited English score less well than those who are proficient. This is what has been commonly known as the "achievement" gap.

In 2005, NAEP released a study reporting trends in the achievement of U.S. students over the past 35 years. There was some promising news: Nine-year-olds in elementary schools today are scoring higher in reading and mathematics since NAEP began testing students in the early 1970s. African American and Latino fourth graders have shown the most impressive gains, and, as a result, the gap between their achievement and that of their white peers is smaller than it has ever been. Thirteen-year-olds have also made gains, and, in most cases, the gaps among various groups are also smaller. However, high school students have not made similar progress. Overall, their achievement is about the same as it was 30 years ago, and the gaps among groups remain almost as wide. These test score gaps become more meaningful when we compare students across ages and racial groups. By the end of high school, Latino and African American students have math and reading skills that are virtually the same as those of white 13-year olds.[37]

High School Graduation and Dropout Rates   Nationally, only 68 percent of those who enter ninth grade graduate from high school with a regular diploma at the end of twelfth grade, according to a recent study by Harvard University and the Urban Institute.[38] The graduation rates are even lower for students of color. In 2001, only 50 percent of African American students, 51 percent of Native American students, and 53 percent of Latino students graduated from high school. However, because the U.S. education system provides second chances for those who leave high school without a diploma, about 87 percent of all 25- to 29-year-olds in 2003 had received either a diploma or some form of equivalency certificate. Even so, African Americans were far less likely than whites to have attained the status of a high school graduate (88 vs. 94 percent), and only 62 percent of Latinos were likely to have done so.[39]

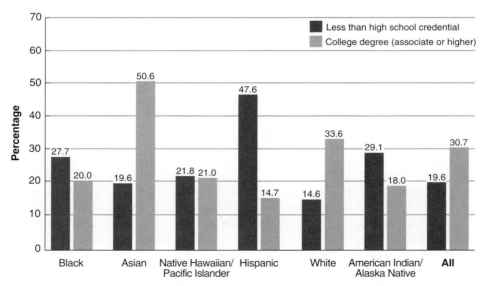

In the U.S. among adults age 25 and over: **20%** have less than a high school credential and **31%** hold a college degree.

FIGURE 1.10 *Highest Level of Educational Attainment, Age 25+, by Race and Ethnicity.*

Source: Sandra S. Ruppert, *Closing the College Participation Gap: A National Summary* (Denver, CO: Education Commission of the States, 2003).

College Attendance   In 2003, more students than ever before from all racial groups were going to college, but the gains among groups were not equal. In particular, the Latino participation rates lagged far behind those of African Americans and whites. In 2003, 57 percent of all 25- to 29-year-olds had completed some college, with whites (66%) more likely than African Americans (51%) or Latinos (31%) to have done so. Twenty-eight percent of all 25- to 29-year-olds had at least a bachelor's degree in 2003. Although the percentage with a bachelor's degree or higher has increased for all three racial/ethnic groups, the gaps between whites and blacks and between whites and Hispanics have actually widened over time.[40] Figure 1.10 shows the gaps in high school and college attainment.

The Struggle for Socially Just Teaching

In the remaining chapters of this book, we will continue to share the experiences and reflections of teachers who identify themselves as teachers for social justice. Many of them are writing at the conclusion of their first year of teaching. Through their teacher education courses, their work in classrooms, and their own life experiences, they understand the inequalities we've described in this chapter, and they've begun their careers committed to teaching in ways that will change the world. Their voices are hopeful and optimistic about the possibilities of education and social justice in a diverse, unpredictable world. These teachers also reveal their struggle to bring their knowledge and values to their practice as they strive to create classrooms and schools where students develop the academic and moral capacities and the commitment to shape their own places in a socially just future.

Four of these teachers deserve a special introduction, since they and their students appear in photographs throughout the book. These four teachers struggle for socially just public schools that forge unity without diminishing difference. They also hold on to the belief that schools and teaching can indeed change a world where lives are marked by poverty, discrimination, and injustice.

Mauro Bautista

Mauro Bautista is a fifth-year teacher who has become the coordinator of bilingual education at his middle school. He lives and teaches in the same Latino neighborhood where he grew up. He sees himself in his sixth-, seventh-, and eighth-grade students, and he sees his own parents in their parents. Mauro and his wife have three young children, and two of them go to one of the neighborhood schools. Consequently, he always treats his students as he hopes his own children will be treated.

※ ※ ※

I define "social justice educator" as someone who identifies inequities in education, builds coalitions with others affected by the inequities, and then takes action to disrupt the reproduction of these inequities. . . . I look at educational practices with critical lenses. Instead of doing certain things longer and stronger, I often take a step back and ask, "How else can we do this?"

There are always questions: "Am I doing justice to my students?" "How do I know that what I am doing is socially just?" "Why do we have to do it this way?" "Can I do it this other way?" "If I can't do it this other way, what does that mean to my students?"

Mauro holds the highest expectations for his students and their parents and he tries to treat them with the utmost respect.

Kimberly Min

Kimberly Min teaches third grade in a diverse, low-income, South Los Angeles community. At the conclusion of her first year of teaching in one of the city's most impoverished neighborhoods, Kimberly dedicated her Masters' degree project to her students. She said that she couldn't have asked for a more endearing, bright and loving group of children, and she thanked them for being incredibly patient with a first-year teacher.

※ ※ ※

Education is viewed by many as an equalizing agent in our society. However, children of color, children of poor working families, and children of immigrants, are still marginalized and victims of an unequal society that privileges rich, white, middle and upper class values. 50 years after Brown v. Board of Education, *inequity, injustice, and compensatory education continue to be the experiences of our children in inner city schools. Although the* Brown *decision marked a turning point in history, the struggle for equality in education continues.*

So it's been 50 years. Now what? Educators must continue to teach students about their history, have discussions about inequity, race, and privilege, and create a space in which students can express what they are thinking, feeling, and learning, as well as share their opinions and perspectives. . . . As an elementary school teacher in South Los Angeles, I empower, engage, and encourage my students to disrupt cycles of oppression and inequity with a curriculum that requires them to read text (literature, media, art, expression) with a critical eye.

Mark Hill

Mark Hill is a first-year high school math teacher. The son of a teacher, and a very good math student, he spent much of his growing up years tutoring other young people. He simply enjoyed helping his peers succeed with their schoolwork. He reports, "It was never my mother's goal for me to follow in her footsteps and become a teacher, but she made no bones about how it was work she enjoyed and found satisfying."

Mark's students live in a racially diverse, working-class community, where more than 30 different languages are spoken. Neither well-off nor the poorest of the poor, the community's average household earns $39,000 per year.

Mark's own experience as biracial person, the son of a white mother and a black father, has had a profound effect on his teaching. He understands the limits that our culture's struggle with race places on students who are not white. He also knows how important it is for students to be seen as more than just their race—as individuals—and to be accepted on their own terms, regardless of preconceived notions of race, gender, or age.

───────────── ⊗ ⊗ ⊗ ─────────────

I see social activism relating to my teaching in a very simple way. I am a role model for students of color and low socioeconomic status. It is my goal that every one of my students leaves my classroom believing in themselves and their ability to reach college. I treat each student with respect, and I hope to teach them to respect each other and themselves in the same way.

Judy Smith

Judy Smith is a third-year teacher, but teaching is her second career. Before obtaining her teaching credential, Judy worked in the private sector—in a high-tech industry. Now she teaches history and government to eleventh and twelfth graders at a comprehensive high school that enrolls more than 3,000 Latino, African American, Asian, and white students. Two-thirds of the students come from low-income families and a third are still learning English as their second language. The school has failed to meet its achievement test-score targets under state and federal law, and it has been identified by the state as being academically "low performing." Nearly half of the students drop out before graduation, and only about 16 percent of those who do graduate go on to four-year colleges and universities. Judy tells us that, as is the case on many urban campuses, "high fences, numerous security guards, and sprawling graffiti sap the school's spirit."

Judy loves her job and the challenge of bringing academic rigor and engaging learning opportunities to her students, despite widespread beliefs that students like hers won't succeed with high-level academic work. As her comments at the beginning of this chapter make clear, her determination to make a difference at her school is driven by extraordinarily difficult questions:

> How does a social justice teacher teach in an urban school where very large class sizes, minimal resources, low expectations, and low literacy affect both students and teachers? What does it mean to be a socially just teacher in a socially unjust world? What do all students deserve?

Judy Smith's answers include such powerful ideas as respectful learner-centered communities, academic rigor, cultural responsiveness, and democratic citizenship. She quotes Dr. Martin Luther King Jr.'s Nobel Prize acceptance speech:

> I refuse to accept the view that mankind is so tragically bound to the starless night of racism and war that the bright daybreak of peace and brotherhood can never become reality. . . . I believe that unarmed truth and unconditional love will have the final word.

Mauro Bautista, Kimberly Min, Mark Hill, and Judy Smith, like many other teachers, differ from Americans who look longingly to a mostly imagined past, when the "good" life meant one without diversity, a life lived with people mostly like "us."

In this sense *us* has typically meant those at the center of society—a location that is white and middle class, with males in authority and women and children safely protected in heterosexual families. These new teachers also differ from some of their colleagues who are intent on returning to an imagined "good" past when children all spoke English and scored above average, and their parents only came to school to deliver cookies. The social justice these new teachers envision does not try to re-create the past. They know they must wrestle with traditions in schools and society that will obstruct their efforts and attempt to persuade them that their idealism is naive or destructive.

What a struggle it is! In the face of cultural diversity, school critics on the political right have openly launched what some call the "culture wars" by attempting to require teaching the mainstream culture and language and none other. They often favor "back to basics" and traditional teaching methods. Political moderates and liberals have sought ways to equalize students' chances for school success by giving them the same opportunities as white, middle-class students. To do this they promote equally high academic standards that depart significantly from traditional views, and they call for all students to have equally well-qualified teachers and other resources. Progressive educators are cautious about the moderates' and liberals' programs unless these programs are accompanied at every step by tough cultural questions: Whose schools are these, and who benefits from them? Whose language may be spoken? Whose knowledge is important to include? Finally, finding no hope in a common education, some individuals—on both the right and left—have carved out separate specialized schools to serve different "monocultural" communities. Many are giving up on public education, emphasizing the democratic right to be separate over the democratic ideal to stay together. This is not a quiet or passive withdrawal of support, but an active, complex, political battle.

This book seeks to help answer the questions Judy Smith and her colleagues raise about social justice teaching in the twenty-first century. Its goal is to provide aspiring teachers with an understanding of the hopeful struggle that these teachers are engaged in. It also aims to provide the knowledge and a sense of possibility that arms new teachers to be effective agents for educational equality—ready to teach to change the world.

🅞 OLC Connections

Additional online and print resources and a set of questions for reflection about the American schooling dilemma can be found at www.mhhe.com/oakes3e/.

▩ Digging Deeper

About Digging Deeper: In this final section, we provide some of the most useful sources of information on the topics we've discussed in this chapter on the American dilemma of diversity, inequality, and democratic values. We call the section "Digging Deeper," because these references are good places to delve into the issues introduced in the chapter in more depth and detail. The scholars, organizations, and websites we list here provide a wealth of factual information, important insights that help explain those facts, and analyses of how educators can think about them and act on them in ways that can promote social justice in schooling. You'll find a "Digging Deeper" section at the end of each chapter.

Facts and Reports about Diversity, Inequality, and Schooling

Childstats.gov (http://childstats.gov/) is a government website assembled by the Federal Interagency Forum on Child and Family Statistics, a working group of federal agencies and private research organizations that collect, analyze, and report data on issues related to children and families. The Forum's annual report, *America's Children: Key National Indicators of Well-Being,* details the status of children and families in the United States.

The Civil Rights Project at Harvard University (CRP), directed by Professor Gary Orfield, is a leading organization devoted to civil rights research. CRP research has been incorporated into federal legislation, cited in litigation, and used to spur congressional hearings. The group's website at http://www.civilrightsproject. harvard.edu/ makes available downloadable versions of many of its reports.

Economic Policy Institute (EPI), a Washington, D.C. think tank, produces regular biennial reports about Americans' economic well-being on a variety of measures—data that enables the book's authors to closely examine the impact of the economy on the living standards of the American people. EPI and the report can be found online at http://www.epi.org/.

Education Trust is an education advocacy organization in Washington, D.C., with a second branch in California (EdTrust West). The Trust assembles a wide range of data about education. Among the useful resources on the organization's website is Education Watch Online, a user-friendly, searchable database that features state and national data showing student achievement and opportunity patterns, kindergarten through college, by race, ethnicity and family income. The site can be accessed at http://www2.edtrust.org.

Inequality.org is a project of Demos, a group that describes itself as a New York City–based online resource "for journalists, activists, scholars and policymakers seeking information on the connection between rising economic inequality, on the one hand, and eroding opportunity and democracy, on the other." Demos describes its mission as "first, to illuminate the causes and multidimensional consequences of America's growing concentration of wealth, income, power and opportunity; and second, to move what we consider an important and neglected problem onto the front burner of American politics and public discourse."

The Lewis Mumford Center at the State University of New York, Albany campus compiles data and produces reports on the implications of changing demographics for American society. The Mumford Center also has an initiative tracking the status and experiences of children in newcomer families, especially those growing up in families from Latin America and Asia. The Mumford Center can be found online at http://mumford.albany.edu.

The National Center for Educational Statistics at the U.S. Department of Education is the primary federal agency charged with collecting and analyzing data about education in the United States. Four recent reports provide the most up-to-date official analyses of school-related data: *Condition of Education*, 2005; *Digest of Education Statistics*, 2003; *Indicators of School Crime and Safety*, 2004; and *Projections of Education Statistics to 2013*. All these reports are down-loadable from the Center's website at http://nces.ed.gov/edstats/.

U.S. Census Bureau provides raw data and publishes regular reports on the U.S. population. Some recent reports are relevant to diversity, inequality, and schooling. For example, a recent report related to segregation is *Racial and Ethnic Residential Segregation in the United States: 1980–2000*. The site also provides easy-to-use data tools that allow users to search for information based on the 2000 census. The U.S. Census Bureau is online at http://www.census.gov.

Scholars Who Investigate the Causes and Consequences of Inequality

Walter R. Allen and **Daniel Solorzano,** professors of education at the University of California, Los Angeles, are sociologists who study the access and participation of African Americans and Latinos in higher education. Their **CHOICES Project** examines these students' experiences moving through K–12 schooling into higher education, graduate and professional school, and careers. The project's website, http://www.choices.gseis.ucla.edu/index.html, provides useful information about re-sources related to increased college access, equity, and opportunity, including links to websites that identify college opportunity resources.

Jean Anyon, professor of urban education at the Graduate Center of the City University of New York, studies the intersection of social class, race, the political economy, and education in two recent books, *Ghetto Schooling: A Political Economy of Urban School Reform* (Teachers College Press, 1997), and *Radical Possibilities: Public Policy, Urban Education, and a New Social Movement* (Routledge, 2005).

David Berliner, professor and former dean of the School of Education at Arizona State University, has analyzed the role of poverty in the failure of schools to reform in ways that increase successful schooling for the nation's most disadvantaged children. See his paper "Our Impoverished View of Educational Reform" (available online at http://www.asu.edu/educ/epsl/EPRU/documents/EPSL-0508-116-EPRU.pdf).

Jonathan Kozol is an education writer who, since the 1960s, has illuminated inequalities in American schools and the devastating impact of those inequalities on low-income children and children of color. His 1991 book *Savage Inequalities: Children in America's Schools* (New York: Crown, 1991) paints a vivid portrait of the discrepancies in resources and opportunities between the schools of rich and poor children. His most recent book, *The Shame of the Nation: The Restoration of Apartheid Schooling in America* (New York: Crown, 2005), brings to life the statistical data about the resegregation in urban schools.

Using national data on kindergartners, University of Michigan education pro-fessor **Valerie Lee** has examined the compounding of out-of-school inequality and within-school inequality in her book with **David T. Burkam,** *Inequality at the Starting Gate: Social Background Differences in Achievement as Children Begin School* (Economic Policy Institute, 2002).

Richard Rothstein is an economist who analyzes the relationships among the economy, the impoverished status of a large segment of the nation's children, and inequalities in school achievement. His book *Class and Schools: Using Social, Economic, and Educational Reform to Close the Black-White Achievement Gap* (Economic Policy Institute and Teachers College, Columbia University, 2004) shows how out-of-school inequalities play a significant part in how well children learn and succeed at school.

Materials for Classroom Use

Fourth R is published semiannually by the Human Rights Education program (HRE) of Amnesty International USA (AIUSA). HRE facilitates the teaching of human rights by supporting teachers of kindergarten through college as well as educators working in nonformal settings. Fourth R provides teachers with information and instructional materials to engage their students in studying topics related to students' educational rights; it is online at http://www.amnestyusa.org/education/4thr.html.

The National Center for Education Statistics includes on its site a **"Student's Classroom"** page that provides statistical information about schools, colleges, and public libraries in an easily searchable format. It allows students (and teachers) to play games, take quizzes, and build skills about math, probability, graphing, and mathematicians. The site is located at http://nces.ed.gov/nceskids/index.asp?flash=true.

Notes

1. U.S. Bureau of the Census, www.census.gov.
2. http://uscis.gov/graphics/shared/aboutus/statistics/IMM03yrbk/IMM2003list.htm.
3. U.S. Bureau of the Census, www.census.gov.
4. http://www.urban.org/content/IssuesInFocus/immigrationstudies/immigration.htm.
5. Between 1979 and 2003, the number of school-aged children (ages 5–17) who spoke a language other than English at home grew from 3.8 million to 9.9 million, or from 9 percent to 19 percent of all children in the age group. U.S. Department of Education, *Condition of Education,* 2005.
6. *How Unequal Are We, Anyway? (A Statistical Briefing Book),* July 2004, http://www.inequality.org/facts.html.
7. Income comparisons measured by purchasing power parity exchange rates, for 2002 at $36,102. Countries in this comparison are: Australia, Austria, Belgium, Canada, Denmark, Finland, France, Germany, Ireland, Italy, Japan, Netherlands, New Zealand, Norway, Portugal, Spain, Sweden, Switzerland, the United Kingdom, and the United States. See Lawrence Mishel, Jared Bernstein, and Sylvia Allegretto, *State of Working America, 2004–2005* (Washington, DC: Economic Policy Institute, 2005), www.epinet.org.
8. Mishel et al., *State of Working America, 2004–2005.*
9. Ibid.
10. *How Unequal Are We, Anyway?*
11. *America's Children: Key National Indicators of Children's Well-Being 2005,* http://www.childstats.org.

12. Ibid.
13. Ibid.
14. Harvard University's Joint Center for Housing Studies, *The State of the Nation's Housing*, 2004.
15. http://www.nationalhomeless.org/families.html.
16. Mishel et al., *State of Working America, 2004–2005*.
17. John Karl Scholz and Kara Levine, "U.S. Black-White Wealth Inequality: A Survey," unpublished paper, Madison, WI, Department of Economics and Institute for Research on Poverty, University of Wisconsin, 2003; forthcoming in *Social Inequality*, K. Neckerman (ed.), Russell Sage Foundation.
18. Mishel et al., *State of Working America, 2004–2005*.
19. Ibid.
20. Harvard University's Joint Center for Housing Studies, *The State of the Nation's Housing*, 2004.
21. http://www.urban.org/content/IssuesInFocus/immigrationstudies/immigration.htm.
22. Mishel et al., *State of Working America, 2004–2005*.
23. *America's Children: Key National Indicators of Children's Well-Being 2005*, http://www.childstats.org.
24. 1997 report of the U.S. Department of Housing and Urban Development (23 June 1997) as cited in Ronald Brownstein, "Cities Still Carry Poverty Burden, HUD Study Says," *Los Angeles Times*, 23 June 1997, pp. A1, A12.
25. Deirdre Oakley, Polly Smith, Jacob Stowell, and Brian Stults, *Separating the Children*, report by the Lewis Mumford Center, December 28, 2001, http://mumford1.dyndns.org/cen2000/Under18Pop/U18Preport.
26. Gary Orfield and C. Lee, *Brown at 50: King's Dream or Plessy's Nightmare?* (Cambridge, MA: The Civil Rights Project at Harvard University, 2004).
27. The analyses in the Ed Trust report use annual financial data from each of the nation's 14,000 public school districts, gathered by the U.S. Census Bureau and the U.S. Department of Education. The calculations are based on the total amount of state and local revenue each district received for the 2001–2002 school year, the latest year for which such financial data are available. Federal revenues (which make up less than 10% of all school revenues) are not included because federal education funds are specifically meant to supplement, not supplant, state and local resources. To calculate funding gaps for each state, we compare average state and local revenues per student in the *highest*-poverty school districts—those in the top 25 percent statewide in terms of the percentage of students living below the federal poverty line—to per-student revenues in the *lowest*-poverty school districts. These quartiles are weighted so each contains approximately the same total number of students. This procedure also is used to compare funding in high- and low-minority school districts. See Kevin Carey, *The Funding Gap*, 2004 (Washington, DC: Education Trust, 2004).
28. Ibid.
29. Ibid.
30. Carey, *The Funding Gap, 2004*.
31. Amy Pyle, "Attacking the Textbook Crisis," *Los Angeles Times*, 29 September 1997.
32. *Williams v. State of California*, complaint filed May 17, 2000.
33. Jeannie Oakes, *Multiplying Inequalities* (Santa Monica, CA: RAND, 1990).
34. Paul E. Barton, *Parsing the Achievement Gap: Baselines for Tracking Progress* (Princeton, NJ: Educational Testing Service, 2003).
35. Ibid.
36. Jeannie Oakes, *Keeping Track: How Schools Structure Inequality* (New Haven, CT: Yale University Press, 2005).
37. *NAEP 2004 Trends in Academic Progress: Three Decades of Student Performance in Reading and Mathematics*, 2005, http://nces.ed.gov/pubsearch/pubsinfo.asp?pubid=2005464.
38. Gary Orfield, Daniel Losen, Johanna Wald, and Christopher B. Swanson, *Losing Our Future: How Minority Youth Are Being Left Behind by the Graduation Rate Crisis*, Harvard Civil Rights Project and The Urban Institute, 2005, http://www.urban.org/url.cfm?ID=410936.
39. *The Condition of Education*, 2005.
40. Ibid.

CHAPTER 2

History and Culture

Wrestling with the Traditions
of American Education

Education is viewed as the equalizing agent in our society, and meritocracy is viewed as the path to achieve that end. According to this belief, anyone who works hard will fare well. However, the ideology of meritocracy has an underlying flaw: It does not take into account the prevalent inequalities in our society.

Inequality, injustice, discrimination, and racism are terms we generally do not associate with school. However, they are real. We must face and define these terms for our children and ourselves, as we try to make sense of what school is and can be. They should not discourage us, but they should challenge us to make positive change within our schools.

The role of education and schooling is to equip students with tools not only to learn how to participate in this society, but also to challenge the oppressing structures that limit their lives. Theories of social justice can move us toward tolerance, awareness, respect, meaning, and fulfillment. Teaching for social justice can occur at any school site. However, teachers and students alike must cast a critical eye upon schooling, and transform it to mirror their realities and aspirations.

—KIMBERLY MIN
Third-grade teacher

Teacher Kimberly Min wrote these words at the end of her first year of teaching. Her students go to school in one of the nation's most impoverished inner-city neighborhoods, and they suffer from all of the inequalities we outlined in Chapter 1. Both in and outside of school, Kimberly's students experience the consequences of poverty and racism. One might think that the nation would respond immediately and aggressively to correct the inequitable distribution of opportunities, but it does not.

Chapter Overview

In this chapter, we tackle the question of why the unequal patterns of school opportunities and results often seem inevitable and expected, if regrettable. Looking historically and through the lens of social theory, we discuss how the events and ideologies that shape our national character also shape schools and classrooms. In the sections of this chapter, we (1) present a very brief outline of seminal events in the history of American schooling; (2) sketch how the expectations that Americans have for schools have increased over the past 200 years; (3) discuss two deeply held, if mostly unconscious, cultural assumptions—meritocracy and white superiority—that have shaped how Americans think about schools and make the inequalities we described in Chapter 1 seem natural; and (4) provide examples of how educators like Kim Min are struggling against the history and culture that constrain teaching and learning in today's diverse schools.

America's history and traditions reflect values that compete and sometimes conflict: from democracy to capitalism, from individual freedom to the common good. Teachers like Kimberly Min sense the omnipresence of these historical expectations and ideologies—including in their own thinking. This cultural awareness enlarges their ability to interpret the world of their schools and to succeed in their daily work.

A History of Increasing Expectations

In every society, schools reflect their history and culture. The knowledge, skills, and dispositions that children learn at school and the ways schools engage them in learning grow out of a society's collective decisions about what adult members need to function well as individuals and to contribute to the common good. These "decisions" emerge historically, as a society's needs evolve and change.

Over the past 350 years, the U.S. experience has been one of ever-increasing expectations; the public schools, originally charged with preparing future citizens to participate in democratic governance, have taken on other critical social roles. These include, in rough chronological order, preserving the predominantly Anglo Protestant culture established in the eighteenth and nineteenth centuries in response to the arrival of diverse immigrants; tailoring the content of schooling to the nation's workforce and economic needs; developing the scientific prowess required for national security; ameliorating social inequalities; and developing the human capital required for international competitiveness. Each of these expectations emerged at a critical historical moment. As each was layered onto the public schools, none of the earlier expectations disappeared. To meet these new expectations, Americans have greatly increased the number of years of schooling thought to be necessary for every American and greatly expanded the content of public education.

Common Public Schools Can Secure Democracy

At the Republic's founding, Americans placed their hopes for democracy on public schools. Thomas Jefferson argued that citizens must deliberate publicly and use their reason to decide among competing ideas for guiding the democracy.[1] Because a free press would circulate the ideas that Americans would debate, citizens must be able to read; therefore, Jefferson claimed that government should provide children with three years of schooling to ready them for citizenship. Jefferson advocated basic literacy—reading, writing, and mathematics—and beyond that,

EDUCATIONAL TIMELINE
Seminal Events in the History of American Public Schools

1647	Massachusetts requires towns of at least 50 families to hire a school-master to teach reading and writing.
1779	Thomas Jefferson proposes a system of public schools for the state of Virginia as a way to ensure responsible citizens.
1787	Confederation Congress's Northwest Ordinance requires that a section of land in every township of each new state be reserved for the support of education.
1821	First public high school, Boston English High School, opens.
1827	Massachusetts requires towns of more than 500 families to have a public high school open to all students.
1837	Horace Mann, advocate of free "common schools" as the foundation of democracy, becomes secretary of the Massachusetts State Board of Education.
1852	Massachusetts passes a first mandatory attendance law.
1885	Sixteen states have compulsory-attendance laws.
1890–1920	The Great Wave of immigration brings southern and eastern Europeans to newly industrialized cities in the United States.
1896	U.S. Supreme Court rules in *Plessy v. Ferguson* that racially separate public facilities, if equal, are permissible under the U.S. Constitution, legitimizing school segregation.
1910	Schools enroll 59 percent of the nation's 5- to 19-year-olds; 10 percent of American youth graduate from high school.
1917	Congress passes the Smith-Hughes Act, providing federal funding for vocational education.
1918	All states have compulsory-attendance laws.
1920s	Congress enacts the strictest immigration quotas in U.S. history, which limited the entry of Italians, Poles, Jews, and Greeks and totally excluded Asians.
1930s	The Great Depression brings reduction in education funding, school closings, teacher layoffs, and lower salaries.
1940	Schools enroll 75 percent of the nation's 5- to 19-year-olds; 50 percent of American youth graduate from high school.
1954	U.S. Supreme Court rules in *Brown v. Board of Education of Topeka* that "separate educational facilities are inherently unequal."
1958	One year after Sputnik, Congress passes the National Defense Education Act (NDEA), increasing funding for scientific research and science education.

1965	Lyndon Johnson's War on Poverty leads Congress to pass the Elementary and Secondary Education Act (ESEA), providing federal funds for educational programs such as Title I, Head Start, and bilingual education targeted at low-income students.
1966	The Equality of Educational Opportunity Study, often called the "Coleman Report," concludes that African American children benefit from attending integrated schools, but not from increased resources.
1972	Title IX, a new amendment to the ESEA, prohibits discrimination based on sex in all aspects of education
1970	Schools enroll 90 percent of the nation's 5- to 19-year-olds; 79 percent of young people are high school graduates.
1974	U.S. Supreme Court rules in *Lau v. Nichols* that, to meet the requirement of equal educational opportunity, schools must offer special help for students unable to understand English.
1975	The Education of All Handicapped Children Act (PL 94-142) becomes federal law, requiring free and appropriate public education for disabled children (in 1997, the law becomes the Individuals with Disabilities Education Act).
1983	The report of the National Commission on Excellence in Education, *A Nation at Risk*, warns of the dangers of "mediocre" schools and calls for sweeping reforms.
1994	Educate America Act requires all states to develop academic "standards" that all children will be expected to meet.
2001	No Child Left Behind Act (NCLB), reauthorizing the ESEA, is signed into law by George W. Bush, holding schools accountable for students' scores on standards-based achievement tests.

students might also learn the rudiments of Greek, Roman, English, and American history.

Jefferson included the education of slaves in his plan for public schooling in his home state of Virginia, but he limited this education to training for industrial work. He thought such an education would prepare them for productive participation in society once they were granted the freedom he believed they should have. However, Jefferson was not confident that Negroes "could be made the intellectual equals of white men," and he did not argue that they needed to be prepared to participate as citizens.[2]

In arguing for public schooling (and in criticizing those who saw no need), Jefferson acted on a view shared by late-eighteenth-century intellectuals: Creative and rational thought must be the foundation of orderly and stable modern societies. Jefferson articulated other ideas about democratic society that continue to shape American education today. Perhaps the most important is that democratic institutions must ensure individual liberties, even as they advance the common good.

The Common School.

Perhaps the ugliest idea, at least partly attributable to Jefferson, is that race provides a meaningful and useful way to distinguish among people.

In the 1830s, Horace Mann augmented Jefferson's vision of public school as the cornerstone of democratic life. Mann argued compellingly that all Americans should be educated in "common" schools that would complement what families taught their children at home. Mann defined the essential characteristic of what would later be called, simply, the "public school." These would be *equal* schools. Of course, as the material in Chapter 1 makes abundantly clear, schools today are not equal (and were not then), but Mann gave the country a goal worthy of pursuing. These common schools were not charity schools for the poor, but free public schools for the sons and daughters of farmers, businessmen, professionals, and the rest of society.[3]

Mann intended common schools to teach the knowledge and habits, as well as the basic literacy, that citizens needed to·function in a democracy. He envisioned the common school as the "great equalizer" and the "creator of wealth undreamed of" and hoped it would eliminate poverty and crime and shape the destiny of a wise, productive country. Like other modern thinkers of the day, Mann believed that social improvement would follow from advances in knowledge and that schooling would extend individual rights and liberties to all.

Mann's ideal of the common school has never been fully realized. Prior to the Civil War, laws in most Southern states forbade the education of slaves. Following the brief Reconstruction period following the war in which schools were opened to freed blacks in the South, the U.S. Supreme Court decision in the *Plessy v. Ferguson* case permitting "separate, but equal" public facilities led to a wave of "Jim Crow" laws establishing dual school systems—one white and one black—throughout the South. It was not until the 1954 *Brown v. Board of Education* decision that these systems were struck down. Outside the South, racially segregated neighborhoods were nearly as effective as Jim Crow laws in creating segregated schools, and they remain so today.

Even so, Horace Mann's ideal for the common school, to advance liberty and democracy, persists. Mann would surely smile if he heard first-year teacher Sarine Gureghian discuss her efforts to teach her mostly immigrant first and second graders the rudiments of democracy.

---------------------------------------88 88 88---------------------------------------

First and second graders can affect the conditions they live in—for at least half the day. . . . Throughout the year, voting and classroom meetings provided a medium for conflict resolution. The voting was not simply a hand poll. We visited polling stations, filled out registration cards, set up polls and an ongoing voting station in our classroom; we voted on specific units to study. I did anything possible to make students realize that they have a voice.

—**SARINE GUREGHIAN**
First-year teacher, grades 1–2

Public Schools Can Preserve "American" Culture

The twentieth century brought rapid industrialization, urbanization, and immigration, all of which brought incredible new demands on public schools.[4] As newcomers flooded into the nation's cities at the end of the nineteenth century, many escaping poverty and persecution, politicians pressed teachers to "Americanize" the children of these newcomers. These new immigrants were not only coming in unprecedented numbers, they were coming from southern and eastern Europe, which made them seem much more "foreign" than earlier waves of northern European immigrants. In response, schools were asked to go beyond teaching the rudiments of citizenship and patriotism and ensure that these young people learned the habits, values, and language of the predominantly Anglo-Saxon Protestants, who considered themselves the trustees of American culture.

Americanization   The push for Americanization responded to both hopes and fears. Most immigrants were eager to learn the ways of their new country. Romantic ideas about a great melting pot suggested that the new immigration would bring a harmonious melding of cultures into a new composite. Yet, fears also abounded. Chief among them was that the Anglo Protestant values thought to be the strength and heart of the nation would be contaminated and compromised by the infusion of alien customs and languages.[5]

Immigrant Children, 1921.

These fears shaped decisions about how the newcomers should be educated. The result was an Americanization process that sought to eliminate home cultures as well as teach the new one. So, when schoolchildren first recited the Pledge of Allegiance on Columbus Day in 1892, their teachers were told to have students follow the Pledge by shouting, "One Country! One Flag! One Language!"[6] President Theodore Roosevelt argued that the United States had room for only one language, English, and urged restrictive language policies.

English Only   Many consider language as the heart of the culture, so it's not surprising that the Americanization campaigns of the early twentieth century included efforts to make clear to "threatening" immigrant groups that English was the language of the United States. Look at the "Languages Policies" timeline for an overview of language policies that have been enacted within the United States. Bilingual education in German and French had been a common practice in the nineteenth century. Yet after the arrival of Italians, Slavs, and Jews from southern Europe, Congress passed the first federal language law in 1906, requiring that those seeking to become naturalized citizens must speak English. With the U.S. entry into

EDUCATIONAL TIMELINE
Language Policies

1839	Ohio is the first state to adopt a bilingual education law, allowing German-English instruction at the parents' request.
1847	Louisiana passes a law similar to Ohio's, allowing French-English instruction.
1848	Mexico and the United States sign the Treaty of Hidalgo, giving Mexicans the right to speak Spanish in the United States. In the second half of the nineteenth century, those who had another language as their primary language were taught in public schools in a monolingual or bilingual setting.
1864	Congress prohibits Native Americans from being taught in their own languages.
1870s	William Harris, the school superintendent in St. Louis schools and later the U.S. commissioner of education, argues for bilingual education, stating that "national memories and aspirations, family traditions, customs and habits, moral and religious observances cannot be suddenly removed or changed without disastrously weakening the personality." Harris establishes the first "kindergarten" in America, taught solely in German, to give immigrant students a head start in the St. Louis schools.
1889–1891	Attempts begin to legislate against German and in favor of English. The 1889 Bennett Act in Wisconsin legislates that children ages 8 to 14 in public or private schools must be instructed in English in the "three R's" and American History. The Illinois legislature passes a similar measure known as the Edwards Act. Both laws are eventually repealed, but damage to bilingual instruction is done.
	Schools in St. Louis, Louisville, San Francisco, and St. Paul discontinue use of German.
1900	Over 15 million children are enrolled in American public schools. Between 1891 and 1900, 3.7 million new immigrants arrive in America. Thirty-three states and the District of Columbia have compulsory-education laws, heightening the issue of language instruction. At least 600,000 elementary students (about 4%) receive some part of their education in German.
1917	The United States enters World War I, spurring a wave of language restriction in schools.
1919	Fifteen more states legislate English as the basic language of instruction. Linguistic uniformity is seen as crucial to rooting out aliens and containing the "radical labor movement."
1959	A renaissance of bilingual education occurs with the arrival of Cubans flocking to Miami after the revolution. New immigrants start their own private bilingual schools and eventually establish a public bilingual school in the Miami school system.
1968	Congress passes the Bilingual Act of 1968, which gives federal funding to school districts to try to incorporate native-language instruction. Many states follow suit, enacting their own bilingual laws.

1970	Chicano students in Crystal City, Texas, demand to speak Spanish, study Chicano history, and be taught by Chicano teachers. After the political takeover of the school board, city council, and county of-fices, the school district inaugurates an unprecedented districtwide policy that calls for bilingual and bicultural education. La Raza Unida (The United People) is born from this struggle.
1974	In a class action suit on behalf of 1,800 students, 8-year-old Kenny Lau sues the San Francisco School District over English-only instruc-tion in a school where most students speak only Chinese. The Supreme Court rules in *Lau v. Nichols* that schools without special provisions to educate language-minority students are not providing equal education and violate the Civil Rights Act of 1964. The federal government publishes new materials in nearly 70 languages and allo-cates 68 million dollars for bilingual education.
1980	The Mariel boatlift brings younger and poorer Cubans to Dade Coun-try, Florida. Dade voters pass the anti-bilingual ordinance prohibiting any voluntary expenditure "for the purpose of utilizing any language other than English, or promoting any culture other than that of the U.S." The measure is repealed in 1993, but the harsh language of the ordinance exposes growing anti-immigrant sentiment.
1994	California passes Proposition 187, making it illegal for children of un-documented immigrants to attend public schools. The federal courts rule that Proposition 187 is unconstitutional.
1998	California voters overwhelmingly (61% to 39%) approve Proposition 227, an initiative that eliminates the state's bilingual education pro-grams and requires that all instruction be conducted in English.
2000	Arizona passes its version of English-only laws, Proposition 203.
2002	Colorado voters reject English-only laws.
2005	Introduced into Congress, the English Language Unity Act of 2005 would require the U.S. government to conduct official business in English.

World War I in 1917, language policies tightened even further. Particularly wary about the loyalty of German speakers, many states enacted English-only instruction laws, and most schools stopped teaching German. In some communities, mobs burned German textbooks.

In the post–World War II Red Scare period, suspicion about foreign languages broadened and deepened. Fifteen states adopted English-only instruction laws in 1919. Driving these new laws was the belief that linguistic uniformity would root out alien conspiracies and stem the emerging radical labor movement. For the first time, an ideological link was established between speaking "good English" and being a "good American." Across the nation, most bilingual education was ended in the 1920s.[7]

Socializing Immigrants Continues Throughout the Twentieth Century

Over the past 100 years, "Americanizing" the children of immigrants has remained part of what society expects of schools, although Americanization is no longer part of the official education vocabulary. As in earlier decades, today's schools are the focus of immigrants' hopes for becoming productive members of their new country; schools also remain the focus of considerable fear and ambivalence about immigration—pitting the principles of an equitable and welcoming society against the fear and hostility that arises out of differences. Today, once again, many Americans (including many whose families were themselves immigrants 100 years ago) perceive the newest waves of Latino immigrants as threatening "American" culture.

Bilingual education was revived in the 1960s, following the arrival of anti-Castro Cuban immigrants and, later, by the civil rights activism. The newest wave of Latino immigrants has made bilingual education controversial once again. Supporters believe in an "addititive" approach, seeking to teach children academic subjects in their native tongue, at the same time as they are learning English as a new language. Critics argue that academic instruction in a child's native language will constrain a child's ability to learn English quickly. Asserting children need to master English and the values of the dominant culture in order to succeed in America, they prefer a "sink-or-swim" approach that, they argue, will help students learn English quickly.

Led and funded by California software developer Ron Unz, the anti-bilingual organization, English for the Children, has mounted successful campaigns in California (1998's ballot Proposition 227) and in Arizona (2000's Proposition 203) to replace bilingual education with English-only instruction and attempted to do the same in Colorado in 2002 and elsewhere.

Progressive educators and critics of English-only concede that bilingual education has suffered from inadequate and sometimes ill-advised implementation and often does not live up to its promise. However, they point to powerful successes when bilingual education has been supported by adequate resources and well-trained teachers. Such educators point out that like so many reforms, bilingual education is necessary, but by itself, it is not sufficient to deliver a good education to non-English speakers.

───※ ※ ※───

Eighty percent of the students at my school are Latino, many of whom are recent immigrants or speak a language other than English at home. The other 20 percent are African American whose English is often discriminated against and devalued. There are many teachers here who believe that students should transition completely into Standard English and, in the process, divest themselves of their linguistic and cultural rights. Several students have complained about teachers who permit no talk in any language other than Standard English. One P.E. teacher publicly humiliates any student who speaks Spanish in her presence. Another veteran advised me that the only way to create a positive classroom environment is to only permit English to be spoken, even in informal small group conversations. Students report that teachers penalize their participation grades. . . . Perhaps the most pernicious aspect of this linguistic repression is that many students have internalized the negative attitudes about their native language. I began

*teaching aspiring to resist the hegemony of English in my classroom by cre-
ating an environment that supported, respected, and valued my students'
first language while developing their academic English. Were it only so easy.*

—MATTHEW EIDE
First-year teacher, high school history

While these language battles are fought out over policies that focus on language and
how it is best learned, the bilingual battles are also tied to more general and negative views about Spanish-speaking immigrants.

Public Schools Can Support the Nation's Workforce and Economy

Prior to the end of the nineteenth century, schools were not thought to have much
relevance to the nation's economy. It's hard to imagine today, but except for a few
"learned professions" (law, the ministry, etc.) that required advanced academic
training, education was not seen as preparation for work. Most jobs were learned
through apprenticeships that were completely unrelated to children's typical five
years of common schooling.

With the manufacturing boom of the early twentieth century, however, the public school took on the role of developing the "human capital" required by the new

Teaching Future Housewives.

industrial economy. Manufacturers and labor unions both asked schools to prepare students with the competencies required by modern workplaces. Thus, by the 1920s, a major role of schools was to teach both specific job skills and the dispositions (e.g., punctuality, following routines) required for factory work.

Not all students were prepared for factory work, however. Industrial employers needed immigrants socialized with the work habits and attitudes required to "fit in" as factory workers (proper deportment, punctuality, willingness to be supervised and managed) and with technical skills. This need coincided with educators' uncertainty about what kind of high school education would be appropriate for the children of the nation's new immigrants. These young people seemed so different—less capable, in fact—from those who had enrolled in secondary schools in earlier times. The traditional academic curriculum seemed a mismatch, particularly for immigrant youth. Thus, the curriculum was differentiated with tracks focused on academic work for some, and industrial (vocational) preparation for others. We describe how this differentiation has shaped students' school experiences and life changes in Chapter 8.

Vocational education aimed primarily at teaching specific job-related knowledge, skills, and attitudes. So constructed, it has been viewed as providing economic benefits both to individual students and to society. Individuals benefit as they acquire the know-how that enables them to command greater economic rewards as they participate in the labor force. Society benefits by having an accessible pool of skilled workers prepared to maximize production, profits, and consumer purchasing power.

The specific tasks that schools have undertaken to serve the economy have changed over time. But the link for individuals between schooling and work has grown increasingly tight, as has the view that the nation's economic health is tied to the quality of the public schools.

So, for example, when the Great Depression in the 1930s made jobs scarce, students began staying in school longer. However, when the once-easy transition from vocational classes to factory jobs disappeared, the conservative response was to cut back on educational spending. As the supply of workers outstripped demand, programs considered frivolous—including vocational education—were dropped.

Political progressives and many educators, on the other hand, banded together to place schools at the forefront of economic reform. These "social reconstructionists" wanted schools to help create a new social and economic order, one that would reduce income inequalities and free the nation from the threat of economic collapse. Educators added social studies courses to the curriculum—some with quite explicit attacks on capitalism—hoping that these courses might prepare students to tackle the social and economic problems of the time.

Whereas many progressive labor groups and social reformers supported these midcentury efforts, conservative political interests and business objected to what they saw as a blatant effort to undermine the free-market economy by indoctrinating students with socialist ideas. The two sides parted company over their views about how schools should connect students to the economy, although neither side doubted that control of the common school was key to shaping the nation's economic life.

As the twentieth century progressed, the expectation continued that schools would prepare young people for work and a strong public school system would make the nation's economy strong. By the end of the century the schools' success in this domain became linked with the nation's international standing, in terms of national security and economic competitiveness.

Public Schools Can Ensure National Security

It was not until midcentury that even a majority of students graduated from high school. But by the 1950s a 12-year education was an important public policy objective. Then, in 1957, when Russia launched the first space satellite, Sputnik, the actual content of those 12 years of school became a national concern. The press and politicians, anxious about falling behind the Russians, lambasted the flabby academic courses in American high schools and thrust upon teachers the job of developing the nation's capacity in science and mathematics to support cold war space and defense technology. As we describe in Chapter 4, the 1960s brought significant curriculum reform, including an overhaul of science and mathematics teaching.[8]

Unquestionably, American schools demanded too little from all its students in the decades before 1957. However, in the crisis of the moment, most critics neglected to see or note that America's universities were the envy of the world, and America's elite (white and wealthy) high schools were producing the best and finest students anywhere. Where it was willing to place its priorities and resources, America was perfectly capable of turning students into well-educated citizens with world-class science and mathematics skills. In fact, the *least* likely explanation for America's lagging in space exploration was that America had too few smart scientists.

Nevertheless, once schools were blamed for the nation's second-place status in the international space race and asked to upgrade the nation's scientific expertise, policymakers and educators swung into action to live up to the new expectations society had for schools. Since the 1960s schools have continued to be blamed for not being academically rigorous enough, with dire societal consequences, and educators continue to seek to meet higher and higher academic expectations. As we describe more in Chapter 3 and 11, we see these dynamics today in federal and state legislation that holds schools accountable for having all of their students meet high academic standards.

Public Schools Can Solve Social Problems

Since the beginning of the twentieth century American society has also expected public schools to help solve social problems associated with poverty, racism, inequality, urban decay, and the cultural unrest those conditions often bring. For example, the press for lengthening the number of compulsory schooling years came, in part, from a need to solve the social problem of youngsters roaming footloose on city streets during parents' long factory hours, as well as from the perception that preparation for adulthood in an industrialized society required more education.

Over the century, schools have been asked to solve other social problems. The National Association for the Advancement of Colored People (NAACP) saw the

Veazy, Greene County, Georgia.
The One-Teacher Negro School in Veazy, South of Greensboro.

public schools as the institution most likely to undo Jim Crow segregation laws that had legalized racial segregation following the Civil War. The schools were the focus of lawsuits over unequal teachers' pay in southern states and, eventually, over the constitutionality of racial segregation itself.[9]

In the 1960s and 1970s these expectations increased. The 1960s federal War on Poverty legislation specified funding for "categorical" programs (special programs targeted to particular types of students). These programs and other legislation that followed them set particular categories of students in national policy by providing financial incentives for identifying and labeling students in particular ways. Title I of the historic Elementary and Secondary Education Act (ESEA) of 1965, for example, provided categorical funding for "educationally deprived" students. Congress saw these students as needing more academic help (most often remedial) than their local schools were currently providing to compensate for the students' impoverished backgrounds.

School boycotts and other protests by Hispanic students and communities in the 1960s led Congress to pass the Bilingual Education Act in 1968, supporting programs advancing Hispanic culture and language for Spanish-speaking students. In 1974 *Lau v. Nichols*—a suit brought on behalf of non-English-speaking Chinese students in San Francisco—required that *all* schools give special assistance to their students whose native language is not English.

By the 1970s, advocacy groups and new legislation increasingly demanded services for students whose learning disabilities were attributable to neurological problems. Advocates argued that these students needed help that was different and separate from low achievers whose troubles were thought to result from cultural or economic disadvantage. In 1975, after a series of court decisions ruled that disabled students have the right to a suitable free education, Congress passed the Education of All Handicapped Children Act (PL 94-142). The Act (which became the Individuals with Disabilities Education Act in 1997) requires schools to provide a "free and appropriate" education to all students with mental retardation; learning disability; impaired hearing or vision; or speech, emotional, or physical difficulties.

Even as the demands on schools grew, politicians and the public had little appetite for addressing the social and economic inequalities outside of school that underlay the problems schools were expected to solve. Some interpreted the continued problems related to race and poverty as evidence that the 1960s and 1970s reforms that brought money and programs to bear on the problems had failed. For example, conservative economist Charles Murray argued in his best-selling book *Losing Ground* that these efforts, rather than helping, had created an unhealthy dependence on government assistance, had eroded families, and had undermined individual effort.

Bolstered by this new line of thinking, the Reagan and Bush administrations of the 1980s shifted course, declaring that the government would no longer "throw money" at correcting the social conditions that had appeared to give rise to social problems and poor school performance. Under the new conservative approach, schools were not to abandon their responsibility for solving social problems, but they were to approach these problems in ways that were consistent with a conservative ideology. A values-based approach, conservatives argued, would restore the moral base to community and family life and enable individuals to solve their own problems. Schools were to emphasize "character education" and teaching "traditional" values, such as sexual abstinence outside marriage, disdain for welfare, exercise of will over the temptation of drugs, hard work, respect for public institutions, traditional definitions of marriage, and so on.

In the early 2000s, the second Bush administration has continued this conservative approach to engaging the schools in solving social problems. With the 2001 passage of the federal No Child Left Behind Act, poverty and racism are no longer considered "excuses" that make low achievement acceptable. The prevailing ideology argued that schools could help the nation overcome the problems of poverty and racism best by teaching all children to reach high academic standards. We will have more to say about this approach in Chapter 3.

Public Schools Can Boost International Competitiveness

In 1983 a government-commissioned report, *A Nation at Risk*, blamed public schools for the faltering U.S. economy and reeling national self-esteem. Arguing that America's education system was "being eroded by a rising tide of mediocrity that threatens our very future as a Nation and a people,"[10] *A Nation at Risk* called for increases in academic courses taken by all high school students—four years of

English, and three years each of social studies, science, and mathematics—and it added computer literacy as a "new basic." In 1991 the Secretary of Labor's Commission on Achieving Necessary Skills specified what graduates need to succeed in the labor market and to enhance the nation's economic competitiveness in the tight global market. These workplace skills closely matched those advanced in *A Nation at Risk,* and policymakers and educators increasingly saw workplace preparation and intellectual development as complementary components of common schooling.

President Clinton elaborated and extended this definition of a competitive American common school. The Clinton-sponsored *Goals 2000: Educate America Act* passed by Congress in 1994 specified that all students will leave grade 12 "having demonstrated competency over challenging subject matter including English, mathematics, science, foreign languages, civics and government, economics, the arts, history, and geography." It decreed that every school must ensure that all students learn to use their minds well, so they may be "prepared for responsible citizenship, further learning, and productive employment in our nation's modern economy." With much opposition, the Act funded the development of academic standards in a whole range of subject areas that specify what all students need to live and work in the twenty-first century.

As we elaborate in Chapters 3 and 4, the current federal No Child Left Behind Act both continues this standards-based approach to schooling, adding to it stringent accountability measures that sanction schools where all children fail to meet the standards.

A Culture of Powerful Ideologies

Today's educational policies and practices embody the various ways policymakers and educators have attempted to satisfy the ever-increasing expectations for public schools. Historians and social theorists argue that the policies and practices selected as the "best" way to satisfy those expectations did not result from either a rational, neutral weighing of all the options or by chance. Rather, these decisions reflect prevailing American ideologies that, over time, shape what the nation considers to be sensible schooling policies and practices.

The term "ideology" can be defined as the collection of ideas that a society takes as common sense. These ideas are so thoroughly accepted that alternative ways to view the world usually remain invisible to most people within the society. This dominant ideology appears as "neutral," while all others that differ from the norm are often seen as radical. Political analysts often use the term "ideology" to mean a self-serving interpretation of reality that powerful groups in societies use to make their dominance seem legitimate and that preserves social cohesion in face of clear inequalities. For an ideology to "work," both the powerful and those without power must believe that the distribution of power (and the benefits that result from power) is legitimate or inevitable.

As we describe next, contemporary social theorists argue that Americans have constructed a mix of ideologies that both support and undermine their commitment to diverse and equitable public schooling. These ideologies, taken together, help explain why, despite Americans' strong commitment to democracy and wish for all children to prosper, our society establishes social structures and practices that create and perpetuate the inequalities described in Chapter 1.

We explore two related ideologies that characterize American culture and schooling's enactment of that culture. Deeply held assumptions about merit and white superiority provide powerful "explanations" about how American society works. On the one hand, we Americans proclaim openly and with great pride that our culture is meritocratic. On the other hand, we seldom notice, rarely speak about, and often deny that being white in America carries with it cultural privileges that others don't enjoy. As we explore these ideologies, we revisit the historical moments already discussed that triggered ever-increasing expectations for schools. The lenses of social theory and social research illuminate how these cultural assumptions shaped the way schools met those expectations. What becomes clear is that these ideologies constrain society and schools from realizing their democratic possibilities.

The Myth of Merit: "Any Child Can Grow Up to Be President"

Historically, Western societies distributed wealth and privilege according to how close one was to an elite or ruling class. Prior to the surge of democratic thinking in the seventeenth century, royalty, church leadership, landowners, and wealthy merchants managed to have more wealth and privilege than artisans, peasants, and slaves. Not everyone thought it was fair, but few with power apologized or felt they had to justify it. A central dilemma of modern and more egalitarian societies is how to explain disparities in wealth and privilege.

Since the colonial period one source of enormous national pride has been that Americans, unlike their more aristocratic European cousins, forged a fair culture in which individual ability and determination, rather than wealth or personal connections, hold the key to success and upward mobility. The earliest American conception of merit was based on Calvinist and Puritan religious ideas. According to these views, those favored by God were prosperous and those not favored had less. Conversely, being poor was a sign of not being favored by God. Another explanation important from the earliest days was that hard work and ambition determined who deserves wealth and social advantage. Again, the unsuccessful could be seen as having less of these qualities.

Throughout our history, the United States has considered itself a "meritocracy"—merit has given moral legitimacy to what might otherwise appear as unfair or undemocratic and explains why some citizens and their children are so well off while others have so little. It also holds out the promise that wealth and power are available to anyone who marshals sufficient determination and hard work. This is what Swedish economist Gunnar Myrdal called the "American Creed" after his study of race in America in the 1940s.[11]

However, contemporary social theorists have cast considerable doubt on the idea of American meritocracy. Jay McLeod describes what he considers to be the *myth* of merit in his book, *Ain't No Makin' It*, which tells the story of the hopes and disappointments of young men growing up in a low-income neighborhood. As McLeod puts it:

> "Any child can grow up to be President." So says the achievement ideology, the reigning social perspective that sees American society as open and fair and full of opportunity. In this view, success is based on merit, and economic inequality is due to differences in ambition and ability. Individuals do not inherit their social status; they attain it on their own. Since education insures equality of opportunity, the ladder of social mobility is there for all to climb. A favorite Hollywood theme, the rags-to-riches story resonates in the psyche of the American people. We never tire of hearing about Andrew Carnegie, for his experience validates much that we hold dear about America, the land of opportunity. Horatio Alger's accounts of the spectacular mobility achieved by men of humble origins through their own unremitting efforts occupy a treasured place in our folklore. The American Dream is held out as a genuine prospect for anyone with the drive to achieve it.[12]

McLeod, of course, notes that "for every Andrew Carnegie" there are uncountable hardworking and able others who fare much less well, and that most Americans wind up in positions similar to their parents.

Ambition and Hard Work Matter, But So Does Inequality   Like most myths, the myth of merit draws its strength from the grain of truth embedded in it. All other things being equal, the more ambitious and hardworking may well go farther than those who simply do okay in school. As we discuss more in Chapter 5, effort and persistence are hugely important to children's school achievement.

The problem with the myth of merit is that it presumes a basic equality of opportunity and resources for success, and that the *only* variable is that of individual merit. However, as we saw in Chapter 1, all other things are not equal. The United States is plagued by inequalities, such as disparities in safe neighborhoods, decent housing, adequate health care, and sufficient school resources; many of these inequalities are in domains that affect children's success in school.

Notably, even the most meritorious schoolchildren have very little control over these structural inequalities. So, although meritorious qualities occur with no less frequency in low-income families and among blacks, Latinos, and immigrants, inequality limits the degree to which members of these groups can parlay qualities like determination and hard work into school success and enhanced life chances. Children's schooling opportunities and achievement in school tend to both mirror and prepare them for the social and economic standing of their parents. What the myth of merit masks is that schooling, within the broad social structure, nearly always favors children from privileged families.[13]

The Civil Rights Movement and the War on Poverty Sought to Repair Meritocracy   Inequalities related to race and social class persist in society and in schools, as the data in Chapter 1 demonstrate so clearly. This comes as a surprise to many Americans who believe that the social reforms of the civil rights movement in the 1960s and the War on Poverty in the 1970s removed the barriers to racial equality and instituted programs that alleviated the worst poverty. As we describe in the following paragraphs, Americans did accomplish significant political gains for African Americans and a strengthened social safety net for poor people, but neither of these eras eradicated the structural problems or the ideologies that underlie inequalities in educational and life opportunity. Moreover, many of the gains achieved during the 1960s and 1970s have been rolled back during the past 25 years.

The post–World War II period was one in which Americans were extraordinarily confident about the goodness of their democracy. Although these years were filled with unsettling discord, including the start of the cold war, America's McCarthy-era political repression, and the Korean War, this was also a time of unprecedented prosperity, growth, and optimism. The nation was in an undisputed position of political and economic world dominance. The dark days of the Great Depression were over, and, many thought that the abject poverty of that period would never be seen again. This was also a period of optimism for those who believed, with Gunnar Myrdal, that racism was an aberration that could and should be removed from the otherwise equitable society.[14] The 1954 *Brown v. Board of Education* enabled those who saw themselves as fair-minded to feel satisfied that any residue of racial prejudice was being addressed.

Given the optimism of the 1950s, most Americans were shocked in 1962 when Michael Harrington's influential book *The Other America: Poverty in the United States* documented a huge underclass of unemployed and working poor.[15] How could it be that such a large segment of society simply did not "earn" better conditions? Harrington argued that this underclass, contrary to popular view, was not an artifact of temporary economic conditions. Rather, increasing numbers of people were locked into lifelong and intergenerational webs of poor education, housing, nutrition and health care, and more. Similar revelations were occurring around race. In reality, by the 1960s the nation had made little progress toward a desegregated society.[16]

Many who read Harrington's revelations were favorably disposed to social action to right the obvious wrongs. Civil rights activism was also gaining support in the American mainstream. By the mid-1960s, it had become clear that regardless of their merit, some people could never overcome the disadvantages with which they began. It was as if they were playing on a field tilted in their opponents' favor—they might kick or throw farther and run faster, but their efforts reaped fewer positive results because the work was all uphill. It was time to fix what ailed the country—to repair the ideology of merit.

Inequalities associated with gender, social class, and age began to shape the social conscience and enrich the climate of social change. Women took stock of their lack of opportunity, their silenced perspectives, their physical domination, their lower wages, and more. College students reacted to what seemed to be a hypocritical gap between their lessons in democracy and the limits that college campuses placed on their free speech. When the student protesters wouldn't back down, they were both confused and energized by the power and force that their college administrators and state governors brought against them. Television viewers were horrified when nightly news programs exposed the dramatic violence of racism and, later, the horrible carnage of the Vietnam War. Nothing in most Americans' experience and little in our national rhetoric prepared the nation to witness how abusive some Americans with power could be. The American social fabric seemed to be disintegrating, and with it, the notion that Americans get what they deserve.

From the mid-1960s until 1980, the federal government pursued social policies designed to make the playing field level. Civil rights activism following the *Brown* decision and War on Poverty legislation sought to remedy the hunger, inadequate housing, and discrimination that diminish the power of ambition, effort, and school achievement. As we've already noted, schools were expected to do much of this work, and a number of measures aimed directly at creating equal educational opportunity and making schools more powerful for disadvantaged children.

These actions paid off. The civil rights movement brought significant political gains, particularly in voting rights. The War on Poverty slowed the widening gap between rich and poor—if only briefly. Programs fed hungry children and provided important learning experiences.

However, these advances barely scratched the surface of the problems of racism and poverty. The 1954 *Brown v. Board of Education* Supreme Court decision may have overturned the *Plessy* decision, ruling that separate is inherently unequal, and ordered schools to desegregate with "all deliberate speed." However, the initial promise *Brown* held for equal opportunity has never been realized. Today, as we described in Chapter 1, black students in the United States remain nearly as racially isolated as before *Brown,* and Latino racial isolation increases steadily. Just as good people look back at the pre-*Brown* days and are angered that a society would allow segregated and unequal schools, that cause for anger remains today.

The impact of the ambitious War on Poverty was also limited. The country lacked experience and expertise in formulating and administering antipoverty programs and equity-minded interventions, and national politics allowed little room for error. When programs faltered or needed reworking, skeptics judged them as failures. Most pernicious of all, many well-off Americans saw "the problem" as poor people themselves rather than the social and economic conditions that made them poor. The country was not prepared to concede that larger social and economic structures, including schools, had to change fundamentally, and that the necessary changes would be costly and difficult.[17]

The Myth of Merit Still Makes Inequality Acceptable   Today, many look back on this short-lived but significant national effort on behalf of African Americans and the poor and interpret its disappointing results using the myth of merit. Some conclude that, if racial minorities and the poor did not lift themselves with the aid of new political opportunities and social programs, then the fault lies with them and with their misguided helpers. Others use the ideology of merit to invoke the argument that, because some African Americans and Latinos achieve stellar successes in school despite the combined burdens of racism and poverty, all have had the opportunity to do so.[18]

Thus, a theoretically possible outcome—hammered home by highly touted examples—obscures what is actually possible for most children. For every Colin Powell, former general and secretary of state, there are thousands of black and Latino men and women whose success and achievements have been diminished by racial and meritocratic thinking. It strains credibility, however, to suggest that the few who manage to succeed under unlikely or miserable conditions are evidence that *anyone* can succeed, and if they do not, it is their own fault. Yet that's exactly where the myth of merit leads.

Why does our culture support the convoluted logic that failure to "overcome" poverty or inferior education proves a lack of merit? The answer may be that people prefer believing that their own wealth stands on a moral platform of merit. Also, like many ideologies, the myth of merit depends on *everyone* believing in the myth just as strongly as those who benefit from it. Many poor and nonwhite Americans also believe schooling benefits are equally accessible to all. Students with dismal schooling experiences typically blame their own lack of ability, effort, or failure to take advantage of opportunities. Describing "the Brothers"—the young African Americans he studied—Jay McLeod put it this way:

> They blame themselves for their mediocre academic performances because they are unaware of the discriminatory influences of tracking, the school's partiality toward the cultural capital of the upper classes, the self-fulfilling consequences of teachers' expectations, and other forms of class-based educational selection. Conditioned by the achievement ideology to think that good jobs require high academic attainment, the Brothers may temper their high aspirations, believing not that the institution of school and the job market have failed them, but that they have failed themselves.[19]

In sum, merit permeates how Americans make sense about schooling—emphasizing the role of the individual, and de-emphasizing the responsibilities of school or society.

Deficit Thinking and White Privilege

—————————————————————————❃ ❃ ❃—————————————————————————

Prior to the first day of school, I had already been told that "these kids are low," and not to worry if the students did not do as well as I hoped because "the entire school is low overall."

—Rosalinda Perez Silva
First-year teacher, grade 1

Rosalinda Silva, who teaches a class of twenty 6- and 7-year-olds in a Spanish-speaking immigrant neighborhood, says that her young students are "brilliantly intelligent" but "already struggling." Certainly, a large part of their struggle is to overcome the judgments teachers have already made about them.

The judgments Silva reports reflect powerful cultural assumptions that young Americans who are not white and middle class come to school with deficits that make their school success extremely difficult, if not impossible. The other side of the coin of deficit thinking is white privilege. White Americans enjoy a set of cultural privileges that are largely unrecognized. The privileges that come with being white allow children to learn and develop unhampered by the vulnerabilities associated with being not white—for example, the negative judgments that Rosalinda Silva's students must struggle against. White privilege allows the most powerful Americans to believe that their ways of knowing and being in the world represent intelligence and merit, and, therefore, they deserve the disproportionate school and life advantages they enjoy.

As we explain in what follows, deficit thinking and white privilege help explain why our culture is far less meritocratic than Americans would like to believe.

A History of Deficit Thinking   From the earliest colonial times, many Americans identified their prosperity with confiscated land and slave labor. Annihilation of Indians and the African slave trade were justified both on economic grounds and biblical explanations of white superiority. After the mid–eighteenth century, a new group of modern natural scientists—craniologists—offered empirical evidence, arguing that white superiority rested on racial differences in skull size, with the larger skulls of Caucasians proving their greater capacities.

When he studied American society in the 1830s, French intellectual Alexis de Tocqueville noted, "The same schools do not receive the children of the black and European."[20] Widespread agreement about the moral and intellectual deficiencies of nonwhites justified denying them citizenship and prohibiting nonwhite landowners from passing property on to their heirs. Many Southern communities had passed "compulsory ignorance" laws that banned schooling for slaves. Communities in the North established segregated schools because it was simply unimaginable that white children could be safe from sexual and other physical threats and moral corruption. Thus, by the time Horace Mann described his vision for a common public school, the country already had deep traditions that allowed the government to limit those it would include in the collection of persons called the "public."

As the nation expanded westward, new groups were added to the American racial hierarchy, and from time to time groups would be reclassified. Whites migrating to the Southwest judged Mexicans to be "half-civilized" (in comparison to the uncivilized Indians) but "white," due to their Spanish language, Catholicism, and the presence of a property-owning elite that bespoke European as well as Indian heritage. On the other hand, Asian men, imported in the late nineteenth century to build California's railroads and work its mines and farms, joined the ranks of the black slave laborers brought from the American South and were disdained for their strange customs, "pagan" religions, and incomprehensible language.

In the mid–nineteenth century, a California court classified the Chinese as Indians and, therefore, "nonwhite." By this time, Darwin's *Origins of Species* had established that all races were human. However, it had also spawned a group of less reputable "social Darwinists" who advanced theories that whites were a more highly evolved, cognitively superior, race. These theories were used to support the segregation of nonwhites. Even after the abolition of slavery, most white Americans viewed African Americans as inferior and supported racial segregation.

Although the U.S. government had declared in 1868 that "compulsory ignorance" laws were illegal and native-born nonwhites were citizens, the states could choose whether or not to fund schools for nonwhite children. Many did not, and it was not until 1910 that the majority of black children attended school. The majority of Mexican, Asian, and Indian children did not attend school until 1920, and after that time most racial minorities attended segregated schools.

The misapplication of Darwin's evolutionary theories to cultural as well as racial groups confirmed for many that immigrant students were less socially and morally developed. The superintendent of the Boston schools warned in 1889: "Many of these children come from homes of vice and crime. In their blood are generations of iniquity. . . . They hate restraint or obedience to the law."[21] Because these immigrants came from different parts of Europe than previous waves, racial and religious prejudices were typically at the core of these worries. Prominent educator Ellwood Cubberly wrote in 1909: "These southern and eastern Europeans are of a very different type from the north Europeans who preceded them. Illiterate, docile, lacking in self-reliance and initiative, and not possessing the Anglo-Teutonic conceptions of law, order, and government, their coming has served to dilute tremendously our national stock, and to corrupt our civic life."[22]

Although many considered these unfortunate attributes biological, and therefore unchangeable, reformers hoped that schooling could turn immigrant children toward more constructive ways. In Cubberly's words, "Our task is to . . . assimilate and amalgamate these people as a part of our American race and to implant in their children, as far as can be done, the Anglo-Saxon conception of righteousness, law and order."[23]

Psychologist G. Stanley Hall's theories also played a powerful role in shaping deficit thinking about immigrants. Hall's notion that children's development followed that of the entire race—that is, from presavagery as infants to civilization as adults—included the argument that environments such as neighborhood and school profoundly influenced this development. The unstable and corrupting environments in city neighborhoods pressed individuals toward depravity. Especially vulnerable were children and adolescents—whom Hall described as being at the developmental stage of savage, vagrant, and nomadic life. Unless adolescents were in homes where "industry, intelligence and thrift prevail, where books and magazines abound, where the library table forms the center of an interested group, where refinement of thought and life prevail," they would surely fall into delinquency and moral depravity.[24]

As children of color and from southern and eastern European immigrant families began attending school in larger and larger numbers, a new "science" of intelligence began offering theories and data that provided seemingly scientific evidence that they had mental deficits that would limit their school achievement. Psychologist Richard Valencia has traced the links between tests, test bias, and widely held conceptions of cultural deficits in students of color.[25]

Among the most well known of those developing the science of intelligence was Lewis Terman, a professor at Stanford University, who developed and promoted intelligence tests for U.S. schoolchildren. Although Terman purported that his IQ tests measured innate abilities, the following items taken from one section of his test make clear that children from educated, culturally mainstream families were more likely to earn high IQs[26]:

   4. Most exports go from
      Boston San Francisco New Orleans New York
   9. Larceny is a term used in
      Medicine Theology Law Pedagogy
  16. A character in *David Copperfield* is
      Sinbad Uriah Heep Rebecca Hamlet

Because children from nonwhite and poor families scored lower than more socially advantaged ones, Terman used his IQ test results to confirm his view that heredity determined intelligence. He also used the test results to support his advocacy of low-level schooling for those who tested poorly as well as population control among the feebleminded. After testing a group of boys who lived in an orphanage, Terman wrote:

> The tests have told the truth. These boys are ineducable beyond the merest rudiments of training. No amount of school instruction will ever make them intelligent voters or capable citizens. . . . Their dullness seems to be racial, or at least inherent in the family stocks from which they came. . . . [O]ne meets this type with such extraordinary frequency among Indians, Mexicans and Negroes. . . . Children of this group should be segregated in special classes and be given instruction which is concrete and practical. . . . There is no possibility at present of convincing society that they should not be allowed to reproduce, although from a eugenic point of view they constitute a grave problem because of their unusually prolific breeding.[27]

Although IQ tests were periodically modified after the 1920s, they would continue to support deficit views similar to Terman's.

The second half of the twentieth century brought significant structural changes that could have altered deficit thinking about Americans who are not white. The 1954 Brown decision overturned laws that separated children in school by race, and the *Lau v. Nichols* decision in 1974 set forth the constitutional requirement that equal educational opportunity demanded that schools must offer help for students unable to understand English.

However, neither these decisions nor the considerable legislation meant to make schools more respectful and inclusive of students of color and immigrants eradicated the deficit ideologies that perpetuate discrimination and disadvantage. The norms and informal practices that keep most neighborhoods and schools segregated and sustain the disparities in prosperity and political among racial and linguistic groups persist.

Mauro Bautista, one of the teachers portrayed in Chapter 1 and in the rest of this book, is committed to turning his firsthand experience with deficit thinking into teaching that defies it.

———————————————————— ⊗ ⊗ ⊗ ————————————————————

I am living one of my life goals by teaching in the neighborhood where I grew up, went to school, and still live. In 1982, my parents and I immigrated into East Los Angeles from Mexico. Unfortunately, I am only one of a handful of students from urban immigrant communities who have the opportunity to pursue higher education. Many teachers and scholars contend that minorities occupy an inferior economic, social, and political status because of some deficiency within the minority groups themselves. As a social justice educator, I want to challenge deficit thinking. I want to challenge the traditional educational practice of holding low expectations of underrepresented students. I expect my students not only to survive in this country, but also to

excel. My students have high career goals and, therefore, I expect them to at
least have the option to attend a higher learning institution in order to pur-
sue those goals. My students' parents also have high expectations of their
children and are interested in their education.

—**MAURO BAUTISTA**
Middle-school bilingual education coordinator

Today's Deficit Thinking about Race   In 1994, just two months after its publication, *The Bell Curve: Intelligence and Class Structure in American Life* had
400,000 copies in print. Richard Herrnstein and Charles Murray's best-selling book
claimed to offer scientific proof that African Americans inherit lower IQs than white
Americans and that these IQ differences are virtually impossible to change. Put
bluntly, Herrnstein and Murray state that the average African American is less well
educated and less wealthy than the average white because he or she is not born with
the capacity to be as smart. Therefore, the authors also claim, social programs that
attempt to close opportunity gaps—programs such as Head Start, compensatory
education, and affirmative action—are costly and useless. They argue that (1) the
programs hurt those people they are intended to help by steering them away from
the lower-level aspirations and occupations that suit their abilities and (2) such programs harm society because they give less intelligent people access to social positions that require greater aptitude. The authors, well-known academics from prestigious universities, bolstered these claims with impressive-looking charts, graphs,
and statistics in their 800-plus-page book.

The *Bell Curve* has profound implications for schools and teaching. It argues
that Americans need to face the reality that "in a universal education system, many
students will not reach the level of education that most people view as basic."
Moreover, according to the authors, efforts to teach groups of children with low IQs
(disproportionately, disadvantaged children of color) more than the most modest
skills will benefit neither those children nor society. Rather, government and educators should shift most of their teaching resources and efforts from the disadvantaged to the intellectually gifted.

Readers of *The Bell Curve* and of the countless magazine and journal reviews
that followed its publication, as well as listeners to TV talk shows and radio call-in
programs about the book, were frightened and enraged. Those who liked the book
were angry because it confirmed their political views about the futility (or worse) of
social programs that aimed at improving the life chances of Americans of color.
People who disagreed were furious because they found the book dishonest, unscientific, and morally offensive.

A book such as *The Bell Curve* appears every few decades or oftener. In 1969
Harvard psychologist Arthur Jensen argued that because national poverty programs
did not appreciably raise children's IQs, children of the poor must be genetically intellectually inferior. Physicist William Shockley reemerged years after co-inventing
the transistor to bring the authority of his scientific credentials to a proposal for re-
imbursing voluntarily sterilized individuals according to their number of IQ points
below 100. What is notable here is the instant popularity of such views. The findings

in these reports made front-page headlines, and they gave eager readers permission to speak aloud their previously private convictions about race and the poor.

Even the most fair-minded teachers did not realize the extent to which *The Bell Curve's* old-fashioned, inaccurate (at best), and racist perspectives were present in the minds and hearts of their fellow Americans, including many of their colleagues at school. Respected scholars instantly refuted the books and reports, but they were consigned to smaller pieces on the editorial pages and to magazines and journals with smaller audiences than television or newspapers.

The theories of race and intelligence that are embedded in *The Bell Curve,* sadly, are alive and well in today's schools. These are not neutral and objective scientific discoveries. Rather, they reflect the beliefs and values of the times and of the Western and American cultures in which they develop. Supported by prevailing racial ideologies, the theories that gain acceptance most quickly and easily nearly always serve the interests of powerful people of the period.

Today's Deficit Thinking about Language   In the past two decades, a growing "English-only" movement has warned that the nation's dominant language is endangered by the encroachment of other languages. The movement's campaign for legal protections for English has resulted in successful "official English" measures in 23 states. The federal government has considered, but has not passed, measures that would make English the federal government's sole language of official business.

James Crawford, longtime analyst of language policy issues and current director of the National Association for Bilingual Education, offers a penetrating analysis of the current deficit thinking about non-English-speaking Americans. Finding no evidence that those in the English-only movement share the ideology of racial extremists—Nazis, for example—he is more troubled by the fact that anti-bilingualism has become a mainstream phenomenon. This mainstream support, according to Crawford, "rests on the absurd claim that the most successful and dominant world language in history is under siege in its strongest bastion."[28]

Crawford argues that, rather than being about language per se, the aversion to non-English-speaking immigrants reveals conflicts over cultural and material supremacy—that is, struggles for social and economic dominance—that lie beneath the surface of the public debate over language. The stakes involved are not merely the cultural symbolism of language, but also resources, power, and status. Crawford's view is that the contemporary English-only movement stems from a determination to resist racial and cultural diversity in the United States and dates from 1983, when former Senator S. I. Hayakawa of California founded *U.S. English.* He argues that language is simply the most respectable basis on which to control the potential cultural degradation from the influx of Latino immigrants whose other deficits include the failure to use birth control, lack of concern for the environment and low "educability." Objections to language mask less readily admitted fears about fundamental deficits in non-English speaking immigrants—a propensity for crime, welfare dependency, and competition for scarce jobs.[29]

White Privilege   In 1988, Peggy McIntosh wrote an essay drawing parallels between what she called "white privilege" and the "male privilege" that she had studied as a professor of women's studies at Wellesley College. In it she recounts her realization that being white brings with it considerable advantages that she had always taken for granted as simply normal features of her life. McIntosh wrote:

> As a white person, I realized I had been taught about racism as something that puts others at a disadvantage, but had been taught not to see one of its corollary aspects, white privilege, which puts me at an advantage.
>
> I think whites are carefully taught not to recognize white privilege. . . . So I have begun in an untutored way to ask what it is like to have white privilege. I have come to see white privilege as an invisible package of unearned assets that I can count on cashing in each day, but about which I was "meant" to remain oblivious. White privilege is like an invisible weightless knapsack of special provisions, maps, passports, codebooks, visas, clothes, tools, and blank checks.[30]

McIntosh made a list of 50 everyday privileges she believes come with the color of her skin. She notes some of the items on her list are "what one would want for everyone in a just society," but that others allow whites to be "ignorant, oblivious, arrogant, and destructive." See Focal Point 2.1 for a selection of her 50 privileges.

McIntosh relates how her recognition of these racial privileges undermines the notion of the United States as a meritocratic society.

> For me white privilege has turned out to be an elusive and fugitive subject. The pressure to avoid it is great, for in facing it I must give up the myth of meritocracy. If these things are true, this is not such a free country; one's life is not what one makes it; many doors open for certain people through no virtues of their own.

Notably, McIntosh realized that these privileges are structural, not simply a matter of individual prejudice. She also understands just how hard such structural arrangements of privilege are to change.

> In my class and place, I did not see myself as a racist because I was taught to recognize racism only in individual acts of meanness by members of my group, never in invisible systems conferring unsought racial dominance on my group from birth.
>
> Disapproving of the systems won't be enough to change them. I was taught to think that racism could end if white individuals changed their attitude. But a "white" skin in the United States opens many doors for whites whether or not we approve of the way dominance has been conferred on us. Individual acts can palliate but cannot end, these problems.

McIntosh's provocative observations have caught the attention of many educators seeking to explain to themselves, colleagues, and students how, decades after the end of legalized segregation and racial discrimination, race plays such a powerful cultural role in enhancing or limiting access to school and life opportunities.

Judy Smith, whom we met in Chapter 1, is one such educator. The diverse community where she teaches high school struggles with multiracial and ethnic tensions compounded by poverty-related problems with gangs, vandalism, transience, and drugs. Conscious of her own white privilege and the deficit thinking about her students of color that pervades our culture, Judy structures her teaching to make the diversity in her classroom an asset to learning, rather than a source of tension.

FOCAL POINT 2.1

The "Invisible Knapsack" of White Privilege (excerpt)

1. I can if I wish arrange to be in the company of people of my race most of the time.
2. If I should need to move, I can be pretty sure of renting or purchasing housing in an area which I can afford and in which I would want to live.
3. I can be pretty sure that my neighbors in such a location will be neutral or pleasant to me.
4. I can go shopping alone most of the time, pretty well assured that I will not be followed or harassed.
5. I can turn on the television or open to the front page of the paper and see people of my race widely represented.
6. When I am told about our national heritage or about "civilization," I am shown that people of my color made it what it is.
7. I can be sure that my children will be given curricular materials that testify to the existence of their race.
8. If I want to, I can be pretty sure of finding a publisher for this piece on white privilege.
9. I can go into a music shop and count on finding the music of my race represented, into a supermarket and find the staple foods which fit with my cultural traditions, into a hairdresser's shop and find someone who can cut my hair.
10. Whether I use checks, credit cards, or cash, I can count on my skin color not to work against the appearance of financial reliability.
11. I can arrange to protect my children most of the time from people who might not like them.
12. I can swear, or dress in secondhand clothes, or not answer letters, without having people attribute these choices to the bad morals, the poverty, or the illiteracy of my race.
13. I can speak in public to a powerful male group without putting my race on trial.
14. I can do well in a challenging situation without being called a credit to my race.
15. I am never asked to speak for all the people of my racial group.
16. I can remain oblivious of the language and customs of persons of color who constitute the world's majority without feeling in my culture any penalty for such oblivion.
17. I can criticize our government and talk about how much I fear its policies and behavior without being seen as a cultural outsider.
18. I can be pretty sure that if I ask to talk to "the person in charge," I will be facing a person of my race.
19. If a traffic cop pulls me over or if the IRS audits my tax return, I can be sure I haven't been singled out because of my race.

20. I can easily buy posters, postcards, picture books, greeting cards, dolls, toys, and children's magazines featuring people of my race.

21. I can go home from most meetings of organizations I belong to feeling somewhat tied in, rather than isolated, out of place, outnumbered, unheard, held at a distance, or feared.

22. I can take a job with an affirmative action employer without having coworkers on the job suspect that I got it because of race.

23. I can choose public accommodation without fearing that people of my race cannot get in or will be mistreated in the places I have chosen.

24. I can be sure that if I need legal or medical help, my race will not work against me.

25. If my day, week, or year is going badly, I need not ask of each negative episode or situation whether it has racial overtones.

26. I can choose blemish cover or bandages in "flesh" color and have them more or less match my skin.

※ ※ ※

The diversity of the 37 students in my first period economics class gives the class incredible energy. They represent countries such as the Philippines, Tonga, Vietnam, Hungary, Egypt, Mexico, Dominican Republic, Guatemala, Peru, and El Salvador. Although 77 percent speak another language at home (Spanish, Arabic, Hungarian, Tongan or Tagalog), approximately half speak English fluently. A quarter of the students are black, but not all are African American. Often students gravitate toward other students of the same race and heritage. Most English learners hesitate to speak in front of their peers.

As a white teacher of students of color, I am aware of white privilege, or what Peggy McIntosh calls an "invisible package of unearned assets." In my classroom, there are two power structures. Not only am I a member of the dominant culture, but I also represent authority as the teacher of the class.

To address these realities, my students and I co-construct a positive, respectful learning community. We discuss openly the benefits of a learning community where we all learn and feel respected and valued. I consciously plan lessons that include a number of activities that ensure that the students' voices and languages are heard. At times I assign heterogeneous groups, as I want to mix skill levels and races. I also encourage students to identify with each other throughout the semester.

The students provide me with the opportunity to learn more about the content, the issues that affect their lives, the truths and the impact of various societal problems, and, most important, the reason teachers teach. Together we make meaning of content, day-to-day issues, and grow as human beings.

Learning does not happen without risk-taking. I have to take risks and encourage my students to take risks. It is challenging to discuss racism, sexism, and homophobia. However, for a truly effective learning community, we must address the very topics that maintain the status quo. My students and I work together to understand the gross economic and social inequities that exist and what we can do about them.

—Judy Smith
Senior high school social studies teacher

A growing number of scholars have also begun to study "whiteness" and white supremacy in an effort to understand and improve opportunities for all Americans, in school and in society generally. One particularly interesting book, *Critical White Studies: Looking Behind the Mirror,* edited by Richard Delgado and Jean Stefancic, pulls together research and essays from scholars and thinkers. The book begins with the conclusion now shared by most scientists that race cannot be considered a valid scientific category because the genetic differences between races are insignificant compared with those within them. These writers grapple with profound cultural questions about U.S. society that people rarely ask: How was whiteness invented, and why? How has the category of whiteness changed over time? Why did some immigrant groups, such as the Irish and Jews, start out as nonwhite and later become white? Why does the "one drop" rule, whereby those with any nonwhite heritage are classified as nonwhite, persist today? Can some individual people be both white and nonwhite at different times, and what does it mean to "pass for white"? At what point does pride in being white cross the line into white supremacy? What can whites concerned over racial inequity or white privilege do about it?

Among the thought-provoking answers Delgado and Stefancic and their colleagues provide is that race is largely relational—that "whiteness" is the norm against which other races are evaluated. As a result, we can only understand what it means to be white in light of what it means to be nonwhite. So, as we have discussed here, white privilege and white superiority become important and understandable in light of the deficit thinking that Americans of color have been so routinely subjected to.

These are not simply academic issues; they affect the lives of teachers and students every day. Another of the four teachers we introduced in Chapter 1, Mark Hill, has experienced firsthand our culture's troubling thinking about race. Mark, like so many of his students, has struggled to make sense of racial categories that place whites in a privileged position and attribute deficits to people of color. His own story makes clear how limited our culture's view of race is and how limiting its effects are on the lives of many Americans.

— ⚙ ⚙ ⚙ —

When I think about culture I feel that I sit in a unique space. While it is a given that as individuals we all have a unique upbringing, I have yet to find anyone's quite as singular as my own. My family consists of myself, my twin brother and my mother and father. When my mother, who is white, married my father, who is black, her family immediately disowned her. . . .

As a person of color I am assumed to have grown up with all the typical assumptions Americans have for black people, but I have few memories of any such experiences. I grew up in a poor, racially mixed neighborhood but I was never allowed out of the house or the walled up backyard, and we never had any visitors. Thus, my cultural identity was formed almost solely based on my mother, a white Jew. I lit the candles of our menorah on Hanukkah, celebrated Rosh Shashana and am sympathetic to Israel in the Middle East conflict. . . . I am a good person and hold no biases that I am aware of, attempting to treat others as I wish to be treated.

Why do I feel guilty that I don't feel the depth of the connection with my black half as I do my white half when I take an honest appraisal of my self identity? It is through no machinations of my own that this is so, I am simply a product of my circumstances. . . . Due to the biology of genetics and the judgment of society I will not only never be white, but also will always be black.

I have found that this experience helps me to relate with all of my students. I remember as a child wanting others to "see" me the same way I saw myself. Because of this, I make a tremendous effort to "see" students as individuals and accept them on their own terms, regardless of preconceived notions of race, gender or age. This is very important for adolescents who are struggling with their identity and are looking for acceptance.

—**MARK HILL**
High school mathematics

Teaching for Democracy in a Contradictory Culture

⚜ ⚜ ⚜

The forces of inequity and democracy are perpetually in tension within our schools. . . . Ignoring the power that lies in our position as teachers, not examining our theories about children and learning, and ignoring the political dimensions of our work perpetuate in our own classrooms the social inequality that plagues our society.

—**LAURA SILVINA TORRES**
First-year teacher, grade 2

In the midst of well-justified worry, concern, and outrage about the nation's contradictory history and traditions, the twenty-first century also brings signs of an energizing hopefulness. Americans are fortunate to have a school tradition that speaks— if not always loudly and clearly—to democracy's core values, and teachers like Laura Torres help the nation keep its democratic tradition alive, as they speak out against the deficit thinking that constrains the diverse young people they teach.

Today, more teachers than ever before are listening to voices like McLeod's and McIntosh's as they seek new ways to enhance the democratic tradition. White teachers whose students are likely to be young people of color are struggling to understand how they can come to terms with the fact that racism affects their own lives, as well as those of their students. They seek to use their awareness of their own taken-for-granted white privileges and of pernicious deficit thinking to move beyond the conventional explanations that blame students, their families, and their cultures for low achievement. They seek to use their privilege responsibly as they seek to make real for their students what has been possible for themselves—being academically successful and retaining their culture, identity, and language—by increasing their knowledge and implementing a curriculum and pedagogy that have been shown to be effective with students of color. They also challenge structural policies that undermine the academic success of students of color. We describe these practices and challenges throughout this book.

We conclude with the words of Matthew Eide who, like every other teacher, has to solve the technical question "What do I teach on Monday morning?" But drawing on his understanding of the history and culture we've described in this chapter, he poses other questions for himself that will ultimately determine the success and satisfaction he finds in his lessons and his career. These are not the questions of beginning teachers but the concerns of every twenty-first-century educator wrestling with the history and traditions of American schooling.

———————————————————❧ ❧ ❧———————————————————

As a teacher, I must question everything I do. All my classroom practices must be open to a critical examination. How do issues of race, class, language, and gender influence what I do? How does my classroom resist and perpetuate the institutional racism, classism, linguicism, and sexism of education and society? I must ask myself who benefits from the structure of my class. Yet with this awareness must also come action. I must commit myself to multiculturalism and a culturally relevant pedagogy that affirms and legitimizes the language and culture of my students. I must try to create a democratic classroom, where students actively construct their own knowledge. Finally, I must be a teacher who helps students discover their possibilities and urges them to claim their role as transformative members of society.

—MATTHEW EIDE
First-year teacher, high school history

⒪ OLC Connections

Additional online and print resources and a set of questions for reflection about education history can be found at www.mhhe.com/oakes3e.

❋ Digging Deeper

To learn more about the social and educational history of schooling and schooling traditions we suggest you seek out work by the following scholars. Some are referenced in the text; others are not. They all provide highly regarded research and theory about American education.

Historical Studies of American Schooling

Raymond Callahan's classic text, *Education and the Cult of Efficiency: A Study of the Social Forces That Have Shaped the Administration of the Public Schools* (Chicago: University of Chicago Press, 1962), still stands as the best work analyzing the impact of scientific management on American public schools.

The late **Lawrence Cremin** wrote the classic history of the pivotal period of huge growth in U.S. schooling. The book, *The Transformation of the School: Progressivism in American Education 1876–1957* (New York: Knopf, 1961), contains wonderfully detailed stories about how American education moved from a small, local activity to a huge national enterprise.

Harvard University historian of education and former dean of the Graduate School of Education, **Patricia Albjerg Graham,** recently published *Schooling America: How the Public Schools Meet the Nation's Changing Needs* (Oxford: Oxford University Press, 2005). Graham's book, like this chapter, traces the history of U.S. schooling from the perspective of society's changing and escalating expectation for public schools.

Norton Grubb's and **Marvin Lazerson's** book, *The Education Gospel: The Economic Power of Schooling* (Cambridge, MA: Harvard University Press, 2005), traces the history of the expectation that schooling is the key to a prosperous economy. They argue that the knowledge and skills acquired in school, and, especially in universities, are a poor match with those required in the workplace.

Diane Ravitch, a senior fellow at the Hoover Institution and research professor at New York University, is the most prominent politically conservative educational historian writing today. Like Lawrence Cremin (above), Ravitch's work examines progressive forces in education. Two of her most widely read books are *The Troubled Crusade: American Education 1945–1980* (New York: Basic Books, 1983) and *Left Back: A Century of Failed School Reforms* (New York: Simon and Schuster, 2000).

Joel Spring is professor of educational history at Queens College (CUNY) and author of numerous educational histories. Spring's work is especially helpful for understanding how schools have worked systematically to support the social, economic, and political status quo, and how the history of peoples of color in the United States connects with educational policies and practices. Of particular interest might be *Education and the Rise of the Corporate State* (Boston: Beacon Press, 1972), *Conflict of Interests: The Politics of American Education* (New York: Longman, 1988), *The American School, 1642–1990* (New York: Longman, 1990), *Deculturation and the Struggle for Equality: A Brief History of the Education of Dominated Cultures in the United States* (New York: McGraw-Hill, 1997), and *Education and the Rise of the Global Economy* (Hillsdale, NJ: Erlbaum, 1998). Spring views the history of schooling through a progressive lens.

David Tyack, Stanford education historian, has written a number of solid and engaging historical texts. Of particular interest is his *The One Best System: A History of American Urban Education* (Cambridge, MA: Harvard University Press, 1974), a history of how modern urban schools were shaped by a coalition of civic elites, reformers, and professional school administrators. Tyack's book with

Elizabeth Hansot, *Managers of Virtue: Public School Leadership in America, 1820–1980* (New York: Basic Books, 1986), traces the goals and methods of those who have headed the schools, from the early nineteenth-century promoters of the common school to present-day urban superintendents. Finally, Tyack's book with fellow Stanford historian **Larry Cuban,** *Tinkering toward Utopia: A Century of Public School Reform* (Cambridge, MA: Harvard University Press, 1997), analyzes the failure of most twentieth-century school reforms to change the basic institutional patterns of schooling.

Web Resources on the History of American Education

The History of American Education Web Project (online at **http://www.nd. edu/~rbarger/www7/**) provides snapshots of the history of education from the perspectives of students in an undergraduate Foundations of Education class. The site includes some interesting historical photographs.

Daniel Schugurensky, professor at the University of Toronto, has assembled a website "Selected Moments of the 20th Century," online at **http://fcis.oise. utoronto.ca/~daniel_schugurensky/,** that includes short descriptions of "educational episodes" such as policy, a court case, a piece of legislation, a scholarly article, a new theory, a research report, an incident, the release of a book, a speech, an empirical finding, a conference, the opening or closing of an institution, a movie, an anecdote, or anything, big or small, that tells us something about education theory, policy, politics, research, or practice during the last century.

School: The Story of American Public Education was a four-part documentary series on public television that chronicled the development of the U.S. public education system from the late 1770s to the twenty-first century. The website of the documentary series at **http://www.pbs.org/kcet/publicschool/** contains historical material, historical photographs of educational innovators and classrooms, a description of the documentary, and resources for parents and teachers, including a curriculum guide, developed by the American Association of Colleges for Teacher Education and the ERIC Clearinghouse on Teaching and Teacher Education, to support educators and others in exploring the themes and questions raised in each episode of the series.

Scholars Examining Merit, Deficit Thinking, and White Privilege

Richard Delgado and Jean Stefancic, professors of law at the University of Pittsburgh, brought together in their book *Critical White Studies: Looking Behind the Mirror* (Temple University Press, 1997) writings from scholars in a number of disciplines about a new field of scholarship that they call "whiteness studies." The book seeks to engage both nonwhites and whites in reflecting on what it means to be white, in terms of the social, political, and economic advantages that accrue to white people because of historical and structural arrangements. The book looks at these arrangements from the perspectives of sociology, law, history, cultural studies, and literature.

Jay McLeod followed two groups of young men—one white, the "Hallway Hangers," and the other black, the "Brothers"—as they made the transition from high school to adulthood in the housing projects and schools of Clarendon Heights. McLeod's ethnography, *Ain't No Makin' It: Aspirations and Attainment in a Low-Income Neighborhood* (Boulder, CO: Westview Press, 1995), weaves a fascinating story. At the same time, it presents insightful analyses of the role of race, class, and the "achievement ideology" of schools in shaping low-income students' ambitions, effort, and life chances. Together the stories and the analysis provide a powerful critique of schools as meritocracies.

Rethinking Schools, a progressive education journal, has interviewed scholars and teachers about white privilege and how it impacts education and social equity, generally. In one interview, "Diversity vs. White Privilege" (vol. 15, no. 2 [winter 2000/2001]), California State University, Monterey Bay professor **Christine Sleeter** discusses the importance of white privilege in the history of education. Among other concepts, Sleeter stresses that multiculturalism, at its core, is a struggle against racism, and must go beyond an appreciation of diversity. In a second interview, "Confronting White Privilege," (vol. 16, no. 4 [summer 2002]), teacher **Dale Weiss** shares her own efforts to struggle against racism in her profession and her life. *Rethinking Schools* is online at http://www.rethinkingschools.org/archive/15_02/Int152.shtml.

Mike Rose, a UCLA education professor, has written two very readable and compelling books about the problems and possibilities of schools for low-income children. His first book, *Lives on the Boundary: The Struggles and Achievements of America's Underprepared* (New York: Penguin, 1990), detailed how low-achieving and minority students have been disregarded and mistreated in schools. *Possible Lives: The Promise of Public Education in America* (Boston: Houghton Mifflin, 1995) gives rich portraits of schools, teachers, and classrooms across the country where similar students engage in socially and intellectually rich learning.

University of Texas at Austin educational psychologist **Richard Valencia** evaluates the validity and reliability of intelligence and achievement tests, particularly for use with Latino students. His work has traced the links between tests, test bias, and widely held conceptions of cultural deficits in students of color. Of particular interest is his book *The Origins of Deficit Thinking: Educational Thought and Practice* (London, England: Falmer Press, 1997).

Cornel West, professor of religion and African American studies at Princeton University, is a noted author, scholar, and social commentator on issues of race and the American culture. West first attained wide public recognition in 1993 with his best-selling book *Race Matters* (Boston: Beacon Press, 1991). His more recent books include *Keeping the Faith* (Boston: Beacon Press, 1993) and *The Future of the Race* (Boston: Beacon Press, 1996), coauthored with **Henry Louis Gates Jr.** Although West's specific focus is on race relations and the struggle of African Americans, he ties issues of race and freedom to questions of philosophy and to a belief in the power of the human spirit. West's website at http://www.pragmatism.org/library/west/ includes several links to his writing and talks.

Notes

1. Most of Jefferson's specific recommendations came in the form of proposals for education in his home state of Virginia. See, for example, Thomas Jefferson, *Notes on the State of Virginia.* For a good collection of Jefferson's writings, see James Gilreath (Ed.), *Thomas Jefferson and the Education of a Citizen* (Washington, DC: Library of Congress, 1999, distributed by University Press of New England).
2. Carter Godwin Woodson, *The Education of the Negro Prior to 1861: A History of the Education of the Colored People of the United States from the Beginning of Slavery to the Civil War, 1919,* The Project Gutenberg EBook, online at http://www.gutenberg.org/etext/11089.
3. David Tyack and Elisabeth Hansot, *Managers of Virtue: Public School Leadership in America, 1820–1980* (New York: Basic Books, 1982).
4. David Tyack, *The One Best System: A History of American Urban Education* (Cambridge: Harvard University Press, 1974).
5. Paula Fass, *Outside In: Minorities and the Transformation of American Education* (Oxford and New York: Oxford University Press, 1989).
6. *Who Built America?* CD-ROM produced by the American Social History Project, City University of New York, as cited in *Rethinking Schools,* Summer 1996. The project also can be located online at www.ashp.cuny.edu.
7. John Crawford, "Anatomy of the English-Only Movement," in *Language Legislation and Linguistic Rights,* ed. Doublas A. Kibbee (Amsterdam and Philadelphia: John Benjamins, 1998).
8. Joel Spring, *American Education* (Boston: McGraw-Hill, 1996).
9. Richard Kluger, *Simple Justice* (New York: Vintage, 1977).
10. National Commission on Excellence in Education, *A Nation at Risk: The Imperatives for Educational Reform* (Washington, DC: U.S. Department of Education, 1983), p. 5.
11. Gunnar Myrdal, *An American Dilemma: The Negro Problem and American Democracy* (New York: Harper and Brothers, 1944).
12. Jay McLeod, *Ain't No Makin' It* (Boulder, CO: Westview Press, 1995), p. 3.
13. See, for example, ibid; Pierre Bordieu and Jean Claude Passeron, *Reproduction in Education, Society and Culture* (Thousand Oaks, CA: Sage, 1990); Samuel Bowles and Herbert Gintis, *Schooling in Capitalist America: Educational Reform and the Contradictions of Economic Life* (New York: Basic Books, 1977); and Raymond Allan Morrow and Carlos Alberto Torres, *Social Theory and Education: A Critique of Theories of Social and Cultural Reproduction* (Buffalo, NY: SUNY Press, 1995).
14. Myrdal, *An American Dilemma.* Myrdal's massive report (more than 1,500 pages) concluded that a deeply troubling *American Dilemma* was the fundamental contradiction between the nation's democratic ideology and its pervasive racism. However, Myrdal also saw racism as a cultural anomaly that Americans could and should excise.
15. Michael Harrington, *The Other America: Poverty in the United States* (1962, reprint, New York: Collier Books, 1997).
16. Gary Orfield and Susan Eaton, *Dismantling Desegregation: The Quiet Reversal of* Brown v. Board of Education (Boston: New Press, 1996); Gary Orfield, Mark Bachmeier, David James, and Tamela Eitle, *Deepening Segregation in American Public Schools* (Cambridge, MA: Civil Rights Project, Harvard Graduate School of Education, 1997).
17. See, for example, Michael Katz, *The Undeserving Poor: From War on Poverty to War on the Poor* (New York: Pantheon, 1989).
18. Stephan Thernstrom and Abigail Thernstrom, *No Excuses: Closing the Racial Gap in Learning* (New York: Simon and Schuster, 2003).
19. McLeod, *Ain't No Makin' It,* p. 126.
20. Alexis de Tocqueville, *Democracy in America,* 2 vols. (New York: 1945, originally published 1835), Vol. 1, pp. 373–374.
21. Stephen J. Gould, *The Mismeasure of Man,* 2nd ed. (New York: Norton, 1996), p. 24.
22. Herbert Kliebard, *The Struggle for the American Curriculum: 1898–1958* (New York: Routledge, 1983).

23. Gould, *The Mismeasure of Man,* p. 190.
24. Ibid.
25. Richard Valencia (Ed.), *The Origins of Deficit Thinking: Educational Thought and Practice* (London, England: Falmer Press, 1997).
26. Excerpted from "Mental Ability Test, Stanford University, Test 1, Information (World Book Co, 1920), as reprinted in Bill Bigelow, "Testing, Tracking, and Toeing the Line," *Rethinking Our Classrooms: Teaching for Equity and Social Justice* (Milwaukee, WI: Rethinking Schools, Ltd., 1994), p. 121.
27. Gould, *The Mismeasure of Man,* p. 221.
28. Crawford, "Anatomy of the English-Only Movement."
29. Ibid.
30. Peggy McIntosh, "White Privilege and Male Privilege: A Personal Account of Coming to See Correspondences through Work in Women's Studies," working paper 189, Wellesley Collage Center for Research on Women (1988).

CHAPTER 3

Philosophy and Politics
The Struggle for the American Curriculum

We respectfully borrow the subtitle for this chapter from Herbert Kliebard, *The Struggle for the American Curriculum: 1898–1958* (New York: Routledge, 1983).

"What does it mean to be a social justice educator?" Prior to my experiences in teacher education and as a full-time teacher, my responses were static, broad, and without theoretical frameworks to support my ideas. Now, however, I realize that there is no one correct answer. Yet, there are several important sociocultural principles that guide my philosophy and practice as a social justice educator.

Sociocultural theory argues that teachers must understand the historical context of our students, the school, and the community. As a social justice educator, I challenge the traditional educational practice of suppressing important "funds of knowledge" urban students possess, such as languages other than English. It is my responsibility to recognize, respect, and use the home languages in order to facilitate learning. The respect I place on the home languages will afford my students greater opportunities to develop a strong sense of self-worth.

As a social justice educator, I challenge the traditional practice of excluding people of color, especially women of color, from the curriculum. I include my students' voices in the curriculum. Many literacy activities revolve around students' personal and family histories. Women of color with professional degrees visited our classroom, including a Latina doctor, Latina professional singer, and two Latina teachers. Their presence in our classroom was critical because they are visual and physical proof that my students' high expectations of themselves are realistic and attainable.

—**MAURO BAUTISTA**
Middle-school bilingual education coordinator

Mauro Bautista is not a traditional teacher. His stance toward curriculum can be characterized as progressive, as he draws on relatively new theories of schooling that challenge a set of ideas that has governed education since the colonial period. Mauro rejects the traditional views that the only knowledge worth teaching is that of the dominant culture and that the primary purpose of schooling is to pass the dominant culture on to society's children. He also rejects the traditional view that other cultural knowledge and languages that students bring with them to school are not worthy of incorporation into the curriculum.

What schools teach, *why*, and *how* they go about it (conventionally called the curriculum) result from deep philosophical commitments that reach deep into every aspect of the culture. When we refer to *philosophy,* we mean systems of beliefs about fundamental matters such as reality, knowledge, meaning, value, being, and truth. These beliefs shape one's views about the purpose of schooling, the proper relationship between school and society, and what type of schools will achieve them.

In a country as culturally diverse as the United States, the journey from philosophy to classroom practices is highly political. When we refer to *politics,* we mean powerful struggles over which views of schooling will set the agenda for what teachers teach and what students learn.

Mauro's stance is both philosophical and political. He challenges traditional systems of beliefs about education, as well as the prevailing power arrangements that disadvantage those whose culture and language are not Anglo-American and English.

Whether teachers are inspired to change the dominant modes of education, like Mauro Bautista, or to maintain them, they should understand the ideas that nourish current practices and the politics that hold them firmly in place. Either way, change or maintain, all teaching is a philosophical and political act. Teachers are often surprised to find, and ill-prepared to negotiate, this philosophical and political terrain.

Chapter Overview

This chapter looks first at how people in Western societies have thought about the human mind and its relationship to knowledge. These philosophical perspectives range from very traditional, European ways of thinking to postmodern ideas. We describe a set of traditional and progressive educational philosophies that have emerged from these basic ideas. We then provide a brief history that shows how Americans have mixed philosophy and politics in their struggles over the curriculum. We conclude with an overview of recent debates about what schools should teach, and the impact they are having on teachers committed to social justice. Chapters 4, 5, 6, 7, and 8 show how these broad debates play out in specific academic subjects and in the practice of teaching.

Basic Philosophies of Education

Reduced to their bare essentials, the centuries-old arguments about education reflect philosophers' differing views on (a) the nature of reality, (b) humans' ability to "know" reality, and (c) what's worth knowing.

The Roots of Western Educational Philosophy

Throughout the world's cultural and intellectual history, people have sought large, overarching organizational principles to help make sense of the world. Whether from God, king, nature, science, humans' own intellect, or political or economic systems, people have looked to consistent systems of thought and rules that freed them from meaningless chaos. American traditions and institutions, including schools, were born out of *modern* systems of thought that developed with the eighteenth-century European period known as the Enlightenment. The nation was founded as Western thought turned increasingly to science and reason as central organizing processes.

The European Renaissance from roughly the fourteenth to the seventeenth century marked a transition from medieval to modern thought—from people as subjects in God's world to people who could initiate astonishing achievements in architecture and art, mathematics, commerce, cities and government, and more. Thinkers began to ask a new set of questions: What it was about humans that allowed those achievements? What or who was the source of knowledge that made the achievements possible?

Even asking questions about the source of knowledge entailed a powerful shift in how people thought; it raised fundamental questions that are not entirely agreed upon today. Enlightenment scholars concluded that *reason,* an inborn human capacity, is partly responsible for people's ability to turn experiences into certain types or categories of knowledge.

The giants of Enlightenment philosophy—including Rene Descartes (1596–1650), John Locke (1632–1704), and Immanuel Kant (1724–1804)—proposed and sought to answer perplexing questions about humans, learning, and knowledge.

Are some forms of knowledge inborn or innate?

What truths can be known through reflection, or by examining our own thoughts?

Is there a mind or soul that is spiritual or separate from the physical body? If so, do they interact?

What is the difference between physical sensations and ideas?

How do smaller bits of experience (I feel cold) turn into broad abstractions (Is it better to conserve energy, or should I turn on the heater and maybe avoid the stiff neck I get from the tension?)?

How do we study something (like the mind) that we can't see?

Each of the preceding Enlightenment thinkers came to different answers, and their answers and reasoning have influenced the centuries that followed.

Descartes emphasized the mind as a region separate from the body that inspects ideas. He argued that some forms of knowledge were inborn and that the mind's reasoning was the most reliable source of that knowledge. Following Descartes, a school of philosophy known as the "idealists" took the position that reality is essentially spiritual, and knowledge is a product of human reason; the most valuable ideas are those that stand the test of time since they are exposed to reason the longest.

Locke, in contrast, questioned the concept of innate ideas and turned to "empirical" evidence for knowledge. Empirical knowledge is that which can be detected by the senses. He argued that the mind is a blank slate (no preexisting knowledge) that only is written on through experience. Following Locke, philosophers known as "realists" have argued that reality (facts, truth) exists "out there," and humans come to know it by carefully examining the empirical world. This knowledge is already organized according to universal laws that govern the working of the universe. The job of scholars is to discover those laws.

Kant, also in the idealist tradition, saw the mind as an organ that was equipped with processes for creating orderly thought and understanding (rather than blankly awaiting experience). The mind mediated, categorized, and represented sensations and ideas, making sense out of chaotic, concrete experience. Unlike Descartes, Kant found the outside world relevant to thinking because it provided the raw material for the mind to organize.

Philosophy in the History of American Schooling

Benjamin Franklin, Thomas Jefferson, and other intellectuals at the time of the country's founding were influenced by deism, a religious perspective that saw God as the rational architect of an orderly world. After the initial work of creation, God had little to do with the day-by-day (or eon-by-eon) operations of the universe. Something like a "Master Watchmaker," God created a perfect mechanism and left the universe to run on its own. God was similarly absent from the daily affairs of people. Deists believed every human was born with all necessary spiritual knowledge, making the teachings of any church unnecessary. Only human reason was necessary to gain access to spiritual and physical truths. Of course, while the universe was complete and orderly, human reason was incomplete and imperfect. Thus, education in the United States was influenced by the beliefs that humans, imperfect though they are, can, through science and reason, discover, organize, and control for their own benefit and enlightenment the mysteries of the universe and human existence.

From the nation's beginning, schools have been at the center of efforts to create social progress out of change and upheaval. The main social task of common schools in the early nineteenth century was to impart to youth values such as honesty, civic loyalty, hard work, and charity—all considered essential for national unity, republican government, and social progress. Although most nineteenth-century American educators had little or no training in how to teach, metaphors drawn from the work of Descartes, Locke, Kant, and other Enlightenment thinkers helped people "understand" the mystery of learning and helped shape classroom instruction.

For example, following Locke and the realists, many educators thought about their young students' minds as "empty vessels" to be filled or as "blank slates" to be written on as they explored the empirical world. Following Descartes, Kant, and the idealists, educators were attracted to the belief that studying certain subjects would strengthen faculties such as memory, reasoning, will, and imagination. It is to this view that we owe the still popular metaphor of the "mind as a muscle" and the notion that the study of classical languages, geometry, and so on causes learners to "exercise their brains" and produces stronger, more capable minds.[1]

These philosophical positions were challenged in the late nineteenth century by two new sets of ideas—pragmatism and behaviorism. Both sets of ideas grew out of philosophers' increasing interest in psychology, an emerging science investigating the mind and mental processes, including learning. The pragmatist John Dewey and his colleagues, like the realists, believed in a reality that exists in the world and in the power of humans to know it through interacting with it. However, unlike realists who placed the greatest value on knowing the unchanging laws of nature, the pragmatists emphasized the importance of understanding how the physical world changes and knowing how to solve problems. Behaviorism emerged as psychologist Edward Thorndike combined the results of his scientific studies of animal learning with philosopher and psychologist William James's theory that systematic exercise and drill could build proper habits of thought in humans.

Both pragmatism and behaviorism saw science as providing benefits to society. In spite of the horrendous social problems and inequality that accompanied industrialization, mass production, and urbanization at the turn of the twentieth century, Americans were optimistic. Bringing more and more of life's variables under control, rational and scientific methods would be the instruments of progress.

At the beginning of the twenty-first century, scholars across many different disciplines now view the linear nineteenth- and twentieth-century habits of thought born of the "scientific method" as just *one* of many ways of knowing, not the *only* way. Thus, we can no longer be so certain (or arrogant) about what is progress for others, and what seems good to others, or even what is real to others. Multiple versions of truth and goodness might be credible not only to different people but also to ourselves. Little by little, formerly unquestioned modern and Western ideas of universal truths, regularity, and progress are giving way to a *postmodern* emphasis on particularity, difference, and unpredictability. As we will discuss later in this chapter, this postmodern way of thinking has influenced educational philosophy and curriculum as well.

Six Philosophies of Education

In the past century, a number of specific philosophies of education have developed from these broader philosophical trends. The following tables depict the usual way that six of the most influential educational philosophies are described. Each position has a somewhat different view of the purpose of schooling, its curriculum, and the roles teachers and students play. Each is manifest in one or more contemporary approaches to schooling, although nearly all educational practices incorporate ideas from more than one of these philosophies. The first three philosophies inform what we consider "traditional" conceptions of schooling (see Concept Table 3.1). They have firm roots in Enlightenment thinking and see the purpose of education as passing on to the young the knowledge, skills, and virtues prized by the culture. These first three also tend to see learning as a process of acquiring knowledge and skills.

The second three philosophies have informed what we consider "progressive" perspectives (see Concept Table 3.2). Their roots lie in pragmatism and postmodern thought. They view the purpose of education as developing knowledge and ways

CONCEPT TABLE 3.1 *Three "Traditional" Philosophies of Education*

Philosophy	Roots	Education's Purpose	Preferred Curriculum	Role of the Teacher	Role of the Student	Examples Today
Essentialism	Idealism	Transmitting the culture from one generation to the next; training the basic intellectual skills	Knowledge and basic skills necessary to preserve the culture and to enable constructive participation in it	The authority in the classroom, the conveyor of knowledge, and the administrator of tests to ensure that knowledge has been acquired	Receiver of transmitted knowledge—i.e., an "empty vessel" that accumulates knowledge	E. D. Hirsch's "Cultural Literacy," standards-based curriculum
Perennialism	Idealism and realism	To cultivate the mind, instill timeless virtues and advance the search for truth	Enduring ideas, universal truths, classic intellectual achievements	Instill virtues; know and teach subject matter to all students; convey received wisdom and knowledge, often through Socratic questioning	Receiver of knowledge—i.e., a mind waiting to be developed; they may think critically, but not challenge intellectual authority	The Coalition of Essential Schools—"habits of mind"
Behaviorism	Realism	Build proper habits of thought	Individualized program; carefully paced, linear instruction	Teacher as trainer—provides stimuli and reinforcement for learning	Respond to stimuli and develops habits of thought and behavior	Direct instruction

CONCEPT TABLE 3.2 *Three "Progressive" Philosophies of Education*

Philosophy	Roots	Education's Purpose	Preferred Curriculum	Role of the Teacher	Role of the Student	Examples Today
Child- and Community-Centered Schooling	Pragmatism	Learning to solve problems of society and democratic living	Problems engaged by society and by children, informed by the academic disciplines	Creates an environment rich with opportunities for student-directed learning and group problem solving	Active engagement in deciding what to study; learning by doing, rather than from listening	Constructivist teaching and learning
Social Reconstructionism	Pragmatism	Solving critical social problems that limit equality, justice, and democracy	Community and societal problems that are amenable to social and political action	Raise consciousness about social problems and provide the tools for social critique and social action	Active engagement in understanding social problems and taking action to solve them	Critical pedagogy
Multiculturalism/ Socioculturalism	Pragmatism/ Postmodernism	Promote a just, multicultural democracy through the recognition of diverse cultures	A broad array of knowledge in the traditional subjects, with an emphasis on respectful understanding of all cultures and people	Build on the "funds" of knowledge students bring from home; provide experiences that allow for diverse ways of learning	Actively construct knowledge by participating in ways that connect home culture and language with school experiences	Bilingual education, antiracist pedagogy

of thinking that will move society toward realizing democracy or social justice. These second three philosophies tend to see learning as a social process of constructing knowledge and an apprenticeship into cultural practices.

Philosophy and Politics in the Struggle for the School Curriculum

With the exception of social reconstructionism and multiculturalism, these educational philosophies are not typically described as being political. It is characteristic of essentialist and perennialist thinkers, in particular, not to see the political elements in their own views. After all, if you see the curriculum as "basic" or as enduring across all time, it is hard to imagine that others might view it differently; therefore, asserting your essential or perennial values and perspectives is not an exercise of power, but a simple expression of truth. However, as the remainder of this chapter makes clear, proponents of all the philosophies try to instill their values and beliefs in the educational system, and by extension, they exclude the values and beliefs of others. In that sense, they are all political.

Interwoven with struggles over which philosophical positions should govern American schooling have been debates about whether all American students should have the same kind of schooling. For most of our history, most Americans have believed they should not. As education scholar Lauren B. Resnick observes, Americans "have inherited two quite distinct educational traditions—one concerned with elite education, the other concerned with mass education. These traditions conceived of schooling differently, had different clienteles, and held different goals for their students."[2]

These "distinct educational traditions"—elite and mass—have also carried with them social and political consequences, as well as educational ones. Elite education has opened up access to universities and professional jobs. Mass education has restricted such access.

Much in our democratic rhetoric—including having public schools for everyone—seeks to diminish the power of social class to determine who gets schooling opportunities and who does not. However, the tradition of separate "mass" and "elite" education clearly has made it much easier for Americans with wealth, power, leadership, and higher education to succeed in transferring to their children these advantages. The political tensions between the rhetoric of equal opportunity and the reality of social power have intertwined with philosophical debates over the purpose and conduct of American schooling for most of its history. They continue today.

Essentialist Mass Education in the Nineteenth Century

In the 50 years following the Revolution, much of America's population either dispersed through westward expansion or concentrated in urban clusters to work in a rapidly expanding trade and manufacturing economy. Fully tax-supported schools were still a long way off, and communities that had compulsory education rarely enforced it. All students, including the masses, were expected to learn their sums and perhaps a little accounting; read well enough to understand the Bible, newspaper, and almanac; understand a smattering of natural history (biology); and be familiar with at least some national, European, and classical stories or history. This emphasis on the basics (or essentials) included the prevailing moral and religious predilections that teachers were expected to transmit—typically, those of northern European Protestant denominations.

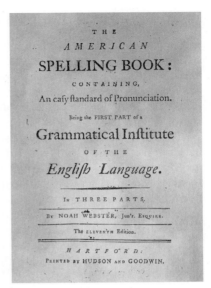

The *Elementary Spelling Book,* a Revision of Webster's Older *American Spelling Book,* First Appeared in 1829.

In the 1780s Noah Webster—of dictionary fame—authored an enormously popular series of textbooks, notably the "blue-backed speller." Commonly referred to as the "Schoolmaster of America," Webster was passionately committed to an America free of decadent European influence and with strong, uniquely American citizenship and institutions. Starting as a schoolteacher himself, he fashioned a system of instruction that, in addition to providing lessons in reading and writing, aimed at developing patriotic Americans and creating a unified national spirit. Webster argued that children should be educated in uniquely American language and social perspectives to distinguish our culture from less acceptable European ones.

The speller attempted to instill respect for hard work and property rights. Its political and moral catechism required students to memorize the following series of questions and answers:

- What is a moral virtue? It is an honest upright conduct in all our dealings with men.
- Can we always determine what is honest and just? Perhaps not in every instance, but in general it is not difficult.
- What rules have we to direct us? God's word contained in the Bible has furnished all necessary rules to direct our conduct.
- In what part of the Bible are these rules to be found? In almost every part; but the most important duties between men are summed up in the beginning of Matthew, in Christ's Sermon on the Mount.[3]

By 1875, 75 million copies of Webster's blue-backed speller had sold. Its incredible popularity both reflected and shaped what people thought children should learn. Once the speller became the standard (there were not many choices), it set an enduring pattern for infusing political and moral content into teaching basic skills.

Essentialist Elite Education in the Eighteenth and Nineteenth Centuries

In the 1800s, schooling beyond the rudimentary basics was available only to those who could pay for private tutors and schools. Most private schools favored a classical European education and prepared students for high schools and universities. Also following an essentialist philosophy, these schools taught the basic knowledge of mathematics, science, Latin, Greek, English grammar, geography, perhaps rhetoric, and so on.

However, some elite private schools took on a more distinctively American character. Benjamin Franklin and other rationalists of the revolutionary period urged a departure from traditional courses in religion and classics and favored useful and practical studies. Franklin, not surprisingly, envisioned an education consistent with his values for self-improvement. These values depended less on mastering facts through rote learning than on accumulating learning processes that would serve, as they did in Franklin's own case, a lifetime of learning. Franklin favored a breadth of utilitarian knowledge such as modern languages and the study of commerce and trade. Thus, Franklin advocated an education for elites that would later hold strong appeal for the masses. He also provided some of the earliest hints of a curriculum that could serve social justice goals—one that is process oriented and focused on complex and practical knowledge.

That the first public high school was not established until 1821, however, bears witness to the prevailing view that an education beyond the most basic literacy and moral training was not of mass public concern. So, when public high schools did begin to appear, schoolmasters patterned them after the private academies, and few children had access to them.

The Common School

In the 1830s and 1840s the idea of the common school, based on principles outlined by Horace Mann, first emerged, and it was to become the dominant symbol of American education. The common school curriculum, including use of textbooks for older youth, paved the way for today's public elementary and secondary schools.

The common school appealed to nearly everyone, but for very different reasons. Working-class people, immigrants, and those outside the dominant culture who lacked resources for their own private schools saw the common school as a path (a narrow one, to be sure) to the American dream. People of greater wealth and status saw their own well-being enhanced by common schools. Everyone would benefit, they reasoned, if schools could turn out productive workers and good citizens. Some literacy and some math were required of all.

However, then as now, when determining "how much" education and "how much for whom," the tradition of distinct mass and elite education prevailed: Private schools would continue to meet the country's needs for educated elites.

A Common Essentialist Curriculum   Essentialist schooling components reinforced one another in the common schools: moral truths, cultural certainty, nationalism, capitalism, Protestant Christianity, and the view of children as "empty vessels" formed a tightly compatible whole. Imagine the overlapping influence of Webster's blue-backed speller and another 122 million copies of *McGuffey's Readers.* Between 1836 and 1920 *McGuffey's Readers* taught rules for reading and proper speech; practical moral precepts; God's active participation in death, nature, and distribution and withholding of wealth; the rules of capitalism; and—in a time before separate textbooks for different subjects—science, history, biography, geography, and more.

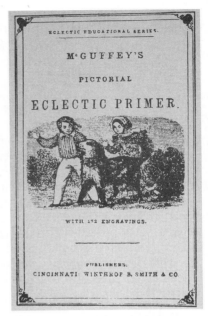

McGuffey's Reader.

McGuffey's Readers did it all. Elites could be comforted since the readers, though educating large numbers of previously uneducated classes, offered academic and social lessons that preserved important social class distinctions. Consider historian Joel Spring's comments and selections from two stories and what both rich and poor children would learn from them.

> In "The Rich Boy," students learned that the rich boy knows "that God gives a great deal of money to some persons, in order that they may assist those who are poor." In keeping with the idea that the rich are elected by God, the rich boy is portrayed as being humble, kind to servants, and "careful not to make a noise in the house, or break any thing, or put it out of its place, or tear his clothes." The reader is also told that this model of virtue "likes to go with his parents to visit poor people, in their cottages, and gives them all the money he can spare."[4]

> In "The Poor Boy," Spring tells us that

> unlike the rich boy wanting to help the poor, the poor boy dreams of earning his own living. He likes his food of bread and bacon and does not envy the rich little boys and girls "riding on pretty horses, or in coaches." At the end of the story, the poor boy states his acceptance of his social position: "I have often been told, and I have read, that it is God who makes some poor, and others rich—that the rich have many troubles which we know nothing of; and that the poor, if they are but good, may be very happy. Indeed, I think that when I am good, nobody can be happier than I am."[5]

During the latter half of the 1800s, Webster's spellers and *McGuffey's Readers* amounted to national textbooks, with the readers remaining popular until World War I. These texts helped unify social, moral, political, and educational values, just as their authors had very pointedly intended. Educational and political leaders educated according to these values retained power and influence well into the twentieth century. Many were active in resisting change or in shaping reforms to keep schools aligned with nineteenth-century educational values. Further, throughout most of the twentieth century, the public, generally, would continue to see as sensible McGuffey's and Webster's rote learning and their heavy-handed political and moral indoctrination with its male, Anglo, and Protestant orientation.

The Scientifically Organized Common School   William Torrey Harris, re-spected scholar and philosopher as well as superintendent of St. Louis schools and U.S. commissioner of education from 1889 to 1906, argued persuasively that schools could best pursue democratic principles through strict discipline, orderly behavior, and mastery of the school subjects that we recognize today as the core of the mod-ern essentialist curriculum: mathematics, geography, literature, art, grammar, and history. Harris also believed that, if schools were scientifically and rationally orga-nized into grade levels of students by age and into ability-grouped classes, this cur-riculum would produce better people for the American democracy. His ideas were taken up by school systems around the nation.

What did such a curriculum look like? In 1893 pediatrician and school critic Joseph Mayer Rice gave the following description of a geometry lesson in a New York City school:

> Before the lesson began there was passed to each child a little flag, on which had been pasted various forms and colors, such as a square piece of green paper, a triangular piece of red paper, etc. . . . Upon receiving the signal, the first child sprang up, gave the name of the geometrical form upon his flag, loudly and rapidly defined the form, and fell back into his seat to make way for the second child, thus: "A square; a square has four equal sides and four corners; green" (down). Second child (up) "A triangle; a triangle has three sides and three cor-ners; red" (down). . . . The rate of speed was so great that seventy children passed through the process of defining in a very few minutes.[6]

Common Secondary Schools   As more and more students began attending sec-ondary schools, the question of what students should learn in secondary education and whether all students should learn the same things became pressing. In 1893 an influential report from the National Education Association's "Committee of Ten" recommended that secondary schools offer more than one curriculum, but that all of the offerings should be highly academic and lead to university training for those who desired it.[7] The Committee argued that all young people—regardless of their future station in life—would benefit from a mix of classical and modern studies that would transmit the western European intellectual tradition.

This approach to secondary schooling incorporated the perennialist ideals into the prevailing essentialist curriculum. Perennialism sought to impart knowledge and habits of thinking of everlasting value for all people. Since facts about the world are always changing, as are vocations and technology, schools should concentrate on teaching universal principles such as scientific reasoning, and they should help students address how humans interact with their natural, physical, and social worlds. Intellectual development, rather than the essentialists' basic skills, was the goal of a perennialist curriculum.

The "Progressive Education" Movement

At about this same time (the late 1800s and early 1900s), still other educators strug-gled to fashion an education that met the needs of a rapidly urbanizing and industrializing society. Educators rooted in science and pragmatism proposed educational responses that went off in a variety of directions—some toward behav-ioral psychology, some toward efficient school management, and others toward child- and community-centered schooling. They all considered themselves part of the "progressive education" movement.

As different as they were from one another, the various groups of progressives held some core beliefs in common. They cared more about applying rational, scien-tific advancements to the effective *delivery* of knowledge and to the organization of schools than the essentialists and perennialists who tended to focus on *what* was taught. In particular, progressives looked to the emerging science of psychology to guide their recommended practices. They were also influenced by pragmatism—asking educators to consider whether and how their efforts would contribute to the long-term benefits of students and society.

Progressives who focused on efficiency and behaviorism retained their commit-ment to traditional views of the purpose of schooling, to traditional conceptions of knowledge, and to the traditional view of learning as acquiring knowledge and skills. Only those moving toward child- and community-centered education assumed what we recognize today as a *progressive* stance on the purpose of schooling, knowl-edge, and learning.

Scientific and Efficient Curriculum   G. Stanley Hall was founder of the "child study movement" at the end of the nineteenth century. Hall argued that each stage of children's development mirrors that of social evolution, and he wanted school to be in harmony with the child's developmental stage. He provided the foundation for the idea of adolescence—a stage of life when children had markedly different needs and required distinctive treatments in school. The invention of the junior high school as a separate institution with curriculum and instruction designed to match the young adolescent's developmental needs and interests followed directly from Hall's science.[8]

Franklin Bobbitt thought that a curriculum designer should be like a "great en-gineer." In 1918, Bobbitt published *The Curriculum,* outlining a scientific ap-proach to curriculum development. In accordance with "machine theory" and be-haviorism, Bobbitt set out principles of curriculum planning that included specifying not only what knowledge was important for students to learn but also the specific behavioral objectives that would be met and activities that lead to accom-plishing those objectives. In 1920, Bobbitt elaborated his theory in *How to Make a Curriculum,* a book that offered 800 curriculum objectives and activities to ac-complish them.

About the same time, W. W. Charters advocated a similar scientific, behaviorist approach in his book *Curriculum Construction.* Mirroring "efficiency experts" in factories, Charters proposed a "job analysis" approach to curriculum planning that began with specific, measurable objectives, analysis of the tasks that would be required to meet those objectives, and activities designed specifically to accomplish those tasks. Together, Bobbitt and Charters established curriculum as the result of an efficient scientific planning process.

Elite and Mass Schooling Under One Roof   By 1918 vast numbers of workers' and immigrants' sons and daughters were attending public secondary schools, where they joined a much smaller group of students from more-established, elite families. Their schools were common. However, the tradition of separate mass and elite education reestablished itself under one roof.

Unlike the Committee of Ten, 25 years earlier, most progressive educational leaders believed that only the elites had the mental capacity to learn a rigorous perennialist curriculum, and only they would occupy the social roles that require such knowledge. Social efficiency advocates, influenced by behaviorism, sought a scientifically designed curriculum that would give students direct instruction in the academic basics and prepare them with the specific skills that they would use as adults.

Thus, children of the elites would have an academic curriculum; children of the masses (including most immigrants) would learn practical and vocational knowledge and skills, infused with a heavy dose of American patriotism. For that vast majority of students, a 1918 National Education Association (NEA) Commission on the Reorganization of Secondary Schools established seven curricular goals: (1) health, (2) command of fundamentals (basic skills), (3) worthy home membership, (4) vocation, (5) citizenship, (6) worthy use of leisure, and (7) ethical character. The Commission tied the loftiest attributes of democracy—especially freedom and self-determination through effort and merit—to schools teaching the mass of citizens practical competencies and sound moral character.

Child- and Community-Centered Progressivism

John Dewey.

Another quite distinct progressive approach also emerged at this time, that of John Dewey, the philosopher and reformer whose name today is most closely associated with the term *progressive education*. Like other progressives of the time, Dewey emphasized the social and pragmatic nature of schooling and learning. However, recognizing that children's development and learning were anything but rational and orderly, he and his followers advocated a child-centered and community-centered curriculum to give students experiences that make rigorous intellectual demands in the contexts of democratic social living.

Child-Centered Schooling   Child-centered reforms emerged as early as 1873 in response to the results of an examination given by the school board in Quincy, Massachusetts.

Historian Lawrence Cremin relates, "The results were disastrous. While the young-sters knew their rules of grammar thoroughly, they could not write an ordinary English letter. While they could read with facility from their textbooks, they were utterly confused by similar material from unfamiliar sources."[9] Shocked by these results, the Quincy board, under the leadership of Superintendent Francis Parker, made a number of changes. Cremin goes on to note:

> [The] set curriculum was abandoned, and with it the speller, the reader, the grammar, and the copybook. Children were started on simple words and sen-tences, rather than the alphabet learned by rote. In place of time-honored texts, magazines, newspapers, and materials devised by the teachers themselves were introduced into the classroom. Arithmetic was approached inductively, through objects rather than rules, while geography began with a series of trips over the local countryside. Drawing was added to encourage manual dexterity and indi-vidual expression. The emphasis throughout was on observing, describing, and understanding, and only when these abilities had begun to manifest themselves—among the faculty as well as the students—were more conven-tional studies introduced.[10]

In short, Parker had introduced a curriculum that "began" with the child's learning and then sought out appropriate content, materials, and experiences to make the learning happen. This differed markedly from conventional approaches that began with inflexible content, materials, and approaches and expected the student to ad-just to them. After only a few years Quincy students achieved excellent scores in reading, writing, and spelling on an exam administered by the Massachusetts State Board of Education.

Parker moved on to train teachers as head of the Cook County Normal School in Chicago, where only a few years later, he stated explicitly that his academic goals had a clearly social character. The school, he argued, should be a "model home, a complete community, and an embryonic democracy."[11] In Parker's experimental school, children created stories that became their "texts" for reading, spelling, pen-manship, and grammar. Science took the form of nature study, including field trips to Lake Michigan, where the students observed, wrote descriptions, and made drawings of what they saw. Back in the classroom, these observations became the basis of "laboratory" work, where the children also learned mathematics as they constructed the "equipment" they would use in scientific study. Teachers intro-duced all subjects by connecting them with activities or experiences that already had meaning for the children.

It was to Parker's Chicago experimental school that University of Chicago philosopher John Dewey sent his own children, and there Dewey gathered ideas for the University Laboratory School that he began in 1896. As at Parker's school, Dewey introduced children to learning through familiar activities of the family. An early account gave this description of Dewey's classroom for 4- and 5-year-olds fol-lowing a trip to a farm:

> Part of the group played grocery store and sold fruit and sugar for the jelly making of the others. Some were clerks, some delivery boys, others mothers, and some made the grocery wagons. The clerks were given measuring cups with which to measure the sugar and cranberries and paper to wrap the pack-ages to take home. . . . A wholesale house was constructed out of a big box.

Elevators would be necessary, a child volunteered, for storehouses have so many floors; and these were made from long narrow corset boxes, a familiar wrapping in every household of the day.[12]

Dewey had such a high regard for knowledge and knowledgeable teachers that he was certain that they could find a way for each child to get to the heart of the academic disciplines. So although many critics accused Dewey of being "child centered" to the exclusion of children learning valued knowledge and skills, this was not the case.

As students grew older, Dewey's teachers guided them through integrated activities filled with increasingly sophisticated opportunities to learn mathematics, science, and the other disciplines. Six-year-olds constructed a model farm and raised wheat. Seven-, 8-, and 9-year-olds explored the history of Western civilization and the United States through concrete human activities, such as occupations, trade, and building cities. Teachers integrated these thematic activities with lessons in the arts, science, music, history and geography, foreign language, and literature. History illuminated human successes and failures; and literature conveyed the hopes of people in various social contexts. The oldest children specialized in a particular discipline, developing in-depth, yearlong projects.

Thus, Dewey's curriculum began with experiences immediately familiar to the child, then moved students to more distant and abstract ideas, and finally led them to grapple with broad social themes. Such an approach, Dewey argued, would prepare students to improve society as well as understand it.

Dewey was no less interested in shaping character than those who preceded him—Webster, McGuffey, or Harris, for example. However, Dewey was less interested than others had been in preventing or correcting undesirable traits. Rather, he sought to develop in students a character that would build democratic and interdependent communities. Logically, given Dewey's emphasis on learning through activity, he argued that schools should themselves be miniature democratic societies—places where children *live,* rather than "only a place to learn lessons."[13]

Community-Centered Schooling   Dewey and other early-twentieth-century reformers also argued for cultural pluralism in the curriculum. In 1899 Jane Addams founded Chicago's Hull House, the best known of the big city settlement houses that helped immigrants adjust to American life. Addams created a community in the Chicago slums that was rich in intellectual and cultural opportunities. Together she and Dewey sought ways to help immigrants adapt to the American culture without losing contact with the cultures they left behind. They argued that while everyone should learn the common culture—English, American history, and the American political system—immigrants should also retain and be proud of their home cultures.

Schooling figured prominently in Jane Addams's reform efforts. She argued that education for immigrants must go beyond the basics of English language instruction and civics, to provide for the social and moral well-being of the poor. That meant attending to their social and aesthetic needs with lectures, discussions, concerts, and art gallery visits; providing vocational training; and giving workers an understanding of the history and significance of the industrial life to which they and their families

Jane Addams at Hull House.

belonged. In 1908 Addams explained in an address to the NEA how schools should address social concerns:

> The schools ought to do more to connect these children with the best things of the past, to make them realize something of the beauty and charm of the language, the history, and the traditions which their parents represent. . . . If the body of teachers in our great cities could take hold of the immigrant colonies, could bring out of them their handicrafts and occupations, their traditions, their folk songs and folk lore, the beautiful stories which every immigrant colony is ready to tell and translate. . . . Give these children a chance to utilize the historic and industrial material they see about them and they will begin to have a sense of ease in America, a first consciousness of being at home. I believe if these people are welcomed upon the basis of the resources which they represent and the contributions which they bring, it may come to pass that these schools which deal with immigrants will find that they have a wealth of cultural and industrial material which will make the schools in other neighborhoods positively envious.[14]

Social Reconstructionism

In the 1920s Dewey and other intellectuals became increasingly outspoken about social and economic injustices. By the 1930s progressive reforms had taken an even more political turn. As the Great Depression made injustice highly visible, George Counts, professor at the University of Chicago, and Harold Rugg of Teachers College, Columbia University, with Dewey's support, captured the curriculum reform spotlight with their calls for a "social reconstructionist" curriculum.

In a manifesto called "Dare the Schools Build a New Social Order?" Counts railed against capitalism's emphasis on property rights over human rights and the culture's overemphasis on the individual. He indicted those trends that he believed had taken a wrong direction, including the traditional essentialist and perennialist curricula and the push for scientific efficiency, calling them ideally suited to cementing the status quo of unequal economic and social power. Counts argued that democracy must exert greater control over capitalism, that the school curriculum must critique social institutions that did not further democracy, and that teachers must act as a militant force for change. It is easy to see how social reconstructionists would be accused of having a political agenda for the nation's schooling. However, the power behind their challenges to prevailing practice never rose to compete with the political power that held the status quo in place.

In sum, the social reconstructionists struck a responsive chord in American social thought, but they barely penetrated the school curriculum. Their main achievement came with the widespread adoption of Harold Rugg's textbooks. These texts were the first that wove together the disciplines of history, geography, civics, economics, and sociology—all previously taught as separate subjects—as integrated "social studies." Rugg believed that a curriculum centered on real social problems, informed by ideas from the social sciences, would lead students to independent thinking and social action. For example, his books described the plight of African slaves and included vivid descriptions of conditions on the slave ships. His unit on economic disparity included photographs of wealthy and poor neighborhoods in the nation's capital.

Rugg's books were very popular during the 1930s but most educators and the public did not sympathize with the social reconstructionists' anticapitalistic ideology. And with World War II bringing both economic prosperity and a resurgence of American patriotism, Rugg's texts came under attack by conservative newspapers and organizations such as the American Legion and the Daughters of the Colonial Wars. Attacked as un-American (one column blasting Rugg in the *American Legion Magazine* was called "Treason in the Textbooks"[15]), the ideas of Rugg and Counts, and even Dewey, stood little chance.

Despite considerable ferment around Dewey's progressivism and social reconstructionism, the dominant curriculum throughout the first decades of the twentieth century remained a combination of basic academics, organized and taught separately and efficiently according to William Torrey Harris's design. This dominant curriculum also included the vocational and life skills training that became part of the high school, following the 1918 Cardinal Principles of Secondary Education argument that elite and mass curriculum tracks should exist side by side in "comprehensive" high schools.

Post–World War II, Sputnik, and Curriculum Crisis

The 1940s and 1950s brought little curricular change. Progressives continued to search for ways to connect students' school learning with the rich and relevant learning opportunities that could be found at home and in the community. Ralph Tyler, the nation's leading curriculum scholar, argued that the highest curriculum priority should be teaching about the practical concerns of daily living, for example, the chemistry of detergents, driving and servicing an automobile, and how local utility services work. This "life adjustment" curriculum suffered the fate of many progressive reforms. A fundamentally sound idea that was only superficially implemented opened itself to sometimes justified ridicule and reaffirmed traditionalists' opposition to reform.

Further, the country had little motivation for changing the schools. The cold war of the 1950s, marked by the virulent anticommunist sentiment of the McCarthy period and the horrific oppressions of Stalinist Russia, made the national climate inhospitable to progressive schooling—even when due thought and resources were devoted to its implementation. It was a time when the vocabulary of progressives, including "reform," "social justice," "democratic," and "progressive," could be (and actually was) labeled as un-American. Finally, complacency brought on by post–World War II prosperity left little room for thinking that schools needed to be improved. All that changed in the late 1950s when the Soviet Union shocked the world and American educators by sending a small ball of steel into space.

The Post-Sputnik Curriculum   The launching of the space satellite Sputnik in 1957 foreclosed further debate between the progressive and traditional camps, at least temporarily. That the Russians—source of cold war anxieties and the ever-present communist threat—could beat the Americans into space could only mean

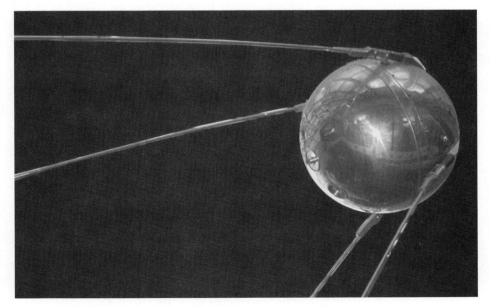

Sputnik: A 184-Pound Satellite Sent into Orbit by the Russians in 1957.

that U.S. schools had failed. Many citizens believed that the nation had fallen from educational and scientific preeminence. Clearly, education was no longer a need only for individual prosperity and an informed citizenry; education, especially in political rhetoric, had become a matter of national security. High school graduation and college entrance standards were raised, and mathematicians and scientists around the country developed rigorous new courses of study for elementary and secondary schools.

Drawing from the new, cognitive learning theories of Jerome Bruner and the developmental theories of Jean Piaget, the "new" math, science, and social studies programs asked students to engage with knowledge in an increasingly sophisticated "spiral" curriculum. Bruner contended that children at every stage of cognitive development could learn some form of the most important ideas of the academic disciplines if the curriculum mirrored the structure and the inquiry processes of the discipline.[16]

Implementation of these new, more academic curricula was spotty, however, and interest in them was short-lived. The Bruner-inspired reforms of the 1960s and 1970s went against the common sense of most Americans. This turn toward rigorous and demanding intellectual work for America's youth was quickly ridiculed with disdain similar to that previously heaped on the life adjustment curriculum. Curriculum materials that encouraged attention to the social nature of learning and knowledge, such as the "new math" and discovery-oriented social studies, attracted a firestorm of criticism that the programs were flaky and neglected familiar facts and skills.

Even less inspiring of confidence were pockets of passionate interest in so-called open classrooms, in which students' interests drove the curriculum. A. S. Neill's 1960 book, *Summerhill,* describing a "free school" in England where young people constructed their own learning experiences in a democratic community, had captured the imaginations of many Americans critical of traditional schools.[17] In some quarters, the briefly and barely implemented curriculum of the new math, new science, and new social studies, together with what was seen as a "do-your-own-thing" approach to schooling, were blamed for many of the country's ills, including the civil rights and anti-Vietnam War student activism that so outraged much of the nation.

Back to Basics

The backlash in the 1970s was a back-to-basics movement, a return to a strong essentialist philosophy and a behaviorist approach to curriculum. Once again, a skills-based curriculum, largely accomplished through memorization and enforced through tests of students' competencies, became the order of the day. With this return to tradition, critics hoped to restore stability and predictability to schools (and society as a whole), as well as to increase achievement of the most disadvantaged children. This trend remains powerful today, as we describe later in this chapter.

Programmed Learning   This "basic" and skills-oriented curriculum quickly found allies among Americans who believed that scientific methods and technology could make skills instruction and learning vastly more efficient. Based on the work of behaviorist B. F. Skinner and educational psychologist Robert Gagne, reading labs sprang up in schools throughout the land. Spurred by reports that President Kennedy endorsed a popular, widely advertised speed-reading method for White House staff, capable readers along with nonreaders were soon exposed to expensive programs that promised to increase reading speed a hundredfold or more. The labs and classrooms filled with "controlled readers"—machines that would flash word groups on a screen to train readers' eyes to take in more words, faster. Tachistoscopes would blink words or numbers on a screen for a similar effect.

"Programmed" and individualized reading and math kits turned teachers into monitors. They spent much of their class time administering diagnostic tests that placed students at the right starting point in the kit, handing out and scoring worksheets in the proper sequence, giving mastery tests, and keeping extensive records of students' progress. The instructions and practice exercises in the kits did the teaching. Not unlike the hoped-for "computer revolution" a generation later, however, this earlier version of technology reform produced limited benefits for student learning.

A Compensatory Curriculum   As usual, the benefits of a back-to-basics curriculum were most loudly proclaimed for students who were poor, of color, had "learning disabilities," or otherwise did not fit in with conventional schooling. And, by the 1970s, the back-to-basics curriculum took on new importance as educators received new federal funding from Lyndon Johnson's War on Poverty. The Elementary and Secondary Education Act sought to remedy low achievement among the nation's poor children.

The cultural deficits ideology, discussed in Chapter 2, was widely embraced by educators. The remedy for young children was to offer preschool programs that would compensate for the cultural deprivation in their homes and help their parents acquire middle-class parenting skills. For older children, school personnel turned to basic academic instruction emphasizing drill-and-practice in orderly, teacher-directed classrooms, supplemented by pull-out programs for remedial instruction.

The "Who's Who" timeline here summarizes the history of the philosophical and political struggle for the school curriculum by highlighting those who profoundly influenced what schools taught, how, and to whom over the first 200 years of American schooling.

By the 1970s, the schools' dilemma was that the chosen "cure" for an undereducated nation was destined to limit the achievement of the nation's fastest-growing demographic sector: children of color, poor children, and children whose first language was not English. Clearly, new thinking was needed. And, in fact, the 1970s also brought a group of educators and education scholars that forged a new progressivism, melding cognitive and sociocultural theory with multicultural and socially just principles and values. Much of this new work has been led by teachers and scholars of color who are deeply sensitive to and knowledgeable about the possibilities for all students to learn well.

EDUCATIONAL TIMELINE
Who's Who of American Curriculum, 1775–1975

1780s–1880s	*Noah Webster* Blue-backed spellers: lessons in reading and writing, aimed at developing patriotic Americans
1830s–1840s	*Horace Mann* Common schools: should teach all the community's children basic literacy, numeracy, and citizenship
1900s	*Francis Parker; John Dewey; Jane Addams* Progressive, experiential, child-centered curriculum: focused on democracy and solving social problems
1900s	*G. Stanley Hall* Child study: curriculum based on scientific study of the stages of child and adolescent development
1918	*NEA Commission on the Reorganization of Secondary Education* Cardinal Principles of Secondary Education: schools should "track" students into different curriculum based on their abilities and interests
1920s	*Franklin Bobbitt: W.W. Charters* Scientific efficiency: curriculum based on a scientific inventory of human life and occupations and formulated as an efficient series of specific objectives and activities
1930s	*George Counts; Harold Rugg* Social reconstructionist: "Dare the Schools Build a New Social Order?" advocated that students prepare to solve social and economic problems
1940s–1950s	*Ralph Tyler* Life Adjustment: curriculum should match the life activities of U.S. citizens
1960s	*Jerome Bruner The Process of Education:* as active problem solvers, children should explore the structure of the academic disciplines; led to "new" curricula in math and science
1960s	*A. S. Neill* Free schools: best-selling book *Summerhill* advocated child-directed curriculum
1960s–1970s	*B. F. Skinner; Robert Gagne* Behaviorism: teaching "machines" and programmed instruction, where each lesson must be mastered in order to go on to the next

The Postmodern Curricula: Critical Multicultural and Sociocultural Perspectives

In the 1970s, multicultural and, later, sociocultural approaches to schooling emerged as alternatives to traditional, essentialist, and behavioral educational philosophies. As extensions of progressivism and social reconstructionism, these new approaches suggested that knowledge is created, rather than simply discovered, and that the purpose of schooling is to make the world better for all. They also signaled a shift from the modern to the postmodern world.

By the start of the twenty-first century, the Internet, a global economy, and population shifts contributed to Americans' deep awareness that they learn, think, and live differently from their regional, national, and international "neighbors." Contact with the broader world, and in some cases fears or threats from that world, exposed Americans to many perspectives different from their own but no less "logical" or "true" to those who hold them. Not only have Americans had to get used to different sorts of knowledge, they have had to accept the idea that different kinds of "truth" could even exist.

Increased ethnic diversity of the population, women's increasing economic and political power, and the reemergence of fundamental constitutional issues such as the meanings of privacy, separation of church and state, legal relationships among gays and lesbians, and so forth all have challenged the dominance of modern thinking.

Increasingly, critical multicultural reformers maintain that the hallmarks of the traditional curriculum—absolute certainties and universal truths as mined from the depths of white, Western culture—are weak and limiting guidelines for deciding what and how students will learn in the twenty-first century. Multiculturalists and socioculturalists press for reform with two main principles in mind: that the curriculum should be culturally democratic, and that the content of the curriculum should suit what we know about learning and cognition. It follows from these principles that social justice in schools and society is a powerful guide for developing curricula that are useful, intellectually rigorous, culturally cohesive, and accessible to all.

Like earlier child- and community-centered approaches and social reconstructionist philosophies, multiculturalists are often associated with political liberalism. And, as we will discuss later in this chapter, it's not surprising that these curriculum ideas have triggered virulent reactions, particularly among political conservatives.

Multicultural Education

Multicultural education developed in the 1970s as part of the nation's growing concern for racism and civil rights and as a reaction to the view that those who are not white or middle class are culturally deprived. Educators seeking to help all Americans learn more about the nation's diverse population sought to extend the ethnic studies curriculum that developed in higher education in the 1960s into elementary and secondary schools and into teacher education. The goal was to establish that being culturally different did not equate to being culturally deprived. Reformers also wanted students in desegregated and racially isolated white schools to develop positive racial attitudes and inter-group relations. Over time, educators have brought multicultural sensibilities into curricula when they sought to help students view the world from the multiple perspectives of diverse groups of people.[18]

A *critical multicultural curriculum,* a more recent refinement of multicultural education, helps students know and value the diverse traditions that enrich and dignify the nation's heritage, and it engages students in learning and maintaining their own heritage and language. It also acknowledges the social and economic power that derives from a command of Anglo-American traditions and Standard

English. Finally, a critical multicultural curriculum confronts the visible and invisible norms that perpetuate racism, classism, sexism, and other "isms" so that students can act on their knowledge.[19]

The Curriculum Is Inclusive   Jane Addams's voice echoes through much critical multicultural and bilingual curriculum today. Like Addams, contemporary multiculturalists press for curriculum that includes the "handicrafts and occupations, their traditions, their folk songs and folk lore, the beautiful stories which every immigrant colony is ready to tell and translate" of nonwhite and immigrant students. We also hear W. E. B. DuBois's passionate plea:

> We should fight to the last ditch to keep open the right to learn, the right to have examined in our schools not only what we believe; not only what our leaders say, but what the leaders of other groups and nations, and the leaders of other centuries have said. We must insist upon this to give our children the fairness of a start which will equip them with such an array of facts and such an attitude toward truth that they can have a real chance to judge what the world is and what its greater minds have thought it might be.[20]

Like DuBois, many of today's multiculturalists engage students with the ideas and "truths" of diverse people.

However, even among some multiculturalists and certainly in most traditional classrooms, what typically passes for a pluralistic or multicultural curriculum is little more than a mention of the "place" of minorities and immigrants in the unquestioned story and content of American culture. For example, schools may celebrate (or simply announce) "ethnic" holidays like Cinco de Mayo and Ramadan. They may use Black History Month to recognize events such as Harriet Tubman's nineteenth-century smuggling of slaves to freedom on the underground railroad or to play a few seconds of Martin Luther King's "I Have a Dream" speech.

Even these modest additions may result only after hard-won curriculum battles against forces who resent the inclusions for diminishing attention to white American cultural icons. And although King and Tubman—as modified by white curriculum writers—are considered appropriate historical representatives of African Americans in American history, W. E. B. DuBois and Malcolm X usually are not. Not only is their social criticism less palatable to mainstream tastes, many teachers and curriculum planners do not have a deep knowledge of their contributions. Without such knowledge and sympathetic understanding, educators cannot represent the most important ideas of nonwhites in ways that people of color can use, or as scholar Sonja Nieto notes, "in their own terms."[21]

The following quote from teacher Kimberly Min shows how social justice priorities can influence curriculum in ways that go far deeper than simple mentions, tributes, and food tastings.

❈ ❈ ❈

In honor of the 50-year anniversary of the landmark Brown *decision, my students examined oral histories to better understand the schooling experiences of people then and their own experiences now. My students interviewed*

adults who were bused or who attended schools that were in the midst of de-
segregation. This examination culminated in a PowerPoint presentation
and play they created about a little black girl who was bused to a desegre-
gated school in the 1960s.

The guiding questions for these investigations were: What was schooling
like then? How is schooling now? Has anything changed? With literature cir-
cles developed around books such as The Story of Ruby Bridges *and* Freedom
School, Yes! *students connected their knowledge of civil rights activists, what*
schools were like in the past, and their own experiences now.

—KIMBERLY MIN
Third-grade teacher

Kimberly Min's lesson shows that individual teachers can make powerful multicultural contributions. Even more ambitious efforts are possible when schools and districts support multicultural reforms. An example is two-way bilingual programs,
where native English–speaking children and those with another primary language—
Spanish, for example—become fully literate in both languages. These programs
don't consider the "other" language as a problem or regard bilingual education as a
way of remediating language deficits of children whose first language is not English.
In a number of cases, these two-way programs have become quite popular with
English-speaking, affluent families who see learning a second language as worthwhile for their children.

A less common approach to curriculum that reflects cultures other than the
white mainstream is an ethnocentric approach that places nonwhite cultures at the
center of the curriculum. Several big cities (e.g., Detroit, Milwaukee, Washington,
D.C., and Baltimore) have developed special Afrocentric elementary schools for
black students—sometimes just for black boys—in racially isolated city centers.
Elsewhere, even without an official "mandate" for an ethnic emphasis, individual
schools and teachers have shifted the school curriculum to reflect the special relevance of the students' culture. Often, this shift takes place under the leadership and
scholarship of the school's teachers of color.

Policymakers have been willing to try these controversial schools and/or willing
to overlook curriculum variations given the overwhelming evidence that the typical
traditional curriculum does not work well in inner-city neighborhoods. Teachers in
these schools hope that their students can break the persistent pattern of low academic achievement and antischool attitudes. The curriculum is a better match to
students' home cultures and provides knowledge of students' own heritage, race,
and culture. For example, teachers at Detroit's Malcolm X Academy wear African
dress; the hallways display African murals, posters, and flags; and the curriculum
gives prominence to African and African American history, culture, and current
events as students learn standard academic skills.

Few secondary schools have adopted ethnocentric curricula wholesale.
However, many in racially mixed as well as racially isolated communities offer
black studies and Chicano studies courses to balance the Western ethnocentric
mainstream. These schools are worth watching. They may reveal new and more

powerful ways to incorporate diverse groups into new expressions of a culturally democratic common school curriculum.

The Curriculum Includes the "Codes of Power"   In her book *The Dream-keepers,* which is about outstanding teachers of African American children, Gloria Ladson-Billings cites teacher Patricia Hilliard, whose multicultural classroom attends to the power of Standard English as well as respects the Black English her students speak outside of school:

> "I get so sick and tired of people trying to tell me that my children don't need to use any language other than the one they come to school with. Then those same people turn right around and judge the children negatively because of the way they express themselves. My job is to make sure that they can use both languages, that they understand that their language is valid but the demands placed upon them by others mean that they will constantly have to prove their worth. We spend a lot of time talking about language, what it means, how you use it, and how it can be used against you."[22]

Hilliard's teaching reflects recent sociological theory and research about how both the content and the structures of schooling connect with social class and race stratification. Perhaps the single most important finding of this research is that possession of what sociologists call *cultural capital* is often used to justify and legitimize the uneven distribution of wealth and power among racial and social class groups. (In the United States, the cultural capital that is most highly prized for high-wealth jobs and professions and for high-status colleges is white middle- and upper-class knowledge, dispositions, and values.) Just as in the market dollars may be exchanged for goods or services, in schools, jobs, and social interactions generally, certain habits and knowledge "buy" acceptance or favored treatment. First-year teacher Kay Goodloe is determined not to perpetuate this pattern.

───────────────────────── ⊗ ⊗ ⊗ ─────────────────────────

As an African American female, and a product of the public school system, I am bi-dialectical. But do not jump to conclusions and assume that Black English was my primary home language. It was not. I learned Ebonics on the playground and on the streets of Los Angeles. Our working/middle-class community expected children to use mainstream English. I use the word community *because all of the mothers shared the duty of policing our language. I have clear recollections of being reprimanded by a neighbor for using "slang" and being questioned as to where I had learned such language. As children, we became adept at code switching. We used mainstream English at home and in the presence of our parents and other authority figures, but we used Ebonics freely among our peers and at school. To be able to talk "jive" became a sign of group membership and demonstrated an individual's level of "coolness." It was also a form of resistance. We could communicate with our peers, ridiculing whites and other authority figures with the realization that they were absolutely clueless.*

I vowed never to deliberately silence my students' voices. This vow is not easy to keep; it is something I struggle with daily. I am committed to

creating a safe environment within my classroom, where my students feel
comfortable expressing themselves regardless of the language that they bring
with them, be it Ebonics, Spanglish, or other English dialects. But, to facili-
tate my students' acquisition of mainstream English, all of their assign-
ments must be written in "standard" English. The majority of the time, I
communicate with my students using Standard English, but I feel that it is
also necessary to model code switching in the classroom.

To achieve success in mainstream American society, bicultural students
need to acquire "mainstream" English. But in exposing bicultural students
to Standard English, we also need to expose the relationships of power inher-
ent in these forms of discourse. When Standard English is discussed as
"proper," society fails to acknowledge the cultural hegemony implicit in this
definition. An effective teacher cultivates a classroom in which all student
voices are valued.

—Kay Goodloe
First-year teacher, history, grade 11

Much cultural capital is wrapped up in students' language. Standard English and formal diction are quickly judged indicators of social class, parental influence, aspirations, school behavior, and academic potential. Cultural capital may be as simple as the good impression a young student creates by knowing and being willing to say "please," and "yes, ma'am" (and knowing when it is not worth the bother). It may be as subtle as a middle-school student's degree of inoffensive confidence when asking why she got a lower than expected grade.

Findings that cultural capital is pivotal in gaining wealth and power have prompted some reformers to reassert the value of teaching nonwhite and low-income students the formal, traditional knowledge and skills of white middle- and upper-class culture as well as the less formal knowledge and skills that privileged children learn at home. These reformers are not reverting to the traditionalist agenda in the usual sense, however. Most of them strongly support a multicultural curriculum. At the same time, they are suspicious of curriculum that cultivates students' own language and culture *to the exclusion* of the mainstream. They also reject the usual approaches to teaching mainstream culture to nonmainstream students as *assimilationist*—designed to obliterate other cultures and preserve white middle- and upper-class privileges.

Researcher Lisa Delpit frames the problem of the usual approach to multiculturalism as well-intentioned liberalism run amok. In her book *Other People's Children* she asks, "Will black teachers and parents continue to be silenced by the very forces that claim to 'give voice' to our children?"[23] Delpit and teachers like Kay Goodloe believe that all children should have access to the knowledge and skills that they will need to participate fully in the culture—as long as they understand that they are learning a particular code of power and not simply the "right" or "best" culture and language.

The Curriculum Includes Social Critique   Critical analysis is a powerful tool for revealing the cultural content in school curricula and in the community.

Students at all grades can use critique as a filter that preserves the best of democratic traditions while it identifies oppression. Teaching critical analysis, most often called *critical pedagogy,* links knowledge of diversity and inequality with actions that can make the culture more socially just. From this perspective, typical multicultural curricula appear superficial because they fail to consider institutionalized racism and other oppressive social structures. For the teacher, critical pedagogy means that classroom procedures and relationships as well as subject matter content are continually subjected to questions designed to reveal bias, favoritism, or single perspectives (usually, not always, those of the dominant culture).[24]

The questions that teachers consider when they plan their curriculum from a critical perspective include: Who benefits from the lesson being taught this way (i.e., the projects, worksheets, lectures, discussions, testing, grading, etc.)?, Who benefits from this version of the story (i.e., manifest destiny, Japanese internment camps, the Bill of Rights, AIDS, Martin Luther King Jr., etc.)?, and Whose prior knowledge and cultural experiences are best matched to the most important principles of the lesson, and whose are excluded? Questions such as these become cultural tools that teachers and students use to examine the fairness and the multiple understandings of the curriculum as they learn and teach what is conventionally understood as "subject matter." Such questions have benefits that can be recognized even by school critics who are not particularly sensitive to cultural or social justice issues: The questions are intensely engaging to all students, whatever their cultural background, and they provide practice in delving beneath the surface of complex issues.

Sonja Nieto and others advocate a critical curriculum that teaches students about the systematic discrimination that people of color have faced in the past and continue to face. The goal is not merely to expose injustice (or to generate guilt among white and affluent Americans). Rather, it is to help students see that possibilities for liberation exist side by side with oppression. Advocates of critical pedagogy argue that the study of liberation and oppression is basic for everyone. Any student who does not experience it is being *mis-educated,* to use the term that African American educator Carter Woodson used when he introduced this idea in 1933. Nieto observes:

> Textbooks in all subject areas exclude information about unpopular perspectives, or the perspectives of disempowered groups in our society. For instance, there are few U.S. history texts that assume the perspective of working-class people, although it is certainly true that they were and are the backbone of our country. Likewise, the immigrant experience is generally treated as a romantic and successful odyssey rather than the traumatic, wrenching, and often less-than-idyllic situation it was and continues to be for so many. . . . And finally, we can be sure that if the perspectives of women were taken seriously, the school curriculum would be dramatically altered. Unless all students develop the skill to see reality from multiple perspectives, not only the perspective of dominant groups, they will continue to think of it as linear and fixed and to think of themselves as passive in making any changes.[25]

First-year fourth-grade teacher Lucy Patrick used a lesson on the gold rush to draw students into taking the perspectives of others.

———————————————————❀ ❀ ❀———————————————————

We also dealt with power and justice. After the excitement of panning for gold, I asked the students, "How do you think the kindergarten children felt when you took over their sandbox, and what happened when they wanted to play, too?" We discussed our greediness and how we can all get caught up with "gold fever," but we had taken over an area that really did not belong to us. When the kindergartners saw us, they were intimidated, and one fourth grader snatched a gold piece from a kindergartner. I asked my students to connect this oppression to our readings about the people from the east taking over parts of California inhabited by the Spaniards, Mexicans, and Indians. My students made some powerful statements:

- *"We took over the kindergarten yard like the forty-niners did from the Indians. In a way, we were greedy, greedy for gold. . . . We were greedy, we didn't care, but we didn't realize whose 'home' we were actually destroying."*
- *"Now I know how the Indians and Spaniards felt when pioneers took over their land."*
- *"Today we went mining for gold in the kindergartners' sandbox. It was just like what the forty-niners did to the Spaniards and Indians. I don't think it was fair!"*

Students considered the issue in depth, exchanged views and opinions, and debated the implications. Through role playing and class discussions, students were able to generalize principles, such as fairness and justice, and apply them to present situations.

—LUCY PATRICK
First-year teacher, grade 4

Lessons like Lucy Patrick's draw on the curriculum theories of Brazilian educator Paulo Freire, as well as a postmodern view of knowledge as a social and political construction. This critical pedagogy asks students to reflect on what they learn by examining its history and politics, by generating alternative explanations, and by acting on what they learn. Freire's curriculum for helping poor Brazilian farmworkers focused literacy instruction on the social, political, and economic circumstances of their lives, particularly on the oppression that kept them poor and made wealthy landowners even wealthier. Applying these ideas to the American culture, critical multiculturalists argue for *praxis*—that is, a curriculum that teaches students the knowledge and skills of recognizing and combating racism and discrimination.

A social critique adds the concept of power differences to commonly accepted meanings of democracy, equal opportunity, and fairness. English teacher Michael Alvarez found ways to infuse critical perspectives into the high school literature curriculum in his school—helping his students to see power relations that they otherwise might have missed.

———————————————————❀ ❀ ❀———————————————————

I made attempts at critical teaching with To Kill a Mockingbird. *If one of the reasons to teach this novel is to expose students to the racism African*

Americans have had to deal with, I think we could find better choices. We see
the effects of racism not through the eyes of someone who has experienced it,
but rather through the eyes of a white narrator and white author. We only see
African American characters such as Tom Robinson and Calpurnia through
the eyes of a young white girl.

I wanted my students to explore issues of race and power by looking
through the eyes of Tom and Calpurnia. Do we think Tom would really be so
pleased to help Mayelia Ewell after she had called him a nigger? What about
Calpurnia? I asked my students how these characters might be different if
an African American had written the novel. My fifth-period class, which has
the largest percentage of African American students of my classes, gave me
some of the most revealing answers. One girl responded that Calpurnia prob-
ably would not be so happy to raise two children other than her own, but
would feel that it was the only job she would be able to get because of racism.
Another student said that while Tom would probably be grateful to Atticus,
he would not act so inferior to him and always refer to him as "Sir."

—**MICHAEL ALVAREZ**
First-year teacher, English, grade 9

Critical pedagogy intersects with a Deweyan view that the curriculum should
require students to enact as well as learn about important ideas. Critical teachers
may incorporate community projects or ask students to participate in local political
processes so students can learn skills and ideas to contribute to social change by
participating, not just learning about what *others* do. For example, first-year
teacher Armi Flores describes how she helped her students act on their growing
knowledge of racism.

— ✿ ✿ ✿ —

In the past year, we have had many bouts with racism in our classroom.
Light-skinned students have ganged up on darker-skinned students. And
those who are more "American" by virtue of the amount of time they have been
in the United States have a higher social status within our classroom. . . .
When I informed them that the entire class was designated "Latino or His-
panic," the majority of the light-skinned students were outraged. They didn't
want to be associated with "Latinos": They believed that they were "white." In
an attempt to create some sort of wall of protection around themselves from
the dark-skinned students, one student called out, "Well, what about Douglas?
He's not Latino, he's black." When I informed the class that Douglas, although
he was dark-skinned, was also Latino, the class fell silent. They couldn't be-
lieve that they were all Latino and not "white."

This discussion launched us into discussions about definitions of race
and ethnicity, and about discrimination. The concepts (i.e., discrimination,
protest, and segregation) were straight out of the social studies book. Then,
the students took part in a simulation. The entire class took a brief math
assessment. One third sat in front and received preferential treatment (i.e.,
clean sheets, candy, privileges, teacher attention, and encouragement). Those

in the back had to share ripped-up copies of tests; I made discouraging com-
ments and gave them little positive attention. Afterward, the students talked
about what it felt like to be discriminated against. Then, I invited the stu-
dents to examine other examples of discrimination they have seen or
experienced.

We discussed issues of discrimination we saw in the media or in our
city. After the simulation and discussion, I was amazed at the range of top-
ics they wrote about. Students raised topics such as slavery, the 1992 LA
riots, gang warfare, and deportation. They were making connections from
history, from the social studies text, from their personal experiences, from
the media, and then wrestling with the issues orally and in writing. Marcos
wrote a letter to the president voicing his concern about the current issue of
the burning of black churches. When I asked him why he thought this hap-
pened he answered, "Well, I'm not sure . . . but I read this book before about
how a long time ago, white people used to buy black people and make them
work for them." I asked him, "Do you think that's connected to the churches
being burnt down now?" He answered, "Yes, I think so." Marcos connected
the content of the lesson, the media, a book he had read and then made a huge
critical jump to posit a historical rationale for the prevalence of hate crimes
today.

Finally, they all wrote letters to influential people who they thought
could ameliorate the problems of discrimination. Students wrote to the presi-
dent, the Marines, the police, a judge, God, or their parents. One student sug-
gested that the answer was within themselves—that they had to take respon-
sibility for discrimination and act against it. They weren't writing
hypothetically.

—**ARMI FLORES**
First-year teacher, grade 4

Much of today's critical multiculturalist curriculum is owed to Professor James Banks, who is widely acknowledged to be the founding father of multicultural education. Over the past nearly 40 years, Banks has led the field as it has developed from ethnic studies to a comprehensive philosophy of education. In Focal Point 3.1, Banks summarizes his current conception of the field.

Sociocultural Perspectives on Curriculum and Learning

As we have seen, critical multiculturalism presses for a curriculum whose content includes the cultural knowledge of diverse groups, including languages other than English. It does not reject the knowledge of the dominant culture that is the content of the traditional curriculum. However, it recasts that knowledge in a postmodern frame, as the knowledge of power in contemporary society. Critical multiculturalism also engages students in social critique and encourages action that grows out of their critical learning.

Those who advocate for critical multiculturalism often turn to sociocultural theories about learning to guide the enactment of multiculturalism in classrooms.

FOCAL POINT 3.1

James Banks on Multicultural Education

The Goals of Multicultural Education

Multicultural education is an idea, an educational reform movement, and a process. As an idea, multicultural education seeks to create equal educational opportunities for all students, including those from different racial, ethnic, and social-class groups. Multicultural education tries to create equal educational opportunities for all students by changing the total school environment so that it will reflect the diverse cultures and groups within a society and within the nation's classrooms. Multicultural education is a process because its goals are ideals that teachers and administrators should constantly strive to achieve.

The Dimensions of Multicultural Education

I have identified five dimensions of multicultural education. They are: content integration, the knowledge construction process, prejudice reduction, an equity pedagogy, and an empowering school culture and social structure. Content integration deals with the extent to which teachers use examples and content from a variety of cultures and groups to illustrate key concepts, generalizations, and issues within their subject areas or disciplines. The knowledge construction process describes how teachers help students to understand, investigate, and determine how the biases, frames of reference, and perspectives within a discipline influence the ways in which knowledge is constructed within it. Students also learn how to build knowledge themselves in this dimension.

Prejudice reduction describes lessons and activities used by teachers to help students to develop positive attitudes toward different racial, ethnic, and cultural groups. Research indicates that children come to school with many negative attitudes toward and misconceptions about different racial and ethnic groups. Research also indicates that lessons, units, and teaching materials that include content about different racial and ethnic groups can help students to develop more positive intergroup attitudes if certain conditions exist in the teaching situation. These conditions include positive images of the ethnic groups in the materials and the use of multiethnic materials in a consistent and sequential way.

An equity pedagogy exists when teachers modify their teaching in ways that will facilitate the academic achievement of students from diverse racial, cultural, and social-class groups. Research indicates that the academic achievement of African American and Mexican American students is increased when cooperative teaching activities and strategies, rather than competitive ones, are used in instruction. Cooperative learning activities also help all students, including middle-class White students, to develop more positive racial attitudes. However, to attain these positive outcomes, cooperative learning activities must have several important characteristics. The students from different racial and ethnic groups must feel that they have equal status in intergroup interactions, teachers and administrators must value and support cross-racial interactions, and students from different racial groups must work together in teams to pursue common goals.

An empowering school culture and social structure is created when the culture and organization of the school are transformed in ways that enable students from diverse racial, ethnic, and gender groups to experience equality and equal status. The implementation of this dimension requires that the total environment of the school be reformed, including the attitudes, beliefs, and action of teachers and administrators, the curriculum and course of study, assessment and testing procedures, and the styles and strategies used by teachers.

To implement multicultural education effectively, teachers and administrators must attend to each of the five dimensions of multicultural education described above. They should use content from diverse groups when teaching concepts and skills, help students to understand how knowledge in the various disciplines is constructed, help students to develop positive intergroup attitudes and behaviors, and modify their teaching strategies so that students from different racial, cultural, and social-class groups will experience equal educational opportunities. The total environment and culture of the school must also be transformed so that students from diverse ethnic and cultural groups will experience equal status in the culture and life of the school.

Source: http://depts.washington.edu/centerme/view.htm.

These theories bear a strong resemblance to those John Dewey posed a century ago. We discuss their origins and their implications for instruction in more detail in Chapter 5. In the following sections, we describe why sociocultural theories are compatible with postmodern views of knowledge and multiculturalism. In essence, a sociocultural curriculum embodies three related ideas: knowledge is constructed; knowledge is meaningful in context; and new knowledge is connected to what students already know.

Knowledge Is Constructed   The main point of departure from centuries-old modern ideas to postmodern ideas—from traditional notions of learning to progressive and sociocultural approaches—is the concept of *construction.* Construction is so central to both learning and knowledge that the two become inseparable. Knowledge (or *subject matter* or *content* contained in the school curriculum) is not fixed, is not the same for everyone, and varies in different contexts and over time. This claim, that knowledge and even what might be called "facts" are human constructions, gives people fits. "What about 2 plus 2 equals 4?" Yes, there are multiple ways to "construct" this simple equation so that it can have different meanings. For this reason, we ask children to find the reasoning and meaning behind even this simplest of additions rather than simply recite the words. "Reasoning" and "making sense" are part of the constructing process.

Traditional schooling typically poses problems that have right procedures to follow and right answers to find. Constructivist-oriented teachers do not dispute that such answers have their place—spelling, math facts, and so on—but they object to a curriculum where attention to narrow, single-answer tasks displaces opportunities for multiple right answers or selecting (reasoning, constructing, making sense of, and so forth) among approaches to solving problems. Constructivist teachers most emphatically do not accept just any answer offered. And they may not accept even a "correct" conclusion until students can reconstruct how they arrived at that answer. Typically, the multiple meanings and reasoning that students offer can be negotiated. When everyone, including the teacher, can reconstruct and accept the sense-making that has gone into a conclusion, the answer can stand.

A constructivist approach challenges students in ways that the traditional curriculum does not. First-year teacher Jeffra Becknell shares how the knowledge demands and intellectual rigor of a constructivist lesson can surpass modernist approaches that prescribe what, when, and how knowledge must be transmitted.

—————————————————※ ※ ※—————————————————

My students are often frustrated when I answer their questions by posing another question and resist telling them the "right" answer. I want them to think. I do not ask them to memorize a lot of names and dates, although they need to refer to events to respond to questions. For example, one question on the Scientific Revolution asked whether it was a good idea for the Church to have so much power in those days. To answer that question students referenced their knowledge that Galileo's theory went against the Church's and that the Church tried him and kept him under house arrest. I am proud to say that my students themselves are able to develop penetrating questions. For instance, one student wanted to know, "If they could, would white people bring slavery back?" When developing questions for the Mexican Revolution, students wanted to know about life after the revolution, women's participation, weapons, and the fate of various participants; their questions reflect their individuality and inquisitiveness.

—**JEFFRA BECKNELL**
First-year teacher, social studies, grade 9

Engaging students in constructing knowledge also acknowledges that, in real life, there is seldom one right resolution to most real problems. Similarly, most real-life problems lack definitive resources like a spell checker or dictionary that gives an answer that is (somewhat) indisputable. Real-life solutions have to be compatible with multiple ideas, fit innumerable contexts, and suit the knowledge and opinions of so many people that two people rarely enact the same resolution. Furthermore, the same person often will not select the same solution twice if given the chance to change her mind or learn from her experience. In the real world, people need to figure things out by using trial, success, and error, as well as by relying on memorized and automatic routines.

Knowledge Becomes Meaningful in Context   In the real world, knowledge is not constructed or used out of contexts. Only in schools are students expected to remember isolated facts—names, events, dates, formulas, and algorithms. Facts are not unimportant, of course, but they only have meaning when they are presented within the context of ideas, narratives, or experiences that already mean something to students. Educational and social critics frequently tout surveys showing that a shamefully low percentage of teenagers know basic historical facts, such as the century in which the American Civil War was fought. It isn't that they were never taught. More likely, they learned the dates outside of any meaningful context and promptly forgot them.

That's the problem that first-year teacher Zeba Palomino struggles with as she helps her ninth graders think about solving algebraic equations—a topic typically taught with even fewer connections to meaningful contexts than history.

As difficult as it has been for me to find or design contextualized math lessons, they have worked much more effectively than boring and meaningless lectures about a rule or algorithm. In the unit on solving equations, my students became very familiar with the idea of balance scales, and with keeping the scales balanced by doing the same thing to both sides of the balance scale. They also became comfortable with the concepts of "variables," "like terms," "distributive property," and "opposite operations" through using manipulatives including teddy bears, number blocks, and visual balance scales. Gradually, all of them, at their own pace, "weaned" themselves off the manipulatives and became comfortable solving equations with just pencil and paper. We did not talk about rules or algorithms such as "to undo an operation you must perform the opposite operation to both sides of the equation." Instead, we discovered easy, logical ways to figure out an unknown amount on a balance scale without throwing the scale off balance.

—Zeba Palomino
First-year teacher, high school mathematics

New Knowledge Connects with What Students Know Students bring to classrooms a store of both formal and informal knowledge. This prior knowledge and experience are a valuable curriculum resource, as first-year teacher Ramon Martinez discovered when he began a geography unit with his first graders.

My students are Latino first graders who have been classified as limited English proficient. All of them come from low-income homes, and most live in the projects. My unit "Donde Estamos?" builds on my students' knowledge of their community to help them understand basic concepts in geography. We made a "mural map" as the centerpiece of the unit. Instead of telling my students what to include, I allowed them to decide. Many students supplied me with details about their community that would have otherwise gone unnoticed. One saw that I had forgotten to put a particular store on the map. I encouraged her to make it and put it where it belonged, which she did in amazing detail. Another noticed that the Chinese restaurant near her house

did not appear. Not surprisingly, she knew exactly where to put it. My stu-
dents began noticing maps everywhere. Once my students realized that I wel-
comed their knowledge, they began to participate more actively. They showed
me maps in the hallway and interrupted during journal time to show me
maps in books. One brought back a map from Disneyland and insisted on
sharing it. After I introduced the cardinal directions, they were constantly
notifying me every time that they saw the cardinal directions in print.

—RAMON MARTINEZ
First-year teacher, bilingual grade 1

One of the strengths of multilingual schools is the potential for using students' prior language as a bridge for understanding new concepts.

———————————————— ⚘ ⚘ ⚘ ————————————————

One day a student who has a lot of difficulty speaking English spoke. I did
not understand him and was reminded of the trouble he had acquiring
English in my class, while speaking mostly Spanish at home and studying
Cantonese at Chinese school. As I often do, I replied to him in his home lan-
guage, saying "What?" in Spanish. He then rattled off a beautiful description
of a bird building its nest on a rooftop, and he connected it to an integrated
lesson we had a month earlier. To the casual observer, it might not have
seemed like any success in developing language. For me, it was poetry—the
student's description of a bird building a nest to take care of eggs that would
someday hatch. He engaged his classmates in a real-life situation and con-
nected it to what we had done in class. He not only got his Spanish-speaking
peers to speak in their home language, the rest of the class became interested.
Despite not being able to understand Spanish, other students were excited
and tried to figure out what was being said. This led the Spanish speakers to
explain in English and Spanish. As I looked at this class at that moment, I
saw 20 smiling faces engaged in a spontaneous language arts lesson led by a
peer who was speaking just two of the languages he was going to master.

—BENJAMIN CHANG
First-year teacher, grade 1

Whereas a traditional curriculum might *enrich* lessons by acknowledging diverse and multiple cultures, sociocultural theory invites teachers to place inclusive and democratic elements at the center of their curricula and from that core let develop the daily learning opportunities. Professor Luis Moll's research at the University of Arizona explains how diverse students bring knowledge and experiences to school that provide a rich and valid basis for learning. Moll contends that the secret to literacy instruction is for schools to investigate and tap into the "hidden" home and community resources of their students. Moll, who studied Mexican American families in Tucson's impoverished barrio, discovered that clusters of these households had developed rich "funds of knowledge" about agriculture, mining, economics, household management, materials and science, medicine, and religion. However, the schools neither knew about nor used this knowledge base to assist students with academic skills.[26]

First-year teachers Wendy Herrera and Megan Ward followed Moll's approach as they created a curriculum for their bilingual K–1 class where learning developed through cultural interactions.

─────────────────────────────── ⚔ ⚔ ⚔ ───────────────────────────────

We chose Dia de los muertos instead of Halloween. We wanted our students to understand better the tradition that stems from their own history and culture, and choose whether or not they want to embrace it for themselves. We asked the students, "Que es el Dia de los muertos?" so we could create a brainstorm web of their ideas. Students responded to the question with a blank stare, and later made comments such as, "Es cuando la gente se muere y los gusanos se los comen" ("It's when people die and the worms eat them"). Another comment was, "Es como Halloween cuando la gente se viste de monstruos" ("It's like Halloween when people dress up as monsters"). So, we asked that parents share what they know with their children, and students drew and wrote about what they had learned from their parents. The students compiled their drawings into a big book.

Because the altar is central to the cultural celebration, we created one in the classroom. Students went home and discussed with their parents what meaningful artifact they would like to share and place on the altar. Each time that a student brought something in for the altar, we would sit in a community circle and the student would share its significance. The altar and the walls were filled with student work, and we encouraged the students to decorate and add their personal objects on the altar that reminded them of someone or something that had passed away. Many students brought in photographs and drawings. Some students placed stuffed animals that reminded them of a pet that had died.

Dia de los muertos was an open invitation for parents and school community members to become a part of our learning process. One woman in the community who knew a lot about the celebration demonstrated making paper flowers for the altar. She also offered insights into the meaning behind items that go on the altar. She gave the students calavera rings that she painted representing an aspect of Dia de los muertos. Throughout the month, we read books that illustrated the various items that could be placed on the altar, and the students brought in flowers, plants, fruit and candles. Mothers gave suggestions and reminded us of things that needed to go on the altar. We painted, colored, and made various art projects, including puppets and masks and even making our own Pan de Muertos. One could walk into our classroom and feel the students' energy.

—**WENDY HERRERA AND MEGAN WARD**
First-year bilingual teachers, grade K–1

───

Wendy Herrera and Megan Ward, like Louis Moll, identified the funds of knowledge in their students' families and communities. In doing so, everyone learned to do far more than simply identify a few features of the *Dia de los muertos* tradition.

Building on *prior knowledge* presents a challenge to many teachers who are not used to valuing all knowledge or in whom it is engrained that classroom knowledge must not depart from the subject matter in texts and curriculum guides. But the outcomes can be impressive, as teachers Martinez, Chang, Herrera, and Ward make clear.

The Curriculum Struggle Today: An Essentialist Backlash to Multicultural and Sociocultural Perspectives

Beginning in the early 1980s, political conservatives have championed a return to an essentialist curriculum, focused on a set of indisputable, unchanging ideas, values, facts, and particular works found in past generations of history, literature, and even science and mathematics instruction. Although many of those arguing for such a curriculum claim to value "higher-order" thinking and interpretation—a perennialist theme—most conservatives today believe that public schools should stick to the basics and avoid a curriculum that questions dominant cultural values or that questions rules governing correct procedures and right answers.

Mounted under such themes as "excellence," "cultural literacy," and "standards," the backlash against critical multicultural and constructivist curriculum has been quite successful over the past two decades, as is evidenced most recently in the philosophical and curricular underpinnings of the current federal No Child Left Behind Act.

Backlash as "Excellence"

Ronald Reagan's 1980 election brought a new and hostile assault on American schools. Consistent with a political agenda to minimize or remove the federal government's involvement in people's lives, Reagan was eager to end the federal role in education and included eliminating the federal Department of Education. The administration consistently attempted to discredit federal efforts to promote equality and provide additional funding for poor children, arguing that such efforts had brought a "rising tide of mediocrity" to American schools. *A Nation at Risk* (discussed in Chapter 2) pointed to declines in SAT scores and the nation's poor showing in international test-score comparisons as evidence that the schools required tough-minded reforms.

The curriculum was the first line of attack. *A Nation at Risk* called on the states to stress traditional academic subjects. All high school students should complete the "new basics" including four years of English; three years each of mathematics, science, and social studies; and a half year of computer science. The report also argued that elementary teachers must spend more instructional time on these subjects. States quickly enacted stringent high school graduation and college entrance requirements and lengthened the school day and year.

In the rush to restore excellence—as well as economic competitiveness and national security—few noticed that the report's authors overlooked data that could have altered their conclusions and recommendations. The shame of America's low ranking was not that schools needed to be told what to teach, but that they taught an "elite" curriculum to a few students and a "mass" curriculum to many more students. Thus, it was not so much a matter of education *policy* that was at fault, as it was education (and political) *philosophy* that restricted the distribution of high expectations. In the end, *A Nation at Risk* may have kept students in school longer and raised requirements, but it did little to address the nation's belief that all students needed the opportunity to receive a high level education.

Backlash as Essentialist Certainty

A Nation at Risk, combined with the considerable discomfort with the spread of multiculturalism, provided fertile ground for the late E. D. Hirsch's essentialist explanation for the nation's educational problems. In his 1988 best seller, *Cultural Literacy,* and his 1997 book, *The Schools We Need, and Why We Don't Have Them,* Hirsch argued that progressive reformers' emphasis in the 1960s and 1970s on projects, "discovery learning," and other "anti-subject matter" methods had brought curricular anarchy and low achievement to U.S. schools. Teachers working from constructivist and social justice perspectives were the primary targets of Hirsch's outrage.

To restore uniformity and predictability to the curriculum, Hirsch outlined the "core knowledge" that all American students should learn. In a series of grade-by-grade books beginning with *What Your First Grader Needs to Know: Fundamentals of a Good First Grade Education,* he specified the essential names, phrases, dates, and concepts that children should learn at each grade. In behaviorist fashion, topics are carefully sequenced in the books so that students can master the supposedly simpler parts of content before they are exposed to more complex knowledge. And rather than having students "discover" this knowledge through a problem-based approach, Hirsch argued that teachers should present the information they expect children to practice and memorize.

Hirsch's ideas proved enormously popular and were widely promoted by the Reagan and first Bush administrations. While Hirsch must be credited for his insistence that all children be given access to "high-status" knowledge, his popularity among political conservatives came mostly from the comfortable familiarity of his lists of content and because his approach keeps teachers firmly in charge of meaning. The lists were appealing not only for what they included, but by implication, what they excluded. So, in literature, for example, what the author of a work intended is far more important than the meanings students might find in it.[27] In a very modernist way, Hirsch argues for an unambiguous, "correct" curriculum that students acquire rather than construct.

Backlash as Preserving the Dominant Culture

Throughout the 1800s, social leaders increasingly used public schools as the battleground on which to wage a cultural war, maintaining that national unity required that immigrants' language and culture be faded into the American background.

In the late 1980s Allan Bloom, author of the influential book *The Closing of the American Mind,* resurrected the notion of the culture wars. Writing that "culture means a war against chaos *and* a war against other cultures,"[28] Bloom declared war on mid- and late-twentieth-century reforms that brought multicultural sensibilities to the college curriculum.

Bloom argued for an undergraduate college curriculum focused on social "truths" embedded in a classical or liberal arts education. This curriculum has come to be called the *canon,* or a binding and unchanging set of core principles and works most highly valuing Western literary classics, capitalism, the practice of American government since its earliest days, the nuclear family, and so on. Without such a curriculum, Bloom argues, American students will continue their decades-long lapse into a relativism that undermines the moral grounding of the nation. If Bloom's prescriptions for what college undergraduates should learn were to be translated into a curriculum for late elementary and secondary schools, it would look quite a lot like Hirsch's *Cultural Literacy* lists.

To be sure, Hirsch's "core knowledge" curriculum includes "contributions" from African Americans and Native Americans. However, it does not see multiple perspectives on knowledge as legitimate or permit debate about the dominant perspective. Rather, the curriculum should enable "others" to adopt the traditional, largely Anglo-American culture (including both facts and interpretations) as their own. So, for example, Hirsch would have all children accept—without deliberation or debate about alternatives—the idea that the land Columbus came to was a "new" world, that manifest destiny was a progressive national expansion, and that civil rights law (though not the civil rights "movement" that brought the laws about) has solved the racial problems in America. Hirsch argued that there are two forms of multiculturalism: the ethical, progressive, and cosmopolitan form that he advocates; and a retrogressive and ethnocentric form that "tends to set group against group" and "hinders the educational excellence and fairness it was conceived to enhance."[29]

The "progressive" form (in Hirsch's usage, as embodied in Hirsch's core knowledge curriculum) considers ethnicity an accident of history, having little to do with defining one's identity and cultural essence. Consequently, according to Hirsch, the desirable form encourages sympathy for other cultures and respect for one's own, but it stresses "competence in the current system of language and allusion that is dominant in the nation's economic and intellectual discourse."[30]

The regressive, undesirable form, Hirsch claimed, emphasizes ethnic loyalty. It allows children to learn a lot, for example, about their cultural past, instead of learning to read, write, solve mathematical problems effectively, and understand natural science. This regressive multiculturalism, he argued, victimizes minority children by preventing them from participating in the mainstream culture. Bilingual education is one of the most disparaged forms of regressive multiculturalism.

Backlash as Standards

In 1989 President George H. W. Bush and the 50 state governors held an educational "Summit" to set goals for the year 2000 that would spur the nation to improve students' academic performance. Among the goals was to make U.S. students first in the world in their mathematics and science achievement. Although the year 2000 has come and gone without those goals being met, Goals 2000 had an enormous impact on the debates around what students should know and be able to do. Perhaps most important, the Summit spawned the "standards movement" that has engaged policymakers, businesspeople, and educators in defining what students should learn in each of the subject areas.

The idea of standards, it turns out, appealed to nearly everyone. Traditionalists like Hirsch believed that they would restore clarity and correctness to the school curriculum. Many progressives—especially those who had fought hard for civil rights—believed that setting high standards for all children and holding schools accountable for reaching them might be the best tool for gaining equitable schooling for minority students.

To establish standards, teachers and subject matter experts gathered throughout the 1990s at national, state, and local meetings to deliberate and write long reports detailing the standards in each subject. These groups offered the results of their work as new standards to guide curriculum and testing programs. But rather than following Hirsch's example or other traditionalist conceptions of the curriculum, these expert groups framed the standards, by and large, in the form of a "meaningful" curriculum that matches cognitive and sociocultural learning theories. As each of these expert-informed consensus reports came forth, conservatives were further outraged. They saw that the new standards for tough, rigorous learning (as they envisioned it) had strayed even further from a familiar fact- and skills-based curriculum. In fact, instead of turning back the direction of "constructivist" or "postmodern" reform, the expert reports encouraged schools to move faster and far beyond where progressive reform had taken most schools.

To stop these standards-driven reforms, conservative advocates campaigned aggressively to persuade policymakers and the public that the standards were dangerous. Their tactics included belittling "expert" involvement in favor of common sense, and then calling upon their own "experts" to support their views. They garnered considerable media attention as they caricatured the social constructivist approach as nothing more than mindless games, "invented" spelling, and math without numbers. Illogically, they blamed these "new" methods for the persistent low standardized test scores of students who had been taught with mostly conventional approaches.

By the mid-1990s, the backlash against cognitively and socioculturally oriented curricula had captured enormous public sympathy and policy clout. Anti-reform advocacy groups such as Mathematically Correct in California and Arizona Parents for Traditional Education began using the Internet as a forum to fight the standards. We describe the battles over the standards in the academic subjects further in Chapter 4.

Backlash in Favor of "One Right Way"

In 2001 curriculum scholar Michael Apple wrote a remarkable book, *Educating the "Right" Way: Markets, Standards, God, and Inequality,* documenting the process by which conservative movements have shaped current school reforms.[31] Apple traces how a disparate set of conservative social movements—including neoliberals committed to markets and competitive individualism; neoconservatives committed to traditional culture, knowledge, and behavior (like Bennett, Hirsch, and Bloom); "authoritarian populists" who promote Christian fundamentalist ideas; and the "new middle class" of professionals and managers—have come together to forge a "mainstream" reform agenda of standards, testing, and choice.

According to Apple, these groups have also redefined how Americans think and talk about democracy, freedom, morality, and culture. These redefinitions support the growing political appeal of vouchers and other strategies for privatizing public education. Apple argues that a "conservative modernism" opposes both a multicultural curriculum and related efforts to create socially just schooling.

A familiar example of this reform direction is the much-touted "Texas miracle" of raising achievement and narrowing the minority-white achievement gap. Indeed, much has happened in Texas that can be admired, such as a surge of grassroots political organizing for better schools in low-income communities. (We explore that dimension of Texas reform in Chapter 10.) Yet beneath the miracle is a less happy story of huge increases in the number of elementary school children being retained, soaring middle and high school dropout rates, and the dominance of a low-level, skill-based, "test prep" curriculum schools attended by poor children.[32]

Backlash as "No Child Left Behind"

By 2005, every state had adopted standards. In some states these standards mirror the national standards constructed by subject matter groups in the 1990s; in other states they conform to conservative views of knowledge and learning. Under the federal No Child Left Behind Act of 2002, every state must assess student progress toward proficiency on those standards as a condition of receiving federal funding for programs supporting the education of low-income students. Most teachers support the standards, but, as we detail in Chapter 6, most also believe that the tests that accompany the standards have had negative effects on instruction. Most also object to the traditional reading curriculum required under the Act's Reading First program that we discuss in Chapters 4 and 11. Nearly all lament that both the federal government and individual states have been far too slow in providing the resources to fulfill the promise of standards—that all children can learn at very high levels. We discuss the tensions in these policy choices more in Chapter 11.

Today's teachers stand at the center of a curriculum battle—a battle shaped by traditional American understandings of merit, efficiency, competition, and progress—that extends far deeper than their classrooms. The traditional curriculum does not match the way students learn, and it favors Americans of wealth and power. But it could be otherwise. Each day American teachers confront and win the curriculum battle, as they engage students with rich and powerful ideas that touch their lives. That is one reason they return to school each day.

⊚ OLC Connections

A list of additional online and print resources and a set of questions for reflection about the philosophy and politics of curriculum history can be found at www.mhhe.com/oakes3e.

▒ Digging Deeper

The educational historians we listed in the Chapter 2 "Digging Deeper" document the events, trends, and themes of American education. Here, we suggest a number of curriculum theorists who emphasize the philosophical and political underpinnings woven throughout past and current school organization and curriculum. We also list a professional organization for multicultural curriculum whose membership includes both university faculty and educators who work in elementary and secondary schools.

University of Wisconsin professor **Michael Apple's** books *Ideology and Curriculum* (New York: Routledge, 1990), *Cultural Politics and Education* (New York: Teachers College Press, 1996), *Official Knowledge* (New York: Routledge, 1993), and others analyze how politics and ideology pervade curriculum. Another book with **Linda Christian-Smith,** *The Politics of the Textbook* (New York: Routledge, 1991), examines how the content of textbooks reflects the dominant perspective in ways likely to maintain the national status quo of power and privilege. Of particular interest is his newest book that we mentioned in this chapter, *Educating the "Right" Way: Markets, Standards, God, and Inequality* (New York: RoutledgeFalmer, 2001), which offers a compelling discussion of the current conservative stance toward education.

Professor **James Banks** of the University of Washington was instrumental in developing the idea of a multicultural curriculum. Banks has edited two of the most complete sources on multicultural education history and research: *The Handbook of Research on Multicultural Education* (San Francisco: Jossey-Bass, 2001) and *Multicultural Education, Transformative Knowledge, and Action: Historical and Contemporary Perspectives* (New York: Teachers College Press, 1996). Additionally, Banks is director of the University of Washington's Center for Multicultural Education, which focuses on research projects and activities designed to improve practice related to equity issues, intergroup relations, and the achievement of all students. The Center's website at http://depts.washington.edu/centerme/home.htm includes information about successful K–12 programs and links to numerous other multicultural education websites.

John Dewey's writings on curriculum provide the foundation for current social constructivist curricula. Especially relevant for this chapter are his 1897 essay, "My Pedagogic Creed," and his books *The Child and the Curriculum* and *The School and Society* (reprinted, Chicago: University of Chicago Press, 1991). Those interested in reading an analysis of Dewey and his influence might try Robert Westbook,

John Dewey and American Democracy (Ithaca, NY: Cornell University Press, 1993).

Professor **Christine Sleeter,** Professor Emerita of California State University at Monterey Bay has written some of the most helpful books for teachers on developing multicultural curriculum. Her 1989 book with Professor **Carl Grant** of the University of Wisconsin, *Making Choices for Multicultural Education: Five Approaches to Race, Class and Gender* (Columbus, OH: Merrill/Prentice-Hall, 1989), is one of the most important conceptualizations of multicultural education. Their most recent book, *Turning on Learning: Five Approaches for Multicultural Teaching Plans for Race, Class, Gender, and Disability* (Upper Saddle River, NJ: Prentice Hall, 1998), translates those theories into a practical guide to planning multicultural lessons. Additionally, Sleeter has recently published a new book, *Un-Standardizing Curriculum: Multicultural Teaching in the Standards-Based Classroom* (New York: Teachers College Press, 2005), that provides guidance teaching academically rigorous multicultural curricula under the current constraints of standards and accountability.

Brazilian adult educator **Paulo Freire** developed "critical pedagogy," an approach to informal adult education that has influenced thousands of grassroots organizations, college classrooms, and, most recently, school reform efforts in major urban areas. Freire's best-known book, *Pedagogy of the Oppressed* (New York: Continuum, 1970), argues that education is a path to permanent liberation; that is, through critical pedagogy, people become aware of their oppression and transform it. His recent book, *Pedagogy of Hope* (New York: Continuum, 1994), reexamines his work in critical pedagogy 25 years after *Pedagogy of the Oppressed*. His posthumously published book is *Teachers as Cultural Workers* (New York: Routledge, 1998).

Henry Louis Gates, Jr., W. E. B. DuBois professor of the humanities and chairman of the Afro-American Studies Department at Harvard, offers some of the most cogent arguments for multicultural curriculum. His book *Loose Canons: Notes on the Culture Wars* (New York: Oxford University Press, 1992) includes a series of essays that argue for a curriculum that respects both the diversity and commonalties of human culture. That curriculum, according to Gates, provides the best hope for forging a civic culture that respects both differences and similarities.

Professor **Andy Hargreaves** of the Ontario Institute for Educational Studies in Toronto, Canada, has written thoughtfully on the conditions of postmodernity and their impact on schooling, and especially on teachers' work. This work can be found in *Changing Teachers, Changing Times: Teachers' Work and Culture in the Postmodern Age* (New York: Teachers College Press, 1994). His many other books and articles, especially recent ones on the emotions of teaching and educational reform, are also worth pursuing.

Herbert Kliebard, a professor at the University of Wisconsin, stands out as the nation's most astute curriculum historian. His book *The Struggle for the American Curriculum: 1893–1958,* 3rd ed. (New York: Routledge, 2004) provides an insightful analysis of the multiple forces that shaped the curriculum in the twentieth century.

UCLA professor **Peter McLaren** is one of the nation's leading thinkers and writers on critical pedagogy. *Life in Schools: An Introduction to Critical*

Pedagogy in the Foundations of Education (New York: Longman, 1998), one of his many books, is an excellent resource for American teachers struggling with how to teach students to question the structures and power relations that limit their lives. McLaren includes a journal of his own teaching in an inner-city school as well as his analysis of that experience. He places both the journal and the analysis in the context of scholarship in the local tradition.

The **National Association for Multicultural Education** (NAME) was founded in 1990 to bring together educators who have an interest in multicultural education. NAME's quarterly magazine, *Multicultural Education,* features sections with promising practices and resources for teachers. The organization's annual conference provides an opportunity for intensive discussion and learning. NAME's Internet address is http://www.nameorg.org.

Professor **Sonja Nieto** is on the education faculty at the University of Massachusetts, Amherst, where she studies multicultural and bilingual curriculum issues. Her book *Affirming Diversity: The Sociopolitical Context of Multicultural Education* (New York: Longman, 2000) is a highly readable overview of the theory and practice of multicultural education. The text comes alive with Nieto's inclusion of case studies of 12 diverse students and how schooling intersects with their lives. Another book, *The Light in Their Eyes: Creating Multicultural Learning Communities* (New York: Teachers College Press, 2000), includes a review of the research on multiculturalism and teachers' powerful reflections on multicultural teaching.

Notes

1. Herbert Kliebard, *The Struggle for the American Curriculum: 1898–1958* (New York: Routledge, 1983).
2. Lauren Resnick, *Education and Learning to Think* (Washington, DC: National Academy Press, 1983), p. 3.
3. Joel Spring, *The American School: 1642–1990* (New York: Longman, 1996), p. 41.
4. Ibid., p. 149.
5. Ibid.
6. Joseph Mayer Rice, *The Public School System of the United States* (1893, p. 34), as quoted in Kliebard, *The Struggle for the American Curriculum.*
7. Kliebard, *The Struggle for the American Curriculum.*
8. For a detailed analysis of these movements, see Kliebard, *The Struggle for the American Curriculum.*
9. Lawrence Cremin, *The Transformation of the School: Progressivism in American Education 1876–1957* (New York: Knopf, 1961), p. 130.
10. Ibid.
11. Francis Parker, *Talks on Pedagogies* (New York: E. L. Kellogg, 1894, p. 450), as quoted in Cremin, *Transformation,* p. 132.
12. Katherine Camp Mayhew and Anna Camp Edwards, *The Dewey School* (New York: Appleton-Century, 1936, pp. 65–65) as quoted in Cremin, *Transformation,* p. 137.
13. John Dewey, *School and Society* (reprinted, Chicago: University of Chicago Press, 1991), p. 28, as quoted in Kliebard, *The Struggle for the American Curriculum,* p. 69.
14. Jane Addams, "The Public School and the Immigrant Child," in *The Educating of Americans: A Documentary History,* ed. Daniel Calhoun (Boston: Houghton Mifflin, 1969), pp. 421–423.
15. O. K. Armstrong, "Treason in the Textbooks," *The American Legion Magazine,* September 1940, pp. 8–9, 51, 70–72, as cited in Kliebard, *The Struggle for the American Curriculum.*

16. Jerome Bruner, *The Process of Education*, (Cambridge, MA: Harvard University Press, 1960).

17. A. S. Neill, *Summerhill* (Oxford, England: Hart Publishing, 1960).

18. See James A. Banks, "Multicultural Education: Historical Development, Dimension, and Practice," in *Handbook of Research on Multicultural Education,* 2nd ed., ed. James A. Banks and Cherry McGee Banks (San Francisco: Jossey Bass, 2004).

19. Barry Kanpol and Peter McLaren, *Critical Multiculturalism: Uncommon Voices in a Common Struggle* (London: Bergen and Garvey, 1995).

20. W. E. B. DuBois, "The Freedom to Learn," in *W. E. B. DuBois Speaks,* ed. P. S. Foner (New York: Pathfinder, 1970), pp. 230–231. This 1949 speech came to our attention because Linda Darling-Hammond uses it to set the tone of her book *The Right to Learn.*

21. Sonia Nieto, *Affirming Diversity: The Sociopolitical Context of Multicultural Education*, 2nd ed. (White Plains, NY: Longman, 1996), p. 312.

22. Gloria Ladson-Billings, *The Dreamkeepers* (San Francisco: Jossey-Bass, 1994), p. 82.

23. Lisa Delpit, *Other People's Children: Cultural Conflict in the Classroom* (New York: The New Press, 1995), p. 46.

24. Peter McLaren , *Life in Schools: An Introduction to Critical Pedagogy in the Foundations of Education* (New York: Longman, 1998),

25. Sonia Nieto, *Affirming Diversity,* p. 319.

26. Luis Moll, "Funds of Knowledge for Teaching: Using a Qualitative Approach to Connect Homes and Classrooms," *Theory into Practice* 31, no. 2 (1992), pp. 132–141.

27. Walter Feinberg, "Educational Manifesto and the New Fundamentalism," *Educational Researcher* 26, no. 8 (1997), p. 32.

28. Quoted in Lawrence W. Levine, *Opening of the American Mind: Canons, Culture, and History* (Boston: Beacon Press, 1996), p. 19.

29. E. D. Hirsch, "Toward a Centrist Curriculum: Two Kinds of Multiculturalism in Elementary School," Charlottesville, VA: Core Knowledge Foundation, 1992; located online at http://www.coreknowledge.org.

30. Ibid.

31. Michael Apple, *Educating the "Right" Way: Markets, Standards, God, and Inequality* (New York: RoutledgeFalmer, 2001).

32. Linda McNeil, *The Contradictions of School Reform: Educational Costs of Standardized Testing* (New York: RoutledgeFalmer, 2000).

PART II

The Practice of Teaching to Change the World

CHAPTER 4

The Subject Matters
Making School Knowledge Meaningful

As teachers we decide what to teach our students. Yet there are times when we do not have a choice. . . . Curricular back to basics, achieved by implementing oppressive language arts and math programs, are used throughout urban schools. This narrow emphasis is a site of contention for many teachers and students. . . . What are teachers to do? How are students to cope? It is in these moments that we must be critical and creative.

We must present the histories of our students, of our country, and of our realities in a context that is critical and truthful. Including marginalized ethnic groups into our curriculum, students of color can identify with powerful histories that mirror their realities. This avenue of identification with the subject matter not only legitimizes students, but also enhances the curriculum by demonstrating the myriad ways that different people have influenced our world.

—KIMBERLY MIN
Third-grade teacher

Chapter Overview

This chapter focuses on what today's teachers spend most of their time teaching—the academic subjects. It describes the debates that swirl around progressive teachers like Kimberly Min as they struggle to make school knowledge meaningful for their diverse students and remain true to their own commitments to socially just schooling.

Today as in the past, debates about what and how to teach are very political. They arouse Americans' interests, passions, and fears about how schooling portrays the culture and how the culture might be changed by what schools choose to teach. Clearly, teachers are not merely knowledge technicians parceling out a preestablished, neutral commodity called subject matter.

As we noted in Chapter 3, on opposing sides of the debates are people we call "traditionalists" (because they hold conservative views of culture, essentialist and behavioral views curriculum and teaching) and those we call "progressives" (because they hold postmodern views of culture and sociocultural or critical multicultural conceptions of curriculum and teaching). Traditionalists tend to be on the conservative end of the political spectrum, and progressives tend to be politically liberal. The establishment of curriculum standards in every state has not reconciled the positions of progressive and traditional educators. Deep disagreements continue about what students should learn in mathematics, in English language arts, in social studies, and in science.[1]

Mathematics

In August 1997 Lynne V. Cheney, who is now the nation's second lady, was a senior fellow at a conservative Washington think tank, the American Enterprise Institute. In an essay about mathematics curriculum reform, Mrs. Cheney used the following story to make a caustic judgment about progressive mathematics curriculum:

> "They lied to me," says Madalyn McDaniel of Atascadero, California. "They completely betrayed me." At parents' night at the local high school, McDaniel was told about a great opportunity for her son: *The Interactive Mathematics Program,* in which he would be learning everything taught in traditional math courses only in a more effective way. But after signing him up, McDaniel realized the program was not at all what it was advertised. Instead of learning rules and formulas, her son and his classmates were presented with problems and expected to invent their own ways of solving them. "He was very frustrated," McDaniel says. "I'd say, 'Look in the book, it will explain.' He'd say, 'Mom, there is not a book.'"
>
> McDaniel had encountered "whole math." Also known as "fuzzy math" or "new-new math," whole math is based on the idea that knowledge is only meaningful when we construct it for ourselves.
>
> . . . The whole-math disaster began in 1989 when the National Council of Teachers of Mathematics issued a set of standards declaring a new approach to be in order. No more "drill and kill," as whole-math people like to call traditional teaching. Instead, from kindergarten on, there would be a calculator in every hand so that young minds would be free of irksome chores like addition and multiplication and thus able to take on higher-order tasks such as inventing their own personal methods of long division.[2]

Cheney's story provides a glimpse of both the substance and the rancor of the debate still raging about mathematics in K–12 schools, and of the dilemmas that debate creates for teachers.

The Math Crisis

In the early 1980s the widely publicized Second International Study of Science and Mathematics Education rocked the math education community and the public.[3] That study showed American eighth graders lagging far behind their counterparts in nearly every other developed nation.

The math and science communities responded to what could only be seen as the deficiencies of existing mathematics teaching. In 1989 the National Research Council (NRC), the research and policy arm of the National Academy of Sciences, published a report, *Everybody Counts,* advising the nation to overhaul traditional mathematics education. That same year, the National Council of Teachers of Mathematics (NCTM) concluded a consensus-building process involving thousands of math teachers and mathematicians and published a set of "standards" defining what Americans should know and be able to do in mathematics. The NCTM believed that these standards would raise the quality of mathematics teaching and learning dramatically.

But soon, traditionalists like Lynne Cheney were engaged in (and, by many accounts, winning) a full-scale war against the NCTM standards, and the controversy continues today. Two additional international studies show that U.S. students continue to lag behind.[4] The NCTM standards have been revised somewhat to make clear that they don't disdain basic arithmetic knowledge and skills, and many states and textbook publishers have used them to guide their approach to mathematics curriculum. However, critics continue to call for a return to traditional math.

What's the Problem?

For many Americans the problem seems straightforward. American teachers aren't pressing students to learn as much math as they could; teachers should have high expectations (standards), upgrade their knowledge, spend more time teaching math, and (along with their schools) experience negative consequences if their students do not perform.

For the most part, the mathematics education community sees the problem differently. Many of these educators believe that trying to improve a fundamentally flawed approach to curriculum and pedagogy will not produce the desired results. They believe that emphasis on memorizing prescribed rules and methods for solving problems keeps students from understanding math principles; and that, in turn, explains why so few students remember and use the mathematics they are taught.[5] They argue that even students who are proficient at remembering facts and performing algorithms—and who score well on tests—actually understand little.

Compared with countries such as Japan and Germany where math achievement is very high, the U.S. mathematics curriculum is fragmented and incoherent.[6] Progressives also point to the U.S. system of ability grouping that keeps many students from ever being taught higher-level math, noting that most high-scoring countries shun that practice.[7] In other words, progressives have argued that the "cure" that the traditionalists were recommending was very close to what schools were actually doing and was responsible for holding down improvements in math education.

Their view upsets many who worry that threats to the age-old order and truths of mathematics are part of a general trend toward a disintegrating educational and social order.

Traditional Mathematics: Skills-Based and Sequential

Mathematics is conventionally considered an orderly, enduring set of facts and logic that describes patterns and relationships in the physical world—arithmetic operations, algebraic manipulations, geometry terms and theorems, and so forth. Traditional math curriculum lays out a hierarchical sequence of topics and skills that allows students, step-by-step, to master this body of mathematical knowledge.[8] For example, a conservative member of California's standards commission argued in 1997: "Mathematics is a cumulative, hierarchical subject; learning new skills and concepts often depends on mastery of previous ones. . . . [Students] must enter each grade in possession of all the prerequisite skills."[9] The prerequisite skills—or the basics—of math are math facts and the rules (or string of rules) known as algorithms. For example, long division is an algorithm composed of orderly steps that include basic mathematical skills such as multiplication and subtraction.

Traditionalists usually argue for "balanced instruction in mathematics: basic facts and skills, conceptual understanding; and problem-solving ability."[10] But "problem-solving ability," like many catchphrases in the curriculum controversies, means different things to different people. For example, traditionalists view solutions as the final operation after the successful manipulation of basic skills, or "building blocks." They accept correct answers as the only legitimate confirmation of a student's mathematical knowledge. Although no progressive would deny that mathematics offers useful and precise solutions, most also see, for example, *estimation* as an integral guide to mathematical reasoning. Progressive mathematics educators try to fathom the student's reasoning and understanding since these, ultimately, are a critical measure of understanding mathematics.

Traditional elementary schools stress the number facts and algorithms necessary to add, subtract, multiply, and divide and to compute fractions, decimals, and percentages. Most middle schools review or reteach these basic operations. Beginning in middle school, however, the curriculum diverges for different students. The "best" math students eventually take courses in trigonometry and calculus. Those who haven't mastered the basics take general math classes, where they continue to review the basic math skills of elementary school. Both progressives and traditionalists have severely criticized these dead-end remedial courses, and many schools now channel low-achieving students through separate and slower pathways that may include first-year algebra.

Progressive Mathematics: Meaningful Knowledge in Context

At the end of her first year of teaching Zeba Palomino wrote a letter to her high school students explaining how she views mathematics and why she teaches it.

———————————————————※ ※ ※———————————————————

Mathematics has a history, and it is deeply rooted in cultures all over the world. Mathematics is logical and controversial at the same time. Mathematics is a beautiful cycle of connections; it is not a linear study of fragmented pieces. Mathematics is connected to, a foundation for, and dependent upon philosophy, communication, art, science, language, and more. Mathematics is not just numbers and letters, and it is not a set of rules to be memorized; it is a world of ideas and patterns to be discovered and played with. Mathematics is not a right or wrong answer; it is an infinite collection of strategies from which to choose to use as we develop our own ideas and make our own sense of the world. It is because these beauties exist within and around the field of mathematics that I choose to use mathematics as a means for critical education.

My intention is to use a constructivist approach to mathematics and the power of collaborative learning to help you develop the intellectual and moral capacities and the commitment to help you shape your places in the world. Through your own construction of mathematics knowledge, you can become

*experts in understanding, reasoning, communicating, analyzing, imagin-
ing, examining, connecting, and proving. And by learning collaboratively,
you learn and achieve more, you respect and care more about each other and
your communities, and you take more pride in your responsibilities and capabilities. As you build these academic and moral capacities, my hope is
that you are opening doors for yourselves to countless possibilities.*

*My biggest struggle is staying true to these goals. I know that I often fall
into just teaching mathematics skills and concepts because it is much easier
to do. I know that many of you would prefer that I continue to do it that
way—just let you sit in rows, give you the algorithms, and give you individual work to practice those new math rules. But, please understand, it is unfair and unjust of me to do that to you. When I "teach" that way, you are not
truly learning or empowering yourselves. You are only "learning" a meaningless concept with no deeper significance to you and which you will soon
forget. You are not building or exchanging ideas, and you are not participating in a critical transformative education.*

—ZEBA PALOMINO
First-year teacher, high school mathematics

Zeba Palomino's views embody much of the reform advice of the NRC report
Everybody Counts. Mathematicians today have achieved (with the aid of computer
technology) breakthroughs in number theory, logic, statistics, operations research,
probability, computation, geometry, and combinatorics that reach far beyond the
traditional areas of mathematics (algebra, analysis, and topology).[11] Such dramatic
changes in the discipline, the NRC reasons, mean that mathematics education must
also change:

> The transformation of mathematics from a core of abstract studies to a powerful
> family of mathematical sciences is reflected poorly, often not at all, by the tradi-
> tional mathematics curriculum. One can hardly blame students if they rarely see
> evidence of its full power and richness.
>
> As mathematics is more than calculation, so education in mathematics must
> be more than mastery of arithmetic. Geometry, chance, and change are as impor-
> tant as numbers in achieving mathematical power. Even more important is a com-
> prehensive, flexible view that embodies the intrinsic unity of mathematics; esti-
> mation supplements calculation; heuristics aid algorithms; experience balances
> innovation. To prepare students to use mathematics in the twenty-first century,
> today's curriculum must invoke the full spectrum of the mathematical sciences.
>
> [C]hildren should use calculators throughout their schoolwork, just as
> adults use calculators throughout their lives. . . . Real measurements from sci-
> ence experiments can be used in mathematics lessons because the calculator
> will be able to add or multiply the data even if the children have not yet learned
> how. Many adults fear that early introduction of calculators will prevent children
> from learning basic arithmetic "properly," as their parents learned it. The expe-
> riences of many schools during the last fifteen years show that this fear is un-
> founded. Students who use calculators learn traditional arithmetic as well as
> those who do not use calculators and emerge from elementary school with bet-
> ter problem-solving skills and much better attitudes about mathematics.[12]

The NRC also identified as a *myth* the common view that "[t]he best way to learn how to solve complex problems is to decompose them into a sequence of basic skills which can then be mastered one at a time." *Everybody Counts* argues that "[t]here is abundant evidence that mastery of necessary skills is rarely sufficient for solving complex problems."[13]

Mathematics as Purposeful Activity   The standards created by the NCTM in 1989 defined mathematics as an active process of using mathematical algorithms and ideas in the course of some *purposeful activity*—that is, across many disciplines and in real-life situations.[14] The standards emphasized that *knowing* math is inseparable from *doing* math.

Computation remains critical in mathematics and in daily life. However, our technological age also allows complex computation to be done by calculators and computers. Having quick mental calculating ability is no longer a prerequisite for success in many daily situations or even in some complex problem solving.[15] It is not necessary for students to be denied opportunities for more advanced mathematics learning because they are slower to develop what had previously been "basic" skills.

The NCTM spelled out in its 258-page document what mathematics teaching and learning might look like. Throughout the grades, mathematical ideas should be embedded in problems that are familiar and meaningful to students. Teachers must show the links between math ideas and procedures rather than teaching a topic and then dropping it, never to be seen again. From kindergarten on, students should engage with the ideas and strategies of whole numbers, fractions and decimals, geometry, measurement, statistics and probability, patterns and functions. Number systems, number theory, algebra, trigonometry, discrete mathematics, and calculus can be added as students' mathematical understanding grows. Computers and calculators should be at the core of instruction instead of being used only as timesaving aides after students prove their proficiency with paper-and-pencil calculations. That calculators and computers are an *escape from* or *a way to avoid* rigorous mathematical work is an idea that begins with adults in our schools and communities who are often less familiar with those technologies.

The math standards made clear that learning mathematics is no more linear or sequential than learning how to dance. Certainly, there are concepts. There are big ideas. There are facts and processes that will be memorized over time and eventually become automatic (i.e., performed without conscious thought). And it is definitely best to approach certain ideas after one is competent with previous ones. That said, learning mathematics through traditional instruction might be compared to learning to dance from a lecture and a book. In both cases, it is not quite the "real thing," and only a few will rave about how much fun they had.

Mathematics for Everyone   On the question of *mathematics for whom?* the standards were unequivocal. The core mathematical ideas are necessary and appropriate for *all* students. Schools cannot use the differences in students' talents, achievements, and interests as excuses for some students not learning math.

In 1999 an NCTM task force found that mathematics achievement is constrained by inequalities in curriculum, instruction, and expectations for student performance. Believing that low-achieving students have low math ability, educators have thought it sensible to teach these students low-level math. This approach has both rationalized the uneven distribution of qualified math teachers and depressed students' math achievement. Progressive reformers have been intent on changing all of this.

Mathematics for Social Justice   As the press for high-level mathematics for all has increased, teachers have looked for materials that will make mathematics accessible to African Americans and Latinos, girls, and other groups that have been underrepresented in mathematics, as well as to those who've been seen as having low ability in mathematics. Educators have also sought ways to connect mathematics with social justice goals.

Mathematics educator Eric (Rico) Gutstein's new book, *Rethinking Mathematics: Teaching Social Justice by the Numbers,* written with progressive educator Bob Peterson, is a valuable resource for such educators. It includes teaching ideas, lesson plans, and reflections that teachers can use to weave social justice principles throughout the math curriculum, as well as to integrate social justice math into other curricular areas.[16] The book's goal is to provide high-level math to all students, and, at the same time, develop students' understanding of society and prepare them to be critical, active members of a democratic society (see Focal Point 4.1).

The Math Standards: The Politics of Mathematics Continues

California's traditional/progressive mathematics battles are representative and possibly instructive for the rest of the country. As the state developed its mathematics standards, Mathematically Correct, a powerful group of traditionalists including some professors of mathematics, established an anti-reform Internet site to marshal opposition to the NCTM standards.

Accusations flew back and forth across the Internet and in letters to newspaper editors. Teachers were attacked for teaching math without numbers, denying children access to conventional ways of multiplying and dividing, and paying more attention to how students feel than to whether or not they can do math. The battle concluded with a policy fight over verbs. The writers of the California standards made generous use of the following: "model, estimate, interpret, classify, explain, and create." They argued that each points to a different strategy for thinking about, learning, and solving problems using mathematics. However, the conservative state board of education, echoing the objections of Mathematically Correct, rejected these verbs in nearly every case. One board member declared that the way to "get children to do more and better and higher math" is with such phrases as "do it, solve it, know it."[17]

The revised standards embodied the traditional view of mathematics learning. An outraged official at the National Science Foundation (NSF) wrote a letter to the California board stating that the board's action "is, charitably, shortsighted, and detrimental to the long-term mathematical literacy of children in California."[18] The standards the board adopted emphasize basic skills, memorizing, and practicing; they discourage invention, estimation, and solving nonroutine problems. They deny the

FOCAL POINT 4.1

Teaching Social Justice by the Numbers

Mathematics: An Essential Tool for Understanding and Changing the World

To have more than a surface understanding of important social and political issues, mathematics is essential. Without mathematics, it is impossible to fully understand a government budget, the impact of a war, the meaning of a national debt, or the long-term effects of a proposal such as the privatization of Social Security. The same is true with other social, ecological, and cultural issues: You need mathematics to have a deep grasp of the influence of advertising on children; the level of pollutants in the water, air, and soil; and the dangers of the chemicals in the food we eat. Math helps students understand these issues, to see them in ways that are impossible without math; for example, by visually displaying data in graphs that otherwise might be incomprehensible or seemingly meaningless.

As an example, consider racial profiling. This issue only becomes meaningful when viewed through a mathematical lens, whether or not the "viewer" appreciates that she or he is using mathematics. That is, it is difficult to declare that racial profiling occurs unless there is a sufficiently large data set and a way to examine that data. If, for example, 30 percent of drivers in a given area are African Americans, and the police stop six African-American drivers and four white drivers, there is weak evidence that racial profiling exists. But if police stop 612 African-American drivers and 423 whites, then there is a much stronger case.

The explanation lies in mathematics: In an area where only 30 percent of the drivers are black, it is virtually impossible for almost 60 percent of more than 1,000 people stopped randomly by the police to be black.

The underlying mathematical ideas—(dis)proportionality, probability, randomness, sample size, and the law of large numbers (that over a sufficiently large data set, the results of a probability simulation or of real-world experiences should approximate the theoretical probabilities)—all become part of the context that students must understand to really see, and in turn demonstrate, that something is amiss. Thus with a large data set, one can assert that a real problem exists and further investigate racial profiling. For youth, racial profiling may mean being "picked on," but the subtleties and implications are only comprehensible when the mathematical ideas are there.

When teachers weave social justice into the math curriculum and promote social justice math "across the curriculum," students' understanding of important social matters deepens. When teachers use data on sweatshop wages to teach accounting to high school students or multi-digit multiplication to upper-elementary students, students can learn math, but they can also learn something about the lives of people in various parts of the world and the relationship between the things we consume and their living conditions.

Source: "Introduction" from Enrico Gutstein and Bob Peterson, eds., *Rethinking Mathematics: Teaching Social Justice by the Numbers* (Milwaukee, WI: Rethinking Schools, 2005). More information about *Rethinking Mathematics* is available at the Rethinking Schools website at http://www.rethinkingschools.org.

early use of calculators and caution about their later use. So, California's third graders memorize the multiplication tables, fourth graders master carrying and borrowing in subtraction without calculators. Seventh graders are expected to do the following:

> Use the inverse relationship between raising to a power and extracting the root of a perfect square integer; for an integer that is not square, determine without a calculator the two integers between which its square root lies and explain why.[19]

In the effort to eliminate what they call "fuzzy math," the traditionalist groups also sought to remove the College Preparatory Mathematics (CPM) texts from the state's classrooms. Some went so far as to argue that, because the texts are more effective with low-income students and students of color, CPM sacrifices the math learning of more-advantaged students on behalf of less-advantaged ones.

Similar campaigns have taken place around the nation. Responding to the pressure, NCTM revised its standards in 2000. Called *Principles and Standards for School Mathematics*, the revised standards place more emphasis on memorizing and rote computation. However, NCTM insists that its revisions remain consistent with the theories of mathematics and mathematics learning that underlay the first set. Most states have used the revised standards as the basis for their own standards; few followed California's more traditional path.

Today the battle continues. In 2005, the politically conservative Fordham Foundation graded every state's mathematics standards. California's traditional standards were given an A, largely because it rejected the NCTM's standards. Eighteen states received Ds and 11 received Fs, largely because they've patterned theirs after NCTM.[20] How have mathematics teachers responded to the politicizing of their subject?

───────────────────────── ❧ ❧ ❧ ─────────────────────────

> *My school has been making strides toward improving the scores on the [standards-based] tests that California uses to rank school achievement, but we are still classified as a "low performing" school. Because of this, there has been a lot of pressure to "teach to the test" and focus the curriculum on the material that the state has decided will be on the tests. The result is a pacing guide that stresses breadth over depth.*
>
> *Many content teachers shy away from teaching critical thinking skills during class due to these intense curriculum deadlines. I experienced this myself. I was often unable to explore a particular concept in depth, even when my students were struggling, in favor of starting the next section in the allotted time frame. I was afraid that if I took time away from my content area to teach problem-solving strategies, I would fall behind the pacing guide. The result was a shallow conceptual understanding by most of my students.*
>
> —MARK HILL
> First-year teacher, high school mathematics

───

Even under the worst political deluge, teachers like Mark Hill weather the storm and teach math well. In Mark's case, he tested various teaching approaches and found that his students actually had an easier time learning the mathematics procedures that are on the state test when he spends time helping them develop critical thinking skills. He concluded,

---◈ ◈ ◈---

Problem-solving strategies enable students to remember and use the procedural knowledge they are exposed to.

Perhaps the best defense, and weapon as well, against politically driven mandates is an articulate and highly competent generation of teachers of mathematics—elementary and high school—who know more about math and how to teach it than their critics. With care and competence such teachers can negotiate traditional mandates and still serve their students well.

English Language Arts

Webster's Encyclopedic Unabridged Dictionary of the English Language gives 28 definitions of the word *read.* The first two sum up traditional notions of what it means to read:

> 1. To peruse and apprehend the meaning of (something written, printed, etc.): *to read a book;* 2. To utter aloud or render in speech: *reading a story to his children.*[21]

Progressive English language arts teachers and theorists also pay substantial attention to the other 26 definitions. A few examples make clear how varied and deep this broader conception of reading really is:

> 5. To make out the significance of by scrutiny or observation: *to read the dark and cloudy sky as the threat of a storm.* 6. To foresee, foretell, or predict: *to read a person's fortune in tea leaves.* 7. To make out the character, motivations, desires, etc. . . . as by interpretation of outward signs. 8. To infer (something not expressed or directly indicated) from what is read or considered . . . : *He read an underlying sarcasm into her letter.* 25. To admit of being interpreted: *a rule that reads two different ways.* 26. (Of an electronic computer) to read data. 27. Read in, to introduce information into a computer.[22]

Webster's gives a similarly long list of definitions for *write.* And just as with reading, traditional educators prefer a narrow conception of writing—rejecting many writing-related activities and competencies that progressives favor.

The traditional curriculum frames reading as acquiring a set meaning off the printed page, and writing as mastering the conventions of spelling, grammar, and form. However, progressive teachers with a sociocultural perspective on learning see young readers and writers as already having—bringing to school with them— the resources, background, personal history, and individual voices that already qualify them as fully literate, lacking only certain skills that have a high "exchange rate" or value in mainstream society.

Traditional Language Arts: Mastering Skills, Rules, and Forms

Traditionally, schools expect young children to learn the rules (and many exceptions) that govern how letters and combinations of letters translate into sounds. Teachers emphasize the skills to decode letters, combinations of letters, and whole words. They work to help students learn a hierarchy of discrete skills—from recognizing beginning consonants, to consonant blends, to reading inexplicable words like *cough* and *height*. They expect students to master the conventions of Standard English by memorizing correct spellings; dividing words into syllables; alphabetizing; capitalizing; punctuating; recognizing synonyms, homonyms, and antonyms; and identifying parts of speech and sentences. They ask students to practice writing sentences, paragraphs, stories, and reports.

Building from Parts to Whole   These basics cycle and recycle throughout the grades. Middle-school and senior high teachers layer on harder spelling, vocabulary, capitalization, punctuation, usage, and grammar lessons. They add new writing algorithms—topic sentences, supporting paragraphs, three and five (but rarely four) paragraph essays, and, finally, the research paper. Students try out the conventions of common writing styles—descriptive, persuasive, analytic, critical, personal, "practical" (business letters), and narrative. College-bound high school students memorize sophisticated vocabulary words—partly to ready them for college entrance exams.

As in mathematics, tradition dictates that reading and writing are composed of parts—essential elements—that combine into wholes. For example, the alphabet is more specific, and therefore more basic, than recognizing the sounds of parts of words, which are more basic than whole words. Letters are analogous to numbers. Phonics, or the sounds of letters and groups of letters, is elemental, perhaps similar to counting or even addition and subtraction. Grammar and sentences are akin to more complex algorithms, such as algebraic formulas. Once students master the basics, they are ready for more adultlike, sophisticated tasks. The conventional curriculum also treats reading, writing, and speaking as universally applicable skills that (like mathematics, in the traditional view) do not change much in different contexts.

Extracting Meaning from Traditional Texts   The traditional curriculum also includes literature. Elementary students learn basic literary genres—stories, poems, newspaper articles, and novels (known to many younger students as "chapter books"). Older students learn Western literary conventions, like plot, setting, characters, theme, and so on, and they read classics and established twentieth-century writers who are part of the cultural canon: William Shakespeare, Charles Dickens, Ralph Waldo Emerson, Emily Dickinson, John Steinbeck, Ernest Hemingway. Teachers ask students to discover or simply tell them the author's intended meaning and students learn to identify conventional literary devices (irony, foreshadowing, metaphor, etc.). This is not to say that traditional approaches *never* allow "contemporary" literature, but, often, what passes for contemporary turns out to be 20 to 50 years old.

Traditional Textbooks   Textbooks form the traditional curriculum's bedrock. Basal readers and language arts texts provide simple stories and practice exercises to support young students' sequential development of decoding, vocabulary, comprehension, and other skills. In later grades, the basal reader merges into the familiar anthology that contains longer and shorter works, fiction and nonfiction, and includes poetry, drama, and essays. Some anthologies feature themes such as exploring life in cities; others focus on particular traditions, such as American, British, or world literature. Like basal readers, anthologies target particular grades and include particular pieces according to their reading difficulty.

Some textbooks supply detailed manuals that offer teachers step-by-step "direct instruction" strategies, including questions to ask, ways to motivate, assignments, tests, worksheets, posters, overhead projections, video recordings and disks, software, websites, and more. Some include complete "scripts" for teachers to follow. State legislatures and local school boards often select traditional texts to ensure that teachers teach reading and writing comprehensively, competently, and uniformly. However, with an increasing shortage of qualified teachers, especially in overcrowded urban communities, many decision makers see scripted approaches to reading as "damage control" in classrooms where teachers know little or nothing about teaching reading. It's not surprising, then, that many urban school districts have adopted these materials.

Progressive Approaches to Language Arts: Developing Literacy

Since the 1960s critics have faulted the traditional language arts curriculum for its inconsistencies with sociocultural theories of literacy development, and for its solid grounding in the elite, white cultural canon. Progressive educators worry that a narrow focus on the basic skills will cause some students to miss the essence of literacy—the pleasure and power of expressing and understanding ideas. They prefer to think of literacy *practices* rather than skills—to think of literacy as something that people *do* rather than learn about and store for future use.

Building from the "Texts" That Children Know   In the past 30 years, research on learning provides English language arts teachers with overwhelming evidence that all students come to school with experiences that prepare them for full adult literacy.

Professor David Pearson, former director of the National Center for the Study of Reading and now dean of the Education School at the University of California, Berkeley, notes: "Even the three year old who recognizes that if an arch is in sight, a hamburger is not far away has learned the basic principle of signs—that our world is filled with things that 'stand for' other things."[23] Similarly, the 3-year-old who sees his parent pick up a book knows that sitting on a lap and being told a story are soon to follow. This child can read the environment long before he can read the book. Also, the child has learned that he is an active agent in determining the full meaning of his "reading." How he sits—still or squirmy—and how he "rewards" his parent—by pointing to the illustration that matches the text being read—show that relationships are inseparable from this and most literacy events.

When teachers build their literacy lessons on their belief that children are already literate, Pearson argues, they are more likely "to engage them in tasks in which they can demonstrate their literacy and use those successes as bridges to even more challenging literacy activities."[24]

Integrated and Authentic Reading and Writing Attention to realistic and useful reading and writing experiences, starting in the earliest grades, is at the heart of "whole language" and "literature-based" approaches to language arts. Teachers also have begun to focus on writing as a multistepped, repeating process of reflection, drafting, editing, getting feedback, more reflection and drafting, and so on. These processes are not linear, have no clearly defined beginning and end, and at their best are intensely interactive.

Central to these new approaches are principles of integration and authenticity.[25] *Integration* means that literacy events and acts are not broken down into subskills (thus the *whole* in whole language); that reading, writing, speaking, and listening are treated as different aspects of the same fundamental linguistic and cognitive processes; and that every school subject makes important literacy contributions. *Authenticity* means that students should engage in literacy activities that allow them to communicate about real things of interest and that have relevance beyond school. From the earliest grades, young children should read and produce real stories and other forms of genuine communication—even if they don't have all of the conventional "skills."

National Standards in the Language Arts

In 1992, the International Reading Association (IRA) and the National Council of Teachers of English (NCTE)—the professional organizations for elementary and secondary teachers—took the lead in developing national standards that establish what students should know and be able to do in English language arts.[26] In 1994 the groups circulated drafts of the *Standards for the English Language Arts* to hundreds of reviewers, including literacy organizations, state departments of education, and scholars and practitioners. Despite the overwhelmingly—but not exclusively—favorable comments from reviewers, the federal government suddenly refused to continue sponsorship of this standards effort. The government cited "nonperformance," but some organizational leaders believed that the problem stemmed from political resistance, similar to what the mathematics community had experienced.[27] With private funds and their own resources, IRA and NCTE continued developing their standards, seeking widespread reviews, and building a consensus. They published their standards in 1996.[28]

The IRA/NCTE standards reflect sociocultural theories and research on how students become literate. These standards press schools to respect, and help students to use, the literacy they have developed elsewhere. Many are expressed in terms of what might be called *practices* ("apply," "adjust" "conduct," "develop," etc.), as distinct from the traditional idea of acquiring *skills*. Whereas skills are typically "taught" or "shown" by a book or teacher, these practices require that students read and write in order to "do" as well as to "learn." The standards ask teachers to engage students actively rather than telling them what they should know.

The standards include many different literary genres, many historical periods, fiction and nonfiction, classic and contemporary works. In addition to asking students to master basic skills of spoken, written, and visual language, they expect students to conduct research through the process of generating ideas and questions, posing problems, gathering information through a variety of technological and informational resources (e.g., libraries, databases, computer networks, video), and synthesizing and communicating what they've learned. They also emphasize literature from the many rich cultural traditions that comprise our American society.

Multicultural Lessons

Using multicultural literature makes the English/language arts curriculum inclusive—important for all American students; it also makes it authentic for students whose languages and traditions are not reflected in the traditional curriculum. As such, the literature can be taught both as valuable examples of human expression, in themselves, and as a bridge to more traditional works. For example, first-year English teacher Kelly Ganzel used Laura Esquivel's novel *Like Water for Chocolate* as a bridge to help her Latino ninth graders gain access to Shakespeare's *Romeo and Juliet*.

———————————————————⊗ ⊗ ⊗———————————————————

Pairing classic texts with contemporary, ethnically diverse, young adult literature is valuable. Such pairing affords the opportunity for teachers to collaborate with their students in choosing a contemporary novel to study. Through multicultural literature, I invite my students to share their knowledge about the history, traditions, and community of their own culture.

Similarly,

———————————————————⊗ ⊗ ⊗———————————————————

As I prepared to teach Harper Lee's To Kill a Mockingbird, *I decided to capture my students' attention through a portrayal of African American women's experiences in the South during the Depression. After showing "I Know Why the Caged Bird Sings," the film version of Maya Angelou's*

youth, Nancy [an African American student with a history of school failure]
was bursting with questions and comments. Her interest was authentic and
consuming. I was ecstatic when Nancy approached me after class with a
smile on her face. "I'll do my homework tonight, Ms. Ganzel. I really like that
stuff." The next day, Nancy entered the classroom eager to know if we were
going to share our writing. She had written a reflection about how she would
have felt had she been in Maya Angelou's shoes.

—**KELLY GANZEL**
First-year teacher, high school English

Multicultural texts like the Esquivel novel and Angelou's filmed biography, Ganzel
believes, allow her students to "celebrate their distinct human experiences" and
"liberate them to find meaning in the literature as they define it." First-year English
teacher Jessica Wingell found a similar way to engage her ninth graders:

———————————————⚛ ⚛ ⚛———————————————

My ninth-grade classes are 50 percent Latino, and I purposely loaded my
curriculum with Latino literature. I taught Cisneros's The House on Mango
Street, *a unit on Latin American magical realism, Esquivel's* Like Water for
Chocolate, *and Rodriguez's* Always Running. *These works are all on the*
ninth-grade reading list, but I decided to forgo some of the traditional
*canon—*Great Expectations *and* Fahrenheit 451, *for example—to accommo-*
date the Latino writers on the list.

I wanted my Latino students, in particular, to see themselves in the lit-
erature. Additionally, there is some Spanish included in many of the works
I've taught this year, and I don't speak Spanish. My students (including stu-
dents who are not Latino but are taking Spanish classes) love to show what
they know, and they have been very helpful with pronunciation. I often ask
my Spanish speakers for help, and I think they appreciate having their bilin-
gualism acknowledged and used.

In the unit on magical realism, I wanted the students to experience the
pure enjoyment of the stories. I also want them to understand what magical
realism is (the imaginary becomes real), and why it originated in Latin
America (according to Gabriel Garcia Marquez, events in Latin America
have been so extraordinary that realism was not adequate to describe people
and events). The culminating project for the unit was a research project on
an author, an event, or a historical figure. They needed to find the connection
between their topic and the events or circumstances in Latin America that
led to the development of magical realism.

The strength of this unit is the material—the students really liked the
stories because they were unusual, lyrical, and challenging. In addition, my
Latino students in particular enjoyed the opportunity to explore aspects of
their heritage that they wanted to know more about (the slaughter of Mayans
and Aztecs were popular topics for the research project). I also think that
this approach is powerful because it combines students' home culture and

> *high-status knowledge in an English curriculum. In an urban school, we*
> *need to acknowledge our students' home communities, but not at the expense*
> *of access to an honors-equivalent curriculum.*
>
> —JESSICA WINGELL
> First-year teacher, English, grade 9

Many traditionalists would object strongly to the literature that teachers Ganzel and Wingell and their students find so compelling. Traditionalists and progressives disagree over whose perspective, whose voice, and whose knowledge belong in the curriculum.

An instructive case in point was the 1998 decision by the San Francisco Board of Education to require teachers to assign books by nonwhite authors to high school students. At the time, the only required books were Chaucer's *Canterbury Tales,* Shakespeare's *Romeo and Juliet,* and Mark Twain's *Huckleberry Finn.* Although no one disparaged these works, board members thought it reasonable to broaden the list of readings, particularly since 87 percent of the district's students are students of color. However, the proposal exploded onto headlines nationwide and became the target of derision by talk-show hosts. The president of a conservative San Francisco think tank told the *New York Times,* "They [students] have to go on to college and the work world, and this would destroy their opportunities." The board member who proposed the new policy described the event as the most difficult time of his life.[29]

Despite the vibrant tradition of black American literature and a growing group of American Latino writers (as well as an extensive body of Latin American literature), U.S. students rarely hear these voices in school. As recently as January 1998, two different Maryland school systems removed books by African American authors from the curriculum—one, Nobel Prize–winning Toni Morrison; the other, poet Maya Angelou—after parents complained that the works were "trash" and "anti-white."[30]

A Conservative Backlash

Shortly after the NCTE and the IRA published the standards in 1996, a professor from Missouri wrote an angry commentary for *Education Week* (a weekly newspaper with wide circulation to those interested in education events and policies):

> One would have hoped that the leading language-arts standards-setting group in the country would have stated in plain English that our schools expect all students to use proper spelling, grammar, and punctuation in written communication. Indeed, any normal person would have assumed that such fundamental matters would have been at the top of the list of concerns treated by language-arts teachers. However, if one reads the roughly 100-page document, one finds virtually no mention of such things.[31]

This critic closed by noting,

> I am a product of the "drill and kill" school of literacy training complete with weekly spelling and vocabulary tests throughout K–12, along with 20- to 30-page research papers done on weekends at the public library (as opposed to the

one- to two-page journal-writing exercises that now dominate English instruction). I, like so many others, somehow managed to overcome this seemingly
"stifling" and "boring" education to develop a love for the written word and to
author several books and numerous other publications.[32]

Another professor of education commented, "I can't imagine any other profession
promulgating a practice that ends up harming literally hundreds of thousands of
children."[33] As had happened in mathematics, these professors joined a rising chorus that attributed all manner of social and educational ills to a supposed departure
from traditional, skills-based instruction.

The debate about how to teach language arts gathered advocates and resources
far afield from the public schools and their mission to educate everyone well. Commercial companies like Sylvan Learning Centers filled the airways trying to "educate" the public to believe that schools have neglected an easy method to improve
reading. Right-wing entities like the Blumenfeld Education Letter and the Eagle
Forum Education and Defense Fund became strong back-to-basics advocates.[34]

The opposition to "whole language" has made its way into policy as progressive
and conservative groups jockey to have their views represented in the new state
content standards. In California, Nebraska, North Carolina, Massachusetts, Texas,
and Ohio, traditionalists mounted concerted efforts to mandate explicit phonics
instruction and to eliminate the use of whole language instruction; some, as in
California, succeeded.[35]

Reading First   English language arts is the one subject matter that No Child Left
Behind addresses directly, and the impact of the new law has been profound. As we
describe in more detail in Chapter 11, NCLB establishes the requirements for states
and schools to receive federal funding for reading instruction of low-income kindergarten through third-grade students. The U.S. Department of Education requires
the funds be spent on materials, professional development, and testing associated
with "scientifically based" reading programs.

Although this sounds both appealing and wise, a limited set of reading programs qualify according to the department's definition of "scientifically based."
Those that do fall squarely into a traditional, behavioral approach to teaching and
learning and reject the constructivist approach to language arts recommended in
the national standards in English language arts.

All approved Reading First programs must demonstrate with scientific studies
that they improve students' test performance in five discrete reading skills: phonemic
awareness; phonics; vocabulary development; reading fluency (including oral reading); and reading comprehension strategies. All must have a coherent design that includes "explicit instructional strategies that address students' specific strengths and
weaknesses, coordinated instructional sequences, ample practice opportunities and
aligned student materials."[36] The department also requires that the programs be
taught in a protected, uninterrupted block of more than 90 minutes per day.

Seeking Balance

What do progressives see as wrong with phonetic decoding, having both a subject
and verb in one's sentences, using conventional spelling, and learning the traditional

protocols for writing research papers? Nothing! Contrary to the fears and accusations of traditionalists, most researchers as well as progressive policymakers and
teachers seek a "balanced approach" to literacy that neither neglects skills nor dis-
counts the knowledge of the past 30 years about literacy and learning.

David Pearson places the search for a balanced approach to language arts instruction in a historical perspective:

> I am convinced that we are capable, as a profession, of developing an approach
> to phonics that is respectful of the journeys we have taken since the early 1980s
> [when] phonics was a major component of literacy instruction. We are not the
> same profession now as we were then. Our views of reading have changed. In
> the 1960s, we regarded reading as fundamentally a perceptual process—taking
> in visual stimuli and recording them into verbal representations. In the 1970s,
> we discovered that reading was a cognitive process. In the 1980s, we added a
> distinctly socio-cultural perspective. And in the 1990s, we discovered a literacy
> perspective. Today we are learning more and more about reading as a political
> phenomenon. We need a phonics that respects these roads we have traveled.[37]

The National Academy of Sciences and other groups agree that the explicit
teaching of phonics is only one of a comprehensive set of strategies needed to assist
young children to become literate. Effective teachers use multiple approaches to
teach content and skills, integrate test preparation into lessons, make connections
between what students learn at school and their lives outside of classrooms, teach
strategies to help students think about their work as they are doing it, and press students to probe deeper into what they have learned. At best, teachers and students
engage in "cognitive collaboration" to "push one another's thinking, challenge one
another, or bounce ideas off one another."[38]

We see this balance at work in first-year teacher Benji Chang's struggle to infuse
his sociocultural understanding of how students construct literacy into the highly
prescriptive, direct-instruction "Open Court" reading program (one of the programs
approved under Reading First) he is required to use with his first graders.

———————————————————— ⚘ ⚘ ⚘ ————————————————————

*Initially, I was overwhelmed and sometimes fell into the trap of just follow-
ing along with what the Open Court teachers' guide told me to do. Because
the program required my students to sit still for extended periods of time, I
found myself thinly disguising its rote phonics drills and dry grammar
lessons as games or with the use of a puppet. Although these strategies did
not put lessons in the context of my students' lives or tap into their background knowledge, they were somewhat successful at engaging my class.*

*By late November, I was more familiar with my students and the Open
Court structure, and I had learned to work my way around the program's
subtractive nature. I developed integrated lessons using multicultural literature. For example, I used* The Legend of Hua Mu Lan *to engage students in
practicing synonyms by trying to retell the story. Because the students were
exposed to different types of literature, by mid-January they were able to
take a critical look at some of the literature provided by Open Court. In the
basal reader, there is a story about an African boy named Jafta. It is one of
the first encounters that students have with a character of African descent in*

the reader and one of the rare stories that identifies the ethnic or racial back-
ground of a character.

   During a shared reading of the story, I asked the students if they thought
the story was fantasy or reality and why. Students said the story was fake
because a little boy would not run around with hippos and elephants in his
underwear. They said that he would probably have to help out his family at
home and do homework because that is what they have to do. My students
were not simply reciting the words on the pages of a story that reinforces
stereotypes of black Africans. They were developing a critical lens through
which to view the world. My students were not just developing literacy, but
critical literacy as well.

—**Benji Chang**
First-year teacher, grade 1

Finally, scholars Gloria Ladson-Billings and Lisa Delpit, widely known as advocates of progressive and critical multicultural curriculum, provide another important reason for a balanced language arts curriculum. They term the traditional skills and conventions of reading, writing, and speaking in Standard English "codes of power." Ladson-Billings, Delpit, and others worry that if teachers don't teach the codes of power to students of color at the same time as they build on students' home languages and cultures, they will further limit the opportunities of those students whose families and communities may speak in some way other than formal Standard English.[39] They argue that nothing in a sociocultural perspective, nothing in a concern for social justice, can ever justify an education that denies students the power to communicate skillfully to all people.

Social Studies

Hannah Cha had just begun teaching first graders in a low-income, Latino immigrant neighborhood in Los Angeles. In the fall, Hannah, like most American first-grade teachers, wanted to teach her students about Thanksgiving and to tie her reading and writing lessons to this historical event. But Hannah's understanding of children's learning led her in an untraditional direction.

———————————————— � ✖ ✖ ————————————————

Thanksgiving is more than just the picturesque scene of European pilgrims
sitting at a table eating turkey with Native Americans standing, almost hid-
ing or blending, into the background. It was not only the first multicultural
event celebrated in this country, it was the beginning of mixing, sharing,
and appreciating one another's differences. My class considered the Pilgrims
as immigrants seeking a life of more opportunities. They concluded that we
are all pilgrims. Our families journeyed here from another country in search
for a better existence. Further, we can celebrate Thanksgiving in our own cul-
tural fashion and not feel marginalized if we do not have turkey for dinner.

   We had just read How Many Days to America? *by Eve Bunting, and*
Marissa strongly identified with the story. It is a book about a Latino family

that underwent many tribulations to immigrate to America. Although
Marissa did not remember [her immigration], the experience was very alive
to her through her mother's stories. She shared some of these stories with
the whole class, and concluded that she is American and Mexican—she is
American even though people tell her that she is not. When a writing activity
followed the story, Marissa went straight to work. Usually she is easily dis-
tracted because her reading and writing skills are so low, but she connected
with this activity and took some risks. She achieved the critical awareness
that she is just as much an American pilgrim as the traditional European
Pilgrims. I believe this was Marissa's start to becoming literate.

—**Hannah Cha**
First-year teacher, grade 1

In Hannah Cha's social studies lesson, first grader Marissa is learning both the traditional story of Thanksgiving and developing a sense that she is not "less than" but
"as good as" American first graders who are Anglo and not immigrants. The stance
Americans take about Hannah's social studies lesson will depend on whether they
take a traditional, a progressive, or multiculturalist perspective. At one end of the
spectrum, traditionalists want social studies lessons to preserve traditional versions
of the past, to teach the basic historical "facts," as they were established in generations past, and to instill patriotism. At the other end, the most progressive and multicultural social studies educators will want Marissa to have access to historical
knowledge about Americans who are Latinos, Indians, Africans, Chinese, Arabs, and
others *in their own terms,* as well as learning how to fit herself into certain historical moments in Anglo-American history.

At the other end of schooling, Judy Smith teaches her high school seniors a required course in economics. As a high school social studies teacher, Judy seeks to
achieve some of the most traditional goals of American schooling, to

———————————————————❈ ❈ ❈———————————————————

educate and guide our students to recognize their potential, provide them
the skills and strategies to be successful after high school and college, and
understand their role in our democratic society to ensure our democracy
continues and thrives. Teachers must educate students that our democracy
should not be taken for granted, and that it requires constant vigilance and
responsibility.

Yet, her lessons are anything but traditional, since she believes that social studies teachers also

———————————————————❈ ❈ ❈———————————————————

need to direct students towards critical consciousness—of their potential, of
their freedom, of ongoing injustices, and of the obligation to ensure our
democracy and improve on it for future generations.

—**Judy Smith**
High school social studies

Like Hannah Cha, Judy Smith approaches her subject in ways that teach both basic concepts and encourage critical consciousness. In a one three-week unit, for example, Judy's students considered the economic and social effects of colonialism and neocolonialism, including how consumer habits and beliefs in wealthy countries have an impact on the environment and on other cultures and other people. In addition to the basic economic concepts, her students grappled with the connections between their own buying habits, business ethics, and social injustices.

Students analyzed economic development indicators and questioned why persons living in the North are the "haves" and people in the South are the "have nots." We discussed racist reasons for colonialism and how it continues in different forms today. Students read about sweatshops and indigenous cultures and how corporations take advantage of people of color. Finally, we talked about what our roles are in the global marketplace, what changes in our own behaviors we could make, and what additional steps could be taken to address some of the social injustices.

Many of my female students love shopping. They want to go into business for themselves or become clothes designers. Some also work at retail stores. Two lessons, a reading that focuses on a popular Los Angeles clothes store and a video called "Zoned for Slavery," showcased brand name stores (Gap Inc., OshKosh, and Eddie Bauer) exploiting female workers in its sweatshops. The brand name recognition makes the content accessible to students. They could feel the pain of the sweatshop workers. They could also look at themselves as consumers and decide if they want to change any of their purchasing habits.

—**Judy Smith**
High school social studies

Traditional versus Progressive, Multicultural Social Studies

As with mathematics and English language arts, the controversy over the social studies curriculum has been intense and highly political. Here, too, traditionalists and progressives have debated what and whose history and culture should be taught to young Americans.

Traditional Social Studies   At the core of the traditional curriculum are the facts about American history and government, appreciation for citizens' rights and responsibilities, and acceptance of the basic values and ideas in the nation's core documents—the Declaration of Independence, the Constitution, and the Bill of Rights. Elementary school teachers engage children in units focused on the Founding Fathers and the Westward Movement. Most middle schoolers take classes in American history and government, including a hefty unit or whole course on state history. Nearly all high school students take required courses in American history and government, supplemented by electives in psychology, world history, economics, sociology, and law.

Traditionalists want students to focus on the traditional disciplines of history, geography, and civics (government). History lessons, for example, should emphasize how government and the values embedded in its founding documents have endured over time, as well as presenting stories about how the values and courage of American leaders and heroes shaped this country.[40] This attention to solutions and victories is consistent with the traditional approach to history as a story of progress.

In a traditionalist curriculum, history is typically taught from the perspective of leaders and the dominant culture. And though some of presidents, generals, tycoons, and inventors did have humble origins and may have improved the lot of "common folks," school history generally provides few insights into what it was like to live an ordinary working-person's life (of all races) during the Reconstruction South, the Great Depression, the 1950s, and so on.

Immigrant and minority groups may be included in the traditional curriculum, but most often the focus is on their assimilation into the dominant culture. The following examples from a fourth-grade California history textbook about the Indians' experience in the California missions reveals how traditional history results in an account that would be considerably different if it had been told from the Indians' perspective:

> Indians helped the settlers, and the settlers helped the Indians. The Indians had better food and clothing than they had ever had. They were more comfortable than they had ever been.
>
> Once in a while a mission Indian had to be punished for something he had done. Sometimes such Indians ran away. Some of them took guns with them. Sometimes they took horses with them, too. The runaway Indians taught the wild Indians how to steal animals and other things from the missions. Once in a while soldiers had to protect the missions from an Indian raid.
>
> The Indians at the missions ate more regularly than they had when they were wild. The padres took care of them in many ways. . . . They learned to do many things as the Spaniards did. They learned many new skills.[41]

This text, published in 1965, was used for many years. Children who learned these facts and attitudes in their fourth-grade classes are now in their midlives, and at the height of their economic, social, and political influence. They are parents of today's students, and veteran teachers and curriculum designers. We must wonder when and how and if they have changed their views of history, conquest, and Indians. We can only hope that their reflections on the California missions do not bring forth images of happy, grateful, wild men who sometimes were very bad and had to be punished.

The traditional curriculum also includes minority leaders, but the predominant focus is on the progress they've made toward solving social problems. Students may learn, for example, that Cesar Chavez was a great Mexican American who led protests to improve conditions of migrant farm workers. However, they often learn little about exploitive conditions that farm workers faced or the poverty that remains. Similarly, students may learn overly simple lessons that Rosa Parks and Martin Luther King ended segregation or that the mistake of the Japanese internment camps won't be repeated.

One recent review of multicultural curriculum in social studies classrooms concluded:

> [S]tudents have little knowledge of the history of race relations in the United States. What they do know is the character of the relations between enslaved African Americans and their White masters. Focusing on the "evils" of slavery— cruel masters, the brutal treatment of slaves, belief in the inferiority of slaves— is important to be sure. But it provides a history that is too narrow and limited to be of much use in discussing contemporary American society. It provides very weak links to issues of racism, discrimination, and the denial of political and civil rights.[42]

In one example, students revealed how the curriculum limited their understanding of African Americans' experiences with racism. For these students, racial segregation and prejudice are not enduring social problems, but anomalies— historical moments that came and went.

> Jean wrote about southern slavery as the "era of racism, prejudice, and slavery"; Eric wrote, "less than ninety years later [after the Civil War], black people were the target of racism once again"; Diana wrote, "that was the past"; and Sue, summing up African Americans' experiences, wrote "in the end, as you know, there is no more slavery anymore."[43]

Finally, traditionalists also prefer that teachers teach about controversial topics from the perspective of dominant values, rather than as issues that students explore, discover, or clarify. AIDS, for example, is rarely presented as having emerged in a historical and political context of homophobia. Drug and alcohol use are typically portrayed as character flaws. These approaches are not invitations to explore issues or to solve problems from a social science perspective as much as they are conclusions and behavioral prescriptions the curriculum asserts unconditionally.

In fact, many traditionalists today lament that today's schools focus on current values and issues while neglecting historic events. They suggest that emphasis on the process of *doing* social science and constructive teaching methods (simulations, projects, etc.) has altered what history instruction is supposed to accomplish. Many object to the term "social studies," because it conveys neglect of the traditional disciplines. Some decry progressive social studies as morally flabby and relativistic. They would be likely to accuse the progressive teachers quoted in this chapter of "tearing down" the country by exposing students to unsolved dilemmas, real or imagined, in the American culture.

Progressive Social Studies   In contrast to traditionalists' emphasis on historical facts, progressives want students to learn to think like historians, political scientists, geographers, anthropologists, sociologists, and economists. Their hope is that students will learn how these social science disciplines construct and understand knowledge. They may ask students to do original research and reenact society's decision making and problem solving around critical social issues. They may ask them to explore their personal and family histories to help make sense of traditionally taught events and historical figures.

Progressives also prefer a curriculum that helps students "place the human story in larger context."[44] Many, like Hannah Cha and Judy Smith, quoted at the beginning of this section, have students use history and social commentaries to observe and make sense of their own lives. In another example, teacher Erik Korporaal's class brought together 10- and 11-year-old Latino Catholics and African American Protestants and Muslims. He connected the standard sixth-grade social studies unit on Egypt with the rich and complex knowledge that the children could share with one another and with him about their own cultures.

———————————————————— ⚘ ⚘ ⚘ ————————————————————

My students were learning about Egyptian burial practices. They researched the burial customs of their own families and cultures, shared information, and compared their own customs with those of other students. The students now had real-life contexts that they could relate to new understandings of Egypt. They were able to critically analyze their burial customs and form deeper understandings about their history and origin.

—ERIK KORPORAAL
First-year teacher, grade 6

Another progressive approach is to challenge students to view history from the perspective of those at the bottom of the social ladder, particularly of those who may not have benefited from the technological advances, territorial expansion, and economic progress that traditional histories highlight history. For example, when first-year teacher Jennifer Garcia taught her eleventh graders about the end of the nineteenth century, she stressed how the industrial age affected workers and immigrants. She included their stories alongside more conventional accounts of the rise of industrialists' power and the making of new economic policy.

———————————————————— ⚘ ⚘ ⚘ ————————————————————

Throughout the unit on "Industrialization, Unionism, and Immigration," I attempted to incorporate critical multiculturalism—not in one or two activities but as a central theme. The goal was for students to be exposed to and appreciate the period's social complexities. Activities and discussions based on themes such as factory life, union organizing, political machines and corruption, and urban living conditions challenged students' preconceived notions about workers, immigrants, and politics. By the end of the unit, students had not only been exposed to the social complexities of the late 1800s but developed a measure of empathy with the people and issues through critically examining social, political, and economic issues.

—JENNIFER GARCIA
First-year teacher, history, grade 11

Moreover, progressive educators stress that *all* students—not just students of color, not just older students—need a multicultural curriculum that goes beyond a more traditional "let's-include-everyone." Jeffrey Madrigal found a way to engage fourth graders in such an approach:

The study of music quickly expanded into a study of international and domestic politics and geography. The class explored the African roots of hip hop and learned about the trials and accomplishments of Nelson Mandela. We used the strong social commentary present in some music to study the politics of South Africa (South African revolutionary music), to learn about the Rastafarian religion of Jamaica (Reggae), and to look at black nationalism in America (Rip Hop). After the lesson, a simple rap song took on historical roots and sociopolitical meaning. We explored social commentary [in] jazz and Middle Eastern music. The levels of understanding by each student varied, but the children were always attentive, and they even learned to take notes.

—JEFFREY MADRIGAL
First-year teacher, grade 4

Critical multiculturalists go even farther. They, like teacher Martha Guerrero, in the next vignette, critique traditional historians, geographers, and anthropologists as men who learned and worked in the tradition of the European Enlightenment. Such teachers believe that students draw energy and optimism from grappling with history and contemporary issues from multiple perspectives. They think that schools have an important activist role in challenging and improving society. They argue that an objective pursuit of social justice does not require one to be dispassionate, passive, or neutral.

My unit on slavery begins with the idea that historical texts give diverse subjective and objective information. My goal is to encourage students to begin questioning information that commonly remains unexamined. Thus, students are asked to consider who writes history, who is excluded from history, and why history is written as it is. We analyze history by looking at slavery as an economic mode of exploitation. Students examine how slavery is depicted by different authors. I explained the difference between primary and secondary sources. In groups students analyzed firsthand accounts of African American slaves. By looking at these primary documents, we validated the history and culture of our ancestors. As a class, we outlined the textbook section on slavery. We then compared the different ways that slavery was presented.

—MARTHA GUERRERO
First-year teacher, high school history

Progressives like the teachers quoted here have had some impact on the social studies curriculum over the past few decades. For example, the 1991 revision of the California social studies text made quite a few changes in its account of Indians at the California missions:

> Although some Indians were content on the missions, many others were unhappy with this new way of life. By living at the missions the Indians gave up their own culture, the way of life they had known in their tribal villages. They could only leave the mission grounds with permission from the padres. They were not free to hunt or to pick berries.
>
> Mission Indians were not allowed to return to their tribes once they agreed to take part in mission life. Some ran away. But soldiers usually brought them back and sometimes whipped them. Others wanted to revolt. They wanted to rise up against their leaders, the Spanish padres and the soldiers at the mission communities.
>
> Sometimes Indians revolted violently. Six years after its founding, the San Diego Mission was attacked by Indians. They set the mission on fire and killed one of the padres.
>
> Many Indians died of diseases brought by the Spanish. When crops failed, Indians didn't have enough to eat. Some became sick from the change in their diet on the missions. By the end of the Mission period, the California Indian population was half the size that it had been when Father Serra raised his first cross at San Diego Mission.[45]

However, even this version, 25 years later, waffles as it portrays the stunning violations of decency and human rights that California Indians endured. The revised text still situates Native Americans in the white American story of the westward expansion that brought progress to the wilderness. Indian deaths seem sanitized, kept a safe distance from the killers; disease, crop failure, and a change in diet reduce the Indian population by half, not theft of land and enslavement. On the other hand, Indians, with *their* offenses, are downright uncivilized; they violently revolt, attack and burn missions, and kill padres. Nevertheless, many traditionalists worried that this most recent California text was too liberal in its depiction of California history.

Seeking a Middle Ground: The National History Standards

The historians and educators at UCLA's National Center for History in the Schools knew they had walked into the middle of the traditional/progressive debate when they launched their project to develop a set of national curriculum standards in history. Hoping to avoid being labeled as part of either camp, the Center included both traditional and progressive groups in the standards-setting process. In 1994, after two years of work, the group had framed standards for teaching U.S. and world history from kindergarten to twelfth grade.

Historical Thinking and Historical Understanding   In an effort to blend traditional and progressive views, the group specified two types of standards. One type focused on the progressive goal of having students develop historical thinking skills. The second focused on the traditionalists' goal of having students acquire knowledge of historical events.

> *Historical thinking skills* [our emphasis] that enable students to evaluate evidence, develop comparative and causal analyses, interpret the historical record, and construct sound historical arguments and perspectives on which informed decisions in contemporary life can be based.
>
> *Historical understandings* [our emphasis] that define what students should know about the history of their nation and of the world. These understandings are drawn from the record of human aspirations, strivings, accomplishments, and failures in at least five spheres of human activity: the social, political, scientific/technological, economic, and philosophical/religious/aesthetic. They also provide students the historical perspectives required to analyze contemporary issues and problems confronting citizens today.
>
> Historical thinking and understanding do not, of course, develop independently of one another. Higher levels of historical thinking depend upon and are linked to the attainment of higher levels of historical understanding. For these reasons, the standards . . . provide an integration of historical thinking and understanding.[46]

However, the Center's effort to forge a middle ground between traditional and progressive camps was futile. The battle over these standards was intense. At the height of the controversy, the standards were condemned by the U.S. Senate.

"The End of History"—Traditionalists Attack the Standards   Two weeks before the public release of the standards, Lynne Cheney (the same Lynne Cheney who railed against the NCTM math standards) published a *Wall Street Journal* editorial, "The End of History." In it, she accused the National Center for History in the Schools of writing standards that promoted a left-wing political agenda. Among other things, she complained that Harriet Tubman was mentioned six times, while Ulysses S. Grant was named only once, and Robert E. Lee not at all—evidence, she argued, of a politically correct emphasis on women and minorities.[47]

Rush Limbaugh, perhaps the nation's most popular conservative radio talk-show host, picked up the attack, saying the standards should be flushed "down the sewer of multiculturalism."

> When you bring [students] into a classroom, and you teach them that America is a rotten place, . . . and they don't have a chance here . . . you have a bunch of embittered people growing up, robbing and stealing and turning to crime because they've been told all their young lives that there's no future for them. . . .

This country does not deserve the reputation it's getting in multicultural classrooms, and the zenith of this bastardization of American history has been
reached with the new standards.[48]

Not all of the criticism came from such politically conservative voices, but the
traditionalist argument was made most vehemently by those with antigovernment,
pro–free market, and fundamentalist religious ideologies. For example, former Reagan White House policy adviser Gary Bauer, now head of the conservative Family
Research Council, declared:

> It is hard to overstate the magnitude of the failure. For the Department of Edu-
> cation, this embarrassing public fiasco is indisputable evidence of bureaucratic
> ineptitude. If we adopt these amnesiac history standards, we will succumb to a
> kind of national identity crisis. We will cease to remember who we are and why
> it matters that there is an America.
>
> [T]here is an anti-free enterprise bias to the history standards. Students are
> encouraged to put John D. Rockefeller on trial for his sharp business tactics.
> But where do the standards lead young Americans to an understanding of the
> most productive and free economic system in history? Nowhere.
>
> It goes without saying that the history standards' emphasis on race, gender,
> and class forces young Americans to accept a secular world view. The history
> standards panel clearly failed to comprehend the influence of religion in Ameri-
> can life.[49]

What called forth such impassioned concern? Were the writers of the standards
that ill-informed, that un-American, and that irreligious? Following is a brief sample
of the kind of language in the standards that set off the critics. Indeed, not only does
it encourage questioning, but questioning values:

> Value-laden issues worthy of classroom analysis include not only those irre-
> deemable events in human history from which students can most easily draw
> clear ethical judgment—the Holocaust, for example, or the Cambodian genocide
> under the Pol Pot regime. These analyses should also address situations of last-
> ing consequence in which what is morally right and wrong may not be self-
> evident. Was it right, for example, for Lincoln, in his Emancipation Proclama-
> tion, to free only those slaves behind the Confederate lines? Because of the
> complicated way values act upon people confronted with the need to decide,
> the full moral situation in a past event is not always immediately clear. Students
> should understand, therefore, that their opinions should be held tentative and
> open to revision as they acquire new insight into these historical problems. Par-
> ticularly challenging are the many social issues throughout United States history
> on which multiple interests and different values have come to bear. Issues of
> civil rights or equal education opportunity, of the right of choice vs. the right to
> life, and of criminal justice have all brought such conflicts to the fore.[50]

Clobbered by the political backlash, the Center agreed to revise the standards
and in 1996 issued a document that fared better with conservatives. The story of
American history was cast in a more positive light, and many previously absent
names were included.[51] The Center dropped the "teaching examples" and some of
the more offensive language.

Unlike the fate that met the English language arts standards, the revised history standards have retained their U.S. Department of Education sponsorship. Even after the controversial standards were vindicated, however, many textbook publishers have shied away from using them as a blueprint for standards and curriculum.[52]

The debate about what social studies and whose history should be taught will not likely be settled soon. The best hope, as always, lies with teachers who acquire the confidence and commitment that comes with training, experience, and scholarship. Teachers who want to press their students to think deeply and ask hard questions about the rhetoric and realities of social life may have to look elsewhere—besides standards and textbooks—for help. Used with care and thoughtful scholarship both by teachers and their students, the Internet can be a rich resource for escaping the chilling effects of curriculum and standards battles.

Science

—⚜ ⚜ ⚜—

My integrated, coordinated science class is centered on a "survivor" theme. The students and I are stranded together on Santa Rosa Island—one of the larger Channel Islands off the coast of California. The first day of class I introduced the situation, showed them a map, and asked them what they wanted to learn. My students brainstormed topics that they wanted to study that would better equip us for survival on the island. They decided on three topics: water, food, and shelter. We decided that we needed to farm in order to sustain ourselves, and that to be efficient farmers we needed to be experts on plants. The students also wanted to study medicinal plants so that we could make medicine. Every lesson we did was tied to surviving on the island.

I wanted my students to be able to describe why humans and plants are dependent on each other, and what a plant needs in order to photosynthesize. If we understood how plants work, then we would be good farmers on the island. My objectives matched the district standards.

My goal for scientific literacy guided many of my activities. I wanted my students to acquire the academic language needed to talk about plant structures and their role in photosynthesis—terms including absorption, xylem, phloem, and glucose. The students learned by doing, and the content was learned as students used materials to test out hypotheses. The experiments forced students away from passive listening to active participation.

Because the students chose their own curriculum, it was relevant to their lives, and they were motivated to learn. Having an overarching theme of "survival" helped my students to understand scientific principles. Facts they learned were not discrete bodies of knowledge, but rather related principles that supported each other. There was always a purpose to learning. Having a theme also helped me to select science concept depth over breadth.

—JENNIE LEE
First-year teacher, high school science

Jennie Lee's science unit would not please everyone. As in the other academic disciplines, long-standing debates also permeate curriculum decisions in science. Some of the most hotly debated questions are these:

- Should the science curriculum focus on depth or breath of coverage of science topics?
- Should schools teach the traditional science disciplines—earth science, biology, chemistry, and physics—separately or integrated around themes or concepts?
- Should lessons connect science with related social issues?
- Should all students learn the same science, and can they learn it?

Traditional versus Progressive Science Curricula

The answers to the preceding questions, and the reaction to Jennie Lee's "survivor" unit, relate directly to theories about knowledge and learning, and they speak precisely to whether or not social justice values are viewed as a legitimate part of the school curriculum.

Traditional Science   Traditionalists stress a view of science as an objective, empirically based, value-neutral explanation of "the way things are." They see teaching as transmitting this knowledge through explanation, demonstration, and practice. They prefer that the science disciplines be taught separately.

The traditional science curriculum is most often organized into orderly sequences of topics, subtopics, and facts, often matched to the table of contents of science textbooks. Students learn scientific terms (e.g., photosynthesis, osmosis, deciduous) and memorize important principles in their briefest form (e.g., plants are green because they contain chlorophyll, plants produce oxygen) and conduct experiments in which they demonstrate the concepts they are learning. This cycle repeats throughout the year until the teacher has covered all the topics. In 2000 the *National Commission on Mathematics and Science Teaching for the 21st Century*, chaired by senator and former astronaut John Glenn, found that students are rarely asked to learn the powerful and fascinating ideas of science. Instead they "spend much of their time learning definitions, or the labels that apply to natural phenomena and scientific processes."[53]

In high schools, the traditional science curriculum typically consists of introductory and low-level general science courses; survey courses in specific disciplines that prepare students for college—most often, biology, anatomy, chemistry, physics; and advanced placement versions of these survey courses for the most able science students. Traditionalists view efforts to integrate the sciences and to place them in a social context as disturbing signs of curricular softness. They fear that such moves both erode the rigor of students' academic studies and undermine the structure of the knowledge that has developed through scientific discovery.

The traditional science curriculum has been widely criticized for skimming the surface of science without promoting in-depth scientific understanding. For example, a 1996 report of an international study, *A Splintered Vision: An Investigation of U.S. Mathematics and Science Education,* found that the average American ninth-grade science student covers nearly 55 topics. Most of the other 50 nations in the study produced much higher achievement in science and offered far fewer topics. The conclusion was that fewer topics studied in depth may result in greater science knowledge.[54]

However, teachers face enormous pressure to provide students a taste of many science topics. One source of pressure comes from the fact that the traditional curriculum is so familiar to us. As we describe next, some very distinguished scientists are extraordinarily suspicious of progressive approaches that depart from the traditional coverage of the disciplines. Textbooks also press teachers toward a traditional approach. Publishers want to include all the topics that different schools might want to teach, so no topic receives treatment in depth. Such texts encourage superficial coverage, especially if teachers' own science knowledge limits their ability to extend lessons beyond what the text provides.

Progressive Science   Some of the nation's most prestigious science organizations, including the National Science Foundation and the American Association for the Advancement of Science, have endorsed progressive approaches of science education.[55]

In contrast to the traditional view, progressives argue that science is a product of human understanding and subject to constant revision. Most contend that scientific "truth" lies on a continuum from pretty good hunches to long-enduring, seemingly unassailable (but always open to reinvestigation) facts.

A progressive curriculum is more likely to be organized as sustained investigations that may cut across the specific science disciplines. Students engage in observation, experimentation, and interpretation of what they find. For example, in a life science unit of study, students might observe and make sense of the processes by which plants grow by cultivating plants. Hands-on work (e.g., altering light, water, nutrients, and other growing conditions) while observing, recording, and forming and testing hypotheses anchor more traditional knowledge sources (lecture, films, textbooks, etc.). Students work cooperatively, share prior experiences, and offer plant growth predictions based on articulated reasons. Many different experiments occur simultaneously, and students follow the progress of those that relate to their own hypotheses. In our progressive curriculum example, students also investigate real-life consequences of plant growth for farmers, the public, the environment, businesses, and government. Each student considers the careers and lifestyles of those whose work centers on plants: farmworkers, growers, wholesalers, retailers, experimental botanists, chemists, conservationists, rangers, teachers, florists, and so on. Each student presents a formal oral report of his or her observations and work and participates in a group effort to present conclusions. The teacher holds all students accountable for core concepts that they can reasonably master (photosynthesis, osmosis, the nature of cells, plant reproduction, etc.) and for the concepts and foundations of their independent research.

Progressive science educators argue strongly that the old distinctions among the science disciplines should no longer drive the curriculum. Paul DeHart Hurd, perhaps the dean of American science education, argues that the move toward integrating the science curriculum reflects important changes in science:

> Disciplines have been replaced by research fields, and most research is done by teams of investigators. A team represents a cognitive system that is phasing out the traditional notion of scientific inquiry. Much of scientific research is strategy or problem oriented rather than theory stimulated. For example, the Hubble telescope has made a wealth of observations, and it may take scientists a century or more to find theoretical explanations for them. A blending of science disciplines is taking place, such as biophysics, biochemistry, and biogeochemistry. The most active areas of research today are cross-disciplinary.
> . . . Changes in the practice and culture of today's science go unnoticed. Professional science educators, as well as most scientists, pay little attention to what these revolutionary transformations in science ought to mean for a citizen's education in the sciences.[56]

In the past decade or so, many secondary schools have integrated their science curriculum—converting the traditional "layer cake" of separate physical science, biology, chemistry, and physics courses into a sequence of integrated classes organized around themes.

National Standards: Deep, Integrated, Socially Relevant Science for All

The federal government charged the prestigious National Academy of Sciences with developing national standards for the science curriculum.

Joining Content and Process   The *National Science Education Standards* specify eight content categories that are necessary for a high-quality science program. Physical science, life science, earth and space science, and science and technology are four categories that sound familiar, and their adoption into school programs would not upset traditional views of teaching science. However, the remaining four categories—unifying concepts and processes, inquiry, societal challenges, and the history of science—would, indeed, turn science education on its head. These "new" conceptions of science content are provocative and exciting:

- The content of science cannot be placed outside of science's unifying concepts and processes.
- Participation in inquiry is scientific content, not just process.
- Scientific knowledge is not distinct from societal challenges.
- The history of science is science content that underscores science as a human and social enterprise.

Each of the standards specifies core skills and concepts. For example, upon entering high school, students will develop and enact the following abilities for scientific inquiry:

- Identify questions and concepts that guide scientific investigations.
- Design and conduct scientific investigations.

- Use technology and mathematics to improve investigations and communications.
- Formulate and revise scientific explanations and models using logic and evidence.
- Recognize and analyze alternative explanations and models.
- Communicate and defend a scientific argument.

In addition to these "abilities to do scientific inquiry," the standards also specify the *understandings* that students should develop. For example, students in grades 9–12 will understand how substances exist in or are represented by "three domains of thought—the macroscopic world of observable phenomena, the microscopic world of molecules, atoms, and subatomic particles, and the symbolic and mathematical world of chemical formulas, equations and symbols."[57]

The *National Science Education Standards* also press for integration across disciplines. Although they don't completely blur the distinctions among physical science, life science, and earth and space sciences, the standards do emphasize the following crosscutting themes—what the document calls unifying concepts and processes:

- Systems, order, and organization
- Evidence, models, and explanation
- Constancy, change, and measurement
- Evolution and equilibrium
- Form and function

These crosscutting ideas "provide students with productive ways of thinking about and integrating a range of basic ideas that explain the natural and designed world."[58]

Science for All   The *National Science Education Standards* authors' make clear their position about who can do science:

> The intent of the *Standards* can be expressed in a single phrase: Science standards for all students. The phrase embodies both excellence and equity. The *Standards* apply to all students, regardless of age, gender, cultural or ethnic background, disabilities, aspirations, or interest and motivation in science. Different students will achieve understanding in different ways, and different students will achieve different degrees of depth and breadth of understanding depending on interest, ability, and context. But all students can develop the knowledge and skills described in the *Standards,* even as some students go well beyond these levels.[59]

Similar statements appear in the reform documents of the National Science Foundation, the National Academy of Sciences, and the American Association for the Advancement of Science.

As described in Focal Point 4.2, Columbia University professor Angela Calabrese-Barton acts on her commitment to science for all by taking standards-based science instruction out of the classroom and into New York City shelters for homeless families.

FOCAL POINT 4.2

Science and Social Justice
Professor Angela Calabrese-Barton Teaches Science to the Homeless

"Since August 1995, I have had an after-school science program for homeless children and their families," Professor Calabrese-Barton said. "I use the setting to provide an opportunity for children in a homeless shelter to play with science and use it productively in their lives." The program considers three questions: How do homeless children construct their identities in science? How can science be used as a productive force in their lives and be created out of their experiences? And, what do teachers need to know to teach children in extreme poverty?

The logistics of being homeless, moving frequently, not having money for basic needs and for daycare, not having a permanent address or immunization records, makes regular school attendance difficult for these children. When they do attend school, children often change schools several times throughout the year. Often they have to repeat grades and are likely to score below grade level in reading and math.

"I wanted to use science as an agency to empower them," she explained. "I wanted to help people who teach science to understand the connection between the larger social context of living in poverty and just surviving in school."

As urban homeless children learn science, she says, they also learn a lot about who they are and what science is. Teachers need to think about how children perceive themselves and the choices they make based on those perceptions, and they need to think about how children perceive science and what they believe they can do or want to do with science.

"Science can be fun, but it has an integral role in our society," Calabrese-Barton noted. "I want to help these children use science in a way to make their lives better."

One long-term study they did concerned pollution and the local community. "The kids hate living at the shelter because of the social stigma and its closeness to a crack house," Calabrese-Barton said. "They never talked to me about the fact that they could learn something about their neighborhood and take that knowledge and make changes."

The project began with the children listing complaints about where they lived and the feelings they associated with those problems. They decided to gather more data from other people in the neighborhood.

"They took a video camera and interviewed people in the area and asked what they thought about the neighborhood," Calabrese-Barton explained. "They studied the quality of the water in their building and the ground pollution in a one-block area and devised a plan to clean up that block and put plants in the area. They took experiences they felt bad about and used science to transform them and to help them act on them."

An important benefit the children receive from science time is the consistency with which Professor Calabrese-Barton returns to the shelter to work with them.

"One of the most psychologically devastating aspects of being homeless as a child is the uncertainty and instability," Calabrese-Barton explained. "When I came back the following week, one of the young boys jumped up, started running around in circles, and screamed to us and his brother, 'I knew they would come! I knew you'd come back! I told you!'"

Source: Excerpted from *TC Today* 23, no. 1 (1997); Professor Angela Calabrese-Barton is the author of *Teaching Science for Social Justice*, 2003.

The Conservative Backlash

As was the case in the other academic subjects, the national science standards generated considerable controversy. Once again, the debate was particularly hot in California.

In the midst of widespread agreement among scientists and science educators, skepticism about "who can do science" prevented a strong unified effort to reform science education. The nuclear physicist who was leading the group writing the state's version of the standards expressed the view that a major problem in science education is that too many students—particularly low-income and minority students—give up and never become scientifically literate. He said that California's standards must change a curriculum that currently leaves behind "all these kids who don't get it."[60]

However, three Nobel laureates, led by Glen Seaborg, protested California's plan to model its science standards on the national standards.[61] They charged that the progressives writing the California document were bent on "dumbing down" science to make science appealing to students. The laureates claimed that the standards expressed a philosophy of science education that would compromise rigor and undercut learning about great, though difficult to understand, scientific discoveries. One charged, "Educational content is continually diluted in a failed effort to produce palatable bits of information for progressively less skilled students. It is essential that we take a stand and insist on educational standards with greater content."[62]

These traditional critics appeared to be judging the quality of the curriculum based on who they expected to master it. At the end of a rancorous process, Seaborg and his group were successful in securing a set of standards far closer to traditional science curriculum than what the national standards had sought to inspire.

Debating Darwin

Perhaps the most enduring controversy in curriculum has been over the science of evolution. Almost 75 years after biology teacher John Scopes was arrested for teaching evolution in violation of Tennessee law, the state board of education in Kansas voted in 1999 to remove evolution from the state's science standards.

Although the board did not ban the teaching of evolution outright, it did eliminate evolution from the topics on which Kansas students would be tested. One argument made by the conservative board majority was that evolution is not a proper science topic. Science, they argued, is the investigation of the natural world, whereas evolution examines mankind's origins—a supernatural topic that falls under the purview of the supernatural. One board member said, "I don't want my children's biology teacher talking about religion."[63]

Kansas governor Bill Graves called the board's decision an "embarrassment," and most school districts ignored it. In November 2000 Kansas voted in new board members who promised to restore evolution to the state's standards, and in February 2001 the new board reversed the anti-evolution decision of 1999.

Following Kansas's lead, however, Nebraska eliminated evolution from its state science guidelines, and Alabama required that science textbooks note that the theory of evolution is "unproven." In other skirmishes, New Mexico banned the teaching of creationism (after voting to allow it four years earlier), and Louisiana upheld teachers' rights to not read a disclaimer that evolution is an "unproven" theory.

The controversy was not settled, and in 2005 again made headlines. This time it was Pennsylvania, rather than Kansas. In 2004, the Dover, Pennsylvania, school board began requiring its high school biology teachers to read a four-paragraph statement to their students that questions the accuracy of Darwin's theory of evolution. This statement points to "intelligent design" as a competing theory for the origin and evolution of life. Intelligent design argues that "gaps" in current scientific knowledge point to an intelligent force (commonly understood to be God) responsible for the life forms we see today. A group of parents took the board to court, claiming that the statement simply tries to "repackage" creationism and interject religion into the science curriculum. And, in fact, the six members of the Dover board who approved the policy were open about their belief that "the origin of life was guided by a heavenly hand."[64]

In 2005, a federal judge ruled that "intelligent design" is a particular religious belief, not a valid scientific theory, and teaching it in public school science classrooms violates the Constitution. However, many expect that the U.S. Supreme Court will eventually rule on this case.

Will Anybody Do Science?

The most serious problem with science may be that schools teach so little of it. For example, a 1987 National Center for Educational Statistics survey found that children in elementary school averaged only two and a half hours a week learning science.[65] More recent evidence suggests that little has changed, despite concern about our nation's increasing need for scientific workers. Part of the problem is that many elementary teachers have little more scientific knowledge than the general public, and they feel uncomfortable teaching science. Similarly, many who teach older students are not science majors or not credentialed to teach science. Because basic reading and math dominate the movement for contemporary elementary school "accountability," science rarely shows up on basic skills tests; thus, teachers may be less motivated to teach it and school policies do not encourage it. Many middle-school students can take science for only one semester, and many senior highs require only one science class for those not planning to attend college.

Often, even skilled science teachers resort to science shortcuts. They may simply *tell* students about science rather than let them *do* science if resources and time are not adequate. When this happens, science can boil down to memorizing names and facts. Given these conditions, the authors of the *National Science Education Standards* proposed standards for the entire science education system. In addition to content standards, the document includes standards for what teachers should know and be able to do, for professional development activities for teachers, for judging the quality of science assessments, for judging the conditions of school science programs (including resources and learning opportunities), and for judging policies related to science education. With this comprehensive set of standards, the science community highlighted crucial needs that apply to all the subject matters. In science, as in all of the disciplines, the content of the curriculum must be considered in light of who teaches the subject, how they teach and assess it, and what conditions prevail for students to learn.

The Struggle for the Subject Matter

Professional responsibility obliges teachers to be articulate participants in *both* the public and professional arenas of curriculum inquiry and debate. Sheridan Blau, president of the National Council of Teachers of English, cautions and advises:

> Our profession as seen from inside teachers' lounges and in the conversations of professionals and in the presentations and workshops at conferences . . . is not a bloody battleground of competing ideas, but it has been made to appear so by a press hungry for dramatic stories and by impatient policy makers and a frustrated public looking for the same kind of simple answers that popular opinion often demands—answers that offer scapegoats and saviors. . . . The true ideological battleground for our profession, then, is not in the field where teacher-educators and teachers debate about the most effective teaching strategies nor in the labs and research sites where scholars offer different theoretical perspectives, different methodological procedures, and competing findings. Disagreements in these arenas can and do lead to dialogue and thereby to the advancement of learning.[66]

Dialogue and advancement of learning in the subjects—in the classroom and out: This is the work of teachers.

OLC Connections

A list of additional online and print resources and a set of questions for reflection about traditional and progressive approaches to teaching subject matter can be found at www.mhhe.com/oakes3e.

Digging Deeper

The authors and organizations in this section detail the issues related to the school subjects described in this chapter. Many also offer specific guidance about translating curriculum reforms into practice.

Mathematics

The Algebra Project, developed by civil rights leader Bob Moses, is a national network of sites striving to improve mathematics achievement for African American and other minority students who have not been reached by existing efforts at education reform. The Algebra Project works through materials development, teacher training, peer education, and school-community partnerships. The project has an activist agenda that demonstrates possibilities for quality education for all children, and they use the success of these local projects to advocate for national education reform. (In 2001 Los Angeles superintendent and former Colorado governor Roy Romer borrowed a phrase promulgated by Moses in the 1960s to characterize algebra as a "civil right" of all his city's students.) The Algebra Project also spun off the Young Peoples' Project, Inc. which trains high school and college-age Mathematics Literacy Workers to create a new culture around math literacy for youth through peer education and mentorship in after-school, in-school, Saturday programs, and summer program settings. The project is described in Moses's book, *Radical Equations: Civil Rights from Mississippi to the Algebra Project* (Boston: Beacon Press, 2001), and it can found online at http://www.algebra.org/.

The **Early Algebra Research Project** began in 1996 under the direction of **Thomas Carpenter,** director of the National Center for Improving Student Learning and Achievement in Mathematics; **Megan Loef Franke,** a professor at the University of California, Los Angeles, and director of Center X: Where Research and Practice Intersect for Urban School Professionals; and **Linda Levi,** researcher at the Wisconsin Center for Education Research. The study, which began in Madison, Wisconsin, found that mathematics instruction could pave the way for elementary school children to begin to reason algebraically. The researchers are now conducting a large-scale experimental study examining the effects of the teacher professional development program on students' algebraic understandings, involving about 5,000 Los Angeles elementary school students and their teachers. A report on the project can be found online at http://www.nwrel.org/msec/nwteacher/winter2005/elementary.html.

For more than 75 years, the **National Council of Teachers of Mathematics** (http://www.nctm.org), the largest professional association of mathematics educators in the world, has been dedicated to improving the teaching and learning of mathematics. NCTM provides professional development opportunities through annual, regional, and leadership conferences and publishes journals, books, videos, and software.

Deborah Schifter, senior scientist with the Education Development Center in Newton, Massachusetts, has written helpful accounts of teachers who use constructivist approaches to mathematics. Her books *Reconstructing Mathematics Education: Stories of Teachers Meeting the Challenge of Reform* (with Catherine Twomey Fosnot, New York: Teachers College Press, 1993) and *What's Happening in Math Class?* (New York: Teachers College Press, 1996) provide narratives from elementary teachers who are shifting their mathematics curriculum away from traditional lessons and focusing more on understanding children's mathematical thinking.

English/Language Arts

Lucy Calkins, education professor at Teachers College, Columbia University, is founding director of the Teachers College Writing Project, a coalition of teachers, teacher-administrators, professors, and writers, which provides professional sustenance and hope—roots and wings—to literacy educators across the country. Her publications include *Lessons from a Child* (Portsmouth, NH: Heinemann, 1983) and *The Art of Teaching Writing* (Portsmouth, NH: Heinemann, 1986, 1994). A "balanced literacy" advocate, Calkins is widely respected for her ideas on how to teach children to read and write, and she has inspired a generation of teachers to help the youngest children become confident writers. Calkins's latest book is *One to One: The Art of Conferring with Young Writers* (Portsmouth, NH: Heinemann, 2005).

The **International Reading Association** (http://www.reading.org/) includes classroom teachers, reading specialists, consultants, administrators, supervisors, college teachers, researchers, psychologists, librarians, media specialists, students, and parents. Association journals include *The Reading Teacher,* directed toward preschool, primary, and elementary school educators, and the *Journal of Adolescent & Adult Literacy,* directed toward teachers of older students. The association's website includes links to resources on such topics as beginning readers, adolescent literacy, comprehension, and struggling readers.

UCLA professor **Ernest Morrell** studies the uses of language and texts across a variety of contexts paying close attention to the relationships between language, literacy, culture and power in society. He also examines interventions designed to facilitate literacies of power and freedom among urban youth, and he investigates strategies for developing effective literacy educators in urban contexts. Morrell directs an annual Critical Research and Writing Seminar for urban teens, teachers and parents in the Los Angeles area. He provides resources for teachers interested in pursing these approaches in *Linking Literacy and Popular Culture: Finding Connections for Lifelong Learning* (Norwood, MA: Christopher-Gordon Publishers, 2004). With colleague, Professor Jeffrey Duncan-Andrade at San Francisco State University, Morrell also studies how hip-hop culture can be a bridge to academic literacy for urban youth.

The **National Council of Teachers of English** (www.ncte.org) provides an array of opportunities for teachers to continue their professional growth throughout their careers and a framework for dealing with issues that affect the teaching of English. NCTE publishes three monthly journals: *Language Arts, English Journal*, and *College English*. It also publishes position papers, teaching ideas, and other documents on professional concerns such as standards.

The **National Writing Project,** established in 1974, brings teachers together in summer and school-year programs around the country. The programs are led by classroom teachers who have been trained to talk with one another about teaching. The Writing Project's teachers-teaching-teachers programs serve over 100,000 teachers annually at 189 project sites across the country. The National Writing Project is online at http://www.writingproject.org/.

Reading Recovery is a widely used program developed by New Zealand psychologist **Marie Clay** in the 1970s. The approach in this program is to intervene early and provide intensive literacy experiences for students who appear to be at risk for failing to learn to read in the first grade. The individualized approach infuses direct skill teaching into sessions where children read real books, write, and play with letters to form words. Marie Clay's book *Reading Recovery: A Guidebook for Teachers in Training* (Portsmouth, NH: Heinemann, 1993) offers practical suggestions for teaching problem solving with reading, teaching writing, vocabulary, and even phonemic awareness. The Reading Recovery website is at http://www.readingrecovery.org/.

Social Studies

Facing History and Ourselves is a nonprofit organization that offers an innovative, interdisciplinary approach to teaching citizenship. It connects history to the day-to-day experiences of students by revealing the way violence and hate can destroy a society, and how the decisions of ordinary people shape an age and ultimately history. Facing History's resource center has a lending library of relevant books, periodicals, and videos. Resource books include *Facing History and Ourselves: Holocaust and Human Behavior, Elements of Time,* and seven study guides. The Facing History and Ourselves National Foundation is on the Internet at www.facinghistory.org.

UCLA's National Center for History in the Schools (NCHS), founded in 1988, develops and provides curricular materials that will engage students in exciting explorations of United States and world history, and it aids the professional development of K–12 history teachers. Many NCHS materials are available on its website, http://www.ucla.edu/nchs. NCHS director, UCLA professor **Gary Nash,** in collaboration with professors **Charlotte Crabtree** and **Ross E. Dunn,** wrote a fascinating account of the political battles over the history standards in *History on Trial: Culture Wars and the Teaching of the Past* (New York: Knopf, 1997).

The **National Council for the Social Studies** is an umbrella organization for elementary, secondary, and college teachers of history, geography, economics, political science, sociology, psychology, anthropology, and law-related education. The group developed *Expectations of Excellence: Curriculum Standards for Social Studies* (Washington, DC: National Council for the Social Studies, 1994), which outlined 10 thematic strands and performance expectations for social studies in the early grades, middle grades, and high schools. Included is a special supplement on powerful teaching and learning. The Council can be found on the Internet at http://www.ncss.org/.

The **National Geography Standards,** Geography for Life, were developed by the National Council for Geographic Education (http://www.ncge.org/), an organization that works to increase the status and quality of geography teaching and learning.

Linda Symcox, historian and teacher educator at California State University at Long Beach, has written a compelling history of the controversy surrounding the National History Standards. The book, *History Under Fire,* provides both an insider's view and a fascinating cultural analysis of how the school curriculum is highly political.

Science

Teachers College, Columbia University professor **Angela Calabrase Barton's** book, *Teaching Science for Social Justice* (New York: Teachers College Press, 2003), written with Jason L. Ermer, Tanahia L. Burkett, and Margery D. Osborne, reports on six years of research on after-school science programs in homeless shelters. Barton shows how urban children and youth come to construct their identities amidst poverty and homelessness.

The late **Paul DeHart Hurd,** former professor of science education at Stanford University, coined the term "science literacy." Throughout his career, Hurd argued that science does not and cannot proceed outside of the societal context. His book *Inventing Science Education for the New Millennium* (New York: Teachers College Press, 1997) elaborates on his claim that the first step to inventing new science curricula is the linking of science and technology to the welfare of students and to the economic and social progress of the nation. Hurd's last book is *Transforming Middle School Science Education* (New York: Teachers College Press, 2000).

Lawrence Hall of Science at the University of California-Berkeley offers an exciting collection of hands-on science and math activities and materials for preschool through high school that emphasize the "learning-by-doing" approach pioneered at the Hall. One project, EQUALS, strives to increase access and equity in mathematics for students in traditionally underrepresented gender, race, class, and cultural groups. FAMILY MATH encourages these groups to pursue mathematics by engaging their families in mathematics activities. FOSS is an elementary-school science program with 27 modules that incorporates hands-on inquiry and interdisciplinary projects, building on recent advances in the understanding of how youngsters think and learn. The Lawrence Hall of Science Internet site address is www.lhs.berkeley.edu.

The **National Science Teachers Association** (www.nsta.org) offers curricular resources based on *A Framework for High School Science Education*, an NSTA publication. The microunits, composed of labs, readings, and assessments for teachers and students, form a complete curriculum that was developed and tested to meet the national science education standards. The NSTA-initiated project—Scope, Sequence, and Coordination of High School Sciences (SS&C)—is a major curriculum project, funded by the National Science Foundation and coordinated with the National Science Education Standards.

Project 2061 (www.project2061.org/) of the American Association for the Advancement of Science has developed books, CD-ROMs, and online links and tools to help teachers work toward science literacy for all high school graduates.

Notes

1. Although we don't discuss them here, the other central disciplines—the arts and foreign language, for example—also matter. No less critical to a democratic education and to social justice, these disciplines are usually the first to be cut when budgets or reading scores are seen as inadequate. And although sound arguments can be made that school graduates and society benefit equally from multilingual citizens who understand and create music and art as they do from citizens who can solve quadratic equations, it is success in algebra that is a social justice

gatekeeper, and it is "verbal analogies" that suppress scores on gatekeeping tests such the SAT. For this reason, we focus our attention here on the subjects that determine which students' schools will consider the "good students."

2. Lynne V. Cheney, "The Latest Education Disaster: Whole Math," *Weekly Standard,* 4 August 1997.

3. Curtis C. McKnight, F. Joe Crosswhite, and John A. Dossey, *The Underachieving Curriculum: Assessing U.S. School Mathematics from an International Perspective* (Indianapolis: Stipes, 1987).

4. International Association for the Evaluation of Educational Achievement (IEA), *Trends in International Mathematics and Science Study (TIMSS),* 2005, online at http://www.iea.nl/; and U.S. Department of Education, National Center for Education Statistics. *International Outcomes of Learning in Mathematics Literacy and Problem Solving: PISA 2003 Results from the U.S. Perspective* (NCES 2005–003). Washington, DC: U.S. Government Printing Office, 2004.

5. For example, K. M. Cauley's study, "Construction of Local Knowledge: Study of Borrowing in Subtraction," in the *Journal of Educational Psychology,* 80 (1988), pp. 202–205, found that third graders lacking conceptual knowledge of the multidigit subtraction procedure were more likely to make performance errors, such as subtracting the top smaller digit from the bottom larger digit.

6. Richard Shavelson, "The Splintered Curriculum," *Education Week,* 7 May 1997, p. 38. Shavelson places some of the blame on textbook publishers who "produce textbooks that are a mile wide and an inch deep" to promote sales across the diverse U.S. market and some on standardized tests that cover a wide range of material. Shavelson's essay draws on material in William Schmidt, Curtis C. McKnight, and Senta Raizen, *A Splintered Vision: An Investigation of U.S. Science and Mathematics Education* (Dordrecht: Kluwer Academic, 1997).

7. McKnight, Crosswhite, and Dossey, *The Underachieving Curriculum.* For a comparable, more recent international comparison and analysis, see the report from the Third International Mathematics and Science Study, William Schmidt, *Facing the Consequences: Using TIMSS for a Closer Look at U.S. Mathematics and Science Education* (Dordrecht: Kluwer Academic, 1999).

8. National Council of Teachers of Mathematics, *Curriculum and Evaluation Standards for School Mathematics* (Reston, VA: Author, 1989), p. 7.

9. "Mathematics Content Standards for Grades K–12," submitted by Bill Evers, Commissioner to California State Academic Standards Commission, September 15, 1997; online at http://www.rahul.net/dehnbase/ hold/platinum-standards/altintro.html.

10. Ibid.

11. National Research Council, *Everybody Counts: A Report to the Nation on the Future of Mathematics Education* (Washington, DC: National Academy Press, 1989), p. 34. The National Research Council is a group established in 1916 by the prestigious National Academy of Sciences, whose own mission is furthering knowledge and advising the federal government.

12. National Research Council, *Everybody Counts,* p. 43.

13. Ibid., p. 60.

14. National Council of Teachers of Mathematics, *Curriculum and Evaluation Standards for School Mathematics*, p. 7.

15. Ibid. pp. 44–45.

16. Eric Gutstein and Bob Peterson, eds., *Rethinking Mathematics: Teaching Social Justice by the Numbers* (Milwaukee, WI: Rethinking Schools, 2005).

17. Richard Lee Colvin, "State Endorses Back-to-Basics Math Standards," *Los Angeles Times,* 30 November 1997, pp. 1, 18, 19, 26.

18. Luther S. Williams, letter to the California State Board of Education, 11 December 1997.

19. California Mathematics State Standards—Grade Seven. California Department of Education, 2000.

20. David Klein, Bastiaan J. Braams, Thomas Parker, William Quirk, Wilfried Schmid, W. Stephen Wilson, Chester E. Finn Jr., Justin Torres, Lawrence Braden, and Ralph A. Raimi, *The State of Math Standards 2005* (Washington: Fordham Foundation, 2005).

21. *Webster's Encyclopedic Unabridged Dictionary of the English Language* (New York: Gramercy Books, 1989).

22. Ibid., p. 1195.

23. P. David Pearson, "Reclaiming the Center: The Search for Common Ground in Teaching Reading"; online at http://ed-web3.educ.msu.edu.cdpds/pdpaper.rtc21197.htm.

24. Ibid.

25. Ibid.

26. International Reading Association and National Council of Teachers of English, *Standards for the English Language Arts* (Champaign, IL: Author, 1996), p. 75.

27. Karen Diegmueller, "English Group Loses Funding for Standards," *Education Week,* 30 March 1994; and Miles Myers, "Where the Debate About English Standards Goes Wrong," *Education Week,* 15 May 1995.

28. Ibid., p. 25.

29. See, for example, "Multicultural Book List Proposed in San Francisco," *New York Times,* 11 March 1998; and "S.F. Board OKs Reading of Works by Nonwhites," *Los Angeles Times,* 21 March 1998, p. 1.

30. Annie Gowen, "Maryland Schools Remove 2 Black-Authored Books," *Los Angeles Times,* 11 January 1998, p. A6.

31. J. Martin Rosser, "The Decline of Literacy," *Education Week,* 15 May 1996.

32. Ibid.

33. As quoted in Karen Diegmueller, "The Best of Both Worlds," *Teacher Magazine,* March 1996.

34. Karen Diegmueller, "War of Words," *Education Week,* 20 March 1996.

35. Ibid.

36. www.ed.gov/programs/readingfirst.

37. P. David Pearson, "The Politics of Reading Research and Practice," a presentation at a conference in Houston, Texas, May 15, 1997; online at http://ed-web3.educ.msu.edu.cdpds/pdpaper.politics.html.

38. Judith Langer, as quoted in Deborah Viadero, "Researchers Flag Six Elements of Good Secondary English Instruction," *Education Week,* 14 June 2000; online at http://www.edweek.org.

39. Ladson-Billings's and Delpit's work is discussed in more detail in Chapter 3.

40. Gary B. Nash, Charlotte Crabtree, and Ross E. Dunn, *History on Trial: Culture Wars and the Teaching of the Past* (New York: Knopf, 1997).

41. California State Department of Education, *California's Own History* (Sacramento: Author, 1965).

42. Hugh Mehan, Dina Okamoto, Angela Lintz, and John S. Wills, "Ethnographic Studies of Multicultural Schools and Classrooms," in *Handbook of Research on Multicultural Education,* ed. James A. Banks and Cherry A. McGee Banks (New York: Macmillan, 1995).

43. John S. Wills, "The Situation of African Americans in American History: Using History as a Resource for Understanding the Experiences of Contemporary African Americans" as quoted in Hugh Mehan, Dina Okamoto, Angela Lintz, and John S. Wills, "Ethnographic Studies of Multicultural Schools and Classrooms," in *Handbook of Research on Multicultural Education.*

44. As quoted in Ron Brandt, "On the High School Curriculum: A Conversation with Ernest Boyer," *Educational Leadership,* 46, no. 1 (September 1988), pp. 4–9.

45. *Oh, California* (New York: Houghton Mifflin Co., 1991) as cited in "Tragic Side of Mission Era Being Told," *Los Angeles Times,* 2 September 1997.

46. National Center for History in the Schools, *National Standards for United States History* (Los Angeles: UCLA National Center for History in the Schools, 1994).

47. Lynne Cheney, "The End of History," *Wall Street Journal,* 20 October 1994, p. A26.

48. Rush Limbaugh, as cited in Nash, Crabtree, and Dunn, *History on Trial,* p. 5.

49. Gary L. Bauer, "National History Standards: Clintonites Miss the Moon," Washington, DC, Family Research Council, 1995; online at http://www. frc.org.

50. National Center for History in the Schools, *National Standards for United States History.*

51. The United States is not the only society that struggles to protect a spotless version of its history. Perhaps we can have a higher regard for teaching new insights into our own past, when we see the dissembling (happily, corrected in this case) of another country. The following appeared

in "Japan's High Court Rules Against Rewriting History," *Los Angeles Times,* 30 August 1997: "[The Japanese Court] ruled that the Education Ministry acted wrongly in ordering a textbook writer to delete accurate descriptions of Japanese atrocities during World War II, including a mention of the notorious Unit 731 that conducted gruesome medical experiments on human guinea pigs . . . and quoted one of Japan's most famous novelists, Ryotaro Shiba: "A country whose textbooks lie . . . will inevitably collapse."

52. Kathleen Kennedy Manzo, "Glimmer of History Standards Shows Up in Latest Textbooks," *Education Week,* 8 October 1997.

53. *Before It's Too Late: A Report to the Nation from the National Commission on Mathematics and Science Teaching for the 21st Century,* chaired by John Glenn, 2000, p. 20; www.ed.gov/ inits/math/glenn/report.pdf.

54. Schmidt, McKnight, and Raizen, *A Splintered Vision.*

55. The AAAS considers science literacy as (1) being familiar with the natural world and recognizing both its diversity and its unity, (2) understanding key concepts and principles of science, (3) being aware of some of the important ways in which science, mathematics, and technology depend on one another, (4) knowing that science, mathematics, and technology are human enterprises and knowing what that implies about their strengths and limitations, (5) having a capacity for scientific ways of thinking, and (6) using scientific knowledge and ways of thinking for individual and social purposes. See AAAS, *Science for All Americans* (Washington, DC: Author, 1989).

56. Paul DeHart Hurd, "Science Needs a 'Lived' Curriculum," *Education Week,* 12 November 1997, p. 48.

57. National Research Council, *National Science Education Standards* (Washington, DC: National Academy Press, 1996), p. 113.

58. Ibid., p. 115.

59. Ibid., p. 2.

60. Roland Otto, as quoted in Richard Lee Colvin, "Spurned Nobelists Appeal Science Standards Rejection," *Los Angeles Times,* 17 November 1997, p. A25.

61. The group, composed of Glen Seaborg, Dudley R. Herschbach, and Henry Taube, filed a formal appeal to the state Commission for the Establishment of Academic Standards in November 1997. See Richard Lee Colvin, "Spurned Nobelists Appeal Science Standards Rejection," *Los Angeles Times,* 17 November 1997, p. A25.

62. Colvin, "Spurned Nobelists Appeal Science Standards Rejection," p. A25.

63. Janet Waugh, as quoted in "Kansas Restores Evolution Standards for Science Classes," CNN.com/U.S., February 14, 2001; online at http://www.cnn.com/2001/02/14/Kansas.evolution.02/.

64. Michael Powell, "Pa. Case Is Newest Round in Evolution Debate: 'Intelligent Design' Teaching Challenged," *Washington Post,* 27 September 2005, p. A03.

65. National Center for Education Statistics, *Time Spent Teaching Core Academic Subjects in Elementary Schools* (Washington, DC: U.S. Department of Education, 1997).

66. Sheridan Blau, "Toward the Separation of School and State," Inaugural address, 1997 NCTE Convention, Detroit, MI, November 20–25, 1997.

CHAPTER 5

Instruction

Classrooms as Learning Communities

In the Round Robin review activity, I gave each group of four students a math problem. Once the group arrived at a solution, I checked their work. If it was correct, I gave the group the go-ahead to copy their problem onto a big sheet of paper and place it on the wall. When every group had finished, each group chose two members to stay at their problem and be explainers, while the other two rotated. Every three minutes the rotators moved in a circle to a new problem, where they would copy the problem on the wall while a group member talked through their solution. Once the rotators had been through all the problems, they switched places and explained their problem solution while the remaining members circled the room.

I listened to student reflections throughout the activity and looked for improvements in the students' abilities to articulate their ideas about the concepts they encountered. Afterward, we talked about how, in order to explain a problem to someone else, you first need a good understanding yourself. As the students reflected on their learning, they were especially confident about the problem that they presented, and said that the activity helped them identify which concepts they were comfortable with and which they needed more practice: "It helps me by sorting out what I know and what I don't"; "I find that the problem I have to explain, I get right on the test"; "It gives me ideas about how to remember the problem."

The students also appreciated the opportunity to get up and walk around.

—MARK HILL
First-year teacher, high school mathematics

Chapter Overview

This chapter focuses on classroom instruction. It begins with a bit of history of how teaching has changed—and how it hasn't changed—over the past 200 years. It then discusses theories of children's learning, and how those theories influence teaching. Following this discussion of theory, we describe six "authentic" instructional principles—so called because they are compatible with the progressive perspectives on schooling and sociocultural learning theories. These principles are (1) teachers and students are confident that *everyone* learns well; (2) lessons are active, multidimensional, and social; (3) new learning builds on students' existing cultural knowledge; (4) assessment enhances learning; (5) relationships are caring and interdependent; and (6) talk and action are socially just.

How Teachers Taught*

Imagine you are a city schoolteacher in the early 1800s; your teaching is nothing like the activity that Mark Hill describes in the opening vignette. Instead of moving around listening to students explain to one another how to solve problems, you likely sit on a raised platform at the front of a cavernous room designed for 450 students of various ages. Below your desk are three rows of monitors' desks and, behind them, rows and rows of students in assigned seats. You direct the monitors who, in turn, instruct and hear recitations from platoons of students who march forward, slates in hand, to the monitors' desks. In precise sequences, students march, listen, and recite—all under your watchful eye. You "motivate" with awards and punishment, including administering the rod, to keep your charges orderly and industrious. Your main interest is not students' intellectual development. You teach basic skills such as arithmetic, reading, spelling, and penmanship, but your "real" job is to steer your charges away from evil influences, train them for good moral conduct, and protect the rest of the city from the crime and disease these children would cause if they continued to cling to their foreign or rural habits.

You were not hired because of your intellectual or pedagogical skills, but because you were "of pure tastes, of good manners, of exemplary morals."[1]

A century later, as a teacher in an early 1900s urban public school, you are following new "scientific" and efficient school reforms. Your pupils are divided by age into grades and by ability into classes, and you have 40 to 50 of them sitting in rows of desks bolted to the floor. Since you have been to a special training or *normal* school for your teacher preparation, you know some theory (e.g., the mind needs exercising as if it were a muscle) and pedagogical skills (drill and recitation) to guide your teaching. But you follow the uniform curriculum and classroom routines dictated by your principal. The rules might be like these expected of Bronx teachers in the 1920s: (1) Size the children and assign seats, (2) make a seating plan of the class, (3) drill on standing and sitting and putting the benches up and down noiselessly, (4) place your daily lesson plan and your time schedule on the desk where you can refer to them frequently.[2]

You help students build strong habits of mind through drill and repetition. You reward correct answers with grades, approval, and preferred seating. You measure progress with tests. Any fact the curriculum specifies as important, your students memorize and recite in unison. However, there are increasing pressures for you to teach silent analyzing and decoding of texts. You are also expected to pay attention to how well students communicate with and persuade others, as these become

---

*The heading for this section as well as much of the content here is from Larry Cuban's book by the same name: *How Teachers Taught: Constancy and Change in American Classrooms, 1890–1990* (New York: Teachers College Press, 1993).

Classroom on the Lower East Side in New York City.

important business skills. You follow popular classroom management methods such as lining students up and marching them with good posture to assigned spots at the blackboard during instruction and to the lavatories at recess. Like your counterparts a century earlier, you are more concerned about developing character than intellect. Your focus is mostly utilitarian, preparing students—many who are immigrants—with the habits, language, and dispositions for industrial urban life.

As archaic as these pictures of past classrooms strike us, something about them is also disturbingly familiar. Tables and chairs may have replaced bolted desks, and desks in U shapes or groups of four may have replaced rows. However, individual teachers still instruct large groups of students, and students mostly work alone. Teachers transmit knowledge to students in an orderly sequence of steps, often prescribed in school or school district policy.[3] Students drill and memorize and recite answers, and the mind-as-a-muscle metaphor still holds sway. End-of-unit tests assess whether learning took place. Mastery is rewarded, mistakes are corrected, and unlearned material is retaught. Then everyone moves on to the next topic or skill.[4] Although today's "time-outs," "behavior cards," and student behavior contracts are improvements over corporal punishment of the past, the rewards and punishment theory of why such controls "work" remains. Teachers stress language, basic skills, and good work habits rather than high intellectual achievement for low-income and culturally and linguistically "different" students. Mostly, children of the wealthy and children of the poor sit in different classrooms, even when they go to the same schools.

If you imagine your own most satisfying learning, in or out of school, you prob-ably picture experiences very different from those just described. Those moments might have been challenging, but they were likely connected to your interests and possibly related to similar adult activities. Adults generally believed that you *could* learn everything you needed to know. They assumed that you would *want* to learn and *would* learn by observing and participating with others. You got help when you needed help. This learning was probably closer to that experienced in societies without mass education, and learned through what anthropologist Jean Lave calls "participation in communities of practice."[5] Today's teachers can tap the power of such relationships but that requires teaching based on up-to-date learning theory rather than theory that guided schools in centuries past.

Matching Teaching to Theories of Learning and Intelligence

For most of the twentieth century, *behavioral* theories of learning shaped how teachers taught. These are theories of how stimuli elicit responses and how, if rewarded, the responses become habitual or "learned." Stimulus-response theory holds that if a child's correct response is rewarded with something pleasant— a smile or candy, for example—he or she is more likely to repeat the response. The teacher's job then is to "transmit" knowledge in small chunks, provide constant rewards or reinforcement, monitor (test) whether the chunks of knowledge have been learned, and reteach whatever was missed. Behavioral theory has some small value for explaining a narrow range of learning; however, the last 50 years of scien-tific research on learning reveals that so much more is possible and necessary. Fortunately, most teachers have never been so mechanical or limited in their actual practice that they never depart from behavioral rules, but nevertheless, behavioral and transmission models for instruction remain at the center of conventional teaching.

Learning Is Developmental, Social, and Cultural

Since the 1960s psychologists, linguists, neuroscientists, and anthropologists have learned a great deal more about intelligence and about how children learn. All now agree that learning is not simply responding to stimuli. Learning is an experience that can be wrapped up in the expression "to make sense" of something. That is, people learn as they interact with others to make sense or *construct* meaning out of the world and their experiences in it. Teachers can do quite a lot to provide appro-priate learning opportunities and good learning environments for children, and that is the starting point for good teaching.

The idea that learning takes place as people interact is not new. In the early twentieth century John Dewey, Jean Piaget, and Lev Vygotsky saw engagement within a social environment as the key to learning.[6] In 1896 philosopher John Dewey wrote an essay for *The School Journal* called "My Pedagogic Creed." In it, Dewey ties children's learning to the social context in which they learn. Dewey wrote:

> I believe that all education proceeds by the participation of the individual in the social consciousness of the race. This process begins almost unconsciously at birth, and is continually shaping the individual's powers, saturating his consciousness, forming his habits, training his ideas, and arousing his feelings and emotions. Through this unconscious education, the individual gradually comes to share in the intellectual and moral resources which humanity has succeeded in getting together. He becomes an inheritor of the funded capital of civilization. . . . I believe that the only true education comes through the stimulation of the child's powers by the demands of the social situation in which he finds himself. . . . Through the responses others make to his own activities, he comes to know what those mean in social terms. . . . I believe that the psychological and social sides are organically related and that education can not be regarded as a compromise between the two, or a superimposition of one upon the other.[7]

Piaget and Vygotsky devoted themselves to understanding how children develop cognitively. Piaget saw the child as very much an independent learner, already equipped to draw in and make sense of the environment, including relationships with others. According to Piaget, children, like "little scientists," investigate and learn pretty much on their own, using the environment as their laboratory. One of Piaget's most important contributions was his theory that children think in fundamentally different ways from adults and that their thinking *develops* as they make sense of experiences. He documented how children represent the world differently as they proceed through developmental stages.

Vygotsky stressed a much more essential and interdependent relationship between child and adult. He blurred the distinction between social experiences and mental processes. He emphasized learning and solving problems as that which happens *between* a learner and others. Social participation does not simply provide external stimulation for one's own thought; it is part of and in some respects indistinguishable from one's own thinking process. Vygotsky claimed that all meanings stem from interactions.

Vygotsky also proposed the *zone of proximal development*. He conceptualized this zone as containing the knowledge that a student can learn when assisted by or collaborating with an adult or more knowledgeable peer. The zone's boundary on one side is the knowledge the student already has or the problems she can solve alone. On the other side of the zone is knowledge and problem solving for which the student is not developmentally ready.

Like Dewey, Vygotsky placed great importance on the teacher's role of arranging activities and social groupings that keep students stretching within their zone. Obviously, students must be challenged beyond problems they can already solve, but they must not be frustrated by problems they cannot learn well in spite of the help available.

Psychologists today continue to explore the fusion between social settings and mental processes. As they do, they have returned to Dewey's notion that children learn as they interact with their culture's *use* of knowledge. This work also shows how cognitive processes differ in cultures that stress different kinds of knowledge, values, social organization, or work. *Sociocultural* and *cultural historical* theories assert that society and culture determine learning and learning is not solely a mental activity, or rather, learning and mental activities *are* cultural.[8] In other words, scholars go beyond simply saying that culture *influences* thinking; they maintain that society and culture are indistinguishable from learning or thinking. For example, Jerome Bruner has become increasingly convinced that people create and transform meanings (learn) as members of particular cultures.

Learning, remembering, talking, imagining: all of them are made possible by participating in a culture. (p. xi)

So, in the end, while mind creates culture, culture also creates mind. (p. 166)

—**Jerome Bruner**
Culture and Education, 1990

People cannot separate *how* thinking takes place from *what* knowledge is available in the place *where* learning happens. Drawing heavily from cross-cultural studies of learning (comparing how people think and solve problems in different societies), sociocultural theories fuse learning, intelligence, and culture into a single entity.

Intelligence Is Learned, Cultural, and Multidimensional

Scholars today have demonstrated quite convincingly that people learn to be intelligent as they interact with others to make sense out of the world and their experiences in it. Intelligence does not operate "inside the head" but develops as people interact using the tools and symbols of their culture.

A number of contemporary psychologists have also developed theoretical models that discount *single* intelligence and emphasize the many mental abilities and intelligences we all use. For example, Robert Sternberg proposes three types of intelligence that vary in strength among people. One intelligence promotes analytical and critical thinking, one leads to the development of creative new ideas, and one enables humans to respond quickly and productively to everyday events and experiences. Howard Gardner identifies intelligences that include but are not limited to language, mathematics and logic, visual and spatial perception, control over one's own movements, sensitivity to others, and knowledge of oneself. Gardner argues that everyone inherits the capacity to develop each of these intelligences, although individuals vary, and he notes that different cultures and subcultures stress certain kinds of intelligence. He also argues that these intelligences are more appropriately considered the mastery of competencies or skills, rather than underlying abilities or the quality of one's mind.

Moreover, although innate and universal predispositions may enhance the development of some abilities, most people are more concerned about whether or not children develop those abilities and values the culture wants. In *Outsmarting IQ,* for example, David Perkins of Harvard contends that the most important mental processes are learned, not inherited.[9] Because different cultures provide children with different learning situations, and because they value the mastery of different tasks, differences among groups of people in IQ actually explain little about what they can and do learn. Whatever else intelligence might be, an especially useful concept for teachers is that intelligence is *distributed* throughout a person's social world—home and community, the workplace, and school.

That children can learn to be smart in school is extraordinarily positive and reaffirming for teachers, and it represents a dramatic shift from older views. Classroom experiences that allow for meaning-making in the variety of ways that students have available to them do help students become smart. Theories of multiple intelligence press educators to develop complex, realistic, multidimensional assignments and projects so all children can discover and combine their particular strengths with areas where they are not strong or lack experience.

Contemporary Theories in the Classroom

Given these new understandings of learning, it's not surprising that most teachers entering the profession today seek community-like relationships within classrooms rather than the factory-like relationships of the past. Understanding that learning is both social and cultural, teachers develop opportunities for participation and relationships that allow students to use information in ways that transform their thinking and help them to participate in and benefit from society's multiple cultures.

As discussed in Chapters 3 and 4, and as will become clearer later in this chapter, subscribing to sociocultural learning theory, to principles of knowledge construction, and to the concept of intelligence as multidimensional and learned does *not* mean that students are set free from learning the valued traditions, facts, and skills of their society. However, these theories do encourage taking a broader view of what different cultures value. They support teachers who believe their job is to help all students develop the intelligence, understanding, and problem-solving skills necessary to fill important roles in a diverse and democratic society. As such, teachers today have a clear alternative to the obvious and documented failures of traditional theory and practice. They can now "answer back" with theory of their own, one that is consistent with their moral and ethical convictions and one that simply works better for having more children learn more than ever before.

In the past several years, researchers and teachers have sought to develop pedagogy that aligns classrooms more closely with the settings where people learn naturally, and, at the same time, to accomplish the academic goals of schooling. Six principles have emerged from this work that teachers can use as guidelines as they construct classroom learning communities. These are summarized in Concept Table 5.1.

Each of these principles draws from a distinct body of research on teaching that is consistent with views of learning as cognitive, social, and cultural. But practices grounded in these principles act together, and each one is necessary for all the

CONCEPT TABLE 5.1 *Six Principles for Classroom Learning Communities*

Teachers and students are confident that *everyone* learns well (Chapter 5).

Lessons are active, multidimensional, and social (Chapter 5).

New learning builds on students' existing cultural knowledge (Chapter 5).

Assessment is integral to learning (Chapter 6).

Relationships are caring and interdependent (Chapter 7).

Talk and action are socially just (Chapter 7).

others to work. Eliminate any one, and competent, socially just teaching collapses like a house of cards. Coupled with deep, worthwhile content, as described in Chapter 4, these principles support students' conceptions of themselves as competent learners, encourage effort and persistence, and promote intellectual rigor and democratic dispositions. In the remainder of this chapter, we explore the first three of these principles. In chapters that follow, we examine assessment, caring relationships, and social justice.

Confidence in a Context of Difference

Whereas traditional teaching often works against confidence, sociocultural learning theories, coupled with a value for social justice, foster confidence, hard work, persistence, and learning. How and why this is so has a great deal to do with how teachers respond to students' differences and how they construct classroom lessons.

Difference Is Normal

Even in schools where everyone pretty much "looks" alike, students are still very different. Much of the delight of teaching comes from observing and interacting with these differences. Prior experiences, attitudes and expressions, charm and sociability, shyness and silliness, mastery of sophisticated knowledge, and astonishing and hysterical misunderstandings and gaps in what they "should" but do not know all vary among the students in any classroom. In many classrooms students also differ in the languages, cultures, and community resources they bring to school. These differences, no less delightful, influence how students approach classroom learning, and they bear no relation to whether or not they are capable learners.

Differences among students are often not neutral, but schools place a positive or negative value on those differences. Traditional teaching makes students acutely aware of how their personal characteristics are problems or benefits for themselves and for the teacher. In fact, traditional teaching *requires* these differently valued distinctions to be made. For example, traditional teaching assumes that all students *should* learn the same things in the same way at the same time. Such lessons make students' differences conspicuous and troublesome, and they virtually guarantee that the teacher and class will lose confidence in at least some students' capacity or willingness to learn.[10]

FOCAL POINT 5.1

How Status Becomes Public in the Classroom

Consider the countless classroom routines that expose students to public scrutiny; for example, the posted grades and other symbols of students' progress—letters, numbers, stars, smiley faces, racehorses, halos, and so on. A glance at student work stuck on the wall immediately tells who are top students and who are not. In addition, teachers sometimes read scores aloud or permit student helpers to return graded papers to their classmates. Gradebooks are often open for students to peruse classmates' grades. Results of aptitude, achievement, and other standardized tests become public when students or their parents offer their scores voluntarily. Student messengers may call other students out of class, and the color of the pass (from the principal's or dean's office) instantly informs everyone if this student is in disciplinary trouble or on his way to a special "gifted" activity. On holidays, students might exchange gifts in the most open and public way. A teacher's public display of annoyance is noted by all; and signals sent by peers are always salient. And all this takes place in the cramped four walls of the classroom where, for a legally prescribed number of minutes per day, students must remain. In the world of these evaluative acts and symbols, students quickly sum up their own ability in a subject and their schoolworthiness in general.

Another way to think about difference is to presume that there is no central "normal" by which others are compared and judged. In this sense, a Muslim and Christian are equally different from one another; black and white students are racially different, but one is not more "normal" than the other regardless of their relative numbers in a particular classroom; and students who learn differently and at different rates are not relatively more or less normal.

In socially just classrooms dimensions of difference can exist in their own right, and differences (and students) do not have to be judged on how close to "normal" they are. Such a classroom becomes a community of very diverse learners where everybody is smart, and differences are the source of rich learning interactions. Teachers make each student's particular competence visible and available to others as learning resources. Social interactions allow students to scaffold one another's learning, and to combine their different knowledge and experiences into the knowledge and experience of the learning community. Such lessons set in motion a positive cycle of confidence, effort, persistence, and learning.

Comparisons Are Avoided

Learning and succeeding (or not) in most classrooms is very public. Who finishes quickly, who gets the most correct answers, who never seems to be able to respond when the teacher calls on her—is obvious to everyone in the room. Even when teachers appropriately challenge students, students risk making mistakes and suffering public judgments. Thus, students' engagement always has an audience of teachers and classmates. Focal Point 5.1 discusses some of the ways children's status becomes public in schools.

Of course, sensitive teachers, even if they follow largely traditional ways of teaching, can mitigate some of the destructive effects of public comparisons. But this is a very large hurdle, and few are entirely successful. More likely, students treat their peers as others treat them. Impressions about individuals soon solidify as a classroom consensus about each student's role and value. Each day brings a greater distinction between those students whom the classroom culture expects to meet the class's highest standards and those from whom that culture expects little. These classroom status differences trigger easy social comparisons of students who are "smart" and those who are not. Then it is only a short step for students and teacher to conclude that some students simply can't or won't learn well.[11] Finally, everyone blames the students' differences (intelligence, race, effort, prior schooling opportunities, etc.) for their failure, not the classroom relationships and routines.

Learned helplessness can be another effect of public comparisons in classrooms. When students do not feel competent and have low status (i.e., their classroom peers also see them as less competent), they may assume that no amount of effort will lead to success. Each time they try to act competently, they risk making their incompetence more visible unless the class is designed so that each student (1) *can* succeed and (2) is convinced that lack of success is a specific and temporary condition and not attributable to an inherent lack of ability.[12] Students who are not so convinced have little reason to work hard or seek help. Their self-doubts develop into global judgments about their overall worth. Students may begin by saying or thinking "I can't understand the problems on the test" and end up believing "I am not smart at math" or "I'm not much of a student."

Finally, the most far-reaching, as well as ironic, effect of public comparisons in the classroom is that these comparisons communicate that school is a place where imminent failure is possible for *any* student, not just those currently out of favor. The very existence of the status hierarchy that comparisons create may affect negatively the highest-achieving students, who may become chiefly motivated by a desire to "not fall" to a level where they are treated like others. Such conditions do not help students become fully engaged in their own learning or care about others' success. No wonder so many students, older ones in particular, spend their time acting on some of school's "real" lessons: Work hard for others' approval, and if that does not produce results, find another "game" you can win—disruption, resistance, or failure.

It's Safe to Be Different

For all students, public comparisons are often dangerous and rarely beneficial. Although prejudice and stereotypes are typically thought of as simple exclusionary rules or hateful epitaphs, often they are more subtle than that—reflecting deep-seated cultural beliefs enacted by well-meaning classmates and teachers. Sociologist Daniel Solorzano refers to *microaggressions* as racially laden attitudes, comments, and actions of peers and teachers who would deny that they were prejudiced or acting hurtfully. Solorzano offers many examples such as these:

"When I talk about those Blacks, I really wasn't talking about you."

"You're not like the rest of them. You're different."

"If only there were more of them like you."

"I don't think of you as a Mexican."

"You speak such good English."[13]

Makeba Jones, an educational researcher at the University of California, San Diego, describes how her identity as an African American woman increased her vulnerability in an environment where those "differences" were not neutral:

> As a teenager, I questioned my abilities in comparison to my peers. Despite the fact that my large public high school was racially mixed, I was the only person of color in my white and affluent Honors level courses. I felt conspicuous and out of place, or rather misplaced. When I did not understand an assignment, I felt sure my peers could see both the confusion on my face, and that I was only pretending to write an essay when I was staring at a blank page.
>
> I accepted the belief that only individual ability and merit would bring high grades and teacher praise. I was naive about race as an adolescent. I am not sure if I felt so inadequate because I was the only black girl in the class, but I felt self-confident outside of my advanced classes. I battled the contradiction between what I knew in my heart was true about me, Makeba, and what I perceived that my peers and teachers thought about me and my "place." This struggle of identity and self-examination pushed me to drop out of Honors English my senior year. I felt relieved the second semester as I passed by the Honors English classroom on my way to a classroom that didn't suddenly fall silent when a student answered a question wrong. But I also felt as though the American Dream only applied to those whose stamina and ability allowed them to flourish under such pressure, and not those, like me, who needed more reassurance and sensitivity.[14]

As Makeba Jones observes, schools do not have to be overtly prejudiced to participate in social stereotypes. For example, a school might not tell girls to avoid advanced mathematics classes, but staff might not make a needed special effort to overcome the stereotype that girls are less well suited for math. When a girl decides to avoid advanced math, the counselor may say (and believe), "OK, that's your choice." On the one hand, it *is* a free and individual choice; on the other hand, it is a choice that is informed by cultural knowledge that translates into limited opportunity. Further, the girl who does decide to take advanced math may be aware that her performance in class not only carries the usual risks of exposing flawed math knowledge but also makes others see her as a representative of girls who take math. Stanford University professor Claude Steele argues that this combined awareness may impinge on a girl's concentration and her confidence, despite other evidence that she is well suited for success in math.[15]

Steele's studies help explain how stereotypes limit performance and opportunities. In one of his experiments, high-achieving African American men and women were given "intelligence tests" and asked to specify their race. They did less well than other similar African American students who were not asked about their race and therefore did not expect to be judged according to a racial stereotype.

Steele also found that everyone is vulnerable to stereotypes. In another experiment, white males—unaccustomed to being intellectually stigmatized—were told that Asians achieved higher scores than Americans on a mathematics test. This group of white males achieved lower scores on that test than a control group of white males who were not told anything about previous test results.

Importantly, like other social science research, Steele's findings are not meant as predictions for what will surely happen in particular cases. That is why his term *vulnerability* is so apt. Although everyone is vulnerable, *how* vulnerable they are probably depends on the prevalence and depth of the stereotype as well as a host of individual, nongroup characteristics. And, clearly, the significance of stereotypes is not entirely about what *other* people think; stereotypes affect everyone's thinking

High Expectations for Everybody

Teachers' beliefs about children's ability to learn have enormous power. This was first documented in Robert Rosenthal and Lenore Jacobson's landmark study, *Pygmalion in the Classroom.*[16] Rosenthal and Jacobson told a group of elementary teachers that a few students in their classes were "late bloomers." They said that although these students were not exceptional now, they would make substantial strides in the future. In fact, the researchers randomly selected students who were neither more nor less ready to bloom than the others. By the end of the year, the students who had been labeled late bloomers and expected to shine academically outperformed their classmates.

The study's central assertion—that teachers' expectations influence students' performance—has held up over the years. Adults respond to initial cues from students about what to expect from them and how much to push or encourage them; in other words, they set expectations high or low and then students meet them. Unkempt appearance, behavior taken as disruptive, and cultural meanings ascribed to a student's use of language or accent can be negative cues. Positive cues can include courteous behavior and a well-groomed appearance.

Teachers communicate expectations in many subtle ways. For example, a teacher may give some students a bit of extra time if they are confident of a correct answer, while quickly moving on from students whose hesitation matches the teacher's view that the student is "slow." Sometimes, to avoid embarrassing a student judged as having little to offer, a teacher will skip over the student or quickly supply a correct answer. Which distracted student gets a good-natured call back to the task and which receives a scolding glare can influence a student's developing concept of himself as a learner.

Myra and David Sadker's research offers fascinating documentation on the extent to which teachers communicate different expectations for boys and girls. Particularly in math and science, teachers, both men and women, enact the larger society's gender stereotypes in subtle ways that, when pointed out, are astonishing to the teachers themselves. For example, teachers ask boys more questions and allow them to dominate laboratory experiments. In addition, when students encounter difficulties, teachers encourage boys to press on and try harder but are more likely to console and comfort girls.[17] Low-income children and children of color face similar expectation barriers.[18] Such responses certainly affect a student's willingness to become engaged, to participate, to take risks, and to work hard.[19]

———————————————————————— ⚙ ⚙ ⚙ ————————————————————————

The first major scholastic improvement I witnessed was in a student who simply did not do any homework or much classwork for that matter. She did not prepare for tests and had a deep "F." I spent the entire semester encouraging her—asking her to come in for extra help during lunch, etc. She finally came in for extra help, did her homework, and received "A's" on the last quiz and test. It was too late for her to pass the semester, but the change in behavior continued during summer school, and she passed with a high "B." What was amazing to me was the change in this student's perception about herself and in her ability to succeed in school. As she began to understand the material and perform better on tests, I could see her confidence increase and her expectations for herself improved.

—**MARK HILL**
First-year teacher, high school mathematics

Sometimes acting on high expectations requires teachers to challenge "normal" procedures that reflect institutionalized low expectations. This is particularly true in the case of English learners where schools often act as if students who speak languages other than English can't learn math, science, social studies, or other school subjects until they master English. As the bilingual coordinator at his school, Mauro Bautista advocates for students he believes should be held to the highest expectations possible. The problem he addresses is the low expectations for "Limited English Proficiency" (LEP) students in "English as a Second Language" (ESL) classes where academic demands are low.

———————————————————————— ⚙ ⚙ ⚙ ————————————————————————

I am forming coalitions with interested people both in and outside school and we are acting on our concern about tracking so many LEP students into low-level ESL classes. Instead of following district procedure, we changed the referring process to account better for the likelihood that limited English students could succeed in more academic classes. This year we have many more grade-level English classes than ESL classes for our LEP students. I hope these more rigorous classes will better prepare them to pursue a higher education.

—**MAURO BAUTISTA**
Middle-school bilingual education coordinator

Lessons to Construct Confidence

Racial and other stereotypes along with perceptions of academic ability and acceptance of diversity are all tightly linked. Most teachers value and want to be sensitive to student differences, but as Laura Torres and Marilyn Cortez have learned, they need experience and support to work productively with the social world of their classrooms.

———————————————❈ ❈ ❈———————————————

I focus on what students can do instead of what they are not doing. Then I give them opportunities to recognize their strengths and support for critical thinking. A colleague of mine, whose deficit thinking is both explicit and subtle, approached me. Frustrated with his students' writing, he asked what we were doing, and I explained my students' analytical writing. He immediately said, "Oh, you guys are doing that? That is way too sophisticated . . . my kids are not going to be able to do it." He glanced over my students' work and asked, "So, what's the trick? If there are any tricks you can tell me, I'd love to hear them." I was upset with his implication that my students could not think at those levels without having some trick taught to them, so I said, "Well, it's not about any tricks, it's starting from a belief that they can do it."

—**Laura Silvina Torres**
First-year teacher, grade 2

———————————————❈ ❈ ❈———————————————

Discussions that focused on logic and reason helped students to make sense out of mathematics. The challenges students faced in my classroom gave them a sense that their math class was no longer a place for "dummies." Rather, it was a place that challenged them to reason things out. I would hear them bragging about this to their friends outside of our class. Although several students would complain about the difficulty of the work, they were proud to be doing it.

—**Marilyn Cortez**
First-year teacher, high school mathematics

Sociologists Elizabeth Cohen and Rachel Lotan worked together for more than 20 years identifying classroom practices that interrupt low expectations for students' performance. Their studies of elementary- and middle-school classrooms affirm fundamental principles for creating lessons that sustain confidence. Cohen and Lotan have taken one of these principles—engaging students with rich and complex knowledge—and made it the foundation for their program called Complex Instruction. (We examine a second principle—a focus on student interactions—later in this chapter.)

Complex Instruction requires lessons that include a variety of student abilities and special attention to students' status as learners and class members. Consider the example, "Read the chapter and answer the questions at the end. Test on Tuesday. Don't forget the vocab." This is not a multiability lesson. Low-level reading comprehension and memorization are the intellectual skills required. The test will measure those skills alone, and who scores high and who scores low is predictable. By the third month of school, the teacher and every student in class will know who is smart on this kind of test and who is not.

A multiability lesson can be short range and relatively simple. However, a richer, more complex lesson is long range, often a project that may involve a number of tasks and subassignments. It has elements requiring distinctly different levels of skills and other elements that all students benefit from. It requires work that students can do individually and work that students must do together. It involves hands-on activity and traditional book-and-paper scholarship and research and makes use of students' informal and prior knowledge. All students participate in all elements of the lesson, and each student can find areas in which she has particular strengths. The teacher or other knowledgeable helpers are ready to step in when some students struggle or others are ready to forge ahead. Clearly, no such lesson ever reaches an ideal. There is always another activity, another opportunity for a student experiment, another theme to explore, more resources to add, and a teacher's wish for just a little more time.

Cohen and Lotan propose that with a multiability approach, teachers can engage the class in discussions that explicitly probe the many different intellectual abilities and other skills the lesson will require. Teachers can assure students that although no one in the class will be "good on all these abilities," each student will be "good on at least one." Cohen and Lotan found that when teachers do this consistently, students begin identifying each other and themselves as "smart" on a wide range of attributes, weakening the power of the more common negative expectations. Of course, the goal of identifying this wide range of abilities is not to assign or label individual students as being good at one thing and not another. Rather, the goal is for students to assume that everyone is competent, that it is everyone's job to help everyone contribute, and that individual competence results from *participating* in the classroom learning community.

As evidence of the success of the multiability approach, Stanford professor Jo Boaler's research in two British high schools documented superior mathematics achievement in multiability high school classes. She describes her study as follows:

> In one [high school], the teachers taught mathematics using whole-class teaching and textbooks, and the students were tested frequently. The students were taught in tracked groups, standards of discipline were high, and the students worked hard. The second school was . . . completely different. Students there worked on open-ended projects in heterogeneous groups, teachers used a variety of methods, and discipline was extremely relaxed. . . . [S]tudents at the second school—what I will call the project school, as opposed to the textbook school—attained significantly higher grades on the national exam. This was not because these students knew more mathematics, but because they had developed a different form of knowledge.
>
> At the textbook school, the students were motivated and worked hard, they learned all the mathematical procedures and rules they were given, and they performed well on short, closed tests. But various forms of evidence showed that these students had developed an inert, procedural knowledge that they were rarely able to use in anything other than textbook and test situations. In applied assessments, many were unable to perceive the relevance of the mathematics they had learned and so could not make use of it. Even when they could see the links between their textbook work and more-applied tasks, they were unable to adapt the procedures they had learned to fit the situations in which they were working. . . .

The students themselves were aware of this problem, as the following description by one student of her experience of the national exam shows: "Some bits I did recognize, but I didn't understand how to do them, I didn't know how to apply the methods properly." . . .

Students from this school reported that they could see mathematics all around them, in the workplace and in everyday life, but they could not see any connection between their school math and the math they encountered in real situations. . . . [T]hey believed that school mathematical procedures were a specialized type of school code—useful only in classrooms. As one girl put it, "In math you have to remember; in other subjects you can think about it." . . .

. . . On the national examination, three times as many students from the heterogeneous groups in the project school as those in the tracked groups in the textbook school attained the highest possible grade. The project approach was also more equitable, with girls and boys attaining the different grades in equal proportions.[20]

Constructing the Competence of Low-Status Children   Cohen and Lotan's and Boaler's work makes clear that a student's degree of competence does not matter as much as her degree of engagement in activities that scaffold her learning. In an ideal participatory setting, everyone's status would be that of a highly competent learner. However, students themselves have much to say about the classroom's learning environment. The combination of their existing self-concepts with their habits of judging others is so powerful that teachers must address status and self-concept issues head-on. Thus, Cohen and Lotan encourage teachers using Complex Instruction to assign competence to low-status students explicitly.

To do this, teachers watch for instances of capable performance on various intellectual tasks relevant to the classroom learning activities from students whose status and/or expectations of themselves are low. The teacher then gives the student a "specific, favorable, and very public evaluation," pointing out to others in the class that the student can serve as a resource to others in that area. First-year teacher Cindy Bell used just this strategy to boost her students' confidence.

※ ※ ※

"Asking a friend" is an important strategy that I encourage my students to use. I've incorporated expert roles throughout all parts of the curriculum so that each student has an expert role in math, writing, and reading. In math we have different experts who explain to the class their strategies for solving a problem. In writing we have editing experts such as "title titans," "main idea masters," "detail detectives," "super spellers," "handwriting experts," and the "capital letter crew" who assist in the second editing of our writing process. Every student is assigned a role because they all have something authentic to contribute. No matter where a student's overall literacy development is, each one plays an important role as an expert.

—Cindy Bell
First-year teacher, grade 2

Assigning competence disrupts students' cycle of low expectations, low status, and low participation. Of course, the assignment must be genuine and credible. Quick praise for something mediocre or not central to the task (such as decorating the cover of a science project with cartoon characters) will not convince anyone of a student's competence. It may well have the opposite effect. Admittedly, these public evaluations carry some of the risks associated with rewards and praise. However, if the teacher has established his role in class as a "broker" of knowledge—one whose main job is not to evaluate but to ask questions and point out knowledge sources— then he can present the student as a resource rather than as a shining example.

Confident Teachers

Finally, teachers' own confidence is critical in constructing a community-like class-room where all students believe they can learn well. Inflexible curricula, fixed time limits, and customary grouping practices can undermine a teacher's efficacy. It is crucial to understand how common practices such as these get in the way of the multiability lessons. Teachers whose own education was in the traditional mold (nearly everyone) may have difficulty identifying and building on student suc-cesses. Tradition-minded colleagues are not much help in this matter. They are more likely to suggest traditional solutions than to show enthusiasm for practices with which they are not familiar. If that sounds like a daunting challenge for a new teacher, it needn't be. There is ample evidence that even first-year teachers can break the mold of traditional teaching while remaining a respected member of a traditional school faculty. We discuss this further in Chapter 12.

The remainder of this chapter and the next two look more closely at the strategies teachers use to make their classrooms places where both they and their students can be confident about everyone's ability to learn.

Opportunities for Active, Multidimensional, and Social Learning

—⚙ ⚙ ⚙—

During our study of civil rights in U.S. History, my students wrestle with essential questions such as "How should we liberate ourselves? How should we gain civil rights?" I number students off, and they become different his-torical figures of the era (in this case, Marcus Garvey, Ida B. Wells, W. E. B. Dubois, Booker T. Washington, etc.). The students have a goal—to convince the rest of the class that their character has the best answers to these ques-tions. Together they read the readings and produce speeches and questions for the other characters. They also create some piece of artwork. Because of the variety of the tasks and singularity of the tasks, the students usually re-main on task and work well together.

—Judy Smith
High school social studies

Many teachers, striving for quiet and efficient classrooms, organize their instruction to control or minimize activity and social interactions. These teachers talk to the whole class at once, and they walk around the room giving individual help. They call on students to read aloud to the class, answer questions, or write on the board. Students quickly learn to identify the behaviors that school adults want from them. Some students learn to listen for the answers that please adults, and they become skilled at repeating them. After only a short time in school, students decide that the real learning is what they do by themselves.

In contrast, the power of active, multidimensional, and social instruction in learning (such as that described in the preceding vignette) is virtually uncontested by research. This research has been summed up by Roland Tharp and his colleagues at the Center for Research on Education, Diversity, and Excellence (CREDE)—a federally funded national research center at the University of California, Santa Cruz. In *Teaching Transformed: Achieving Excellence, Fairness, Inclusion, and Harmony,* Tharp and his colleagues offer five principles that describe the characteristics of lessons that promote academic excellence for all students. These principles are (1) teachers and students producing together, (2) developing language and literacy across the curriculum, (3) making meaning by connecting school content to students' lives, (4) teaching complex thinking, and (5) teaching through conversation. These principles require teachers to create settings where diverse activities occur simultaneously. Working in small groups, students' out-of-school experiences become integrated with new learning, and all students can be appropriately challenged. Following these principles, the teacher can draw on students' diverse backgrounds and experiences so that difference becomes a strength rather than a problem; in the process, these classrooms are active and multidimensional.[21]

Students Learning Together

Kimberly Min's third-grade students in the photo on the next page are counting each other's teeth in an investigation designed to help them meet one of California's third-grade science standards. They are constructing knowledge about human development.

The traditional view, however, is that teaching is all about transmitting knowledge—in other words, *telling* students facts such as humans begin a long process of acquiring their set of 32 adult teeth at about age 6. Similarly, traditional classrooms focus on getting students to approach learning as a solitary effort. Schools abound with admonitions that reflect individualistic values, such as "Be sure to do your own work," "You need to become an independent thinker," and "He's just not a self-starter."

In contrast, sociocultural theories lead teachers to structure classroom lessons that are active and social. Many teachers, following Vygotsky, think of their classrooms as "learning communities" where they pay special attention to activities and relationships that give students access to adults and knowledgeable peers who support one another's learning.

Two Lessons   Consider how two different teachers might approach the teaching of measurement to upper-elementary-school students. The first teacher—one who

is grounded in traditional theories and practice—explains to the class how to add feet and inches and demonstrates the process by working through several sample problems step-by-step on an overhead projector she keeps at the front of the room. As she goes through the examples, she elicits students' ideas about what comes next, and as much as half the class gets to respond at least once. A handful of students is clearly enthusiastic and would answer every question if allowed.

The teacher then gives the students a few minutes to do a problem by themselves at their desks and asks two volunteers to come to the board to model how they worked the problem. She corrects any errors they make and asks the rest of the class if they understand. Seeing mostly positive head nods, she assigns a page of 20 practice problems (e.g., $6'4'' + 2'10'' = ?$) for them to work on quietly for the rest of math time, while she circulates and monitors their work.

The second teacher proceeds quite differently. She had a measurement lesson planned, but she modified it two days earlier, after one of her students came late to class, having been delayed in the school office while getting his cut knee bandaged. On the way to school the student was running across a littered empty lot and fell. The class talked about the problems of the lot (it was ugly, dangerous, a waste of space), and the teacher asked them to imagine what could be done with it to solve the problem and improve the community. The students decided that a playground would be nice, with benches for old people to sit on. However, their interest was not just self-serving or charitable; they marshaled their anger and social consciousness to add energy to their project with some wondering why they had no nice parks close by.

Enlisting the supervision help of two parents, the teacher took her class, organized into teams, to the lot to measure its dimensions and locate and sketch topographical features (a small hill, an abandoned refrigerator, etc.). Back in the classroom the students designed and located play equipment, paths, perimeter fencing, and other features. They calculated amounts of materials and costs—in some cases enlisting the help of parents with construction experience—telephoned and visited lumberyards, and so on. They figured costs and prepared a budget.

To some degree, this teacher used the same instructional strategies as the first teacher: lecture/demonstration, question/answer, drill and practice. But these strategies were used more sparingly and in the context of solving real problems. Never did she allow them to become ends in themselves or to dominate large blocks of time. Often she used them with just a portion of the class.

Learning as a Community Activity   If the preceding second lesson doesn't seem entirely strange, it's because many teachers do use strategies in their classrooms that intuitively or purposefully are very consistent with cognitive, sociocultural, and social justice perspectives. Advocacy for classroom learning as an active and social process has a long, if not dominant, history in American schools. For example, early in the twentieth century John Dewey not only theorized about learning and curriculum, he also pioneered progressive approaches to teaching that were consistent with his view that learning happens as students experience and interact with the world.

Dewey believed that classroom learning activities should prepare children to solve the problems of a democratic society. What's more, he maintained that classrooms themselves should be democratic. Rather than places where adults retain all of the authority and dictate to students, classrooms must allow students' active learning in the context of a cooperative, democratic community.

Dewey's presence has been felt in education throughout the century. Although some Dewey-like practices have become commonplace—such things as field trips and science projects, for example—few schools or teachers promote lessons like the preceding one on measurement. And fewer still contemplate a social action project outside the school.

By teaching lessons such as the preceding one, the teacher allows the students to become members of a mathematical community. As members of that community, students see themselves as math-using specialists in a real and practical math-using world. The lesson invites instructional assistance, encourages the relationships and support that one finds in caring communities, and allows the class to enact social justice behaviors and values.

Many elements of active and social classrooms make them consistent with cognitive and sociocultural learning theories and principles of social justice. Three explored here stand out as particularly important: multidimensional tasks (of the sort recommended for authentic lessons and Complex Instruction), instructional assistance or scaffolding, and cooperative group work.

Multidimensional Tasks

The more elaborate measurement lesson just described, unlike the first teacher-at-the-board lesson, provides mathematical tasks in abundance and allows all students to succeed with what they know. The multiple tasks permit students to tackle problems, with help, just beyond their abilities to solve independently—in their zone of proximal development. Opportunities for the teacher to explore what and how much students learn (called "authentic assessment," a topic we discuss at length in Chapter 6) are embedded within the tasks themselves.

The following lesson that Kim Pham describes has similar advantages. Her class had just finished investigating how the United Farm Workers Union fit into the Chicano movement, and they were working in small groups preparing to present to the class what they'd learned.

───────────────────────────────❈ ❈ ❈───────────────────────────────

The room is alive with activity. Desks are pushed to the edge of the classroom, accommodating various groups. Some students discuss how to share their recent experience of working with migrant farmworkers in the fields. One student patiently charts a graph showing the economic breakdown of maintaining a large farm. Two students and I plan the presentation order. Other students complete a poster on the United Farm Workers, focusing on the leadership of Cesar Chavez and Philip Vera Cruz. Their photographs, news clippings, and markers are sprawled across the floor. Laughter erupts from the back of the room where four students debate the idea of dressing up as fruit while presenting information on the movement of farmworkers across the state following the peak harvest times of the fruit and vegetable season. Someone asks me if she can give her classmates a test after the presentation. "Certainly," I reply, "but consider—'What do you want them to know?'" The student thinks about the question while slowly returning to the group. Activity continues unabated until the final minutes. I remind students to document progress with a short journal entry highlighting individual concerns and feelings. Students write until the end of class.

—KᴵᴹMᴀɴ Tʜɪ Pʜᴀᴍ
First-year teacher, history, grade 11

───

Elizabeth Cohen has drawn the following characteristics for multidimensional tasks from her own and others' research. Such tasks

include more than one answer or more than one way to solve the problem;

are intrinsically interesting and rewarding;

allow different students to make different contributions;

use multimedia;

involve sight, sound, and touch;

require a variety of skills and behaviors;

require reading and writing; and

are challenging.

Cohen's examples include role playing, building models, drawing a "mind map" of the relationship among ideas, and discovering and describing relationships by manipulating equipment or objects—activities like those Kim Pham planned for her students. Cohen notes how "hands-on" science lessons that ask students to observe, carefully manipulate, collect and record data precisely, hypothesize causes and effects, and write up the report fit her notion of multidimensional. She also believes that basic skills are an important part of multidimensional classrooms, but she notes that learning these skills can be enhanced by multidimensional tasks. According to Cohen, if tasks have a single right answer, can be done more quickly and efficiently by one person than by a group, and involve simple memorization or routine learning, teachers can be pretty sure the tasks are unidimensional and will inhibit many students' learning.[22]

Scaffolded Participation

Classroom social interactions include all the ways students and the teacher relate to one another about academics, behavior, and social matters. The teacher's role is to support, or *scaffold*, students as they move through their zone of proximal development, defined as the knowledge and skills that the student cannot learn on his own but can learn with the assistance of someone who is more capable. As with an apprentice's relationship to an accomplished member of the community, these relationships value any contributions a novice might make—no matter how small.

For example, as Mauro Bautista works to help one of his students still learning English with writing skills, he might ask a question such as, "This sentence says, 'ran home' but I could understand it better if it told who or what ran home." As his student's skills develop, Mauro will ask him increasingly sophisticated questions and encourage him to try increasing complex problem solving strategies. Some call this learning relationship scaffolding because it provides a temporary structure around the "construction" of the student's learning and helps hold concepts together during the early stages of "sort of" knowing something, but not having it "all together."

Math teacher Juliana Jones, quoted next, is mindful of these interactions as she guides her students through social learning. Her work underscores how a teacher's active involvement has to rest on both her specific lesson preparation and her on-the-spot reliance on theory. There is no way for a teacher's plan alone to prepare her for the spontaneous and idiosyncratic questions and responses her students are likely to offer. Theory without preparation (and subject knowledge) will fall flat. Experience helps, too.

———————————————————— ⚋ ⚋ ⚋ ————————————————————

No matter how student-centered the classroom may be, I still have an important job to facilitate discussion and cognitive conflict by asking a tough question or challenging their conjectures. I must know how to support the "stretching of their minds." I need experience to do this effectively, but it also takes preparation. Before a lesson, I brainstorm ways to extend understanding, or compose questions to push students a little farther. I think about questions they may ask and devise ways to help them come to an understanding.

One never knows how students will respond—that is the excitement of teaching.

I have gotten the students to volunteer ideas, and some of them ask the most wonderful questions. However, I must ask rich mathematical questions and pose interesting problems. I must field their wonderful questions (and by wonderful I mean they stop me in my tracks and leave me wondering how in the world I can answer them) by using a counterexample and asking questions, or articulating why what they say is correct or incorrect. And I must rely on what I know about the student's personality and prior struggles to figure out where they are getting lost, ask them a question that lets them rethink the situation, use a manipulative or drawing to clear something up, or tell them, "You know, that is a really good question, and I'm not sure how to answer it, so let's explore some possibilities. What does the class think?" I learn so much as I facilitate mathematical discourse. The fodder for years of reflection lies in these class discussions.

—JULIANA JONES
First-year teacher, middle-school mathematics

By setting classroom norms to guide math talk, Jones has developed a community of math learners whose members scaffold one another's understanding of mathematics strategies, explanations, and algorithms. These norms are consistent with Vygotsky, who proposed that learning occurs "out there" as much as inside the head. More precisely, Vygotsky viewed thought as the internalization of experiences in the social context. Thus the "location" of Juliana Jones' students' mathematical learning and knowledge cannot be specified as being in individual students' heads, in the classroom culture at large, or in the relationship among students. It is, in a word, sociocultural. The internalization of the social interaction *becomes* the cognitive process.

Three Research-Based Scaffolding Strategies

As we described in Chapter 3, there is considerable interest in teachers using instructional strategies for which there is support from scientific research. The following three strategies are not teaching recipes but they have been the subject of rigorous research demonstrating that students' achievement increases when teachers emphasize active and social learning.

Substantive Conversation   A team of researchers headed by Fred Newmann at the University of Wisconsin spent five years studying hundreds of classrooms, trying to understand what particular classroom conditions enhance the intellectual quality and the authenticity of students' schoolwork.[23] Newmann and his colleagues found that one of the most powerful strategies was the *substantive conversation*. By that, they meant "students engage in extended conversational exchanges with the teacher and/or their peers about subject matter in a way that builds an improved or shared understanding of ideas or topics."[24] They stress that such subject-matter conversations go far beyond reporting facts, procedures, or definitions; they focus on making distinctions, applying ideas, forming generalizations, and raising questions.

Teachers do not script or control substantive conversations. Rather, they flow from a sharing of ideas among the participants who are working to understand a concept or finish a project. The teacher's skill, art, and knowledge of both the students and the subject guide the conversation, return it to the teaching goals, and extend important themes and principles. These conversations may appear to be self-sustaining—requiring little more than the students' interest and urge to partic- ipate. But the teacher's role is no more "effortless" than that of skilled athletes (say, a diver, a golfer, or a tight end) at the peak of their performances. Again, knowledge, experience, and relationships are what lie behind these lessons.

Reciprocal Teaching   The late Ann Brown and her husband, Joe Campione, both professors at the University of California-Berkeley, and Annemarie Palinscar, pro- fessor at the University of Michigan, developed strategies that use cognitive and so- ciocultural learning theories as a basis for teaching reading. These research-based principles have great relevance for adolescent and adult learning as well as for ele- mentary students. One of their strategies, *reciprocal teaching,* teaches children to ask for assistance when they encounter unfamiliar words, to stop and summarize the text periodically, to ask questions about the content, and to predict what they expect to find next. Students work in groups of six or so. Each member takes a turn leading the discussion about an article, a video, or other material they are using to gather information. The leader begins by asking a question and may ask the group to make predictions. Clarifying and summarizing help ensure comprehension.

Brown, Campione, and Palinscar believe this strategy works because it "provokes zones of proximal development within which readers of varying abilities can find support. Group cooperation, where everyone is trying to arrive at consen- sus concerning meaning, relevance, and importance, helps to ensure that under- standing occurs, even if some members of the group are not yet capable of full participation. . . . The task is simplified by the provision of social support through a variety of expertise, *not* via decomposition of the task into basic skills."[25]

Cognitively Guided Instruction   A third approach comes from Tom Carpenter and Elizabeth Fennema, University of Wisconsin researchers, and from Megan Franke, at UCLA. *Cognitively Guided Instruction (CGI)* is not a teaching strategy per se. Rather, the researchers provide groups of teachers information about cogni- tive theories of learning that help them investigate students' thinking about mathe- matics. In other words, teachers learn all they can about how students are making sense or facing obstacles as they use various strategies for problem solving. From this understanding of *how* students are thinking about mathematics (rather than simply assessing "what they know"), teachers plan their lessons.

CGI teachers develop their skills to make explicit the knowledge and strategies the students use to solve problems. Teachers ask students to explain, to show how, and to suggest different ways that might work. As the teachers focus less on what they are transmitting to students and more on how the students are thinking, in- struction becomes more closely aligned with the help that students need. Also, the classes become alive with mathematical talk and activity as "figuring out" becomes an interactive or relational rather than an individual experience. In fact, "figuring out" becomes the heart of mathematics and replaces the old paradigm of "doing problems."[26] CGI has its origins in mathematics teaching, but its principles apply to teaching generally.

Productive Group Work

In the first activity of the Pythagorean theorem unit, I gave students a chance to explore the relationships in the theorem. Working in pairs and trying to convince each other of their responses, students helped each other see things from different perspectives. It was interesting to watch and listen to students claim their version had more area. It was more interesting to hear their reasons why. Because they were required to explain why and how they knew, students needed to fully analyze the situation while forming their final responses. They were confronted with situations where problem solving was difficult to do alone. I saw students working together and expanding each other's ideas. There appeared to be both a competitive spirit and a cooperative one at the same time. Although students worked together on finding solutions, they still wanted to be the first ones to discover them and explain them to the class.

—**Marilyn Cortez**
First-year teacher, high school mathematics

Considerable classroom research documents the advantages of students working together in small groups.[27] In fact, although vigorous disputes remain over how and when groups ought to work and how groups ought to be formed, there is simply no disagreement among researchers and education policy advisers over whether a substantial amount of group work should occur in classes. Sharing, talking, and working with others should be central to lessons, not by-products. As students work together, they take charge of the assignment. They help divide the lesson into tasks and decide how, when, and who will do each task. In such group work, each student has an opportunity to make valuable contributions to classmates' work. All students can have their work appreciated by others. Despite (or perhaps because of) all the interactions among students, any one student's strengths and weaknesses need not become fodder for comparison or embarrassment. When working with others, students can safely watch and learn how others become successful. Not surprisingly, students in these kinds of classrooms learn more.

Shared Expertise Ann Brown and Joe Campione combined the idea of cooperative group work with Vygotsky's and Piaget's theories of cognitive development. In a project called "Fostering a Community of Learners," Brown and Campione used the following "jigsaw" group strategy to develop expertise that is both individual and shared by the class. Students select a topic for their own "research" that is related to the scientific idea that the class is learning. One class of second graders studied the animals in their habitat. Some students became experts on how animals protected themselves from predators; others studied animal communication or reproduction. Then design teams composed of experts in each of the areas shared their knowledge to design a habitat or invent an "animal of the future." The teacher's role is that of a more knowledgeable person who guides the individual and group activities with questions and prompts.[28]

In a similar vein, high school teacher Douglas Pollock assigns heterogeneous groups in his twelfth-grade composition classes to write a documented critical essay on a single author. Students in a group read different combinations of, for example, James Baldwin's works. Each student is responsible for his or her own independently produced paper, but the group develops a shared online database of research and support articles brought in from library research and from the Internet. Students reading these articles are quick to point out useful information for others' projects, and considerable common knowledge and cross-fertilization of ideas take place. Various editing, critiquing, and interim reporting requirements keep students in tune with others' ideas and progress. Students are quickly and easily impressed with the power and extent of their group's literary "intelligence," and how that intelligence becomes the most important resource for their own work. Pollock's conversations with students help them articulate their problems and frustrations and formulate questions that the data or other students can help answer.

Cooperative Learning   Well-designed cooperative lessons offer a variety of tasks and paths to success, so they stand a good chance of accommodating students' differences. Since the mid-1970s researchers have developed and studied different approaches to cooperative learning. In addition to Elizabeth Cohen's Complex Instruction, strategies popular with teachers include "team learning" developed by Robert Slavin and his colleagues at Johns Hopkins University, "learning together" strategies developed by David and Roger Johnson at the University of Minnesota, and "jigsaw" methods developed by independent researcher Spencer Kagan. Although all these approaches differ in their particulars, they all enact a common set of principles, which are summarized in Concept Table 5.2.

Regardless of the particular strategy, good cooperative lessons must contain knowledge that is complex and rich in meaning. Simple group goals such as memorizing a list of terms do not necessarily serve all students well, since there are bound to be some who can memorize better on their own, some who already know the meanings, and others who need more time to learn than the group can allow.

Productive cooperative groups must seek rewards from achieving a group goal that students cannot reach unless each group member does his or her own best work. Such lessons challenge better-skilled students more than competitive lessons do. Just doing better than others no longer brings easy rewards. All students, regardless of skill level, are able to contribute in areas of their strength, and all can receive help in areas in which they do less well. When lessons include these opportunities, the commonly expressed fear that groups slow down the progress of better students is unwarranted. Even the strongest students make considerable intellectual gains when they work with students of all skill levels.

CONCEPT TABLE 5.2 *Principles of Cooperative Learning*

Small groups	Students engage together in groups of three, four, or five—large enough for diverse perspectives; small enough so that everyone can engage fully.
Positive interdependence	Students engage in a task that cannot be successfully completed without cooperation, and each individual's success is dependent on the success of the group.
Talk	Asking questions and providing explanations to one another about what is being learned is central to the learning process.
Group social skills	Knowing how to work together is not taken for granted but is an explicit part of what students must learn.
Debriefing	Students discuss and evaluate how well they have worked together as a group, as well as judging how well they have learned.

However, organizing students for productive group work requires attention to details, to sociocultural principles, and to very particular skills that make the experience different from what most students, parents, and teachers are familiar with. Most students, even those who have spent lots of time in groups, need a specific induction into cooperative groups. All members, not just the most skilled, have to help others, risk exposing their mistakes, feel safe with their peers, and be able to receive help from them. Everyone has to find value in what others offer and view their own success as interdependent with theirs. New social skills are needed to resolve the inevitable conflicts that occur. Teachers cannot simply tell students to move their chairs and work together. Absent these steps, group work may not be an improvement over working alone. Eric Korporaal recognizes that developing social skills is essential to support learning.

——————————————————————❧ ❧ ❧——————————————————————

I began by having my students work on simpler, shorter activities in teams of two. For instance, the small groups worked on math problems that they were already familiar with. I did this so that they could focus on working together rather than struggling to understand the problem. Gradually, I increased the difficulty of the tasks as well as the size of the groups. I reinforced positive behavior and pointed out the types of interactions that led to successful groups. Over time students began to realize the sorts of interactions (e.g., effective communication, listening, delegation of responsibilities, and attention to each member's contributions) that needed to occur in order for their group to succeed.

—**Erik Korporaal**
First-year teacher, grades 4 and 5

What does an academic and socially productive cooperative lesson look like? No single lesson can cover the entire range of possibilities, but the literature unit briefly sketched in Focal Point 5.2 illustrates some essentials. In a ninth-grade English class, groups of four students had worked together for nearly 10 weeks. They had practiced the necessary social skills—how to ask for help and give explanations, share ideas and not dominate, withhold judgments and not put down their class-mates and others—and, although certain groups still had problems to work out, most had achieved easy familiarity. The teacher had balanced each group as far as possible, mixing students who differed in race, boys and girls, highly skilled and less-skilled students. She also had mixed high-energy social students with shy, quiet ones.

Work in small cooperative groups will not solve all the problems that ail typical classes. Nonetheless, successful cooperative groups enable learning to take place while presenting the fewest limits to students, and they help ensure many essential conditions for learning. When cooperative groups are successful, it is likely that there is a teacher who has a deep knowledge of the subject, who has designed rich and complex multiability lessons, who models scaffolding, who deals openly with his values of treating others with respect and dignity, and who frequently engages students in democratic participation and decision making.

Technology as Scaffolding

Technology clearly has become a fundamental part of education. Not only does nearly every school across the nation see computers and the Internet as basic equipment for teaching and learning, students increasingly use computers to learn at home In the 2003–2004 school year, 77 percent of public schools reported that a majority of their teachers used the Internet for instruction, up from 54 percent in 1998–1999.[29] A national survey of 6- to 17-year-olds in 2004 found that nearly 90 percent of school-aged children reported that a broadband connection like DSL was either important or very important for completing school assignments.[30]

Electronic technologies can serve either traditional or progressive approaches to teaching and learning. Many software packages for classrooms, or "distance learning" offerings, provide nothing more than traditional instruction wrapped up in electronic packages. On the other hand, used in the context of authentic and active learning communities, these same technologies can scaffold learners' explorations beyond the bounds of their current knowledge and provide multidimensional routes of investigation.

The North Central Regional Educational Laboratory (NCREL) provides tech-nology guidance to teachers and schools around the country. Their charge is to translate the best research on the educational uses of technology into practical guidelines for schools. One of their online publications, *Plugging In,* helps teachers' judge whether a technological offering will promote students' active engagement.[31] Their indicators of engaged technology, some of which are in-cluded in Concept Table 5.3, tap into the dimensions teachers should seek when they attempt to create active, multidimensional lessons that scaffold students' learning.

FOCAL POINT 5.2

A Cooperative Learning Lesson
To Kill a Mockingbird

The class read *To Kill a Mockingbird,* an engaging and intellectually demanding classic that is nearly always on high school reading lists. The novel includes themes of racism (including whether the book's treatment of racism is itself racist), justice, early education, one-parent families, small-town life, courage, sexism, maturation, assuming the perspectives of others, and more. Soon after the class started the novel, the special-education resource teacher (who had several students "mainstreamed" in the class) arranged a lunchtime showing of the movie adapted from the novel. Most students didn't want to give up their lunch periods, but several did—including all the special-education students. These students had an easier time reading the book after they had seen the movie. Furthermore, because they had an overview of the novel, they could make valuable contributions in their groups.

After reading one-third of the book, each group member adopted a different character to follow. As they finished reading, the students wrote short compositions describing their characters and linking them to the book's themes. They took notes on their reading and exchanged ideas with "expert groups." That is, they conferred with their classmates from other groups who had chosen the same character. Although the students could get help and ideas from their classmates, the teacher held all students individually accountable for their brief composition.

The next part of this assignment emphasized group interdependence; that is, no student could successfully complete his or her own work without the participation and cooperation of the student's groupmates. The students wrote a longer composition, entitled "Exploring Themes in *To Kill a Mockingbird* through Four Characters," using the short pieces that each of the four group members had written as source materials. In the longer assignment, the most-skilled students found sophisticated differences and commonalties as they explored the characters and themes. They practiced research conventions by attributing ideas to their sources—quoting from both the novel and their classmates. Less-skilled students stretched beyond their first inclination simply to summarize their group's four papers and attempted to do what their more highly skilled classmates did.

Throughout, the interaction was intense—questioning, explaining, and arguing. The students had pragmatic reasons for engaging others and expecting good work from their fellow group members. As the individual compositions neared completion, the students grew increasingly interested in what their peers were writing. After all, their own ideas were being represented. It's hard to squelch your curiosity when you see your own name in the text or footnote!

When they had finished their compositions, each group wrote a skit loosely based on their characters. Each picked a common conflict at school that concerned them. The groups selected such problems as social cliques, dating, drug use, grade pressure, intimidation and violence, and parent-student trust. Then each student

(continued)

conjectured about how his or her character would fit into the school conflict. (They could take liberties with the character's age or gender.) Each student wrote the dialogue for his or her own character. Finally, the groups performed the skits for the class. Because the skit had a group rather than an individual goal, the group shared a single grade. As with the compositions, each student achieved something by working with others that could not have been achieved by working alone.

CONCEPT TABLE 5.3 *Educational Technology That Engages Students*

Purpose of technology	Examples
Provides challenging tasks, opportunities, and experiences	Complex problems and cases; links to unique resources such as museums and libraries; opportunities to examine contrasting events or databases
	Access to experts, peers, and community members who can guide, mentor, tutor, broker, share, inform, and involve students in meaningful ways
	Access to rich media sources for data manipulation or presentations
	Tools for interactive browsing, searching, and authoring
Allows students to learn by doing	Engages students in planning, reflecting, making decisions, experiencing consequences, and examining alternative solutions and ideas
Provides guided participation and content customized to suit the particular needs or interests of students	Socratic questioning
	Intelligent tutoring
	Diagnosing and guiding an analysis of mistakes
	Adaptations or changes that respond to students' actions

Source: Adapted from Beau Fly Jones, Gilbert Valdez, Jeri Nowakowski, and Claudette Rasmussen, *Plugging In* (Oak Brook, IL: North Central Regional Educational Laboratory, 1995).

One example of technology that provides rich, multidimensional tasks and scaffolds students' learning is the *Adventures of Jasper Woodbury* series developed by cognitive psychologist John Bransford and his colleagues at the Cognition and Technology Group at Vanderbilt University. The Jasper adventures are a series of 12 multimedia adventures designed for students in grades 5 and up. Each consists of a videodisc and supporting materials that center on a short video adventure that ends in a complex challenge. For example, in one adventure, Jasper travels upriver to buy an old boat that has no running lights and a small, temporary fuel tank. Students help Jasper determine whether he can make it home before dark without running out of gas. In another adventure, Larry's grandfather has been kidnapped but is able to get a message out, which students must decipher. They help rescue Grandpa by using algebra to decode the note that tells the location of the secret hideout.

The designers of the Jasper adventure series followed the model of good detective novels where all the data necessary to solve the adventure (plus additional data that are not relevant to the solution) are embedded in the story. Jasper adventures also contain "embedded teaching" episodes that provide models of particular approaches to solving problems. The materials are consistent with the National Council of Teachers of Mathematics (NCTM) standards. Teachers can use the adventures as tools to help students develop cognitive skills such as planning, formulating problems, finding and constructing information, mathematical calculation, and decision making. The Jasper series also seeks to bridge the gap between natural learning environments described by sociocultural research and school learning environments. The adventures provide a common context for instruction, an authentic task, and a chance to see that school knowledge can be used to solve real problems.[32]

The Digital Divide   As with many other things, however, the widespread and creative use of computers in education is not evenly distributed across students and schools. Even though studies suggest that schools serving low-income students and students of color have nearly as many computers and Internet access as schools serving more-advantaged students, the actual use of technology in high-poverty, high-minority, and academically failing schools lags behind technology used in more advantaged schools.[33]

One study in an urban midwestern high school found that the computing lab was claimed by a group of white, gifted boys who used it as an informal clubhouse.[34] They were encouraged by teachers who often relied on these students to help set up equipment, troubleshoot, and teach. Girls and African American students did not feel welcomed in the lab. Other evidence suggests that teachers tend to infuse technology into lessons much less with low-achieving students than with high achievers and that computer use is often limited for students learning English.

K–12 schools' failure to make high achievement in technology expected for all students has enduring consequences. UCLA researcher Jane Margolis and her colleagues studied college students for four years and found that both male and female students, as well as teachers, expect males to be better at computing. Their study also found that these expectations damaged girls' confidence.[35] Expectations and opportunities are clearly linked: If, for example, schools don't expect girls or poor students to achieve, they won't provide opportunities for success. By holding high expectations for all students, schools are more likely to recognize students' existing strengths and resources on which to build their success. Students' culture and language are among those strengths and resources.

Building on Students' Culture and Language

First-year history teacher Matthew Eide could have had his diverse high school students memorize important facts about turn-of-the-century immigration but instead chose an approach that built on what they and their families already knew.

⚝ ⚝ ⚝

I had students interview a recent immigrant, ideally a family member or a close friend. About 80 percent of my students were able to interview a family member. The students asked how the immigrants navigated a new life in a sometimes hostile environment, and specifically how they used their family and social networks to survive. The students then wrote essays comparing the experiences of the immigrants they interviewed with those of the turn-of-the-century immigrants. This essay had the highest completion rate of any I had assigned. I believe that's because they used their cultural and linguistic knowledge in a way that was legitimate in the classroom.

—MATTHEW EIDE
First-year teacher, high school history

Chapter 1 described the increasing diversity of U.S. schoolchildren, in particular, students from Asia and Latin America. Providing scaffolding for these children requires strategies that connect the culture they bring to school with the academic content of the curriculum. Students must be able to use their own social and cultural thinking knowledge and processes to make sense of *any* new knowledge, whether it is knowledge derived from their "home" culture, the larger societal culture, or some combination. But schools often send the message that a student's existing cultural tools for learning and solving problems are inferior to those of the dominant (or school) culture. If we do not encourage students to develop and use all the cultural background they possess, we deny them, according to sociocultural theories, a substantial part of their available intelligence.

All Students Bring "Funds of Knowledge" and Cultural Competencies

Researcher Luis Moll, whose work we discussed in Chapter 3, assessed the enormous knowledge resources that Mexican American children had available to them *outside* their school. Because of the low expectations held for children of poor and working-class parents, these Tucson, Arizona, children performed "as expected." They had low achievement, and they found in school little relevance to their lives.

As Moll studied the children's extended families, however, he found rich funds of knowledge. Each household was a place that developed expertise in particular domains (Moll identified nearly 50, including soil and irrigation systems, minerals, renting and selling, budgets, design and architecture, first aid, folk cures, moral knowledge and ethics, etc.). Children participated in doing tasks and chores, all the while observing, asking questions, and being assisted by adults. Although the child's help may be minimal, more difficult tasks are also allowed and help is available when needed; thus, there is no need for failure.

Moll believes (as does the teacher in the following quote) that schools could use these cultural funds of knowledge and practices to enrich both culture and intelligence, instead of the current practice, which is to see cultural knowledge as not useful or as an obstacle.

─────────────────────────────────── ⊠ ⊠ ⊠ ───────────────────────────────────

Neither my students nor I enter our classroom empty-handed. We come, as Luis Moll says, "con nuestras mochilas llenas, no estan vacias (with our backpacks full, not empty)." I not only carry pedagogical theories about teaching and learning, but I also carry assumptions and ideas about people: what learning looks like, what a teacher looks like, what schooling looks like and why. . . . No classroom practice exists in isolation of a social and cultural history.

—**Cindy Kauionalani Bell**
First-year teacher, grade 2

First-year teacher of English as a Second Language Maria Hwang used students' local knowledge to help them learn about Mexico in light what they know about where they live.

─────────────────────────────────── ⊠ ⊠ ⊠ ───────────────────────────────────

My curriculum on Mexico begins in Los Angeles, a point of reference for the students. They explore and rediscover the familiar in order to establish a foundation for new information that will be introduced in their [studies about] Mexico. Understanding the influences of Mexico manifested in Los Angeles, students can absorb the authentic source from which the influence derives.

—**Maria Chiping Hwang**
First-year teacher, high school ESL

"Additive" Instruction for English Learners

Connecting students' home culture to the academic content of the curriculum is especially important when students' primary language is not English, particularly in schools where there are "English only" policies. Judy Smith (shown in the photo here), who teaches high school students who are still learning English, uses her own fluency in Spanish to make these important connections.

Because language is at the very heart of culture, educators must pay attention to both first and second language learning. Vygotsky made clear that learning language and literacy is a never-ending process of communicating with others and internalizing content, meaning, and feelings. Drawing on Vygotsky's ideas, linguist Jim Cummins

has developed the principle of "additive bilingual enrichment," based on the theory that language is learned in contexts where communication is meaningful, purposeful, and has social value.

Additive bilingual enrichment argues that primary languages are essential and authentic aspects of culture and means of communication in communities and families. Thus, children can best learn second languages in highly interactive social contexts where they learn a new language as they simultaneously strengthen and enrich their primary language. In other words, students use the experiences and meanings in their primary language to scaffold their learning of the new one. Cummins contrasts this approach with a "subtractive" approach in which one language *replaces* the other and often results in little more than minimal literacy in either language.

Cindy Bell, whose classroom is in a Latino immigrant community, used this work to guide interactions and learning in her classroom.

———————————————————————❈ ❈ ❈———————————————————————

When my students talk to each other, they engage in purposeful conversation. Whether to help a friend find a word in the dictionary or to discuss what game they will play at recess, they talk to communicate. They know that they must speak to be understood and they must listen to understand. The students develop their speaking and listening skills by developing conversational strategies. They ask each other questions. They repeat the most important points. They emphasize words and give them meaning. They also identify their audience and tailor their words by switching between English and Spanish depending on with whom they are talking.

This last practice is most obvious when we welcome new students into our classroom's Community Circle. Lali, who recently arrived in the United States from Mexico, joined our classroom in November. As our class introduced ourselves to her, the students immediately changed from their usual English welcomes to Spanish greetings, because, as they discussed, Lali wouldn't understand if they spoke in English. Even Maria, my one monoliterate English student, recognized the value of communicating for meaning and asked someone to translate so Lali would understand. In this group interaction and in many others, language acts as a functional social skill that develops oral literacy skills. My students understand that both English and Spanish are social tools because they are valuable and meaningful forms of communication.

—CINDY KAUIONALANI BELL
First-year teacher, grade 2

Learning theorist Steven Krashen has studied students' feelings when they are learning a new language, especially if their primary language itself is disparaged. Referring to "affective filters," which constrain students' learning new language and other knowledge, Krashen argues that students must feel secure and hopeful before they can open themselves to the risks of failure.

First-grade teacher Benjamin Chang describes the learning challenges he faced in his first year in his diverse classroom, and how his understanding of affective filters supplemented other theories of learning as problem solving, understanding, and participation.

─────────────────── ❈ ❈ ❈ ───────────────────

Two days before school started, I finally received my class roster. Four of my students are African American with roots in Texas, Georgia, and Alabama. Seven are Latino, with parents born and raised in Guatemala, El Salvador, and Mexico. Other families come from countries in Asia and the Pacific, such as Vietnam, Cambodia, Thailand, Hong Kong, the Philippines, and China. Six of my students are biracial or triracial, with families from all of these areas, as well as Belize and Puerto Rico. Within each category of race and ethnicity, I also learned about substantial linguistic diversity in my class (10 languages). . . . I was surprised, but it was a challenge I was eager to take.

    One idea that supported my effort to research and access my students' languages and cultures is Krashen's concept of the "affective filter." As I have come to know more about my students and their families, I have been able to connect what I learned outside the classroom with what we are doing in the classroom. For example, to learn about nouns and adjectives, I asked students to pretend they were going to the store with their lola *(Tagalog for grandmother) or some other family member. With all of the different domestic practices and foods in my students' homes, this context for learning about different word types also became a social studies lesson.*

    The end result was a group of engaged students learning about and appreciating their differences as well learning the official language arts curriculum. A simple assessment lets me know if I have been successful in lowering affective filters. It is the twinkle in their eyes, and the smiles on their faces. Their faces light up in a way that is unlike anything else. Neither ice cream, nor stickers, nor extra recess minutes can produce the expression on my students' faces when I ask them how to say a high-frequency word in their own language or when they answer questions in the context of their homes and families.

—**Benjamin Chang**
First-year teacher, grade 1

───

    When teaching an "English-only" class, Kimberly Min noted that her African American students spoke a variety of English that schools often interpret as incorrect. However, she understands that her students must feel secure with their home language and culture as they risk engaging in new learning at school.

─────────────────── ❈ ❈ ❈ ───────────────────

Mainstream Academic English (MAE) is not only considered the standard language, it is also a code of power. African American Language (AAL) is also a legitimate form of language, with a sociocultural history that is culturally significant for African Americans.[36] The majority of my students use AAL, which most teachers deem as slang or as an unacceptable form of

English. There is a great deal of neglect in terms of language acquisition be-
cause many teachers do not acknowledge that African Americans are stan-
dard language learners.

I counter this by allowing my students to express themselves in both
AAL and MAE, while I teach the contexts in which to use both languages ap-
propriately. Once students have an understanding of when it is appropriate
to use either AAL or MAE, they are successful "code switchers." During writ-
ing assignments and oral language activities, these students demonstrate
that they can successfully use MAE. For instance, Aaron is aware of his lan-
guage use and the language use of his classmates, as he constantly reminds
them of the rules of MAE. Yet, on the basketball court, Aaron successfully code
switches back to AAL to convey his anger or happiness to his peers. This
ability to switch languages depending on their contexts is what I hope to
teach my students.

—KIMBERLY MIN
Third-grade teacher

Cheng and Min have found ways to help students feel secure and hopeful enough about the language competencies they bring from home to take the risks necessary to develop new language competencies at school.

No Easy Recipes

This chapter has focused on important characteristics of classrooms that are consistent with sociocultural theories of learning—confidence in the context of difference; active multidimensional learning opportunities; and connections between school knowledge and students' culture and language. How teachers enact these theories in their classrooms profoundly influences students' willingness and ability to apply their natural learning processes to formal school learning and makes a critical difference in allowing all students in a diverse society to succeed at school.

Basing classrooms on cognitive and sociocultural learning theories and principles of social justice is an ideal in much the same way that democracy is an ideal—something to be pursued, but something never quite good enough to suit us. And so it's not surprising that teachers who act on what they know about learning and what they believe about social justice are often dismayed by the gap between their ideal and their classrooms. Even so, such teachers do create environments far closer to their ideal than to the world outside, and that ideal serves well their commitment to social justice.

OLC Connections

A list of additional online and print resources and a set of questions for reflection about constructing classrooms as learning communities can be found at www.mhhe.com/oakes3e.

▒ Digging Deeper

Some of the following scholars and resources can provide readers with a deeper understanding of instructional theories based on sociocultural perspectives on learning. Others provide practical, research-based ideas and strategies for teaching.

Association for Constructivist Teaching, housed at Old Dominion University and online at http://www.odu.edu/educ/act/, is dedicated to the growth of all educators and students through identification and dissemination of effective constructivist practices in both the professional cultures of teachers and the learning environments of children. The association membership is open to anyone who is interested in the field of education, including classroom teachers, administrators, supervisors, consultants, college and university personnel, students, parents and retired educators. The association's journal, *The Constructivist,* is available online at http://www.odu.edu/educ/act/journal/.

Jo Boaler, professor of mathematics education at Stanford University, specializes in mathematics education and teacher education, with particular interests in the effectiveness of different teaching environments, the inequitable nature of mathematics classrooms, and situated analyses of learning. Her 2002 book, *Experiencing School Mathematics: Traditional and Reform Approaches to Teaching and Their Impact on Student Learning* (Mahwah, NJ: Lawrence Erlbaum) presents, in a highly readable fashion, the results of a carefully conducted study of the teaching of mathematics in two high schools.

John Bransford, professor of education at the University of Washington, was formerly codirector of the Learning Technology Center at Vanderbilt University. He and Vanderbilt colleagues developed the Jasper Woodbury problem-solving series in mathematics, the Scientists in Action series, and the Little Planet Literacy series— programs that have received many awards. Bransford is also coeditor with Ann Brown of *How People Learn: Brain, Mind, Experience, and School* (Washington, DC: National Academy of Sciences, 1999), one of the best books available on learning.

Professors **Ann Brown** (deceased) and **Joseph Campione** of the University of California-Berkeley have studied learning in inner-city classrooms. The goal of their research has been to transform grade-school classrooms from worksites where students perform assigned tasks under the management of teachers into communities of learning and interpretation, where students are given significant opportunity to take charge of their own learning. A recent description of this work can be found in the book Brown coedited with John Bransford, *How People Learn: Brain, Mind, Experience, and School* (Washington, DC: National Academy of Sciences, 1999).

Jerome Bruner, research professor of psychology and senior research fellow in law at New York University, has a long and distinguished career. His work investigates how cognitive psychology and child development can inform teaching so that all children can become highly competent and fully participating members of their cultures. Books you might want to read include *The Process of Education* (1960), *Toward a Theory of Instruction* (1966), *The Relevance of Education* (1971), *Acts of Meaning* (1990), and *The Culture of Education* (1996)—all published by Harvard University Press.

The late Professor **Elizabeth Cohen** and her colleague Professor **Rachel Lotan** at Stanford University have published several books exploring how schools can teach at a uniformly high level when their students vary tremendously in terms of achievement, proficiency in the language of instruction, and social status. Cohen's most recent books include *Designing Groupwork: Strategies for the Heterogeneous Classroom* (New York: Teachers College Press, 1997) and, with Rachel Lotan, *Working for Equity in Heterogeneous Classrooms* (New York: Teachers College Press, 1997).

Larry Cuban spent 14 years teaching social studies in inner-city high schools and 7 years as a district superintendent before becoming a professor of the history of U.S. education at Stanford University. His book *How Teachers Taught: Constancy and Change in American Classrooms 1890–1990* (New York: Teachers College Press, 1993) traces the history of teaching in U.S. schools.

Cognitively Guided Instruction was developed by a group of mathematics education researchers, including Professors **Tom Carpenter** and **Elizabeth Fennema** of the University of Wisconsin and Professor **Megan Franke** of UCLA. Their book *Children's Mathematics: Cognitively Guided Instruction* (Portsmouth, NH: Heinemann, 1999) provides an introduction to this work. Other information about Cognitively Guided Instruction can be found on the Promising Practices site, http://www.promisingpractices.net, developed by the RAND Corporation to highlight educational programs that are proven to be effective.

Harvard education professor **Howard Gardner's** many books range from explications of his own theories of multiple intelligence (e.g., *Frames of Mind* [New York: Basic Books, 1983, 1993]), to a history of the cognitive revolution (*The Mind's New Science* [New York: Basic Books, 1985]), a textbook providing a comprehensive overview of intelligence (*Intelligence,* with Mindy L. Kornhaber and Warren K. Wake [Orlando, FL: Harcourt Brace, 1995]), to the implications of cognitive psychology for teaching (e.g., *Multiple Intelligences: The Theory in Practice* [New York: Basic Books, 1993] and [New York: Basic Books, 1991]).

Jean Lave and **Etienne Wenger** have developed the idea of learning as occurring within a "community of practice." Lave, a professor of anthropology at the University of California-Berkeley, has developed theories of "situated" cognition, and learning as identity development. A book particularly interesting for educators is Lave and Wenger's *Situated Learning: Legitimate Peripheral Participation* (New York: Cambridge University Press, 1991). Wenger's book *Communities of Practice: Learning, Meaning, and Identity* (Cambridge, England: Cambridge University Press, 1999) provides a comprehensive framework for learning in social contexts and the relationship between learning and identity, drawing on his extensive studies of people interacting and learning at work.

Deborah Meier was principal of one of the most remarkable public schools in the country, Central Park East (CPE) in East Harlem, for 20 years and then became the founder and principal of the Mission Hill School, a K–8 Boston Public Pilot school serving 180 children in the Roxbury community. In her book based on the CPE experience, *The Power of Their Ideas: Lessons for America from a Small School in Harlem* (Boston: Beacon Press, 1995), Meier argues for teaching that connects learning to real-world activities. You can learn more about Deborah Meier at her website, http://www.deborahmeier.com/.

Luis Moll, an education professor at the University of Arizona, studies learning and knowledge in the lives of working-class Mexican American students and their families in the barrio schools of Tucson. You may find the following articles particularly useful: "Bilingual Classroom Studies and Community Analysis: Some Recent Trends," *Educational Researcher* 21, no. 2 (1992), pp. 20–24, and "Funds of Knowledge for Teaching: Using a Qualitative Approach to Connect Homes and Classrooms," *Theory into Practice* 31, no. 2 (1992), pp. 132–141. Moll has also edited a helpful collection of articles by leading sociocultural theorists, *Vygotsky and Education: Instructional Implications of Sociohistorical Psychology* (Cambridge, England: Cambridge University Press, 1992).

Fred Newmann, professor and researcher at the University of Wisconsin Center for Educational Research, and his colleagues professors **Gary Wehlage** and **Walter Secada** developed the concept of authentic pedagogy based on their studies of teaching that emphasizes higher-order thinking, supports the learning of low-income students of color, and fosters high levels of engagement and interaction. A description of authentic instruction can be found in Fred Newmann, ed., *Authentic Achievement: Restructuring Schools for Intellectual Quality* (San Francisco: Jossey-Bass, 1996).

Professor **Annemarie Palinscar** of the University of Michigan developed reciprocal teaching, a dialogue between teachers and students to summarize, generate questions, clarify, and predict the meaning of text. Her book *Teaching Reading as Thinking* (Alexandria, VA: Association for Supervision and Curriculum Development, 1984) describes the procedures of reciprocal teaching, modifications of the basic strategies, and means of evaluating its effectiveness. Other information about reciprocal teaching can be found on the Promising Practices site, http://www.promisingpractices.net, developed by the RAND Corporation to highlight educational programs that are proven to be effective.

At Yale, psychologist **Robert J. Sternberg** develops models of multidimensional intelligence. His triarchic theory of intelligence includes "componential" intelligence—the linguistic and logical-mathematical abilities that most traditional intelligence tests assess; contextual intelligence (the source of creative insight), and experiential intelligence (the "street smarts" of intelligence). His books include *Beyond IQ: A Triarchic Theory of Human Intelligence* (1985) and *Metaphors of the Mind: Conceptions of the Nature of Intelligence* (1990). Cambridge University Press published both.

The book *The Dialogic Curriculum: Teaching and Learning in a Multicultural Society* (New York: Boynton/Cook, 1995), by **Patricia Lambert Stock** of Michigan State University, provides a detailed portrait of inquiry-based, integrated language arts teaching in two twelfth-grade classes where she and her colleagues taught literature by asking students to read and write about subjects that mattered to them. Stock's book describes teachers' planning and students' reading, writing, and talking in ways that expand their experiences and literacy.

Roland Tharp, retired professor of education and psychology at the University of California-Santa Cruz, has studied cultural forces in psychological development and change in a variety of settings, focusing particularly on effective educational programs for minority children. His colleague, UCLA Professor **Ronald Gallimore**

has extended the work he and Tharp began in Hawaii with teachers in a low-income, largely Latino district in the Los Angeles area. Tharp and Gallimore's essential ideas are found in *Rousing Minds to Life: Teaching, Learning, and Schooling in Social Context* (New York: Cambridge University Press, 1988). Tharp's most recent book, *Transforming Teaching: Achieving Excellence, Fairness, Inclusion, and Harmony* (Boulder, CO: Westview Press, 2000), translates these findings into specific strategies for teachers.

Notes

1. As quoted in Joel Spring, *The American School, 1642–1990* (New York: Longman, 1990), p. 120.
2. Larry Cuban, *How Teachers Taught: Constancy and Change in American Classrooms, 1890–1990* (New York: Teachers College Press, 1993).
3. Philip Jackson, *The Practice of Teaching* (New York: Teachers College Press, 1987).
4. Cuban, *How Teachers Taught.*
5. Jean Lave and Etienne Wenger, *Situated Learning: Legitimate Peripheral Participation* (New York: Cambridge University Press, 1991).
6. John Dewey, *How We Think* (Boston: D.C. Heath, 1910); Jean Piaget, *The Science of Education and the Psychology of the Child* (New York: Orion Press, 1970); and Lev Vygotsky, *Mind in Society. Cambridge, England: Cambridge University Press, 1978.*
7. John Dewey, "My Pedagogic Creed," in *The School Journal,* 1896, reprinted in John Dewey, *Early Works* (vol. 5) (Carbondale, IL: Southern Illinois University Press, 1989).
8. See, for example, Jerome Bruner, *Culture and Education* (Cambridge: Harvard University Press, 1996); Michael Cole, *Cultural Psychology: A Once and Future Discipline* (Cambridge: Harvard University Press, 1996); Jean Lave and Etienne Wenger, *Situated Cognition: Legitimate Peripheral Participation* (Cambridge, England: Cambridge University Press, 1991); Barbara Rogoff, *Apprenticeship in Thinking: Cognitive Development in Social Context* (New York: Oxford University Press, 1990); and Etienne Wenger, *Communities of Practice: Learning, Meaning, and Identity* (Cambridge, England: Cambridge University Press, 1999).
9. See, for example, David Perkins, *Outsmarting I.Q.* (New York: The Free Press, 1995).
10. See Elizabeth Cohen and Rachel Lotan's book *Working for Equity in Heterogeneous Classrooms* (New York: Teachers College Press, 1997) for an elaborated discussion of these issues.
11. Cohen and Lotan's *Working for Equity in Heterogeneous Classrooms* includes a nice review of the sociological literature in this area.
12. See Carol Dweck, "Motivational Processes Affecting Learning," *American Psychologist* 41 (1986), pp. 1040–1047, on learned helplessness.
13. Daniel G. Solorzano, "Critical Race Theory, Race and Gender Microaggressions, and the Experience of Chicana and Chicano Scholars," *Qualitative Studies in Education* 11, no. 1 (1998), p. 121.
14. Makeba Jones, "Rethinking African American Students' Agency: Meaningful Choices and Negotiating Meaning" (Ph.D. diss., Los Angeles, UCLA Graduate School of Education and Information Studies, 1998), pp. 1–2.
15. Claude Steele, "Race and the Schooling of Black Americans," *Atlantic Monthly,* April 1992, pp. 68–78.
16. Robert Rosenthal and Lenore Jacobson, *Pygmalion in the Classroom* (New York: Holt, Rinehart & Winston, 1968).
17. Myra Sadker and David Sadker, *Failing at Fairness: How America's Schools Cheat Girls* (New York: Macmillan, 1994).
18. One of the first and best-known studies documenting these patterns is Ray Rist, "Student Social Class and Teacher Expectations: The Self-Fulfilling Prophecy of Ghetto Education," Challenging the Myths: The Schools, the Blacks, and the Poor. Reprint Series no. 5 (Cambridge, MA: Harvard Educational Review, 1971).

19. See, for example, Jere Brophy and Thomas Good, *Looking in Classrooms*, 7th ed. (New York: Longman, 1997), especially Chapter 3.

20. Jo Boaler, "Mathematics for the Moment, or the Millennium?" *Education Week* 18, no. 29 (31 March 1999), pp. 52, 30.

21. Roland Tharp, *Transforming Teaching: Achieving Excellence, Fairness, Inclusion, and Harmony* (Boulder, CO: Westview Press, 2000).

22. Elizabeth Cohen, *Designing Groupwork: Strategies for the Heterogeneous Classroom* (New York: Teachers College Press, 1994).

23. Fred M. Newmann, Walter G. Secada, and Gary Wehlage, *A Guide to Authentic Instruction and Assessment: Vision, Standards, and Scoring* (Madison, WI: Wisconsin Center for Education Research at the University of Wisconsin, 1995).

24. Ibid., p. 35; see also, Fred M. Newmann (Ed.), *Student Engagement and Achievement in American Secondary Schools* (New York: Teachers College Press, 1992), p. 8.

25. Ann L. Brown, Kathleen E. Metz, and Joseph C. Campione, "Social Interaction and Individual Understanding in a Community of Learners: The Influence of Piaget and Vygotsky," in *Piaget-Vygotsky: The Social Genesis of Thought*, ed. Anastasia Tryphon and Jacques Voneche (East Sussex, UK: Psychology Press, 1996), pp. 145–170.

26. Thomas P. Carpenter, Megan Loef Franke, and Linda Levi, *Thinking Mathematically: Integrating Arithmetic and Algebra in Elementary School* (Portsmouth, NH: Heinemann, 2003).

27. See, for example, Robert Slavin, *Cooperative Learning: Theory, Research, and Practice* (Englewood Cliffs, NJ: Prentice Hall, 1995).

28. Ann Brown and Joseph Campione, "Guided Discovery in a Community of Learners," in *Classroom Lessons: Integrating Cognitive Theory and Classroom Practice*, ed. Kate McGilly (Cambridge, MA: MIT Press, 1994).

29. "Technology Counts," *Education Week*, 2005, online at http://www.edweek.org/ew/articles/2005/05/05/35tracking.h24.html.

30. The survey was conducted on behalf of SBC Communications Inc. by Opinion Research Corporation's Pre-Teen Caravan and Teen Caravan omnibus surveys, as reported on http://www.prnewswire.com/.

31. Beau Fly Jones, Gilbert Valdez, Jeri Nowakowski, and Claudette Rasmussen, *Plugging In* (Oak Brook, IL: North Central Regional Educational Laboratory, 1995), online at http://www.ncrel.org.

32. More information about the Jasper series can be found online at http://www.erlbaum.com/jasper.htm.

33. "Technology Counts," *Education Week*.

34. Janet Ward Schofield, Computers and Classroom Culture (New York: Cambridge University Press, 1995), pp. 134–190.

35. Jane Margolis and Allan Fisher, *Unlocking the Clubhouse: Women and Computing* (Cambridge, MA: MIT Press, 2002).

36. The terms AAL and MAE were coined by Dr. Noma LeMoine; see Noma LeMoine, *English for Your Success: A Language Development Program for African American Children Grades PreK–8* (Saddle Brook, NJ: The Peoples Publishing Group, 1999).

CHAPTER 6

Assessment

Measuring What Matters

In my classroom, we do presentations, tests, simulations, projects, quizzes, seminars, quick writes, debates, etc. I am always on my feet talking to students, looking at their work as they do it, spontaneously adding more questions/thoughts for them to wrestle with. I try to read their work every evening. I am constantly adjusting my teaching plans because, as I read quick writes or other class work or listen in on group and partner dialogues, I know whether I need to go back and review or I can push ahead. Recently, I postponed a test for three days because I knew the students weren't ready (everything from their body language to a practice test were dead giveaways). I worked with them to teach each other the material and explain how they would study for the test.

—JUDY SMITH
High school social studies

What most people think of as "testing" is just one of the many techniques that Judy Smith uses to keep track of what students are learning, to evaluate the success of her instruction, and to figure out what she and her students should do next. Teachers like Judy Smith, committed to social justice and high levels of learning, use assessment to actively inform their daily classroom practice.

Chapter Overview
—⌘—

We begin this chapter on assessment by defining a few of the concepts associated with it. We then give a brief history of assessment, focusing, in particular, on the nineteenth- and early-twentieth-century development of testing to determine intelligence. Next, we turn to the modern descendants of early IQ tests, today's standardized achievement tests, and we describe their construction, meaning, and uses in twentieth-century education. This leads to the current "high-stakes" testing policies—so called because of their significant consequences for students, teachers, and schools. Finally, we focus on classrooms, illustrating how, despite all the current emphasis on standardized testing, assessment can foster learning and social justice.

A Few Definitions

Testing, evaluation, and test-based accountability are assessment-related practices used to measure and judge the performance of students, their teachers, and their schools. Because we refer to these concepts throughout the chapter, we begin with a few definitions.

Assessment is a process of gathering, describing, or quantifying information about performance. The purpose of student assessment is to support learning and teaching by identifying students' academic strengths and weaknesses; informing instruction and the provision of supplemental intervention and support; and tracking students' learning over time.

Assessments can be divided into two major categories: *classroom assessments* used by teachers to support learning and evaluate achievement; and *large-scale assessments* developed by experts, "standardized," and administered to individuals or groups in schools and classrooms across the country. Classroom assessments may be teacher-made or produced commercially and packaged with textbooks or other instructional materials. Large-scale assessments are mandated, designed, conducted, and reported outside the classroom. Teachers are only one of many intended users, and the results of such assessments are often used to make important administrative decisions about students, such as grade promotion, placement in classes, identification of the need for special education, or high school graduation.

Assessments can be classified as traditional or alternative. *Traditional assessment* typically includes forced-choice measures, such as multiple-choice questions, fill-in-the-blanks, true-false, and matching test items—all of which have a predetermined "correct" answer. Students' knowledge is assessed by demonstrating their recall of information by selecting or producing the correct answer. Traditional assessments may be standardized or created by teachers, and they may be administered in classrooms or across schools, states, or countries. The assumption underlying traditional assessment is that learning consists of acquiring knowledge and skills that have been taught as part of the curriculum, the behaviorist view we described briefly in Chapter 3 and will explain more later in this chapter.

Tests, which are the most common form of traditional assessment, are specific, formal procedures by which a teacher or other test administrator obtains a sample of what a student knows or can do and generalizes from this sample to the student's broader knowledge—as when a few multiplication problems indicate whether the student understands multiplication or when a composition reveals the student's writing skills.

Alternative (also called *authentic*) *assessments* usually consist of projects, demonstrations, or other cumulative products such as portfolios. Students are expected to show that they can apply skills and knowledge they have learned—for example, writing skills necessary to produce a high-quality newspaper, research skills as revealed in a debate, math skills as needed to complete a science experiment, and so forth.

Assessments that compare student performance on a simulated, real-life task with the performance of an already accomplished person are called *performance* assessments. For example, a student group designs and maintains its own stock market "mutual fund," gaining specific economic and investor knowledge; at the end of the semester they prepare a prospectus to report on their fund and convince new investors to join. Or more simply, the teacher has students write a letter to the principal complaining about cafeteria hamburgers and evaluates writing skills exhibited in this "real" activity.

CONCEPT TABLE 6.1 *Contrasting Traditional and Alternative Assessment*

	Traditional	**Authentic (Alternative)**
How does a student display competence?	Selecting or supplying a response	Performing a task
Is the type of activity contrived or similar to real life?	Contrived task	Real-life task
What type of knowledge or skill is measured?	Recall/recognition	Construction/application
Who determines what is offered as evidence of competence?	Teacher structured	Student structured
What type of evidence is the basis of judging competence?	Indirect evidence (infer from a response that was selected)	Direct evidence (infer from a performance of the knowledge or skill)

Alternative assessments typically include a *rubric,* or listing of the criteria by which the performance should be judged. Although there are not predetermined correct responses, the rubric specifies characteristics of performances at various levels of competence, along with guidelines for scoring. For example, one rubric item for an essay asking students to combine scientific evidence for global warming with suggestions for solutions might be "Relates evidence to conclusions." A student might receive all or partial credit for that item. A portfolio rubric might list all assignments to be included, with subcriteria for further evaluating those elements. A team project rubric might include items for both group and individual contributions and specify maximum values or "points" that correspond with particular learning goals evidenced in the project.

Psychology professor Jon Mueller at North Central College in Naperville, Illinois, offers a useful set of contrasts between traditional and alternative assessments. (See Concept Table 6.1.) Like many educators, Mueller uses the term *authentic* to describe the alternatives.[1]

One other important distinction is that alternative assessments are much less easily *standardized*—making them less useful for many traditional testing purposes. Increasingly, educators prefer alternative assessments, as they match with sociocultural perspectives on learning and they accommodate students' diversity. Yet policymakers tend to favor traditional assessments, partly because they are easier to administer, score, and report over very large groups of students. This tension is a theme that we explore throughout this chapter.

Evaluation, which is usually the end product assessment, is the interpretation of the student's response and a judgment about its quality, value, or worth. Evaluation involves the application of established criteria to determine whether the performance being assessed or tested is *good.* Grades are one example of evaluations, since they convey whether a student has done well, average, or poorly; but they say nothing about the particulars of what he or she has learned.

Test-based accountability refers to the provision of assessment results to officials and the public in order to demonstrate whether schools and teachers have fulfilled their responsibility for using resources to promote student achievement. Increasingly, large-scale student assessments of student achievement are used for accountability by states and the federal government, with the No Child Left Behind Act being the most visible example today.

The History of Educational Testing

Because tests have dominated educational assessment for more than a hundred years and continue to do so, a bit of history is useful for seeing tests as human constructions, created and used in particular contexts, rather than as "natural" or inevitable parts of teaching and learning.

Testing in Early China

Large-scale tests took place in China, starting around 1100 B.C. A system was devised to select the very best people to hold high public office and, thereby, become part of the elite class. By about A.D. 1100, most of the population was eligible to take the exams, although those in a few occupations and their children were excluded, including watchmen, executioners, torturers, laborers, detectives, jailers, coroners, play actors, slaves, beggars, boatpeople, scavengers, and musicians.[2] Throughout the Chinese empire, thousands of candidates took a series of rigorous examinations hoping to qualify for important government posts. Those taking the exams subjected themselves to grueling conditions, as described by anthropology professor F. Allan Hanson in his fascinating analytic history of testing:

> Examinees were crowded into huge, walled compounds that contained thousands of tiny cells. Huddled in his cubicle for three days and two nights, under the scrutiny of guards who prowled the lanes and watched from towers, the candidate would write commentaries on the Confucian classics, compose poetry, and write essays on subjects pertaining to history, politics, and current affairs. No one could enter or leave the compound during an examination, a rule so strictly enforced as to cause certain inconveniences on occasion:
>
> If a candidate died in the middle of an examination, the officials were presented with an annoying problem. The latch bar on the Great Gate was tightly closed and sealed, and since it was absolutely never opened ahead of the schedule, the beleaguered administrators had no alternative but to wrap the body in straw matting and throw it over the wall.[3]

Hanson also reports some of the lore that surrounded the testing process:

> Numerous stories circulated of candidates going insane during the examination, or being visited by ghosts who would confuse and attack them in retaliation for evildoing, or assist them as a reward for some previous act of kindness. Accounts of miraculous events in examinations dramatized the Buddhist principle of preserving all living things: an examiner finally passed a paper he had

twice rejected when, each time he discarded it, three rats brought it back to his desk. It was later ascertained that the candidate's family had not kept cats for three generations. Another candidate received the highest pass after an ant whose life he had saved posed as a missing dot in one of the characters in his essay—a flaw that would have been sufficient for disqualification.[4]

To "pass," candidates had to score well on a sequence of increasingly difficult examinations, each lasting a few days. Very few did. The examinations began as oral assessments and later—about 200 B.C.—became written exams. The topics included law, military, agriculture, finance, geography, and Confucian classics, and handwriting was weighed heavily.[5]

Testing developed much later in the West. Medieval European craft guilds required those seeking to attain the status of master craftsman to submit their work to juries who would judge whether their workmanship qualified them. Similar processes were used in universities where students took oral examinations to prove their mastery of knowledge.

Despite this long history of examinations, educational tests did not appear on the U.S. schooling scene until the mid-nineteenth century, and the technology of large-scale standardized testing was not refined until early in the twentieth century.

Testing in Nineteenth-Century U.S. Schools

In colonial times, teaching and learning was quite individualized, and so was assessment. In small village schools, teachers taught students of all ages, providing different instruction to individuals and small groups. Generally, they knew what their students had learned and what they had not. Students were often called to the schoolmaster's desk individually or in small groups to demonstrate their learning by reciting what they had memorized. Teachers communicated this informally to parents, most of whom they knew well.

Recitations   In the large urban "monitorial" schools in the early 1800s, recitations to demonstrate mastery of knowledge and skills were an established part of the school routine. Monitors under the supervision of the schoolmasters listened to recitations as students marched by their desks. For much of the nineteenth century, the end of the school day was the time for recitation and oral quizzes. And, at the end of each school term, public "recitation days" provided parents and community members a chance to witness what children had learned in spelling, grammar, rapid arithmetic, geographical and historical knowledge, and displays of penmanship.

The quest for efficient and fair ways to assess large numbers of students drove the development of large-scale examinations in nineteenth-century American schools. As schools were divided into grades, the expectation came that all the students in the same grade should master the same material. Visiting examiners conducted annual oral examinations in many city elementary and secondary schools to ascertain whether students should be promoted to the next grade.[6] Those who failed were held back, regardless of their age.

Recitation for Inspectors in a Nineteenth-Century Common School.

Written Examinations   As urban systems grew in the mid-nineteenth century, oral examinations were no longer practical. So, for example, in 1845, when Boston enrolled over 7,000 children in 19 schools, the system turned to written examinations.

> It was our wish to have as fair an examination as possible; to give the same advantages to all; to prevent leading questions; to carry away, not loose notes, or vague remembrances of the examination, but positive information, in black and white; to ascertain with certainty what the scholars did not know, as well as what they did know.[7]

Anthropologist Hanson relays an amusing anecdote about the early administration of written examinations in Boston schools in 1845.

> There were a few practical wrinkles at the beginning. The same test was given in all schools, and although it was printed, it did not occur to the committee to have it administered in all schools simultaneously. Instead they gave it in the schools one at a time, rushing as quickly as possible from one school to the next in an effort to prevent knowledge of the questions reaching some schools before the test did.[8]

Nineteenth-century school leaders saw these examinations as a major advance in American education. In 1845, for example, Horace Mann praised the tests as uniform and impartial tools for evaluating students and schools. Written tests reduced the risks of bias or for teachers' offering suggestions during the exam or showing favoritism to some students. He also welcomed them as a means for permitting a

Huge Classroom Taking Test, San Jose, 1920s.

more thorough understanding of what students have learned and documenting it for evaluation against objective standards.

Systemwide written tests soon became common practice in cities across the nation. Schools in San Diego, California, based students' promotions and graduation on annual exams developed by the county board of education. Teachers gave the tests and graded the students' responses, but the answers were all predetermined, and students had to answer 75 percent of the items correctly to be promoted. When San Diego ended its countywide annual examinations in 1891, the school board authorized teachers to administer exams for promotion.[9] In New York, the statewide Regents exams began in 1878.

Report Cards Nineteenth-century schools also developed more systematic and efficient ways to report the results of tests and other assessments to parents. By the 1890s, teachers were less likely to know their students well, and increasing numbers of parents didn't speak English. So teachers began to report students' accomplishments graphically, with letter grades. Report cards sent home several times a year became standard, and they evolved only slightly over the twentieth century. Most often, teachers assigned letter or number grades in the various subjects, although as the twentieth century proceeded, many schools substituted phrases for grades, for example, "exceeds expectations," "satisfactory," or "needs improvement." Also, schools added comments to describe behaviors such as effort, conduct, and personal habits.[10]

All these forms of assessment relied heavily on behavioral theories of human learning. Recitations and written tests were the "end" of a transmission process in which knowledge began with the sender (teacher) and finished with the receiver (student). This model resembles a straightforward one-directional conduit or pipeline. The process asks the teacher to break down and organize the facts (curriculum and lesson planning), send the facts (teaching), and monitor whether the facts have been received (testing). Although faulty transmission could occur anywhere along the pipeline, the fact that *some* students learned made it seem logical that those who didn't learn well were entirely responsible for their own failures.

The Development of Scientific Testing

Today's professionally developed standardized aptitude and achievement tests are direct descendants of nineteenth- and early-twentieth-century attempts to understand and measure intelligence. As we discussed in Chapter 3, the nineteenth-century fascination with empirical investigation included a "scientific" understanding of humans. Understanding mental functioning was one of the most appealing quests, even though the mind could not be observed directly. In finding ways to represent and measure the mind, and in particular, "intelligence," psychology left its previously philosophical roots and sought to adopt the methods and elevated status of the natural sciences. As history makes clear, this new science of experimental psychology was trapped in the prevailing racism of the time.

Early Behavioral Psychology: Measuring the Observable   The first scientific studies of the human mind were a curious mix of crackpot invention and increasingly sophisticated study of learning and intelligence. Phrenology, for example, represented an attempt to make practical use of an early version of psychological theory. Yes, some believed that they could feel the bumps on one's skull and know something about that person's mental faculties and character traits. But Franz Gall, a noted nineteenth-century phrenologist (a practitioner of bump analysis), combined his nonscience with a systematic study of anatomy. Other investigators studied the brain and brain functions—sometime correctly identifying parts of the brain that had specific functions such as speech or sight.

What is most significant about these studies is that they signaled the beginning of the scientific study of behavior and, eventually, learning. No longer limited to thought scenarios, general scholarship, and study of the classics, scholars were becoming systematic in their observations, recording their findings, and building on, or refuting, the work of other observers.

Throughout the 1800s enthusiasm mounted about the prospect of knowing with precision a person's mental and behavioral characteristics. Might scientists predict who was a person of compassion, a murderer, crazy, intelligent? Could there be certainty about how people come to know (learning), and could they compare their knowledge and reasoning to others (intelligence)? By the end of the century, a new science was born, psychology, focused on investigating the mind and mental processes, including learning. Much early psychology was a blend of folk wisdom, philosophy, anthropology, introspection, and biological science.

Trying to rise above this ill-formed anarchy, psychologists in the early years of the twentieth century strove mightily to bring order and respectability to their discipline. In brief, they wanted a "scientific" field of study. In 1913 American psychologist John Watson argued against an approach being pioneered by European psychologists, where human participants might "cooperate" with investigators by reporting about their mental processes. He maintained that since impartial investigators could not observe the working of the mind, asking people about their own thinking produced unreliable, unscientific information. Therefore, Watson contended that psychologists should stick to examining observable behaviors.[11]

Following Watson's caution, much of psychology in the first half of the twentieth century followed two traditional lines of scientific inquiry: (1) laboratory experiments with animals, often investigating response times and other physiological responses (blood pressure, respiration, eye blinks, etc.), and (2) psychological study with humans that was psychometric, that is, involving tests that could be scored and converted to statistics.

Assessment and testing in nineteenth-century schools had been focused on measuring what and how much knowledge students acquired. Psychologists had somewhat different goals. They wanted to understand the learning process itself and to measure intelligence—the mental power that psychologists believed to govern human capacity to learn. As we describe next, intelligence was of particular interest to psychologists because they wanted to assess the "differences" among people. That is, they were not as interested in whether any one person was intelligent as they were in measuring how much *more* or *less* intelligent various individuals and groups are.

The Science of Intelligence   Charles Darwin (1809–1882) had argued that the human species transmitted intelligence along with other traits, and natural selection favored its most intelligent members. Darwin's nephew, Sir Francis Galton (1822–1911), used Darwin's notions to study how intelligence was revealed in his contemporary times. He gathered data about the British royal family and concluded that intellectual capacity runs in families. He also developed tests of sight, hearing, reaction time, and sensitivity to touch to measure intelligence. Galton's studies were empirical; they relied less on subjective judgments and more on objectively recorded observations. Galton's pursuit of a way to measure inherited abilities sparked a search that dominated psychology in the first decades of the twentieth century.

At the end of the nineteenth century, the American school population swelled. In 1890 only 10 percent of young people pursued schooling beyond the basic primary years. But by 1920 that percentage had nearly quadrupled. Similarly, France had instituted mass education and expanded its educational goals to reach many more students. Both American and French schools continued to educate children from prosperous families who learned easily; at the same time, both countries began struggling to teach children from families who had never attended school and who seemed unable to learn or behave. The French devised a way to help cope with diversity among students—the intelligence test.

The French government asked psychologist Alfred Binet (1857–1911) to devise a test to help schools identify those students who might benefit from greater help and attention in school—thus increasing their chances of succeeding in school. Binet's test included a range of questions designed for different-aged children. An 8-year-old who could pass most of the questions designed for a 12-year-old was said to have a *mental age* of 12. The reverse was true as well—a 12-year-old could have a mental age of 8, thus indicating a child who required special help. Binet cautioned that the test was strictly a screening device, not for use with "normal" children or to be applied broadly in schools.

Americans imported Alfred Binet's intelligence test, although American educators were primarily looking for educational efficiency and were less motivated by sentiments of helpfulness or fairness. Within a few years, the field of psychology made intelligence the cornerstone of a new scientific respectability. Many refinements of Binet's original tests followed, each one giving the test more power in the minds of the test givers and more power over the test takers. A significant change was to report the "result" (e.g., a 5-, 6-, or 7-year-old mental age) as a ratio of mental age to chronological age (actual age in years). Thus, a 6-year-old who scored a mental age of 4 received a score that was the quotient of 4 over 6, or a 67 intelligence quotient (after getting rid of the decimal). A 4-year-old with a mental age of 6 would have an IQ of 150. Of course, the test results did not really say anything more about a child than how many questions he or she could answer relative to other children of the same age. However, the convenient shorthand created the impression that IQ captured the essence of the child's prospects for school achievement, occupational fitness, and adult success.

Once imported to the United States, Binet's test did not remain a neutral device to identify a small population of students. The test immediately linked progress-minded, scientific authority to existing social power and prejudices. At the center of this process were men of high regard in the world of science. Their views and work employed statistical analyses along with novel, often twisted, interpretations of Darwin's evolution theories and those of another profoundly influential scientist, Gregor Mendel (1822–1884), who established principles of biological inheritance. In particular, H. H. Goddard (1866–1957), Lewis Terman (1877–1956), Charles Spearman (1863–1945), and others took theories of evolution and inheritance to fashion a progressively precise and scientific theory of eugenics. *Eugenics* was the use of selective breeding, including who should not be allowed to breed, to improve the mental and moral qualities of the human race.

Intelligence Is Inherited: H. H. Goddard   Prior to World War I, psychologist H. H. Goddard used a version of Binet's tests on youngsters in a large New Jersey mental institution, as well as on their relatives, to explore whether "feeblemindedness" ran in families. His work was responsible for popularizing Binet's ideas in the United States. But Goddard went much further than Binet, by applying Mendel's ideas of biological inheritance to intelligence. Binet's scale provided Goddard a single number to represent how much intelligence a person inherited. Goddard concluded that the poor and criminals had low intelligence—a trait they passed on to their children:

> Our thesis is that the chief determiner of human conduct is a unitary mental
> process which we call intelligence: that this process is conditioned by a nervous

mechanism which is inborn: that the degree of efficiency to be attained by that nervous mechanism and the consequent grade of intellectual or mental level for each individual is determined by the kind of chromosomes that come together with the union of the germ cells: that it is but little affected by any later influences except such serious accidents as may destroy part of the mechanism.

How can there be such a thing as social equality with this wide range of mental capacity?[12]

Low-IQ Children Are Mostly Non-Anglo and Poor: Lewis Terman   Despite Binet's admonitions, educators worked intelligence testing into the very structure and ideology of American schools. Terman, a professor at Stanford University, developed and promoted intelligence tests for U.S. schoolchildren.

Although Terman purported that his Stanford-Binet IQ tests measured innate abilities, the following items taken from one section of his test make clear that children from educated, culturally mainstream families were more likely to earn high IQs:[13]

4. Most exports go from Boston to
   San Francisco New Orleans New York
9. Larceny is a term used in
   Medicine Theology Law Pedagogy
16. A character in
   David Copperfield is Sinbad Uriah Heep Rebecca Hamlet

Because children from nonwhite and poor families scored lower than more socially advantaged ones, Terman used his IQ test results to confirm his view that heredity determined intelligence. He also used the test results to support his advocacy of low-level schooling for those who tested poorly as well as to promote population control among the feebleminded. After testing a group of boys who lived in an orphanage, Terman wrote:

The tests have told the truth. These boys are ineducable beyond the merest rudiments of training. No amount of school instruction will ever make them intelligent voters or capable citizens. . . . Their dullness seems to be racial, or at least inherent in the family stocks from which they came. . . . [O]ne meets this type with such extraordinary frequency among Indians, Mexicans and Negroes. . . . Children of this group should be segregated in special classes and be given instruction which is concrete and practical. . . . There is no possibility at present of convincing society that they should not be allowed to reproduce, although from a eugenic point of view they constitute a grave problem because of their unusually prolific breeding.[14]

Although IQ tests were periodically modified after the 1920s, they would continue to support views similar to Terman's.

IQ Explains Almost Everything: Charles Spearman   Spearman, an English military engineer before he was a psychologist, tested schoolchildren with a wide variety of measures to determine whether people who were good at one thing tended also to be good at others. Through statistical analysis of the results of the tests of different abilities, Spearman inferred an entity that he called *g*, for general intelligence. He conceived of *g* as a kind of inherited energy or power within the brain that activated other entities he called *s*, which referred to more specific abilities for which one could be trained. Without going through Spearman's inventive statistical methods, suffice it to say he made a big mistake. Stephen J. Gould, who does explain the methods very well, calls Spearman's g "the theory of intelligence as a unitary, rankable, genetically based and minimally alterable thing in the head." He also calls it "a bankrupt theory."[15] According to Spearman, in 1927:

> The general conclusion emphasized by nearly every investigator is that as regards "intelligence" the Germanic stock has on the average a marked advantage over the South European. And this result would seem to have had vitally important practical consequences in shaping the recent stringent American laws as to admission of immigrants.[16]

A Prejudicial Construct Becomes a Real Thing   Many late-nineteenth-century scientists were attracted to the study of intelligence because they sought rational and scientific explanations to explain and justify the social class differences between racial and other groups. They had previously traced the lesser merit of the poor and of "other" races to their smaller brains, nefarious eyes, recent descent from apes, parents who were eastern or southern European, or religion.

Very soon, psychometrics—the measurement of mental traits, abilities, and processes—was applied quickly and widely throughout the country. IQ became firmly entrenched as the scientific measure of a real human attribute—the substance or quality of mind that defines the upper limits of learning ability. It had a home: the brain. It had origins: heredity. It was precise: a person could have an IQ of 110 or of 78, and racial groups could, on average, possess more or less. Because psychologists considered intelligence to be a natural endowment—like hair color or height—people were thought to be more or less stuck with the intelligence with which they are born. For many, grounding merit in the concepts of intelligence and achievement—measured by scientifically developed standardized tests—was attractive because it did not upset the prevailing distribution of wealth and privilege.

Attempting to accommodate the role of nurture (parenting, early childhood experiences) as well as nature (inherited abilities), psychologists also argued that families influence whether and how children use their intelligence for learning. Consequently, a highly intelligent child born to a supposedly culturally impoverished family might not blossom intellectually because the parents would not provide intellectual stimulation. By the time children reach age 5 or 6, schools, supposedly, could do little to alter the predetermined upper limits of what these children could accomplish in school. What began as Binet's highly specialized construct and measure (idea and tool) for recognizing severe cognitive deficiencies had become a real thing.

Intelligence had become, in a word, *reified* as IQ and defined as a score on an IQ test. Reified ideas are not real in any material sense. Rather, they are ideas and abstractions about human attributes and behaviors—what social scientists call *constructs.* According to researcher and measurement expert Kenneth Sirotnik, many educational constructs begin as narrowly defined, highly specialized measures that researchers and theorists use for very limited purposes. Then, as these constructs make their way from research to professional journals and teacher preparation programs to popular media to the everyday talk of policymakers and the public, they lose their narrow definitions and specialized uses. "Pretty soon," Sirotnik notes, "people talk and make decisions about other people's *intelligence, achievement,* and *self-concept* as if these attributes really existed in the same sense as, for example, people's height and weight."[17]

Sirotnik argues that this reification (treating abstract social constructs as if they have concrete, material reality) distorts people's thinking about education. Once reified, categories such as "gifted," "high ability," "average," and "retarded," whether they began with specific and technical definitions or as loose and informal concepts, become deeply embedded features of students' identities—in both their own and others' minds. Often, educators and others fail to examine the origins and limits of the specialized meanings of these labels, and they exaggerate and overinterpret them. The dangers of intelligence-related constructs have plagued makers and users of intelligence and similar tests from their beginning.

For example, in 1927 Harper and Brothers published a book, *Tisn't What You Know, But Are You Intelligent?* The book's back cover proclaims, "Rate yourself on the actual tests used in the Department of Applied Physiology at Yale University."[18] The preface explains that intelligence is the "capability to do productive thinking" and that intelligence is not knowledge, but "an inborn capacity of the mind." In the section on feeblemindedness, the author declares, "By the principle of heredity, two feebleminded parents have nothing but feebleminded children and usually in large numbers."[19] Although no claims are made about the racial basis of intelligence, there are some rather amazing assertions about gender:

> The introduction of a strain of low mentality into an intelligent family sometimes shows up in later generations. This strain of feeblemindedness is usually introduced into the family on the female side. This statement is not one of misogyny. Its reason lies in the fact that many of the qualities in the male which make him a desirable mate, his abilities and his earning capacity for example, are related to intelligence. These qualities are not always expected in the female. A girl of moron intelligence may have the physical beauty and grace that lead quickly to matrimony even though her conversation is limited to, "I've had a perfectly glorious time"; "Isn't it too wonderful"; "You dear"; and, "Oh, anything you say—!"[20]

The book consists of intelligence tests and a preface by a Yale psychologist explaining the concept of intelligence. A table provides the intelligence ratings that correspond with the test scores and a list of the average number of correct answers given by members of different occupations—from laborers at the bottom with "low average intelligence" to accountants and doctors at the top with "superior intelligence."

What were the questions on the Yale tests like? Much like those included in Terman's early tests, and, perhaps not surprising, some are quite a lot like the questions that turn up on today's aptitude tests like the SAT. Here are some examples:

1. It is wiser to save some money and not spend it all, so that you may (a) gamble when you wish? (b) prepare for old age and sickness? (c) collect all the different kinds of money?
2. How long will it take a man to walk 42 miles if he walks at the rate of 3 miles per hour?
3. The Percheron is a kind of (a) goat, (b) horse, (c) cow, (d) sheep.[21]

IQ and Scientific Schooling   As we described in Chapter 5, educators found great use for behavioral psychology and intelligence tests. It helped make education more scientific at a time when being scientific brought increased respectability and higher status. Psychologists and educators alike agreed that scientific tests enabled teachers to address students' particular mental capacities and prepare them for particular social roles based on those capacities.

The American public bought into the idea that IQ and IQ tests gave educators an expert's authority to measure any student's capacity for thinking and learning. For several decades, group IQ tests were routinely given to American students as the basis of determining their intellectual potential and assigning them to "appropriate" classes and programs.

As this brief account makes clear, the twentieth-century Western world invented a peculiar way of thinking about a person's capacity for learning: Intelligence represented an upper limit, a ceiling, on how successful a student might become. Especially important for Americans who always must balance democratic equality with the preservation of privilege, the tests appeared to be scientific and fair: The same tests were administered under the same conditions, with impartial mathematical formulas used to produce the final representation of a person's intelligence. In an even more potent development, groups of children now could be compared by averaging individual intelligence quotients. Such averaging gave the broader society an explanation and justification for inequalities across many social domains beyond education, including income, jobs, housing, healthy lifestyles, and so forth.

As we discussed in Chapter 2, the idea of IQ remains a powerful construct in contemporary society. The serious reception given to the 1994 book, *The Bell Curve: Intelligence and Class Structure in American Life,* claiming that African Americans disadvantaged circumstances stem, in part, from lower inherited IQ, is just one example of how persistent such deficit ideas are, despite the considerable advances in our understanding of intelligence and learning that we'll discuss later in this chapter.

Contemporary Large-Scale Testing

In recent years, the widespread use of IQ tests in school has fallen into disfavor. When they are used today, for example for identifying students with special needs, they are used far more carefully than in the past. However, IQ tests have also spawned large-scale aptitude and achievement tests—the SAT, ACT, and a wide array of tests of basic skills tests that are simply variations of the IQ tests themselves. Like IQ tests, these contemporary tests shape judgments about students' abilities, and they play an important role in rank ordering students and deciding what their future schooling opportunities will be. So, although most students today are unlikely to be tested for IQ, their schools will have something very similar by which to judge them.

Although it is difficult to obtain exact data on the extent of standardized testing in schools, an estimate in 1990 of 200 million per year probably vastly underestimates the number of standardized tests given today.[22] The nation looks to scores on such tests as the single most important indicator of whether students and schools are doing well.

In addition to state and local tests, the National Assessment of Educational Progress (NAEP) is a national test that every few years provides new data and trend lines to document the educational achievement of American students. Recently, the NAEP test has been nicknamed "the nation's report card," and when the NAEP scores are released, they make the front page of newspapers across the county. International tests, given once a decade, provide rankings of nations according to how well their students do in reading, writing, math, and science.

All of the scores make headlines. Federal officials decry the nation's standing in international math and science tests; state policymakers proclaim a crisis when their state's achievement scores are lower than other states; federal and state government threatens to withhold funds when a school's test scores indicate that it is "low-performing"; the real estate salesperson compares the local school's test scores; advantaged parents trumpet high-achieving scores as irrefutable proof of their children's merit.

Standardized Testing

Today's standardized tests follow the same logic and statistical procedures in their design that were pioneered by IQ test developers. They are all designed to obtain a "sample" of students' behavior that will allow more global judgments about their ability, in terms of either general aptitudes or particular subject areas. As *standardized* tests, they are uniformly developed, administered, and scored, so that all individuals are assessed under the same conditions. In their development, they have met technical requirements of test *validity* and *reliability*. If the test is not administered according to the standard conditions, the results are invalid.

Also, like IQ tests, most of these tests compare a students' performance with that of other students of their same age or grade. That means that the score on the test reports, not what or how much a student actually knows, but how well the student did in relation to the performance of other students. However, a new breed of achievement tests, developed in conjunction with curriculum standards, compares students' performance against a fixed standard. We describe these tests later in this chapter.

Norm-Referenced Standardized Tests   Like IQ tests, most standardized tests are *norm referenced;* that is, the test development process included a national sample of students—called the "norm" group. The scores of this group comprise the standard against which the performance of subsequent test takers is compared. The scores on norm-referenced tests don't reveal what or how much a student actually knows, but, instead, tell how he or she compares to the norm group.

There is no good, everyday synonym for "norm," probably because most people are not accustomed to thinking in strictly statistical terms, and that's what a norm is—a statistical artifact that combines some elements of "normal," or "usual," or perhaps, "most common," but it is really quite different from these ideas. For example,

500 on the SAT is an average score, just like 100 on an IQ test. A student's percentile score tells what percentage of the "norm group" he or she did better than; someone who scores in the 80th percentile got more answers correct than 79 percent of the students in the norm group. Grade-level scores work the same way. A student who scores at grade level did about as well as the average person in his or her grade, but someone who is above grade level did better than most of his or her peers.

Because norm-referenced tests need to be able to place students precisely within their peer groups, the tests are designed to spread the scores out over a wide range. That way, there will be enough difference among test takers to rank them. Therefore, the tests must be constructed so that most people score in the average range, with fewer getting scores above and below average, and even fewer at the two extremes. This is why the scores on these tests can be described with a *bell curve*. The large number of average scores form the highest point of the bell, and the smaller number of extremely high and low scores flatten out the curve on either side.

Aptitude Tests   The SAT (formerly known as the Scholastic Aptitude Test) and the ACT, the American College Testing Program's college admissions test, are *aptitude* tests. Their goal and claim is to predict how a student is likely to perform in the future. Specifically, both of these tests are used to predict the grades that high school students will earn when they get to college.

The SAT and the ACT have some questions that are closely aligned with the school curriculum, but, like IQ tests, they purport to measure very general knowledge and skills. The SAT argues, for example, that studying for the test is not really worthwhile because the test measures very general competencies—verbal and mathematics aptitudes—not specific subject knowledge. On their website, the College Board that administers the SAT cautions:

> Coaching companies' current estimates of the benefits of coaching for the SAT are much too high. Coached students are only slightly more likely to have large score gains than uncoached students. In addition, about 1/3 of students experience no score gain or score loss following coaching.[23]

In short, as aptitude tests, the SAT and ACT tests claim to predict future school success, but they do not claim to measure accurately what students have learned.

The following SAT "mathematical reasoning" question is an example of the blending of school knowledge (math), reading ability (with a focus on vocabulary), cultural knowledge (familiarity with playing cards, and perhaps prior experience solving problems for no practical reason), and reasoning:

> Seven cards in a pile are numbered 1 through 7. One card is drawn. The units digit of the sum of the numbers on the remaining cards is 7. What is the number of the drawn card? (The choices are numbers 1, 3, 5, 6, or 7.)[24]

Achievement Tests   Most standardized achievement tests assess how well students have acquired knowledge and mastered certain skills that are taught in school, compared with others at the same grade. However, because many of these tests have important reading comprehension components, such as the CTBS and the Iowa Test of Basic Skills, they measure very similar skills as the SAT. In fact, since scores on reading comprehension tests typically correlate strongly with scores on IQ tests, the reading tests are often used to substitute for IQ tests. In other words, a high reading score is taken to mean high general ability—just as a high score on an IQ test is taken to mean high intelligence. This includes kindergarten reading readiness or prereading tests.

Claims Made for Standardized Tests   Standardized tests rely on a particular "technology"—a defined set of practices, rules, and standards for test construction and administration. Whether norm referenced or standards based, standardized tests claim to be objective, valid, and reliable.

Objectivity in testing means that the answers or judgments are not open to interpretation, bias, or dispute and that test performances can be reduced to statistical representations, such as scores, grades, and averages. The scoring process should guard against the influence of irrelevant factors (e.g., background, language, etc.) or personal bias. Most of all, an objective test should provide each student with a fair opportunity to show what he or she has learned.

Test *validity* refers to whether the information being collected and analyzed is trustworthy for the assessment purpose. Does a high score mean that the student is really good at what is being measured? Will it lead to correct decisions? Does it provide information about all important aspects of the performance being assessed? Does the format allow students to show what they can do? Do the instructions make clear what the student is expected to do?

Reliability refers to whether the results of the assessment can be trusted to be consistent. Will the results be similar if the assessment is repeated at another time? Will the score be the same if another person administers or scores the test? Do students answer questions seeking to measure the same knowledge or skill consistently?

Critiques of Standardized Tests   Standardized tests have become increasingly controversial, even as they continue to be the most influential assessments in American schools. The most serious criticisms are that these tests are out of step with contemporary scholarship on learning, and they share the misuses and abuses of their highly discredited ancestor—the IQ test. Of course, test makers and sophisticated users would claim that abuses stemming from standardized tests are not *inevitable*. Unfortunately, although the better tests can provide sophisticated and highly nuanced information, in the real world of schools and politics, tests are very blunt tools, indeed. It is extraordinarily difficult to find a school district that actually complies with testing experts' and the test makers' own recommendations for how the tests should be used. Policymakers are inclined to be ignorant of the problems inherent in standardized testing or to make excuses for why these flawed instruments are better than alternatives.

Reflect Flawed Theories of Learning   Standardized tests embody nineteenth-century behavioral psychological theories and ignore much new scholarship on learning as sense-making and connecting new information and experience to what is already learned. The assumption behind the use of standardized tests is that the student acquires a fixed body of knowledge that has been transmitted by a teacher, and that learning (the knowledge already acquired or a prediction of future learning) can be represented by selecting a predetermined right answer. Other assumptions for using tests are that knowledge can be broken up into small bits that can be assessed bit by bit and that learning can be assessed accurately in a situation with a *test giver*—powerful with knowledge and licensed to judge others—and a *test taker*—without power and submitting to judgment. As testing expert Robert Mislevy succinctly put it in 1993, "The essential problem is that the view of human abilities implicit in standard test theory . . . is incompatible with the view rapidly emerging from cognitive and educational psychology."[25]

Grounded in the Flawed Logic and Technology of IQ Tests   Rather than seeing learning abilities as global attributes, scholars now generally believe that intellectual competence is a far richer and deeper collection of abilities than the technology of standardized testing can measure and explain.

Yale psychologist Robert Sternberg, for example, argues that the most important intelligence for success at school and on the job is poorly revealed by standardized IQ-like tests. Further, many of these skills and intellectual processes can be taught "to at least some of the people, some of the time."[26] Howard Gardner offers evidence that the kind of intelligence that IQ represents—and that many of today's standardized tests measure—pales in importance compared with other, more reflective mental processes. Gardner suggests the most successful corporate CEO, schoolteacher, or surgeon may have gotten the best test scores in school, but neither school success nor standardized tests typically predict one's ability to seize a business opportunity, ask a good question at just the right moment, or hold a scalpel steady.[27]

Critiques levied at the technology of standardized tests often focus on the presumption of the "bell curve" that underlies their construction. As we noted earlier, like IQ tests, standardized aptitude and achievement tests are designed to produce a wide range of scores; that's the only way that people can be ranked and grouped into percentiles. So the test makers must develop and include items that range from easy to very difficult to answer. As a result, the tests don't show what the test takers have learned about the subjects being tested. Finally, the questions that do the best job of *distinguishing* or separating different test takers—especially those who get higher scores—are those that few people know the answers to. As a result, life decisions and opportunities can be unduly influenced by one's possession of arcane and rarified facts that have little real-life import.

Embody Cultural Biases   Scholars almost universally agree that IQ and standardized test scores do not provide evidence that people of different cultural groups or races inherit more or less ability. Because different cultures provide children with different learning situations, and because they value the mastery of different tasks, it is unimaginable that a standardized test, useful for schooling purposes, could be designed to work *across* cultures. Much attention has been given to so-called *culturally sensitive* or *appropriate* standardized tests, but these represent faulty notions of culture as much as they suggest inflated ambitions for the tests.

Poverty and oppressive social conditions (factors that do vary in the United States according to race) significantly relate to people's performance on IQ and other standardized tests, but that is more reflective of those conditions than of intelligence. In a cross-cultural example of this, Jerome Bruner reports on the interplay between social conditions and IQ: Korean immigrants to Japan score 15 points lower on average on IQ tests in Japan than Korean immigrants score in the United States. Bruner attributes this gap to the two cultures' treatment of the Korean immigrants: In Japan, they are denigrated as ignorant; in the United States, they are stereotyped as smart.[28]

Moreover, Stephen J. Gould details the scientific and statistical flaws of intelligence testing and traces the links between IQ, bigotry, and oppression in his richly documented history *The Mismeasure of Man.*[29] Yet, these same problems plague many of the tests that today show gaps between racial groups in aptitudes and abilities. Even those tests that purport to measure what's been taught at school are usually what analysts call "instructionally insensitive." That is, they tell more about students' economic status and culture than about what students have learned at school.

Middle-class Americans often associate problem-solving speed with intelligence, and speed is a prized attribute when taking most standardized tests; Ugandan villagers, however, describe intelligence with words such as *slow* and *careful.* The Chinese place a high value on the ability to memorize facts; Australians consider this trivial. Middle-class Americans consider intelligence to encompass technical and abstract skills; Kenyans and Maylans see intelligence as comprising social and personal responsibility as well as cognitive skills. Ugandans and the Ifaluk people of the western Pacific consider intelligence to include both knowing socially responsible actions *and* actually acting that way. Interestingly, this global tour exposes different learning *values* that we all share. So the pressure to succeed on narrow, fact-based, speed-prized standardized tests can burden anyone in a culture that uses standardized testing to judge or quantify intelligence.

Standards-Based Testing

Many of the more recent achievement tests, particularly those administered by states, are intended to determine whether students have become proficient on the state standards. Although they are not constructed to compare students to one another, aggregated scores are inevitably used to compare and even rank schools. Unlike general aptitude tests or basic skills tests, these tests purport to measure whether students have acquired the knowledge in the curriculum for their grade level. Tests that compare student performance against a standard of particular knowledge and facts are called *criterion-referenced* tests, or more recently, just standards-based tests.

Students' test performances are reported as whether or not they've reached a level of mastery of the standards, such as *below basic, basic, proficient,* and *advanced.* Unlike norm-referenced tests that require a spread of scores from highest to lowest, it is possible with standards-based tests that all students or none will score at a particular level. The federal No Child Left Behind legislation requires all students to reach the proficient level in reading and mathematics on their state test by the year 2014.

The following is a sample question from a standards-based test, in this case the New York State's Regents test in biology:

> The excretory organelles of some unicellular organisms are contractile vacuoles and
> A) Cell membranes
> B) Cell walls
> C) Ribosomes
> D) Centrioles
> (Study guide for the 1995 New York Regents test in high school biology)

The question is technical and specific, it seems intellectually challenging, and it appears to be measuring knowledge contained in the state's biology standards.

Even though standards-based tests avoid some of the problems of norm-referenced standardized tests, they, too, are seriously flawed. They focus narrowly on limited academic goals and do a poor job of measuring them. Further, instruction must prepare students to understand the subjects in a way that produces good results within the traditional and narrow testing format. To a large degree, this creates pressure for teachers and schools to continue their traditional teaching methods, a subject we'll delve into in Chapter 11.

Most standards-based assessments are paper-and-pencil tests consisting of traditional items in which students either select or supply a predetermined correct response. As a result, although items like the preceding biology question may seem intellectually challenging, they display what researcher Linda Darling-Hammond calls "trappings of intellectual rigor." Like the school examinations of the nineteenth century, this question measures nothing more than whether a student has memorized definitions of words unique to the discipline (i.e., *organelles, ribosomes*). Darling-Hammond argues that the tests actually crowd out students' opportunities and motivation for making knowledge meaningful and useful.[30] Such questions do not measure whether students actually understand and can do science at all.

A second problem with standards-based tests is that most states have established far too many standards for any test to measure. That means, the test results don't provide any overall sense of which standards students have met and which they have not. High scores only mean that students could answer questions correctly about those standards that were represented on the test. Together, these two problems mean that inferences about whether students have actually met the standards are based on insufficient information.

A final problem with standards-based tests is that they are used increasingly to make decisions about students and schools that carry with them serious consequences. Students can be retained in grade and denied high school diplomas; schools can be reconstituted or taken over by the state. Despite all the critiques, in the past decade, the "high stakes" attached to standards-based tests have become the single most popular policy instrument for raising academic standards in schools. We will return to these standards-based testing policies and their effects in Chapter 11.

Professional Guidelines for Using Large-Scale Tests

In 1999, the American Educational Research Association, American Psychological Association, and National Council on Measurement in Education came together to develop professional standards to guide the use of standardized tests. (See Focal Point 6.1.) These guidelines seek to set limits on the tests so that their flaws, described in the complaints above, don't harm the individuals being tested or contribute to unwarranted educational decisions.

Although testing experts have universally endorsed these standards, they have not been effective in halting some of the harmful practices experts cite. As we discuss in Chapter 11, for example, policies in more than 30 states currently use a single "high-stakes" graduation test as the basis for denying high school diplomas. In some states, English learners must take tests in English, and test accommodations for students with special needs are lacking.

Large-Scale Alternative Assessment

Over the past two decades, assessment experts have sought to develop large-scale tests that match current conceptions of learning and intelligence and avoid the problems with traditional tests. Although some have the goal of eliminating traditional standardized tests altogether, most seek to augment conventional tests with multiple ways to assess learning. Some of these development efforts have shown great promise, but they have also been plagued with practical, technical, and political problems—problems serious enough to severely limit the use of large-scale alternative assessments.

In the 1990s, California, Kentucky, Maryland, and Vermont all developed alternative assessment strategies as part of their state testing programs. In California and Maryland, for example, students wrote essays and laboratory reports, and explained their mathematical reasoning instead of taking multiple-choice tests. Vermont and Kentucky had students do group activities, conduct hands-on science tasks, and use tools and manipulatives. They developed portfolios of their work and identified what they thought were the best examples of their work. In some states, teachers helped score these assessments; in others, professional contractors did the scoring.

Although teachers generally liked these new assessments because they fit better with complex curriculum and multidimensional teaching, they consumed far more of students' classroom time than traditional standardized tests and cost more to develop, administer, and score. The fact that these assessments had far fewer actual "items" than multiple-choice tests raised technical questions about whether they could actually measure validly a broad enough scope of the academic subjects they were assessing. Some critics raised concerns that the administration (wording of the instructions, time limits, etc.) of these assessments couldn't be standardized as well as multiple-choice tests, so they might not be fair. The performance assessments also turned out to be difficult to score. In Vermont, for example, different scorers didn't always rate students' performances in the same way, compromising the reliability of the scores. In Maryland and California, strong

FOCAL POINT 6.1

Standards for Educational and Psychological Testing

In 1999, the American Psychological Association, the American Educational Research Association, and the National Council on Measurement in Education created a set of professional standards for *educational and psychological testing*. These standards set out several important principles designed to promote fairness in testing and avoid unintended consequences. They include:

- Any decision about a student's continued education, such as retention, tracking, or graduation, should not be based on the results of a single test, but should include other relevant and valid information.
- When test results substantially contribute to decisions made about student promotion or graduation, there should be evidence that the test addresses only the specific or generalized content and skills that students have had an opportunity to learn.
- For tests that will determine a student's eligibility for promotion to the next grade or for high school graduation, students should be granted, if needed, multiple opportunities to demonstrate mastery of materials through equivalent testing procedures.
- When a school district, state, or some other authority mandates a test, the ways in which the test results are intended to be used should be clearly described. It is also the responsibility of those who mandate the test to monitor its impact, particularly on racial and ethnic-minority students or students of lower socioeconomic status, and to identify and minimize potential negative consequences of such testing.
- In some cases, special accommodations for students with limited English proficiency may be necessary to obtain valid test scores. If students with limited English skills are to be tested in English, their test scores should be interpreted in light of their limited English skills.
- Likewise, special accommodations may be needed to ensure that test scores are valid for students with disabilities. Not enough is currently known about how particular test modifications may affect the test scores of students with disabilities; more research is needed. As a first step, test developers should include students with disabilities in field testing of pilot tests and document the impact of particular modifications (if any) for test users.

Source: American Educational Research Association, American Psychological Association, and National Council on Measurement in Education. *Standards for Educational and Psychological Testing* (Washington, DC: American Educational Research Association, 1999).

political objections were raised to the practice of only giving a few performance tasks to each child and then assigning the scores to schools, rather than giving each child a score.

In all of these states, concerns were raised about the lack of national norms for alternative assessments, which meant that they couldn't compare the performance of their children to those in other states. In some cases, California, for example, the charge was also lodged that the nontraditional performance items pried too deeply into students' personal beliefs and paid too little attention to their mastery of core knowledge.

Each of these states has now reverted to their former practice of using more conventional standardized tests, including norm-referenced tests, in their state assessment systems.

Contemporary Classroom Assessment

—⚙ ⚙ ⚙—

I have come to believe that assessment is one of the most overlooked challenges, especially if one departs from the multiple-choice/pencil-and-paper/procedural tests that are nicely provided in the Teacher's Edition. Do I just walk around the room and give grades based on content of discussion? How do I respond to the author of a journal entry who already understood the concept versus the hardworking author who finally achieved some degree of understanding? Do I respond differently? Will it take me a solid week to grade the test with open-ended questions? What if a good student does a poor job when editing another student's paper? How do I use the results of assessments to guide my teaching or grade student achievement?

As a new teacher, I tried a variety of methods to begin learning how to assess my students' mathematical understanding and use the information to inform my instructional practices. I used writing as an assessment tool as much as I could. Students had to write about their process of solving the problem. Strategies, false starts, steps they took, diagrams that helped—all these items and more were part of the process about which I wanted students to write. Not only did I want to know what they were doing and why, I wanted them to have to reason and justify their thought process. I did learn an incredible amount about how students think about mathematics. By giving students an opportunity to articulate their internal thought processes, I was able to assess understanding of the problem. I could identify strengths or weaknesses in their logic and help them, or comment accordingly.

—JULIANA JONES
First-year teacher, middle-school mathematics

In the midst of all the current attention to large-scale assessments, it is important to remember that most of the assessments that students experience are chosen or made by their teachers and are administered in their classrooms. In the remainder of this chapter, we turn to the day-in and day-out assessment practices that teachers use in classrooms. Doing so, we return to the social and cultural conceptions of intelligence and learning we described in Chapter 5. We also revisit the concept of alternative assessments. We offer examples of how assessment can support the work of teachers who see learning as social and cultural, who reject the traditional conception of intelligence, and who are changing classroom assessment traditions.

Shifting from Traditional to Alternative Classroom Assessments

Since the dawn of behavioral psychology and scientific testing more than a century ago, classroom teachers have used assessment to gather samples of students' knowledge in order to make inferences about the extent to which they have learned the whole curriculum. Like behavioral psychologists, teachers have focused their assessments on what they could observe *after* learning has taken place—whether students can recall what they've learned—and, they have paid less attention to processes that occur at the moment of learning. Their methods mimicked large-scale tests with teacher-made tests and those taken from textbooks typically including multiple-choice, true/false, and fill-in-the blank items.

Like commercial test makers, teachers call such tests "objective." However, teachers' decisions to include particular questions, the grading scale, the amount of time given for instruction and to take the test, and the weight or importance given to the test are all subjective decisions. In the classroom, teachers typically do not have formal "norm" groups against which to judge their students' performances, but they may have an informal protocol (or "curve") for giving the top few performances A's and the lowest scores D's and F's—based as much on how the class as a whole performs as on the student's actual number of correct answers.

Of course, teachers have also always used assessment strategies that we now call "alternative" or "authentic," scrutinizing students' essays, performance, and projects to assess how well students can apply what they've learned. But, in the tradition of scientific efficiency and behaviorism, these assessments have often been treated as samples of students' knowledge that can be objectified. Thus, the teacher's reading of the essay test may be translated into points (87), the points into a grade (B plus), the grade into a class grade (B), which goes back into points before it can be averaged into a grade point average.

Principles to Guide Assessments That Promote Learning

Despite the long tradition of behavioral forms of classroom assessment and all of today's pressures around standardized testing, many teachers are turning to alternative assessment practices that match new theories of intelligence and learning. To help with this shift, the National Forum on Assessment, a coalition of education and civil rights organizations, came together in 1995 to develop a set of principles to guide assessment. Although they hoped to influence large-scale testing programs, their primary commitment was to help educators make classroom assessment consistent with new understandings of student learning, to integrate assessment with curriculum and instruction, and to make sure that assessments are fair to all of the nation's diverse students.

Concept Table 6.2 includes the seven principles of assessment that the Forum believed would help achieve these goals.

CONCEPT TABLE 6.2 *Principles of High-Quality Assessment Systems*

	Principles	Characteristics and Actions
1	Assessments' primary purpose is to improve student learning.	• Organized around improving student learning. • Provides information about students' progress toward learning goals. • Employs practices and methods consistent with curriculum, instruction, and learning. • Integrates with curriculum and instruction. • Uses methods such as structured and informal observations and interviews, projects and tasks, tests, performances and exhibitions, audio and videotapes, experiments, portfolios, and journals. • Limits use of multiple-choice methods. • Limits use of assessments intended to rank order or compare students.
2	Assessment used for other purposes also supports student learning.	• Bases important decisions, such as graduation, on information gathered over time, not a single assessment. • Uses information for accountability and improvement that comes from both regular, continuing classroom work and from large-scale assessments. • Uses sampling procedures in accountability assessments to minimize burden on students. • Applies rigorous technical standards to ensure high quality assessments. • Monitors the educational consequences of the particular assessment tools.
3	Assessment systems are fair to all students.	• Doesn't limit students' present and future opportunities. • Allows for multiple methods for students to express knowledge and understanding. • Reflects a student's actual knowledge. • Is adapted to meet the specific needs of particular populations, such as English language learners and students with disabilities. • Uses methods that student have been taught. • Studied and approved by bias review committees.
4	Professional collaboration and development support assessment.	• Helps educators understand the full range of assessment purposes. • Helps educators use a variety of methods appropriately. • Ensures that educators collaborate. • Has the support of states, districts, and schools. • Improves educators' capability as assessors. • Prepares teachers to assess diverse student populations. • Allows educators to score student work at the district or state levels.

(continued)

CONCEPT TABLE 6.2 *(continued)*

	Principles	Characteristics and Actions
5	The broader community participates in assessment development.	• Draws on the community's knowledge. • Includes parents, community members, and students in the development of the system. • Discusses assessment purposes and methods with wide range of people who help shape the assessment system.
6	Communication about assessment is regular and clear.	• Educators discuss assessment system practices and student and program progress with students, families, and the community. • Educators (and experts) communicate, in ordinary language, assessment purposes, methods, and results. • Reports provide information about what students know and are able to do, what they need to learn to do, and what will be done to facilitate improvement. • Reports discuss achievement in terms of agreed-upon learning goals. • Reports are translated as needed. • Reports include examples of assessments and high-quality student work. • Reports include contextual information such as education programs, social data, resource availability, and other student outcomes.
7	Assessment systems are regularly reviewed and improved.	• Seek to make assessments more educationally beneficial to all students. • Adapt to changing conditions and increased knowledge. • Focus cost-benefit analyses of the system on the effects of assessment on learning.

Source: National Forum on Assessment, *Principles and Indicators for Student Assessment Systems*, FairTest: The National Center for Fair and Open Testing, 1991, http://www.fairtest.org/princind.htm.

Undergirded by these principles, classroom assessments can promote learning and social justice because they support students' beliefs that their hard work will result in learning. The assessments can reinforce instruction that is increasingly rich, complex, and full of meaning and enhance lessons that offer authentic tasks with a variety of routes to success. Further, such assessments help teachers avoid the easy comparisons made possible by grades, numbers, and rankings, which everyone in the classroom and throughout the school can transform into destructive judgments about who is smart and who isn't. The remainder of the chapter shows how teachers are using assessments in just these ways.

Assessments That Promote Learning

High school social studies teacher Judy Smith uses assessment throughout her lessons to enhance learning, not just at the end to see what students have learned. For example, she began her global economics unit on sweatshops by assessing what her students already knew.

---—❈ ❈ ❈—---

I introduced students to the concept of sweatshops by having their teams analyze pictures and cartoons of sweatshops. During this "write around" activity, the students analyzed the pictures, wrote comments, questions, thoughts, and feelings about what was in the picture. When they finished, each group explained the images to the class. Then, on the back of the "write around" sheet, I asked, "Now that you have an image of a sweatshop, how would you describe one? What goes on in a sweatshop?" We played with the word sweatshop *and with the interpretations of the pictures. Students wrote for a while as a way to learn and understand more from the images, their group's knowledge, and classroom discussion.*

This informal assessment of their prior knowledge was useful to me. I learned that the students had very little knowledge about actual sweatshop conditions although they did gain some initial impressions.

—Judy Smith
High school social studies

During the unit, Judy constantly assessed her students' learning. On one occasion, she asked them to write a letter to a CEO of a company that supports sweatshops, so that she could assess how the students' knowledge about global economics was developing.

In another example, first-year history teacher Jennifer Garcia uses concept maps to simultaneously push her students' thinking about the content and gather good information about what her students know and need to know.

---------------------------------⊗ ⊗ ⊗---------------------------------

*I used concept maps in a variety of circumstances—from a quick compre-
hension check to an alternative way of assessing at the end of my unit on
World War I and Progressive Politics. Concept maps allow teachers (and
students) to determine whether critical historical connections are being
made. They test comprehension, not facts, and focus on what students know
and the connections they can make, instead of what they don't know. They
ask students to demonstrate historical understandings at a deeper level
than a more traditional objective form of assessment (i.e., multiple choice,
matching) because they must relate concepts to each other.*

   *One student, for example, connected the events of World War I pre–U.S.
involvement to events in World War I post–U.S. involvement. However, his
concept map told me that while he was able to recall many specifics from this
historical period, he did not address the larger concepts.*

   *This format leaves plenty of room for individual differences; students
realize that there is no one "correct" answer and that there is room for
individual interpretation and analysis. Allowing for this type of
maximum freedom (as much as is possible in a formal assessment
situation) allows students of all abilities and types of intelligence to
succeed academically.*

—**JENNIFER GARCIA**
First-year teacher, history, grade 11

Assessment that promotes learning is not limited to traditional academic content. Mauro Bautista used assessment throughout a college and careers unit he
taught his middle-school students who were still learning English. Many of his
students had high career aspirations, and Mauro wanted to be sure they had the
knowledge they needed to navigate successfully toward their goals. He also
designed the unit to meet his school district's language arts standards. As he introduced the unit, he began with a lesson that engaged students in writing about
careers and allowed him to assess what his students already knew about careers.

---------------------------------⊗ ⊗ ⊗---------------------------------

*Taking into account that students are generally more engaged when their in-
terests guide instruction, the "big idea" in this lesson was to identify my students' career goals, so that their interests could guide the rest of the unit. I
asked students to answer the following question in a free write: Where will
your life be in 15 years? Students had the option of using their home language to document their ideas in detail.*

Mauro provided scaffolding to his students to support their efforts to develop their
knowledge, even as he was assessing it.

---------------------------------⊗ ⊗ ⊗---------------------------------

*I provided the following support questions: What occupation do you want to
have in fifteen years? Why do you want to have that occupation? Do you*

know anyone who has that occupation? If yes, who? What do you need to do in order to have that occupation? These questions helped me further assess what students knew about their future career goals.

—**Mauro Bautista**
Middle-school bilingual education coordinator

Mauro noted that very few of his students understood that they would need to pursue higher education if they wanted to achieve their dreams of being teachers, doctors, and architects. He used that information to design learning activities that would allow them to both understand and feel competent about what they needed to do, and he assessed their developing knowledge at every step of the process.

In each of these examples, assessment is seamlessly integrated with students' learning; that is, assessment is indistinguishable from the scaffolding by which the student and teacher co-construct the student's knowledge. These assessments focus on the moment of learning, rather than on what students can do afterward.

Assessments That Provide Multiple Routes to Success

In Chapter 5, we described multidimensional instruction that allows students to learn and demonstrate their learning in multiple ways. We provided the list of characteristics of multidimensional tasks that researcher Elizabeth Cohen derived from research. We repeat that list here, as these are the very characteristics of assessments that allow for student differences and avoid narrow definitions of competence or mastery. Assessments that provide multiple routes to success

- include more than one answer or more than one way to solve the problem;
- are intrinsically interesting and rewarding;
- allow different students to make different contributions;
- use multimedia;
- involve sight, sound, and touch;
- require a variety of skills and behaviors;
- require reading and writing; and
- are challenging.

The examples that Cohen gives of instructional tasks are equally good examples of assessments—role playing, building models, drawing a "mind map" of the relationship among ideas, and discovering and describing relationships by manipulating equipment or objects. Many of these strategies are used by the teachers we cite here. For example, Jennifer Garcia describes the open-ended task she used to assess her student understanding of important historical concepts and events.

———————————————— ⊗ ⊗ ⊗ ————————————————

I created a demonstration project assessment to assess students' historical understandings of the connections between the concepts of industrialization, unionism, and immigration (i.e., how they could tie together themes such as immigration trends, political machines, early union efforts, factory conditions, production changes, changes in gender roles, etc.). I did not set limits on the format, but I suggested some possible ideas.

Students created immigrant journals, posters and advertisements, and original songs that showed they were able to incorporate both the historical evidence and creativity and originality at a deeper intellectual level. In the immigrant journals, students assumed the persona of an immigrant who came to the United States during the 1880s. Common themes included descriptions of what countries they immigrated from, why they immigrated, their immigration journey, the processing (Ellis Island), living conditions in urban areas, factory working conditions (union vs. nonunion), and so on.

These journals were not re-creations or copies of texts/outside resources— they were original stories that students developed from lectures and their impressions of what experiences real people went through. This was a new form of assessment for many students and I was unsure about how seriously students would take it. I was impressed with the success, particularly for those who do not test well. I learned that it is a good teaching strategy to give students a variety of ways to be assessed so that each student can succeed, allowing their individual strengths to shine through.

—**JENNIFER GARCIA**
First-year teacher, history, grade 11

Mauro Bautista asked his students to demonstrate their understanding of careers and the pathways to them by constructing collages using a wide range of resources and materials. Mauro observed that, "The collages offered an opportunity for students who are artistically inclined to excel. They also provided visual scaffolding for the writing and oral presentations."

First-year teacher Christopher Yusi also found that students became engaged in and learned a great deal from assessments where he asked them to demonstrate their understanding of elements of literature in forms other than paper-and-pencil tests.

———————————————— ⊗ ⊗ ⊗ ————————————————

As a final project, the class made mobiles to hang around our room. Each mobile consisted of two main characters, two settings, and one plot. Each piece of the mobile was shaped and illustrated on one side to match what they represented, and on the other side students wrote a description or narrative. This was a great final project, because it afforded students the opportunity to use different modalities to show what they had learned. Most of the unit consisted of reading and writing, with too few creative, artistic exercises. But when we developed the rubric for the final mobile project, some students' motivation seemed to skyrocket.

—**CHRISTOPHER YUSI**
First-year teacher, grades 4 and 5

Assessments That Are Interactive

As students construct logical answers that include descriptions, facts, experiences, and problems, they *use* their knowledge to sort, form, and conclude. This process makes their knowledge richer and more complex than if they had simply repeated facts or tried to recognize and choose the correct answer on a paper-and-pencil test.

When teacher and student go back and forth during assessments, the teacher can adjust on the spot to help the student express what he knows. Only in a spoken exchange can a teacher sense when it is appropriate to say, "Take a few more seconds to think about it" or "Let's skip that for now; we can come back to it later." Interactions can be open-ended. When teachers ask students probing questions like "What do you think of that?," "What will you do next?," "Why did you do it that way?," and "How did you figure that out?," they get as close as they can to the heart of the students' learning. Then students' responses will reveal their sense-making—not just their conclusions.

Interactive assessments generate responses that guide teachers as they help, explain, and provide feedback. Both teachers and students can make "course corrections" when students get stuck. These exchanges can help students become more comfortable with assessment and increase their efforts to do better. Students can begin to see assessment as a process by which a friendly person helps them identify and overcome roadblocks to learning. Jennifer Garcia used journals as a forum for such "informal and comfortable" dialogues.

───────────────────────────── ✄ ✄ ✄ ─────────────────────────────

I used journal entries as a continuous form of informal assessment, and as a means of communicating more personally with students about what they were learning and how they felt about it. The goal was not to elicit any particular "correct" response, but to allow students to find their own voices and write about what interested them in that historical unit. Keeping the journal provided an opportunity for students to take time to reflect and opened up an informal and comfortable dialogue between the students and me (particularly for those learning English as a second language who are often reluctant to participate in other ways). Many commented that they appreciated time to reflect and ask questions in a private way, and even that they appreciated the response comments by me. This form of informal assessment can help develop self-confidence and student voice.

—Jennifer Garcia
First-year teacher, history, grade 11

If students receive feedback in the form of new questions and subtle encouragement, it prompts them to explore beyond their first hunches. Unlike conventional testing, or classroom question-response teaching—where a common first inclination is to give up, to say "I don't know," or to select any answer just to get over the discomfort—students raise their own questions as they explain what they have learned. The next steps in learning become more clearly focused and continue from where these questions end.

Teachers can keep interactive assessment nonthreatening and nonjudgmental, in part, because it can be negotiable. That is, teachers don't need to ask all students the same questions. Furthermore, they can accept many answers at many different levels of sophistication, depending on the question and on students' prior knowledge. For example, students often seem to know very little when their teachers or classmates first ask a question. If the teacher (or the test) accepts the first response as the final answer, this may confirm that the student knows very little. Given the chance to think about the question and receive some clarification, however, the student might reveal more knowledge than anyone thought he had, including himself. Such interaction invites follow-up questions and additional elaboration. Not only do teachers gain more insight into the student's knowledge, they also elicit important misinformation that can create obstacles if not corrected.

Assessments That Are Personalized

Teachers can assess individual students' progress and avoid public comparisons. However, most teachers still work in schools with policies that require traditional evaluations and record keeping. A goal, then, is to use authentic assessments while promoting a classroom culture that both cares about students' progress and protects privacy. One high school teacher discussed privacy concerns with his class, and the class agreed to this policy: "*Do* inquire about classmates' grades if you are genuinely interested in their progress, if you have worked with or helped them on the assignment, and you care about them. If you do inquire, do so outside of class. *Do not* sneak a look at someone's grade or shout out 'Wadja get?'"

Increasingly, teachers are balancing traditional evaluations and grades with

strategies for students to demonstrate to others their growing competence. When others can witness and then respond to one's work, assessment occurs *and* learning continues. For example, when Mauro Bautista's English learners gave their oral presentations describing the collages they had developed to show their careers and what it would take to reach them, he engaged the rest of the class in developing a set of questions that they could answer collectively about the substance of the work. Clearly, in spite of some of their very rudimentary English language skills, the students were learning much unfamiliar content, how to gather academic knowledge, and classroom interactions and expectations.

———————————————— ✂ ✂ ✂ ————————————————

The presenters consistently spoke confidently, referring to their collages as
necessary. The "audience" also did an excellent job. We created a personal-
ized chart for each presenter that incorporated the students' personal goals.
The audience filled out the chart as their classmates were presenting. The
charts kept the audience actively engaged in the presentations.

For instance, when Julie presented, the three questions on her chart
were: What is one thing on Julia's chart? What are two things Julia needs to
do to become a doctor? What did you like best about her presentation? Jose
answered the questions accordingly, "One thing on Julia's collage is doctor
allundando a un paciente [doctor helping a patient]." "Good grades and
graduate school." "Me gusto como ella read [I liked how she read]."

—**Mauro Bautista**
Middle-school bilingual education coordinator

Many teachers personalize evaluation by asking their students to collect samples of their work over time in a *portfolio*—like artists who keep samples of their
work. Students might include a series of writing samples, experiments, lists of books
they've read, math problems they've solved, and more. Portfolios work well when
they go beyond simple collections of all of the student's work and instead allow students to assess and select work that represents their best achievements and growth.
Here, too, Judy Smith's assessments of her global economics unit provide a useful
example.

———————————————— ✂ ✂ ✂ ————————————————

On the last day of class, students turned in their portfolios. In the folder,
they wrote me a letter reflecting on their learning during the unit. I could
see whether the students achieved the unit learning goals: learn about
international trade and the economic and social results of colonialism and
neocolonialism and learn how their individual consumer habits and beliefs
impacted the environment, other cultures and peoples, and themselves.

The reflection included three parts. First, the students picked one assign-
ment that they felt best demonstrated what they learned and explained why
they picked that assignment over other assignments, what it made them think
about, and how it demonstrated their learning. Second, they wrote an essay
in which they reflected on their performance during the role-play and on the
responsibility we have for what is happening to indigenous groups and rain-
forests in places like Ecuador. Finally, they reviewed their entire portfolio
and wrote about their personal habits of consumption and what they might
change. I asked what they thought they would remember in ten years and
why. I requested that they document a question that the unit raised for them.

—**Judy Smith**
High school social studies

Such assessment strategies allow teachers, parents, classmates, and students
themselves to reflect on and discuss what's been learned.

Assessments That Include "Authentic" Tasks

Linda Darling-Hammond proposes that assessments should be based on "meaningful performances in real-world contexts," and that these performances should be so "closely entwined as to be often inseparable" from the curriculum itself.[31] She points to schools that engage students in demonstrating their learning in exhibitions and portfolios with "products like mathematical models, literary critiques, scientific experiments, dance performances, debates, and oral presentations and defense of ideas." In such performances, rich conceptual knowledge, understanding, and problem-solving skills do not have to be broken up into small bits that can be easily measured with conventional testing.

Researchers at the University of Wisconsin have also established criteria for high-quality authentic assessment. In their view, students should be engaged in an assessment task that has them construct knowledge through the use of disciplined inquiry that has some value or meaning beyond success in school.[32] By *disciplined inquiry*, they mean that students work within the conventions of the scholarly discipline of the topic they are studying. Thus, the biology student would present her findings as a biologist might, by writing her findings in a report or demonstrating and discussing an experiment (this, of course, during and after her authentic learning/instruction, in which she learned as a biologist learns—reading, working collaboratively, reporting and checking findings, etc.).

Judy Smith describes a debate that simultaneously engaged students in deepening their learning and allowed her the opportunity to assess it. It is a task that illustrates what Darling-Hammond and the Wisconsin researchers mean by authentic.

With one week left to go in the unit, I introduced the final project—the role play. I hoped that students would debate progress versus tradition. I also wanted them to experience the ethical dilemmas that corporations face when pursuing profit. Students represented one of six roles—Indigenous Indians, Oil Company, Workers, Missionaries, Environmentalists, and the System of Profit. Fulfilling these roles by writing interior monologues, building alliances, and then debating, students made meaning of the issues and demonstrated their learning in an intellectual space. Students had already learned about profit, capitalism, power, gross domestic product, and neocolonialism. The two-day debate, in which almost every student participated at least once, allowed the students to enact a real dilemma that continues to plague our global community today.

—JUDY SMITH
High school social studies

As they participate in these tasks, Judy and other teachers like her take note of the knowledge and skills students display. They observe how students interact and how they solve problems. They follow closely the nature and appropriateness of students' reasoning as well as the correctness of their answers. They analyze students' responses to uncover gaps and errors in students' thinking about what they are learning and to help frame new strategies for pushing that thinking further.

Authentic tasks also include performing of the real-world tasks that their learning makes possible. As the culminating project in his career and college unit, Mauro Bautista assessed his students' understanding of successful pathways toward college and careers by having his students fill out college applications that included calculating their grade point average, writing their personal statement, and submitting letters of recommendation.

A Culture of Authenticity

Ongoing authentic assessment challenges students to go beyond the usual classroom study habits of skimming the chapters, doing problems, and studying before a test, and never again bothering with the material. Interactive assessments keep students working. Nobody gets off the hook by giving perfunctory, if correct, answers. Moreover, reasoning and figuring out take place *as a part of* the learning and assessment process, not at the end of the unit and just before the test. Authentic assessments make it difficult for students to excuse themselves by quietly accepting a bad grade *before* the exam even takes place. Personalized methods of evaluating and reporting student learning also communicate substantive and meaningful information to parents about what their child has learned, and how well.

Such assessments also have a way of permeating the classroom culture. Students' interactions among themselves begin to take on many of the teachers' values, habits, and skills for authenticity that contribute to a learning-assessing community. Fundamental to all of these assessment practices is that teachers see all students as extraordinarily capable learners. With that understanding in place, the other principles for assessment that supports learning make good sense, and they prompt extraordinarily creative classroom assessment strategies.

🔵 OLC Connections

Additional online and print resources and a set of questions for reflection about assessment can be found at www.mhhe.com/oakes3e.

🟦 Digging Deeper

The scholars and works listed in this section should provide readers with a deeper understanding of assessment practices in today's schools. Some of the scholars listed here have investigated the historical and philosophical roots of assessment; others speak more to actual assessment practices.

CRESST is the National Center for Research on Evaluation, Standards, and Student Testing, funded by the U.S. Department of Education. Housed at UCLA, the center conducts research and development that improves assessment and accountability systems and helps schools and districts respond to the many accountability demands of the No Child Left Behind Act. The CRESST website, at http://www.cse.

ucla.edu/index.htm, includes a page for teachers with articles and assessment tools, as well as a page for parents. The site also contains research reports and other related resources.

Stephen Jay Gould's *The Mismeasure of Man* (New York: W. W. Norton, 1996) traces the history of efforts to classify and rank people according to their supposed genetic gifts and limits. This revised edition includes a new introduction telling how and why he wrote the book and tracing the subsequent history of the controversy on inherited characteristics, right through *The Bell Curve.* The book also includes five essays, dealing with *The Bell Curve* in particular, and with race, racism, and biological determinism in general.

Asa Hilliard is an educational psychologist and professor of urban education at Georgia State University in Atlanta. Hilliard served as an expert witness in several landmark federal cases on test validity and bias, including the *Larry P. v. Wilson Riles* IQ test case in California—a case that outlawed the use of IQ tests for classifying African American students as mentally retarded. His book *Testing African-American Students* (Chicago: Third World Press, 1996) explores issues of educational equity in assessment, particularly regarding the use of IQ tests with African American students.

Alfie Kohn's book *Punished by Rewards: The Trouble with Gold Stars, Incentive Plans, A's, Praise, and Other Bribes* (Boston: Houghton Mifflin, 1995) argues against the use of rewards in raising children, teaching students, and managing workers. Kohn also looks carefully at how behavioral approaches to learning and external motivation undermine students' intrinsic motivation to learn. Kohn's personal website is at http://www.alfiekohn.org/index.html.

Journalist **Nicholas Lemann**'s 1999 book *The Big Test: The Secret History of the American Meritocracy* (New York: Farrar, Straus & Giroux) tells a fascinating story of testing and meritocracy in the United States. His revealing history of the SAT makes clear that American conceptions of meritocracy that lead to unequal and unfair opportunities are neither natural nor inevitable.

George Madaus is a professor of education and public policy and a senior fellow with The National Board on Educational Testing and Public Policy at Boston College. He has analyzed the testing industry for more than 30 years. In an interview on PBS's *Frontline* on May 24, 2001, Madaus argued that tests can and should be used to hold schools accountable, but not students, and that it is "bad practice" to judge a student's performance on the basis of tests scores alone (online at http://www.pbs.org/wgbh/pages/frontline/shows/schools/interviews/).

Elaine and **Harry Mensh**'s book *The IQ Mythology: Class, Race, Gender and Inequality* (Carbondale, IL: Southern Illinois University Press, 1991) reports a comprehensive, well-documented study of bias in mental testing and in IQ tests in particular.

Jon Mueller, a professor of psychology at North Central College, Naperville, Illinois, has created a useful website, the Authentic Assessment Toolbox, which he calls a "how-to" hypertext. The Toolbox includes step-by-step help for teachers about creating authentic tasks, rubrics, and standards for measuring and improving student learning, as well as a discussion of how authentic and traditional assessment compare. The Toolbox is online at http://jonathan.mueller.faculty.noctrl.edu/toolbox/.

Steven Selden, who teaches and coordinates the program for curriculum theory and development at the University of Maryland, has studied the eugenics movement in American history and traces how this strange mix of racism and science has influenced our conception of human abilities. His book *Inheriting Shame: The Story of Eugenics and Racism in America* was published in 1999 by Teachers College Press at Columbia University.

Leila Zenderland's book *Measuring Minds: Henry Herbert Goddard and the Origins of American Intelligence Testing* (Cambridge, England: Cambridge University Press, 1998) is a well-documented history of the development of IQ tests in early twentieth-century America.

The National Center for Fair and Open Testing (FairTest) is an advocacy organization working to end the abuses, misuses, and flaws of standardized testing and ensure that evaluation of students is fair, open, and educationally sound. The center emphasizes eliminating the racial, class, gender, and cultural barriers to equal opportunity posed by standardized tests and preventing their damage to the quality of education. FairTest publishes a quarterly newsletter, *The Examiner,* plus a catalog of materials on both K–12 and university testing to aid teachers, administrators, students, parents, and researchers. FairTest can be found online at http://fairtest.org.

As past president of the American Educational Research Association, University of Colorado professor **Lorrie Shepard**'s presidential address at the group's 2000 annual meeting in New Orleans provides an explanation of the role of assessment in classroom learning. In her talk, "The Role of Assessment in Learning Culture," Shepard gives a historical overview of testing that shows the connections among tests, ideas of scientific management, and behavioral learning theories; she provides a contrasting framework grounded in cognitive, constructivist, and sociocultural perspectives; and she argues for changes in assessment practices that are consistent with this alternative framework. Shepherd's article is published in *Educational Researcher* 28, no. 7 (October 2000), pp. 4–14 (online at http://35.8.171.42/aera/pubs/er/arts/29-07/shep01.htm).

Grant Wiggins is the president of Authentic Education in Hopewell, New Jersey, and a nationally recognized expert on assessment. His 1998 book, *Educative Assessment: Designing Assessments to Inform and Improve Student Performance* (San Francisco: Jossey Bass), reviews the principles of high-quality assessment design and provides guidelines for developing performance tasks that meet rigorous educational standards. He also covers such critical topics as how to score assessments fairly and how to structure and judge student portfolios.

Notes

1. "What Is Authentic Assessment?" Authentic Assessment Toolbox, http://jonathan.mueller. faculty.noctrl.edu/toolbox/whatisit.htm.
2. C. T. Hu, "The Historical Background: Examinations and Control in Pre-modern China, *Comparative Education* 20 (1984), p.17, as cited in F. Allan Hanson, *Testing Testing: Social Consequences of the Examined Life* (Berkeley: University of California Press, 1993), p. 191, http://ark.cdlib.org/ark:/13030/ft4m3nb2h2/.
3. Ibid.
4. Ibid.

5. Hanson, *Testing Testing.*
6. Ibid.
7. Isaac L. Kandel, *Examinations and Their Substitutes in the United States* (New York: Carnegie Foundation for the Advancement of Teaching, 1936), as quoted in Hanson, *Testing Testing.*
8. Hanson, *Testing Testing.*
9. Rudolph T. Shappee, "Serving the City's Children: San Diego City Schools, The First Fifty Years," *The Journal of San Diego History* 37, no. 2 (spring 1991), http://www.sandiegohistory.org/journal/91spring/schools.htm.
10. Larry Cuban, *How Teachers Taught: Constancy and Change in American Classrooms 1880–1990* (New York: Teachers College Press, 1994).
11. Pioneering German psychologist Wilhelm Wundt introduced what might have become in America a third line of inquiry—the systematic analysis of the perceptions, interpretations, and judgments that people report. Wundt was influential in Europe, but American investigators found Wundt's procedures—talking to people and recording what they report—less than scientific.
12. Stephen J. Gould, *The Mismeasure of Man,* 2nd ed. (New York: Norton, 1996), p. 190.
13. Excerpted from "Mental Ability Test, Stanford University, Test 1, Information (World Book Co, 1920), as reprinted in Bill Bigelow, "Testing, Tracking, and Toeing the Line," *Rethinking Our Classrooms: Teaching for Equity and Social Justice* (Milwaukee, WI: Rethinking Schools, 1994), p. 121.
14. Gould, *Mismeasure of Man,* p. 121.
15. Moreover, Gould calls *The Bell Curve,* published in 1994, "little more than a hard-line version of Spearman's *g.*" In Gould, *The Mismeasure of Man,* p. 35.
16. Gould, *Mismeasure of Man,* p. 301.
17. Kenneth Sirotnik, "Equal Access to Quality in Public Schooling: Issues in the Assessment of Equity and Excellence," in *Access to Knowledge: The Continuing Agenda for Our Nation's Schools,* rev. ed., ed. John I. Goodlad and Pamela Keating (New York: The College Board, 1994), p. 162.
18. *Tisn't What You Know, But Are You Intelligent?* Preface by Howard W. Haggard (New York: Harper and Brothers, 1927), p. 8.
19. Ibid.
20. Ibid.
21. College Board Online, "Test Question of the Day," 16 March 1998 (online at http://www.collegeboard.org/tqod/bin/question).
22. Noe Medina and Monty Neill, *Fallout from the Testing Explosion: How 100 Million Standardized Exams Undermine Equity and Excellence in America's Public Schools,* 3rd ed. (Cambridge, MA: FairTest, 1990).
23. http://www.collegeboard.com/prof/counselors/tests/sat/scores/data_tables.html.
24. College Board Online, "Test Question of the Day," 16 March 1998 (online at http://www.collegeboard.com).
25. Robert J. Mislevy, "Foundations of a New Test Theory," in *Test Theory for a New Generation of Tests,* ed. Norman. Frederiksen, Robert J. Mislevy, and Isaac I. Bejar (Hillsdale, NJ: Lawrence Erlbaum, 1993), pp. 19–39.
26. Robert Sternberg, "Myths, Countermyths, and Truths About Intelligence," *Education Researcher* 25 (March 1996), pp. 11–16, 13; excerpted from "Mental Ability Test, Stanford University, Test 1, Information (World Book Co, 1920), as reprinted in Bill Bigelow, "Testing, Tracking, and Toeing the Line," *Rethinking Our Classrooms: Teaching for Equity and Social Justice* (Milwaukee, WI: Rethinking Schools, 1994).
27. Howard Gardner, *Frames of Mind* (New York: Basic Books, 1983, 1993).
28. Jerome Bruner, *Culture and Education* (Cambridge: Harvard University Press, 1996), p. 77.
29. Gould, *Mismeasure of Man,* p. 24.
30. Linda Darling-Hammond, *The Right to Learn* (San Francisco: Jossey-Bass, 1997), pp. 59–60.
31. Darling-Hammond, *Right to Learn,* p. 115.
32. Fred M. Newmann, Walter G. Secada, and Gary Wehlage, *A Guide to Authentic Instruction and Assessment: Vision, Standards, and Scoring* (Madison, WI: Wisconsin Center for Education Research at the University of Wisconsin, 1995), p. 8.

CHAPTER 7

Classroom Management

Caring, Respectful, and Democratic Relationships

I think about classroom management. I have a very structured classroom, and we go bell to bell. My agenda is on the board. I have a booklet where I record every day's lesson. Absent students know to look at it to find out what they missed. I put up the basic announcements and things they need to know for extracurricular activities or college.

I am flexible, too. I say "yes," when appropriate, to almost every personal student request. I go with teachable moments, such as when my all-Latino class wants to know more about blacks and gives me a chance to address tensions, stereotypes, and history. I have posters that represent lots of different communities. I put up student work and pictures of students from their presentations. I greet the students and talk to them and check in with them as frequently as I can.

Classroom management and social justice are compatible ideas because society runs on spoken and unspoken norms. Teachers are not doing students any favors by not having clear guidelines. Students want a well-run classroom. How would they succeed if they didn't know both academic and behavior expectations?

I've observed that some first-year teachers talk about social justice but don't know how to do it when it comes to classroom management. What does social justice look like in the everyday classroom? I think it starts with respect and clear guidelines—when we are together, we learn. We have fun, and we respect each other. This is what we do.

—Judy Smith
High school social studies

I think that classroom management is relevant, not as a means to empower the teacher in terms of controlling the class, but rather to empower students to feel that they belong and are safe in the class. I start off the year by asking the students what they think the rules should be. Every year, the students give me a laundry list of NO: "No running, no gum chewing, no lighters (that was Jameon's comment my first year teaching), no name calling, etc." After I write down every comment, I ask the students what we are allowed to do. The students then change their language to: "Be nice, take turns, love, etc."

The words take on new meaning and the students see the rules of the class as rules that we should abide by as humans. The students are not told "no no no"; rather, "love, be kind, etc." I think it shifts the perspective. I have never had a list of "rules" in the class posted on the door before students have walked in. I think it is important to listen to their ideas and incorporate what I want to see and what they want to see in the class. The students also begin to see the classroom working in a democratic manner and see that I respect their voices.

—KIMBERLY MIN
Third-grade teacher

When we asked Judy Smith and Kimberly Min about classroom management, they did not tell us about special programs designed to keep students under control. They told us about their approach to teaching, their caring and respectful relationships with students, and their deep commitment to learning. For Judy and Kimberly, these are the hallmarks of social justice.

Chapter Overview
───※───

This chapter surveys the traditional behavioral legacy of management, discipline, and control as well as a nontraditional perspective—creating caring and respectful relationships. This is not to suggest that the latter perspective is somehow a "new" invention of constructivist educators. Today's school officials and teachers often accept the logic, research findings, and quite a lot of personal and intuitive experience that support this second perspective, but, in practice, many cannot imagine abandoning the behavioral approaches that pervade American schools. Without a critical perspective on the history, philosophy, and politics that underlie rewards, punishments, threats of failure, and so forth, traditional discipline remains common sense.

We begin with three other teachers who, like Judy Smith and Kimberly Min, illustrate the connection between social justice and classroom management.

Three Caring, Respectful, and Democratic Classrooms

Like most first-year teachers, Erik Korporaal was worried about classroom management. Could he control his rambunctious 9- and 10-year-old fourth and fifth graders? These children lived in a pretty rough urban neighborhood, and tensions between his African American and Latino students often spilled over into the classroom. Many of Erik's more-experienced colleagues used behavior modification systems that meted out rewards and punishment to train the students to follow classroom rules. As a new teacher at the school, Erik was expected to do the same. However, his knowledge of learning and development made him cautious about these strategies—even if they might "work" in the short term to make the children behave. His commitment to social justice also compelled him to bridge the racial differences in his class rather than masking them with firm control. He was determined to build a community in his classroom where students' "good behavior" grew from engaging lessons, from their reflections about ethical actions, and from the caring and respectful relationships that he fostered.

As the year progressed, I saw a definite change. Students were much more polite to each other and exhibited far more respect. The class atmosphere began to change. I have fewer problems with students not getting along. Instead of bickering or competing, they feel responsible for the success of their peers. Success to them is no longer an individual competition, or even a competition between groups. Rather, it means doing well as a whole class. When students have questions about assignments in class, other students jump at the opportunity to help them out. They feel better about themselves for helping a classmate.

This increased cohesion also changed the way many of my Latino students participate. They seem to feel more comfortable in activities and discussion. I believe that their silence at the beginning of the year was a sign that they did not feel connected.

The change also manifested itself outside the classroom. No longer did race and gender strictly define peer groups. Students of different races were friends and began to associate with each other. A much broader peer group also formed that consisted of the entire class. No longer would students split themselves into separate groups on the playground. They began to play together every day during recess and lunch. What I found most remarkable was the group's reaction when somebody felt isolated. Most of the students would take the initiative and try to include this person, and the whole group would become noticeably upset and disturbed if they could not find a way to include someone who felt excluded. The playground monitors were thrilled to see that the students monitored each other's behavior, reminding and keeping in line those students who were breaking the rules.

When I look back to the beginning of the year, I would never have guessed my class could be so close. They are individually and collectively remarkable people. My students' success gives me hope (and higher future expectations) that classrooms, even those divided by powerful social forces such as race, can become communities of learners. By no means are all the problems solved, but every day my students learn more about respecting and relating to one another. I am very proud of the progress they have made.

—**Erik Korporaal**
First-year teacher, grades 4 and 5

First-year teacher Amy Lee's sixth-grade class included several children with serious out-of-school problems as well as in-class misbehavior. Hector, for example, had been placed in his aunt's care when the county children's protective services agency decided that his drug-addicted mother was not fit to care for him, and his anger often erupted in the classroom. Amy's school, like Erik's, expected her to follow a discipline system that included a series of increasingly severe consequences for misconduct. The first consequence for misbehavior is that students post cards with their names on them in the front of the class. Hector posted his nearly every day.

In the beginning, my students didn't trust me. They were sixth graders on the verge of junior high school; many of them were already hardened and embittered toward school and their teachers. Many had been ridiculed, silenced, demeaned, and misunderstood, and to them, I was just another teacher who would continue to do the same. They waved their attitude like a red flag, challenging me to play their game. They expected me to live up to their low expectations of what a teacher should be. I was determined to prove them wrong.

I wanted to build relationships with my students—authentic relationships. Much of what I had read stuck with me: Be fair; allow your students a voice; teach with care, respect, and kindness. I struggled to be tolerant, giving each student the opportunity to voice his or her side. I touted fairness and mutual respect, always telling my students how much I valued their ideas and insights. However, I had to prove to them through my actions that I was sincere. I gave second chances, and when proven wrong, admitted that I was at fault. At first, none of my efforts made any impact. I think the students believed it was a facade and that soon I would show my true, mean colors. They were wary and did not respond to any of my attempts to know them.

Hector was my biggest challenge. From the first day, he was in my face, resisting any attempts at kindness. Other teachers, some of whom had never even had him in their classrooms, came and warned me about how awful he was.

Every day Hector stayed with me after school for misbehaving. He seemed surprised that I talked with him. His answers were usually short and inexpressive, or he sat like a stone and said nothing. So, at first, I did all of the talking. I told him that no matter how hard he pushed me away, I would not give up on him. I think that this was the key—not giving up. So many of his teachers in the past hit such a point of frustration with Hector that they threw up their hands and walked away. I was very close many times to doing exactly the same. He yelled at me, threw his binder through the air, and sat in class refusing to do the intelligent work that he was capable of. I quietly but firmly reprimanded him in class, and then in our conversations after school shared with him all of the good things that I saw from him during the day. I called his aunt frequently to praise him, and I visited his home.

Slowly Hector came to realize that I was real, and that I really did care. He gradually let me into his world. He started to change. He no longer sat like a stone after school and said nothing. In class, instead of reacting quickly and irrationally, I found him expressing himself and calmly telling others "how frustrated I got when . . ." instead of yelling and screaming like before. It was a miracle. Over the next few months, Hector blossomed. He became a real class leader and role model, and the other students noticed. "Wow, Ms. Lee, Hector hasn't posted his card in a whole month. He is really different from last year." He made friends and strengthened his "PR" at school. I was really proud of him; he was proud of himself.

Hector is one of the many students who touched me deeply this past year. I believe that it was the time and effort in building caring relationships that made all the difference. I had many moments filled with frustration, anger, disappointment, and apathy, but fortunately, when I was ready to walk away, the pure joys of teaching revealed themselves. I fell in love with my job this year, because I fell in love with the students I teach.

—AMY LEE
First-year teacher, grade 6

Jennifer Garcia's high school brought diverse students together, including many immigrants. Often, her students had part-time jobs and family responsibilities; some were engaged in gang activities; and many considered dropping out as a real option to continuing their education. Like Amy and Erik, Jennifer relied on trusting relationships and a community-like atmosphere to create a suitable environment for learning.

—⚜ ⚜ ⚜—

By developing a classroom where students help construct the curriculum, I hope to diminish the power issues. In our unit on industrialization, immigration, and unionism, my goal was to bring to life a time period that is often overlooked—one that focuses on poor ethnic immigrants, workers, government scandals, and inner-city living conditions—and to acknowledge the experiences and contributions of a variety of people. This critical multiculturalism acknowledges the contributions and experiences of groups that have been marginalized historically and encourages students to question and challenge the status quo and traditional power relationships.

Hands-on, student-centered activities drew students into the historical theme and time period. They simulated factory life by creating an assembly line along which students constructed, piecemeal, paper airplanes, negotiated a union contract, and reenacted a political machine election. They gathered and analyzed information in cooperative learning groups (e.g., analyzing political cartoons). The students worked well together— supporting each other and offering help when needed. They were able to express their opinions and feelings in the journals they kept. Activities allowed students to empathize with diverse people and challenge their preconceived notions about workers, immigrants, and politics.

—JENNIFER GARCIA
First-year teacher, high school history

Like Judy Smith, Erik, Amy, and Jennifer have no formula or system that guarantees picture-perfect deportment—that no "Hector" will toss a notebook in the air or that no racial epithets will be heard.

Why should Erik, Amy, and Jennifer expect students to behave well in class, listen to instruction, do homework, study for tests, and so on? Because students enjoy class? Enjoy behaving? Because some external payoff motivates them? Because an authority (a teacher) told them to? Because they want to please? Because they want to avoid punishment? No, because they are engaged in caring, respectful and democratic relationships that are at the core of learning.

Management, Discipline, and Control: Lasting Legacies

As Erik, Amy, and Jennifer would attest, school administrators and experienced teachers often place enormous importance on first-year teachers' ability to "control" their classrooms. As a consequence, many new teachers think that without traditional discipline, their reputations will suffer as their classrooms disintegrate into chaos.

Traditional methods may bring some short-term relief from noise or disruption, but the fact that discipline problems are a constant source of school aggravation clearly indicates that, over time, rewards, punishments, and controls simply do not produce good results. Neither learning nor "discipline" are easily achieved if an hour-long silent classroom is taken as proof of "good discipline" and good learning. Trusting relationships, cooperation, and a sense of classroom community and caring take some time and require steady attention.

Traditional discipline has a long history. St. Thomas Aquinas argued in the thirteenth century that schools should shape character and foster moral development, including training the wills of the young, as well as their minds. That is pretty much what America's earliest white settlers thought. So, from the beginning, American public schools were as much or more about socializing children to act right as they were about academic learning.

Classrooms as Smooth-Running Factories

Recall the description in Chapter 5 of early-nineteenth-century schools, which were composed of large classrooms with students moving in orderly groups to recite their lessons with monitors. Beginning at this early time, schools tried to match the organizational efficiencies of factories that were producing such abundant manufactured goods.[1] These efficiencies required smooth-running classrooms where many students would all do the same academic work at the same time. In such settings, little movement could be tolerated, and materials other than the most rudimentary texts, slates, tablets, pens, and pencils were either not available, too costly, or thought unnecessary. Neither children nor adults could be left to follow their own propensities to learn and teach. Coercion was a central feature of these public school classrooms.

FOCAL POINT 7.1

Classroom Management 100 Years Ago

"One who studies educational theory aright can see in the mechanical routine of the classroom the educative forces that are slowly transforming the child from a little savage into a creature of law and order, fit for the life of civilized society."

Source: William Bagley, *Classroom Management* (New York: Macmillan, 1907); we are indebted to historian Howard Zinn for bringing this quote to our attention.

Training Dutiful Workers   As we noted in Chapter 2, teachers in the late 1800s and early 1900s were expected to transmit to students the values and approved behaviors of the industrialized society: respect for authority, punctuality, following directions, performing tasks with precision, tolerating the boredom of repetitive activity, and so on. The expansion of large-scale, assembly-line production made equal sense for schools and factories. In either setting, the benefits were not directed to individual workers or students but to the larger enterprise of training students to become workers who would match well to the predominant mode of production.

Between 1907 and 1927 William Bagley's teacher education textbook, *Classroom Management,* was enormously popular. Bagley made explicit connections between classroom order and assembly lines, and he advised teachers to develop rigid classroom routines to build good behavior habits.(See Focal Point 7.1.) For example, Bagley suggested that teachers have students practice packing and unpacking their desks in a particular order, marching to the blackboard, and marching through the cloakroom to get their coats as they left the classroom. He urged teachers to march the children in lines through the lavatories before recess to develop good habits related to "bodily functions," and to teach them to assume on command a formal pose of attention.

Bagley and other educators turned to the expanding field of psychology for help in designing strategies that would produce students' compliance. For example, Edward Thorndike's behaviorist theories led many teachers to reinforce good behavior with rewards that included conveying approval with talk, facial expressions, and gestures. This approach became seen as "scientific," especially as behavioral animal research like that of Pavlov's promised that a regular schedule of reinforcement could actually control behavior.

Throughout the twentieth century, systems for producing student learning and for producing goods and services followed parallel paths. Today, changed patterns of production, employment, and school enrollments all make traditional discipline attitudes even less appropriate—or possible—than they were. Teachers have lost or rejected controls over students that had previously supported the factory model of schooling. For example, "firing" students (expulsion or permissible dropping out to a waiting job) is a less available option. Gone too is the widespread acceptance of physical punishment and public humiliation, although the latter remains evident as a control mechanism.

Managing for High-Quality Work   In the 1970s and 1980s, as America's unquestioned dominance of world markets eroded, particularly in those areas that
hit closest to American pride—electronic technology and automobiles—much of
America's faith in the infallibility of traditional business practices diminished. Some
business analysts looked to other countries, particularly Japan and Scandinavia, for
their "secrets" and discovered that more cooperative and humanistic production
models could produce greater job satisfaction and commitment along with efficiently manufactured, high-quality products. This emphasis on respect for the
dignity and worth of workers and students struck a chord with many Americans.
Respect and dignity also seemed like good business, and that was a combination too
good to resist.

William Glasser is notable among those who have borrowed from and added to
the enlightened management perspectives for managing students' classroom behavior. He argues that students will act to meet basic human needs (which he asserts are survival, love, fun, power, and freedom) and will prefer productive choices
if those choices are available. The key for Glasser is to give students the responsibility for choosing those actions that will fulfill their own needs—to empower them
by helping them understand that they can control their lives by experiencing both
the benefits and consequences of their choices. Glasser's "choice theory" (originally
called "control theory") emphasizes that the successful teacher should provide
students with a "satisfying picture of that activity," "empower" them, and stress
cooperation, rather than punishing, telling, overpowering, and enforcing rules.[2]

Drawing from the work of W. Edwards Deming, a widely respected consultant
to corporations, Glasser makes his choice theory of discipline an integral part of
what he calls "the quality school." In these schools, as in the most successful business organizations, teachers-as-managers help students understand the nature of
high-quality work and understand that they can meet their needs by doing such
work. In this way, better teaching, which is really better managing, can make all students eager to participate.

Glasser's approach is a great improvement over many of the overtly behaviorist
classroom management programs finding their way into schools. However, his emphasis on students' choices to meet basic needs within carefully managed classroom
environments falls short. Glasser connects the social environment (such as working
in groups) directly to its usefulness in meeting student needs. In doing so, he neglects many mediating processes that would explain some of the underlying
strengths that led to Amy Lee's effectiveness with Hector, as well as those that
would explain why Hector's struggles are far from over.

It was indeed important for Amy Lee to persevere in allowing Hector to make
continuously better choices over time, rather than trying to control him through
punishment. However, she was also acutely aware that Hector's decision making is
far more complex than basic need fulfillment. Hector's decision making was powerfully connected to social *structures* and the school *culture,* two dimensions of his
life that neither he nor Amy Lee had entire control over. To some degree, Hector and
Amy Lee negotiated acceptable parameters for Hector's behavior; to some degree,
Hector gradually allowed additional scaffolding from his teacher and classmates; and
to some degree, Hector continues to be in for a rough time at school.

As a social justice teacher, Amy Lee is aware that other teachers' classes were, and will continue to be, places that Hector influences—not always positively. Hector is sure to try to prove to his next teacher that Amy Lee was an exception, a mistake. Others will just as surely respond to him in characteristically unfriendly ways (unless one wants to believe that Hector is forever "cured" of feeling at odds with his environment). Amy Lee is constrained in how influential she can be, but she can continue to struggle on Hector's behalf. She can share with other teachers how she managed to gain Hector's trust, and she can try to maintain a continuing relationship with him. Depending on the school culture, other teachers will be more or less receptive to learn of their colleague's success with a troublesome student, especially when the colleague has spent extraordinary time and energy in the effort.

Classrooms as Socializing Agents

From the beginning, schools punished students to manage their behavior. In the early-nineteenth-century public schools that used the "monitorial" method, teachers placed a wooden log around the necks of children who talked too much or didn't do their schoolwork. They punished more serious offenders by hanging them in a sack or basket from the school roof in a place where their classmates could see them. Other schools used a simple "spare the rod, spoil the child" approach. Many viewed strictly enforced behavioral controls as the best way to achieve the common school's goal of suppressing crime and unrest among the lower socioeconomic classes.

Socializing Immigrants   Strict classroom discipline took on a more patriotic tone at the end of the nineteenth century. As we noted in Chapter 2, by that time society wanted schools to Americanize a flood of newcomers with the habits, manners, and loyalties necessary for a proper social life. By 1909, 58 percent of the students in the nation's 37 largest cities were foreign born, and many longer-standing residents feared a wholesale corruption of the culture. Schools responded by adding a considerable dose of patriotism to the curriculum, but Americanization was far more about behavior and discipline than about learning the substance of the American culture. Through character training and strictly enforced discipline, schools were expected to extinguish the threatening foreign ways that immigrant children brought to school.

Taming the Unruly   The widespread adoption of compulsory education laws in the first half of the twentieth century brought more and more unwilling students into classrooms—immigrants and nonimmigrants alike—making strictly imposed classroom controls seem all the more necessary. Schools couldn't simply fire recalcitrant students the way industry could dismiss unwanted workers, and modern parents and educators increasingly regarded the harsh physical punishment of earlier times as inhumane.

The economic trauma of the Depression in the 1930s and World War II in the 1940s dampened quite a lot (certainly, not all) of the country's worries about wayward, troublesome youth. But by the 1950s, popular films like *Blackboard Jungle* heightened fears of an increasingly belligerent younger generation—particularly in city schools. The concept of "juvenile delinquent" gained currency. While favoring minorities, this was a cross-cultural class of antisocial, antischool, antiauthority disruptive youth, vaguely disaffected with modern society. Their lot was to stay in school and be bothersome, drop out to no one's chagrin, or be sent to a variety of "reform" schools, widely understood as one step before prison.

Remedying Cultural Deprivation   By the 1960s, teachers were taught in their teacher education programs that poor children were "culturally deprived," in part because they came from disorganized families that failed to teach such basics as punctuality, obedience, cleanliness, respect for personal property, or a value for education. In short, the stereotypical judgments that had previously been associated with race or nationality were partly stripped of their most blatant and odious prejudice.

Instead, society adopted a new construction of social science—a nongenetic theory that attributed minorities' huge gaps in education achievement to their faulty "culture." In fact, *poor* in the 1960s was also a powerful code word for *race,* and when policymakers referred to "the poor" or "the culturally deprived," they often meant blacks and other minorities or people from isolated rural areas.

Culturally deprived became one of those terms that took on a life of its own. Thus, teachers and the public generally came to see children who were not white, urban, or middle class as requiring a special set of treatments in schools in order to bring them up to the schooling standards that white, middle-class children learned at home. Such children, social scientists and educators reasoned, needed classrooms with fixed routines, unambiguous rules, and firm disciplinary policies.[3]

Using Behavioral Psychology to Control Student Behavior

Since the 1970s college courses, school district workshops, and training from profit-making corporations have offered teachers a range of detailed plans and programs for controlling classroom behavior.

Some go so far as to suggest techniques to scare or intimidate disruptive students, based on crude behavioral theories of using punishment to extinguish unwanted behavior. Teachers might use the "stony stare," verbal reprimands, nonverbal signals (e.g., pointing one's finger or moving close to an offender), and threats of a failing grade. Many schools bought the services of "Scared Straight," a program that brought teenagers in contact with hardened, jailed criminals who verbally intimidated the students with horror stories of prison life. Like nearly every other plan to threaten, scare, and punish, this one didn't work and didn't last.

Nevertheless, most of the commercially developed classroom management and discipline programs have built on B. F. Skinner's developments in behavioral psychology to provide more-refined "scientific" methods for using rewards and punishment to shape students' classroom behavior. These behavior modification approaches offer carefully prescribed and scripted lists of foolproof techniques that guarantee correct behavior through conditioning of students' behavior.

Assertive Discipline   Today, *Assertive Discipline,* developed by Lee and Marlene Canter, is perhaps the most popular of the commercially available, behaviorally grounded discipline program.[4] The Canters' strategy starts with the premise that teachers have the right to define and enforce rules for student behavior that allow them to teach. Teachers communicate clear expectations for students' behavior and clear classroom rules. They let students know the set of escalating "consequences" (punishments) for undesirable behavior, and that misbehaving students will be identified publicly.

Whole-class rewards (parties, candy, etc.) for everyone's good behavior are meant to reinforce those behaviors, as well as to bring social control to bear on individual students who might prevent the class from getting its reward. Proponents claim that the preestablished punishment scheme, along with the proper arrangement of classroom time and space, enables teachers to manage disruptive behavior in a routine way, without diverting either their or the class's attention from the lesson.

Focal Point 7.2 provides an example of Assertive Discipline in the elementary school serving Weir, Kansas, a community of 750 people. The school system sent the following letter home to parents explaining their system for controlling students' behavior.

Systematic programs like Assertive Discipline may suppress misbehavior in the short term, but the research on this is not clear. Even if punishment strategies do "work" in this way, however, they don't teach acceptable behavior or even reduce difficult students' desire to misbehave.

What we do know about behaviorally oriented discipline schemes is that the "lessons" learned from punishments and rewards tend to be very specific, and they can be lost if either the punishments or rewards change slightly. Thus, students learn to make judgments based on what they can get away with—rather than learning to read the environment and make choices that are appropriate for themselves and for the classroom community.

In more recent years, Glasser and the Canters have embraced more community-like and cooperative classrooms. Yet their approaches remain intensely individualistic—individual students make behavioral choices; the teacher is the center of moral and behavioral authority. Other similar systems that rely more on rewards than punishments, for example, Token Reinforcement or Contingency Contracts, may be somewhat less mechanical and rule-bound while offering more opportunity for cognitive sense-making. However, they, too, have been widely criticized for emphasizing teachers' power and control in the classroom rather than students' learning and problem solving. Substantial evidence exists that giving external rewards for good behavior can actually diminish students' intrinsic motivation to learn or to conform to the social norms of the classroom.[5]

First-year kindergarten teacher Javier Espindola thought that the Assertive Discipline strategies used by many veteran teachers in his school would help him motivate his young students. Before long, he changed his mind.

FOCAL POINT 7.2

Assertive Discipline in Weir, Kansas

Weir Attendance Center
Assertive Discipline Policy (Grades 3–5)

March 30, 2005

Dear Parents:

In order to give your child and the students in our classrooms the learning climate that they deserve, we will be initiating the following discipline plan.

OUR PHILOSOPHY

We believe that all students are capable of behaving appropriately in the classroom. We will not tolerate a student stopping us from teaching and other students from learning.

CLASSROOM BEHAVIOR

The students will:

1. Follow rules of behavior and instructions the first time they are given.
2. Talk only with permission.
3. Keep feet, arms, and hands to themselves.
4. Stay in their seats except with permission to leave.

DISCIPLINE CONSEQUENCES PER DAY

If a student chooses to break a rule:
FIRST—one check—warning
SECOND—two checks—lose five minutes of recess
THIRD—three checks—lose ten minutes of recess
FOURTH—four checks—lose one recess
FIFTH—five checks—sent to principal's office
-ISS* remainder of day—parents notified

Any student accumulating fifteen (15) checks for the week will serve one (1) day ISS

SEVERE CLAUSE—This goes into effect when there is a severe disruption. Examples: fighting, profane language, severe disobedience/disrespect. Any of these violations will cause a student to be sent to the principal's office immediately.

POSITIVE BEHAVIOR: Students may earn rewards for positive behavior. These will be given on an individual and classroom basis. Examples: movies, parties, mini-golf, afternoon recess, etc.

   *ISS: In-school suspension
   Source: http://www.usd247.com.

—⚓ ⚓ ⚓—

When my students were sitting quietly and listening to me or when they were on task writing in their journals, I would give them a sticker or happy face to motivate them to continue that behavior. When I saw them talking with peers and not working, I would put their names on the board or give them a sad face.

At first, these strategies worked. Over time, however, I noticed negative effects. Students . . . began to refuse to follow classroom directions, work productively, and respect and listen to their peers and me if they did not receive any rewards. Labeling was another problem. For example . . . [e]very time Steve broke the classroom rules and directions, I placed his name on the board with a check mark or under the sad face. Soon Steve received a reputation and was labeled as a troublemaker by his peers. One day during a lesson, one of my students was shouting out the answer without raising his hand. I asked my students "Who is shouting out the answer without raising their hand?" A few students shouted out Steve's name, even though he was absent that day! It was evident that Steve's peers had labeled him as the classroom troublemaker, and whenever someone was to blame, they chose Steve. Finally, I felt limited in the activities I could do with my kindergartners. I worried that I would lose control of my students if they were interacting, sharing, and working with each other during group activities.

The first step in removing Assertive Discipline from my classroom was discussing it with my students. I told them that they were no longer going to receive happy faces, stars, stickers, and candies when they were behaving and performing well or consequences such as check marks, sad faces, or names on the board when they were behaving inappropriately. I removed from the chalkboard the chart where I posted check marks when students misbehave and stars when they behave well. The students were extremely happy that the chart was gone. Steve said, "No more checkmarks," with a big smile. The next step was to let students know how we were going to solve problems when the classroom rules were not followed. I let them know that we would have discussions after classroom activities to decide what needed improvement.

I no longer feel the need to have complete control of my students. I have implemented group activities that encourage my students to interact, share experiences, and work with their peers. . . . Steve became interested and intrinsically motivated; many of the behavior problems he had displayed earlier in the school year disappeared. Steve is no longer seen as the classroom troublemaker but is now a valuable resource in the classroom. By being patient and not labeling Steve as "troublemaker," I have proven to his peers and myself that everyone is capable of improving his or her academic and social skills in a comfortable environment.

—JAVIER ESPINDOLA
First-year teacher, kindergarten

Zero Tolerance   The most extreme forms of nonphysical behavioral controls on student behavior are "zero tolerance policies." Originally intended to address blatant safety threats such as weapons, the policies trigger automatic suspension or expulsion. The policies are sometimes interpreted to include all manner of forbidden objects and behavior, some of which is clearly not threatening, but subject to the severe consequences. In line with behavioral psychology, the idea is that if students know that these violations will automatically bring severe consequences, they will be deterred from committing them. This commonsense logic holds well for students who are not at all inclined to be a threat, but it has little influence over students who are so disturbed as to want to bring great harm to others. Research on these policies makes clear that they are not only ineffective, but also lead to increased rates of school dropout and discriminatory application of school discipline practices. Perhaps most serious is that zero tolerance may create an illusory feeling of security and well-being without addressing conditions that actually impact on a safe school environment. As a result, the National Association of School Psychologists has concluded: "Systemic school-wide violence prevention programs, social skills curricula and positive behavioral supports lead to improved learning for all students and safer school communities."[6]

Corporal Punishment   At the ultimate extreme of methods used to control students' behavior is corporal punishment, or paddling. As of 2000, 22 states still permitted the use of paddling as a means of punishing misbehavior. Figure 7.1, constructed by the National Center for Effective Discipline, shows that although the numbers of student who have been struck in school for disciplinary reasons has declined in the last two decades, in 2000, more than 300,000 American students were subjected to corporal punishment.

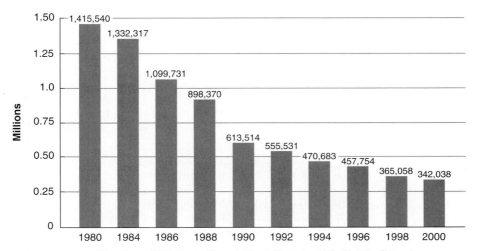

FIGURE 7.1 *Number of Students Struck Each Year in U.S. Public Schools.*

Source: Center for Effective Discipline, 155 W. Main Street, Suite 1603, Columbus, Ohio 43215, tel: (614)221-8829, www.stophitting.com.

Can Effective Teaching Prevent Disruption?

The notion that classroom management and discipline will take care of themselves if teachers use effective instructional techniques emerged in the 1970s. The vast majority of classroom management problems were attributed to instructional short-comings, with claims that mindless curriculum and boring pedagogy added to the need for elaborate management and discipline strategies. Certainly, not all discipline problems can be attributed to inadequate lessons or teacher skills; however, sound instruction and strategies allow teachers to address individual behavior problems productively while continuing with the instructional plan.

Teachers Who Are "With It"   In one of the best-known series of studies on classroom management, Jacob Kounin studied thousands of hours of classroom videotapes. Kounin found that teachers in smoothly running classes consistently used instructional strategies that seemed to prevent disruption. These teachers displayed what Kounin called "withitness." By monitoring students' behavior constantly, they nipped problems in the bud and didn't hesitate to identify miscreants publicly. They managed multiple activities simultaneously and responded to individuals' needs without disrupting the rest of the class (e.g., moving to stand near an inattentive student without stopping instruction). These teachers also maintained what Kounin called "signal continuity"—that is, a consistent focus for students' attention. They didn't confuse students with "false starts" or disorderly presentation of material, and they provided independent seatwork that was easy enough for students to do alone but challenging enough to hold their interest.[7]

Other experts have elaborated on Kounin's initial findings. For example, when teachers convey a personal interest and liking for students, it prompts them to imitate a teacher's behavior, adopt her attitudes, and be sympathetic if others misbehave. When teachers are credible—that is, their words and actions are consistent—students will be less likely to "test" teachers with misbehavior. Other general guidelines include having teachers plan rules and procedures in advance; making those rules and procedures very clear to students; letting students assume some responsibility for determining rules and consequences and lessons; returning to the rules occasionally to discuss new understandings and revisions, developing cooperative relationships with students; minimizing disruptions and delays; and planning independent activities as well as whole-class lessons.[8] Most emphasize the importance of starting the year off in a friendly but business-like way, quickly establishing rules and routines.

Very few people would dispute all these principles. Why, then, are they so often absent from the classrooms of well-intentioned and hardworking teachers? What other conditions exist that make a teacher *not* convey a personal interest and liking, *not* plan adequately, or *not* establish cooperative relationships with students?

Perhaps the problem begins when teachers see these practices as discipline strategies rather than teaching and learning strategies. When the purpose of cooperation is, for example, behavior control rather than learning, then the quality of the lesson is likely to suffer. When students sense that their participation in making classroom rules is more about managing their behavior than it is about their learning, goodwill and a genuine feeling of community may not develop. And students can surely tell the difference between the teacher who stands beside them to "redirect attention" or forestall disruptive behavior and the teacher who stands nearby ready to answer a question or encourage. In short, teaching strategies and management strategies are very different even though they may look similar on the surface.

Teachers Who Make Lessons Interesting   Offering the simplistic solution of "make the lesson interesting" hardly addresses the complex problem of student discipline. However, decidedly *un*interesting lessons make any problem, including discipline, worse.

Purdue University researcher Jeff Gregg investigated whether traditional conceptions of curriculum and pedagogy might be at the root of teachers' behavior management.[9] He conducted a fascinating yearlong study of how discipline and control problems came to dominate the "general" (lower-track) mathematics class of a first-year high school teacher.

The teacher began the class aware that the students were not "college bound," and she lowered her expectations for their academic performance. However, she still set high (strict and traditional) standards for their behavior, and she pledged to teach them in the same way that she taught the college-bound students in her upper-level geometry class. Yet, unlike that class, the general math students had little inclination to comply with her rules, listen to her during instruction, remain silent during seatwork, and do homework each night. They didn't find the math interesting, and they didn't believe that math would have some payoff for them later.

Worried about the students' potential to be troublesome, the teacher decided not to joke, "be nice" to students, or give them risky opportunities to participate in "fun" activities. In return, they were even less eager to please her. Together, she and the class entered a cycle of the teacher clamping down, the students misbehaving more, followed by a stronger teacher reaction. Eventually, she gave up trying to enforce her rules, blamed the negative attitudes students brought from home, and decided that she didn't care if they learned or not.

This teacher did not consider that the problems she and her students faced might originate in what Gregg calls "the school mathematics tradition." That is, both she and her students thought that "general" mathematics was little more than (usually boring) rules and procedures. They did not consider that math could be learned outside the usual routine of (a) teacher leads the class as they check their homework, (b) teacher provides instruction on the next topic, and (c) teacher assigns practice problems that the students work on quietly and individually for the remainder of class and finish as homework. Gregg considers the very nature of school knowledge as one root of the problem; a good rule of thumb is that good teaching cannot be based on knowledge or teaching methods that the teacher herself finds boring.

This teacher would have needed far more knowledge and commitment to break from the subject matter tradition that she followed. Mathematics and other subjects stripped down to remedial algorithms and presented without any further inducements (no talk, no fun) are almost certain to create discipline problems. In Chapters 3 and 4, we described some curriculum approaches that can keep knowledge-loving teachers engaged and enthused in helping students direct their energy to learning.

Caring, Respect, and Democracy: A Second Set of Legacies

Traditional schooling has had its critics—reformers always looking to make schools better—since the early nineteenth century. A big part of that criticism has implicated schools' need to encourage desirable and prevent undesirable behavior. For example, Horace Mann believed that physical punishment, generally accepted at the time, undermined character development. Nineteenth-century Boston schools sought women teachers because many progressives believed that women would bring their child-rearing nature into classrooms and make them more nurturing. (Not incidentally, women were cheaper to employ and were thought to be more likely than men to remain in teaching.) Turn-of-the-twentieth-century progressive reformers, including John Dewey, argued for "child-centered" rather than subject-centered schools. Advocacy for caring, child-centered classrooms remains a strong force in American schooling today both to foster a well-educated and civic-minded populace and to avoid the consequences of disaffected youth and adults.

Child-Centered Schooling

As we noted in Chapter 3, some school reformers throughout the nineteenth and twentieth centuries argued that students' essentially good nature would cause them to behave well in school if their needs were met. Jean-Jacques Rousseau theorized that humans are naturally good, and that it is society that corrupts. Since discipline represents society's efforts to impose goodness on the child, Rousseau's followers argued that it has no place in education. Instead, progressive reformers believed that schooling practices should match children's needs at their current stage of development, rather than preserve the social order.

Johann Pestalozzi (1746–1827), a Swiss educator, translated Rousseau's ideas into pedagogy, and Pestalozzi had a strong following in the United States throughout the nineteenth century. Pestalozzi wrote about the virtues of "domestic education," explaining that students learn best when schools help them develop self-respect and emotional security. According to Pestalozzi, rather than learning abstractions while sitting obediently at a desk, academic learning should follow from students' engagement, exploration, and activity that connect ideas to real-life objects and events—all under the maternal guidance of a teacher. "Maternal love," in Pestalozzi's view, promised to ensure trust and obedience, elevate moral character, and improve the lot of poor children.

Friedrich Froebel (1782–1852) built on Pestalozzi's ideas and developed the first kindergarten curriculum aimed at promoting children's development through self-expression and cooperative play. Froebel saw the classroom as a miniature society, wherein the cooperation children learned at school would make them cooperative members of adult society.

What a contrast these ideas were to the dominant mode in early-nineteenth-century schools! Educational historian Herbert Kliebard recounts that in 1913, Helen M. Todd, a factory inspector, surveyed 500 child laborers and asked if they would prefer to go back to school or "remain in the squalor of the factories." Kliebard notes, "Of the 500, 412 told her, sometimes in graphic terms, that they preferred factory labor to the monotony, humiliation, and even sheer cruelty that they experienced in school."[10]

Meeting Social as Well as Academic and Vocational Needs   At the turn of the century, the settlement house movement developed an ethic of social service and democratic community that merged political, social, and educational purposes. Jane Addams's Hull House and other settlement houses were more like extended families and communities than like schools. Over time, the settlement house reformers persuaded many schools to appoint school physicians and offer classes for handicapped children; they initiated school lunch programs and school libraries in a movement they called "socialized education." John Dewey's friendship and support of Jane Addams's work influenced his thinking that schools might themselves become social centers that modeled themselves after the community at Hull House.

John Dewey also wanted schools to provide for the multiple needs of immigrants and especially to respond to the devastating effects of their disconnection from their Old World cultures. But Dewey wanted schools to go further than just administering to needs. The key to social progress, he believed, was for schools to develop in children the dispositions and skills to serve society. Dewey wanted schools to turn immigrant children into "good Americans, public-spirited citizens, and members of the 'great community.'"[11]

"Open" Schools and Classrooms   Caring and community were counterpoints to the dominant theme of management and control throughout the twentieth century. In the 1970s the theme of caring and community emerged perhaps more strongly than it had since the turn-of-the-century progressive reforms, in a movement called *humanistic education.* Spearheaded by a group of humanistic psychologists, most prominently Carl Rogers, Abraham Maslow, and Lawrence Kohlberg, reformers proposed that if schools treated students humanely and respectfully, these qualities would prevail in classrooms.

Closely related to the humanistic movement were the more radical, existential ideas of A. S. Neill, whose school (and the book by the same name), Summerhill, featured "open" classrooms. At Summerhill, students were free to discover and choose for themselves meaningful ways to behave and interact with others in the classroom, and teachers facilitated and mediated students' freedom.[12] These ideas inspired numerous attempts to instill humanist ideas and replicate Summerhill's features in what were and still are often called *alternative* schools.

For humanistic reformers, values, moral development, self-discipline, and personal responsibility assumed a major role in students' learning and behavior. A popular method was a technique called "values clarification," wherein students engaged in discussions and simulation exercises to help them discover and examine the principles by which they choose to live.

Interestingly, in the 1990s an emphasis on values would be advocated by another group, also called humanists—though they occupy a niche at the opposite end of the political spectrum. These other humanists, including former secretary of education William Bennett, prescribe fundamental, universal, human qualities and specify how schools should promote them. Often using the term *character education,* these contemporary conservative theorists and educators emphasize telling over guiding, control over freedom, and correcting children's errors over teaching them to examine and inquire with confidence.

As a final note, much of the alternative and humanistic experimentation, although never widely popular, has taken place in middle-class and suburban schools. It has had less appeal and practice in poorer, urban communities.

An Ethic of Care

A compelling exploration of schools and classrooms as caring communities is found in the work of Nel Noddings, a Stanford University professor of educational philosophy. Noddings wants an "ethic of care" to shape the social, emotional, and academic conditions in classrooms. She believes that "schools should be committed to a great moral purpose: to care for children so that they, too, will be prepared to care."[13] Because caring encompasses the moral and cultural values of how people relate to others, caring is an alternative to traditional discipline and classroom management. She proposes that behavioral control strategies like Assertive Discipline destroy care. In her view, not only are these strategies manipulative, but in their effort to free teachers from having to talk or interact with students about their behavior, they also foreclose the opportunity to help students learn to be "healthy, competent, moral people."[14] Noddings believes that even in a math or language lesson or on the playing field, the child-philosopher, the child-scholar, the introspective child, and the humanitarian child must be kept together to make a whole child—exactly what does not happen under mechanized discipline systems with predetermined and automatic consequences for undesirable behavior.

Noddings explains that care includes far more than "a warm fuzzy feeling that makes people kind and likeable."[15] Rather, care implies a "continuous search for competence" and includes fostering in students the knowledge and skills "necessary to make a positive contribution" in whatever field of study or work they might choose. Thus, a caring search for competence has curricular as well as interpersonal implications. Students grapple with questions that are at the core of human existence. According to Noddings, "As human beings, we care what happens to us. We wonder if there is life after death, whether there is a deity who cares about us, whether we are loved by those we love, whether we belong anywhere; we wonder what we will become, who we are, how much control we have over our own fate."[16]

The Power of Relationships

Contemporary reformers like Nel Noddings offer a philosophical perspective that emphasizes caring to fulfill the social and moral purposes of schooling. This work connects in interesting ways to that of psychologists who focus on how relationships are inseparable from cognitive and social development. Consequently, a caring classroom relationship is part of a "search for competence," and, as it is a relationship, there are two people searching. The student's search is his own discovery of what he knows and how he knows it. The teacher's search—an act of care and

respect—is also discovering what the student knows and how he knows it. Teachers express care by searching for their students' competence. Far from offering automatic approval for whatever knowledge or interpretation the student arrives at, we can say that the teacher co-constructs the student's competence as he searches for it. And by a wonderful turn of perspective, we can also say that teachers' competence is co-constructed by their students.

—————————————————— ❆ ❆ ❆ ——————————————————

My approach to classroom management and the way I treat students now as an English Learner (EL) coordinator was and is influenced by my own two sons. My two boys attend a local LAUSD elementary school (Breed Elementary) that feeds into Hollenbeck. When dealing with students, I often ask myself, "How would I want an adult at a school setting to treat my own son in this situation?" Thus, if it is a celebratory occasion, I make sure to praise. If it is a situation where a student needs to be reprimanded, I make sure to do it in a respectful manner. If I need something from a student, I make sure to say "please." If a student does a favor for me, I make sure to say "thank you." Students, like adults, appreciate being treated with respect. In turn, they will treat you with respect.

In the classroom, I had the greatest expectations of my students academically and behaviorally. I made my expectations clear at the beginning of the year and I often reminded them of those expectations throughout the year. If something occurred that was not in line with the expectations, I made an effort to look at my practices first. Many times classroom management issues occur when a lesson is not properly thought out. Thus, instead of blaming the students, teachers need to look at themselves and ask, "How can I change the lesson to engage all students?"

—MAURO BAUTISTA
Middle-school bilingual education coordinator

Relationships, Meanings, and the Search for Competence   In his 1993 book *Developing Through Relationships,* psychologist Alan Fogel explores how relationships are crucial to all development.[17] Fogel's work is primarily with young children, but there are learning implications for everyone. Each new bit of information is understood personally and differently within each social setting and relationship.

For example, even a teacher's simplest utterance, "Take out your pencil," means different things to different students—in large part based on their relationships with the teacher: "I'm in trouble, no pencil"; "Great, we are having the quiz I prepared for"; "How rude, he never says please"; "Como?"; "I don't care if I do fail"; "Another 45 minutes to go"; "Should I just get up to sharpen this or raise my hand and ask for permission? Either way some teachers get mad." None of the preceding meanings is independent of the classroom culture or the relationship with the teacher. In this sense, the information "received" is different for everyone in the class, and since the teacher spoke the same four words to everyone, everyone must have created his or her own different meaning.

Students do not *independently* construct their own meanings. The sociocultural perspectives taken by Vygotsky, Fogel, and others emphasize that meanings are *co*-constructed (or, in Fogel's term, co-regulated) in the relationship. In our preceding example, it was *this* teacher, not another, who spoke *these* words in *this* class where she expected students to have pencils. The teacher and different students share histories of what these words mean. This history might include the teacher's annoyance if students do not have a pencil, the amount of time she waits for students to fish the pencils out of their backpacks, and so on. These are different from the histories the same students might share with other teachers in other classes.

There are simply too many meanings in action to try to fix or control most of them. Learning individuals must be willing to accept guidance and expertise from others, and be willing to change.

Beyond Rules and Routines   In classrooms that are rigidly structured and bound to the rules of behavioral discipline systems, teachers dispense consequences for "misbehavior" almost automatically. In fact, sometimes these systems advise teachers to avoid "unnecessary" interactions with students. Such teachers might try to assure students, "It's not personal, the punishment is strictly a consequence of your behavior." We think that this is an extreme message to send, because it forecloses the possibility of classroom communities in which students develop their own tools for interaction, interdependence, and problem solving. All classroom interactions are in some way personal.

The relationships among people in and out of classrooms are not incidental to learning. And the importance of relationships goes far deeper than our conventional sense that if a teacher has a "good" relationship with students, students will try harder and learn more. No one would fault the teacher who has the capacity to be popular and friendly. However, these clearly desirable relationship strengths mean far less if the teacher neglects the interactive teaching strategies and cooperative activities that join cognitive and social learning.

Caring Teachers   Complementing Fogel's work are psychological studies that show the importance of relationships between teachers and students who are coping with the difficulties of urban poverty. For example, UCLA researchers Carollee Howes and Sharon Ritchie examined how teachers were able to construct positive classroom relationships with children who lived in difficult circumstances. Some students were homeless, and they all brought to the classroom the behaviors and assumptions about relationships that they developed in response to difficult and sometimes tragic experiences. These children had a very poor learning prognosis. Furthermore, they were often "hostile, aggressive, and distrustful, and not easy to have in a classroom."[18] The teachers established trust with the children in much the same way that Amy Lee did with Hector.

The researchers noted that novice teachers sometimes feel that they must be consistent in their responses to different students to show that they are not playing favorites. However, establishing trust with students who have few safe or reliable relationships with adults requires a teacher who is "sufficiently flexible to individualize" his or her interactions.[19] Also, teachers who repeat key relationship phrases— for example, "I'm going to help you," "Do you need me to help you?," and "I'll help you"—seem to engender trust. Such repetition signals and establishes a whole category of positive attention that might otherwise be lost as isolated (and meaningless) exchanges.

Expert teachers in the study gave students positive attention and communicated clearly that they believed the children were worthy of affection. However, flexibility and a lack of rigid, behavioral structures should not be mistaken for confusing, inconsistent, or unpredictable classroom practices. Howes and Ritchie's research shows that trusting, mutually satisfying relationships and a sense of community at school create conditions where all children—even those in quite desperate circumstances—can learn and develop well.

George Noblit and his colleagues studied how two highly experienced teachers, Martha and Pam, constructed caring relationships with their students in their racially mixed, inner-city school. The two had quite different classroom manners. Pam, an African American teacher, kept her classroom interactions formal and polite, while Martha, a white teacher, encouraged lots of informal exchange. Yet both exercised what Noblit calls a "dogged determination" to develop trustful, caring relationships with troubled students.

Like Erik Korporaal and Amy Lee and the teachers that Howes and Ritchie observed, Pam and Martha used "no magic tricks, no technical fixes—just consistent day-in and day-out, hour-to-hour, even minute-to-minute" attention to creating opportunities for these children to succeed and attain social competence.[20] For example, Martha established daily rituals to communicate her care for Robert, a student who had recently transferred from a special school for students with severe problems. She waited at the door to say "hello" to him; she made sure that she took a few minutes to chat with him about nonschool matters, such as television programs; and she said "good-bye" when he left each afternoon. Martha also insisted that Robert participate in class activities. In time, her regular and obvious commitment and attention helped create a classroom context for Robert that allowed him to behave appropriately, make friends, and achieve more than he ever had before.

In accordance with her style, Pam used a somewhat different approach to developing a caring relationship with John, a painfully shy special education student who had been mainstreamed into her class (see Chapter 8 for a discussion of the terms *special education* and *mainstream*). In response to John's efforts to avoid interacting with her by "hiding" behind other students or his desk, Pam insisted in a stern, but reassuring way that he sit up and participate. She moved his desk so he would be close to her, and she made a practice of standing nearby when he worked in groups with other students. She also often touched his shoulder to show her support. Pam's constancy and her obviously caring actions over the school year helped John feel safe enough to participate and learn.

Martha's and Pam's students recognized the concrete ways that their teachers showed that they cared. Students told Noblit that they knew Martha and Pam were caring because they helped them with their schoolwork "without demeaning them for needing help"; they talked with them and showed respect by listening; they were confident about students' abilities; they tolerated mistakes; and they encouraged them.[21]

Making Classrooms Communities

—————————————————— ⚙ ⚙ ⚙ ——————————————————

At the time that I chose to teach the book Bridge to Terabithia, *I had become quite concerned by a general lack of compassion in the classroom and school communities. Discussions of local violence and death were often glorified with naive excitement. Many of my students had lost loved ones to violence in the community or in their native countries. In addition, my fourth and fifth graders had trouble finding common ground and seemed to have very different notions of friendship. I felt that I needed to address these issues through the curriculum, and this core literature book offered the collective experience that I thought would most benefit our classroom community.* Bridge to Terabithia *is primarily about relationships. The plot centers on the friendship of a fifth-grade boy and girl who learn to show compassion.*

—CHRISTOPHER YUSI
First-year teacher, grades 4 and 5

In *Beyond Discipline: From Compliance to Community,* former teacher Alfie Kohn describes class meetings during which students agree on how they will work together to solve the inevitable problems that arise in class.[22] By pondering such questions as "What makes school awful sometimes?," "What can we do this year to make sure things go better?," "Suppose you hurt someone's feelings, or did something even worse. How would you want us, the rest of the community, to help you then?," and "What if someone else acted that way? How could we help that person?" students can construct a safe and caring learning community. Kohn argues that such conversations, combined with lots of collaborative work on academic and social issues, can turn classrooms into places where discipline problems rarely happen.

Kohn draws extensively from the Child Development Project in Northern California, a research group that developed and studied community-like classroom practices. The project emphasizes that core values must be experienced, not just taught; thus, participating teachers learn to reflect on their own practice and ask questions that elicit students' thinking. Students are given and accept increasing responsibility for their own learning. Teachers learn how to maintain order without extrinsic rewards and to de-emphasize competition by having students set learning goals and establish classroom rules. Teachers and students collaborate on a curriculum in which they investigate—through literature, science, and history—what it means to be a principled, caring person. Class meetings and problem solving are classroom community routines, rather than a response to extraordinary crises.

Project researchers Eric Schaps and his colleagues studied sixth graders who had participated in the program since kindergarten. Compared with peers of the same social class and achievement who had attended conventional classrooms, these students behaved more considerately toward their classmates and worked better together. They also better understood others' perspectives and could better solve interpersonal conflicts. Two years later when the students were in junior high, the positive effects of the program were still evident. Other schools in the project have noted substantial decreases in discipline problems, as well. Research by this group also provides evidence that these strategies work well in central city schools enrolling low-income children of color, as well as in more affluent suburban schools with white and middle-class children.[23]

First-year teacher Cicely Benninger provided her African American and Latino kindergartners a series of experiences to establish a culture of care in her classroom that would help them extend caring to the often harsh world outside.

———————————————————⚌ ⚌ ⚌———————————————————

The Peace Builders antiviolence curriculum helps teachers teach social, emotional, and thinking skills to help students avoid violence and give them a strategy for handling conflicts peacefully.[24] Using a combination of stories, role plays, discussions, writing activities, projects, positive reinforcements, and exhibitions, the curriculum addresses the causes, effects, and alternatives to violence at both a global and local level. Peace Builders is organized around four principles that serve as guides for how to develop into an effective peace builder: (1) praise people; (2) give up put-downs; (3) notice hurts and right wrongs; and (4) seek wise people. Lessons and activities focus on these ideas.

CICELY BENNINGER
First-year teacher, kindergarten

To enact these classroom norms, Benninger's students discuss peace and violence in their own lives, brainstorm ways to support peace, invent a pantomime to accompany the class-adopted theme song, "I've Got Peace Like a River," and read big-book stories like "Tillie and the Wall," "an allegorical tale of a young mouse who bravely crosses a long-accepted wall that separates her community from another." The students consider walls in their lives and whether they "fear what is beyond these walls." Benninger creates a bulletin board to recognize students' peace-building activities and has the students construct links of a giant "peace chain" to help them visualize peaceful acts.

─────────────────────────── ✗ ✗ ✗ ───────────────────────────

> *Some may argue that bringing the unpleasantness of surrounding violence to the fore of a curriculum for 5-year-olds is ill-timed and casts a dark shadow on what ought to be the most carefree time of a child's life. This assertion might hold up if these young children did not already suffer from exposure to violence. Several of my students speak very candidly about witnessing domestic violence, homicide, and gang activity. A teacher's silence on these issues is irresponsible. Expecting young children to interpret the violence they witness and extricate themselves from violence in their own responses to conflict [without the help of adults] is a disservice.*

Benninger's approach echoes that of Chicago kindergarten teacher Vivian Gussin Paley. In her book *You Can't Say You Can't Play,* Paley probes the moral issue of children excluding others in the classroom, especially those whom they see as different. According to Paley, schools reinforce children's rejections of others. Sometimes adults accept rejection as a natural behavior and only intervene or take a moral stance in cases of blatant physical or psychological harm. Because acts of rejection are so familiar and frequent (usually painful and cumulative pinpricks rather than violent attacks), teachers may choose to ignore what they see as mild negative behavior.

Tolerating rejection is not a minor discipline issue. Unchecked, it lets students develop social attitudes that affect their own and others' well-being and safety. To prevent her students from developing this habit of rejection, Paley implemented a rule that her students proposed when they discussed this problem. That rule forbade them from turning away any student who wanted to play in their group: "You can't say you can't play."

Socially Just Classrooms: Doing Democracy

Throughout the nineteenth century, small and often marginalized reform groups worked to make schools instruments of social justice. Particularly interesting are the efforts of African American women educators, often assisted by black churches and sometimes by liberal white groups like the Quakers, to use the schools to improve the social, economic, and political circumstances of the African American community. These women used their classrooms and their leadership to teach reading and writing not only to their students but to community adults as well—a daring act in the nineteenth century.

For example, teacher Fannie Jackson Coppin organized tuition-free classes for freedmen coming north and founded a school for children of emancipated slaves. Believing that knowledge is power, Coppin intended her teaching to "uplift" the race. Other well-educated black women educators such as Anna Julia Cooper and Mary McLeod Bethune also went far beyond teaching their students technical skills and attempted to teach in ways that would bring about social and political change. At the root of their efforts was the conviction that education was not about individual gain, but about strengthening the community, a view captured eloquently in the motto of the National Association of Colored Women—"Lifting as We Climb."

In the educational mainstream, first Horace Mann and later John Dewey envisioned schools as agencies of social reform and the democratization of American society. Dewey stressed that classrooms are a part of life, not merely preparation for it, and that to make society more democratic, students must participate in classrooms that are themselves democratic societies. Teachers must give students a chance to learn how their actions affect the success or failure of the group. And students must develop their sense of civic-mindedness by sharing both the pleasant and trying tasks that complex group projects require. "Doing one's part" as a member of a classroom project prepares children to be both leaders and followers.

Beginning with the 1960s' civil rights movement, the struggle for equal educational opportunity has brought structural changes in schools: racial desegregation, bilingual education, inclusion of handicapped children in regular classrooms, and heterogeneous (or mixed-ability) grouping. Each of these changes met with intense and continuing opposition, and much work remains before their goals are achieved. To accommodate these changes, researchers and teachers began developing cooperative small-group learning to improve social relationships and ease tensions in racially mixed and otherwise diverse classrooms. Reformers today speak less about overcoming the "problems" of diverse classrooms than they do about unleashing the power of diversity as a resource.

Critical Pedagogy Responds to Students' "Resistance"

At the end of the twentieth century, critical pedagogy emerged as a theory of education that calls for classrooms to be democratic and socially just communities. Critical pedagogy, introduced in Chapter 3, begins with the assumption that schooling is not Horace Mann's "great equalizer." Rather, schools help privileged families pass on their advantages to their children, and they make it likely that low-status and low-income children will also follow in their parents' footsteps. When teachers use a critical pedagogy, they ask students to examine historical and contemporary events, institutions, and relationships in order to expose otherwise invisible mechanisms of advantage and disadvantage. This endeavor requires listening to different voices, versions, and interpretations typically kept out of official versions of school knowledge and culture.

Even though her students are very young, Kimberly Min understands that their engagement in school will depend on whether they see the connections between what they are learning in classrooms and their lives in their low-income community of color. Kimberly's following comments illustrate her logic in presenting a unit surrounding the landmark *Brown v. Board of Education* case.

---⚗ ⚗ ⚗---

As a critical pedagogue, I strive for my students to be interested and invested in what they are learning and provide a space for my students to have opportunities to create knowledge. The lessons I have developed encompass California state standards and fulfill my goal to actively engage my students in rigorous knowledge-making around the implications and the outcomes of the Brown *case.*

Students discussed how history has affected their current educational reality and although only 8 years in age, they can recognize and express their discontent with their educational experiences. The students also shared their discontent with the type of curriculum, lack of school supplies, and diversity on campus.

—**Kimberly Min**
Third-grade teacher

Critical pedagogy is a tough and unforgiving view of the world that relentlessly seeks liberation of the oppressed by identifying the rawest social sores and refusing to be polite about them. For some, it is difficult to get beyond the vocabulary of critical pedagogy to examine the merits of the ideas. Critical pedagogues tend to use words that approximate how people are affected by ideas and social processes, rather than how democracy-minded, socially concerned people intend society to work. Thus, if there are people oppressed by their economic conditions, there must be *oppressors*. If there are less powerful segments of society, there must be *dominant* ones. If people find themselves on the margins of society (and they did not place themselves there), others have *marginalized* them. On the other hand, critical pedagogy is far from a fearsome, subversive perspective bent on destroying the social order. It is a philosophy that seeks to bring clarity to injustice and unjust processes.

Critical pedagogy asks the teacher to remove himself or herself from the role of oppressor—however benevolent. Brazilian educational theorist Paulo Freire, for example, argued that students must never be manipulated or controlled. And perhaps the most pernicious form of control is in using one's power (authority, charisma, language, etc.) to cause students or their parents to think that they have made unimpeded choices on their own behalf. Rather, critical pedagogues involve students in a constant dialogue that allows students to examine their experiences and act to improve the conditions of their lives—in school and out.

School traditions make critical teaching seem strange, if not incendiary. However, even in the midst of institutional requirements—cover the curriculum, assign grades, enforce discipline policies—teachers can work steadily to empower their students. Teachers who struggle to break free from oppressive relationships will benefit their students in many ways as well as find their own practices enormously satisfying. Of course, the point of being a critical teacher is to empower critical students—students who reflect and question the common sense that underlies issues of race, class, gender, and the often invisible privileges of white, middle-class people, and of men. To do this well, teachers should not "go it alone," but find others with similar views to help find age- and content-appropriate opportunities to bring critical perspectives to students.

Critical perspectives about their schooling help students find identities as transformative actors rather than the disaffected or resistant students they might be labeled. Students are thoroughly capable of *unpacking* commonsense ideas about learning, knowledge, classroom activities and relationships, and the common schooling issues of authority, discipline, and control. Such activities, a form of literacy in their own right, can also bridge to students' acquiring the conventional literacies that are demanded for mainstream school success.

Although critical educators would never frame their approach as a form of classroom management or discipline (and it surely is not), they do believe that their practices moderate the thinking, structures, and routines that cause many students to be "discipline problems." Further, this shift may cause many teachers to reevaluate what they perceive as a problem.

The theory of "resistance," developed by Paul Willis and Henry Giroux, embarks from anthropological studies of schools and classrooms. Both Giroux and Willis found that lower-class students often behave "badly" as an expression of resistance. The students knew, at least on some level, that the way schools responded to them doomed them to limited life chances. Thus, in this view, antischool attitudes and behavior can be seen as logical (if usually unproductive) rebellion against an oppressive institution, rather than as individual psychological problems—lack of self-discipline, laziness, low ability, and so on—or problems that stem from poor parenting or a disorganized neighborhood. Although critical educators do not believe that all "oppositional behavior" has this political quality, they do believe that many students act to assert their own power over their destiny.

Democratic Classrooms and Diversity

Resistance theory, "oppositional behavior," and other facets of critical pedagogy exist on two levels. As social, political, and learning theory, critical pedagogy enables scholars to step back and understand human relationships from the broad perspective of power relationships, historical contexts, and more. On another level we can find many examples of educators whose actions embody these theories. In very practical and down-to-earth ways their teaching helps children preserve, enrich, and value their own culture by contributing to and challenging the schoolwide and community culture. As Professor Gloria Ladson-Billings has said, the classrooms of such educators are "culturally relevant."

Culturally Relevant Classrooms   It is easy to have a commitment to "cultural relevance" *as a value* but difficult to act on that value—especially when your students have cultural backgrounds other than your own. However, teaching only those students who share your background is neither desirable nor likely to happen. And teaching all students only from your own perspective is unacceptable. Most teachers of color and teachers for whom English is not their first language have had extensive experience with white, middle-class, mainstream culture, as well as their "own" racial, ethnic, or language group. White teachers are more likely to be mono-cultural. But whether teachers are monocultural, bicultural, or multicultural, there are both generic and specific dimensions to culturally relevant teaching that they all must acquire. Acquiring these dimensions as part of one's own teaching can be, like foreign travel, daunting at first; but the discovery and adventure are soon difficult to resist. And even though, in our travels, we will not be "natives," we can learn and earn respect.

The generic elements to culturally relevant teaching are really what this book is all about—approaches to schooling, learning, curriculum, and so forth, that are friendly to difference. The specific dimensions to culturally relevant teaching, how-ever, require cultural knowledge that can only be gained by knowing your particular students and their community.

In her book *The Dreamkeepers: Successful Teachers of African American Children,* Ladson-Billings describes the practices of eight teachers (three white and five African American) who created wonderful caring and democratic class-room communities with their inner-city students. These teachers viewed them-selves as artists who "mined" knowledge from very capable students, rather than technicians who put knowledge into them. They saw and valued their students' "color," working constantly to help them see how their identity as African Ameri-cans connects with national and global ideas and events. All eight teachers saw themselves as part of and "giving back" to the communities where they taught.

In a style that Ladson-Billings calls "we are family," the teachers structured classroom social interactions so that students worked together in ways that we de-scribed in Chapter 5. For example, teacher Margaret Rossi used her students' racial identity to accomplish something sixth-grade teachers everywhere struggle with—having students see how "current events" connect with their own lives. At the out-set of the Gulf War, Rossi pressed her California students to figure out how events in Kuwait and Iraq affected them. Notice in Focal Point 7.3 the several concepts Rossi manages to weave through this culturally relevant lesson, including "disproportionality"—basic to mathematics and statistics—language appropriate to cultural groupings, and respectful affirmations of students' contributions to the group.

With Rossi's skillful guidance, the "current events" session evolved into a rich, culturally relevant lesson for students. Ladson-Billings describes the students work-ing busily together by the end of the lesson to create casualty charts revealing how various events in the news might impact their community.

Being responsive to cultural style is always more subtle than teaching tips can account for. Teachers can be open about their desire to connect better with their students and overcome handicaps imposed by their own difference. They also might acknowledge this cultural difference (which is undoubtedly obvious to all) and invite parents or other members of the students' community into the class to offer

FOCAL POINT 7.3

Successful Teachers of African American Students
The Dreamkeepers

Denisha, a small African American girl who was a diligent student but rarely spoke up in class, raised her hand.

"Yes, Denisha."

In a soft and measured voice, Denisha said, "Well, I think it affects us because you have to have people to fight a war, and since they don't have no draft, the people who will volunteer will be the people who don't have any jobs, and a lot of people in our community need work, so they might be the first ones to go."

Before Rossi could comment, an African American boy, Sean, chimed in, "Yeah, my dad said that's what happened in Vietnam—blacks and Mexicans were the first ones to go."

"I'm not sure if they were the first to go," remarked Rossi, "but I can say they were overrepresented." She writes these words on the board. "Do you know what I mean by this?"

None of the students volunteers a response, so Rossi proceeds with an example.

"If African Americans are 12 percent of the total U.S. population, and Latinos are 8 percent of the total U.S. population, what percent of the armed services do you think they should be?"

"Twenty percent total," calls out James, beaming at his ability to do the arithmetic quickly. "Twelve percent should be black, and 8 percent should be Mexican."

"Okay," says Rossi. "However, I would call that 8 percent Latino rather than Mexican, because we are also including Puerto Ricans, Cuban Americans, and other U.S. citizens who are from Latin America. But in Vietnam, their numbers in the armed services far exceeded their numbers in the general population. Often they were the first to volunteer to go. Does it seem as if Denisha's comments help us link up with this news item?"

Source: Gloria Ladson-Billings, *The Dreamkeepers: Successful Teachers of African American Children* (San Francisco: Jossey-Bass, 1994), pp. 50–51.

their impressions of how the teaching could be more effective for these students. For example, parents might observe that these students would do better with a friendlier, more gentle tone, or they might suggest a more formal and directive approach. Similarly, teachers might observe several successful teachers and note how they "reach" the students.

Gender-Fair Classrooms   Culturally democratic classrooms also consider gender differences. In their book *Failing at Fairness: How America's Schools Cheat Girls,* researchers David and Myra Sadker examine the role that gender plays in the way teachers treat children and the way children treat one another. The Sadkers sent "raters"' to observe fourth, sixth, and eighth graders and their teachers in more than a hundred classrooms in inner cities, rural areas, and affluent suburbs. They studied routine classroom phenomena by asking the following questions: Whom did the teacher call on? How did the student get the teacher's attention? By raising a hand? By calling out? Did the teacher designate the student? What did the teacher say after she or he called on students? What level of help or feedback were students getting? If the teacher praised a student, what was the praise for?

The Sadkers detail how "schoolgirls face subtle and insidious gender lessons, micro-inequities that appear seemingly insignificant when looked at individually but that have a powerful cumulative impact." These "hidden lessons" take many forms and begin early. In elementary school classrooms, girls were shortchanged in class discussion, on the playground, and in the curriculum. Boys received more of four reactions from teachers: praise, correction, help, criticism—all reactions that foster student achievement. "Girls received less time, less help, and fewer challenges. "Reinforced for passivity, girls' independence and self-esteem suffer."[25]

David Sadker noted in an interview, "It's not good teaching to reinforce with the boys the idea of 'Act out, threaten to act out, and I will shower you with instructional time to keep you on task.' To girls, teachers say silently: 'Do what's expected, and I'll ignore you.'"[26] The Sadkers suggest that teachers can keep boys from dominating the classroom by waiting longer for answers after asking a question, monitoring cooperative-learning groups, and making comments to girls that encourage academic progress.

Taking this work to heart, first-year high school science teacher Lisa Trebasky considers gender as she makes curriculum and instruction decisions.

It is not only what I do but also what I do not do that has a tremendous impact. I have high expectations for all of my students, not just the boys. If I challenge a boy to figure out the answer to a scientifically engaging problem for himself, and then go and give the answer to a girl, I send an unconscious message that I do not think my female student can figure it out by herself. I encourage the girls' active participation when it is easy for them to be drowned out by the louder and more aggressive boys. I encourage girls to ask questions and help them use scientific methodology to find answers. I challenge them to think about why there are more men who do science than women.

—LISA TREBASKY
First-year teacher, high school science

Democratic Classrooms and Power

In the introduction to this book we pointed out that multiculturalism is not a philosophy or a strategy or, for that matter, a choice. In a society where there are many cultures, *multicultural* is simply a description. Similarly, as resistance theory makes clear, the power of students is not something for adults to bestow or deny, or debate whether it is a "good idea" to have. Where there are students, they have power—although that may be power to act out and disrupt; power to shut down and withdraw; or power to learn, care, and contribute. The question worth asking, then, is "What shall students and teachers make of these multicultures and this power?"

Schools typically respond to students as if personal problems were the cause of students not fitting in, not conforming, and causing disruptions. The alternate view here is to affirm and find new power within diverse cultures and to find the learning and social power in students' legitimate cultural attributes. Importantly, we should not be so naive as to think that inattention to cultural difference explains all school problems, or worse, to use that difference to excuse behaviors (teachers' or students') that would be unproductive in any culture.

Classrooms as "Apprenticeships in Democracy"   Critical theorists such as Peter McLaren, Ira Shor, and Antonia Darder emphasize the role of culture-related power in the classroom. These educators grapple with the dual dilemma of how to turn resistant students' energies in directions that will benefit them instead of asking students to give up what makes them different. In a probing and comprehensive argument, Antonia Darder, for example, calls for classrooms to be "apprenticeships in democracy." Darder stresses the need for teachers to take seriously student participation, solidarity, common interest, and voice.[27]

In *Culture and Power in the Classroom: A Critical Foundation for Bicultural Education,* Darder alerts teachers to immigrant and nonwhite students' right and need to develop and maintain bicultural identities. Darder wants teachers to create a culturally dynamic environment to help students construct and determine how they fit into (and apart from) the dominant culture. Given the students' different experience and cultures, there can be no formulas, no "best" cultural curriculum. The curriculum of culture begins within the students themselves, and all other learning (such as literacy, science, etc.) will take place in the context of this culture. If students' bicultural identities are not valued, then all other curriculum will be fragmented and resisted.

First-year teacher Ramon Martinez decided that his first graders who lived in poverty in public housing projects were not too young to confront in the classroom some of the conditions they experienced in their daily lives. Using Darder's approach, he sought to counteract the resistance that his students, as young as they were, had already begun to exhibit.

———————————————————————————————⊠ ⊠ ⊠———————————————————————————————

I witnessed firsthand the way that my students' cultural contexts influence their attitudes and actions in our classroom. Since academic and economic success are uncommon in their community, my students are likely to dismiss academic and economic aspirations as unrealistic. In fact, some of my students seem to have already done just that.

The challenge for me is to use my theoretical understanding of students' behavior to provide a more effective learning environment. In particular, I have been influenced by the notion that student participation and the development of student voice are essential components of a culturally democratic learning environment.

My students' familiarity with alcoholism, drug abuse, and gang violence; their mastery of "Spanglish" and code-switching; and their skillful ability to communicate the subtle nuances of everyday life in the projects might not be perceived as knowledge or intelligence by many teachers. However, my students have much to contribute to the construction of knowledge in our classroom. Group discussions, weekly "sharing time," and interactive journals are three ways that I have attempted to validate my students' lived experiences. I have tried to communicate to them that their thoughts, ideas, and experiences are important and worthy of discussion in the classroom. My goal has been for them to feel that they are experts when it comes to their neighborhood and themselves.

For example, although most of my students live in the projects, [when we made our "mural map" of the neighborhood] many of them chose to create large, colorful homes with sloped roofs. Interestingly, one student depicted her building extremely realistically. When I smiled at her house, she insisted that that was how it really looked. I agreed with her and recruited her to make more buildings to fill some of the empty spaces on the map. After she had completed her task, I noticed that one of the buildings had "PR" written on it in large letters. When I questioned her about what the letters were for, she was silent and even seemed a little embarrassed. After an extended pause, she told me that that was what they spray painted on the walls of her building. I quickly realized that she had attempted to imitate the graffiti of "PF" ("Primera Flats"), one of the eight gangs that reside in the housing projects. I realized that her embarrassment was due to her uncertainty as to how I would react to the graffiti. I reassured her that it was perfectly all right to depict things as she saw them.

To a very large degree, these strategies have been successful. My students share their thoughts, ideas, and experiences with me and with their classmates. They seem to perceive that our classroom is a forum for them to share freely and openly. I feel that I have contributed to their empowerment by encouraging them to express and define themselves.

—RAMON MARTINEZ
First-year teacher, grade 1

Building on Students' Powerful Resources   Obviously, to help students gain access to their own power, teachers have to be able to recognize it as Ramon Martinez did. This is not always easy, given schools' inclination to interpret hints of student power as negative or valueless. This is a matter about which Ira Shor is very helpful. In his 1992 book, *Empowering Education: Critical Teaching for Social Change,* Shor identifies empowering resources that are worth every teacher's efforts to look for and support. In some respects, the measure of a caring and democratic classroom is revealed by this power in action. In the following list, we offer and build on Shor's specification of 10 "student resources for empowering education and critical thought."[28]

1. *"Students have extra cognitive and affective resources" that caring and democratic classrooms allow to bloom.* [S]tudents "can read, write, listen, and debate with more care than they habitually demonstrate; they feel more deeply

about experiences and ideas than they let on . . . they are brighter, more articulate, and have more emotional depth" than the typical teacher-centered classroom allows them to risk showing.

2. *Students will talk wonderfully well in caring and democratic classrooms.* Shor notes: "[T]hey can speak passionately about themes that are important to them . . . [and] student speech is rich and colorful when they let teachers hear their authentic voices; they display lively imaginations, interesting thoughts, deep feelings, and humor; city life also makes them verbal in their daily relationships, if not in class; they are used to talking a lot in their private life; their talkative habits can become academic tools in class."

3. *Students will tell their "life and work experiences" in caring and democratic classrooms.* Shor points out that teachers must be aware that students' experiences in "school and family life, in street life, and in relationships . . . are worthy of inquiry, like teenage pregnancy, abortion, drugs and alcohol, suicide, . . . racism, sexual harassment . . ." and, as we have heard from first-year teachers, neighborhood and family violence."

Of course, not all is so grim. Students also have warm and enriching experiences—minor satisfactions and major triumphs—to share. Many classrooms take none of this seriously, the grim or the joyful. Importantly, with exceptions for students whose words can dominate or be hurtful, to foreclose the expression of any one student's experience must necessarily dampen the expression of everyone else. The class never loses just one story or one student's insights.

4. *Students desire self-esteem and can find it in caring and democratic classrooms.* Self-esteem is typically seen as a "need," and we may be more accustomed to associating needs with deficits than with power. However, when classrooms support students' confidence, they become powerful actors on behalf of themselves and their classmates. Confidence allows one to ask for help and to help others. "I listen carefully . . . and take notes in class from their comments; I ask them to repeat their statements and to reread their papers aloud . . . so that other students can focus on the words of a peer as serious material for discussion; I also start a class hour with some reference to what students said before . . . to reinforce the importance of their words; I use their themes as problems for dialogue, to indicate the value of their perceptions and lives."

5. *Students have a curiosity that is powerful when it is supported in caring and democratic classrooms.* What makes curiosity powerful also makes it risky. It leads into places unknown and reveals vulnerabilities that are intolerable in public settings that threaten, ridicule, or ignore.

6. *Students have powerful democratic attitudes that can be developed in caring and democratic classrooms.* Shor offers a virtual catalog of powerful dispositions that students bring to class. They have "a healthy dislike for bosses, big shots, politicians, and arrogant pundits; they are sensitive to indignity and don't like to be pushed around by arbitrary authorities, haughty supervisors, and bureaucratic chiefs; they resent following rules they did not make; their democratic values include beliefs in justice, equality, tolerance for differences, fair play,

and free speech. [T]hese values compete with antidemocratic ones developed by community and mass cultures, like male superiority, white supremacy, homophobia, narrow-minded ethnocentrism, competitive self-reliance, environmental disregard, excessive consumerism, and glory in military force," and more.

Before we float away with the democratic glories of youth, Shor keeps us earthbound. He reminds us of some social conditions that explain why not all power develops positively, and why democratic classrooms are so essential: "[T]hey [students] don't see individuals and groups winning improvements through concerted democratic action, so their orientation to activism is virtually nonexistent; students express cynicism about moneyed power in society but want to live like the rich; they believe in democracy despite few democratic experiences in school, at work, at home, in the street, and in their traditional classrooms."

7. *Students bring differing views of race and racism to school; as a topic, racism is a powerful democratic tool in a caring and democratic classroom.* But ignored, racism destroys a classroom. Perhaps there is no other student attitude that is more futile and dangerous to try to "control" or suppress than racism. We sketch here just a few of Shor's many views and practices as examples of how one democratic teacher approaches racism. (Other places to look for ideas are included in "Digging Deeper" on this book's website.) Shor tells us, "I intervene with questions, comments, exercises, and readings, to raise the profile of the pervasive discrimination faced by people of color and not by whites, and to encourage unprejudiced students to speak up and question their peers; so that I don't remain the leading antiracist voice in class. . . . I try not to lecture students on good and evil; I cannot moralize or sermonize them as if I am a superior teacher who considers them awful or dumb; any superior attitude on my part will only make the racist students defensively cling to their beliefs; . . . I try to treat all students as intelligent people who want to do the right thing; students are generally reluctant to discuss racism while listing it often as a big problem in society needing discussion; one pedagogy I found helpful in regard to racism uses a problem-posing format beginning with a dialogue around the question 'What is "racism"?' . . . What causes racism? What can reduce racism?'"

8. *Students are willing to apply their considerable power to overcoming sexism and homophobia (their own and others) in caring and democratic classrooms.* We are so surrounded by differential treatment of men and women—in schools and out—that most teachers will go days or months (some manage an entire career!) without noticing or responding to the misapplication of gender privilege. Whether it is a matter of boys dominating the microscope in science class (while the girls write up the lab notes), a middle schooler calling his neighbor a "fag," or a group of high school freshmen girls passing along rumors about a classmate's recent date, *not responding* to sexist and homophobic behaviors denies students the opportunity to use their power to change the culture that tolerates these behaviors.

9. *Students are able and eager to explore felt, but usually unspoken, reservations about the American dream, in caring and democratic classrooms.*

Students whose families benefit less from American capitalism have no more facility with its critique than those who benefit more have. Although many students doubt whether they will personally benefit, nearly all seem to have considerable faith that an economic system exists that benefits those who are smart enough, good enough, hardworking enough, or even crooked enough. Much of what eventually surfaces as "resistance" may have its origins in the cumulative weight of students' unarticulated sense that America (or simply, school) works in others' favor but not their own. Culturally democratic classrooms help students explore how culture and identity interact with conceptions of worth and merit and how the doctrines of capitalism define worth and merit.

10. *Students express humor and emotion in caring and democratic classrooms.* Shor writes, "[Students] often react with surprise, delight, or shyness when class dialogue is emotional, not just analytic, and when texts convey intensity . . . from humor to sadness to outrage to hope; some take a while to laugh or express strong emotion in class because it is new to them, that intellectual life in classroom should have emotional qualities." Of course, when controlling students is a matter of concern, expressing humor and emotion (especially the noisy kind, like laughter) is the first to emerge as a problem.

Creating Classroom Communities Is a Struggle

—————————————————⊗ ⊗ ⊗—————————————————

Community and community building were important aspects of my educational philosophy, so I knew they had to be part of my practice from day one. I spent the first week of school doing community-building activities. We did people hunts, made and wore nametags, wrote first-day-of-school creative essays, and did other getting-to-know-you activities. By the second week, I felt my students were getting to know each other and me and were developing a sense of trust and security.

As the days passed, I began to wonder when and if my kids were ever going to "learn." I felt such pressure to make sure my students were academically prepared that, by the third week of school, I had placed the idea of community building on the back burner. I did not see any behavior problems in those first weeks, so I felt comfortable that the time we spent building our community was probably enough. I was ready to get down to "business." I watched them work in partners or in groups, and the work was getting done. That was all that I cared about. What I failed to realize, however, was that they were simply completing the work independently, while sitting next to their partners. There was no negotiation, communication, or interaction taking place. It was every student for him- or herself.

By the fifth week, my students were out of control. They were tattling, bullying, name calling, poking, and excluding one another from activities. They did not value or respect one another, and their antics were affecting the lessons and activities. I spent more time mediating fights than mediating knowledge. I was miserable and angry.

I decided to incorporate a community circle into our schedule. I called the circle to share what I had observed in the classroom and the yard. I used a story, "A Sense of Goose," from A Second Helping of Chicken Soup for the Soul *as a discussion starter. The story describes how geese function as a community, uplifting one another as they fly in a V formation. Interwoven through the story are italicized messages that make the connection between how geese live and how humans should live. But my students spent more time trying to figure out the vocabulary than to comprehend the meaning. Many did not even know what geese looked like or anything about geese. (I marked this as failure number one.) I found myself losing patience with them because they weren't "getting it." I could not believe that my students were not able to take the meaning from the story and apply it to life and our classroom. I could not imagine taking thirty-two students outside and making them flap their arms in a V formation for them to construct understanding. So I tried to draw it on the chalkboard. (I marked this as failure number two.)*

Eventually, after a couple of readings a few students understood the meaning, but I didn't want to push it. The idea of community and our classroom as a community of learners was as foreign as another language. I placed the story back into my lesson plan book, feeling defeated. I had my students put the story in their binders, in hopes that one day we would come back to it and really understand its meaning and relevance. They complied and silently sat with bewildered looks as if to say, "What was this crazy lady talking about?" We held a few more community circles before winter break, but we never revisited the story.

Over winter break, I finally had time to read Alfie Kohn's book Beyond Discipline: From Compliance to Community. *It could not have come at a better time. I began to find answers to why the "A Sense of Goose" story did not make sense to my students. Whatever form of community we had was enforced by me. I was running a very teacher-centered classroom, where all the power of decision making and conflict resolution rested in my hands.*

As the year progressed, my students and I began to realize a democratic classroom community. It was an incredible and sometimes difficult evolution from a teacher-centered and controlled environment to a community created and strengthened by students. "Guess what the teacher wants" (under the guise of democracy) evolved into "What should we do?" under guidelines I determined, and then into "I can't/don't need to do it myself, what do you guys think we should do?" Over the next couple of months, my students and I developed and maintained a wonderfully strong community.

Then, once again, I put our community building on autopilot, just as the "change" in sixth-grade students that my colleagues had warned me about occurred. Slowly things crumbled. Best friends were no longer best friends. Rumors and gossip were "destroying" reputations and tearing down trust. Four of my students were put into in-school suspension! I was barely sleeping at night. The "Goose story" began to nag me from the recesses of my mind.

I raced to my classroom and created a space big enough in the center for the thirty-three chairs to be formed into a circle. I stopped the students before they entered and told them to take a seat in the circle. The looks on their faces were priceless. The expression was not the same "What is this crazy lady talking about" look; it was a "something big is about to happen" look. They did as they were told. I sat down, took a deep breath, and let them know we needed a community circle. I then passed around "A Sense of Goose." Expressions of familiarity washed over their faces. Their responses to the story were incredibly insightful. They understood how the geese worked together in communities, took care of and looked after one another. They shared wonderful examples of how humans should work together. They shared relevant and meaningful stories that revealed how profound their connections were with one another and how deeply those connections had been damaged. We sorted through issues in our classroom community by engaging in dialogue, and began the long and difficult process of making change.

—JANENE ASHFORD
First-year teacher, grade 6

Creating a caring and democratic classroom takes time, experience, and patience. Even when teachers gain skill and confidence, and their classrooms are more safe and caring than they might have hoped for previously, new challenges will arise. Next year, Janene Ashford and other teachers like her will be calling upon themselves for even greater measures of care and skill than they thought possible this year. Educational researcher Andy Hargreaves, in his book *Changing Teachers, Changing Times,* offers a valuable perspective on creating better classrooms and a better society. He suggests to us that over the span of a teaching career, teachers' work is not about *solving* learning and social problems, but allowing ourselves to struggle with a "better class of problems." We believe that struggling to care is a better class of problem than struggling to discipline.

🅞🅛🅒 OLC Connections

A list of additional online and print resources and a set of questions for reflection about classroom management can be found at www.mhhe.com/oakes3e.

▩ Digging Deeper

The group of scholars and educators in this section all explore new theories and practices for making classrooms more caring and socially just. The organizations provide networks for educators working with these approaches in classrooms.

William Ayers is a distinguished professor of education and a senior university scholar at the University of Illinois at Chicago, where he teaches courses in urban school change and teaching for justice and democracy. Four of his books offer vivid portraits of teachers' struggles to create democratic schools and classrooms. *To Teach: The Journey of a Teacher* (New York: Teachers College Press, 1995) reveals Ayers's inspiring firsthand experiences. *To Become a Teacher: Making a Difference in Children's Lives* (1995) is an edited collection filled with practical, concrete advice for new teachers (and experienced teachers who are rethinking their practices). *City Kids, City Teachers: Reports from the Front Row* (New York: The New Press, 1996), written with **Patricia Ford,** contains more than 25 essays from educators and writers exploring the realities of city classrooms from kindergarten through twelfth grade. His most recent book, *A Simple Justice: The Challenge of Small Schools,* edited with **Michael Klonsky** and **Gabrielle H. Lyon** (New York: Teachers College Press, 2000), includes essays that use history, philosophy, cultural criticism, and pedagogy to make explicit the connections among small schools, social justice, and educational equality.

Professor **Antonia Darder** is a member of the education faculty at the College of Education at the University of Illinois, Urbana-Champaign. In *Culture and Power in the Classroom: A Critical Foundation for Bicultural Education* (Westport, CT: Bergin & Garvey, 1991), Darder offers principles for a critical practice of bicultural education. Darder's critical perspective helps teachers evaluate their current practices. Darder's most recent book is *Reinventing Paulo Freire: A Pedagogy of Love* (Boulder, CO: Westview Press, 2002). In it, she explores the legacy of Freire, interviews eight of his former students who are now teachers themselves, and reflects on Freire's own teaching practice.

The **Developmental Studies Center** is a nonprofit education organization headquartered in Oakland, California. Center researchers **Eric Schaps, Victor Battistich,** and **Marilyn Watson** have developed comprehensive school-change efforts to help elementary schools become inclusive, caring communities and stimulating, supportive places to learn. Teachers can learn strategies in Marilyn Watson's book, *Learning to Trust: Transforming Difficult Elementary Classrooms Through Developmental Discipline* (San Francisco: Jossey Bass, 2003). The Center also publishes materials for teachers, including *Ways We Want Our Classroom to Be: Class Meetings That Build Commitment to Kindness and Learning,* available online at (http://www.devstu.org/about/articles.html).

McMaster University professor **Henry Giroux** has theorized extensively about the connections between culture, student resistance, and critical pedagogy. Of his many books, teachers might find the following especially interesting: *Schooling and the Struggle for Public Life: Democracy's Promise and Education's Challenge* (Boulder, CO: Paradigm Publishers, 2005) *Pedagogy and the Politics of Hope* (Boulder, CO: Westview Press, 1996); *Postmodern Education: Politics, Culture, and Social Criticism,* with **Stanley Aronowitz** (Minneapolis: University of Minnesota Press, 1991); *Theory and Resistance in Education* (South Hadley, MA: Bergin & Garvey, 1983); and *Ideology, Culture, and the Process of Schooling* (Philadelphia: Temple University Press, 1981).

Education writer and social critic **Herbert Kohl,** a former teacher, has written many engaging books that tell compelling stories about teachers' work with students in difficult life circumstances. One of his early best-selling books,

36 Children, relays his own experience teaching in an inner-city school in the 1960s. A more recent book, *I Won't Learn from You and Other Thoughts on Creative Maladjustment* (New York: The New Press, 1994), includes essays and stories about responses to situations where, in Kohl's words, "students' intelligence, dignity, or integrity are compromised by a teacher, an institution or a larger social mind-set." In *Should We Burn Babar?: Essays on Children's Literature and the Power of Stories* (New York: The New Press, 1994), Kohl provides new perspectives on well-known children's stories, highlighting instances of racism, sexism, and condescension. He offers powerful ideas for better ways to tell children stories.

Alfie Kohn is also a former teacher who now works with educators across the country. In addition to his writing on assessment, noted in the Digging Deeper section of Chapter 6, Kohn has written about democratic and respectful communities in schools and classrooms. Teachers may find the following especially useful: *The Schools Our Children Deserve: Moving Beyond Traditional Classrooms and "Tougher Standards"* (New York: Houghton Mifflin, 1999); *What to Look for in a Classroom . . . And Other Essays* (San Francisco: Jossey-Bass, 1998); and *Beyond Discipline: From Compliance to Community* (Reston, VA: Association for Supervision and Curriculum Development, 1996).

Gloria Ladson-Billings is professor of education at the University of Wisconsin-Madison. Her best-selling book, *The Dreamkeepers: Successful Teachers of African American Children* (San Francisco: Jossey-Bass, 1994), describes, through narratives about real teachers in urban classrooms, the success of culturally relevant pedagogy. In 2001, Ladson-Billings published *Crossing Over to Canaan: The Journey of New Teachers in Diverse Classrooms* (San Francisco, Jossey-Bass), a book about preparing novice teachers to succeed with all students in multicultural classrooms.

University of North Carolina at Chapel Hill professor **George Noblit** studies caring and community building in schools. Although he grounds his work in a philosophical discussion about morality in schooling, he also provides rich descriptions of teachers developing relationships with students. With **Van O. Demise,** Noblit wrote *The Social Construction of Virtue: The Moral Life of Schools* (Albany, NY: SUNY Press, 1996), which examines the history of two southern elementary schools that merged when segregation ended.

Education professor **Nel Noddings** of Stanford University wrote *The Challenge to Care in Schools: An Alternative Approach to Education* (New York: Teachers College Press, 1992). In it, she lays out the conceptual underpinnings for viewing teaching as creating cultures of care.

Vivian Gussin Paley, a kindergarten teacher to whom the MacArthur Foundation gave one of its prestigious "genius" awards, published her first book, *White Teacher,* in 1979. It has been followed by several others, each addressing fundamental issues of classroom life—children's development, racism, gender, and what it feels like to be the outsider, to be "different." These highly readable books (all published by Harvard University Press in Cambridge, Massachusetts) include *You Can't Say You Can't Play* and *Kwanzaa and Me.* The books describe her compelling strategies for building the curriculum and classroom community around the knowledge and traditions of her students' families and neighborhoods.

Rethinking Schools publishes a newspaper regularly, books occasionally, and other materials for teachers seeking practices that match social justice values. Of particular relevance for the issues in this chapter is the organization's book *Rethinking Our Classrooms: Teaching for Equity and Social Justice.* Begun by a group of Milwaukee-area teachers who wanted to help shape reform, Rethinking Schools has become a nationwide resource that is committed to equity and to the vision that public education is central to a humane, caring, multiracial democracy. It emphasizes problems facing urban schools, particularly issues of race. *Rethinking Schools* is online at http://www.rethinkingschools.org.

Myra Sadker (deceased) and **David Sadker,** professor of education at The American University in Washington, D.C., began studying gender bias against women and girls in the classroom as doctoral students in the 1960s. Since that time the Sadkers completed several studies and wrote widely on this issue, including a popular book that summarizes their and others' findings, *Failing at Fairness: How America's Schools Cheat Girls* (New York: Macmillan, 1994).

Ira Shor is a professor of English at the College of Staten Island, City University of New York. His books *Empowering Education: Critical Teaching for Social Change* (Chicago: University of Chicago Press, 1992) and *When Students Have Power: Negotiating Authority in a Critical Pedagogy* (Chicago: University of Chicago Press, 1996) suggest ways for teachers and students to transform traditional classrooms into more democratic ones. Another of Shor's books, *Critical Teaching and Everyday Life* (Chicago: University of Chicago Press, 1980), can also be helpful to elementary and secondary school teachers. Shor's most recent book, *Education Is Politics: Critical Teaching Across Differences (K–12)* (Portsmouth, NH: Heinemann, 1999), is a book of classroom practice influenced by the late Paulo Freire.

Teaching Tolerance is a project of The Southern Poverty Law Center. This organization offers a wide range of educational tools including current events, classroom activities, videos, written material as well as a magazine for teachers interested in teaching racial tolerance. The site also has resources for parents, teenagers, and kids. Teaching Tolerance is online at http://www.tolerance.org.

Tribes: A New Way of Learning and Being Together, by Jeanne Gibbs, now in its seventh edition (2001), provides teachers with practical strategies to develop cooperative and safe classroom communities. The text presents a process that develops inclusion (caring and support), influence (a sense of value—meaningful participation), and community (positive expectations). The Tribes group provides professional development for districts and schools. The book and other materials are available online at http://www.tribes.com.

Joan Wink, a professor of education at California State University-Stanislaus, wrote *Critical Pedagogy: Notes from the Real World,* third edition (New York: Longman, 2005). A primer really, the book introduces the ideas and theorists of critical pedagogy in everyday language, provides examples from Wink's and her students' teaching, and offers practical guidelines for creating lessons. Although it is not a substitute for reading Freire, Darder, McLaren, and others in the original, Wink's book provides a highly accessible overview.

Notes

1. Joel Spring, *The American School* (New York: Longman, 1990), pp. 56–57.
2. William Glasser, *The Quality School* (New York: HarperCollins, 1992).
3. See for example, Frank Riessman's *The Culturally Deprived Child* (New York: Harper & Row, 1962) and Harry Passow, Miriam Goldberg, and Abraham J. Tannenbaum (Eds.), *Education of the Disadvantaged* (New York: Holt, Rinehart & Winston, 1967).
4. See, for example, Lee Canter and Marlene Canter, *Assertive Discipline: Positive Behavior* (Santa Monica: Lee Canter & Associates, 1997).
5. See, for example, Alfie Kohn, *Punished by Rewards* (Boston: Houghton Mifflin, 1993).
6. The National Association of School Psychologists, "Zero Tolerance and Alternative Strategies: A Fact Sheet for Educators and Policymakers," 2001, http://www.naspcenter.org/factsheets/zt_fs.html.
7. Jacob Kounin, *Discipline and Group Management in Classrooms* (New York: Holt, Rinehart & Winston, 1970).
8. Thomas Good and Jere Brophy, *Looking in Classrooms* (New York: Longman, 1997).
9. Jeff Gregg, "Discipline, Control, and the School Mathematics Tradition," *Teaching and Teacher Education* 11, no. 6 (1995), pp. 579–593.
10. Herbert M. Kliebard, *The Struggle for the American Curriculum: 1893–1958*, 2nd ed. (New York: Routledge, 1995), p. 6.
11. Alan Ryan, *John Dewey and the High Tide of American Liberalism* (New York: W. W. Norton, 1995), p. 153. Ryan notes that Dewey was far more nationalistic than Addams; he, far more than she, wanted such settings to bring immigrants into the American community, not simply to create community-like settings per se.
12. A. S. Neill, *Summerhill* (New York: St. Martin's Press, 1995, originally published in 1960).
13. Nel Noddings, *The Challenge to Care in Schools: An Alternative Approach to Education* (New York: Teachers College Press, 1992), p. 65.
14. Noddings, *The Challenge to Care in Schools.*
15. Nel Noddings, "Teaching Themes of Care," *Phi Delta Kappan* 77 (May 1995), p. 676.
16. Noddings, *The Challenge to Care in Schools*, p. 20.
17. Alan Fogel, *Developing Through Relationships* (Chicago: University of Chicago Press, 1993).
18. Carollee Howes and Sharon Ritchie, *A Matter of Trust: Connecting Teachers and Learners in the Early Childhood Classroom* (New York: Teachers College Press, 2002).
19. Ibid.
20. George Noblit, "In the Meaning: The Possibilities of Caring," *Phi Delta Kappan* 77 (May 1995), p. 682.
21. Ibid., pp. 680–685.
22. Alfie Kohn, *Beyond Discipline: From Compliance to Community* (Alexandria, VA: Association for Supervision and Curriculum Development, 1996), pp. 114–115.
23. Child Development Project, *Ways We Want Our Classroom to Be: Class Meetings That Build Commitment to Kindness and Learning* (Oakland, CA: Developmental Studies Center, 1994); and Victor Battistich, Eric Schaps, and Nance Wilson, "Effects of an Elementary School Intervention on Students' 'Connectedness' to School and Social Adjustment During Middle School," *The Journal of Primary Prevention* 24, no. 3 (2004), pp. 243–262.
24. Peace Builders is a commercially available curriculum (Tucson, AZ: Heartsprings, 1995) based on Dennis D. Embry's work in conflict resolution.
25. Myra Sadker and David Sadker, *Failing at Fairness: How America's Schools Cheat Girls* (New York: Macmillan, 1994).
26. David Sadker, as quoted in Millicent Lawton, "Girls Will Be Girls," *Education Week*, 30 March 1994.
27. Antonia Darder, *Culture and Power in the Classroom: A Critical Foundation for Bicultural Education* (Westport, CT: Bergin & Garvey, 1991), p. 67.
28. Ira Shor, *Empowering Education: Critical Teaching for Social Change* (Chicago: University of Chicago Press, 1992), pp. 223–232.

CHAPTER 8

Grouping, Tracking, and Categorical Programs

Can Schools Teach All Students Well?

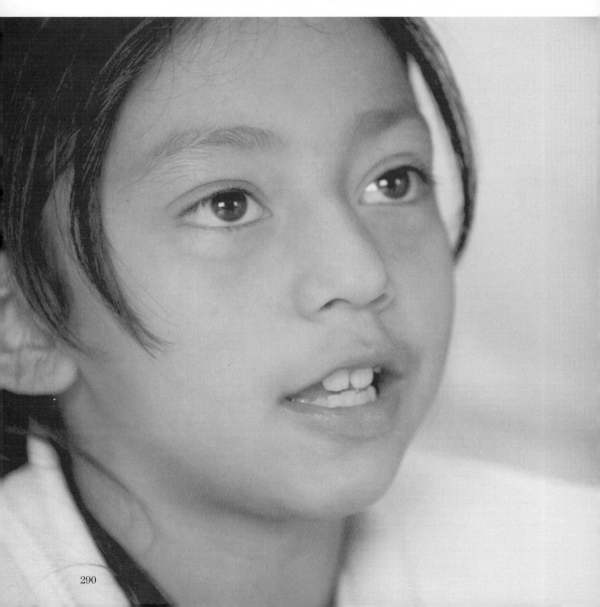

I consider myself a huge advocate for English Learners (EL). Language clas-
sification guides tracking in the twenty-first century. If a student is classified
Limited English Proficient (LEP), it is very difficult for her or him to be re-
classified as a fluent English speaker and be placed in a class where grade-
level curriculum is taught. As the EL coordinator, I helped my school do two
significant things to help EL students have access to rigorous curriculum.
One, we've changed the way that graduates from the fifth grade who are clas-
sified as LEP are placed into our sixth-grade classes. If an LEP student can
perform in grade-level classes (which most can because they rise to the expec-
tations), she or he is placed into regular sixth-grade English and put on
track to take college preparatory English in high school. Two, we have been
reclassifying kids as fluent English speakers by the handful. Last year, we re-
classified over 250 students, which allows them to be placed in grade-level
English. This year we are looking to surpass that number and become the
first large Eastside Middle School to go under 1,000 LEPs. Moreover, we want
to continue to lower our LEP population each year.

—**MAURO BAUTISTA**
Middle-school bilingual education coordinator

Mauro Bautista struggles with one of the most entrenched practices in American education—labeling students according to the schools' judgments about their competencies and deficits and placing them in classes and programs tailored to meet their needs. Although most people rarely question such practices, they can do at least as much harm as good. The exclusion from rigorous curriculum that Mauro worries about has long-term consequences for students' future educational opportunities.

Chapter Overview

This chapter describes how and why schools categorize and group students into separate classrooms and programs for instruction. It focuses both on ability grouping and curriculum tracking[1] and on the multitude of special classes and programs created to respond to differences among students—special education, gifted, compensatory, bilingual. We explain how the categories and labels schools assign to students are social and cultural constructions, and we provide some of the history of how the practice of labeling and sorting became part of American schooling. We then review some of the evidence showing that these practices often do as much to *create* differences as they do to meet students' special needs. Finally, we describe the work and theory of many educators who seek to avoid labels and grouping and use multidimensional, developmental, and socially just approaches to teaching in diverse classrooms.

Labeling and Sorting in Today's Schools

School systems throughout the United States routinely use assessment and evaluation strategies to compare, rank, and assign value to students' abilities and achievements in relationship to one another and to students in other schools, states, and countries, as we described in Chapter 6. Within schools, students are regularly identified as gifted, high achieving, below average, learning disabled, limited English proficient, and more. These labels guide educators as they sort students into instructional groups, classes, and programs that they hope and expect will meet students' learning needs. These grouping practices are highly controversial.

Today, ability, previous achievement, postsecondary aspirations, English language competence, and disability status have all become culturally sensible ways to group students. Furthermore, "individual choice," "talent," "motivation," various course prerequisites, and other criteria are also used. However, nearly all grouping assignments are ultimately made and justified by the school's prediction of the student's *ability* to succeed in a particular group. Generally, the intention is to place students in, or encourage students to take, the most demanding courses in which the school thinks they can succeed. These predictions are fraught with inconsistencies and are often just plain wrong.

Although the labels differ from school to school, most schools have ways of publicly identifying students and differentiating their opportunities. First-year teacher Kimberly Aragon's experience, described next, is not unusual.

---------------------------------------⊗ ⊗ ⊗---------------------------------------

Grouping pervades almost every area of my K–8 school. Some students enter a "VISTA" (gifted according to various intelligences) program as early as second grade, and, as those students progress, there will be at least one VISTA class in every grade. Every grade, 2 to 8, also has what is called a "SHARP" class. SHARP is an acronym for "Students with High Achievement in Reading Program." Students are placed in a SHARP class based on their previous years' test scores and their grades in English. Although the rest of the students at my school are not labeled as "DULL," the implication of the "SHARP" name is obvious.

Moreover, some grades are divided further by placing the Limited English Proficient (LEP) students in one class and all of the rest of the students in another class. In addition, approximately 20 students in grade 1 are pulled out of class for one-on-one Reading Recovery instruction [Title I program]. One-third of the way through this year, the school instituted a middle-school reading elective, which requires 10 students who scored in the

bottom quartile on the previous year's standardized test to receive extra
reading instruction from a credentialed teacher. Those students are then not
able to participate in the other electives offered, such as drama, Spanish,
communications, art, and computers.

  Furthermore, the school's reading philosophy requires that each teacher
create ability groups in his or her classroom, based on reading and math
levels. As an English teacher, I am required to give each of my 70 students a
"Running Record" three times a year and, based on the records, place stu-
dents in groups in which they are reading material at their instructional
level. For instance, if a student's Running Record showed that he could de-
code 93 percent of the words in a fifth-grade passage, his instructional level,
according to the program, is fifth grade, and he should be placed in a reading
group that is reading a fifth-grade book.

—**Kimberly Aragon**
First-year teacher, humanities, grade 8

Sorting by Academic Ability and Achievement

Ability grouping (also commonly known as tracking) is the routine sorting of all students into homogeneous groups and classes of "high," "average," and "low" students
(or any of the creative euphemisms in vogue, such as "advanced," "accelerated,"
"opportunity," "basic," "SHARP," "VISTA," etc.). Such sorting typically begins early
in elementary school—sometimes even in kindergarten—and it continues throughout the grades.[2]

Many elementary schools provide separate classes so that students spend the
entire day with others judged to be at the same "ability level." Other schools group
students by ability for part of the day for specific subjects such as reading and math.
This "regrouping" might include students from more than one class or grade, or,
more likely, it may consist of small ability groups (such as reading or math groups)
within a classroom. Sometimes ability groups follow a staggered schedule. A kindergarten class may be divided into early- and late-birds (separating the more and less
precocious readers) so that each group has time each day to be alone with the
teacher.

Nearly all middle schools and senior high schools ability group some or all academic subjects (typically English, mathematics, science, and slightly less commonly, social studies) based on students' past grades, test scores, and teacher
recommendations. Schools sometimes assign students to blocks of classes all at the
same ability level. This typically happens when schools assign a label to the student
himself; a high-ability or low-ability student would then go into all classes that
match his designation.

In recent years, most schools deny this type of block assignment exists, and
most policies call for assigning students one subject at a time. However, national
survey data indicate that 60 to 70 percent of tenth graders who were in honors math
also enrolled in honors English. A similar degree of overlap exists between remedial
math and remedial or low-level English.[3] Because some subjects like math follow a

sequence, students' assignments in earlier grades determine how far they can progress by the time they graduate.[4] Typically, students who will be in the top math classes all through high school are identified by the sixth grade or before. Students not placed in the uppermost ability class by the sixth grade stand only the slimmest chance of completing calculus in high school.

This type of sorting persists even as reforms attempt to interrupt it. For example, the current push to have all students take algebra in the eighth grade is often implemented by sorting students into different levels of algebra, often with different names such as "basic algebra" or "honors algebra." These and many other dilemmas associated with grouping are discussed later in this chapter.

Sorting by Postsecondary Prospects

In addition to grouping students by their academic ability or prior achievement in various subjects, high schools also prescribe different sequences of classes, or tracks, for students with different futures. Thus, students heading for college and those expecting to take jobs right after high school will be in different tracks. In some schools, students enroll in programs of study—such as college-preparatory, general, or vocational—that dictate their entire array of courses. The vocational or general (noncollege) track usually coincides with the lower academic levels. College-bound students enroll in the high-ability tracks, since the lower-level courses typically don't satisfy college entrance requirements. Increasingly, however, schools are recognizing the importance of preparing all students for college entrance. Aware that classes in the vocational track often have low status, low quality, and limited value for gaining college admission, many vocational educators are now working to upgrade these classes. Finally, even *within* the college-prep designation, different course sequences often emerge—designed to prepare some students for the most competitive universities, some for less competitive ones, and some for two-year community colleges.

Most senior high schools offer some advanced placement (AP) classes for exceptionally high-achieving eleventh and twelfth graders bound for the most competitive universities. These courses allow students to pursue college-level study in nearly all the academic subjects. The content of AP courses is similar nationwide, since a major objective is to prepare students for the AP examinations, a national test administered by the College Board. This is the same organization that gives the Scholastic Aptitude Test (SAT) that many colleges require for admission. Most colleges give automatic credits to students who receive high scores on AP tests and excuse them from beginning courses in those subjects. AP classes often overlap with gifted and talented programs at the senior high level and with honors-level courses. Increasingly, schools further distinguish these highest-level courses by giving extra weight to grades earned in them when calculating grade point averages.

In the past decade, taking AP classes—multiple AP classes—has become critical for students wishing to attend the nation's most competitive universities. In many states the days have passed when "all A's," or even being "class valedictorian," could assure admission to any university "of choice." Many universities are not just looking for "college prep" courses but are requiring specified numbers of courses in the honors or AP track. Students who have not been programmed for these courses stand little chance. Recent studies in California reveal that most of the state's poor Latinos and African American students attend schools that offer only a small fraction of the courses that wealthier schools offer. It took the settlement of a lawsuit for the state to agree to add a minimum number of advanced courses to the poor schools, but wealthy schools are already gearing up to add even more. This will perhaps raise the standards for everyone while maintaining the traditional unfair distribution of opportunity. A few colleges and some high schools are bucking the trend for more AP classes and claiming that they can maintain their high quality without relying on the College Board's determination of the most worthwhile curriculum; however, these institutions must feel especially secure, and typically their status as elite institutions is unquestioned.

Sorting by "Giftedness"

In the past, exceptionally precocious students often skipped grades if they outdistanced their peers academically. If they remained with their peers, they may have made very exceptional progress, or, if the class offered little intellectual stimulation or opportunity, they may have been discouraged and bored along with the rest of their classmates. Federal funding supports state and local efforts to improve services for gifted and talented students. The National Association for Gifted Children reported that in 2005, 32 states provided special funding for gifted and talented students, and most schools had prominent gifted programs where the highest-achieving students were grouped together for enrichment or accelerated instruction, either in separate classes, in *pull-out* programs, or in gifted *clusters* within regular classrooms.

Although IQ is the most commonly used criteria for identifying gifted students, *giftedness* is defined in many different ways in different states and by different organizations. Joseph Renzulli, director of the National Research Center on Gifted and Talented, defines giftedness as high ability (including high intelligence), high creativity (ability to formulate and apply new ideas), and high task commitment (motivation and the willingness to stick with a project until it is finished).[5] In many schools, to ensure that "talented" students without strong academic skills can qualify for gifted programs, IQ scores or achievement tests may be augmented by teachers' observations of leadership, creativity, or other special abilities and, sometimes, by parents' nominations.

Sorting by Disabilities

New disability categories surface and old ones disappear as educators, psychologists, and physicians refine their definitions of conditions that fall outside the normal range in physical, sensory, behavioral, or cognitive characteristics. The 2004 federal Individuals with Disabilities Education Act (IDEA) specifies 13 categories of disability, and it provides funding to states and local school districts for special programs and services. In 1997 the National Academy of Science reported that 5 million students—about 10 percent of the U.S. school population—qualify for assistance under IDEA. About 90 percent of these students fall into four categories: speech or language impairment, mental retardation (MR), severe emotional disturbance (SED), and specific learning disabled.[6]

Once school personnel determine that a student qualifies for special help, the school is required by law to develop a written individual educational plan (IEP). The IEP states the child's needs, outlines specific learning goals, specifies the help the school will provide, and may detail a role for student and family. Students with speech and language problems may need one-to-one instruction provided outside the classroom. Students with long-range illnesses might receive teaching at home or in a hospital. Large school districts often support their own schools for the severely mentally retarded and for the vision- and hearing-impaired. Others may contract with private centers and provide transportation so that students get the help and equipment that typical classrooms can't offer. Students with less-debilitating cognitive and emotional disorders spend all or part of their school day in *resource classrooms*. These are places where small groups of students with disabilities spend time away from the regular classroom receiving assistance from teachers trained in special education and from teachers' aides. However, the law also requires that schools provide special help for disabled students in the *least restrictive environment*. This provision presses schools to *mainstream* students with disabilities into classrooms with peers who have no disabilities for as much of the day as possible.

Cognitive Disabilities   Students often lag behind in some school skills. In most cases, this lag is within the normal range of individual developmental differences. However, a growing number of students of normal intelligence who have difficulties, particularly in reading, are identified as *learning disabled (LD),* and about half of all of those receiving special education services now fall into this category.[7] Students identified as having a learning disability have unusual and specific cognitive disabilities thought to result from an organic cause, such as the brain's inability to process information with the same efficiency as other children.

The key to identifying a learning disability is not so much how a student performs in any one area as the discrepancies among different areas of performance. Such students, try as they may, have great difficulty accomplishing certain skills, such as copying correctly, spelling accurately, reading fast, or memorizing details. However, these same students may be skilled at expressing ideas orally and solving problems. Others have more serious difficulty with language, short-term memory, or visual perception. Identified LD students spend varying amounts of their school time in the resource room.

Students with mental retardation are those who score substantially below the normal range on intelligence tests. Categories of retardation range from Mildly Mentally Retarded to those who are designated Severely and Profoundly Retarded. Their disability so restricts their intellectual functioning that they will never reach adult levels. Like LD students, however, those identified as retarded differ widely. Specific intellectual capabilities can differ markedly among students with the same IQ scores. Some students with retardation develop strong social skills that enable them to get along and even learn far better than others who test higher. Seriously cognitively disabled students might join other students for physical education or some electives. For the most part, however, they are taught separately.

Behavioral and Emotional Disorders All students experience occasional mild behavior problems. Some, though, are consistently at odds with their peers and with adults. Sorting typically takes place only when these students are bothersome to others or there are critical concerns about their own well-being. Such misbehavior can result from the complete range of emotional and psychological conditions that affect students. Chronic problems may also result from a mismatch between the behavior standards in class and those of a student's home or play group. Students who seem unable to pay attention are often the first to capture the teacher's notice. Students who fidget and squirm, run around the room, or doze off during a film are hard to ignore. The chronic inability to pay attention, sit still, be quiet, and act cooperatively can be a disability with serious consequences. These students are unable to concentrate on their studies and fall behind academically. Other students often shun them. And they can hardly escape the effects of disapproving and exasperated teachers.

In earlier generations, schools may have labeled older students who consistently acted badly at school "incorrigible" or "juvenile delinquents" and sent them to reform schools, but most such students simply dropped out of school altogether. Today schools categorize many habitually misbehaving students as disabled. For example, attention-deficit hyperactivity disorder (ADHD) now qualifies students for assistance under federal law. Researchers reporting in the *Journal of the American Medical Association* estimate that the disability affects between 3 and 6 percent of the school population.[8] Many advocates view ADHD as a discrete genetic disorder, while others see it as a catchall label for the behaviors just described.

Educators categorize more dangerously unruly and violent students as having other disabilities, for example, as being severely emotionally disturbed (SED). Though such behavior disorders are not themselves cognitive deficits, they often go hand in hand with learning difficulties.

Most students with behavior disorders remain in regular schools, where educators assign them to resource or "opportunity" rooms for a portion of the day or to special daylong classes. Federal law provides guidelines so students with behavioral disabilities are subject to different, and usually less severe, forms of discipline at school than nondisabled students. For example, schools might not be allowed to expel students for behavior that is related to their disability, even if the offense were warranted under the school's expulsion policy.

Sorting by English Language Competence

From colonial times, American schools have struggled to educate non-English-speaking populations. The increasing numbers of immigrant students in the early 1970s fueled support for federal and state assistance for English language teaching and learning. Although the law doesn't require that schools separate students who speak little or no English from their English-speaking peers, *English as a Second Language (ESL)* and bilingual programs nearly always do so.

ESL programs typically take the form of special classes in which non-English-speaking students learn English as a foreign language—without the use of the students' primary language for instruction. Supporters of ESL programs believe that students will do better, both academically and socially, if they use English exclusively for their schoolwork. ESL classes usually occupy one or two hours a day. For the remainder of the time, students attend "regular" classes and learn their other subjects in English. This may mean that these students are in special academic classes where teachers use "sheltered" English and other strategies designed to make instruction in English comprehensible for those with limited English competency. Because ESL and sheltered academic classes use English for instruction, students with different native languages often take these classes together. Finally, the regular classes that these students attend are far more likely to be the low-ability classes (for English speakers) than high-ability classes.

Bilingual education is based on research showing that students do better in both academic learning and acquisition of the new language if they develop and maintain their native language skills. Advocates of bilingual education argue that students can keep up with their peers in subjects like mathematics and science at the same time that they are learning English. That can best happen if students learn these subjects using their primary language until they can understand those subjects in English. Bilingual classes group students with the same primary language where bilingual teachers teach in the students' language while gradually introducing English.

Most bilingual programs include an ESL component as well as academic instruction in other subjects in the student's native language. Several models of bilingual education rely on separate classes. Bilingual programs called *maintenance* have three goals—learning English, learning academics, and developing literacy in the native language. *Transitional* bilingual programs, in contrast, have only the first two goals, English and academics. Their intent is to shift the student away from the primary language to English as quickly as possible.

Why Do Schools Label and Sort Students?

The conventional explanation for labeling students and placing them into groups, classes, and programs with others like them is that, once the school identifies educationally relevant differences, teachers can teach groups of students with meaningful similarities, and students will benefit from instruction in these groups. However, below this superficially sensible explanation are cultural and historical patterns that reveal how sorting students is embedded in cultural conceptions of racial and social class differences.

The Social Construction of Difference

The way we cut up the world clearly affects the way we organize our everyday life. The way we divide our surroundings, for example, determines what we notice and what we ignore . . . the way we classify people determines whom we trust and whom we fear. . . . The way we partition time and space likewise determines when we work and when we rest, where we live and where we never set foot. Indeed, our entire social order is a product of the ways in which we separate kin from nonkin, moral from immoral, serious from merely playful, and what is ours from what is not.[9]

Documenting and explaining variation has been a controlling purpose of Western science. Humans cannot resist noticing and attempting to make categories for people and things to "fall into." And, as sociologist Eviatar Zerubavel notes in the preceding extract, our categories affect how we see the world, how we act, and what we value.

Every culture uses such constructs to make sense and organize their world, but all cultures don't necessarily create and use the *same* ones. And, even if they have the same constructs, cultures often assign different meanings and importance to them. It is tempting to accept the categories, explanations, and values that one's own culture has constructed as real, true, and "common sense," but clearly they are not. As anthropologists remind us, each culture's meanings and values represent that group's particular way of understanding and preserving their society.

Life in schools is also a world of categories and distinctions. Some deep differences among students are certainly real: Some students have problems so severe that they interfere with learning or social interactions at school; some students have astonishing memories or musical talents. However, most of the educational categories that guide grouping practices in school—practices that impact *all* students, not just a few—bear little resemblance to the wholly justifiable practices that target individual learning problems or talents.

Researchers Harold Stevenson and James Stigler illustrate how intellectual capacity is constructed differently from culture to culture. Comparing American, Chinese, and Japanese cultures, Stevenson and Stigler found that American culture constructs intelligence as a function of innate ability far more than do Asian cultures that emphasize effort and persistence in explaining what accounts for being "smart." Partly because of the powerful role that intelligence has played in our culture historically (as described Chapter 6), Americans typically consider a "good" student to be a "bright" or "smart" student. In contrast, a "good" student in Asian cultures is more likely to be "hardworking." Of course, there is no "correct" answer to the question of what makes students good, even though both cultures treat the categories they construct and the meanings they assign to them as "common sense." Although today, intelligence rarely is the only construct used to categorize students in U.S. schools, it remains a powerful signifier of students' merit, and it often overshadows other constructs that schools use to categorize students: achievement, creativity, motivation, ability, leadership, aspirations, self-concept, and more.

Americans have also believed for more than a century that once schools have identified, and to a large degree created, differences, they should respond to the differences by separating students for instruction. Thus, most schools group students homogeneously (i.e., with others thought to be like them), not only by age but also according to academic "ability," educational "disadvantage," learning and behavioral "disabilities," language "proficiency," educational "aspirations," and

college "potential." This, too, differs dramatically from how the Japanese, for example, treat differences. Until high school Japanese schools rarely separate students
into groups or classes with others who are similar to them. The idea of teaching all
types of students in the same classrooms seems perfectly normal and ordinary to
Japanese teachers.

"Ability" labeling and sorting in U.S. schools has always had strong statistical
overlaps with students' race, ethnicity, and social class. White and wealthy students
are far more likely to be labeled as high ability or gifted and placed in high-level
classes and in programs for those assumed to be college-bound. At the same time,
low-income students, African Americans, and Latinos are disproportionately identified as less able and placed in lower-level groups and classes.

Because of these overlaps, no discussion of grouping can take place without
paying careful attention to the racial and social class characteristics of the resulting
labeled groups. Defenders of ability grouping practices sometimes claim that group
assignments are "objective" or "color-blind," and they attribute the disproportionate
assignments into college-prep or learning-disabled classes to unfortunate differences in students' backgrounds and abilities. But these claims of scientific and bias-
free objectivity are not supported when viewed in the context of historical and
current sorting practices.[10]

The History of Biased Sorting

The labeling and grouping of students began in earnest in the late nineteenth century. Once schools' classrooms were organized into grades, educators wanted to
teach students all the same things at the same time and in the same way. Very soon,
normal differences among children became a bothersome obstacle to this efficient
plan. Grouping students into different classrooms by their ability was seen as a way
to overcome this obstacle to efficient teaching.

As we described in Chapter 2, by the early 1900s, schools were expected to
solve a whole array of social concerns that were quite distinct from students'
learning of mathematics, literature, science, and so forth. Diverse immigrants
needed to learn English and American ways. Factories needed trained workers.
Footloose urban youth required supervision. Future professionals, nearly always
the children of the most advantaged, needed to be taught the high-status knowledge that would prepare them for universities. Despite the rhetoric about schooling as the great equalizer, schools were also expected to help maintain the
current social and economic order with its uneven power and privilege. Policymakers and educators saw homogeneous grouping as a way to help them meet all
of these expectations.

Furthermore, the early-twentieth-century culture generally was one in which
it made perfectly good sense to dislike people who were different. Established
American families often did not think much of immigrants; some immigrants often
thought of themselves as better than other immigrants from different homelands,
and better than anyone more recently arrived in this country. Although some
individuals were free from prejudice, every group at that time thought itself
superior to African Americans, and most of the wealthiest Americans thought

themselves superior to everyone else. Thus, schools had to teach students to get along while remaining separate—teach everyone well, but teach some students to be better.

By the early twentieth century, industrializing democracies sought to combine the efficiencies of assembly lines without losing the fairness of democratic principles. Differentiating among citizens by using the old indicators of race and family background was functional but belied the American creed and dream. Gradually, schools settled on a new view of democratic schooling. They defined *opportunity* as the chance to fulfill, productively and with dignity, a position predetermined by one's race, gender, and social class.

Elwood Cubberly, a prominent educational scholar of the time, wrote, "Our city schools will soon be forced to give up the exceedingly democratic idea that all are equal, and our society devoid of classes . . . and to begin a specialization of educational effort along many lines in an attempt to adapt the school to the needs of these many classes."[11] Two increasingly popular ideas bolstered Cubberly's definition of democratic schooling: that IQ tests could assess students' "potential" for learning, and that scientific efficiency should guide educational practice. We discussed these ideas in Chapters 2, 3 and 6, and in what follows, we show their specific influence on grouping practices in school.

IQ and Grouping   The idea of IQ and the development of IQ tests allowed schools to label and sort students "scientifically" according to their intellectual merit, without involving parentage, race, or wealth directly. Since intelligence tests were increasingly accepted as scientific, accurate, and impartial, there could be no claim of unfairness. However, IQ actually served as a proxy for these older ways of sorting, since the questions selected for the tests were those that privileged test takers would be much more likely to get correct. The result was that sorting according to the scores resulted in ability groups made up of students with similar family background, wealth, and race.

As we described in Chapters 2 and 6, testing helped institutionalize prevailing stereotypes of race and class differences. Test results were consistent with the popular view that poor, minority, and non-English-speaking students were intellectually, morally, and even biologically inferior to Anglo-Americans. Many people who tried to understand school problems adopted a popular distortion of Charles Darwin's evolution theories that explained how darker-skinned, recently arrived immigrants from southern Europe were on a lower rung of the evolutionary ladder. Recall from Chapter 2 intelligence-test pioneer Lewis Terman's words, "Their dullness seems to be racial. . . . Children of this group should be segregated in special classes. . . . They cannot master abstractions, but they can often be made efficient workers." Although these views did not go uncontested, schools enacted the prevailing belief that inherent group differences caused enormous variation in students' potential for school learning. Grouping practices corresponded.

Most current grouping practices don't rely on IQ, at least not exclusively, but the early practices and views set a pattern that continues today. Standardized achievement tests, which help divide students into ability groups based on their potential, are central to qualifying students for compensatory education programs. Standardized language proficiency tests determine the appropriate class level for limited-English students. IQ, in conjunction with other measures, remains basic in identifying students who are gifted as well as those who have cognitive disabilities. Intelligence persists as a widely respected marker in a society that wants to see itself as just and equitable. However, because intelligence has been constructed in a culture characterized by race and class discrimination, using intelligence as an indicator of merit also produces a distribution of power and opportunity that is strikingly familiar to the overt racial and social class sorting of earlier times.

Scientific Management and Grouping   Identifying, separating, and treating students differently fit well with turn-of-the-twentieth-century notions of scientific management. As educators embraced the "scientific" methods being used by managers in the expanding manufacturing sector of the economy, grouping made wonderful sense to school leaders and to boards of education. Educational managers conducted "time-and-motion studies" (picture efficiency experts with stopwatches and charts noting every aspect of school activity, including the passing out and collecting of materials), centralization, authority concentrated at the top, rules for best methods, and so on. Following the model of the efficient factory, schools increasingly saw children as raw materials out of which they would fashion their product, productive adults.

Homogeneous grouping furthered specialization, a division of labor, and mass-produced learning. As in the factory, managers did not value individual differences along the assembly line—differences were defects in the product.

The Press for Universal Education and Grouping   Over the course of the twentieth century, compulsory education laws and the increased necessity of a high school diploma in the job market drew more and more students to school—even those previously considered uneducable. In less-enlightened times, affluent families closeted away children who had serious physical and mental problems or sent them to special schools—often boarding schools. Charitable institutions cared for some of the others. Poor children were often sent to asylums. Frequently, they were an embarrassment and the object of strangers' curiosity, fear, and ridicule.

Milder problems simply went unrecognized or were dismissed as unimportant. When students had trouble fitting in at school, they quit—often with the school's active encouragement. Until midcentury, most of them found jobs and led productive lives. Adults chalked up students' unexplained difficulties at school to their backwardness, having a bad character or upbringing, maladjustment, or just being odd. As the century progressed, however, these attitudes changed, and states and local school systems developed an array of special programs for students who were different.[12]

Categorical programs for low-income children and English learners came out of the War on Poverty, as we described in Chapter 2. Advocates for the "gifted" piggybacked on the trend for categorical funding with the rationale that these students had such significant differences that they could not be fully educated alongside "normal" students. Their efforts were bolstered by faulty views of intelligence—for example, that an IQ of 100 was a real representation of "normal" students. Parents, policymakers, and educators alike became convinced that deviation from the norm *in either direction* gave students disadvantages in proportion to the number of points they were from 100. Relying on the appeal of the "bell curve," they reasoned that a student with an IQ of 68 had a similar degree of disability as a student with an IQ of 132 had "extra ability." Borrowing equity-minded arguments used to justify additional services for students disadvantaged by physical or cognitive handicaps, advocates succeeded in reifying "gifted"—changing it from a metaphorical abstraction to a legal and educational category.

Educators responded in culturally predictable ways to the new laws and court decisions providing categorical funding and protections for student differences. They scientifically diagnosed students' differences and assigned them to a category. They then grouped students for instruction with others in the same category and tailored curriculum and teaching to the "abilities" of each group, according to what educators thought the groups needed. The increasing importance of legally defined groups increased schools' grouping consciousness, and additional groups have proliferated beyond legal requirements.

Grouping Dilemmas

Grouping as a school policy is neither efficient nor effective; it never was and is not now. Students who are assumed to be similar to one another are actually different in such important ways that they do not benefit from any environment that ignores those differences. This array of differences within groups holds true for all groups—high or low. Further, in the twenty-first century, homogeneous grouping will have to meet an even stricter test. The standards movement has made the idea of educating students to very different levels no longer acceptable because the best evidence about learning indicates that these predictions are consistently and needlessly low. Based on this evidence, policies such as No Child Left Behind are now demanding that schools educate every student to high academic standards, regardless of presumed intellectual ability, disability, social status, gender, or race. Grouping practices must be judged by whether they help teachers meet this goal.

The Arbitrariness of Labels and Sorting

States, school districts, and individual schools differ so widely in their definitions of "high," "average," and "low" ability that a student identified as belonging in any one of these categories in one place might wind up in a different category someplace else. Our own research found wide disparities in the cutoff scores that high schools use to decide which students should be admitted to honors, regular, and low-level classes.[13] For example, a student in a generally low-achieving school may require a lower score on a standardized test to get into an honors class than a student in a higher-achieving school. Similarly, California once raised its qualifying score for a gifted designation by two IQ points and instantly disqualified thousands of students who would have been gifted the year before.

Joseph Renzulli, a strong advocate for programs to develop students' talents, argues against "gifted" as a label both because it excludes so many students and because it creates a misleading (and sometimes detrimental) identity for those included. Renzulli told an interviewer that the use of the gifted label is something that he rejects outright, and he relayed his frustration with parents who approach him about their "gifted child": "When a parent comes to me and says, 'I have a gifted child,' I say, 'Wait a minute. Tell me what your child does. Talk to me about their writing, their science, their music. If you begin our conversation by telling me you have a gifted child, you are creating a gulf between us.'"[14]

Disparities in special education categories are also documented widely. Some states require an IQ score of 69 or less for a student to be *mentally retarded (MR)*, while others classify as MR any student with a score of 84 or below. Consequently, the proportion of students identified as disabled ranges from 7 to 15 percent among states.[15] For example, in 1996, Georgia identified only about 3 percent of its students as learning disabled while Massachusetts identified more than 9 percent; Alabama identified more than 10 times as many students as mentally retarded as New Jersey.[16] Connecticut classified students as severely emotionally disturbed (SED) at 40 times the rate that Mississippi did.[17]

Categories come and go, and each change is thought to represent progress and the triumph of enlightened views. For example, in the 1930s educators began using psycho-medical explanations of deviant behavior, such as *minimally brain injured*. These labels lasted well beyond midcentury. When research could not bear out a relevant class of defects to support that label, other diagnoses appeared. Today, the categories of "attention deficit disorder" and "disabled" stand alongside "at risk," "disadvantaged," and others.

The LD category is an example of shifting meanings and questionable usefulness (for teaching and learning). It achieved national status in 1963, with the founding of the Association for Children with Learning Disabilities. The organizing parents did not want their low-achieving children identified as mentally retarded, but they did want their children to have extra help. By 1979 LD had become the largest special education category. Christine Sleeter argues that this surge did not result from a scientific discovery of a previously unknown biological disorder but from advocacy by white, middle-class parents who wanted to differentiate their low-achieving children from lower-class children and children of color.[18] These more privileged families did not want their children's learning problems to be attributed to low IQ, emotional disturbances, or cultural deprivation. And, in fact, the vast majority of students labeled as LD during the first 10 years of the classification's existence were white and middle class. Once established, however, the LD category soon included most students of all racial and economic groups whom schools would formerly have identified as mildly retarded or retarded.

Many people respond to all the unfairness and imprecision of grouping and categories as if grouping systems were ill-functioning machines that needed a tune-up and more careful operators. They call for more exacting diagnosis of students, more precise categories, and more specialized teaching methods and curricula to suit the different groups. However, many researchers agree with Louise Spear-Swerling and Robert Sternberg, who argue in their book *Off Track: When Poor Readers Become*

Learning Disabled that the construct of learning disabilities probably causes more problems than it solves.[19] They believe that LD students and others would be better served if teachers and other learning specialists were allowed to address students' specific cognitive difficulties, such as in reading, and not become distracted by labels. Other researchers make parallel arguments about the validity and usefulness of behavioral categories like ADHD.[20]

The Illusion of Homogeneity

—⁂⁂⁂—

In my school, reading groups are based on ability. Students cannot progress to another basal reader or transition to English until they pass test after test. This has become a nightmare. Teachers must accommodate large numbers of students who are "not reading at grade level" because they have not been able to pass the tests. I have been able to successfully "test out" four of my third-grade students who were considered to be reading at the second-grade level. I believed them to be at grade level, but the question remains: Were these students labeled as below grade level based on their ability to pass the test, rather than on their actual reading ability?

—YVETTE NUNEZ
First-year teacher, grades 3 and 4

Classes designed for specific ability, disability, and language levels are actually filled with a wide variety of students who display noteworthy differences in learning speed, learning style, interest, effort, and aptitude for various tasks. Furthermore, substantial evidence demonstrates that schools often disregard their own placement criteria—allowing, for example, parent preferences or student behavior to influence academic placements. Thus, schools may actually encourage teaching very different students all the same instead of responding to students' inevitable differences.

—⁂⁂⁂—

Placing students in the correct math class was something I assumed was done with very little discrepancy. I found out over the course of the year that many students had been misplaced and were not aware of it. They knew the course name and number, but they did not know the type of content that would be covered. They just assumed that counselors placed them correctly. Misplaced students are plentiful in my "sheltered" class. It was not until late in the year that I asked students individually whether they spoke Spanish fluently, and if so, whether they considered it their primary language. Three students! Only three students in my entire sheltered course considered Spanish their primary language, and only four others spoke it fluently.

—MARILYN CORTEZ
First-year teacher, mathematics, grade 9

As Marilyn Cortez discovered, many school systems designate classes for students at a particular ability level but then enroll students whose measured ability ranges far above or below the stated criteria.[21]

Still other powerful factors make group assignments prone to error and unfairness, including tests, placement criteria, parents' and students' own activism, the school's master schedule, and more.

The Fallibility of Testing   Schools risk enormous unfairness when they use tests to sort students. The most common guideline for identifying a student's learning disability is if her achievement lags two years behind her grade level. Schools use achievement tests, school performance, or both to arrive at a student's achievement level. If her IQ scores show that her intelligence is normal, a low achievement score would indicate a learning disability. (If the student has a low achievement and a low IQ, she may not qualify for some special programs. The reasoning is that she is performing at the anticipated level for a student with low IQ and that special attention would not help her.) However, these test results do not prove that a student has or does not have a neurological disability. Neither do they provide information about what the disability might be.

Difficulties also arise with the measures schools use to identify "gifted" students. Although there is vigorous debate about who is gifted and who isn't, technically, the gifted student is one who meets the state's or the school's criteria. Those criteria often include an IQ score and an array of other criteria, such as artistic talent and leadership qualities. In recent years, many states have expanded the criteria even further in the attempt to make sure that students of color get included in gifted programs. The students who qualify comprise a highly diverse group on many dimensions. Complicating matters further is that intelligence tests are less accurate at the upper end of the curve where one would expect gifted "candidates" to be, and a given student's IQ may vary from day to day, year to year. On a good day, the student might be gifted. If tested on another day, he could fall short.

Other Attributes Influence Placement   Educators claim to base placements on merit—that a child's school achievement alone, not irrelevant characteristics like race and social class, determines whether he or she is in a high, an average, or a low class. Some acknowledge that students' own choices, character, and motivation influence track placements, and social indicators such as maturity and cooperation can sway decisions.

Each category has its unique opportunities for inconsistent placements and placements that have little to do with the stated criteria. For example, since the process of identifying gifted students often begins with the teacher's recommendation, students who are outgoing and mature are more easily noticed than shy, immature ones. Similarly, schools frequently fail to follow state criteria when identifying students as disabled.[22] Often schools place capable but bothersome, poorly behaved students in low-ability groups. Although this behavioral criterion is rarely stated explicitly in policy guidelines, it results in high-ability groups being shielded from disruptive and disaffected students.

Parent Activism and Choice   Another reason for homogeneous groups not really being homogeneous is that parents can interfere with the criteria that the school sets. The distortion of homogeneity that results from this activism is not random, but skewed to the advantage of white and wealthier families.

Most states and schools provide for parent nominations of potentially gifted students as early as kindergarten. As students get older, parents participate in selecting classes and programs for their children. Often, savvy parents who want their children enrolled in the "best" classes and special programs pressure educators.[23] In a competitive system that offers a small number of high-track opportunities, knowledgeable parents have few options but to pit themselves against others to get what they see as the best educational services. Middle- and upper-income families are especially active in seeking a gifted designation for their children. The *Washington Post* reported that a third of the students in an affluent Maryland County school district are now in gifted classes: "[I]n Howard, parents can bypass all other criteria by insisting their children be allowed into the more challenging classes. School officials sometimes try to talk parents out of doing so, if they think it's inappropriate, but parents usually get their way."[24]

Gifted students form a quite visible and elite group in the school. Many schools encourage gifted students to associate with one another, since much of the advocacy literature argues that they feel most comfortable and thrive in one another's company. Often schools or parent associations distribute rosters with telephone numbers to parents of gifted students, and educational meetings for parents (who are usually among the more active in the schools) further support the socializing of gifted students with one another. Because these students often come from the ranks of social and economic elites, it's no wonder that many parents work hard to have their children included.

Organizational Constraints   Schools often compromise grouping criteria in the face of other organizational constraints. Particularly in secondary schools, administrators juggle many factors that may override accurate placements. For example, they must make sure that each student has a class every hour. Those who want football, beginning string class, or second-year computer drafting often get those classes, even if the student winds up in an inappropriate high- or low-level English class. In addition, since each class must have approximately the same number of students, schools may place borderline students, those who enroll late in school, or others in a higher or lower class. As Hugh Mehan, Jane Mercer, and Robert Rueda observed, "If there are 30 slots for LD students in a school, then there will be 30 kids to fill those slots."[25]

Race and Social Class Bias

First-year teacher Matthew Flanders, who teaches at a very diverse high school, reveals how sorting practices mirror societal biases about the intellectual potential of low-income students and students of color.

—⊗ ⊗ ⊗—

My teaching assignment is one of the most diverse that I have ever heard of—two sections of United States history (grade 11), two sections of math (grades 10–12), one section of driver's education (grades 9–12), one section of tutorial (grades 9–12), and the head coach of the men's and women's water polo teams (grades 9–12). The math and tutorial classes are the lowest-level classes in the school.

I see inequities that I had not perceived when I attended high school years before but that, on further reflection, I now realize were present. This high school contains "two schools" even though they are not formally distinguishable. First, there is the advanced placement division. This "school" is composed of the "cream of the crop" of the high school's students. Highly motivated, adequately supported and taught, most of the students are white and are expected to go to college. Then there is the second "school" that is not expected to go on to higher education. These students are not motivated or engaged at all by school, are not given the best resources or teachers, and are overwhelmingly Latino and African American. This school's dropout rate is significantly higher than the first school's.

I teach almost exclusively in the undermotivated and unsuccessful school. These students have lost faith in themselves, in school, in peers, in families, and, in some instances, in life itself. They have to confront their failure every day at this school. Hearing how many students had been accepted to university, how many teams had won championships, how our music program was second to none, and not participating in these activities because of a lack of previous opportunity or deficient grades/units would keep anyone's self-confidence extremely low. They frequently tell me "I can't do this" or "This is too hard for us."

I could not believe this attitude. When I was given a challenge in school I would complain about it, but I would attempt to do it and would usually succeed. These students would not even try. The most frustrating part of this situation was that I was no more intelligent than these students; I just had learned more about how to make school work for me.

—**Matthew Amato Flanders**
First-year teacher, grades 9–12

As Matthew Flanders discovered at his high school, African American, Latino, and low-income students are consistently overrepresented in low-ability, remedial, and special education classes and programs. Racially isolated schools serving low-income and minority students typically have smaller academic tracks and larger remedial and vocational programs than do schools serving predominantly white, more affluent students.

In desegregated schools, like the one where Flanders teaches, African American and Latino students are assigned to low-track classes more often than white (and Asian) students, leading to two separate schools in one building—one white and one minority. For example, in a 1990 study for the National Science Foundation, we found a pattern of "racially identifiable" math and science classes in racially mixed schools. That is, one would expect to find in any particular math or science class a similar proportion of white, black, or Latino students as in the whole school. Instead, higher-tracked math and science classes had much larger percentages of white students in classes, and lower-ability classes had far larger percentages of black and Latino students.[26]

Our more recent studies of racially mixed school systems revealed that the lower participation of African American and Latino students in high-level classes could not be explained simply by the students' prior learning opportunities or achievement. These students were much less likely than white or Asian students *with the same test scores* to be placed in high-ability classes. For example, in one West Coast school system, white and Asian students with average scores on standardized test scores were more than twice as likely to be in "accelerated" classes than Latino students with *the same scores.* The discrimination was even more striking among the highest-scoring students. Whereas only 56 percent of very high scoring Latinos were in accelerated classes, 93 percent of whites and 97 percent of Asians with *comparable* test scores were. In three other school systems, we found similar discrepancies between African American and white students.[27]

For the past several decades, researchers have warned that schools often classify and treat students *with identical IQ scores,* but with different racial and social class characteristics, very differently.[28] By the late 1970s the misidentification problem triggered both federal and state court decisions requiring that potentially disabled students receive due process. And in a far-reaching decision, the California courts ruled in *Larry P. v. Riles* that schools could no longer use intelligence tests to identify minority students as mentally retarded. However, substantial problems remain and new ones emerge, including recent evidence that African American boys are disproportionately identified as having attention deficits or hyperactivity.[29] The Office of Civil Rights 1990 data showed that black students were two and one half times more likely than white students to be classified as mildly mentally retarded (MMR).[30]

Parents and students themselves can tilt selection processes to gain placement advantages that an unbiased system would otherwise prevent.[31] High-achieving, affluent, white parents and students are much more knowledgeable about grouping practices. They are more willing to "push the system" if they are displeased with their course assignments, while parents of low-achieving and midrange students (often nonwhite and lower-income) are frequently less comfortable and skilled at challenging the system, and their lesser "clout" can mean that officials feel that they don't have to pay attention to them. Well-off parents might pay a private psychologist to retest their child if the child missed a "gifted" cutoff on the school's test. Or they might seek private diagnoses of LD for their children when they think that the identification will help children succeed; for example, by requiring extra teacher attention or allowing extra time to take tests. Sometimes a disability designation is sought out so that a struggling student in a high-ability class will be able to remain in that group.

In all cases, however, the process of discovering a student's disability, identifying it, and deciding what to do is a complex and emotionally wrenching experience for any parent. Parents who are poor, not native English speakers, or cautious about public institutions face additional obstacles. They are the least likely to be active advocates in ways that prompt schools to act on their children's behalf. Consequently, their children may not receive the same careful screening (or repeat diagnostic services) as the children of white, middle-class parents.

Ties to Behavioral Learning Theory and Transmission Teaching

Grouping students according to estimates of their abilities creates a high-stakes cycle that makes it even harder for the schools to break away from behavioral theories of learning and teaching. First, homogeneous grouping requires placements in classes that can chart the entire pathway or trajectory of the student's school outcomes and life chances. Consequently, educators rely heavily on standardized testing to make these potent decisions seem legitimate. As we discussed in Chapter 6, the tests themselves, then, call for behavioral approaches that may be effective for mastering the small units of information and discrete skills that standardized tests require, but do not reflect the true learning values that most educators and parents believe serve high-level knowledge or a robust democracy.

Because homogeneous grouping assumes that students in a class are very similar in nearly all respects, teaching can appear misleadingly simple—a matter of delivering (transmitting) facts to waiting minds. Teachers, then, have little reason to develop multidimensional lessons or pay much attention to individual students' learning strengths. For these reasons, homogeneous grouping can discourage an otherwise highly qualified and multifaceted teacher from matching instructional practices to students' diverse abilities and learning needs. Multiple criteria for success and rewards benefit all students, but make little sense if all students are presumed to be the same.

Self-Fulfilling Prophecies and Processes

———————————————————⊗ ⊗ ⊗———————————————————

My students believe they are in classes for stupid people. They say things such as, "We can't do this. We're only '103' [low-ability class] students." Most of them ask if they can move up, and some even say they are in the retarded classes.

It is important for me to not treat these students as if they cannot handle difficult work. The novel Always Running *is not that easy of a read for ninth-grade students. Many complex topics are dealt with, and most of the teachers at my high school would tell me it is too difficult for these kids. Yet I pushed them along and helped them get by certain spots. I try to treat these students the same as I do my "college-prep" kids.*

One thing that has limited my effectiveness in trying to teach with the same expectations of all my students is the culture of the school. Many teachers believe not only that low-track students will not do the work but that they cannot do the work. Any readings I assign for them to do at home I have to photocopy since they are not allowed their own books. There is only a class

*set because someone has decided that they will not do any homework any-
way, and they will probably just lose the books. Because of this, students
rarely get any homework. Many of them tell me I am the only teacher that
gives homework.*

*First semester, I taught my English classes in the print shop. My next
room turned out not to be a classroom at all. My students had nowhere to sit,
and one of the kids said, "Mr. Alvarez, they always give you the cheap classrooms." She sure was right. Finally, with 10 weeks to go in the year, I moved
into a [third] room. . . . The room has one window that does not open, no air
conditioner, and only one door to let in air. It has been close to 90 degrees
every day.*

*The students are being cheated out of a quality education, and they are
seeing a school system that is willing to just throw them anywhere. I look at
all the classes that have to endure this environment, and I see they all have
one thing in common: They are lower-track classes. The four teachers who
were in the print shop and now in the windowless bungalows for the most
part have "103" students. I teach all lower-track classes except for one class,
the other two English teachers have lower-track classes, and the fourth is an
ESL teacher. The school decided that the kids who need the most attention,
the most help, should get the worst environment in which to learn. There is
no way that the school would put honors kids in these rooms. Many people
feel that these kids are already lost so we should not waste any time or resources on them. It is for this reason that I have asked to continue teaching
the "103" students. They need someone who has not given up on them.*

—**Michael Alvarez**
First-year teacher, English, grade 9

Experiences like Michael Alvarez's reveal how the differentiation that accompanies homogeneous grouping can limit students who are not in the uppermost
track. And if the school and teachers "buy into" the idea that these students are
"less able," then the students will also. The result is that not all students are seen as
warranting similarly engaging learning experiences and opportunities—including
access to teachers with reputations for being the most experienced and highly
skilled.[32]

Labeling (even if it is masked in local codes such as "103" students) translates
into lowered self-confidence and lowered expectations for all students not graced
with the highest status label. Placement in a low, middle, or almost-but-not-quite-
top class often becomes a self-fulfilling prophecy—a cycle of lower expectations,
fewer opportunities, and academic performance that, at best, can match (but not
exceed) the expected performance.[33] In every aspect of what makes for a quality
education, kids in lower tracks typically get less than those in higher tracks and
gifted programs.[34] Some of the well-documented differences between high- and
low-level classes are listed in Concept Table 8.1.

As described next, when schools adopt heterogeneous or mixed-ability classes,
these classes tend to look more like the high- than low-ability classes. To understand why this might be so it's worth looking at what typically happens when

PT TABLE 8.1 *Grouping-Related Differences in Learning Opportunities*

roup Advantages	Lower-Group Disadvantages
Curriculum emphasizing concepts, inquiry, and problem solving	Curriculum emphasizing low-level facts and skills
Stress on students developing as autonomous thinkers	Stress on teaching students to follow rules and procedures
More time spent on instruction	More time spent on discipline or socializing
More active and interactive learning activities	More worksheets and seatwork
Computers used as learning tools	Computers used as tutors or electronic worksheets
More qualified and experienced teachers	More uncertified and inexperienced teachers
Extra enrichment activities and resources	Few enrichment opportunities
More engaging and friendly classroom atmosphere	More alienating and hostile classroom atmosphere
"Hard work" a likely classroom norm	"Not working" a likely classroom norm

Source: Jeannie Oakes, *Multiplying Inequalities* (Santa Monica: RAND, 1990).

teachers are assigned to work with "low-ability" or disabled students in a setting that includes only those students. Under these circumstances, teachers may have special training and skills, but they may not be required to be subject matter specialists. And yet, a strong background in and enthusiasm for math, science, literature, and so forth enables any teacher to find multiple ways to make a subject accessible and come alive for all students—especially those with learning disabilities.

Further, resource teachers are often called upon to support teachers with mainstreamed LD students. Lacking both knowledge and credibility, a resource teacher with a weak subject matter foundation is limited in the help he can give to establish successful heterogeneous instruction. With a commitment to heterogeneity, students stand a much better chance of exposure to high-level knowledge as well as the support services they need to master it. Finally, there is abundant evidence that the "nondisabled" students are not at all disadvantaged by learning with their LD peers.

Limited-English-speaking students in separate programs also tend to have fewer opportunities. Although the evidence is clear that they learn better with support in their own language, the shortage of qualified bilingual teachers frustrates this approach.[35] Many students in these programs must learn from teachers who are not fully able to teach either English or academic subject matter using the students' language. Other students work mostly with paraprofessional teachers' assistants.

These assistants may be fluent in the language, but typically they won't have either the subject matter or pedagogical knowledge of a fully qualified teacher.

Grouping practices help shape students' identities, status, and expectations for themselves. Both students and adults mistake labels such as "gifted," "honors student," "average," "remedial," "LD," and "MMR" for certification of overall ability and sometimes personal worth. These labels teach students that if the school does not identify them as capable in earlier grades, they should not expect to do well later. Everyone without the "gifted" label has the de facto label of "not gifted." The resource classroom is a low-status place and students who go there are low-status students. The result of all this is that most students have unrealistically low self-concepts, and schools have low expectations. Few students or teachers can defy those identities and expectations.

Of course, these labeling effects are not just a student phenomenon. They permeate the entire school and social culture. Thus, we have frequent references to "gifted parents." Teachers talk about "my low kids." Parents and educators alike confer greater status on teachers of high-achieving students. For example, at public and professional meetings, a teacher may be more likely to identify herself as an AP calculus teacher than as a teacher of basic math or of average algebra students, even though she might teach all three classes. Teachers of low-ability classes may be admired for how "tough" their job is, but it is often assumed that they are not—or don't need to be—as well qualified. Even highly qualified special education and bilingual teachers are not typically thought of as having the background and training needed to work with highly able students.

First-year teacher Lucy Patrick saw the dynamics of homogeneous grouping at work in an unexpected place—her and a colleague's experiment with creating homogeneous groups within their gifted fourth-grade classes.

———————————————————————————※ ※ ※———————————————————————————

Though my teaching partner and I were both teaching gifted fourth graders, we saw a wide range of abilities in both our classes. I especially saw a large discrepancy between students in the area of mathematics. Wanting to address individual differences and needs, I was frustrated, not knowing what to do for a group of students who learned a mathematical concept, while another group of students needed additional explanation or practice.

I felt like the class was a three-ring circus, with one group doing a handout, another group working independently, and the last group still not ready to do their class work. Feeling ineffective, my teaching partner and I decided to divide our classrooms based on math test scores. It seemed like a great opportunity to have two separate groups and teach toward their needs.

Before long we saw the discrepancy between the two groups widening, and I began to reconsider the advantages and disadvantages of having homogeneous grouping based on ability. By separating students, we isolated many of the student leaders into one group, while the other group contained disruptive students. I was meeting my objective to provide additional help to the group that needed it most, yet time spent on management took away from their review or practice, and they fell more and more behind.

Another concern was the effects on their emotional and social well-being.
Though we never made it known how we divided the students, the students
themselves understood the differences. In my mind, all the students are capa-
ble. Yet I am not certain what message the students received, especially when
the class work and homework were not the same for the two groups. I saw an
elitist attitude building within the higher-track group. I would hear students
say, "I already know this," "This is easy," or "The other group isn't doing
this." This attitude disturbed me because I had tried to create a fair and sup-
portive learning environment in my classroom and I felt that I had failed.

What I had done with my classroom was create a microcosm of the
tracking used in our school in my gifted classroom. I had managed to track
the students even more!

As an educator, I want all my students to reach their potential with het-
erogeneous grouping instead of more homogeneous grouping. I do not think
that I would attempt homogeneous grouping again.

—LUCY PATRICK
First-year teacher, grade 4

Simply by rejecting the "solution" of ever-greater homogeneity, Lucy Patrick did
not solve her original concern. She still must grapple with what to do with a roomful
of highly individualistic and competitive youngsters whose various skills, styles, and
personalities seemed to create academic and social chaos. Her failed experiment redi-
rected her to think about multidimensional lessons and working with the class to
improve their skills at helping their classmates work both independently and in groups.

Disappointing Outcomes

Over the years of schooling, students who are initially similar in background
and skills become increasingly different in achievement when schools put them
into separate, ability-grouped classes. Students placed in lower-level courses—
disproportionately Latino and African American students—consistently achieve less
than classmates with the same abilities whom the schools put in higher-level classes.
Students with both high *and* low test scores do better when they are in higher-level
courses.[36] Clearly, low-ability classes do not promote learning, even if teachers believe they are tailoring instruction to students' ability levels and academic potential.

Achievement gains from compensatory Title I programs are also disappointing,
at least partly because most compensatory programs work like low-ability classes.
That is, they classify students as low achievers, create a separate pull-out structure,
and provide a low-level, remedial curriculum.[37]

Bilingual and ESL programs have generated similar criticisms. First-year bilingual teacher Yvette Nunez observes that separate programs restrict students' access
to the natural, real opportunities to interact with native speakers of English.[38]

───────────── ✄ ✄ ✄ ─────────────

I am struggling to ground my teaching in my philosophy of learning and
still meet the expectations of the district. I want to tear down the system of

isolating Spanish speakers from their English-proficient counterparts. I believe in developing primary language skills, not only because these skills will transfer to English, but also because becoming biliterate and bicultural helps one understand the world.

We do not have high enough expectations for all our students to learn a second language. Students are able to learn language when it is applied in meaningful contexts, and an optimal environment includes lots of native-speaking peers.

—YVETTE NUNEZ
First-year teacher, grades 3 and 4

Students' hopes for the future rise or fall in ways that are consistent with their placements. Like achievement differences, this self-fulfilling prophecy accumulates until high school, when wide differences among students are most obvious. One reason for this long-term effect is that placements rarely change. Most students placed in low-ability or even average groups in elementary school continue in these tracks in middle school. Senior high schools usually place these students in non-college-prep tracks or "low" college-prep tracks that offer access to less-competitive colleges or majors, to two-year colleges, or to remedial classes as college freshmen. Being in a low class most often fosters lower achievement, poor self-concepts, lowered aspirations, negative attitudes, and even dropping out.[39]

Certainly, there are exceptions to these patterns. Many teachers know of students who get inspired and catch on despite their labels and classroom placements. Some, by sheer grit, pull themselves out of low-ability classes and succeed in higher classes. However, exceptions occur in spite of group placement, not because of it, and those who do succeed in spite of the odds often carry bitter memories of their struggle.

Homogeneous grouping is not necessarily good for high achievers, either. In fact, students can become destructively competitive among a very small population of the highest-achieving students—particularly in classrooms that stress individual achievement and grades. Those who are not in the very top sometimes feel like failures when they compare themselves with better students. For other exceptionally bright students, the perception of being gifted as a birthright impedes their discovery that effort and persistence matter more than high scores on tests. Moreover, many studies show that highly capable students do as well in mixed classes as in homogeneous groupings, particularly when teachers use the instructional strategies described in Chapter 5.[40]

Controversy Surrounds Homogeneous Grouping

One highly publicized grouping story came out of Selma, Alabama, in 1990 when Rose and Hank Sanders's high-achieving daughter was put in a low-track class. Rose went to school to straighten out the mistake, as most parents would. It took some negotiating, as it often does, but the principal finally agreed to change the girl's placement. Ordinarily, the matter would have ended here. But the Sanders are not an ordinary family. Graduates of the Harvard Law School, they have a practice together in Selma, and Hank serves in the state legislature. Their daughter's class placement seemed suspiciously like a civil rights violation to them, so they investigated further. When they discovered that nearly all of the school's African American students were in the low track, Rose got on the telephone. She advised every black parent to ask for a class reassignment.

African American school superintendent Norward Roussell agreed to make the grouping system fairer, and he instituted new graduation standards that require all students to take Algebra 1, Biology 1, Geography, and Computer Sciences—courses from which many students had previously been excluded. But Roussell lost the support of white residents and was fired when he tried to make a change. A white city councilman told a reporter that members of the white community feared that the new system would harm their children: "The basic position of the white community was that they wanted an honest program for the gifted students—for the best students. When they saw that being eliminated and the curriculum being watered down, theoretically, to a different level, they objected."[41]

Before it was over, African American protesters held daily marches, boycotted white-owned businesses, and occupied city hall. Students boycotted and closed down Selma High School. Rose Sanders was arrested, and 91 of the students who staged a "peaceful protest" in the cafeteria were reassigned to an alternative school. Since that time Rose and Hank Sanders have mounted a statewide campaign against tracking and educational inequality in Alabama. More recently, Sanders was appointed the first African American woman judge in the state of Alabama.

Efforts to dismantle homogeneous groups usually trigger controversy. Many educators resist detracking because, despite all of the evidence against tracking, they still believe it helps (or it can help) most students. It is also difficult for many educators to imagine how heterogeneous grouping could work, since so many school traditions and other school practices depend on homogeneous groups. Additionally, as in Selma, many parents of high-achieving students—often the most powerful and active parents in the community—oppose any suggestion to change grouping practices because they fear losing advantages the current system provides their children. And, if resistance to ending tracking is not *caused* by racial attitudes, it is indisputable that most resistance has racial consequences.

To Change or to Fix

The usual response to well-supported charges that current grouping practices don't work and aren't fair is to fix, adjust, or modify homogeneous grouping practices so they achieve educators' intentions.[42] Certainly, many schools that take this route are constantly changing criteria, adding or eliminating classes, "recruiting" students of color for the high-track and gifted programs, improving the low-track curriculum, and so forth. For example, a school could assign its most qualified English teacher to the low-ability English class and provide that class with the kind of enrichment typically found in gifted programs.

These suggestions have merit, but educators who have tried them report enormous difficulty in making them stick. Many educators have spent their careers trying to beef up the low-track curriculum, to adopt a more positive disposition toward the capacities of low-track students, and to alter the reward systems that work against teaching these students. They find it extraordinarily difficult to cancel out the negative impact of low-track students' quite accurate perceptions that schools have low regard for their ability and prospects for school success. The argument that educators can fix the technology of grouping underestimates the cultural and political pressures to resist these modifications.

Accommodating Diversity without Sorting

My students represent a wide range of abilities. A dozen of the students are English language learners (ELL). In the beginning, they did not participate in class discussion. They remained quiet until they worked with a partner or group where they often felt more comfortable to ask questions, voice opinions, and grapple with the material. These same students, along with about half of the other students, were struggling readers and writers. Concurrently, one of my students received a silver medal at the Academic Decathlon and several will attend UCLA this fall. There is 1 resource student and 13 gifted and talented students, some of whom are also English language learners. As I plan lessons for this class, I take into account their diversity.

To address diversity and individual needs, I have to think about what I want my students to know and learn and what I want them to be able to do. How can I ensure that all students have access to the information, and that they learn and feel successful? As I put together a unit, I focus on the students (identity and voice), the languages they speak (language acquisition), literacy, and cultural relevancy.

At times I assign heterogeneous groups, as I want to mix skill levels and races. I want students to work with different people because I know that once they graduate, they will not get to choose whom they work with. Sometimes I have students give me names of people they want to work with. I pair them with one of the persons on their list, and then I pair the pairs. I attempt to mix skill levels and ethnicities so that students will experience working with both diverse skill levels and diverse people. I always tell them that they are not marrying the people in their group but they must figure out how to work

with each other in class. We talk about how to communicate well when they
are unhappy with their team contribution.

—JUDY SMITH
High school social studies

Like many other educators today, Judy Smith is part of an effort to make schools more equitable by grappling with differences without classifying and sorting.

Since the late 1980s policymakers and educators have responded to the problems with homogeneous grouping by recommending that schools begin to dismantle them. The most recent critical voices are those of the directors of the Third International Mathematics and Science Study who conclude that tracking "fails to provide satisfactory achievement for either average or advanced students."[43] They join an impressive list of tracking critics.

In 1989 the Carnegie Corporation's prestigious and influential report *Turning Points* identified heterogeneous grouping as a central feature of reforming middle schools.[44] In 1990 the National Governors' Association proposed eliminating ability grouping and tracking as a strategy to help meet the nation's education goals. The College Board, which criticized grouping in middle and senior high school mathematics because it erects barriers to minorities' access to college, aims in its Equity 2000 project to eliminate mathematics tracking in two hundred racially diverse high schools. Most publishers of standardized achievement tests offer cautions about using their tests to group students.

In addition, the NAACP Legal Defense Fund, the Children's Defense Fund, the ACLU, and the federal Government Accounting Office have all raised ability grouping, gifted programs, and special education as a second-generation segregation issue. Throughout the 1990s, the U.S. Department of Education's Civil Rights Division targeted tracking as critical in determining whether racially mixed schools are complying with Title VI requirements for receipt of federal allocations.

Today's standards-based education reforms and No Child Left Behind's requirement that all children reach proficiency make ability grouping and tracking quite obsolete. Nothing in schools leaves children behind more systematically than tracking and ability grouping. Additionally, the Pathways to College Network is an alliance of 30 national organizations and funders working collaboratively to promote college access for underserved students at national, state, and local levels. Notably, the network's first priority is to "encourage schools to make a rigorous college preparatory curriculum the standard course of study for all students, so they will have the skills and knowledge they need to be successful in both postsecondary education and the workplace."[45]

These policy recommendations reflect growing support for heterogeneous grouping as necessary to ensure that all students have access to high-quality curriculum, teachers, and learning experiences. More and more educators and policymakers believe that schools cannot teach or achieve social justice unless they eliminate discriminatory grouping practices. However, this goal will not be accomplished quickly, and policy reports will simply gather dust unless enlightened teachers understand and act to change the norms and political relations these grouping practices embody. This will require teachers to become very competent in ways that are now less familiar to them and to their communities. They must be articulate spokespersons and persuaders to gather support from their colleagues and communities. There is a long, hard road ahead.

Implementing Heterogeneous Grouping

Many schools around the country have altered their grouping practices. The most common reforms include reducing or eliminating ability grouping, adopting school-wide reform instead of targeting groups of students for compensatory education, including gifted and disabled students in regular classes, and developing two-way bilingual programs.

"Detracking"   First-year teacher Kay Goodloe and her teaching partner have joined a large group of educators attempting to "detrack" their schools.

―――――――――――――――――――――❧ ❧ ❧―――――――――――――――――――――

I have ideological problems with the entire advanced placement (AP) program. It is discriminatory and elitist and does not accurately assess a student's academic potential. My AP students received a much more comprehensive education than my other students did. I find this very disturbing. Every student should have access to a college preparatory education. By tracking students, we limit their future choices, and that is the true crime. Every student should be allowed to choose whether they pursue a college education, but by denying them college preparatory classes, we rob them of that choice. My experience with the AP program has strengthened my resolve to provide such an education to all of my students. My partner and I will be detracking our classes next semester and offering a curriculum based on AP to everyone.

—KAY GOODLOE
First-year teacher, high school history

Most educators' first step toward mixed-ability classes is to do away with low-level groups and classes. Some of these schools require all students to take a set of core heterogeneous courses in addition to some that remain tracked. Many schools open honors programs to all students who wish to take them—or almost all. Some schools adopt specialized programs like AVID and The College Board's Equity 2000 that provide schools with strategies for including lower-achieving middle- and high school students in classes that prepare for four-year universities.

Other schools explore ways for students to earn honors credit within heterogeneous classes (e.g., by doing supplemental assignments and activities). Many schools rearrange their schedules so that students having difficulty keeping up academically can get extra help to master the more challenging curriculum. Some offer "backup" classes, tutorial periods, homework centers, and intensive summer programs intended to provide a "double dose" of instruction.

Many racially mixed schools develop multicultural curricula to make knowledge more accessible to all students. Some high schools, for example, diversify their elective offerings to include such classes as African American or Mexican American history, African American or Latin American literature, ethnic literature, and women's literature. Affiliation with educational groups that have high status among community leaders such as the College Board and local universities is often useful.

Many teachers in detracking schools adopt the classroom strategies described in Chapters 5 and 7. These help teachers align their teaching with sociocultural perspectives on learning, and they help students to show their ability in previously unrecognized ways. Socratic seminars, experiential curriculum (e.g., project-based science and interactive math), reduced reliance on textbooks, and cooperative small-group learning promote instructional conversations and scaffolding. Multidimensional assignments challenge students of varying abilities. Assessments that provide students with useful and interesting information support their inclinations to work hard. Multicultural content makes knowledge accessible.[46] A critical pedagogy that draws on students' own backgrounds and experiences can confer expertise on all students in the class. With this equality of status as a common starting point, students with different technical skills in reading, writing, and mathematics can view different skill levels as normal and possibly temporary.

Evidence from a carefully studied project in Philadelphia shows that when detracking is accompanied by such changes in curriculum, instruction, and assessment, both low- and high-achieving students fare very well. The National Center for the Education of Students Placed at Risk has established a set of urban "Talent Development" middle and senior high schools. The Talent Development schools offer a rich, academic curriculum (such as great literature), provide ample opportunities for students to assist one another, and use authentic assessments in heterogeneous classrooms. Middle-school students in the project showed significantly higher achievement gains than did tracked students in the project's "control" schools. To many observers' surprise, the students with the strongest academic skills seemed to benefit most.[47]

High school students in the Talent Development schools made substantial gains in attendance, academic course credits earned, and promotion rates during students' first year of high school, and the improvements in credits earned and promotion rates for ninth graders were sustained as students moved through high school. Improvements in student performance on the eleventh-grade state standards assessment also began to emerge, and there are early indications graduation rates will also improve.[48]

High-Track Classes for All   The standards movement and the goal of leaving no child behind has pressed many school districts to eliminate their lowest-level courses and, at the high school level, to put all students in college preparatory classes. For example, in 1998, the Board of Education of San Jose Unified School District approved new high school graduation requirements that match the courses required for admission to California colleges. In June 2005, a similar policy was adopted in Los Angeles.

Of course, policymakers can't expect that simply putting all students into high-level classes will by itself bring about high achievement, universal school success, and social justice. Implementing such a policy well requires additional supports for both students and teachers. As illustrated in Focal Point 8.1, Rockville Centre

FOCAL POINT 8.1

Detracking in Rockville Centre

In 1990, Rockville Centre School District, a diverse, suburban school district located on Long Island, New York, began replacing its tracked classes with mixed-ability classes and teaching everyone the curriculum formerly reserved for the district's high-track students. Previously, the high school had three tracks—school level, Regents, and honors—and the middle school had two or more in each subject. As in many districts, African American and Latino students were enrolled disproportionately in the lower track. Superintendent William H. Johnson's and the Rockville Centre Board of Education's ambitious goal was to have 75 percent of high school graduates earn a New York State Regents diploma and to close the district's racial and social class gaps. Achieving the superintendent's goal meant that students must pass at least eight examinations in mathematics, laboratory sciences, social studies, English language arts, and foreign language, examinations tied to the curriculum in the higher-track courses. Tracking stood in the way.

The district decided that all students would study the accelerated middle-school math curriculum, since the Regents math test posed the greatest challenge. So the middle school put mixed-ability groups in the math class formerly reserved for the district's highest achievers. It provided support classes and after-school tutoring to help struggling students keep up. The results were astonishing. The following year, over 90 percent of the incoming freshmen, excluding the special education students, entered the district's South Side high school having passed the first Regents math examination. The achievement gap dramatically narrowed, as the percentage of African American or Latino students passing the algebra-based Regents exam in the eighth grade tripled, rising to 75 percent. The percentage of white or Asian American regular education students who passed the test at the end of the eighth grade also increased dramatically—from 54 percent to 98 percent. Not satisfied with those results, the district pushed further. The following year, the special education students were included as well; detracking expanded to other subjects, and in 1999 it followed students into the ninth and tenth grades. Enrollment in South Side's advanced placement (AP) and International Baccalaureate classes was opened up to everyone who wanted to enter them.

During the decade of detracking reform, the school became a U.S. Department of Education Blue Ribbon School of Excellence and one of *Newsweek* magazine's "100 Best High Schools in the United States." By 2003, the gap among Rockville Centre graduates had nearly disappeared. Eighty-two percent of all African American or Latino and 97 percent of all white or Asian American graduates earned a Regents diploma. In 2004, the overall Regents diploma rate increased to a remarkable 94 percent, with 30 percent of the graduating class also earning the International Baccalaureate diploma. In sum, detracking raised the bar for all students. Every group improved at the same time that the achievement gap narrowed dramatically in Rockville Centre.

Source: Jeannie Oakes, "Democracy's Canaries," *Keeping Track: How Schools Structure Inequality.*[49]

Schools in New York were careful and thorough in the supports they provided as they enrolled all students in the state's high-level Regents curriculum.

Carol Burris, South Side High School's principal (South Side is one of the schools in the Rockville Centre School District), now spends a great deal of her time helping other schools create heterogeneous classrooms with rigorous college preparatory curriculum.

Schoolwide Improvement Rather Than Remedial "Pull-Out" Programs

The federal No Child Left Behind legislation governing compensatory education presses schools to use their federal funding to improve regular programs, rather than create separate ones. This eliminates the need to test and classify students as low achievers in order to qualify for the program. With the extra funds, teachers can adopt fundamentally different approaches to the "regular" classroom that make high-quality curriculum, teaching, and learning available to poor students.

Inclusion of Disabled and Gifted Students

Since the early 1990s a movement called "inclusion" has advocated placing students with disabilities in regular schools and classrooms, integrating the special supports these students need into regular education. Such supports (e.g., another teacher or an aide) are available to all students, not just those identified as disabled. Similarly, many, including advocates for the gifted, have argued that gifted students can be well served in regular classrooms if the curriculum is differentiated, and that the activities shown to be effective for gifted students can be extended to other students in the class.[50]

My special education students sit in the front. They get additional time on assignments, projects, and tests. For my gifted students as well as the students whose English is a lot higher than the English of my other sheltered students, I try to have more than one instruction on the board so they can move ahead at their faster pace.

—JUDY SMITH
High school social studies

Purposefully heterogeneous classrooms, advocates argue, do not ignore individual differences and needs but can acknowledge and respond to them in shared, more community-like contexts, such as those we described in Chapter 7. Janet Kim's middle-school students developed such communities.

He didn't speak a word at the beginning of the year. With the support of the special education teacher and a comfortable, caring classroom, he was able to stand up in front of the class during Author's Chair time. He took about 10 minutes reading a five-sentence paragraph. He did it on his own with nobody forcing him. He allowed himself to be vulnerable with a class that had a reputation for put-downs and nonstop torment. He read that paragraph with every pair of eyes fixed on his face—everyone wanting and

hoping that he would finish reading successfully no matter how long it took.
That was one of the most memorable and amazing moments. We were all
so proud.

—**Janet Kim**
First-year teacher, English, middle school

Supporting English Learners without Language Tracking   Beyond providing primary language instruction in the early stages of English fluency, bilingual specialists support a variety of approaches according to their particular philosophy and
the resources that are available at the school. The most important resources may be
skilled bilingual teachers, who are fluent in the student's language, and lots of
English-speaking peers. In the following quote, Mauro Bautista describes how he
uses the diversity of English language facility in his classroom and school as a
resource for learning instead of as a teaching problem.

As a beginning ESL teacher, the zone of proximal development (ZPD) was
constantly on my mind. My classes were made up of students who were di-
verse in their knowledge of English. Thus, in grouping students I would try
to group students whose English skills were low with students who had
greater English skills. This was beneficial for the students who were limited
in English because they could learn from their peers. This was also great for
the more advanced students because they could take on the roles of experts. In
addition, I would attempt to use the ZPD with more advanced students by
encouraging them to join extracurricular activities. Remember, these are
students who just recently arrived from another country. I would encourage
them to join Students Run L.A., Mariachi, Art, and Leadership. Several of
my beginning ESL students were elected class officers. These extracurricular
activities placed these students in settings where they had to further practice
their English. In retrospect, I feel I did a decent job of helping both my low
students and my high students.

—**Mauro Bautista**
Middle-school bilingual education coordinator

One very effective method of providing students the primary language support
they need without segregating them from English speakers is *two-way bilingual*
education. This approach brings native English speakers together with students
whose primary language is not English. Formalized two-way bilingual programs aim
to develop bilingual proficiency in all of the students, as well as promote academic
achievement and cross-cultural knowledge and regard. Available evidence suggests
that these programs are quite successful. For example, a study of 160 schools with
two-way programs (most of them Spanish and English) found these programs to be
effective with both English-speaking students and those who are speakers of other
languages.[51]

Technical Skills, Norms and Beliefs, Politics and Power

Few teachers entering the teaching profession today have had personal experience in heterogeneous classrooms, and few teaching mentors have "answers" for how to make such classrooms work. But some teachers are powerfully equipped to study the challenges and not settle for replicating the familiar. First-year teacher Frank Divinagracia found this challenge engrossing and his profession exciting.

—————————⚔ ⚔ ⚔—————————

The Environmental Careers Academy expects innovative and reform-minded teaching. This, in itself, pushes me to be more hands-off and more creative. Also, the socioethnic background of my students provides for some dynamic group mixes. In a nontracked class with 25 percent African American, 45 percent Latino/a, and 30 percent Asian, I have the chance to create a challenging learning experience for all of us. In choosing the Discovering Geometry book, I had a geometry curriculum that would be centered around investigations and students' conjectures. I wanted to challenge my students to think on their own and in groups. Also, I wanted to give the students more control over the curriculum.

The geometry lessons allowed students to speak and listen to one another and create their own knowledge. As a facilitator, I want them to think for themselves, defend their ideas, and be confident enough to stick to their beliefs. The beauty of it is they have to make their own conclusions and use them for further study. They have to design what they learn in order to apply

*it. I could see deliberateness in my students' actions, a true yearning to un-
derstand. The atmosphere was free and relaxed. They still struggled to learn,
but they did so without fear of being wrong.*

*One young man had a hard time conceiving how to make two angles ex-
actly the same. I began asking questions about the steps he took. Eventually a
young woman in the group explained how she was able to [solve the prob-
lem]. The young man started to understand. I believe he trusted her observations, and her explanations were probably better than mine.*

*Because these students are getting a good dose of group work in all their
classes, they are used to being challenged and engaged in both their individual projects and their group work. They have been extremely creative and
have designed projects such as researching and painting murals, starting a
garden, producing a recycling project on campus, and more. The students
are thinking critically about their environment and [acting on] its
problems.*

—FRANK DIVINAGRACIA
First-year teacher, high school mathematics

Nearly all advocates of ability grouping, in particular those who favor
"gifted"/high-track classes, would prefer classes (and teachers!) such as Frank Divinagracia. For example, Sandra Berger of the Council for Exceptional Children summarized research on curriculum and instruction for gifted students and concluded
that gifted learners are served best by the very same types of educational experiences that make all students successful in heterogeneous classes. Berger advocates
"thematic, broad-based, and integrative content" because "concept-based instruction expands opportunities to generalize and to integrate and apply ideas." She
points to the need for gifted learners to be challenged by "open-ended questions
that stimulate inquiry, active exploration, and discovery" and argues that they learn
best in a "receptive, nonjudgmental, student-centered environment that encourages inquiry and independence, includes a wide variety of material, provides some
physical movement, is generally complex, and connects the school experience with
the greater world." She also emphasizes that teachers must provide multiple ways
for gifted students to demonstrate what they have learned: "For example, instead of
giving a written or oral book report, students might prefer to design a game around
the theme and characters of a book."[52]

Those who advocate heterogeneity conclude that commonly touted benefits
of separate gifted classes are attributable to these and similar classroom and
instruction characteristics. Similarly, the most common criticisms of mixed-
ability classes—that the classes hold back or are boring for high achievers—
can be attributed to the *lack* of these characteristics, not to the particular mix of
students.

Confronting Norms and Values   Educators attempting heterogeneous grouping must come to terms with deep American values for competition and individualism. These norms bring a winners and losers frame of mind to education, and they
imply that "good" education channels the most deserving students toward even

better education and then higher income, power, and status. If heterogeneous grouping is to work well, schools and classrooms must move toward more democratic norms of cooperation, support, and community. Conversely, if Americans want a society that values cooperation, support, and community, then heterogeneity must begin in schools.

Why is this so? Conventional conceptions of knowledge, language, and culture harbor deep-seated attitudes about race and social class. Extensive procedural and ideological "filters" such as curriculum guides, textbooks, legislative oversight, and typical teacher training, to mention a few, keep the curriculum consistent with mainstream Eurocentric, male, and white versions of valued knowledge. These filters can prevent alternative or competing versions of knowledge from reaching students. Educators trying to create heterogeneous grouping need to rethink how curriculum can include all students.

Sociocultural theory demonstrates that teachers need to create a social context where students' personal and social lives are important in their classroom interactions. If students worry about being humiliated because their differences and disabilities are known to others, they won't take the intellectual and social risks that learning requires.

Attention to the Political   The discussion throughout this chapter makes clear that grouping, indeed, nearly all educational policies, is highly political. Homogeneous grouping in particular has consequences with meaning and exchange value beyond school. After all, schools and groups are accompanied by public labels, and status differences, and they signal which students should gain access to the university and the status and life chances that higher education can bring. Thus, ability grouping and tracking become part of the struggles for comparative advantage in the distribution of school resources, opportunities, and credentials that have exchange value in the larger society. Efforts to move away from homogeneous grouping nearly always engender resistance from those whose children are advantaged by it.

Educators also worry about the political consequences of abandoning homogeneous grouping: In particular they worry about losing the support of parents of high-track students. In local forums such as school board meetings and in popular practitioner journals, advocates for categorically funded gifted programs lobby strongly against policy changes that may threaten special opportunities now available to high achievers. In many communities, as the story of the Sanders family in Selma, Alabama, illustrates vividly, this political dimension encompasses highly charged issues of race and social class stratification. Increasingly, a variety of school "choice" policies such as charters, magnets, vouchers, and homeschooling are offered, and at least part of their attractiveness is the desire to create more homogeneous environments than what public schools offer.

The challenge is daunting. Successful heterogeneous grouping will inevitably require that those who may now see themselves as competing—such as advocates for the gifted, for disabled students, for the disadvantaged, and for students of color—make common cause around serving all students well. Building coalitions among these divergent constituencies (and maintaining political credibility) will require that educators guarantee that their new practices will provide all students with opportunities that are at least as rich and rigorous as those they previously enjoyed. No parent would sensibly agree to less. But some parents will also object to changes that take away the *comparative* advantages their privileged children enjoyed with homogeneous grouping—no matter how good the new approach might be. Confronting these issues is a political process that requires astute political leadership by educators.

The Struggle for Heterogeneous Grouping

—————————————————————————————————————— ⊗ ⊗ ⊗ ——————————————————————————————————————

At our school, the "magnet-gifted" and "resident" classrooms are physically set apart from each other. I have heard my magnet students argue on the playground with resident students. The resident students had been calling the magnet students "nerds" and "dorks," while the magnet students counter by saying that they are "smarter" and that the resident students were "stupid." There is the attitude in my classroom—that they are smarter and better because they "got in" to the gifted program. Others go so far as to say that there are students in our classroom who do not belong in the magnet.

Some staff "joke" about the magnet teachers, "Oh, the magnets are having a meeting" or "We're not good enough to be magnet teachers." Some tension between the two schools centers around resources. As a magnet school, there are more funds available for extra materials or needed equipment.

A main concern for the magnet program is how they can differentiate the gifted program from the regular one. The magnet has special out-of-town field trips and experts who come in and teach (art, music, PE, science, opera). Teachers within the magnet program make it a point to be different from the resident school, regardless of what is best for students. For example, when we were deciding which publishing company to choose for our new language arts program, teachers suggested that we choose a series that is different from the resident school in order to explain to parents how the program is different.

Only after intense and honest dialogue about what is best for all students will this two-school system change. Next year, I would like to bridge the two schools by having students interact more on a social level. Perhaps I can combine magnet students with resident school students in classes. As long as the school is based on merit and "ability," those in power will push for the status quo. It will take the combined efforts of students, teachers, administrators, parents, and community members to come together and engage in thoughtful reflection.

—LUCY PATRICK
First-year teacher, grade 4

This chapter has explored how sorting students into categories based on students' presumed abilities requires a school culture that is behavioral and individualistic in its orientation. And in schools where grouping practices position white and privileged students as those with the most merit, Eurocentric versions of valued knowledge dominate. These orientations limit all students' learning, *regardless* of how extensive and well intentioned are the services provided to any particular "special" categories, such as "regular," "gifted," and so forth.

Our educational system has witnessed few events or trends that have required the changes in thinking and attitudes as much as changes in grouping practices will require. Changes of similar magnitude might be the social shifts the country has witnessed in the slow breaking down of legal racial segregation, or gender discrimination, or norms regarding cigarette smoking. For a very long time, knowledge alone about the damage the practices cause was not enough to budge the practices, and now that they have budged, everyone recognizes what a long way we still have to go. But slowly, coalitions of people who see the harm in these practices are finding some success in challenging the status quo. Those who have professional knowledge and those with credible moral standing in the community are joining in. Ultimately, those who benefit from these practices will not be able to marshal political power to hold the practices in place. The status quo does change—by slow, painful degrees, to be sure, but it changes.

⬤ OLC Connections

A list of additional online and print resources and a set of questions for reflection about grouping can be found at www.mhhe.com/oakes3e.

▨ Digging Deeper

The scholars, educators, and projects listed in this section conduct research and develop practices to help schools move away from conventional classification and grouping practices.

Arizona State University education professor **Alfredo Artiles** writes about the social construction of special education and the overrepresentation of students of color in special education classifications. Of particular interest to teachers are two of his recent books. One, written with **Alba Ortiz,** is *English Language Learners with Special Needs: Identification, Placement, and Instruction* (Washington D.C.: Center for Applied Linguistics, 2002); it summarizes research and best practices from the past 30 years into a guide for making appropriate referrals of English learners to special education. A second, written with **Grace Zamora-Durán,** is *Reducing Disproportionate Representation of Culturally Diverse Students in Special and Gifted Education* (Reston, VA: The Council for Exceptional Children, 1997).

Jo Boaler, Stanford professor of mathematics education whose work we described in Chapter 5, is particularly interested in how tracking undermines the effectiveness and equity of mathematics teaching and learning. Her book

Experiencing School Mathematics: Traditional and Reform Approaches to Teaching and their Impact on Student Learning (Mahwah, NJ: Lawrence Erlbaum, 2002) presents, in a highly readable fashion, the results of a carefully conducted study of the teaching of mathematics in two high schools, one tracked and one untracked.

Indiana University professor **Ellen A. Brantlinger**'s book *Dividing Classes: How the Middle Class Negotiates and Justifies School Advantage* (New York: Falmer Press, 2003) is a fascinating report of her study of how highly educated professional, middle-class parents work the tracking system at their schools to advantage their own schoolchildren. She documents how these middle-class tracking advantages come at a cost to children from less-wealthy families.

Dr. **Carol Burris,** principal of South Side High School in Rockville Centre, New York, has led a detracking reform at her school that has almost eliminated the achievement gap among graduates. Carol has written about her school and the research documenting its success with **Kevin Welner** in "Closing the Achievement Gap by Detracking," in *Kappan,* April 2005, pp. 594–598.

James Cummins, a professor in the Modern Language Centre at the Ontario Institute on Educational Studies and the University of Toronto, writes about bilingual education and empowering language-minority students. His research focuses primarily on the challenges educators face in adjusting to classrooms where cultural and linguistic diversity is the norm. His most recent book, *Negotiating Identities: Education for Empowerment in a Diverse Society,* published in 2001, is available from the California Association for Bilingual Education.

Hugh Mehan, professor of sociology at the University of California-San Diego, studies the processes by which constructed categories affect students' schooling experiences. With **Alma Hertweck** and **J. Lee Meihls,** Mehan is the author of *Handicapping the Handicapped: Decision-Making in Students' Educational Careers* (Stanford: Stanford University Press, 1986). His most recent book, *Constructing School Success: The Consequences of Untracking Low-Achieving Students* (with Irene Villanueva, Lea Hubbard, and Angela Lintz), was published by Cambridge University Press in April 1996. It discusses the educational and social consequences of a successful educational innovation, AVID, that successfully "untracks" low-achieving ethnic and language minority students by placing both low- and high-achieving students in the same rigorous academic program.

Jeannie Oakes, a professor of education in the Graduate School of Education and Information Studies at the University of California-Los Angeles, studies inequalities in the allocation of resources and learning opportunities in schools, and equity-minded reform. Her book *Keeping Track: How Schools Structure Inequality* (New Haven, CT: Yale University Press), first published in 1985 and in a second edition in 2005, describes how tracking and grouping students by ability in school affect the classroom experiences of low-income students and students of color, most of whom are identified as having "low" academic ability or as "slow" learners. It also describes research and best practices for detracking. With colleagues, including Professor **Amy Stuart Wells** and **Martin Lipton,** Oakes has also written about middle and senior high schools engaged in detracking reforms. Her book *Becoming Good American Schools: The Struggle for Virtue in School Reform*

(San Francisco: Jossey-Bass, 1999), written with **Karen Hunter Quartz, Steve Ryan,** and **Martin Lipton,** relates the experiences of middle schools engaged in these reforms.

Joseph S. Renzulli is a professor of educational psychology at the University of Connecticut, where he also serves as director of The National Research Center on the Gifted and Talented. A focus of his work has been on applying the strategies of gifted education to the improvement of learning for all students. He has written about developing all students' talent and proposes the "schoolwide enrichment model" as a substitute for narrow and specialized programs for gifted students. He details these ideas in his book *Enriching Curriculum for All Students* (Thousand Oaks, CA: Corwin Press, 2001).

Professor **Maria Sapon-Shevin** at the State University of New York at Syracuse studies and writes about disabilities and gifted education. A proponent of inclusive education, she has investigated classroom strategies to promote learning in mixed-ability classes. Her book *Playing Favorites: Gifted Education and the Disruption of Community* (Albany, NY: SUNY Press, 1994) examines the ways in which gifted programs can inhibit inclusiveness in classrooms, deskill teachers, and limit their willingness to meet individual needs. A more recent book, *Because We Can Change the World: A Practical Guide to Building Cooperative, Inclusive Classroom Communities* (New York: Allyn and Bacon, 1998), is a good resource for preschool through middle school teachers who want practical strategies for creating and maintaining classrooms that support diversity and help students learn to act powerfully.

The Center for the Social Organization of Schools directs the **Talent Development Middle and High School** projects. The projects combine a carefully constructed, research-based design for schools with rigorous data collection and analysis strategy. Talent Development Schools establish separate learning communities of 200 to 300 students. These small learning communities are traditionally organized into vertical, untracked houses with teaching teams (two or three teachers) being responsible for fewer than 100 students. The resulting small, stable learning communities encourage students, teachers, and families to establish strong bonds and close, caring relationships. More information can be found online for the middle-school program at http://www.csos.jhu.edu/tdms/ and for the high school program at http://www.csos.jhu.edu/tdhs/.

Tom Skrtic is a professor in the University of Kansas Department of Special Education. Skrtic's work focuses on the changes taking place in education and special education and how these changes connect to the challenges of postmodernism. He is editor of *Disability and Democracy: Reconstructing (Special) Education for Postmodernity* (New York: Teachers College Press, 1995).

Professor **Carol Ann Tomlinson** at the University of Virginia's Curry School of Education has done research and written widely about teaching in mixed-ability classrooms. She also works nationally and internationally with teachers and administrators who want to develop classrooms and school that are actively responsive to academically diverse student populations. Among her books that are very useful to teachers are *How to Differentiate Instruction in Mixed Ability Classrooms*

(New York: Prentice-Hall, 2004), *The Differentiated Classroom: Responding to the Needs of all Learners* (Reston, VA: Association for Supervision and Curriculum Development, 1999), and *Fulfilling the Promise of the Differentiated Classroom: Strategies and Tools for Responsive Teaching* (Reston, VA: Association for Supervision and Curriculum Development, 2003).

Kevin Welner, professor of education policy at the University of Colorado, Boulder, studies the links among education rights litigation and educational opportunity scholarship. His past research studied detracking efforts reforms aimed at benefiting those who hold less powerful school and community positions (primarily Latinos, African Americans, and the poor). His book *Legal Rights, Local Wrongs: When Community Control Collides with Educational Equity* (Buffalo: State University of New York Press, 2001) reports these studies. A second book with **Jeannie Oakes,** *Navigating the Politics of Detracking (*Arlington Heights, IL: Skylight Publications, 2000), provides practical advice for educators seeking to detrack their schools. See Welner's website at http://education.colorado.edu/faculty/welnerk/ for a free download of this book.

Education policy writer **Anne Wheelock**'s book *Crossing the Tracks: How "Untracking" Can Save America's Schools* (New York: The New Press, 1992; distributed by W. W. Norton, New York, 1992) describes the knowledge, tools, and philosophies that have been generated by schools that are attempting to develop a "culture of detracking" that works against the traditional tendency to separate students into homogeneous groups. Wheelock and **Leon Lynn** edited a special issue of the *Harvard Education Letter* (13, no. 1 [January/February 1997]) on detracking. Wheelock also writes about issues related to special education identification in urban schools.

Notes

1. Ability grouping and "tracking" are often used interchangeably to describe both ability-grouped classes and differentiated programs of study in which schools place students of different abilities. Some make a distinction by suggesting that "tracking" only applies to permanent assignments to a pathway leading to college or work. In practice, assignment to various ability levels is quite permanent and often extends to all of a student's academic subjects, K–12.
2. Although the labels don't always convey it, everyone at a school knows the "ability level" of various groups.
3. Adam Gamoran, "A Multi-level Analysis of the Effects of Tracking" (paper presented at the annual meetings of the American Sociological Association, Atlanta, GA, 1988).
4. Michael Garet and Brian DeLany, "Students, Courses, and Stratification," *Sociology of Education* 61 (1988), pp. 61–77; and Brian DeLany, "Allocation, Choice, and Stratification Within High Schools: How the Sorting Machine Copes," *American Journal of Education* 99, no. 3 (1991), pp. 191–207.
5. Joseph Renzulli and Sally Reis, "The Reform Movement and the Quiet Crisis in Gifted Education," *Gifted Child Quarterly* 35 (1991), pp. 26–35.
6. Lorraine M. McDonnell, Margaret J. McLaughlin, and Patricia Morrison, eds., *Educating One and All: Students with Disabilities and Standards-Based Reform* (Washington, DC: National Academy Press, 1997).
7. Hugh Mehan, Jane Mercer, and Robert Rueda, "Special Education," in *Encyclopedia of Education and Sociology* (New York: Garland, 1997).

8. Larry S. Goldman, Myron Genel, Rebecca J. Bezman, and Priscilla J. Slanetz, "Diagnosis and Treatment of Attention-Deficit/Hyperactivity Disorder in Children and Adolescents," *Journal of the American Medical Association* 279, no. 14 (April 8, 1998), pp. 1100–1107.

9. Eviatar Zerubavel, *The Fine Line: Making Distinctions in Everyday Life* (Chicago: University of Chicago Press, 1993), pp. 1–2.

10. Kevin Welner, *Legal Rights; Local Wrongs: When Community Control Collides with Educational Equity* (Buffalo: State University of New York Press, 2001).

11. Elwood Cubberly, *Changing Conceptions of Education* (Boston: Houghton Mifflin, 1909), pp. 18–19.

12. For a fascinating, detailed history of the links between the growth of universal, compulsory education and special education, see John G. Richardson, "Common Delinquent, and Special: On the Formalization of Common Schooling in the American States," *American Educational Research Journal* 31, no. 4 (1994), pp. 695–723.

13. Jeannie Oakes and Gretchen Guiton, "Matchmaking: The Dynamics of High School Tracking Decisions," *American Educational Research Journal* 32, no. 1 (1995), pp. 3–33.

14. Joseph Renzulli, in an interview with Anne Turnbaugh Lockwood, "Beyond the Golden Chromosome," in *Focus in Change,* a publication of the National Center for Effective Schools at the University of Wisconsin, Madison (no. 11 [fall 1993]), p. 3.

15. McDonnell, McLaughlin, and Morrison, eds., *Educating One and All.*

16. Mehan, Mercer, and Rueda, "Special Education."

17. Donald L. MacMillan and Daniel Reschly, "Overrepresentation of Minority Students: The Case for Greater Specificity or Reconsideration of the Variables Examined," *Journal of Special Education* 32 (1998), pp. 15–24.

18. Christine Sleeter, "Learning Disabilities: The Social Construction of a Special Education Category," *Exceptional Children* 53, no. 1 (1986), pp. 46–54. Also, "Why Is There Learning Disabilities? A Critical Analysis of the Birth of the Field in Its Social Context," in *The Formation of the School Subject Matter: The Struggle for an American Institution,* ed. T. S. Popkewitz (New York: Falmer Press, 1987).

19. Louise Spear-Swerling and Robert J. Sternberg, *Off Track: When Poor Readers Become Learning Disabled* (Boulder, CO: Westview Press, 1996).

20. See, for example, the special issue of *Phi Delta Kappan* (February 1996), and Thomas Armstrong, *The Myth of the ADD Child* (New York: Dutton, 1985).

21. Mehan, Mercer, and Rueda, "Special Education."

22. MacMillan and Reschly, "Overrepresentation of Minority Students."

23. For example, researcher Elizabeth Useem found that middle-school students' placement in math classes was "not necessarily based on some objective, highly accurate assessment of students' 'ability' by school professionals" but rather on parents' willingness to take steps to ensure that their children were enrolled in upper-level classes even when school personnel recommended against it or their children resisted it. Elizabeth Useem, "Student Selection into Course Sequences in Mathematics: The Impact of Parental Involvement and School Policies," *Journal of Research on Adolescence* 1, no. 3 (1991), pp. 231–250; also see Susan Yonezawa and Jeannie Oakes, "Making All Parents Partners in the Placement Process," *Education Leadership* (April 2004).

24. "A New Mix of Gifted Students," *The Washington Post,* 27 July 1997.

25. Mehan, Mercer, and Rueda, "Special Education."

26. Anamaria M. Villegas, "School Failure and Cultural Mismatch: Another View," *The Urban Review* 20, no. 4 (1988), pp. 253–265.

27. Jeannie Oakes, *Multiplying Inequalities* (Santa Monica: RAND, 1990); Oakes and Guiton, "Matchmaking."

28. Mehan, Mercer, and Rueda, "Special Education."

29. Luanna H. Meyer, Beth Harry, and Mara Sapon-Shevin, "School Inclusion and Multicultural Education," in *Multicultural Education: Issues and Perspectives,* ed. James A. Banks and Cherry A. McGee Banks (Boston: Allyn & Bacon, 1996).

30. MacMillan and Reschly, "Overrepresentation of Minority Students."

31. Oakes and Guiton, "Matchmaking"; Susan Yonezawa, *Making Decisions About Students' Lives* (Ph.D. diss., Los Angeles, UCLA, 1997); and Annette Lareau, *Home Advantage: Social Class and Parental Intervention in Elementary Education* (London: Falmer, 1989).

32. Jeannie Oakes, *Keeping Track: How Schools Structure Inequality* (New Haven, CT: Yale University Press, 1985/2005); Oakes, *Multiplying Inequalities.*

33. Oakes, *Multiplying Inequalities.*

34. This is not to say that *particular* classes for lower-ability students are not given wonderful facilities, a solid curriculum, and well-qualified teachers, but such situations are clear exceptions to the rule.

35. Jay P. Greene, *A Meta-Analysis of the Effectiveness of Bilingual Education* (Claremont, CA: The Tomas Rivera Policy Institute, 1998).

36. Jeannie Oakes, "Two Cities: Tracking and Within-School Segregation," in *Brown Plus Forty: The Promise,* ed. La Mar Miller (New York: Teachers College Press, 1995); and Kevin G. Welner, *Legal Rights, Local Wrongs: When Community Control Collides with Educational Equity* (Buffalo: State University of New York Press, 2001).

37. David J. Hoff, " Chapter 1 Aid Failed to Close Learning Gap," *Education Week,* 2 April 1997, pp. 1, 29; Robert E. Slavin, "How Title I Can (Still) Save America's Children," *Education Week,* 21 May 1997, p. 52; and Thomas Kelly, "The 4 Percent 'Structural Flaw,'" *Education Week,* 11 June 1997, p. 44.

38. Jim Cummins, "From Multicultural to Anti-Racist Education: An Analysis of Programmes and Policies in Ontario," in *Minority Education: From Shame to Struggle,* ed. Tove Skutnabb-Kangas and Jim Cummins (Philadelphia: Multilingual Matters Ltd., 1988).

39. Jeannie Oakes, Adam Gamoran, and Reba Page, "Curriculum Differentiation," in *Handbook of Research on Curriculum,* ed. Phillip Jackson (New York: Macmillan, 1992).

40. There is considerable disagreement in the academic community about whether or not high-achieving students benefit academically from high-track placement. Most, however, agree that what benefits might accrue come about because of the enriched opportunities in these classes, not because the students are separated per se. See, for example, the series of articles in the November 1995 issue of *Phi Delta Kappan.*

41. William Snider, "Schools Are Reopened in Selma Amid Continuing Racial Tension," *Education Week,* 21 February 1990.

42. For example, researcher Maureen Hallinan argues that "a more tempered response" is for schools to make grouping practices more consistent with the theories behind those practices, and to balance the inherently negative features of grouping with countervailing policies and practices. See Maureen Hallinan, "Tracking: From Theory to Practice," *Sociology of Education* 67, no. 2 (1994), pp. 79–84. See also, Adam Gamoran, "Alternative Uses of Ability Grouping in Secondary Schools: Can We Bring High-Quality Instruction to Low-Ability Classrooms?" *American Journal of Education* 102, no. 1 (1993), pp. 1–22.

43. William Schmidt, "Are There Surprises in the TIMSS Twelfth Grade Results?" *TIMSS United States,* Report No. 8 (East Lansing, MI: TIMSS U.S. National Research Center, Michigan State University, April 1998), p. 4.

44. Carnegie Council on Adolescent Development, *Turning Points: Preparing Youth for the 21st Century* (New York: Carnegie Corporation of New York, 1989).

45. http://www.pathwaystocollege.net/aboutus/index.html.

46. Jeannie Oakes, Amy Stuart Wells, Susan Yonezawa, and Karen Ray, "Equity Lessons from Detracking Schools," in *Rethinking Educational Change with Heart and Mind,* ed. Andy Hargreaves (Arlington, VA: Association for Supervision and Curriculum Development, 1997).

47. Douglas MacIver, Steven B. Plank, and Robert Balfanz, "Working Together to Become Proficient Readers: Early Impact of the Talent Development Middle School's *Student Team Literature Program,*" Report of the Center for Research on the Education of Students Placed at Risk (Baltimore: The Johns Hopkins University Press, 1998).

48. James J. Kemple, Corinne M. Herlihy, and Thomas J. Smith, *Making Progress Toward Graduation: Evidence from the Talent Development High School Model* (Washington, DC: MRDC, 2005).

49. Jeannie Oakes, *Keeping Track;* see also, Carol C. Burris, Jay P. Heubert, and Henry M. Levin, "Accelerating Mathematics Achievement Using Heterogeneous Grouping," *American Educational Research Journal* (in press).

50. Joseph S. Renzulli and Sally Reis, *The Schoolwide Enrichment Model: A Comprehensive Plan for Educational Excellence* (Mansfield Center, CT: Creative Learning Press, 1985); Carol Tomlinson, *How to Differentiate Instruction for Mixed-Ability Classrooms* (Alexandria, VA: Association for Supervision and Curriculum Development, 1995); and Carol Tomlinson, "Differentiated Instruction in the Regular Classroom: What Does It Mean? How Does It Look?" *Understanding Our Gifted* 14, no. 1 (2001), pp. 3–6.

51. Donna Christian, *Two-Way Bilingual Education: Students Learning through Two Languages* (Santa Cruz, CA: National Center for Research on Cultural Diversity and Second Language Learning, 1994).

52. Sandra L. Berger, "Differentiating Curriculum for Gifted Students," *ERIC Digest #E510* (Reston, VA: Council for Exceptional Children, ERIC Clearinghouse on Disabilities and Gifted Education, n.d.).

PART III

The Context of Teaching to Change the World

CHAPTER 9

The School Culture

Where Good Teaching Makes Sense

Our school provides an excellent environment for inquiry, advancement, and staff development. This is due to the largely supportive administration and the strong influence of educated teachers. Just as is the case with students in classrooms, a critical mass of educators will dictate the school's philosophy and culture. Either a "woe is me" or a "can do" attitude will prevail. There is no middle ground. Our site is most definitely a "can do" atmosphere. My colleagues feed off of each other, and defeatism doesn't have a place to gain traction. Whether it is a challenge dictated to us by the district or state, a lack of basic skills by students coming into the school, difficulties at home for the students, or a lack of the appropriate methods and techniques by a teacher, our site focuses on solving the problem. We are highly collaborative within individual departments, and we are working on greater interdepartmental collaboration. We also have a high level of collaboration with other schools during staff development days. The district encourages teachers to participate as workshop leaders, and it provides strong new teacher training and continued support through departmental "coaches."

—MARK HILL
First-year teacher, high school mathematics

Students need committed and capable teachers, a clean and safe environment, and up-to-date books, computers, and facilities, but they need more. The school's organizational arrangements and routines, attitudes and beliefs, and the relationships among everyone in the building also shape what students accomplish in school. In other words, students need a school culture that makes it inevitable that all students receive a socially just and excellent education. So do teachers.

Chapter Overview
❈

This chapter focuses on the school culture—one of the most important contexts for teaching to change the world. We describe, first, how schools have distinctive cultures that have a powerful influence on the quality of teaching and learning. We then elaborate four features of the school culture that consistently appear on research-based lists of the characteristics of "good" schools. School cultures that foster both high academic quality and social justice (1) press everyone toward learning and social justice; (2) provide broad and deep access to learning; (3) build an environment of caring relationships; and (4) support teachers' inquiry and activism. Chapter 10 considers a fifth essential characteristic of a healthy and socially just school culture—respectful connections between schools and the families and communities they serve. Together, these conditions—obvious, perhaps—allow teachers and their students to teach and learn in ways that can change the world.

In addition to teachers' observations about their own experiences, this chapter also includes several descriptions by new teachers of other, more-experienced teachers from whom they have received valuable guidance, modeling, and mentoring. But the mentors also benefited from the new teachers—drawing on their enthusiasm and reflecting on their difficult questions, and discovering new allies for constructing socially just and academically rich school cultures.

Schools as Cultures

One new teacher described the cultures at two different senior high schools where she has taught. In many ways, the two schools are similar. Both are large comprehensive urban high schools in medium-sized school systems. Both have racially mixed student bodies, and many students who struggle academically. Nevertheless, this teacher was struck by the contrast between the cultures at the two schools.

———————————————————— ⊗ ⊗ ⊗ ————————————————————

Wow. I am still adapting to Jefferson High. The culture is very different from Lincoln where I taught last year. First off, Lincoln High had many well-trained teachers and administrators. Teachers formed small communities among themselves, and one hosted a monthly inquiry meeting. Teachers felt free to speak out at the large monthly staff meetings. We could also give anonymous feedback and ask questions of the principal, and we were given typed-up answers.

I always felt supported at Lincoln. There was a tardy policy. There were discipline procedures. Social justice was not only spoken of, it was absolutely expected. When I wanted to do a community volunteer project, the principal supported me. When I went outside the norm and barely used the textbook, I felt supported. There was a community liaison and a bilingual newsletter for parents and students. Lincoln's leadership was diverse. I definitely found a social justice community of teachers at Lincoln. I also met old-school teachers too. I had no patience for them, unless it was very apparent that they really cared about the students.

Jefferson, in contrast, has had six principals in the last eight years. There is high teacher turnover, and the administration has had a very difficult time finding substitute teachers. Many students sit in the cafeteria waiting for a solution. Because of the lack of consistent leadership, it feels the students run the school in some ways. It is an open campus. There is little to no schoolwide tardy policy. Few discipline procedures seem in place. The school is run by three to eight loudspeaker interruptions a day (management by loudspeaker, I call it). I think there needs to be stronger leadership on what is expected and what is appropriate. I don't think Jefferson is caring enough.

After only six weeks at a pretty dysfunctional school, I can see why teachers burn out quickly. I have four different types of classes I have to prepare for. I am limited on the tools I can use to create a challenging and fun learning experience for my students. Each teacher gets $300 a year for supplies and photocopying. I am worried I will run out by November. Finding a community of social justice teachers has been difficult but I hope it will eventually happen.

—**Name Withheld**
First-year high school teacher

Lincoln and Jefferson High Schools are dissimilar in many respects, but the heart of their differences lies in their school cultures. School cultures help shape what people see, how they feel, and what they think is possible. Within a culture, people do not tend to see culture as something that shapes or limits; culture is just what is normal. In fact, most people only become aware of culture when they come face-to-face with cultural differences.[1] Teachers who are new to a school may be more sensitive to the power of the culture than "old-timers" for whom daily practices and attitudes are simply, "the way we do it here." New teachers can make use of their heightened perception, but they also need to be aware that the existing culture does not take happily to those who challenge it abruptly. After all, the culture is normal; challengers are not.

That said, new teachers, even one who moved from a Lincoln to a Jefferson High, can be assured that patience and struggle do change cultures, and changing the culture is first among the career goals of a teacher who wants to change the world. The last time we spoke to the teacher now at Jefferson High, she told us that she had already begun.

— ❧ ❧ ❧ —

As a new hire in a new school, I had planned to be somewhat quiet but I am finding it increasingly difficult after my Lincoln experience. I have already been a voice of dissent in some meetings (for example, suggesting that we make advisory periods more about the students and their goals and less about creating mottoes and logos). I am seeking out a new network. I would love to locate an inquiry group, or if I knew of enough like-minded teachers, I would host one.

Cultures Shape Sense-Making

Yale University psychologist Seymour Sarason has studied the power of the school culture for 30 years.[2] He first realized how much school culture matters when his studies of school change in the 1960s showed that schools rarely took reforms seriously. The cultural "regularities"—the kinds of opportunities that schools made available to students, the expectations they held for students, and the relationships within the whole school community—blocked any genuine change in most schools.

These patterns were so deeply ingrained in the schools he studied, few people questioned them. Sarason suggested that a visitor from Mars might ask "Why do you do it this way?" but that few people at the schools would ask such a question. If they did, fewer still would be able to answer.

When reforms were proposed, educators and communities saw the way they did things—their cultural regularities—as normal. So, instead of changing their schools to fit the reforms, it made more sense for administrators and teachers to reshape the reforms to fit their schools. Usually, that meant following along with the outward appearances of change, but changing little inside the classroom or in the school relationships in the hopes that the urge behind a particular reform would pass. Usually it did.

Little has changed over the past 40 years, and many studies have echoed Sarason's analysis that few reforms ever take hold in ways that produce the intended results. However, essential reform dilemmas are becoming clearer, and there are hopeful signs that reformers are looking at school cultures to understand what goes wrong and what goes right when schools try to make fundamental changes in their practices. In 1996 the National Commission on Teaching and America's Future issued a challenge, to redesign the nation's elementary and secondary schools. The report, *What Matters Most: Teaching and America's Future,* argued that without a fundamental overhaul of the school culture, teachers cannot teach well, and students cannot learn well.[3]

Some regularities—for example, course offerings, parent conference schedules, and teachers' supervision responsibilities—are matters of formal policy. But some of the most powerful regularities are not formalized; that is, rarely does anyone consciously decide, "Let's do it this way." For example, at one school the faculty stay late to give students extra help. At another, the parking lot empties shortly after the last bell. At one school the principal freely drops by classrooms and participates in lessons. The students love it, and it pleases the teachers that the principal knows about the class activities. At another school the principal steps into classes and meets a cold reception. Here, the teachers feel the principal is nosy and that she doesn't trust him. Even the students "shape up" and appear to concentrate, waiting for the principal to leave before they and the teacher relax. At some schools, teachers follow the required curriculum to the letter; at others they expand upon the curriculum to meet students' needs better. At some schools, teachers pitch in to help their colleagues—preferring to work on teams and with partners; at others teachers jealously guard their ideas and materials and prefer to work alone.

Sarason and other sensible critics of schools emphasize that trying to change individual practices such as these, one by one, is not productive. Broader perspectives are necessary to understand and change schools.

Cultures Where It Makes Sense to Teach All Students Well

Good schools have cultures where it makes sense for faculty to teach all students well and for all students to learn well. That doesn't mean that all good schools are alike. A central tenet of the Coalition of Essential Schools, a network of schools that has become one of the largest school reform movements in the United States, is that "good schools do share powerful guiding ideas, principles that are widely accepted even as they take different shapes in practice when people put them to work in their own settings from day to day."[4] So rather than prescribing lists of ideal practices for schools to follow, educators need to understand that there are critical features of a school's culture—guiding ideas—that will move the school toward high achievement and social justice. The different reform groups that we mention in the Digging Deeper section at the end of this chapter all include the key principles we discuss in the sections that follow:

- A press for learning and social justice
- Broad and deep access to learning
- Caring relationships
- Teacher inquiry and activism

A Press for Learning and Social Justice

Press is a cultural imperative, an alignment, a social consensus, an inevitability that each member of a society, a group, or an institution will be immersed in particular cultural values. Some may rebel, some may not "get it," but all will be touched—not just occasionally, but hourly. Schooling is inevitably pressed by the values, beliefs, and commitments of the larger culture, and schools, in turn, create a press of their own on the adults and young people in them.

Some examples are helpful to understand the concept of cultural press. During World War II American schools were shaped by the strong *press* for victory in the war, which was manifest in nearly every aspect of the daily life in schools. Geography and history made sense to students in terms of the war. Students brought money to school to deposit toward their own federal savings (war) bonds. Clothing, energy use, and meals at school were all influenced by war rationing—not complied with reluctantly, but as a matter of civic responsibility. Games were war games. Conversations often focused on young people who were at or about to go to war.

In the 1970s the popular culture, later labeled the "me generation," was inordinately concerned with self-awareness and personal expression. Encountering one's own and others' feelings and personal revelations were values in the broader culture that also permeated schools. Thus, the curriculum and teaching at many schools reflected, more or less, these cultural values; students were asked to look inward, to "find themselves."

Looking back, we can see how schooling in each decade was influenced by the predominant cultural features of that "age." It's the same today. Prevailing cultural norms—concerns about global economic competition and increasing threats of violence in the United States, for example—are reflected in today's schools. They emerge in the pressure to have American students outscore those in other nations on standardized tests and in the increased presence of metal detectors and "zero tolerance" discipline policies on school campuses.

School cultures also exert a *press* on students to behave in characteristic ways, and, if the culture is strong enough, it can press in ways that counter some of the larger cultural press. Private religious schools offer a clear example of a distinct cultural press that emerges from the religious norms at the school's core. At most of these schools, not everything is religious, but religious values are ever-present reminders in students' daily lives and shape how everyone acts. Adults and usually other students respond very quickly to violations of these norms.

Most schools around the turn of the twenty-first century have crafted statements of their purpose or "mission." All express a value for high levels of learning, and almost all voice commitment to social justice goals of opportunity and equity. In many ways, both of these values run counter to the larger culture that is decidedly anti-intellectual and increasingly egalitarian. However, a mission statement isn't enough to create a strong institutional press for learning and social justice. That requires a culture where academics and equity are simply normal, unquestioned, and reflected in the details of everyday life.

Learning Is the Top Priority

All schools say that learning is their top priority. But schools differ enormously in how strongly this priority is translated into a press for students' daily and hourly academic accomplishments. In some schools, no matter where one turns—student or adult—there is another reminder that learning is "what we do here and nothing else can take its place."

At other schools, however, there is stiff competition for norms of achievement and social justice. Quiet halls and a litter-free lunch court, high attendance at sports events, or a concentrated attention to raising test scores are all worthy-enough goals, but they do not constitute a press for achievement or for social justice. Order and security are essential for a well-functioning school, but some schools can't seem to get beyond their success at "keeping the lid on." Some schools in wealthy communities point to their high average test scores to silence critics that some student groups do far less well than others; and some faculties act like gatekeepers, making sure that students don't get advantages they don't deserve.

The Learning Priority Is Convincing   Listen to principals talk about what makes them proud. Do they describe in specific detail the rich learning experiences going on in many teachers' classrooms? Can they tell you about innovative practices in many courses? Or do they make self-effacing comments about how *they* really don't understand the math being taught or how they are "not good" at English? Are school leaders most comfortable talking about sports, clubs, and social events?

Consider the following description of a fairly well off suburban high school. This school is not "at risk," yet its press for learning seems quite low:

> The bell has rung and the last few eleventh graders are sauntering into their
> second-period class. Several students present "absence slips" to the teacher,
> confessing truancy or documenting their real or invented illness or family
> emergency. Three others present passes, respectively, from the school nurse,
> the counseling office, and the student government adviser. Another student has

forgotten her pass, and the teacher sends her to the office. There are seven students absent. A couple might arrive late. Others will receive summonses from various corners of the school. Only two-thirds of the students actually attend the entire class two days in a row.

Over the public address, a student recites the Pledge of Allegiance without error today, though that is not always the case. Another student reads announcements. The senior class advertises, as it will each day for two weeks, its fund-raising computer-dating dance. Two students perform a hastily written skit. They are too close to the microphone, and their garbled speech is nearly unintelligible. However, a few adolescent sexual innuendoes manage to get through, and the class receives them with exaggerated, uproarious appreciation. A single academic announcement—the scholarship society will offer tutoring at noon—arouses no apparent interest. An announcer praises a winning sports team and commends the losers for a great effort. The vice principal issues a warning about lunch passes. He adds that makeup testing for the state achievement test will take place in the library, and therefore the library will be closed for the next two days.

Announcements over, instruction begins.

The students at this school score well on standardized tests, and many gain admission to top-rated colleges. Some students, particularly those in the highest college-preparatory tracks, undauntedly pursue outstanding education. There is some palpable disdain, however, for many of the top students, especially those with less social appeal. Even some adults at school are cautious about spotlighting their achievements. The youngsters held in highest esteem by their peers are better-than-average students, but they are as notable for their good looks, cars, and general sociability as for their academic achievements. All students, particularly the large group that simply gets by, would achieve more if their school made its real business seem more important.

Learning Time Is Precious   Individual teachers vary in their values and methods. And yet, stepping back from these individual differences, schoolwide differences influence the school's culture beyond any particular faculty member. For example, one national study in the 1980s found that elementary schools scheduled from 18 to 27 hours per week for instruction.[5] This range reflects an important difference in learning opportunities. Furthermore, the study found that most classrooms spent only 70 percent of the 18 to 17 scheduled hours on learning activities—the rest of the time was spent getting ready, cleaning up, disciplining, and socializing. Thus, while an organized and focused teacher will provide more learning opportunities to his students than a disorganized and ill-focused teacher at the same school, the organized, focused teacher will provide more or fewer opportunities depending on what school he is at. The culture makes the difference.

Middle schools and high schools also reveal this combination of individual teacher volition and the school culture. Do teachers hold students until the dismissal bell rings, or do students wander out of class a few minutes early? Does the school generally support "supervised reading" and getting started on homework drills as legitimate classroom activities, or are students fully engaged in discussion, group activities, research, and other activities that can be done only in the class-room? Are videos and films judiciously selected, edited, and discussed, or, at the start of the period, do the lights go out and the movies go on? Are teachers absent rarely or frequently? When teachers are absent, are substitutes carefully selected to follow well-designed instructions, or are substitutes selected for their willingness to put up with abuse and expected to "baby-sit" the students? Again, each school may have teachers who display the full range of concern for keeping students engaged in learning, but each school will also display a cultural tendency to value student engagement more or less.

Currently, many schools are experimenting with alternatives to traditional schedules in order to provide more focus and concentrated learning time and, in secondary schools, to free teachers from the constraints of 50-minute lessons. For example, many schools now use "block scheduling," in which each team of teachers has a large chunk of time each day that they can use flexibly, varying the time students spend on particular learning activities and in particular groups.[6]

Not only the schedule matters, however; the prevailing norms about what's most worth spending time on are also important. Some junior and senior high schools ex-cuse students from class for all kinds of reasons. Their sports team may need to get ready for a game or the auditorium may need decorating for a dance. An elementary-school student body may get to spend school time watching cartoons as a reward for having met their candy-sale goal. And there is no end to the ways that schools can spend time on routines. Taking the roll, tardy checks, lining up properly, and prac-ticing good behavior are just a few. Students can lose as much learning time in the teacher's pursuit of quiet and orderliness as they lose because of noise and disorder.

It's a mistake to think that schools can easily limit these time-consuming activ-ities. Each has its roots in school traditions and societal expectations. Americans see social activities and athletics as ways for common schools to help students prepare for community participation. Schools view athletics as a vehicle for teaching fairness, competition, and cooperation. We sometimes justify sports as opportunities for poor, minority, and academically unsuccessful students to find their niches in school (although the only reliable payoffs for schooling come from academic achievement). Bureaucratic routines and record keeping are often a response to legal requirements schools can do little to change.

It's Normal When *Everyone* Learns Well

All schools *say* they are committed to all of their students' learning; and some schools do translate this spoken value into a school-defining theme. When schools offer all students an intellectually rich curriculum and expect all of them to perform well, students get the message "We believe you can do it." They learn how smart the school thinks they can be. If a school staff believes that all its students can learn challenging subject matter, then schools will work very hard to provide conditions that will enable all students to learn. These efforts pay off.

Unfortunately, many school cultures press in the opposite direction. They assume and behave as if high achievement just wouldn't be normal at their school. Sometimes a caring faculty intentionally maintains low expectations for children in poverty, thinking they are being kind, even though there is considerable evidence that students learn more—even those in the most-distressed urban schools—when they are offered a challenging curriculum.[7] Kimberly Min's first teaching job was in just such a school.

⚙ ⚙ ⚙

Deficit thinking permeates our school culture. A majority of the teachers describe our students as "poor performing." The danger is that the teachers believe they are merely describing reality. They do not recognize that they are instructing the students in a way that is disrespectful. My school is 45 percent African American and 55 percent Latino. Because our staff is mostly of color, when they believe that our students cannot achieve, the students may view their position in society as natural and unchanging. Unless we disrupt these beliefs, we participate in an insidious cycle.

—**KIMBERLY MIN**
Third-grade teacher

Unfortunately, most school cultures foster the belief that, although some students can and will learn very well, many will not, and that anything else would be abnormal. Fourth-grade teacher Jeffrey Madrigal had such an experience. His high expectations for all his students were dismissed as the naïveté of a beginner.

⚙ ⚙ ⚙

During the first days of teaching, I was incredibly self-conscious about ignoring convention, constantly experimenting, and changing every week.

After the first month, however, it was awesome. I seemed to be making progress every week. I nailed some brilliant lessons and produced new ideas. We did group work, hands-on math, and visual social studies; made models, wrote stories, and wrote letters; and did a fascinating unit on the workings of the brain.

Then it all began to slip away. Much to my dismay I discovered that my students had not learned much. My test results were fairly standard for the school: 30 percent of the class did very well, 30 percent did passing work, and 30 percent failed. The big question was why. Were my lessons confusing? Was the test too hard? Perhaps I should have given more frequent evaluations.

The school's answer lay in a conversation I had with one of the older teachers soon after the test. I told her about my result and how discouraged I was over the lack of mastery. She chuckled one of those annoying know-it-all chuckles and said, "We all get those same results. That is just how it is." This immediately reminded me of a similar conversation I had with a teacher during my student teaching. This woman had warned me not to expect to "reach them all." "Take off those rose-colored glasses," she said. I sat at a crossroads. What kind of an educator would I be?

—**JEFFREY MADRIGAL**
First-year teacher, grade 4

Low expectations are not simply inert beliefs. They press people to take particular actions that are consistent with those expectations—to translate low expectations into practices that make it impossible for students to succeed. As the following example shows, this is readily apparent in middle-school and high school tracking. However, the values and assumptions that lie behind tracking also influence decisions about what students can and should learn at every schooling level.

If we assume certain students will fail mathematics, we are not giving all students equal opportunity to succeed in math. If we allow students to fail math because it is not their "strength," we risk having a population illiterate in mathematics. We risk broadening the socioeconomic gap between the privileged and the not so privileged.

I have found this to be a major issue at my school. Students who have the choice to take higher math are encouraged by counselors to take lower-level math courses. The goal is not to get students into college; rather, the goal is to get students to graduate. I began to encourage my students to take higher math. We constantly talked about moving on to algebra next year. I expected them to continue taking math classes beyond the requirements. By the end of the year, many wanted to move on to algebra, and several ninth graders signed up for summer school to "get ahead."

—Name Withheld
First-year teacher, mathematics, grade 9

In sharp contrast, some school cultures, even in the most disadvantaged communities, have an incredibly strong press for learning that translates into powerful actions that enable learning to occur. Teachers are convinced that, if a student does not succeed, the *least* likely explanation is that the student can't. Notably, such teachers concentrate less on what students are lacking and more on what instruction can press all students to achieve. They emphasize and model for their students the hard work and persistence it takes to succeed.

Sometimes such teachers become emblematic of their school and community, and over time they define the culture as much as they work within it. First-year middle-school teachers Lily Kim and Suzanne Markoe found an inspiring mentor in veteran teacher Yvonne Hutchinson, who helped them translate their beliefs about students' abilities into rich classroom learning experiences. Here is what they wrote about their mentor:

Yvonne Divans-Hutchinson teaches eighth- and ninth-grade English at Edwin Markham Middle School in Watts, California. Yvonne was born in Little Rock, Arkansas, in 1943, during the height of racial segregation. When she moved to California, she lived in the Imperial Courts Housing Project in Watts and became a member of the first graduating class of the school where she now teaches. She chose to return to her alma mater and has been teaching

*there for the past thirty years. As one of her respected colleagues stated,
"Yvonne is the gatekeeper to Watts. If you want to get out of Watts, if you
want to go to college, you need to pass through Ms. Hutchinson; you need to
be touched by her."*

*Yvonne prepares her students for real life by setting high standards and
expecting her students to rise to them. Her nickname, "Killer Hutch," came
about because of a fight that she broke up, but it has since evolved to describe
the type of curriculum that she teaches. One of her students aptly noted that
"Ms. Hutchinson helps you to see the deeper side to everything. She makes
you think on a higher level." Yvonne challenges her students with engaging
literature and demands that they go beyond the literal in analyzing what
they read. The students know that they dare not write about what is obvious
in what they read. A former student, now a student at the University of
California-Berkeley, remarked: "Even now I check all my papers and ask
myself if they are good enough for Ms. Hutchinson."*

*Providing an emotionally safe classroom is also vitally important to
Yvonne. To promote respect of different cultures and ethnicities, her students
follow a specific routine in calling on each other. When one student wishes to
call on another student, he or she must choose someone who differs from him
or her in race, ethnicity, gender, or in some other way. Yvonne regularly
reminds her students of this policy, and it promotes a respect of diverse
cultures in her classroom. Whenever a student dares to utter a racial slur or
other form of disrespect to another student, Yvonne will stop the entire class
at whatever they are doing because she believes a more important lesson
needs to be taught. By the time the class is over, the student and class know
not to disrespect another student or culture again.*

*Instead of seeing her students as so many people see them ("at risk,
poverty-stricken, poor, disadvantaged"), Yvonne sees the "thousands of
possibilities" that the students possess.*[8]

As we discussed in Chapter 6, powerful support for anyone's learning is their
opportunity to make use of their own experiences and cultural backgrounds. In a
school with a strong press for learning and social justice, the use of students'
experiences and backgrounds sends a powerful cultural message: We value what
you bring to school as the foundation for high-level learning. That message presses
both for learning and for social justice.

The school described next does just that. This school's principal, Nancy
Parachini, sees culture as a toolkit for learning that is located not only within
individuals, but also within a social context. To separate individual learning from
culture is to diminish both.

New teachers at the school where Nancy Parachini is principal encountered a
culture that supported their social justice commitments. Teaching multiculturalism or applauding children's various backgrounds and beliefs "has to be at the
center of everything," according to Parachini. She has worked with the staff to
change the way the school perceives multiculturalism, "even though it might

have been done before, it was fragmented, it wasn't a unified focus, a vision." For Parachini multiculturalism means respecting what students bring with them to the classroom; it means planning curricula that suit the strengths and interests of the school's children.

In a school where many cultures are represented, Parachini helps the children in her community to know their roots. She holds that it is important for students to learn to appreciate diversity by understanding first their own uniqueness: "I think that once they can start with themselves, then it becomes a more valuable experience." Nancy Parachini believes that understanding must translate into social action. "It's not just tolerance. It's understanding and a knowledge base that will translate into power [and] social action. Because when there is an imbalance of power, that creates the inequity." By incorporating these ideas into the curriculum, children learn to look at themselves and their surroundings differently. They develop the ability to analyze their relationships and understand the implications of inequity in society at large.[9]

The students at this school, in researcher Linda Darling-Hammond's words, are pressed every day to "find and act on who they are, what their passions, gifts, and talents may be, what they care about, and how they want to make a contribution to each other in the world."[10]

The following questions can reveal a school's press for learning. Can students get by without trying very hard? Is the knowledge that students bring with them to school treated as a powerful springboard for high-level learning? Are all students—girls as well as boys, students of color as well as whites, poor students as well as more affluent ones—expected to study rigorous subjects like algebra, a foreign language, and advanced science? What percentage of students does the school expect to go to college? (This is a good question for elementary schools as well as high schools.) Does the school keep records of how many students complete college (or even high school)? In what way do the people at this school see questions such as these as relevant to what they do every day?

Broad and Deep Access to Learning

—————————————❊ ❊ ❊—————————————

The school district is in such dire straits that the teachers can't make photocopies, we don't have overhead projectors, nor do we have enough space for the children. The lack of resources has actually made me a very creative teacher. I learned this year that I didn't need an overhead nor did I need a chalkboard! I've learned that my students don't need paper or pencil. And I've learned to creatively manage and teach a class without these staples of American education.

—STEVEN BRANCH
First-year teacher, grade 5

Sufficient Resources

It has become fashionable, especially in politically conservative quarters, to argue that the problems of American schools cannot be solved with money. Tell that to first-year teacher Steve Branch. Despite his ironic bravado in the preceding quote about teaching creatively without resources, Branch knows better than most the dual truth that teachers can teach well with very little and that money matters a great deal.

Certainly, upper- and middle-class parents throughout history have understood that if their own children are to become readers, they need classrooms and libraries full of books. Their science learning requires equipment and laboratory space. Their physical development requires things to climb on, toys and sports equipment, and open space in which to play. Their classrooms should be suited to the work the teachers try to accomplish, and students themselves should have suitable work-spaces: clean, well-lighted, well-heated, and air-conditioned classrooms with plenty of room for productive activity.

When people ask me why I think my school is low performing, I can rattle off a list that people expect to hear: (a) lack of resources (I have worked without textbooks, broken chairs, and broken desks. Last year a desk collapsed on two students who were writing and it was reported to the office. It took the office three days to respond); lack of supplies (there is a shortage of supplies and many teachers have to purchase their own materials. Teachers cannot rely on the school to have the items that they need to teach); (b) lack of teacher training and professional development (teachers sign in at meetings and sign out and you are considered "professionally developed"); (c) lack of this and that. All these things are true, but I think people do not want to acknowledge that we still operate in a racist school system where schools of color are not only neglected but set up to fail. There needs to be a paradigm shift where schools that need the resources receive them.

—Kimberly Min
Third-grade teacher

In spite of the well-known and well-documented knowledge that high-quality resources are essential for all students, Americans have a high level of acceptance for obviously unequal school resources, as teacher Kimberly Min notes. Those who resist an equal distribution of resources seize on some very narrow and traditional research perspectives that allow them to conclude that resources (and the money spent on them) do not matter. Yet researcher Ronald Ferguson's studies of the impact of expenditures on student achievement show clearly that not only does greater school spending yield higher student achievement, spending on teachers matters most.[11] Of course, school spending is more or less effective depending on many other factors within the school culture.

High-Quality Teaching

In addition to basic facilities and materials, students need enough teachers—qualified ones. Too few teachers means classes will be large and difficult to manage.

Hiring less-qualified teachers for less money means that students are unlikely to have teachers with the expertise to teach well. Both matter for student learning. In November, 2005, 500 students from Los Angeles's South Gate High School boycotted their classes to protest receiving their quarter grades when many students had only had a string of unqualified substitutes for their math and other subjects, and many did not have textbooks for their courses. The school district quickly arranged to supply the requisite teachers and books, but many observers were left shaking their heads and wondering why it took a two-day student walkout and media exposure to get those results.

Enough High-Quality Teachers   The notion of teacher quality is tricky. There is nothing to say that the newest teacher at the school is the least competent or that "credentials" make a good teacher. However, there is a strong likelihood that highly trained and experienced teachers are valuable resources. Similarly, teachers with good reputations across the school and in the community are not guaranteed to be the best teachers, but they are sure a better bet than those with the worst reputations. All this adds up to the legitimacy and pitfalls of talking about "better" and "the best" teachers.

All students at a school—not just the highest-achieving ones—need access to the best teachers available. A not-so-well-kept secret in many school cultures is that teachers are tracked as well as students. The most-experienced and knowledgeable teachers are often rewarded with the "plum" teaching assignments. New teachers often end up with the classes that the others don't want—usually the low-ability classes or those with lots of behavior problems. However, schools are increasingly making an effort to distribute teacher talent evenly, recognizing that low-achieving students are further disadvantaged when they are consistently placed in classes with less-qualified teachers.

-------------------------------------❈ ❈ ❈-------------------------------------

The dismal conditions of schools in poor, urban communities of color have been well documented, and the disparity between rich and poor schools is brought to life for my students by the geographic proximity of my school to areas of Los Angeles such as Palos Verdes and Beverly Hills. The unequal distribution of resources not only perpetuates the existing system of social, political, and economic inequality but sends the message in a very direct way to my students that they don't count as much as the students who have access to computer labs, planetariums, and books! Well-meaning teachers (such as myself) can attempt to compensate for these material deficiencies and be relatively successful in the short run, but it is the long-term effects of an inherently unequal system that will ultimately serve to undermine our good intentions.

—**Jennifer Garcia**
First-year teacher, high school history

Conditions That Permit High-Quality Teaching   Good teaching also depends on the conditions under which teachers are expected to teach. Considerable research shows that 15 students, or fewer, per class is optimal at the elementary level.[12] Unfortunately, classes that small are rare in any but the wealthiest private schools. Secondary school classes should probably not exceed 25 students, although most do. Smaller classes in themselves do not cause more learning, but they strongly affect how teachers can design and carry out lessons. The number of students in a class not only affects the time teachers have available to spend with individual students, but also influences teachers' flexibility in experimenting with teaching strategies.

Though it might sound mundane, teachers also need basic supplies and materials to work with. Books for their students, audiovisual equipment in good working order, hands-on materials, a decent copy machine, access to a computer and a telephone, and whatever might be found in the office of any well-functioning business can make the difference between a teacher feeling able to do her job well and feeling quite overwhelmed.

A Rich, Balanced Curriculum

If a school has no French class, no one will learn French at school. No music? No computers? Then no one learns about music or computers at school. When some students take a subject and others do not, the limits on opportunity are just as apparent. These are obvious examples of lack of opportunity. Most are more subtle. For example, all third graders receive reading instruction. Even so, the quantity and quality of that instruction vary. Good sense tells us what will happen when a group of able readers reads stories, and a low group does only worksheets. The latter will have fewer opportunities to read stories. Likewise, if the advanced high school history class requires a research paper and the regular one doesn't, some students won't get to practice research skills.

It matters whether academically rich instruction is available and which students have access to it. Many secondary schools have taken a crude but often effective first step and simply eliminated low-level academic classes. Some require all students to take courses previously considered advanced—for example, algebra in middle school. Other schools open up their honors programs to everyone or provide gifted and honors activities within heterogeneous classes. These actions are supported by considerable evidence that all students—rich, poor, black, Latino, Asian, white, high- and low-achieving—learn better when they are provided rich and challenging curriculum.[13]

While individual teachers may be sensitive to cultural differences and try to bring in academically challenging content that makes use of students' experiences and background, the broader school can do little or much to make this possible. Department, grade-level, and whole-school commitments can enable individual teachers to diversify literature; tell multiple versions of history, economics, and other social studies; teach high-level conceptual math; and so on.

A new teacher will not change a school's curriculum single-handedly, but new teachers often find more-experienced teachers in their school who support their efforts (and veteran teachers for the new teacher to support). Like Yvonne Hutchinson, who was described earlier, and Pat Cady, described next, these veterans are not just single teachers whose influence is confined to their classrooms. They are, themselves, cultural features. Their "presence" often creates the space and reveals the possibilities for offering the richest possible curriculum. For example, first-year social studies teacher Kate Castleberry found a mentor in veteran teacher Pat Cady, who scaffolded Castleberry's efforts to create a culturally relevant curriculum in her classes.

———————————————————————————⚙ ⚙ ⚙———————————————————————————

Pat Cady has been a social studies teacher for more than twenty years. He agrees with Noel Ignatiev's ideas in Race Traitor *that although people look white, acting and participating in the "white club" only furthers racial segregation, degradation, and depression. He therefore is a white Irishman on the outside, yet his actions and beliefs indicate his affiliation with the entire human race. In his teaching, Pat Cady addresses historical perspectives from many points of view and includes innovative scholars who are also concerned with social justice. His unit on the Vietnam era begins with a study of the African American soldier. He has explored Richard Takaki's* A Different Mirror *and James Loewen's* Lies My Teacher Told Me *with his eleventh-grade class. Both books focus on the multicultural historical perspective. By sharing his standpoint and his approach to teaching, Cady continually sends the message that white is not "best" and that all students should share and represent themselves in our history.*[14]

Extra Help When Needed

In many schools, both teachers and students expect that some children just won't keep up with their classmates. But some supportive school cultures are determined not to let students fall behind. In fact, it would be nice if we could think less about "falling behind" and more in terms of "still learning." Ideally, in the elementary grades extra help comes within the classroom during regular class time. The routine scaffolding available in daily instruction and student groups should blur the distinction between help and extra help. However, it is normal for situations to occur when students just need extra time with a "knowledgeable other." A special resource teacher, a paid aide, or a parent volunteer may provide an extra boost. Or a peer tutor, either in the same class or from a higher grade, may provide one-on-one assistance. Extra help should supplement classroom lessons and should not substitute a remedial program for the regular one.

Many secondary schools give extra help to master the more challenging curriculum. Some offer "backup classes" for low-achieving students; students enroll in both an advanced academic courses and a backup class in place of an elective. The backup class provides them with additional instruction and time on the material in their advanced course—especially if the backup classes are kept small. Some schools call this a "double dose" of teaching. Other schools operate homework centers or Saturday schools, staffed with teachers, community volunteers, or more-advanced students who provide tutoring to those who need help. Some operate summer programs specifically designed to give students the opportunity to skip to higher-level courses in the fall.[15]

Helping students keep up with the regular curriculum, despite its undisputed benefits, conflicts with some common ideas about standardization and efficiency. It may disrupt schools' orderly progression through the curriculum. It may cost more. On the other hand, not helping students keep up is also costly and inefficient. When schools have students repeat a grade, it adds an additional year's cost for that child's education. And since grade retention does not boost students' school success (in fact, retention likely contributes to dropping out of school), the extra expense is money wasted. If students who don't keep up are simply passed along, schools must provide low-level classes to accommodate them—another ineffective use of school resources. Providing extra help so that students can keep up with the "regular" curriculum is money well spent.

Support for a Multicultural, College-Going Identity

Teachers express a cultural value when they tell all their students, "You can go to college." But too often they leave unspoken their belief, ". . . *if* you act like someone else." Just who that "someone else" might be will vary, but it often conforms to a familiar stereotype of who is a "successful" college student. The profile of such a student is complex, but it likely includes someone who scores high on standardized tests; someone whose parents went to college; someone whose main language is mainstream, unaccented English; someone who has middle-class perspectives and financial support; and so on.

Perhaps schools' biggest challenge is to create a school culture that supports college attendance for students whose lives do not conform to this profile. The school culture must position college success as expected and inevitable not just for students who change or for students who are *exceptions* to stereotypes, but for students who have no need or intention to slight their family's background and culture as they acquire the skills and knowledge that are genuinely useful for college success.

For college preparation to be genuinely accessible to students, students must see their cultural identities as integral to college preparation and attendance—not as something they must "overcome." They must develop the confidence and skills to negotiate college preparation without sacrificing their own identity and connections with their home communities. In contrast to commonly held views that low-income students devalue education, studies suggest that they more likely turn away because of a real or perceived lack of opportunities.[16] A study of low-income high school graduates who were eligible for the University of California, but chose not to attend found that the students were most deterred by their beliefs that the university is "not for people like me," and that they weren't prepared for the university's high demands.[17]

In Chapter 5, we pointed to what Claude Steele terms "a stereotype threat" whereby internalized negative labels assigned to racial and cultural groups have deep consequences for how students perform.[18] Students are further affected by aware-ness that their individual performance will reflect on other members of their race or culture. To develop college-going identities among diverse students, teachers, communities, and students must confront explicitly all the hidden beliefs and assumptions about who is fit to go to college. Of course, "confronting" means a lot more than talking—for teachers it means entering into the worlds students inhabit and identifying supports, creating programs, and exploring among students, teachers, communities, and colleges every real and potential opportunity for finding and developing students' college-going competence.

Access to Care

A group of student teachers visited the school where first-year teacher Jessica Wingell was teaching. Struck by the caring relationships they found among many teachers and students, they made the following observation:

> Liam Joyce, a white man, is the counselor for "at-risk" students (mostly students of color) at the high school. The night before we talked with him, Mr. Joyce had been at a student's home until 11:00 P.M. talking with the student and her parents. During our conversation, he stopped five or six times to have brief conversations with students. At one point, a student stuck his head in the door and said, "Mr. Joyce, can I talk to you for one second?" Without a hesitation or a question, Mr. Joyce immediately stepped outside his office. For him, students come first. Mr. Joyce dedicates 99 percent of his time and energy to students and achieving social justice, and the rapport he has developed with his students is amazing.
>
> When one of us asked Mr. Joyce how white educators can bridge the gap between themselves and students of color, he immediately pulled a Latino student in from the hallway. "Michael, I want to ask you some questions." Mr. Joyce then asked Michael questions about whether he trusted him. "Yeah, I trust him," Michael told us. He said that he trusts Mr. Joyce because he "does stuff" for him and shows he cares. "Does it matter that Mr. Joyce is white?" we asked. "No, it don't matter," Michael responded and went on to explain which teachers are "good" teachers. None of what he said had to do with skin color. "Ms. Wingell is good because you know she really wants you to do good," he said, "and she spends time helping you."[19]

Every Student Known by Name

Many schools are attempting to become caring communities—places where teachers can act on their deep commitments to knowing and caring for students. This attention to caring drives other changes in school programs and organization, as well as changes inside classrooms.

Many secondary schools have tried to replace their large impersonal structures with teams, smaller schools-within-schools, and actually "breaking up" very large schools into smaller schools that operate independently of one another—often on a separate campus. This last alternative is what some people envision as a "small schools movement." Focal Point 9.1 illustrates how the small-school concept has been successful in Harlem, New York. These arrangements contrast with the typical bureaucratic structures of secondary schools where students drift through

FOCAL POINT 9.1

Deborah Meier on Small Schools
Creating Democratic Schools

If we're talking about the creation of a thoughtful school culture, size becomes decisive—especially if we're trying to create a changed culture. Thoughtfulness is time-consuming. Collaboration is time-consuming. The time they both consume can't be private time, late-at-night at-home time. To find time for thoughtful discussion we need to create schools in which consensus is easy to arrive at while argument is encouraged (even fostered) and focused on those issues of teaching and learning close to teacher and student experiences, rather than on procedural rules and processes, elections and nominating committees, building-wide disciplinary codes, detention policies, filling out forms and checklists, scheduling, etc.

Only in a small school can deep ongoing discussion take place in ways that produce change and involve the entire faculty—and even there, it's tough to sustain. For teachers to start thinking through the task before them, collectively and collaboratively, schools must be so small that governance does not become the topic of discussion but issues of education do, so small that the faculty as a whole becomes the decision-making body on questions of teaching and learning.

We bragged for years that the Central Park East (CPE) schools didn't have a single permanent committee. We were a committee of the whole; the time we spent talking had immediate repercussions affecting the way we thought and felt about children, classroom life, our teaching practices. If an issue arose we could meet with almost no notice, and gather together in one room, around one table or one circle, and hear each other out. We didn't need complex governing structures, committees of committees, representatives of representatives, differentiations of staff, classes and subclasses.

And even though on the high school level we now do have one permanent committee (our Cabinet), anyone can join any of its meetings—even kids if they wish. (It would be nice if they did more often.) A third of the faculty is in the Cabinet, which only occasionally takes a vote. Mostly we argue it out and find a solution that all can live with for the time being. We avoid deciding issues better decided elsewhere. And anyone can insist that decisions made by the Cabinet can be reviewed at a schoolwide meeting.

This continuing dialogue, face to face, over and over, is a powerful educative force. It is our primary form of staff development. When people ask me how we "train" new teachers, I say that the school itself is an educator for the kids and staff; it's its own staff development project. And it is by this same token always accessible to the outside world as well as to our students; the school itself is a public deliberative body whose existence is a reminder of the power of reasoning, reflecting, assessing, revising, and planning. The habits of mind, our five essential questions, and the habits of work we encourage in our students are thus exemplified in the daily life of the staff. We too weigh evidence, explore alternative

(continued)

viewpoints, conjecture about other possibilities, make connections, and ask, So what? We too must meet deadlines and keep our word and communicate clearly. We're "demonstrating" the value of what we preach—daily.

The staff spends all year reviewing its 14 graduation requirements, and each fall comes up with new versions of one or another of them. The experience of our alumni/ae, of external visitors, the work of our colleagues across the nation, as well as our own daily practice, all lead to such revisions. At various steps along the way the latest drafts are circulated and debated by students and teachers. We added a new section on computer literacy after considerable debate on whether it should be a part of our requirements or a separate one. Recently we added an emphasis on experimental science and redrafted the math requirements to reflect the latest National Council of Teachers of Math (NCTM) standards.

Similarly, issues of behavior, school management, and student-teacher relations occupy our attention. We spend a good deal of time—even an embarrassing amount of time—debating student "dress codes," mostly shall they or shan't they be allowed to wear hats. But even this issue was argued on terms that allowed students to join us. People brought in articles about the impact of clothes and raised issues about the importance (or not) of worrying about how others see us and whether our informality would make it harder for kids to shift to more formal ways of dressing in more formal workplaces. The opponents of dress codes eventually won, but supporters occasionally still submit interesting pieces of evidence for their side.

In a small school we can dare to experiment without feeling we are treating kids like guinea pigs. After all, what doesn't work isn't irreversible. We can reschedule one afternoon and put a new agenda into practice the next morning. We can undo them just as fast. Changes don't require Herculean coordination or time-consuming bureaucratic arranging. In short, smallness makes democracy feasible, and without democracy we won't be able to create the kind of profound rethinking the times demand.

Source: Deborah Meier, *The Power of Their Ideas: Lessons for America from a Small School in Harlem* (Boston: Beacon Press, 1995).

classes without developing stable relationships with teachers or, often, other students. For example, an important middle-school and high school organization is the familiar academic department—social studies, math, English, and so on. School academic departments are simply not designed for teachers to accommodate students' personal and social needs. When teachers must single-handedly manage large numbers of individual students, only the most visible and highly skilled students can compete successfully for attention.

Many middle schools divide students into teams—smaller groups that stay together during the day and connect with an interdisciplinary team of teachers. Large senior highs are increasingly experimenting to give students sustained contact with teachers and other students. One example is an "advisory" class where students and a teacher connect every day for support as students negotiate the complexities of school.[20]

In some elementary and secondary schools students and teachers stay together for two or three years. Many elementary schools combine students into multiage, multiyear classes where only the youngest students are new to the group each year. Some middle schools use a strategy called "looping," where a team of teachers begins with a group of students as they enter the school at fifth or sixth grade and remains with that group until they move on to senior high.

Caring can be part of the whole school's curricular and extracurricular focus. Many schools have "service learning" programs that engage students in community work—for example, tutoring younger students, working in homeless shelters, and so on. First-year teacher Matt Flanders created a most unusual site for a caring community—his water polo team. Since Flanders took over the team it has become one of the more racially diverse settings on campus. Flanders has sought to create space within this extracurricular activity for students to grapple with issues of success, difference, and common cause. He has also created an ethic of care that not only allows but also draws team members toward helping others.

Most of my unsuccessful students felt no connection to the campus community. They did not feel that school was important because they were not involved in it. They did not feel as if their presence mattered, so they sank into the shadows of nonengagement.

I tackled the problem of noninvolvement right away. Water polo had kept me in high school and college, so I knew the value of team involvement in education. My team had been a source of support and friendship for me. Coming full circle, I became head water polo coach. I wanted to do for my student-athletes what my coach had done for me years before. I hired a group of young, energetic assistant coaches to help me out.

We proceeded to coach our team not only in the art of water polo, but in the game of life as well. We provided a place that students could be comfortable as well as mentally and physically challenged. We connected them to the campus, to the school community; both the boys' and girls' teams had winning seasons. However, our involvement with our students did not stop in the pool. We dealt with the issues of alcoholism, drug abuse, pregnancy, sexually transmitted disease, child abuse, and jail time that our student-athletes faced. We helped two team members secure admission to college. We became a big part of our students' lives.

Our teams now include about 5 percent of the student body. Our program is one of inclusion; we do not cut. Our goal is to make the best team and the best group of young people we can. I think that is what draws students to our program. In addition, we have started a middle-school water polo team for our district. Thirty-five children participate twice a week, and they are coached by my senior high school players. Not only are we strengthening our athletic stance for years to come, we are reaching into the broader community and connecting with students to help them be successful in high school.

—MATTHEW AMATO FLANDERS
First-year teacher, high school history

Safe Zones: It's OK to Be Different

As long as one person does not feel safe—experiences or fears abuse by others—no one can be safe. There can be no distinction between the school's failure to respond to a hurtful act and its approval of that act.

Confronting Racism First-year teacher Kate Castleberry found herself in a very diverse high school with a faculty that has been vocal about its commitment to create a school culture where differences among students are acknowledged and respected. Kate, the pep squad coach as well as a history teacher, decided to act.

Capitalizing on some of the cheerleaders' interest in promoting better race relations among the school's diverse student body, she and her students proposed Racial Harmony Day. What they wanted was a day of serious inquiry into all aspects of school life. The school principal and most of Kate's faculty colleagues encouraged her to act on her social justice commitment, and they lent their strong support. The Day became a source of pride and of ongoing schoolwide efforts to improve the racial climate.

Racial Harmony Day was not a day to join hands and sing "Kumbaya." It was a time to explore how we thought of others, and our fear and knowledge of different races. Racial harmony is a commitment to stand up for our people and for our brothers and sisters when they are not present.

Racial Harmony Day began as a dream of two juniors. One hundred and sixty students were separated into homogeneous racial groups—African American, Asian/Pacific Islander, Caucasian, Latino, and Middle Eastern.

[Pairs of groups met to share] and discuss feelings and questions about stereotypes. Students tearfully faced peers and friends and questioned why their "people" held certain thoughts and beliefs. After each group met with the others, the students broke into small, heterogeneous dialogue groups with a facilitator to discuss unresolved feelings. The day ended with an outpouring of willingness to continue the struggle and journey to racial understanding. A core group of students formed a steering committee to help develop more activities. A week after the event, a lunch meeting reacquainted students who suggested further dialogue at a retreat or sleep-over.

Racial harmony will not happen overnight, but students have taken the first steps toward a society that is fair and accepting of all.

—KATE CASTLEBERRY
First-year teacher, high school history

Third-grade teacher Kimberly Min saw firsthand how racism undermines the learning culture at school, even when children are very young and even when the adults and students are of color. Kimberly's school was plagued with racial tensions between African Americans and Latinos and with the deficit thinking about low-income students of color that poisons the thinking of members of disparaged groups themselves. Unlike Kate Castleberry, Kimberly didn't have a racial harmony program to help her think through how to change a school culture where the problem was with the staff as well as the students. Like many teachers, Kimberly showed amazing courage and skill as she worked with her students and colleagues.

———————————————————————⊠ ⊠ ⊠———————————————————————

Misperceptions of race and ethnicity permeate the speech and actions of the staff and students, to the detriment of the whole community. The staff generalizes about African Americans and Latinos—the African American kids are "louder and more physical," whereas the Latinos are more "obedient and reticent." Because I teach African Americans, I receive sympathy from teachers who teach mostly Latino classes. This thinking puts the students in a precarious position, since, when there are tensions or yard fights the African Americans are perceived as the aggressors while the Latinos are seen as the victims. My students at age 7 begin to define what it means to be African American or Mexican in this context.

I use culturally responsive literature to help my students identify with the struggles, successes, riches, and hardships of their collective history. As we read biographies of African American leaders, pictures of segregated drinking fountains brought about genuine interest. I began to ask questions about how segregation began, and Latisha responded, "They [white people] drink out of different water fountains because the black people were sick and the white people didn't want to get sick." Terrell suggested, "The black people must have put something in the white people's water, so they didn't want to drink out of the same place." I found it fascinating that students rationalized segregation with negative views of African Americans, and I began to question their responses. Once I helped them see the injustices that King and Parks sought to reform, they eventually began to see that they didn't always have to associate negative things with the African American community. More important, they saw that African Americans could be agents of change.

Recently we had a discussion after one of my African American students, Jerald, called another student in the yard "nigger" in a demeaning way. Immediately after recess we met in Community Circle and discussed the meanings of this epithet and the ramifications it has in our society. I asked students what "nigger" meant. Ebony stated, "That word is from the olden days when black people were slaves." I asked how we could deter people from using this word. Jerald insisted that change was difficult because the word has passed from generation to generation. He said matter-of-factly, "that word was used by great grandparents who said it to their kids, and then they say it to their kids, like my momma be saying it in front of me. And I will use it in front of my kids."

The discussion made clear that the students knew that they played a role in perpetuating deficit terms. I kept shifting the conversation to how change could start with them. Unfortunately, many of the teachers at the school, including those of color, do not think that students have anything to say about these issues. If one is aware of how racism is shaped and perpetuated in society, these topics must be discussed. Without continual reflection and dialogue, the racial divide and deficit practices will persist at our school.

—**Kimberly Min**
Third-grade teacher

Confronting Homophobia   It is difficult for teachers to confront honestly and out loud the racism that American students have been raised with. It may be even more difficult to acknowledge differences in sexual orientation—a source for bigotry that exists in every community and that educators typically ignore. Of course, students have not been silent about this issue; in schools across the country, "fag" is one of the most common and often tolerated epithets hurled across playgrounds and corridors.

According to research of the American Civil Liberties Union, "[f]or lesbian and gay teens, school is often a nightmare. Harassment from classmates is commonplace, particularly in many schools where teachers and principals tolerate it."[21] A study of Massachusetts high school students published in the journal *Pediatrics* reported that more than 25 percent of self-identified gay teens said they had recently missed school because of fear for their safety, a sharp contrast to the 5 percent of heterosexual teens who had. Nearly one-third of gay teens had recently been threatened with a weapon at school, compared to 7 percent of heterosexual students.[22]

Peer support is difficult to find because lesbian and gay student groups are often discouraged or even prohibited. Survival often means painful self-denial for lesbian and gay youth. It is little wonder, therefore, that the *Pediatrics* study revealed that more than one-third of all gay teens reported having attempted suicide, three times the 9.9 percent for self-identified straight teens.

Indeed, schools rarely offer supportive programs for gay youth. Comprehensive information on sexuality, AIDS/HIV, and other lesbian and gay teen concerns is desperately needed, yet schools choose instead to tolerate, if not actively foster, environments hostile to the development of healthy gay youth. For instance, in one recent study, 53 percent of high school students report hearing homophobic slurs such as "faggot" from *teachers* and other school adults.[23]

The impact of addressing homophobia or anything else that bears on social justice and oppression goes beyond a single "issue" and benefits the overall school climate. For example, the Gay-Straight Alliance Network "supports young people in starting, strengthening, and sustaining" local school gay-straight alliances and helps build their capacity to

> create safe environments in schools for students to support each other and learn about homophobia and other oppressions,
>
> educate the school community about homophobia, gender identity, and sexual orientation issues, and
>
> fight discrimination, harassment, and violence in schools.

Appropriating existing school structures can sometimes create a safe, "normalized" space to counter an oppressive school culture and struggle for social justice. One veteran teacher, adviser to his school's gay-straight alliance, reports that his group addresses campus homophobia, as one would expect, but the group otherwise functions very much like any other campus club—electing its officers, navigating administrative approvals, organizing social activities such as bowling night, and so forth.

After Columbine—Care in a Violent Culture

We are used to schools being very safe places. And, in fact, they are. Without denying the very real emotional hurt inflicted on students by the full range of insensitivity that people are capable of, schools are generally safe places—physically safe places. According to the Surgeon General's 2001 report on youth violence, the perception that schools are dangerous is unfounded. Schools are generally safer than homes and neighborhoods. Of course, any violence is unacceptable and particular concern must be raised at the Surgeon General's finding "senior high school students from racial or ethnic minorities who attend schools in urban districts," are at greatest risk.[24]

What then are we to make of the headlines and on-the-spot television reporting of school violence, of students and teachers suffering injury and even loss of life? Well, it is certainly not acceptable to pass it off by saying, "It doesn't happen that often" or "It probably won't happen here." If there are lessons to be drawn from the shootings at Columbine High School and other well-publicized acts of violence at schools, they are these:

> School violence reflects a violent society, in which violence is a tool available to those who are angry and hurt. When students are helped to talk about these aspects of society and to understand them, then teachers are *doing* something about violence both in and out of school.

> Although watchfulness and security are important, prevention is best accomplished in caring school cultures—cultures that find it intolerable to diminish the dignity or security of anyone for whatever reason. Caring teachers are trusted teachers, and the best safeguard against violence in schools may be students who can approach teachers and report actual or potential violence.

> All physical abuse is violent, and calling it *minor, bullying,* or *normal* does not diminish the violence done.

> There are lots of programs, lots of resources, and lots of caring people.

By working each day to ensure school cultures of care, teachers help to make schools safe as they help students learn more.

After September 11 and Katrina—Care in a Fearful Culture

The shattering enormity of some events, the September 11, 2001, destruction of the World Trade Center in New York, and the devastation to New Orleans from Hurricane Katrina, for example, cannot be left for students to resolve with their limited resources and experiences—perhaps third-hand accounts of the news, a little commentary heard on television, and some youthful maturity. Young and old alike must find ways to explain and express their anger and fears.

Further, the effects of these events are not "local," but resonate across the entire country; and neither are the events in question strictly "national" since the effects of wars, genocides, and natural disasters across the globe can (and should) penetrate deeply into everyone's consciousness. At best we hope that our schools help channel these emotions into productive understandings and action. Good teachers will not be immune from anger, fear, and bafflement when horrifying things occur, and we should have no illusions that teachers can know the "correct" ways to respond to these events and then easily turn their personal response into a coherent and healing pedagogy. And yet that must be our goal, our struggle; our surest guide is to listen persistently, question students, bring them information, and demonstrate care.

After the attacks of September 11, third-year high school teacher Mary Hendra made the observations in Focal Point 9.2 in an article for the *Christian Science Monitor,* published September 25, 2001.

FOCAL POINT 9.2

A Third-Year Teacher on September 11, 2001

I was on my way to school when I heard the news that would rivet the nation, and the world. . . . [M]y reaction went from shock to sorrow. But, there was another thought that went through my head that morning: "What will I teach my students today?"

. . . How could I teach about the Industrial Revolution in world history, and the Gilded Age in U.S. history, and ignore the events of this day? I wondered how I would respond to my students' questions, how we could talk about the event without exacerbating fear?

. . . I have urged my students to question—to think critically, to read critically, and to ask questions about the world around them. So they continue to ask me, "Why would people in other countries be celebrating? Why would people want to cause this destruction? How has the United States created these enemies?"

I also have questions. How do we as a nation critically look at why this might have happened, without being seen as "unpatriotic"? Shouldn't it be a sign of patriotism that we seek to improve our nation? The U.S. has certainly not led a pure and perfect existence, but our democracy has been strong enough to change with the challenges brought by women, African-Americans, social activists, and many others. How can the events of Sept. 11 be molded into an opportunity for humanity's progress?

I wonder, if this tragic event was possible in part because of the freedom and openness of our society, whether restricting that freedom could be the best response. My students, many of whom are first- or second-generation Americans themselves, would probably be among the first to complain of heightened immigration controls. They already ask me, "Why should the U.S. restrict immigration? Immigrants are only looking for a better life."

And if my students look to history for understanding, as I frequently tell my them to do, what can they—and we—learn from Israel's unsuccessful war on terrorism over the past years?

Can we root out terrorism by government-sanctioned violence, regardless of the magnitude of that violence? The more the U.S. is seen as an aggressor, the more resentment it will engender from around the world—and hence the greater commitment it will foster among thousands of individuals who will become willing to put their own lives on the line?

And that implies a question for my classroom: How can I explain to critical teenagers that violence by a government is OK, but violence by an individual is not? What about the violence that was used by imperialist nations to subdue and exploit the African continent?

. . . I believe that asking these questions helps my students understand. I hope they will see adults around them asking questions, too, as we all work through these events and their repercussions. On September 11, my class talked about

(continued)

questions no one yet knows the answers to, but are worth asking anyway. I gave students space to reflect, to put the events outside on "pause" for a few moments.

One student articulated what was probably one of the underlying reasons for much of the questioning that day. "I'm not ready to go to war," she said.

Adapted from an article by Mary Hendra (third-year teacher, high school) in the *Christian Science Monitor,* September 25, 2001.

If teachers confined their teaching in the aftermath of September 11, or the Southeast Asia earthquake and tsunami, or the Katrina hurricane to questions that they knew the answers to, these would be very short lessons indeed. Certainly, there was a need for age-appropriate politics and science to be brought to students, but the humanitarian crises and emotional shocks could never be anticipated in anyone's prepared curriculum.

Further, a common response to shock and a feeling of crisis is to keep things as "normal" as possible: maintain schedules, continue assignments, not intrude on students' highly personal responses. In fact, after the September 11 attack, many teachers were encouraged to proceed with extreme caution—to acknowledge briefly this "current event" and, for the sake of the children, continue with business as usual.

However, a wiser and more humane alternative is to do as Alfie Kohn urges, ". . . help children locate themselves in widening circles of care that extend beyond self, beyond country, to all humanity."[25] This is a tall order in a social and political environment rife with fear and calls for revenge. Such an environment makes it hard for teachers to feel confident about the appropriate developmental level for such lessons and discussions. They worry about acquiring the range of knowledge and perspectives necessary to be responsive to students' questions and concerns. They wince at their potential vulnerability if they truly encourage students to extend their thinking "beyond self."

For example, after September 11, older students quickly became engaged in discussions and arguments surrounding racial profiling, and even the youngest struggled to form impressions about who the bad people were and what they looked like. Politicians, media sources, and others scrambled to learn about the Muslim faith and about the historical and cultural context in which to place and not place the tragic events. Critical thinkers around the world searched for ways to penetrate the meaning and causes of the events without seeming to excuse them. Teachers were no different.

Many teachers are interested in educating their students about the dangers of racial profiling and stereotyping of Arabs and people of Muslim faith and about the historical and cultural context in order to explore the tragic events. Fortunately, many teachers have found help for grappling with these issues from one another and from the many resources from education and social justice organizations— much of it on the Internet.

Inquiry and Activism

Professional teaching carries with it the burdens of its history, and it suffers from the low status that society gives to its clients—children. Historically, society has not valued children highly. Neither has it valued those who spend their lives with them. Servants, not professionals, cared for the children of the middle and upper classes. And for most of the twentieth century, teaching was women's work or, in segregated schools, minorities' work. Community leaders saw women as being dependent on their husbands or other male authorities for leadership—not suited for making important decisions. The feminization of teaching also fit well with scientific management theories. Women and minority teachers provided schools with a class of low-status employees—those who occupied the bottom positions on the organizational chart. They carried out the decisions made by those at the top—male administrators.

In 1908, Felix Arnold published *A Text-Book of School and Class Management,* which explicated theories and practices that should guide school administrators and teachers. Among teachers' duties and responsibilities, Arnold listed these obligations to the principal:

> All instructions, when given by the principal, should be rigidly followed. They may be wrong. They may harm the children. They may be against high ethical standards. But they should be followed. The moment a principal delivers his instructions he becomes responsible for whatever happens when they are carried out. Remonstrance and protest are allowable. But as long as the instructions hold, they should be followed.[26]

Mr. Arnold's advice leaves little room for teachers who want to change the world.

Developing school cultures that enhance learning and social justice requires teachers' long-range involvement, rather than their participation in a primarily technical and rational process—for example, sitting on a committee that will disband as soon as a specific policy has been written or a problem "solved." Teachers must be able to engage with one another in an ongoing process of inquiry where they examine the assumptions and values that underlie their own practice as well as the school's.[27]

Teachers' primary visible task is teaching students in the classroom. This typically occupies five to seven hours a day, five days a week, but teachers must also spend time grading, completing administrative paperwork, supervising, tutoring, preparing for classes and parent conferences, cleaning, and telephoning parents. These activities must take place when teachers are not teaching.

If attending to students and simply keeping up with lessons consume all of a teacher's time, little time or energy remains for professional activities. And a professional school environment should require that teachers have time for creative, energizing inquiry and learning. Time to read, to work with colleagues, and to participate in inquiry and reform activism may be structured into a teacher's working day, but it is more likely that teachers themselves will have to make the tough decisions on how to squeeze in the time for inquiry and activism.

—⚏ ⚏ ⚏—

When I began my first year, I knew that teaching involved more than just planning and delivering a lesson, managing a classroom, grading, and reporting the progress of the students. Teaching included administrative tasks; developing relationships; communicating with fellow teachers, administrators, and parents; and continually striving toward better lessons and instruction. However, I did not understand the constraint that these activities would have on my teaching. With so many constraints, pressures, and demands on teachers, no wonder the profession seems to be conservative and resistant to change. Even though I consider myself one who would like to see changes, I feel pushed toward conservatism because I have so much work. What I want to do on the inside becomes compromised as I deal with the day-to-day reality of the job.

I am finishing my first year of teaching, and these questions are only a few among a mountain that I still ask. Although I have not completely answered them, I know that they are important issues that I need to address if I am to achieve my goals for education. They suggest that in order to achieve my goals for education, I must continue to reflect on my teaching practices through a method of inquiry.

—**Jasper Hiep Dang Bui**
First-year teacher, English, grade 8

Regular meetings with a group of new teachers gave Mark Hill the opportunity to reflect on his practices. Frustrated by his students' seeming lack of critical thinking skills, he conducted a study of whether his students might be more effective mathematics problem solvers if he taught them to monitor their own thinking strategies—a process that psychologists call "metacognition." Mark gave students a pretest to determine the extent they were aware of their thinking and learning processes, taught them some metacognitive strategies, gave them a posttest, collected students' reflections about the lessons, and conducted a focus group to discuss the study and its results with his students.

In the photo here, Mark shares his methods and findings with colleagues for their review. He found that students organized their knowledge more effectively when they use metacognitive techniques, but that all sorts of other social and cultural factors also came into play. These, he says, might be the subject of his next inquiry.

Conducting a formal study, like Mark did, is simply one way of engaging in inquiry and reflection on one's practice. Teachers who teach together often do this as a matter of course. And, in many schools, teachers have joined together in inquiry groups or study groups where they examine a wide range of issues at the heart of their teaching and the school culture. We describe some of these inquiry practices in what follows.

Teaching Together Can Foster Inquiry and Learning

In schools, as in any professional workplace, the most potent force for high levels of performance is a close association and identification with peers. This can take many forms for teachers; a common arrangement is team teaching, as described in the following quotes.

At first, I thought that sharing a room with someone was a horrible thing. I wanted my own class, and I wanted to practice all of the wonderful theories I had learned over the past year. All of my plans were ruined because of a lack of space and because I had to compromise timing, scheduling, and work with this other woman. But, before long, I began to see that we had similar beliefs about how children learn and how we should teach.

The most wonderful thing about it was that we learned an incredible amount from each other not only about teaching, but about every aspect of teaching, including relationships with students, parents, and other teachers. I also learned that two is better than one. We have not only shared ideas and resources, but we are there to constructively criticize and encourage one another as we deal with the many aspects of being a bilingual teacher. It has been so valuable to my students to see that we two teachers are able to work cooperatively and learn from each other. This is consistent with my belief that teachers are not a source of all knowledge, but, like our students, we are learning and changing daily. We have also been able to build a great sense of community among all of our students. They know that there are two adults who care about them, and a whole other class of students who care as well.

—Susie Shin
First-year teacher, grade 1

Team teaching is an unbelievable experience. It is not easy; it requires more time to plan (or maybe Megan and I just have not figured it out yet). It requires patience and good listening skills. There are some days that we wake up on the wrong side of the bed, but that is normal. We have learned to deal with it.

Being able to work so closely with Megan makes me realize how important it is to interact, collaborate, and share with other teachers. We were able to work so well together because we believe in the same things about

schooling, learning, and community. We have done really great and engaging
activities with the kids. We can spend more time doing individual assess-
ments (i.e., running records) while one of us is doing something else. We
have a lot of fun together and I think that the kids do, too. It is just really
nice to have another adult in the classroom. Our parent meetings are much
more successful because there are two of us.

Megan and I have developed a truly special relationship. She has been an
awesome person to work with. She has been my shoulder to cry on, my journal
to reflect in, my partner in crime, and one of my most influential mentors.

—WENDY HERRERA
First-year teacher, grades 1 and 2

Both Susie Shin and Wendy Herrera convey both the personal satisfaction and the professional enrichment that comes when teachers work closely together.

Faculties as Inquiring Communities

A productive school culture requires teachers who have the willingness, skills, and opportunities to continuously examine every aspect of their teaching. This inquiry goes beyond the familiar search for "what works" to make conventional school practice "better." It is an inquiry that mirrors the teacher's own sociocultural teaching. Just as students focus on issues that are important to them, teachers' inquiry focuses on their professional life, including their underlying beliefs and their understanding of school values. Enduring democratic change is possible when people are accountable to each other, express themselves authentically, examine aspects of schooling that are typically taken for granted, and negotiate common understandings that support collective action.

One first-year teacher was lucky enough to experience a culture of inquiry at the school where she student taught. We don't use her name because the school where she now teaches has a culture that sees such inquiry as a waste of time.

— ❧ ❧ ❧ —

Northern's district used its professional development and reform funds to
conduct student and teacher inquiry sessions to address the school's
concerns. . . . [T]he guiding focus of these discussions was the "two schools"
issue—why do different segments of the student population perform and
succeed at different levels?

. . . One English teacher condemned the AP test as the "ultimate canon."
He argued that, for teachers, "there are conflicting priorities. Is our goal to
build a sense of self—for students—or is our goal to push as many kids into
Harvard as possible?" A math teacher responded with his frustration with
the current emphasis on testing and how his priorities have been altered.
"I refuse to believe that passing a test is a measure of one's intelligence.
Let's face it, some of our kids are being prepared to succeed and others are
overlooked. I won't be a part of that system anymore."

Several staff members recognized that without reform in how teachers used assessments, the cycle of educational inequality would be perpetuated. A counselor for "at-risk" students explained that not changing would be "most damaging for lower-achieving students—those who don't see themselves as smart because they don't relate to the school environment and don't 'buy into the system.'"

The most striking aspect of Northern's inquiry was the level of comfort in discussing issues of culture and the ways in which teachers' practices can negatively impact students. These are not easy topics to discuss in a group, because individuals tend to become defensive about their teaching practices. I was surprised that this was not the response. Participants explained their frustrations and distress about the impact of some of their classroom practices (particularly assessment). But they did so in a way that demonstrated that they were struggling with these issues and open to change.

At Northern, people honestly want to exchange ideas and hear what others have to say. The environment is safe and supportive enough to deal with these very difficult issues. Teachers are not blaming administrators, and administrators are not blaming teachers. All are working as a group toward addressing how curriculum, school culture, and assessment impact students. Reform is everyone's priority and everyone seems to believe that these issues can and will be addressed in a meaningful way to improve the learning environment for students.

—NAME WITHHELD
First-year high school teacher

Some forms of teacher inquiry are quite specifically focused on curriculum and instruction. For example, teachers in elementary and middle schools who participate in Cognitively Guided Instruction (CGI) projects meet regularly in inquiry groups to examine samples of the mathematics work done by students in one another's classes. A central dynamic of CGI inquiry is the sharing and examination of teachers' own prior knowledge and beliefs about children's thinking and mathematics.

Over time, teachers learn about children's mathematical thinking.[28] As teachers focus instruction on asking students how they solve problems, the teachers become skilled at using children's talk to guide, or target, subsequent instruction. Teachers respond to the children's descriptions with appropriate requests for new information. This pedagogy rests upon sociocultural conceptions of learning—both for students in the classroom and teachers who are learning CGI. As teachers examine these conversations with their colleagues they replicate the same describing/questioning process that occurs in classroom instruction.

These inquiry processes are quite different from the typical "in-service" or workshop to which teachers are exposed. Traditional staff development replicates transmission models of teaching. There is little scaffolding over time. Scant attention is paid to the relationships among colleagues who may learn something about innovative practices but may not easily share doubts, expose difficulties, or lend support to colleagues.

Other inquiry approaches are much broader in their reform goals. For example, the Accelerated Schools Project began at Stanford University in 1986 as a comprehensive approach to school change, designed to improve schooling for children in at-risk situations by providing all students with challenging activities.[29] The hope is to counteract the traditional practice of reserving such activities for only those students identified as gifted and talented. Accelerated school communities use a systematic inquiry process to transform their entire school.

The transformation begins with the entire school community taking a deep look into its present situation through a process called "taking stock." The school community then forges a shared vision of what it wants the school to be—the kind of dream school that everyone would want for his or her own child. By comparing the vision to its present situation, the school community identifies priority challenge areas. Cadres, which are formed around priority challenges, study the problem, generate and test hypotheses, recommend changes to the whole school community, and assess the results of those changes. Importantly, the change process is a learning process—one that acknowledges and uses the unique cultural backgrounds, interests, and talents of all the people directly involved with the school.

Inquiry and Power

It is not easy to define *inquiry*. At its broadest, inquiry is the way of democracy—a way to learn what other people believe and to struggle for common understandings. For similar reasons, inquiry is the mechanism of sociocultural learning—a way to find out what one another know and to construct, with them, new knowledge.

Some people use the term *critical* inquiry. This adds a political dimension—the dimension of power. Power is always present in relationships, even in the non-coercive, cordial, and cooperative relationships among friends. Typically, when there is a very strong commitment to co-construct understandings (as there often is among close friends), power imbalances do not greatly disrupt the democracy of the relationship. But schools exist in a world of immense status differences associated with gender, race, age, employment, wealth, background, physical power, physical attractiveness, and so on.

The goals of inquiry and social justice are closely tied to diminishing the effects of this power when teaching and when teaching decisions take place. Since we live in this world (where people do not and cannot simply leave their status and power "at the door" and proceed to learn and solve problems as equals) it becomes necessary to purposefully, perhaps self-consciously, create the conditions in which people can explore democratic teaching and learning relationships.

Critical inquiry invites and requires the explicit consideration of the power differences that exist in the room and in the broader community. This agreement to consider power and its effects—one could call it a ground rule—lends a different standard of *practicality* to the discussions and problem solving. Typical "practical" approaches result in a quick agreement to follow a program or solution. However, such problems are often "selected" precisely because people can agree to a solution that they (or someone) may already have in mind—usually a course of action that requires fewest changes with the least discomfort. Critical inquiry looks first to the knowledge, routines, and values that exist in the school community and asks what new knowledge is needed and what alternative values might be explored.

A critical perspective is practical because it seeks to change the culture. Critique of this sort proceeds on the hope (as much as a specific time line) that when people inquire freely and democratically, caring will increase, status differences will diminish, and everyone's full willingness to participate will, over time, address serious problems.

⚔ ⚔ ⚔

Participating in an "inquiry group" has provided an opportunity for me to reflect with other staff members. I am part of the "Wednesday Inquiry Group" that meets every other Wednesday, from 12:15 P.M. until 3:00 P.M. During this time an "Inquiry Sub," trained in the arts, teaches my class. My group consists of seven teachers, the school nurse, and a site coordinator. The teachers involved represent all grade levels, kindergarten through fifth, and special education and bilingual teachers. The teaching experience of group members ranges from first-year teacher to those who have taught over ten years. The site coordinator is an "external critical friend" to the school who participates in all three inquiry group sessions and serves as the facilitator for the group.

Inquiry has allowed me to reflect on my teaching practices with a group of teachers with whom I typically would not have the opportunity to sit and talk. Topics of discussion centered around our school's two "essential questions": (1) "What can I do to ensure that the inequitable pattern of student achievement no longer exists?" and (2) "What can I do to ensure that there is student and parent voice in my classroom?" Still, the topics of discussion are extremely diverse: racial and ethnic issues, creating and sustaining a learning community, critical pedagogy, teaching tolerance, discipline, the school structure, parent involvement, and teaching "growth and development." The group also reads and discusses professional articles and books and agrees to take action as a result of these discussions. For example, at one meeting we agreed to pay attention to how we used "choice" in the classroom. At another meeting, we agreed to pay attention to how we call on students in class. After every agreement [on what the group will observe] we report back our findings at the following meeting. The results create a new springboard for discussion.

As the youngest member of the group, I am in no way made to feel like I am the least experienced. My opinions and viewpoints are listened to and validated. I feel safe expressing my views, even if I think that they will not be embraced by all of the members of the group. Because this is my first year in the school community as a credentialed teacher, inquiry is a good place for me to express my opinions. I am much more comfortable talking in small, intimate settings. This experience has given me an opportunity in a safe setting to reflect and find my "voice."

> *When I contribute to my inquiry group, I bring with me the experiences*
> *of my recent courses saturated in theory. This theoretical grounding has*
> *positively influenced my development as a reflective professional because I*
> *am able to approach and evaluate my classroom practice from a multitude of*
> *perspectives. I have had the opportunity to share books, articles, and my*
> *research papers with the group. The positive reaction and interest expressed*
> *in my contributions have enhanced my comfort and feeling of inclusion.*
>
> —Chrysta Bakstad
> First-year teacher, grades K, 1, and 2

Inquiry sessions like those Chrysta Bakstad participated in give educators regularly scheduled time away from their classrooms to talk about their collective understandings and create new initiatives. The sessions Chrysta describes allowed her and her colleagues to pose questions ("What can I do to ensure that the inequitable pattern of student achievement no longer exists?" and "What can I do to ensure that there is student and parent voice in my classroom?") that give practical help in selecting appropriate teaching practices. The group forged a sphere of rough equality, where each group member was viewed as someone who could elevate the group's understanding. Although the conversations ranged broadly, the core concerns stayed with learning and the struggle for equity. Inquiry, as Chrysta describes it, can alter relationships among teachers, alter classroom pedagogy, and foster new inquiry settings around the school.

Chrysta Bakstad teaches at a school with a well-established structure for inquiry. Yvette Nunez, however, is at a school that is just beginning to make inquiry a part of its institutional and professional life. Yvette's role in introducing inquiry to her school is just as vital as Chrysta's role in sustaining inquiry at hers.

———————————————— ⌘ ⌘ ⌘ ————————————————

> *Bureaucratic nightmares greatly affect my classroom instruction and*
> *student learning—testing students out of reading groups, attempting to*
> *transition students into English, and ensuring that students are not further*
> *distanced from social interaction with native English speakers. I have*
> *argued, using sociocultural theory, for doing what is best for my students.*
> *But because of the bureaucracy, I have also had to play the game to make*
> *sure my students get past the gates. In many instances where the assessment*
> *did not reflect the students' capabilities, I had to learn the system to use it to*
> *my students' advantage. The next step in my development as a social justice*
> *educator is to join the Placement Committee that studies how students are*
> *placed in classrooms, so I can express my strong beliefs about the necessity*
> *of mixing language speakers in one classroom and bringing more students*
> *of various cultural and linguistic backgrounds into our school.*
>
> —Yvette Nunez
> First-year teacher, grades 3 and 4

Inquiry groups confront (mostly) taken-for-granted conceptions of intelligence and ability, racial differences, merit, and deeply entrenched traditions of what is valued curriculum and appropriate practice at the schools. At every school, the efforts of inquiry groups to move toward more effective and socially just practices are countered not only by those who actively resist reform but also by well-intentioned educators whose everyday commonsense actions unwittingly reconstruct the dominant culture and schooling ideologies. Inquiry thrives on opportunities to act, and that action takes many forms. Becoming informed about one's own and others' practices, connecting practices with theory, and developing trusting relationships with colleagues are all examples of powerful actions. These are not "getting ready," or warm-ups, or first steps—these are themselves practical achievements that promote excellent learning opportunities and social justice for students.

Creating Cultures Where Good Teaching Makes Sense

It's become quite clear to most observers that, if we want to achieve the goals of high levels of learning for all students, cultural changes are required. It's also clear that, although each of the separate elements we've described is helpful, they are far more powerful working synergistically as a school culture. When the school extends important knowledge to all students and focuses its resources and energy on high-quality learning, more students learn better. Caring school environments help keep students and teachers more engaged in school. One analysis of nearly a thousand schools undergoing reforms found that schools where faculties developed structures to promote long-term caring relationships, extended a rich curriculum to all students, and emphasized teachers working collaboratively made greater gains in student achievement than schools with more traditional practices.[30]

The question that remains, however, is how might we create such schools on a large scale? We end with a brief discussion of "small schools"—the reform idea that many educators and policymakers see as being most likely to make the good school cultures we describe in this chapter normal, even ordinary. One piece of evidence for just how powerful the idea of small schools has become is the investment that the Bill and Melinda Gates Foundation has made in this idea. By the end of 2005, the Gates Foundation had spent 2.5 billion dollars on education since 2000, and much of that money supported the creation of new small schools and the conversion of large high schools into several smaller ones.

Will "Small Schools" Provide the Solution?

In the 1990s, award-winning teacher and school principal Deborah Meier began writing and speaking about the incredible experience that she and a group of teachers had over 20 years, creating a handful of small schools in Harlem, New York, where test scores were the lowest in the city (refer back to Focal Point 9.1, where Meier's work in Harlem is discussed). Meier's approach was to create democratic communities in small schools where teachers, parents, and students all helped create a culture of academic challenge, rich learning opportunities, and caring.

Meier provides compelling examples in her book *The Power of Their Ideas: Lessons for America from a Small School in Harlem* of how teachers working together in small schools "generate powerful ideas" that result in school cultures where teachers teach well, students learn well, and social justice is the norm.[31]

Meier's inspiring stories of the culture of the Central Park East schools, along with impressive rates of achievement and college going among the schools' graduates, captured the imagination of educators, policymakers, and philanthropists like Bill Gates. Today, through the processes of creating new schools and converting existing ones, the small schools movement has taken hold in nearly every large city in the United States, and in many other places as well. By Gates's count, its foundation has supported over 2,000 such schools, and nearly every major urban area in the country has a Gates-supported "small schools" project.

Will small schools change the culture of American schooling? The safest answer is maybe. What we know for sure is that, like many good things, small is necessary, but not sufficient in itself to change the culture of schools.

Necessary, But Not Sufficient

Around the country, a number of networks and supporting groups in universities and community organizations have developed programs to support the development of democratic small schools. These programs all stress that just going small is not enough. For example, the Stanford School ReDesign Network has a wide range of supportive programs and materials to assist small schools, not only to get established, but to incorporate into their cultures the multiple features of good schools that we've described above. The Stanford group has developed a set of 10 principles, all of which must be acted upon in the creation of small schools (see Concept Table 9.1). You'll notice that they bear a strong resemblance to the elements of school culture we've discussed in this chapter.

Is "small" enough to change the culture of schools? Before answering, it's helpful to ask a parallel set of questions. Will a faculty that tries to keep its expectations high for all students have the smartest students? Will a school that has lots of laboratory science equipment have students who learn science better? Maybe, maybe not. Will those who connect respectfully with students have students engaged in learning? Will faculties who participate in inquiry develop the most powerful strategies for working with students? There are no guarantees, but evidence indicates that schools whose reform efforts press in these directions are seeing positive outcomes for students.

The same is true for small schools. In her introduction to the 10 principles of effective design in small schools, listed in Concept Table 9.1, Stanford Professor Linda Darling-Hammond warns:

> Yet we must proceed with caution. "Small" is not synonymous with successful. There are ineffective small schools, some of which replicate the very problems they were seeking to solve. Small size is a necessary condition for effective schooling, but it is not enough.[32]

As Darling-Hammond cautions, research makes clear that smaller schools and classes won't result in more learning if nothing else changes. Smaller schools may be

CONCEPT TABLE 9.1 *Effective Design for Small Schools*[33]

Principle	Description
Personalization	Smaller classes and reduced teacher-pupil loads help to personalize learning.
Continuous relationships	Advisory classes and looping allow relationships to develop over time.
Standards and performance assessment	High expectations and performance-based assessment help students learn.
Authentic curriculum	In-depth learning with real-world connections leads to higher achievement.
Adaptive pedagogy	Teachers adjust their teaching modes to meet students where they are.
Antiracist teaching	Schools that seek out diversity can provide a caring, respectful community for all students.
Qualified teachers	Qualified teachers make a difference.
Collaboration and development	Time provided for teachers to work together develops their expertise.
Family/community connections	Relationships built with families and communities strengthen student learning.
Democratic decision making	Shared governance allows for the creation of a common vision.

necessary for improved education, even though they may not be sufficient to overcome all the rest of what ails schools. Certainly, all of the conditions that we've described in this chapter are necessary for a high-quality education. However, any one of these conditions, especially one standing alone, will not do the job. That's the hardest, but most important, lesson for advocates of small schools or any other effort to change the culture of schools.

OLC Connections

A list of additional online and print resources and a set of questions for reflection about school culture can be found at www.mhhe.com/oakes3e.

Digging Deeper

The resources listed below include scholars whose research provides a solid understanding of the school culture, as well as some innovative education reform projects. Each is struggling to bring high-quality teaching and learning and a spirit of democratic education to schools.

The Coalition of Essential Schools, a reform movement that links hundreds of schools around the nation and was founded by **Theodore Sizer,** is currently based at Brown University in Providence, Rhode Island. Information about the Coalition can be found online at http://www.essentialschools.org, including many useful resources and information about the network of small schools that has emerged from its work. Ted Sizer has written about the ideas behind the Coalition in *Horace's Compromise: The Dilemma of the American High School* (Boston: Houghton Mifflin, 1985), *Horace's School: Redesigning the American High School* (Boston: Houghton Mifflin, 1991), and *Horace's Hope: What Works for the American High School* (Boston: Houghton Mifflin, 1996).

Linda Darling-Hammond is a professor of education at Stanford University and director of the Stanford School ReDesign Network. Her research, teaching, and policy work focus on issues of school restructuring, teacher education reform, and educational equity. Her award-winning book *The Right to Learn* (San Francisco, Jossey-Bass, 1997) provides a comprehensive overview of research and a compelling analysis of how schools can work for all students. The online resources of the Stanford School ReDesign Network at www.schoolredesign.net provide a wealth of resources for creating good school cultures.

The **Forum for Education and Democracy** is devoted to supporting educational policies and practices that prepare the young for a life of active and engaged citizenship and advance a system of strong public schools for a strong American democracy. George Wood, the director of the Forum for Education and Democracy; the principal of Federal Hocking High School in Stewart, Ohio; and author of the book *Time to Learn: How to Create High Schools That Serve All Students* (Portsmouth, NH: Heinemann, 2005), is joined in the Forum by researchers and leaders in school reform, educational policy, and advocacy for equitable access to quality schools for all American families. The site at http://www.forumforeducation.org/ provides free, downloadable materials in the areas of equitable access to educational resources, progressive school practices, and educational decision making.

Michael Fullan, former dean of the Ontario Institute for Studies in Education at the University of Toronto, is a leading authority on educational change. Books of particular interest to teachers about school culture and reform include his *Change Forces: Probing the Depths of Educational Reform* (London: Falmer Press, 1993) and *What's Worth Fighting for in Your School?* written with **Andy Hargreaves** (New York: Teachers College Press, 1996). *What's Worth Fighting For?* provides action guidelines for teachers and for principals. One of Fullan's most recent books, *The Moral Imperative of School Leadership* (Corwin Press: 2003), focuses squarely on the role of the principal in creating good school cultures.

Andy Hargreaves is professor of education in the Lynch School of Education at Boston College. His book *Changing Teachers, Changing Times: Teachers' Work and Culture in the Postmodern Age* (New York: Teachers College Press, 1994) addresses the challenges to teachers posed by changes in the culture of schools related to the conditions of postmodernity. Hargreaves pulls together his and other researchers' work in the *1997 ASCD Yearbook: Rethinking Educational Change with Heart and*

Mind (Alexandria, VA: Association for Supervision and Curriculum Development, 1997). His most recent book is *Teaching in the Knowledge Society* (New York: Teachers College Press, 2003).

Ann Lieberman, an emeritus professor from Teachers College, Columbia University, is now a senior scholar at the Carnegie Foundation for the Advancement of Teaching. She studies and writes about the importance of teacher networks for teacher learning and school change. Teachers might be especially interested in reading *Teachers, Their World and Their Work: Implications for School Improvement* (New York: Teachers College Press, 1992).

Making Schools Safe is a training program designed to help educators create a safe and open environment for lesbian and gay students and combat antigay harassment in local schools. The program is not about sex, it is not about morality, and it is not "Gay 101." Instead, it is about safety, equal access, and equal protection. It is about making sure that every student feels that they can achieve their best in school in an environment free of hostility. And it is about taking proactive steps to prevent the antigay attitudes that may exist in a school from turning into harassment and escalating into violence. Making Schools Safe is an initiative of the ACLU Lesbian and Gay Rights Project. Materials related to the project can be found online at http://www.aclu.org/getequal/scho/index.html.

The **National Center for Accelerated Schools** at the University of Connecticut (http://www.acceleratedschools.net) continues the work of Professor **Henry Levin,** who founded the **Accelerated Schools Project** at Stanford University in 1986 when he introduced the philosophy and process to two elementary schools in San Francisco. The National Center provides leadership and coordination in the development and implementation of accelerated schools across the country. It develops and tests innovations in training, evaluation, coaching, and troubleshooting and studies the workings of the accelerated schools process. Now under the direction of Gene Chasin, the center is located at the University of Connecticut.

Seymour Sarason, professor emeritus at Yale University, first analyzed schools as cultures in the early 1970s. Recent books of his that provide valuable insight into the power of school culture, especially as it relates to school reform efforts, are the following: *Revisiting 'the Culture of the School and the Problem of Change'* (New York: Teachers College Press, 1996), *The Predictable Failure of Educational Reform: Can We Change Course Before It's Too Late?* (San Francisco: Jossey-Bass 1993), and *Parental Involvement and the Political Principle: Why the Existing Governance Structure of Schools Should Be Abolished* (San Francisco: Jossey-Bass, 1995). Sarason's latest book is *Letters to a Serious Education President* (Corwin Books, 2005). In it, he offers his latest analysis of why school cultures are so hard to change, and how current education reform falls short.

Teaching for Change provides teachers with the tools from a wide variety of sources to transform schools into socially equitable centers of learning. Teaching for Change is a not-for-profit organization based in Washington, D.C. The Teaching for Change online catalog is a unique source for books, videos, and posters for the classroom. It can be found at www.teachingforchange.org.

Online Resources Related to September 11, the Iraq War, Hurricane Katrina, and other fear-inducing events. Increasingly, Internet sites provide teachers with resources to help their students grapple with violent crises, tragedies, and world tensions. For example, in the wake of the September 11 attacks, several established organizations added resources for teachers—including background information, lesson plans, and links to other Internet sites. Here are just a few of the many helpful sites addressing September 11, terrorism, Katrina, and other crises:

- *Rethinking Schools* (http://www.rethinkingschools.org) has a nice collection of lesson plans and resources that provide teachers with different perspectives and factual information for teaching in the context of these world events.
- Educators for Social Responsibility (http://www.esrnational.org/) provides teaching resources regarding the violence in the world, including *Talking to Children About War and Violence in the World*. It includes suggestions for when and how to talk to children, ways to respond to revenge and retaliation fantasies, ideas for collective action, anti-Arab sentiment, rage, fear, and more. The group also lists a set of resources and activities to support teachers as they try to explain the tragedy of Hurricane Katrina.
- The National Association of School Psychologists (http://www.nasponline.org/NEAT/crisis_0911.html) has posted some useful materials for helping students cope with crises, particularly crises related to terrorism. Particularly helpful is that some resources have been translated into Arabic, Farsi, Korean, Spanish, Urdu, and Vietnamese.
- Advice to Educators from the American-Arab Anti-Discrimination Committee (http://www.adc.org/education/advice.htm) offers the ADC's help to school officials, student groups, and others who want films, speakers, or other help in discouraging hate speech, harassment, and other action that is anti-Arab and/or anti-Muslim. It also provides some valuable resources for teachers of Arab students who may be suffering anxiety and confusion.
- The Center for Contemporary Arab Studies (http://ccas.georgetown.edu/outreach.cfm) at Georgetown University offers answers to "Who Are the Arabs?" on their website, along with lesson plans to help teachers educate students on the Arab culture.
- The United Nation's "Cyberschoolbus"—a children's website (http://www.un.org/cyberschoolbus/peace/index.asp)—has a wonderful Peace Education component, including theory and curriculum.

Notes

1. Cultures permit a broad range of acceptable behavior in some matters, and in other matters, only a very limited range of behaviors is acceptable. A university's culture, for example, may tolerate a wide range of dress for attending class but sharply limit where students can smoke cigarettes. Both of these ranges or limits derive from the culture's general system of beliefs regarding what it must do to preserve its most important values and ways of life.
2. Seymour Sarason, *The Culture of the School and the Problem of Change,* 3rd ed. (Boston: Allyn & Bacon, 1996).

3. National Commission on Teaching and America's Future, *What Matters Most: Teaching for America's Future* (New York: Author, 1996).

4. From the Coalition of Essential Schools Internet site, http://www.essential schools.org.

5. John I. Goodlad, *A Place Called School* (New York: McGraw-Hill, 1984).

6. Jeannie Oakes, Karen Hunter Quartz, Steve Ryan, and Martin Lipton, *Becoming Good American Schools: The Struggle for Virtue in School Reform* (San Francisco: Jossey-Bass, 2001); and Theodore Sizer, *Horace's Hope: What Works for the American High School* (Boston: Houghton Mifflin, 1996).

7. Council of the Great City Schools, *Charting the Right Course: A Report on Urban Student Achievement and Course-Taking* (Washington, DC: Author, 1998).

8. This is the first of several excerpts in this chapter from a booklet compiled by UCLA teacher education students to honor educators and citizens struggling to promote social justice in and through Los Angeles area schools: John Rogers and Carolyn Castelli, eds., *Building Social Justice for a New Generation: Profiles of Social Justice Fellows from UCLA's Teacher Education Program, 1997* (Los Angeles: UCLA, 1997).

9. Rogers and Castelli, *Building Social Justice for a New Generation* .

10. Linda Darling-Hammond, "The Right to Learn and the Advancement of Teaching: Research, Policy, and Practice for Democratic Education," *Educational Researcher* 26 (August/ September 1996), p. 5.

11. Ronald F. Ferguson "Paying for Public Education: New Evidence on How and Why Money Matters," *Harvard Journal on Legislation* 28, no. 2 (summer 1991), pp. 465–498. Ferguson's studies are supported by other recent analyses showing that money does indeed make a difference, including a 1994 study by Larry Hedges, Richard D. Laine, and Rob Greenwald, "Does Money Matter? A Meta-Analysis of the Effects of Differential School Inputs on Student Outcomes," *Educational Researcher* 23, no. 3 (1994), pp. 5–14; see also Bruce J. Biddle and David C. Berliner, *What Research Says About Unequal Funding for Schools in America* (Tempe, AZ: Arizona State University, Education Policy Studies Laboratory, Education Policy Reports Project, Winter 2002).

12. See Gene Glass, Leonard Cahan, Mary Lee Smith, and Nikola Filby, *School Class Size: Research and Policy* (Beverly Hills: Sage, 1982); Jeremy Finn and Charles M. Achilles, "Answers and Questions About Class Size," *American Educational Research Journal* 27 (fall 1990), pp. 557–577; and Alan B. Krueger, "Understanding the Magnitude and Effect of Class Size on Student Achievement," in *The Class Size Debate* , ed. Lawrence Mishel and Richard Rothstein (Washington, DC: Economic Policy Institute, 2002).

13. See, for example, Michael Knapp, Patrick Shields, and Brenda Turnbull, *Teaching for Meaning in High-Poverty Classrooms* (New York: Teachers College Press, 1995); Jeannie Oakes, "Two Cities: Tracking and Within-School Segregation," in *Brown Plus Forty: The Promise,* ed. LaMar Miller (New York: Teachers College Press, 1995); and new analyses of the impact of academic coursework on college entrance test scores reported in "Study: Hard Courses Help Urban ACT's," *New York Times,* 15 January 1998.

14. Rogers and Castelli, *Building Social Justice for a New Generation.*

15. Jeannie Oakes, Amy Stuart Wells, Susan Yonezawa, and Karen Ray, "The Politics of Equity and Change: Lessons from Detracking Schools," in *1997 ASCD Yearbook: Rethinking Educational Change with Heart and Mind,* ed. Andy Hargreaves (Alexandria, VA: Association for Supervision and Curriculum Development, 1997), pp. 43–72.

16. See Laurence Steinberg, *Beyond the Classroom* (New York: Simon & Schuster, 1996).

17. Cathy Krop, Dominic Brewer, Susan Gates, Brian Gill, Robert Reichardt, Melora Sundt, and Dan Throgmorton, *Potentially Eligible Students: A Growing Opportunity for the University of California* (Santa Monica: RAND, 1998).

18. See Claude Steele, "A Threat in the Air: How Stereotypes Shape the Intellectual Identities and Performance of Women and African-Americans," *American Psychologist* 52 (1997), pp. 613–629.

19. Rogers and Castelli, *Building Social Justice for a New Generation.*

20. One of many recent books exploring these concepts for high school reform is Theodore Sizer's *Horace's Hope: What Works for the American High School* (Boston: Houghton Mifflin, 1996);

also see Oakes, Hunter Quartz, Ryan, and Lipton, *Becoming Good American Schools: The Struggle for Virtue in School Reform.*

21. From the American Civil Liberties Union website at http://www.aclu.org.
22. As cited in Beth Reis and Elizabeth Saewyc, "Eighty-Three Thousand Youth: Selected Findings of Eight Population-based Studies as They Pertain to Anti-gay Harassment and the Safety and Well-being of Sexual Minority Students" (Seattle, WA: Safe Schools Coalition of Washington, 1999).
23. *Making Schools Safe for Gay and Lesbian Youth: Report of the Massachusetts Governor's Commission on Gay and Lesbian Youth,* 1993.
24. Surgeon General's 2001 report, *Youth Violence: A Report of the Surgeon General,* http://www.surgeongeneral.gov/library/youthviolence/report.html.
25. As cited in "September 11 and Our Classrooms," *Rethinking Schools* 16, no. 2 (winter 2001/2002).
26. Felix Arnold, *Text-Book of School and Class Management: Theory and Practice* (New York: The Macmillan Company, 1908), p. 22.
27. Considerable research has documented the power of collaborative work among teachers in the process of school change and improvement. See, for example, Michael Fullan, *Successful School Improvement* (Philadelphia: Open University Press, 1992); Judith Warren Little, "Norms of Collegiality and Experimentation: Workplace Conditions of School Success," *American Educational Research Journal* 19 (1982), pp. 325–340; Judith Warren Little and Milbery McLaughlin, eds., *Teachers Work: Individuals, Colleagues, and Contexts* (New York: Teachers College Press, 1993); and Karen Seashore Louis and Sharon D. Kruse, *Professionalism and Community: Perspectives on Reforming Urban Schools* (Newberry Park, CA: Corwin Press, 1995). Many of the ideas about inquiry presented in this section emerge from our collaborative work with UCLA colleague John Rogers.
28. More information about Cognitive Guided Instruction is found in Chapter 5.
29. See, for example, Michael Fullan and Andy Hargreaves, *What's Worth Fighting for in Your School?* (New York: Teachers College Press, 1996); Michael Fullan, *Change Forces: Probing the Depths of Educational Reform* (London: Falmer Press, 1993); John S. Rogers and Robert Polkinghorn, "The Inquiry Process in the Accelerated School: A Deweyan Approach to School Renewal" (paper presented at the annual meeting of the American Educational Research Association, Boston, 1990); and Christine Finnan, Edward St. John, and Jane McCarthy, eds. *Accelerated Schools in Action: Lessons from the Field* (Thousand Oaks, CA: Corwin Press, 1995).
30. Valerie Lee, Julia Smith, and Frank Croninger, "Another Look at High School Restructuring: More Evidence That It Improves Student Achievement and More Insight into Why," *Issues in Restructuring Schools* (Newsletter, Center on Organization and Restructuring of Schools, University of Wisconsin, 1995), No. 9, pp. 1–9.
31. Deborah Meier, *The Power of Their Ideas: Lessons for America from a Small School in Harlem* (Boston: Beacon Press, 1995), p. 4.
32. Linda Darling-Hammond, "Overview" to "Ten Features of Effective Design," http://www.schoolredesign.net.
33. Stanford School ReDesign Network, "Ten Features of Effective Design," http://www.schoolredesign.net.

CHAPTER 10

The Community

Engaging with Families and Neighborhoods

Genuine parental involvement is something we struggle with at my school. Recently, we've begun working with the activist community group Inner-City Struggle because we want to move beyond monthly parent meetings and teacher-parent conferences. Inner-City Struggle supports parents in two important ways. One, they provide workshops on basic information that parents need to make sure that their children are receiving a rigorous college preparatory education. For instance, in January they will offer a workshop on the high school graduation requirements. Two, they work to establish a type of student and parent involvement that can lead to social and educational change within the school and the community. For example, Inner-City Struggle sponsors a school service club called United Students Junior. Last year, Inner-City Struggle involved the students and their parents in a successful organizing campaign to ensure that all high school students are enrolled in college preparation courses.

—MAURO BAUTISTA
Middle-school bilingual education coordinator

Administrators and teachers are professionals whom the public entrusts with creating classroom practices and school cultures where all students can learn well; their actions determine the quality of students' opportunities. However, educators are not the only adults who influence whether schools actually become academically rigorous and socially just learning communities. Administrators, teachers, parents, and community members must all work toward this goal. In the best schools, educators reach out, welcome, guide, and respond to families and community members to make sure that their participation is authentic and meaningful.[1] As Mauro Bautisa's story illustrates, this reaching out can extend far beyond traditional efforts to have parents help with students' homework or attend parent meetings at school.

Dozens of studies attest to the benefits of parent involvement on children's school achievements and outcomes. Likewise, parental "noninvolvement" gets much of the blame when schooling does not go well. When parents participate in their children's education, students' attitudes and achievement improve. Increased attendance, fewer discipline problems, and higher aspirations also are correlated with an increase in parent involvement. So, too, is teachers' confidence about teaching diverse groups of young people. A stronger curriculum and more positive school and community relations are associated with parent involvement. These positive effects seem to hold regardless of students' socioeconomic status and prior academic achievement.[2]

Given these findings, many states and the U.S. Department of Education have mandated parent involvement programs to be introduced into schools' daily operations as a condition for receiving certain state and federal funds. Yet, in spite of near unanimous agreement on the broad principle of "parent involvement," there is no consensus and little deep understanding about what involvement has to mean if it is really going to further the goals of rigorous learning and social justice.

Chapter Overview

In this chapter, we look at a number of parent and community involvement strategies and examine whether and how these strategies share power in addition to sharing responsibility. We begin by considering two dominant (and contradictory) complaints about parents:

- Parents neglect their responsibilities to participate and support their children's schools.
- Parents are disruptive and overly involved in schools.

We then examine four types of constructive engagement:

- Parents supporting the work of schools
- Schools serving families' and communities' need for health and social services
- Bridging the cultures of home and school through curriculum
- Receptivity to and partnering with community groups that have organized parents for community and school improvement

Each of these strategies has the potential for helping to build a supportive and respectful synergy between teachers and parents, but they each take considerable work and patience. Parent "involvement" means so much more than parents' acting as supporters, helpers, or compliant clients for the schools' services. Parents must be equal partners in their children's schooling; this is not to say, however, that parents and teachers are supposed to perform one another's "jobs." Instead, the entire community needs to get straight how its various members both do their job and work together. This isn't easy, because the best distribution of work and power in order to create a good school is not familiar or comfortable to most people.

Complaints about Parent Involvement: Too Little and Too Much

A common complaint in schools serving high-poverty neighborhoods is that parents just don't care—evidenced by their failure to show up at school events, to return paperwork to the school, or to respond constructively to phone calls eliciting their help with academic or discipline problems. Often this lack of caring is framed more sympathetically, as when educators also note that poverty constrains the participation of many families. The schools lament that their influence cannot compete with negative influences such as alienated peer groups, drugs, and "dysfunctional" families. Many educators levy a different, but equally powerful, complaint about parents—parents who are too demanding—who are too involved, care too much about every little thing (and often the wrong things).

We discuss these two parent involvement problems in what follows.

Too Little Involvement: Low-Income Parents Who Don't or Can't Care

Whether portrayed with anger or sympathy, school failure is often attributed to improper parenting or a lack of commitment to education or to a variety of other causes that are beyond the school's ability to influence. And, as we described in Chapter 2, deficit thinking about the families, culture, and even the genetics of low-income children and children of color has shaped Americans' explanations for racial and social class gaps in achievement and school success. As recently as the 1980s, parents' failure to care enough to provide sufficient support for learning has been a high-profile, political explanation for students' failure to achieve at school. George Herbert Walker Bush's education secretary Lauro Cavazos publicly admonished Latino families for their children's high dropout rates.[3]

Studies of parents' attitudes toward schooling consistently show something quite different, however—that education is a top priority for low-income, culturally and linguistically diverse families. These parents are unmistakably clear in their belief that schooling provides the crucial hope for their children's move into meaningful work and lives undistorted by poverty.

Why is there such a large gap between common perceptions and actual commitments to education? Part of the answer lies in the different ways that educators and families in culturally diverse communities define an involved parent. Whereas educators stress participation in organized school events and parents who keep up with the details of lessons, parents often see the care, support, encouragement, and cultural values they give their children as the foundation for their success in school.[4]

Poor parents and wealthy parents share the exact same assumption about schools: "The school's job is to see that my child succeeds." Where parents differ is in the kind of critique and empowerment that they bring to their relationship with the school. Wealthy parents have enormous social capital and leverage, and they believe that they are entitled to use it. Schools respond to them. Poor parents, for a multitude of reasons, do not have that sense of empowerment and entitlement, and it makes little sense to equate the respectful "distance" they keep as not caring. The result may be a school view that parents don't care about education and a parent view that schools don't care about kids.

How can educators and families, who want the same thing for students, stop misreading one another's intentions and connect their efforts? Teachers and schools must gain confidence that new, culturally sensitive understandings and roles can further high standards and rigorous learning.

When Mauro Bautista began teaching at a middle school in a mostly Latino community, he was cautioned by some of his colleagues that he shouldn't count on parents being involved. However, because he had grown up in the neighborhood, he knew that the parents did care, even if they didn't spend much time at school. He set out to overcome that obstacle by reaching out to parents in ways they would see as welcoming.

⊗ ⊗ ⊗

I invited all my students' parents to the classroom the first Friday of the year. I introduced myself, gave them my home phone number, and invited them to visit the classroom any time. I spoke Spanish because most of the parents spoke limited, if any, English.

When parents visit the classroom, I approach them as soon as possible and we discuss their goals for the visit. Some come to find out how their children are doing. A few ask me how they can help their kids at home. Several invite me to eat at their homes. One parent invited me for a beer, and I was very humbled by this sign of camaraderie. My parents' respect for the teaching profession is very evident.

In addition to meeting with parents at school, I meet with them in their homes. I would love to visit all of my students' homes. I always try to give positive reports by emphasizing the progress and showing them examples of their child's work. Parents enjoy hearing that their children are doing well in school.

My connections with parents clearly disprove some teachers' belief that parents do not care about their children's success in school.

—**Mauro Bautista**
Middle-school bilingual education coordinator

Hard work and patience are essential. Parents may not respond immediately to teachers' goodwill and invitation to become an active part of their children's success in class. In this way, parents are no different from their students. They may have few prior experiences where they were treated with respect and where their participation was valued. Often low-income parents who grew up in the United States have unhappy recollections of their own schooling that dampen their enthusiasm for getting involved with schools.

Teachers may have few resources and little time to pursue parents who work more than one job, who have no telephone or transportation, or who don't speak English. Ugly racial histories in many communities make some parents of color reticent to be a visible presence at school. Immigrant parents may understand little about American schools—they may mistakenly (or correctly) assume that parents are neither wanted nor needed at school, or trust that their children and the school will make all appropriate educational decisions. For many, language barriers make it difficult or impossible to communicate with teachers.

Students in low-income communities are lucky to have teachers like Mauro whose own life experiences bring a deep understanding of these constraints. But most teachers, even those whose life experiences are very different from the communities where they teach, can acquire the understanding they need to see parents as allies and to advocate for their inclusion.

Too Much Involvement: Middle- and Upper-Class Parent Power

In some neighborhoods, typically middle and upper class, nervousness around grades, test scores, and traditional indicators of success (such as scores on weekly spelling tests) emerge even in the earliest grades, and worried parents can make children's, teachers', and their own lives difficult. The following anecdotes appeared in a 2005 story about parent involvement in *Time* magazine.

> An Iowa high school counselor gets a call from a parent protesting the C her child received on an assignment. "The parent argued every point in the essay," recalls the counselor, who soon realized why the mother was so upset about the grade. "It became apparent that she'd written it."
>
> A sixth-grade teacher in California tells a girl in her class that she needs to work on her reading at home, not just in school. "Her mom came in the next day," the teacher says, "and started yelling at me that I had emotionally upset her child."
>
> A science teacher in Baltimore, Md., was offering lessons in anatomy when one of the boys in class declared, "There's one less rib in a man than in a woman." The teacher pulled out two skeletons—one male, the other female—and asked the student to count the ribs in each. "The next day," the teacher recalls, "the boy claimed he told his priest what happened and his priest said I was a heretic."[5]

Such parents' involvement and worries about their children may do more than create distractions and burdens for teachers. They may also threaten educational programs and approaches for all students. And in schools with social class or racial diversity, misguided parental involvement can undermine high-quality learning opportunities for students of color, students whose families are poor, and students who have not been designated as destined for high achievement.

Few educators or researchers openly discuss this side of parent involvement because it runs counter to the ubiquitous plea for parents to be involved. Because schools need political support—not only for funding and physical resources, but also for credibility—they often acquiesce to parents' demands, even if it means giving special privileges or reining in a reform.[6] Many parents who themselves did well with traditional instruction become apprehensive if their children experience nontraditional classrooms.[7]

The best response to the community members when their "involvement" is tense, critical, and inappropriate is to remain open to their concerns and steadfast in bringing high quality and socially just learning to their children. It is rare that parents—of children in a class or at the entire school—fail to recognize deeply caring, competent, hardworking, and united faculty and administrators. Hypercritical parents can soon find themselves isolated in their complaints and see little to gain from continuing their disruptions. However, in the absence of a unified and competent faculty and school administration who are intent on bringing the best schooling to all the children, these parents may play one teacher or administrator against another and continue their behavior until they get their way.

In Chapters 3 and 4, we discussed the "wars" over curriculum that triggered many such parent complaints in recent years. We witnessed this recently in an affluent community, when a highly acclaimed principal became the target of parents because she instituted a progressive mathematics curriculum.

Importantly, the principal took many of the recommended steps for parent involvement that *should have* smoothed the way for reform.[8] She convened a "transformation" study group of 25 community members, teachers, and administrators, paying much attention to developing a process for openly discussing difficult school and social issues. This group read and talked about research, including the literature on corporate and other ideas familiar in the business world.

Despite the principal's efforts to include her vocal, upper-middle-class community, some of these parents formed an ad hoc group for "educational accountability" and petitioned the board of education to return the school to traditional teaching and curricula. Some parents demanded that specific books be read, and others prescribed specific amounts of time for certain lessons. The innovative math curriculum became a lightning rod for a group of fathers—many with degrees in science and engineering—who blasted the program as failing to prepare their children for the rigors of university. One former student, now attending an Ivy League college, wrote to the local paper blaming the principal for his average math grades in his college class. The principal conceded to parents' demands for more traditional curriculum, but that was not enough. She was fired.

Parent involvement can reflect the racism and classism in the rest of the culture. Some white and middle-class parents' respond to their children's classmates of color or poverty with fear and prejudice. One first-year teacher found herself and her teaching partner in just such a situation.

Last summer, the district decided to install three portable classrooms to absorb the increasing number of children in the district. A group of white, middle-class parents immediately and adamantly opposed the new bungalows, fearing that they would bring transient children of low socioeconomic status from other, less desirable neighborhoods into their children's classrooms (which indeed happened). When the bungalows were installed over their protests, they attempted to rally the neighborhood to turn our school into a charter school. The dissatisfied parents derided teachers in public meetings and sent out inflammatory fliers to convince homeowners without school-age children to vote to change our school to a charter school. The fliers indicated that property values would rise if the measure passed.

Although the charter school proposal died—most teachers and other parents were happy with the school—the problems continued. My teaching partner had one of these parents come to her requesting her child's seat be changed because it was located in the same group as Rosa, a Spanish-speaking child who had recently moved here from Mexico. Rosa always completed her work and had not been a source of problems in this group. The school climate affected our decisions most profoundly during a unit on the migration of groups of people—in this case slaves in the American South. . . . Excitedly, my teaching partner and I prepared everything for the simulation, including

*a paper rendition of the Ohio River; then, as we were taping it to the floor,
she said, "What about the parents? I don't want any more phone calls to our
principal. I just know they're not going to go for this." We canceled the
simulation.*

—NAME WITHHELD
First-year teacher, grade 2

Even when diversity is not an issue, parents often seek educational advantages
for their children. In schools with ability-grouped classes, tracking, or with pull-out
programs for gifted students, for example, savvy parents invariably (and under-
standably) want their children enrolled in the "best" classes. Because so many
schools permit only a small percentage of student slots in high-track classes, many
parents feel they have few options but to push to have their children better educated than others.

We know of no strategies or programs that directly address the problem of
parents who exercise a disproportionate amount of influence over the schools'
programs and over decisions advantaging their own children. We have observed that
teachers or principals rarely can "manage" these parents unless *enough* parents are
involved and their involvement represents the entire school. In such a case, parents
may effectively subdue the most bothersome, intrusive, or self-serving individuals
and cliques, and the experience of working together can lower the distrust and fear
that different groups have of one another.

Removing barriers to participation is the most effective way to solve both
problems: parents not being involved enough, and parents who are inappropriately
involved. The remainder of this chapter provides an overview of strategies
educators have used to involve parents.

Removing Barriers to Constructive Parent Engagement

Schools have traditionally treated parents as helpers or clients—enlisting parents'
support or services *for the school,* and providing support *for families.* Parents are
asked to give to the school as the school sees fit, or receive from the school as the
school can best provide. This relationship is also consistent with the mainstream
culture in which it makes most sense for parties in different social classes to have
either a subservient or dominant role. At the same time, certain *counter*cultural
traditions have persisted without becoming widely popular: Some schools have
tried to retain their academic and social missions while becoming more compatible
with minority cultures, and that has resulted in blurring traditional power distinctions. In some cases outside groups or schools themselves have organized parents
for broad-based social and educational change within the school and in the community itself. All four traditions—parents supporting the school, the school supporting
parents, bridging the cultures between the school and communities, and organizing
for school and social change—have a role in promoting both learning and social
justice.

Parents Supporting the School's Agenda

Schools are most active when it comes to getting parents to support the school's agenda for students. Through all manners of communication—letters sent home, pleas at parent meetings, websites, and so on—the theme is that schools can't do it alone; parents must take an active role in their children's schooling. This traditional parent involvement seeks to have parents make sure that children come to school ready to learn—rested, well-fed, with proper materials, and with supervised homework completed. It emphasizes attending parent conferences, back-to-school night, PTA meetings, and other school events. It solicits parents' help at school—all the way from the proverbial bake sale, to making photocopies and supervising on the playground, to organizing and contributing to significant fund-raising activities that supplement the school's budget. More recently, it has included parents as participants in school governance and other decision-making activities.

Joyce Epstein, a prominent researcher on schools and families, concludes that educators need help in developing strategies for involving parents. Recognizing that families and communities are essential components of school and classroom organization is not a public relations activity. Such a rethinking of parents' roles, Epstein argues, requires more time, organization, and effort than schools are used to committing.

Epstein has developed a typology of parent involvement for developing partnerships with families and communities. (See Concept Table 10.1.) She argues that each type of involvement has particular challenges that must be met and that each leads to different results for students, families, and teachers. Note that most of these strategies focus on having parents and communities support and enhance the work of schools.

Joyce Epstein's work became extraordinarily popular in the last decade of the twentieth century and has done much to refine the traditional ways that schools have engaged parents. Types 1 and 2 in her typology echo a century-long effort to strengthen families' capacity to improve student learning, school behavior, and socialization into mainstream American culture. Types 3, 4, and 5 focus on teaching parents about and engaging them in the actual work of the school—whether it be the content of the curriculum or the procedures of school life.

These strategies have grown in popularity since the 1980s when, not coincidentally, political leaders began to emphasize families as children's first and most important teachers. The U.S. Department of Education reinforced just this view in a 1987 publication, *What Works,* outlining practices that promote school success. In it, federal officials asserted that no school can be effective without parental help. The National PTA has used Epstein's typology as the basis for national parent involvement standards. Today, schools that qualify for federal funding under the No Child Left Behind Act are required to have a written policy encouraging active parent involvement, and parents must be consulted in the writing of the plan. NCLB also includes funding to help parents learn more about standards and testing, and it requires that parents be consulted about how those funds should be spent.

CONCEPT TABLE 10.1 *Joyce Epstein's Parent Involvement Typology*

Parent Involvement Type	What Do Schools Do?
Type 1—Parenting	Assist families with parenting and child-rearing skills, understanding child and adolescent development, and setting home conditions that support children as students at each age and grade level; assist schools in understanding families.
Type 2—Communicating	Communicate with families about school programs and student progress through effective school-to-home and home-to-school communications.
Type 3—Volunteering	Improve recruitment, training, work, and schedules to involve families as volunteers and audiences at the school or in other locations to support students and school programs.
Type 4—Learning at home	Involve families with their children in learning activities at home, including homework and other curriculum-linked activities and decisions.
Type 5—Decision making	Include families as participants in school decisions, governance, and advocacy through parent-teacher organizations, school councils, committees, and other parent organizations.
Type 6—Collaborating with community	Identify and integrate community resources and services to enhance school and family practices and promote student achievement.

Source: Joyce Epstein, Lucretia Coates, Karen C. Salinas, Mavis G. Sanders, and Beth S. Simon, *School, Family, and Community Partnerships: Your Handbook for Action* (Thousand Oaks, CA: Corwin Press, 1997).

Despite these new requirements, most schools do not allow parents a deep influence over the core practices or resources of the school. Further, most parents have nowhere to learn about the school or their rights to participate, except at the school itself. Even when schools are entirely welcoming of parent participation, as many are, schools are not likely to actively teach parents how to question conventional practices. Perhaps it is too much to ask of any institution that it teach potential critics how to challenge the institution's own practices.

To manage the contradictory goal of encouraging parent participation that does not disrupt the status quo, schools often draw a clear line between the "professional" work and expertise of teachers and administrators and the "support" role that parents are expected to play. As one school administrator told us recently, "Parents are welcome when educators want them there."

"Low" parent involvement is usually explained in terms of individuals' attitudes, cultural deficits, or lack of knowledge. Epstein's sixth type of parent involvement suggests that schools can involve communities, as well as individual parents. This sixth type of involvement brings community resources into the school.

However, the sixth type is a limited step if the essential relationship between those who have power and those who do not remains the same. In other words, if schools, working together with community agencies, maintain the role of experts diagnosing problems and developing remedies, they are likely to help families "fit in" to existing structures and cement the status quo. Later in this chapter we consider two opportunities for parents, communities, and schools to consider profound changes in the distribution of power among all those who are needed to make schools just.

Teacher Mauro Bautista, whose work with parents is featured throughout this chapter, connects with families and neighborhoods in all six of the ways Epstein notes. He does so in ways that reflect his sensitivity to community norms. Like all teachers, he doesn't always get it right the first time. But his conviction that parents do care and want to be involved pushes him to try various ways to engage parents. Here's an example that probably fits into Epstein's second category—communication:

Not all of my home visits are planned. Recently, I visited the home of one of my students who had missed class six times. I handled the situation poorly at first. I made the student stay after school to do his work and "pay back" the hours he missed. When his mother came to pick him up, she was very upset. She asked me to let her know the punishment in advance, if he ever skipped class again. It was a very awkward conversation.

After he missed again, I handed him a letter that asked his mom to verify his absences. He refused to take the letter and ran out the door. That afternoon, I visited his house.

My student's mom received me very respectfully and offered me something to drink. After I explained why I was there and my strong interest in helping her son receive a good education, she asked him why he had not shown up to class. He answered that he does not like my classes because I give too much work. The mom made it perfectly clear that she did not approve of either his answer or his actions. She emphasized the importance of working hard in school. She thanked me for coming and asked me to keep her informed.

Now, this mother and I frequently talk about her son's progress. And, seeing that his mother and I had formed an alliance, this student has not missed a single day of class since my home visit. The conversations have not only improved his behavior, but also the quality of his academic work. The power of these interactions is evidence of the great care that many parents of low-income children of color have about their children's progress in school.

—Mauro Bautista
Middle-school bilingual education coordinator

In the photo on the next page, Mauro displays the T-shirts that parent volunteers wear at his school. The shirts not only identify the parents on campus, they also make those parents feel that their presence and help is valued—that they have an "official" role to play in the education of the neighborhood's children, not just their own.

Schools Meeting Families' Needs

One hundred years ago, approximately 2 million American children lived in poverty. Today the number approaches 14 million. Then and now educators seek ways to respond to the multiple problems poor children and their families face.

A Legacy of Services in Low-Income Communities

In the early 1900s, reformers advocated for public schools becoming "social centers" that would provide social and educational services to the broader community. Social reformers appealed to mainstream community interests and established programs that brought some relief to many poor, often oppressed, urban dwellers. Urban centers were polluted, unhealthy, dangerous, and congested, and residents had few common spaces to gather. In cities throughout the Northeast, schools and other public buildings began keeping their doors open for recreational and educational activities, sometimes dispensing health information and care, food and clothing, and perhaps job information.

Today, many low-income area schools offer children, but rarely adults, before- and after-school recreation programs, and perhaps government-subsidized breakfast and lunch. Often, school faculties, public health officials, social workers, police, and probation officers join forces to help students in various kinds of trouble or need. Sometimes teachers make regular home visits or lead activities at community centers to get a better sense of students' lives and to become known as members of the community.

Pathetic, needing charity, helpless, and a threat to the health, safety, economy, and morals of established citizens—this was the widespread view about poor and immigrant city dwellers at the start of the twentieth century. Schools and social service agencies (such as orphanages and other community relief agencies) often acted with compassion, but it was a compassion closely tied to the self-interests and perspectives of the emerging middle class. One turn-of-the-century reformer declared that "society must, as a measure of self-protection, take upon itself the responsibility of caring for the child."[9] Similar ties mark today's social and school services. Compassion, limited perspectives, and narrow self-interest all guide the charity we dispense. For example, the second-grade teacher quoted earlier whose school's decision to bring in portable classrooms evoked parent protests reported just such a mix of motives.

❀ ❀ ❀

One mother approached me a number of times with concern about the cleanliness of a child in our class. It was true that Steven often came to school dirty, wearing the same or ripped clothes. This mother came into our classroom, and, while I was occupied with a group of students, put a pair of new shoes on Steven's feet. Steven came up to me and said, "Look! Mrs. Wilson gave me new shoes!" Her behavior was totally unacceptable to me, considering the possible reaction Steven might get from his parents when he walked through the door in these gleaming new shoes. My experience with his parents made me worry about several things: Would his mom suspect him of stealing them? Would she get angry, when her son told her that another parent had given him the shoes, that other people had meddled in their business? Would she see this action as criticizing her for being a bad parent and provider? All kinds of scenarios entered my mind. While Mrs. Wilson might have meant this gesture in the kindest of ways, I saw potential for hurt feelings and conflict.

—**Name Withheld**
First-year teacher, grade 2

Individual acts of charity are just that: individuals acting on behalf of other individuals—often providing critical, even lifesaving, help, but perhaps offering only short-range help while diminishing another's dignity. Schooling is a public responsibility, and an increasing number of school projects are exploring ways to make schools places where low-income families can access health and social services routinely and with dignity.

Today's Full-Service Schools

In 1994 researcher Joy Dryfoos published a book that became enormously popular among school reformers: *Full-Service Schools: A Revolution in Health and Social Services for Children, Youth, and Families.*[10] Dryfoos documented a growing interest in formal collaborations among schools, social services, and health agencies to serve the multiple needs of low-income families. She argues that schools should use the resources of families, communities, and social service agencies to meet simultaneously students' academic, social, emotional, and health needs.

Full-service community schools provide necessary services such as child care, health care, nutrition, and counseling—crucial supports for both parents and children. Some full-service schools are part of national projects, like those affiliated with the Children's Aid Society and Schools of the 21st Century. Others, like the Molly Stark School in Bennington, Vermont, or the Polk Brothers Foundation Full Service Schools in Chicago, Illinois, are local initiatives. However, all such schools enlist the aid of various community members and groups to provide health and social services for youth and their families, so educators can spend more time focusing on teaching. They engage students in community service and service learning. Most are open most of the time—before school, after school, weekends, and summers—and see themselves as family resource centers.

Comer Schools   One of the most fully developed strategies for creating full-service schools is the School Development Project created by Yale psychiatrist James Comer. Recalling his own childhood experience as an African American growing up in a community that, while very poor, surrounded him with a safety net of watchful and caring adults, Comer has sought to create this experience for young people today. Because few such low-income communities of color have weathered the past few decades of urban decay, Comer has given the school the role of the supportive community he remembers.

Comer's "School Development Process" proceeds from a set of key assumptions. First, due to a lack of developmental support in their homes and communities, many of today's children come to school with developmental gaps and "experience deficits" that impair their ability to learn. Second, although the School Development Program recognizes and addresses the *experience* deficit that can inhibit development, it does not accept the *academic* deficit theory that leads to tracking and lowered expectations of minority and ESL students. The third premise is that students can and are entitled to reach high levels of academic achievement. Fourth, academic learning rests on a foundation of development in six critical areas of human development: physical, psychological, language, social, ethical, and cognitive. Fifth, students with experience deficits will reach their highest potential only if schools provide them with the developmental opportunities they lack. And, finally, schools cannot meet this challenge alone but must mobilize other adults, including parents, to help meet the developmental needs of the students.

Schools following Comer's approach mobilize community adults to support students' learning. Parents, teachers, and administrators are coequal members of a School Planning and Management Team that develops a comprehensive school plan; sets academic, social, and community relations goals; and coordinates school activities, including staff development programs. This team creates critical dialogue around teaching and learning and monitors progress to identify needed adjustments to the school plan as well as opportunities to support the plan.

A Student and Staff Support Team, composed of the principal and staff members with expertise in child development and mental health, such as a counselor, social worker, psychologist, or nurse, promotes desirable social conditions and relationships. This team connects all of the school's student services, facilitates the sharing of information and advice, addresses individual student needs, accesses resources outside the school, and develops prevention programs.

Finally, a Parent Team helps develop activities to support the school's social and academic programs. Studies of Comer Schools have found significant positive effects of the process on school climate, student attendance, and student achievement.[11]

21st Century Community Learning Initiative   During the Clinton administration, the full-service community school movement gained considerable momentum because it suited the national agenda for education reform. This movement speaks to concerns about high-risk youth and those with behavior problems while incorporating high academic standards. Following the examples of Comer and similar community-school projects, the Clinton administration and private foundations gave support to rural and inner-city public schools—in collaboration with other public and nonprofit agencies, organizations, local businesses, postsecondary institutions, and scientific/cultural and other community entities. As of 2005, the Initiative was serving 1.2 million children and 400,000 adults in 6,800 schools in 1,587 communities across all 50 states, D.C., and most U.S. territories.

The goal of the 21st Century Community Learning Initiative is to provide youth, parents, and community members with engaging and healthy activities in safe community settings. Schools can stay open longer, providing a safe place for homework centers, intensive mentoring in basic skills, drug and violence prevention counseling, helping middle-school students to prepare to take college prep courses in high school, enrichment in the core academic subjects as well as opportunities to participate in recreational activities, chorus, band and the arts, technology education programs, and services for children and youth with disabilities.

Proponents argue that this massive program gets us back to basics, back to active community involvement in raising and educating all of our children. An often espoused goal is to create a safe after-school and summer haven for children, away from the violence, drugs, and lack of supervision of children that permeate many low-income communities. Although it is unclear whether the program is reaching all its goals, parents of participants were more likely to attend parent-teacher organization meetings, after-school events, and open houses, and help with homework. There is some evidence that the students did their homework more consistently and, in some cases, achieved higher grades.[12]

Individual Teachers Reaching Out   Although it's far easier for teachers to support their students' broader set of needs when their schools encourage that support, some teachers can make strong contributions on their own. For example, one first-year mathematics teacher found his teaching role entirely compatible with his concerns for students and their families.

———————————————————————— ✂ ✂ ✂ ————————————————————————

My wife, a law student, and I visited a student's family to discuss immigration paperwork. They truly appreciate that we are trying to help them gain legal residency in the United States. Our conversation ends with so much appreciation and warmth. After we shake hands or kiss each other on the cheek (the way Latino families do) and exchange genuine words of thanks

and love, we walk away with mutual trust, or what Luis Moll more meaning-
fully calls "confianza." I look forward to building more of these trusting
relationships as I become a more experienced teacher.

—**NAME WITHHELD**
First-year teacher, high school mathematics

Across the country and each day, many individual teachers connect with families and communities to help them navigate complicated social processes such as obtaining health care and social services, negotiating the juvenile justice system, and grappling with immigration regulations.

Service, Power, and Deficits

Often, service-oriented schools, programs, and individual efforts are energetic, even heroic attempts to empower families to be effective participants within schools. They are guided by an underlying assumption that the physical, educational, and social health of families and communities must be self-determining and self-sustaining, which is to say that people must actively shape their own destinies.

But something is missing from this picture of service providing. It has to do with the oxymoron—the contradictory concept—of *empowering others*. This concept of empowerment can presume that one party has no power until it is bestowed by another. In fact, the concept can communicate the exact opposite of what it supposedly intends because "giving" power reinforces the idea that the giver is more powerful (and can also take away or *dis*empower).

Similarly, some people associate the service-providing model with a "deficit view" of teaching and program design. We prefer a "bridge-building" model. Whereas "service" and "empowerment" are directional—that is, they typically flow from the direction of those who have to those who need—"bridge" implies no such direction. A bridge does not guarantee a two-way flow of respect, of valuing one another's cultures, and of mutual adaptability; but it can allow these processes and dispositions to thrive.

Bridging the Cultures of Schools and Families

———————————————— ❧ ❧ ❧ ————————————————

As I pass through my community day and night, I feel proud of the countless
strengths and positive characteristics it has. I observe hard workers. I see peo-
ple who have so much imagination. I see a beautiful culture. I see so much life.

—**MARTHA GUERRERO**
First-year teacher, high school social studies

Recognizing individuals' and communities' assets, strengths, and beauty does not mean that one is blind to their needs. Likewise, recognizing that parents have enormous competence does not mean that they have the resources or power to act on behalf of their children when faced with complicated school structures and bureaucracies in addition to their everyday challenges. The ideal solution is to construct parent involvement that builds on the cultural strengths and educational resources found in local communities.

—❀ ❀ ❀—

Many teachers use Parent Night as a forum to address such concerns as lack of homework assignments, but it can also be used to connect teachers and the parents. We conducted two Parent Night sessions over the course of the school year. Both nights, parents waited in line while I communicated my desire to partner with them to ensure their child's success.

Because I speak Spanish, I am better able to bridge two cultures, the school culture and the student/parent home culture. Often, immigrant parents treat teachers with such reverence and respect that the concept of building a partnership seems foreign. However, each time I send letters home, call parents, and conduct conferences in Spanish, the partnership grows.

—**JUDY SMITH**
High school social studies teacher

Judy Smith's bilingual skills give her greater access to the strong loyalties and pride her students and their parents have in their culture. It is clear also that Judy's ability to communicate with *all* of her parents is not exclusively a "service" to them, but greatly enhances her satisfaction with her work as a teacher.

"Bridging," as we are using it here, emphasizes the mutual satisfactions of respect, collegiality, and family that teachers can develop within their school communities. This perspective—building bridges to people and their strengths—has roots in the work of Jane Addams and other early-twentieth-century urban reformers. Addams's "settlement house" built on and developed the strengths of immigrant cultures. She and a group of well-to-do young women established Hull House and spent their days providing tangible and very much needed services. They cared for children, taught, nursed the sick, and helped immigrant families grapple with horrendous problems in their new lives. But simultaneously, dozens of classes and clubs met at Hull House with the goal of maintaining the immigrants' expression of their cultures, alongside easing them into knowledge of American ways and language.

The settlement house tradition went beyond the pragmatic "basic skills" of reading and writing and included essential cultural tools of mainstream middle-class life and dignity—including the arts, discussion, and political action. Rather than pitying her immigrant neighbors, fearing them, or treating them with a detached professionalism, Addams worked within the community, visiting her neighbors' homes and workplaces. Her personal interaction with her neighbors strengthened her belief that social equality is a foundation for community life and individual expression.

Learning with and from Communities

The lesson we draw from Jane Addams's work is that connecting with low-income families is a virtue that includes, but is greater than, providing services for the less fortunate. Addams drew together disparate individuals and groups to form a community with community-minded norms. Hull House was a central gathering place, a community center, an education and research community, and a forum for political action. The norms and ethics of Hull House engaged immigrants in ways that fit their strengths, perspectives, and capacities to serve others. The distinctive feature of Hull House was not that it was a "haven" in a deficient community, but that it was a place where community members could strengthen their own community life.

Contemporary educational philosopher Nel Noddings would probably say that Addams's approach embodies an "ethic of care," in contrast to the "ethic of service" that drives many schools' interactions with families, especially in low-income communities. Importantly, an ethic of care expects all participants to understand the conditions that affect them, even if this understanding exposes the faults of local institutions such as schools, law enforcement, social services, and so forth. While an ethic of service focuses on providing prescribed benefits, an ethic of care fosters competence in students', families', and communities' unique needs and aspirations. Caring teachers and administrators listen carefully and act respectfully in response to knowledge they acquire about the experiences, meanings, and preferences of community members. This empathetic relationship frees educators from the common judgments made about families and communities, such as *incapable, uninvolved, not caring,* and so on.

Researcher Angela Valenzuela explores care as it relates to the schooling of Mexican immigrant students. She calls attention to the Mexican idea of *educación* and how it is relevant to teachers' work with all groups of students. For Mexican American students, for example, care includes relationships and school content that affirm their worth as culturally Mexican, and this affirmation helps teachers bridge the cultures of home and school. Without this careful attention, teachers can actually *subtract* students' culture from them, rather than adding the new U.S. ways of schooling to their already rich cultural repertoire. Strong communication between school and home, teachers who are deeply knowledgeable about the students' home language and culture, opportunities for personal and authentic interactions between teachers, students, and their families could all help to dismantle "subtractive schooling" practices.[13]

Learning from families and community members enhances teachers' capacity to care, but care is not only about "knowing"; it requires doing as well. W. E. B. DuBois addresses this crucial element of *care.* He instructs teachers to reach back in time and acknowledge the history of their students' and community's social circumstances. In his 1935 article "Does the Negro Need Separate Schools?" DuBois argued:

> The proper education of any people includes sympathetic touch between teacher and pupil; knowledge on the part of the teacher, not simply of the individual taught, but of his surroundings and background, and the history of his class and group; such contact between pupils, and between teacher and pupil, on the basis of perfect social equality, as will increase this sympathy and knowledge.[14]

With his notion of *sympathetic touch* DuBois captures three qualities of care that, taken together, bridge schools and communities. First, an empathetic understanding allows educators to know the experiences and aspirations of those for whom they care. Second, because understanding alone is not enough, educators must act in ways that respond to their understanding. Finally, "surroundings and background" and history are not simply artifacts of the past but a scaffold and guide for the future. Caring teachers help students and their parents convert their competence and histories into resources for building their futures.

Unfortunately, few comprehensive school and community engagement projects evoke images of Hull House or establish conditions for teachers to exercise a *sympathetic touch*. Nevertheless, many teachers, on their own and with the support of like-minded colleagues, do reach out in caring and sympathetic ways. They work to establish relationships that allow them to gain a deep understanding of their students and communities, and they respond by demonstrating that knowledge in their lessons and relationships. Kimberly Min chose to be just this kind of teacher in a neighborhood quite different from the protected, middle-class one she grew up in. Her view is that her work benefits not only her students, but her own family as well:

---------------------------------⚹ ⚹ ⚹---------------------------------

I chose to teach at a school in the heart of south Los Angeles. When I told my friends and family where I was teaching, many were very concerned about my safety. My only response was that I wanted to be in an area where they needed more credentialed teachers. In fact, this is not the safest place to be.

However, it is my school, and I love to teach here. Once I saw my students for the first time, my full concentration and energies were placed on them. I was able to set aside my anxiety about the school and focus on social justice teaching. I began to explore the community. As a class we took a walking field trip to the library and the fire station, which took us past the park, the banks, and stores. This was a part of the community I had never seen, and I felt more empowered by familiarizing myself with the area.

I visited students' homes early in the day so I would feel safer in the neighborhood. Over the winter break, I visited 16 homes. My brief visits strengthened my communication with parents. I understood better how the harsh conditions in their neighborhoods affected both children and parents. Parents explained their concerns about "gang bangers" down the street, the lack of "safe places" for their children to go, and their reasons for "no open windows or doors." Many parents see the school as "okay," but see their neighborhood as "unsafe, dirty, and full of gang bangin.'"

I felt empowered by knowing that I was welcome and accepted in any of my students' homes. In spite of our cultural and ethnic differences we are together in wanting the best for the children that we share. Many parents say they pray for me, they send their good wishes, their hugs, and kisses of gratitude for the work that I am doing.

Many families have lived in the area for generations. Many of my students' parents are graduates of the school. The roots of the community run deep, and the wisdom and love from the parents and grandparents I encounter give me a surge of energy and a sense of inclusion.

I continue to feel the community's tension, but I am also increasingly grateful for the families' support during the year. I have learned and grown so much. What is so great about this experience is that the people close to me—family and friends—who once thought so poorly about this community, have changed their perceptions as they see my work and hear my stories about what my students and school mean to me. I am not the only one growing from this experience.

—**KIMBERLY MIN**
Third-grade teacher

Bridging Students' "Multiple Worlds"

Bridging the cultures of neighborhood and school is one of the joys of teaching. However, the bridge is not one that is anchored in cement on two sides of a chasm; there are multiple bridges, and they are movable and flexible. Since educators are not necessarily more skilled at connecting with other people's communities than families and students are at connecting with schools, we need one another's help.

The wish to bridge the worlds of school and families is clear in the relationships that first-year teachers Mary Ann Pacheco, Zeba Palomino, and Benji Chang developed with parents.

———————————————❈ ❈ ❈———————————————

Generally, Latino parents hesitate to approach or question teachers because teaching is highly respected. I made myself very accessible and expressed my interest in their understanding bilingual education, student learning, and the importance of their voices in public education. I also built personal relationships, made phone calls and home visits. I reinforced their cultural beliefs but made them aware of certain characteristics that they might want to help their children develop. For example, during parent conferences, some parents were concerned with their child's tendency to talk excessively. Many times, I reminded them that in higher education, the willingness to initiate conversations, participation in group projects, and dialogue were required of students and highly valued. I told them about the endless number of oral presentations, speeches, and debates I had to deliver throughout my educational career. I emphasized that they should not discourage their child's talk, but that together we could empower their children by helping them be responsible in [their speech].

—**MARY ANN PACHECO**
First-year teacher, grade 2

———————————————❈ ❈ ❈———————————————

Most of my immigrant students come from low-income families, have parents who speak little or no English, and have little or no high school education. Lack of education, language barriers, and time constraints prevent them from making meaningful connections to their children's school. This does not mean, however, that parents do not value education. They simply do not know how to get involved. For example, when I called parents to invite them to Back to School Night, quite a few were surprised and pleased to speak with a teacher in Spanish. The school had never contacted them before. They were not aware of Back to School Night, and they had no idea of their power as parents in their children's education. They rely on their children to relay information about school, but often the students themselves do not have enough information about how to steer their education or they choose not to talk to their families about it.

My job is twofold: I must provide students with the support they need to learn math as they develop their English skills, and I must help students connect their home culture with their school culture so that they can understand and succeed.

—**Zeba Palomino**
First-year teacher, high school mathematics

———————————————————— ❈ ❈ ❈ ————————————————————

I went to work right away to become familiar with my students' back-grounds. I observed and asked questions. I wanted to communicate a sense of respect for my students' diverse communities and put their backgrounds in the forefront of my lessons. I made it a point to be visible off campus, and before and after school. From day one, I talked with parents and guardians outside of class, and sent home the first of my weekly home letters, explaining and requesting a home visit. I eventually visited, and usually shared a meal, at 18 of my 20 students' homes. In these visits I forged stronger home-school connections and uncovered invaluable information that would shape my curriculum and instruction. I communicated to parents and guardians that they were the experts on their child. I asked about their child's strengths and areas needing improvement.

I used to picture collaboration with families as parents coming to class to help out or at least helping students with their schoolwork every day at home. I now realize that this model was shaped by my middle-class back-ground. My model did not account for working-class families or families at the poverty level, where parents and other family members are always working and cannot "collaborate" with me. My old ideas did not account for families who do have time but do not understand assignments because they were not educated in English. Now I realize that there are many ways to collaborate. Although they may not come in the way that I expected, these collaborative relationships support students in powerful ways.

—**Benji Chang**
First-year teacher, grade 2

Like Mauro Bautista, Judy Smith, and Kimberly Min, all three of these teachers have gone far beyond typical "parent involvement" strategies to find ways to bridge their students' multiple worlds.

Bridging through the Curriculum

Teachers can design lessons that connect students' schoolwork and "official" curriculum to their experiences in the world, community, and home. Finding and solving real problems that matter to students make schoolwork less abstract and detached. These might be similar to the type of lessons referred to in Luis Moll's documentation of "funds of knowledge" in poor Mexican American homes and neighborhoods and those of two teachers who used community resources to develop elaborate lessons (see Chapter 5). In Chapter 7, we described the work of teachers who developed culturally relevant classrooms by connecting parents and community with lessons.

Veteran kindergarten teacher Vivian Paley, in *Kaawanza and Me,* shows how middle-class white teachers can talk directly and honestly with nonwhite parents, colleagues, and children about their experiences. Paley's work also reveals that bringing community-based curriculum into classrooms means that teachers need to learn about and confront the racism and discrimination that many families experience in communities and schools.

Paley's racially and culturally sensitive kindergarten classroom practices began with a conversation with a former student. This young African American woman, now in college, shared her painful recollections of loneliness and worry in Paley's kindergarten class. Paley, on the other hand, remembered her as a happy member of her racially integrated classroom. What had Paley missed? Paley began a series of honest conversations about racism with her students' parents. Their stories were so rich and powerful, revealing enormous joy and sadness, that Paley invited parents to bring the stories of family traditions and daily life into her diverse classroom. The *Kaawanza* stories that emerged became the basis for students bridging their multiple worlds with each other and their schoolwork.

First-year teacher Christina Haug made stories like Paley's an important part of her curriculum.

---------------------------------⚬⚬⚬⚬⚬⚬---------------------------------

Kenny, a Latino student, has a close relationship with his grandmother who tells him stories about family members, folk tales, and cultural legends. He is a valuable resource for oral storytelling. He also learns that his culture is not being ignored in the classroom, particularly since he is a racial minority. As he shares family stories, he becomes a teacher for our class, educating us about his home culture and language.

—CHRISTINA HAUG
First-year teacher, grade 2

High school social studies teacher Judy Smith also integrates family and community knowledge into the curriculum of her economics course:

———————————————————❈ ❈ ❈———————————————————

In my economics class, students used their parents' knowledge and experience to help them. For the project "How to Make a Living," students asked parents about utility bills, late rent payments, and car buying procedures. Students generated a six-month budget to live financially independently. In their write-ups many of them referenced their parents as a source of information.

In the international economics unit, students compared consumer habits now with economic life 20–30 years ago. Many students realized that they own more and have freedoms their parents did not have.

In still another class assignment, students create their own businesses. I pushed students to think like producers rather than consumers. They create a business plan and discuss business ownership with their parents. Many students used their parents' work experience to write their plans. One student modeled her business after her father's boat repair business. Another student opened a business that competed with his father's spark plug store. A third student, familiar with her mother's work in a beauty salon, documented her plan for opening a nail shop.

Our field trips exposed students both to opportunities and social problems in the larger community. We traveled to downtown Los Angeles to Homeboy Industries [a community-based organization that engages gang members in running a thriving bakery business] and the Los Angeles Central Library. At the library they attended "Choosing to Participate," a Facing History exhibition that emphasized the individual's power to make a difference.

—JUDY SMITH
High school social studies

Our own experience for nearly a decade with the Futures project in Southern California showed several ways that senior high school students and their families bridge the worlds of home and school to increase students' likelihood of going to college. The Futures project began in the fall of 1997 when our research team joined with Anthony Collatos, a local high school teacher, in developing a ninth-grade humanities class into a four-year program that would help students navigate the pathway to college. Although the high school was very diverse, and included lots of middle-class white students, this class was made up entirely of low-income, underrepresented students, mostly Latino and African American.

Over four years, in addition to completing their college preparatory coursework, the students joined UCLA researchers in studying issues relevant to their own high school experiences and future plans. They investigated questions of student resistance in high school, hip-hop and popular culture, the influence of parents on education, as well as the influence of language on educational access. They examined patterns of school success and failure, including how students are tracked into different social and academic groups.

In the summer of 2000, the students conducted research at the Democratic National Convention. This experience put them in contact with many national and local leaders. Students interviewed community, political, and media leaders on topics of access to education, access to media, the living wage movement, urban civic engagement, and social justice. This community-based work was supported by classroom study and research, and vice versa. The student-researchers have presented their research to university faculty, graduate students, administrators, teachers, community members, and teachers in training.

The project also helped bridge the students' worlds of family and school. Monthly meetings, called "Futures and Families," brought greater family awareness of college pathways, and at the same time, eased parents' feelings of isolation from the school. These bilingual programs helped parents learn about college access for their children and included discussions of admissions requirements and financial aid options, hands-on workshops on deciphering school transcripts, and searching for colleges on the Internet. Parents increased their awareness of the social and political obstacles to college (such as tracking and SATs). Personal stories of students and alumni of color, as well as school staff, brought useful strategies to these parents. Perhaps most important, the parents learned that they were not alone in their goals for and struggles with their children. As one mother said, "If I didn't have that program, I would have felt like I was by myself [in trying to get her child to college]."[15]

The Futures students have graduated from high school, and most moved on to college. Several now have bachelor's degrees. The connections among them, their teacher, and their families remain very strong.

Bridging through Community Liaisons

Our Futures project would have been far less likely to succeed in building bridges if it were not for the support of Tere Viramontes, an extraordinarily knowledgeable community liaison. Viramontes, a longtime community member and former parent at the high school, could deftly navigate homes, churches, and community organizations, as well as the school because all of these settings were hers as well.

When schools involve parents and community members in connecting families and schools, they are taking advantage of essential knowledge and relationship opportunities that are unavailable elsewhere. Further, the liaison workers contribute enormously to teachers' understanding of and capacity to work with families. Such respectful links between home and school help students develop academically, socially, and personally.

Gina Rodriguez and Miriam Rogers are two school-community liaisons who were colleagues of Viramontes. Their stories do much to dispel deficit-laden assumptions about members of low-income communities of color while supporting the school's mission of educating all students well (see Focal Point 10.1).

FOCAL POINT 10.1

Bridging Schools and Communities
Gina Rodriguez and Miriam Rogers, Parent Liaisons

Gina Rodriguez was born in Tijuana, Mexico. Her family immigrated to the United States when she was five. Gina eventually attended and graduated from college, where she majored in political science and was active in a Chicano political organization called MEChA that focuses on gaining access to quality education and other resources. Gina now serves as a facilitator/coach for both parents and teachers at her elementary school. She aids in strategic planning, goal setting and gaining access to resources. She also bridges the language and cultural gaps between parents and teachers.

Gina helped parents to realize that they had a right to be involved in their child's education and helped them create a parent center on the school campus where they can come to work on current concerns and issues. One of the strengths of the parent center is that the leadership is shared among all parents. The parents meet weekly and organize major fund-raisers. They also organized the sale and promotion of school uniforms as a way to deal with safety issues. The school staff has become more accepting of parent involvement both inside and outside the classroom. Parent concerns and ideas are now welcomed, respected, and taken seriously, and Gina played a significant role in this transformation.

Miriam Rogers is the parent of a fifth grader and president of the Will Rogers School's African-American Parents group (WRAAP), in addition to her official job as the school's community liaison. Last year, when troubling statistics showed [low academic achievement among] African American students, Rogers brought parents and teachers together to form WRAAP. In addition to promoting academic achievement, WRAAP's goals are to provide parent voice, seek parent vision, strengthen relations between teachers and parents, and provide a place where parents can feel connected to the school. WRAAP is working to foster relationships of respect and tolerance between African American and Latino children on campus. WRAAP has set up a bicultural parents' meeting and plans to create other bicultural events, forums, and social exchanges. WRAAP has a hotline number for students' questions or concerns.

WRAAP also strives to empower students with information about historical and contemporary African American leaders and current events. Weekly, students receive the WRAAP Sheet that includes a quote for the week, a profile of one important African American leader and his or her contributions, as well as vocabulary pertaining to that leader's field. Recently, students performed at a Teacher Appreciation Breakfast sponsored by the WRAAP group. Students read poetry and literature written by African American authors, and they beamed in the spotlight as they performed. Miriam has helped some of the students in this performance who are thought of as problems in the classroom to express themselves in a more positive and creative light.

Source: From John Rogers and Carolyn Castelli, *Building Social Justice for a New Generation,* UCLA IDEA Occasional Paper, 1996.

Partnering with Families and Communities in Educational Activism

An activist approach to improving school opportunities draws from the collective power of residents to solve public problems; this power to solve comes from critically examining community issues and taking action to solve them. Parents who are community activists can be especially effective in bringing socially just schooling to all of the neighborhood's children. Parent activists are also uniquely well positioned to bridge families and schools. Parents who have organized to promote social change do not see themselves as *em*powered by others; their empowerment is derived from their collective actions and "wins," whereby each successful activity informs and emboldens them. By contrast, typical school-controlled support projects may speak of empowering parents, but they often place limits on parents' "power" if parents' goals differ from the school's agenda.

This fourth way of connecting with parents and communities is probably the least mainstream, the least understood, and the most worrisome to traditional educators—but it also has a long tradition in American schooling.

A Tradition of Parent Activism

Parent activism is not a recent phenomenon. It began more than a century ago, and its roots are found in what are now the most traditional parent organizations.

The PTA   The forerunner of the PTA—the National Congress of Mothers—can be traced back to 1897. The Congress was founded to act on behalf of children in the home, at school, and in the world. From the beginning, this group's advocacy extended far beyond having parents help out with schoolwork or supporting their local schools. That early group voiced public concern over the juvenile justice system, the need for child labor laws, and for federal aid to schools. It promoted cooperation between parents and teachers, advocated for sex education, and lobbied for a national health bureau. By the early 1900s fathers were also urged to join.

In the early twentieth century, the PTA and the National Congress of Colored Parents and Teachers (the latter formed to serve children in segregated states) were well known for advocating for reforms in health, safety, and nutrition. By mid-century they had secured health programs, school lunches, and regulations governing school bus safety. In the second half of the century the groups (not integrated until the 1970s) addressed drug addiction, the effects of smoking, child protection and toy safety, violence on television, automobile safety belt and child restraint legislation, the circumstances of children and families in the inner cities, and HIV/AIDS education.

Today, the national PTA continues to take progressive stands on many of these issues and tries to have its membership reflect the changing demographics of the country.[16] On the other hand, local PTA groups are often far more conservative in their activities, content to raise money and solicit volunteers to help the school carry out its agenda.

Community Schools   A second long-standing activist tradition comes out of the "community schools" movement described earlier in this chapter. Broadly speaking, community schools began as local efforts to blur the distinction between communities and schools. Only recently has local community activism around schooling coalesced into national groups that support and inform one another's efforts. We discuss these more recent efforts in a later section of this chapter. For the most part, however, community schools have bucked the national century-long trend toward bureaucratic state and national education policies, and away from grassroots control.

It is not surprising that wherever one finds an emphasis on community activism, empowerment, improvement, and local control of schools, there is a good chance of finding political activism as well. In the early 1900s many of the "social centers" included political activities. Much of this activity—to the consternation of the elites who supported these centers—focused on socialist causes and advocacy for minority political views. Some progressive schools—particularly private and special laboratory schools—developed curricula that engaged students in studying community problems and advocating for solutions.

During the Depression years, public schools purposefully began taking up social causes. The social reconstructionist curriculum movement, discussed in Chapter 3, argued strongly that schools should develop community-based curricula that engaged schools and students in bettering local conditions. For example, Leonard Covello's tenure as principal of East Harlem's immigrant community's high school was marked by curricula designed to investigate and shape policies in the local neighborhoods, including a campaign for public housing.

By the late 1960s community schools began to focus on local communities' power over the school itself. In the midst of social activism around civil rights and civic unrest in many cities, some local communities—particularly African American communities—sought to wrest control from the education professionals and politicians whom they viewed as part of an oppressive government that had frustrated the quest for equal educational opportunity.

The best-known example of the struggle for local control of schools took place in the Ocean Hill–Brownsville neighborhood of New York City. There, activists employed lessons about civil disobedience and power learned from the civil rights movement. Only direct community participation, these leaders believed, would allow schools to shift from being a source of inequality to being a solution to it. Only if local community members were involved in selecting school personnel and curriculum would the schools be accountable for shaping the next generation in ways that would advance the community itself.

Although the Ocean Hill–Brownsville experiment collapsed in the face of opposition from traditional power bases, including political interests, business, and unions, it sowed the seeds for a new type of parent and community activism. Today, low-income communities increasingly seek to hold schools accountable for providing high-quality education to their children. And while teachers and community members were clearly at odds in New York's struggle over who would control the schools, increasing numbers of teachers today are making common cause with activists in the communities where they teach.[17] In the twenty-first century, this new way of connecting with families and communities may prove to be a powerful strategy for social justice school reform.

Contemporary Organizing for School Reform

—————————————————— ✂ ✂ ✂ ——————————————————

Truly transformative teaching must be coupled with activism and resistance in the larger community. I have been involved with an activist organization that fights for equitable school reform. Such organizations represent opportunities to create meaningful alliances with other educators, parents, and students. It is not enough for me to encourage my students to become more active. I must walk the talk myself.

MATTHEW EIDE
First-year teacher, High school history

Community organizing, generally, can be defined as "the work that occurs in local settings to empower individuals, build relationships, and create action for social change."[18] It entails building relationships that can sustain people through difficult struggles and support political action. In the photo here, Mario Bautista holds a flier distributed by Inner-City Struggle, a parent group he supports in his school. The flier advertises a program that includes teachers and students from East Los Angeles advocating for better college preparation in local schools.

Grassroots community organizations are influenced by several traditions. Saul Alinksy's "self-interest"-based model is one of public confrontation between organized "have nots" and powerful, more advantaged "targets" whose concessions can provide solutions to community problems.

Other, less confrontational traditions come from women's work to extend caring into communities beyond the confines of families and home. For example, African American women maintained networks of communication and support during slavery; these were precursors for women's success during the civil rights movement when they were able to transform that tradition into a political force for social change. At the turn of the twentieth century, Jane Addams and other white women saw social networks, social services, and enriching community life as key to supplementing the protections afforded by families in low-income and immigrant neighborhoods. These feminist organizing traditions have contemporary counterparts in mobilization efforts for safer neighborhoods, child care, and youth programs.

Despite their great variety, however, most community organizing shares the perspective that power for change exists within networks of people who identify with common ideals and who can engage in social action based on those ideals.[19]

In the past decade, many local grassroots organizations—focused originally on issues of housing, jobs, and public safety—have turned their attention to school improvement. Perhaps the best known of these efforts has taken place in Texas, where the Industrial Areas Foundation (IAF) joined forces with educators to improve achievement in public schools in low-income neighborhoods. The IAF, a national group begun over 50 years ago by Saul Alinsky, is a network of broad-based multiethnic interfaith organizations. IAF reveals the possibilities of educators and parents joining forces and exercising power over schooling.

Relationships, Common Understandings, and Action   Former civil rights and farmworker organizer Marshall Ganz synthesizes this work into three components of grassroots organizing: relationships, common understandings, and action. Each of these components helps to create bridges among schools, families, and communities.

First, organizers of community-school initiatives spend considerable time talking with parents and educators to learn about their personal concerns for their children's school. Then, within this culture of conversation, people form *relationships* based on common concerns. IAF organizers, for example, conduct a "situational audit" that has everyone in the school community identify its positive and negative aspects. They identify areas of overlapping self-interest with other parents and, if possible, with educators at a school. Organizers also sponsor "neighborhood walks," in which parents and educators gather at a school and then go out to visit parents at home; the aim is to engage families in conversation about their concerns for the school and community.

Organizers also develop relationships through new and existing networks, often churches or other community-based groups. Individuals draw confidence and knowledge from the networks—a power often described as social capital—and, in turn, they contribute to the power of the networks. This power can begin to counter or balance that of the existing leadership and power in communities and schools, which might include voters, powerful and/or wealthy people, "old boy" and other networks, loyal employees, and so forth. Only when underserved families speak with a unified and coherent voice can they grab and hold the attention of the people who currently hold power. In this way a collective voice becomes power, and power exercised on behalf of all children becomes a social action.

A number of theorists have proposed that belonging to a community creates norms of reciprocity. That is, when people belong to the same social circle, they can count on one another to keep commitments and work on one another's behalf. Leadership development is another key to developing power in these relationships. As networks grow and mature, organizers let go of the leadership. The goal is to locate the responsibility for solving problems in the group and in the leaders within it. Steady attention to relationships makes it safe for people to trust one another—

especially during those important stages when new members might not know one another well or understand fully one another's backgrounds and strengths.

Common understanding—a second key feature of community organizing— develops as people engage in dialogue about their situations and generate more hopeful alternatives. Such dialogue is constructive. That is, participants are not rushed into accepting others' descriptions, analyses, and solutions for problems; they build and rebuild their new understandings while adding to the knowledge and insights of others. Through this collective effort, problems initially experienced by individuals are reframed as community, social, or collective problems. As people share their common interests, they develop a collective identity that actually strengthens their individual "agency." No longer helpless against insurmountable odds, they experience a growing sense of personal power over their own futures. They know that when they speak from their heart and their personal experiences, they are also representing the feelings and experiences of others.

Acting together, then, is not a strategy for accomplishing individual concerns; rather, joint action makes sense because the groups' interests and individual interests are seen as indistinguishable. The dialogic pedagogy developed by Paulo Freire in his work with Brazilian peasants, described in Chapter 7, is probably the best example of such generative dialogue. Groups construct a story of who they are, what they do, and why they do it. That "story" points to ways for the group to realize the more hopeful possibilities they've framed.

Third, the emergence of an *activist* community begins when groups pursue a particular objective—often small at first. Often the group acts on a grievance long held by individuals but newly articulated as a jointly held claim. Now the community can strategize about how to use resources at the right moment to achieve its goals. These focused campaigns achieve what the community might call tangible "progress," but they also develop the community itself and increase its capacity to take on larger goals.

All three of these dimensions—relationships, new understandings, and actions—enable communities to gain and use new resources. They both create and result from networks, they frame a story about the network's identity and purpose, and they develop a program of action that mobilizes and expends resources to advance the community's interests.

Ernesto Cortes, former director of the Texas IAF project, explains what he witnessed as parents became organized activists:

> When parents and community members are truly engaged, they are organized to act on their own values and visions for their children's future. They do not just volunteer their time for school activities or drop their opinions in the suggestion box. They initiate action, collaborating with educators to implement ideas for reform. This kind of engagement can only happen through community institutions— public schools, churches, civic associations. These institutions provide the public space where people of different backgrounds connect with one another, listen to each other's stories, share concerns; this is where they argue, debate, and deliberate. In these institutions, individuals transcend the boundaries of their private lives to form public relationships. In the context of these public relationships, parents and community members can initiate conversations

around their core concerns and values. These conversations go beyond the discussion of surface problems and complaints. Through these conversations, people develop the trust and consensus needed for action.[20]

Community and parent activism for better schools is increasing. A recent study of 29 community-based organizations working on education reform in California found that these groups have an impact both in local schools and communities. These organizations have improved the safety of school facilities and successfully advocated for increasing the equity of school and district policies and practices. Activist young people, parents, and community members have won seats on school boards and other decision-making bodies. Parents and community members expanded their base of members in both local organizing and in a statewide movement. This sustained organizing has led to an increased awareness of educational inequality and has advanced an equity agenda across the state.[21]

UCLA's Parent Curriculum Project   Former math teacher Dr. Laila Hasan, now a teacher educator at UCLA, has implemented an approach to parent organizing that combines the principles of community organizing with helping parents gain a solid understanding of high-quality teaching and learning. Teachers are allies and partners in this work.

Hasan works with parents in very low-income neighborhoods where the once African American community is being rapidly replaced by immigrant, Spanish-speaking families. These communities have some of the state's most dismal schools. Large numbers of underqualified teachers, constant turnover in the ranks of school administrators, and limited curriculum offerings limit students' and families' capacity to grapple with problems of poverty, unemployment, gang- and drug-related violence, and racial tension. School dropout rates are extremely high, achievement rates are extremely low, and college going is rare.

During a 10-week seminar and after, Hasan and the parents engage in processes explicitly aimed at developing relationships, constructing a collective story of who they are and what they hope to accomplish, and taking action on behalf of their children and their children's schools. Throughout, the parents themselves become the initiators and leaders of the work, rather than acting like traditional students or clients.

Hasan's project begins by engaging 20 to 30 parents at a time in the seminar in which parents examine the practices at their children's schools. Teachers play a key role, coming to meetings and demonstrating what high-quality lessons in various subjects are like. The parents become the "students" as these teachers teach. That means that the parents, many for the first time, have firsthand experiences with very high-quality teaching and learning in academic subjects. In English and Spanish, expert teachers guide the parents through the writing process, science laboratory experiments, algebraic thinking, and historical inquiry. They learn about standardized testing, as well as grading and tracking practices. They learn what to look for when observing in classrooms, and they practice asking hard questions of teachers and principals. They gain experience comparing what they learn in the seminar with what occurs in their children's classrooms. As a culminating project they design and carry out an action project that includes other parents also committed to gaining high-quality teaching and learning in the community's schools.

With over 300 program graduates, modest beginnings have developed into a significant activist parent presence. The group became its own nonprofit, community-based organization. Many project members now hold influential positions on school-leadership committees, and a Latina mother recently won an election for a seat on the school board. Through the efforts of the group, overcrowded schools that had been operating on year-round schedules that shortened the school year for each child by 17 days have now been returned to traditional school calendars.[22]

The theory at work in these parent groups, much like that in other community organizing for school reform, is that parent advocacy must be based on a good understanding of state and local policy, high standards for learning, and high-quality teaching. As parents come to understand what a really good school looks like and what their rights as parents are, they are likely to set out to accomplish needed changes.

Cross-Class and Cross-Race Parent Activist Groups—Parents for Public Schools Both the Texas IAF and the UCLA Parent Project focus exclusively on communities and schools that are low income and of color. That's not surprising, since these are the types of neighborhoods where parents are least likely to be involved at school, and where activism for school improvement is most desperately needed. However, there are some examples of cross-class and cross-race organizing efforts for school reform. Perhaps the most notable is Parents for Public Schools (PPS), which began as a local initiative in 1989 in Jackson, Mississippi. A group of 20 parents decided to mobilize parents who reflected the full diversity of their town to build strong public schools and a healthier, more vital community out of their southern city that had been badly torn by school segregation, desegregation, and white flight.

The Jackson group began by recruiting families one by one. Through information sessions in their homes, they began to cultivate a new sense of the importance of strong public schools to the community and to create an awareness of the sound education being offered in the public schools of Jackson. Over time PPS brought racial balance to four primary schools in northeast Jackson and promoted a $35 million bond issue—the first to pass since desegregation.

Soon after the Jackson victory—which was featured in the national news media—parents in other communities began forming PPS chapters, and the organization now has a organizational presence in 15 states. While individual chapter activities and goals vary, all are committed to public school enrollment, meaningful parent and community involvement, and districtwide improvement.

What's most striking is that the first PPS chapter has brought parents together across race and class lines to combat white, middle-class flight from the public schools and to publicize the economic, social, and business development benefits that come to cities with strong public schools. In other cities—large and small, urban and rural—PPS chapters have addressed issues such as school safety, building racial and economic bridges, improving facilities, expanding and strengthening curricula, and increasing positive media coverage. Binding these groups together is their belief that parents must become committed owners of, rather than passive consumers in, public schools. Moreover, PPS members commit to advocate for the improvement of public education for every child, not just their own.

Teachers as Community Activists   Teachers are rarely leaders of these organizing approaches to parent and community involvement in education. Yet, increasingly, community organizations are reaching out to teachers who are committed to social justice education to add their voices and their power to that of parents. Many teachers have also discovered that the strategies of community organizing— building relationships, forging common meanings about teaching and learning, and taking action together—are powerful ways for forging connections with parents. First-year teacher Martha Guerrero describes how she integrates such activities into her work as a teacher.

———————————————————— ⊗ ⊗ ⊗ ————————————————————

I am not new to East Los Angeles. I have established a relationship with the community as an organizer. I hope that the relationships that I cultivate with my students and parents will allow me to organize community members in the future. I believe that teachers should develop these genuine relationships with the community in order to make changes in the educational and political system.

I interact frequently with my students and their families outside of the classroom. I do countless home visits. I take my students to conferences and work with them on community-related issues. I helped organize [one conference] with the theme "Rights Now Youth Conference: Speaking Truth to Power." At the conference students attended workshops related to education and the criminal justice system. We also attended a Coalition for Educational Justice conference that focused on overcrowding in inner-city schools and high-stakes standardized testing.

—MARTHA GUERRERO
First-year teacher, high school social studies

The relationship with Inner-City Struggle that Mauro Bautista described at the beginning of this chapter is another example.

Whose Agenda Is It?

An organizing approach to parent involvement stems from and leads to recognizing that schools belong to poor parents and communities, as much as they do to wealthier and more powerful ones. This is a difficult task. But it is ultimately neither respectful nor effective for educators to ignore the potential power of families as advocates for children. Community liaisons like Gina Rodriguez, and projects like the Texas IAF and the UCLA Parent Curriculum Project, along with individual teachers have all developed strategies to help parents of lower-status students speak with as much confidence and sense of entitlement about what they want for their children as the parents of high-status children usually have when they speak.

Such efforts enable parents—poor, middle class, and rich—to exercise their rightful power over schooling as citizens who are responsible for the education of all children, not simply as parents looking out for their own children's interests. This means that parents whom educators consider to be *too* involved, as well as those who seem not involved enough, must develop a very different concept of involvement. They must do more than express their willingness to meet at the same table with parents of different racial groups and socioeconomic positions. Simply coming together to talk isn't enough. People at the table must learn. And then they must act—as citizens.

None of this means that there is no longer a legitimate role for professional educators. In fact, even the most activist citizen parents do not easily develop the knowledge and pedagogical expertise that we've outlined in this book as essential to high-quality and socially just education. That is the purview of professional educators who, in partnership with activist citizens, make sure that all voices are represented and heard in ways that are inseparable from good teaching, a safe campus, social justice, and other absolute schooling basics.

OLC Connections

A list of additional online and print resources and a set of questions for reflection about working with families and communities can be found at www.mhhe.com/oakes3e.

Digging Deeper

The scholars, educators, and organizations listed all combine research and activism in the attempt to craft positive relationships among families, communities, and schools.

Martin Blank is the director for community collaboration at the Institute for Educational Leadership. He leads the Coalition for Community Schools (CCS) that brings together many partners to make schools the center of communities in which children, youth, and families have access to an array of supports and opportunities that improve student learning, strengthen families, and build community. For more information about CCS, visit http://www.communityschools.org/. The group's report, *Partnerships for Excellence,* presents the Coalition's vision of a community school, describes the common principles shared by various community school models, and offers profiles of nine community schools moving toward that vision and how they are improving the conditions for learning.

The **Center for Community Change** in Washington, D.C., was founded in response to the racial political tension in the 1960s. The Center's purpose is to help establish and develop community organizations across the country, "bring attention to major national issues related to poverty," and "help insure that government programs are responsive to community needs." **Leigh Dingerson,** the Center's director of education, has initiated a number of community-related projects, including Partnerships for Change, which brings community organizations and local teachers unions together to learn from each other and to support improvements to public education, particularly for low-income students and children of color. The Center's website is http://www.communitychange.org/issues/education.

James Comer, a professor of psychiatry in the Yale Medical School, has written a number of books and articles that outline his rationale and approach to the Community Development School process. In *Child by Child: The Comer Process for Change in Education* (edited by James P. Comer, Norris M. Haynes, Edward T. Joyner, and Michael Ben-Avie [New York: Teachers College Press, 1999]), community members, business leaders, school board members, superintendents, principals, teachers, and parents across the country share their experiences as they have tried to create school communities in which all adults help young people develop and learn. Comer's latest book about the project is *Leave No Child Behind: Preparing Today's Youth for Tomorrow's World* (New Haven, CT: Yale Press, 2004). The Comer project website is http://info.med.yale.edu/comer.

Catherine Cooper, a psychology professor at the University of California-Santa Cruz, directs the Bridging Multiple Worlds project focused on how youth forge their personal identities by coordinating cultural and family traditions with those of their schools, communities, and work. Cooper and her team have built a "toolkit" for educators to use with students to enhance the schools' and students' successful bridging of multiple worlds. The toolkit is online at http://www.bridgingworlds.org/toolkit.html.

Good Schools Pennsylvania (http://www.goodschoolspa.org) is a statewide grassroots campaign to promote greater equity across Pennsylvania's schools. Good Schools PA works with the support of faith-based groups and/or individuals who have affiliations with such groups. Their campaign has some 150 Groups of 10 around the state that meet monthly. These groups study a curriculum about school conditions and the need for greater equity and then take action throughout the year to highlight their interest in change. Actions range from writing legislators and local press to attending vigils around the state.

Joyce L. Epstein is the director of the National Network of Partnership Schools at Johns Hopkins University (http://www.csos.jhu.edu/p2000/). Through the Network, Epstein and her colleagues conduct and disseminate research, development, and policy analyses that produce new and useful knowledge and practices that help families, educators, and members of communities work together to improve schools, strengthen families, and enhance student learning and development. Dr. Epstein's *School, Family, and Community Partnerships: Your Handbook for Action* (Thousand Oaks, CA: Corwin Press, 1997) guides schools, districts, and states to develop and maintain programs of partnership. Another book, *School and Family Partnerships: Preparing Educators and Improving Schools* (Boulder, CO: Westview Press, 2000), is designed for preservice and advanced education courses.

GiveKidsGoodSchools.org is a project of the Public Education Network, which seeks to build public demand and mobilize resources to provide quality public education for all children. Resources on the website include ways for parents and community members to take actions for better schools, including influencing federal policy through online actions, public forums, writing letters to the editor, and more. The site also provides examples of activist community groups around the country and lists of resources that individual parents can use as they try to work constructively with their schools to ensure that their child is getting the best education possible.

New York University's **Institute for Education and Social Policy,** directed by Professor **Norm Fruchter,** conducts research, evaluation, policy studies and technical assistance aimed at strengthening public education, particularly in urban communities. The Institute's website at http://www.nyu.edu/iesp has a number of very informative reports, scholarly publications, policy briefs, and newsletters featuring information about the role of community-based parent and student groups in school reform.

Pedro Noguera is a professor in the Steinhardt School of Education at New York University. Noguera's research focuses on the ways in which schools respond to social and economic forces within the urban environment. One of the themes in Noguera's work is that community and church organizations can attempt to compensate for deficiencies in schools through after-school and summer school programs. See, for example, *The Trouble With Black Boys*, www.inmotionmagazine. com, 2002. His articles on these topics have appeared in several leading research journals and edited volumes. Noguera's latest book is *City Schools and the American Dream: A Blueprint for Reforming City Schools* (New York: Teachers College Press, 2003).

Parents for Public Schools. Parents for Public Schools is a national organization of community-based chapters working in public schools through broad-based coalitions of parents. Invigorated by its diverse membership, PPS mounts proactive campaigns to help public schools attract all families in a community by making sure all schools effectively serve all children. Parents for Public Schools is online at http://www.parents4publicschools.com/.

The Right Question Project, Inc. (RQP), a nonprofit organization based in Cambridge, Massachusetts, has developed, field-tested, refined, and shared a different strategy that assists parents and local advocacy groups to learn the skill in formulating questions that focus their advocacy efforts with public institutions. The Right Question Project believes that its strategy—now used in many communities— helps low- and moderate-income people in their encounters with the various outposts of government (including public schools, welfare agencies, the health care system, housing programs, homeless shelters, job training centers, and many other publicly supported agencies, programs, and institutions) in ways that traditional parent involvement does not. The Right Question project is online at http://www. rightquestion.org/.

Dennis Shirley is associate dean and a professor of Teacher Education at the Lynch School of Education at Boston College. His book *Community Organizing for Urban School Reform* (Austin: University of Texas Press, 1997) traces the IAF community-organizing work in Texas schools. His newest book, *Valley Interfaith and School Reform Organizing for Power in South Texas* (Austin: University of Texas Press, 2002), explores how community organizing and activism in support of public schools in one of America's most economically disadvantaged regions, the Rio Grande Valley of South Texas, has engendered impressive academic results. Uniting gritty realism based on extensive field observations with inspiring vignettes of educators and parents creating genuine improvement in their schools and communities, this book demonstrates that public schools can be vital "laboratories of democracy," in which students and their parents learn the arts of civic engagement and the skills necessary for participating in our rapidly changing world. It persuasively argues that the American tradition of neighborhood schools can still serve as a bedrock of community engagement and academic achievement.

Mark Warren is a professor of education at Harvard University. Warren's projects focus on parent and community involvement in schools, but in ways that, as he says, go "beyond the traditional notion of the PTA bake sale." Warren's book, *Dry Bones Rattling: Community Building to Revitalize American Democracy,* reports on the Texas Industrial Areas Foundation, the nation's most prominent faith-based community organizing network. The book shows how the IAF network works with religious congregations and other community-based institutions to teach those most left out of school politics how to participate and lead the way toward better schools.

Notes

1. A recent California study found that, although efforts by schools to reach out to parents make a contribution to school success, these activities did not predict higher school achievement scores as strongly as four key school practices: implementing a coherent, standards-based curriculum; analyzing student assessment data from multiple sources; ensuring instructional resources; and prioritizing student achievement—practices we've described in earlier chapters. EdSource, *Similar Students, Different Results: Why Do Some Schools Do Better?* Sacramento: EdSource, 2005, (http://www.edsource.org/pub_abs_simstu05.cfm).

2. For a review of this research see Joyce Epstein, Lucretia Coates, Karen C. Salinas, Mavis G. Sanders, and Beth S. Simon, *School, Family, and Community Partnerships: Your Handbook for Action* (Thousand Oaks, CA: Corwin Press, 1997); and, more recently, Ronald F. Ferguson, "Toward Skilled Parenting and Transformed Schools: Inside a National Movement for *Excellence With Equity*" (paper prepared the First Educational Equity Symposium of the Campaign for Educational Equity, at Teachers College, Columbia University, October 24 and 25, 2005).

3. Roberto Suro, "Cavazos Criticizes Hispanics on Schooling," *New York Times,* 11 April 1990, p. B8.

4. Guadalupe Valdez, *Con Respecto: Bridging the Distances Between Culturally Diverse Families and Schools* (New York: Teachers College Press, 1996); Angela Valenzuela, *Subtractive Schooling: U.S.-Mexican Youth and the Politics of Caring* (Albany: State University of New York Press, 1999); and Ricardo Stanton-Salazar, *Manufacturing Hope and Despair: The School and Kin Support Networks of U.S.-Mexican Youth* (New York: Teachers College Press, 2001).

5. Nancy Gibbs, "Parents Behaving Badly, *Time,* February 21, 2005.

6. For a more complete discussion of this issue, see Amy Wells and Irene Serna, "The Politics of Culture: Understanding Local Political Resistance to Detracking in Racially Mixed Schools," *Harvard Educational Review* 66, no. 1 (1996), pp. 93–118.

7. Jan Nespor, "Networks and Contexts of Reform," *International Journal of Educational Change* 3 (2002), pp. 365–382; Jeannie Oakes and Martin Lipton, "Struggling for Educational Equity in Diverse Communities: School Reform as Social Movement," *International Journal of Educational Change* 3 (2002), pp. 383–406; Joan Talbert, "Professionalism and Politics in High School Teaching Reform," *International Journal of Educational Change* 3 (2002), pp. 277–281.

8. This case is described in Jeannie Oakes, Karen Hunter Quartz, Steve Ryan, and Martin Lipton, *Becoming Good American Schools: The Struggle for Civic Virtue in Education Reform* (San Francisco: Jossey-Bass, 2000).

9. John Spargo, *The Bitter Cry of Children* (New York: Macmillan, 1906).

10. Joy Dryfoos, *Full-Service Schools. A Revolution in Health and Social Services for Children, Youth and Families* (San Francisco: Jossey-Bass, 1994).

11. See, for example, Geoffrey D. Borman, Gina M. Hewes, Laura T. Overman, and Shelly Brown, "Comprehensive School Reform and Achievement: A Meta-analysis," *Review of Educational Research* 73, no. 2 (2003), pp. 125–230.

12. Thomas J. Kane, *The Impact of After-School Programs: Interpreting the Results of Four Recent Evaluations* (working paper of the William T. Grant Foundation, 2004).

13. Angela Valenzuela, *Subtractive Schooling: U.S.-Mexican Youth and the Politics of Caring* (Albany: State University of New York Press, 1999).

14. W. E. B. DuBois, "Does the Negro Need Separate Schools?" *Journal of Negro Education* 4, no. 3 (1935), p. 328.

15. Susan Auerbach, "Engaging Latino Parents in Supporting College Pathways: Lessons from a College Access Program," *Journal of Hispanic Higher Education* 3, no. 2 (2004), pp. 125–145; and Susan Auerbach, "Why Do They Give the Good Classes to Some and Not to Others?" Latino parent narratives of struggle in a college access program, *Teachers College Record* 104, no. 7 (2002), pp. 1369–1392.

16. Linda Jacobson, "PTA Seeks to Raise Number of Hispanic Members," *Education Week,* 11 June 2003.

17. For a discussion of the community schools movement, see John Rogers, *Community Schools: Lessons from the Past and Present* (Los Angeles: UCLA's IDEA Paper Series #1, 1998).

18. Susan Stall and Randy Stoecker, "Community Organizing or Organizing Community? Gender and the Crafts of Empowerment," *Gender and Society* 12 (1998), pp. 729–756 (accessed at http://comm-org.wisc.edu/).

19. For a fuller discussion of community organizing for school reform, see Jeannie Oakes and John Rogers, *Learning Power: Organizing for Education and Justice* (New York: Teachers College Press, 2006).

20. Ernesto Cortes, Jr., "Making the Public the Leaders in Education Reform," *Teacher Magazine,* 22 November 1995.

21. Mamie Chow, Laurie Olsen, Ruben Lizardo, and Carol Dowell, *School Reform Organizing in the San Francisco Bay Area and Los Angeles, California* (Oakland, CA: California Tomorrow, 2001), p. 106.

22. See Oakes and Rogers, *Learning Power.*

CHAPTER 11

Policy and Law
Rules to Make Schools Effective,
Efficient, and Equitable

No Child Left Behind has had a pronounced impact on the mathematics department at my school—both good and bad. With No Child Left Behind, each high school gains or loses points based on what percentage of students are at grade level and scoring at high levels on the tests given at the end of those courses. Our school was losing points for the ninth graders taking the Introduction to Algebra class. Therefore, the district decided to eliminate that class and place all ninth graders in algebra or higher. This policy has worked to the benefit of the students, as many of them are able to handle the curriculum and benefit from the higher expectations.

To help struggling students the district created a support class. This is a class the students take in addition to their regular algebra class that provides additional time to fill the gaps in their knowledge or allow them additional time to process the material. Sounds good, in theory. However, the class was not designed for the students most at need. Rather, the "middle third"—the students deemed to have the greatest chance of reaching "Proficient" status on the algebra state test—were placed in the support class. This decision was made to maximize state scores to avoid being placed on the dreaded "schools in need of improvement" list.

The net effect is that No Child Left Behind has led to one policy that provided students access to algebra, but it also led to another that denied them additional support to succeed.

—**MARK HILL**
First-year teacher, high school mathematics

In the preceding quote, Mark Hill describes the impact that the federal No Child Left Behind Act (NCLB) of 2001 is having on mathematics teaching and learning at his school. The George W. Bush administration and a bipartisan coalition of legislators agreed in 2001 that the federal government should use the funding provided under the Elementary and Secondary Education Act (ESEA) to entice and pressure educators to raise student achievement and close the "achievement gap" among racial and economic groups.

So, in a major change from the older ESEA, the federal government decided to "hold schools accountable" for increasing students' achievement test scores. Specifically, the government would require every state, as a condition of receiving their federal funding, to do the following: (a) test every student in grades 3 through 8, (b) set a numerical target for each school that specifies how many points their scores must increase each year (called Annual Yearly Progress); (c) require that the school increase the scores of every group of students at their school (racial, ethnic, income, disability, and grade level); and (d) levy sanctions and intervene in schools that fail to meet their targets.

Many applaud NCLB for insisting that schools focus on achievement and equity; many others blame it for undermining high-quality curriculum and teaching, particularly for low-income students and students of color. Perhaps the only point of agreement is that NCLB is having a huge impact on states, schools, and classrooms across the country. As Mark Hill reports in the case of his school, NCLB has pushed many schools to provide more students with a rigorous academic curriculum. It also has the perverse effect in many schools of targeting resources and support toward students who are most likely to help the school meet its numerical target (students nicknamed the "bubble" kids), to the detriment of the lowest achievers.

The government uses laws and policies to encourage, support, and require that schools meet the public's expectations. They range from the overarching federal NCLB to local decisions such as whether students will wear uniforms, whether music will be taught, which bus company will get the contract for transporting students, and so on. The early education goals of the Republic described in Chapter 2 (educating citizens with the literacy skills and values for democratic governance) have expanded greatly. Today, we expect our laws and policies to ensure that schools will meet the needs of the workforce and the economy, solve social problems, ensure the brainpower necessary for national security, and keep the nation competitive in a global economy.

Chapter Overview

We have described a number of education policies in earlier chapters—policies governing curriculum, testing, discipline, categorical programs, and parent participation, to name just a few. In this chapter, we describe the roles and responsibilities of local, state, and federal government in moving public schools toward their goals. Because policymakers' decisions are shaped by their various political ideologies, we explore those ideologies to help explain certain predictable patterns in the laws that govern the kind of schools we have. These ideologies and patterns can be seen in policies regulating large-scale testing, high school graduation and grade retention, and the use of "scientifically based" curriculum—all elements of the federal NCLB Act. The chapter concludes with a brief discussion of the courts' role in protecting the rights of the nation's most vulnerable students. Desegregation and school funding are the most prominent examples, but there are many others. Throughout, teachers explain how various policies shape their efforts to teach to change the world.

We focus in this chapter on public policies for public schools. Of course, in 2001, about 5.3 million students (approximately 10 percent of the total) attended private schools. However, private schools, unlike public schools, are exempt from all but a few government policies.

The Complex Education Policy System

In Chapters 2 and 3, we noted the growth of public schooling in the United States during the nineteenth century. For much of the century, these schools were what education historian David Tyack has called "village schools."[1] That is, they were governed by their local communities. The U.S. Constitution made no mention of education as a function of the federal government, so, in accordance with the Tenth Amendment to the Constitution, the authority for education belonged to the states.[2] For the most part, however, states delegated the running of schools to local communities. Typically, community members joined together in local school boards or committees decided where schools should be built, selected the teachers and told them how to behave, and determined the curriculum. Local taxes paid the bills.

By the middle of the nineteenth century, all this had begun to change. As the nation shifted from a rural to a more urban society, city school districts formed, and many states pressed rural schools to consolidate into larger districts. In these larger districts, local community school boards began to give way to centralized district boards and professional superintendents. At the same time, states and the federal government became more involved in schooling.

Increasingly, state leaders looked for uniformity in their rapidly expanding school systems. Massachusetts led the way by establishing a state board of education in 1837 (with Horace Mann appointed as state commissioner) and passing the nation's first compulsory attendance law in 1852. In the South in the 1830s, Louisiana, Georgia, Virginia, Alabama, South Carolina, and North Carolina all passed laws that prohibited teaching slaves to read.

Federal involvement in education began during the Civil War. Using the rationale that the Constitution's Preamble required the federal government to "promote the general welfare," Congress established the Bureau of Education in 1867. The Bureau's stated mission was to collect data and report the "condition and progress of education." For some, however, the real impetus behind its creation was a concern that the Southern states would not comply with the "equal protection" provisions of the Fourteenth Amendment without pressure from the federal government. In fact, the Bureau did not push aggressively for equal education, and in 1886, the Supreme Court decision in *Plessy v. Ferguson* made it legal to maintain segregated school systems. Nevertheless, the U.S. Bureau of Education remained a small agency that did little more than survey and write annual reports about the nation's schools.

Three Levels of Educational Governance

Today, the U.S. educational system has grown into a huge and complex enterprise, in which federal, state, and local government all play powerful roles. Although the division of decision making differs somewhat in every state—since each state system is independent—there are common patterns of policymaking among the three levels of government.

What Do Local School Districts Do?   There are approximately 15,000 local school districts in the United States. Most of these districts are governed by elected school boards who hire a superintendent or a commissioner to lead the day-to-day administration of the system. In recent years, mayors in some large cities like New York, Chicago, and Detroit have "taken over" responsibility for the schools and either appoint the board members or the superintendent.

Now as in the past, local school districts raise funds to support their schools, and they develop and manage their own budgets. They build their own schools, hire teachers and other staff, and negotiate with teachers' and other employees' unions to set salaries and working conditions. They decide how to group students for instruction, what curriculum to offer, and what textbooks to use. They set policies about homework, discipline, and extracurricular activities.

Technically, because state governments are responsible for maintaining schools, local school districts can only do what the state government has delegated to them, and districts are accountable to the state for carrying out their responsibilities according to state laws and regulations. In practice, for most of our history, local school districts have had considerable autonomy over their schools, and most observers still characterize schooling in the United States as locally controlled.

However, since the 1970s the states and the federal government have become increasingly involved in determining policies and practices in local schools, as we describe in the following.

What Do States Do?   States have the primary authority for providing education, and, as long as they do not violate the U.S. Constitution, they are free to run their schools as they like. Nevertheless, the school systems across the states are far more similar than different.

Every state has a state school board and a chief state school officer (a superintendent of public instruction or a commissioner of education). In every state, these officials make rules about how districts should be organized and governed, and they establish standards for educational programs, instructional materials, graduation requirements, and achievement testing; attendance rules; the length of the school day and school year; teacher credentialing, certification, tenure, and pensions; the construction and maintenance of school buildings; school district finances and budgets; school safety; and parents' and students' rights and responsibilities.

Every state also delegates most of the day-to-day operation of schools to local school districts (except Hawaii, which has only one statewide school system). At the same time every state has steadily increased its control over local school policies and programs. In California, the State Education Code, which contains all of the state laws and regulations governing education, is 14 volumes long.

The states' current high level of involvement in local school policies and practices began in the late 1960s when the federal government gave states the responsibility for administering a collection of federal categorically funded programs related to the War on Poverty and civil rights. The relationships between state education officials and local school systems changed as well. The rather unobtrusive technical assistance that the state had provided previously, predominantly to rural school systems, was replaced by a far more assertive role as overseer of programmatic and funding mandates. The state's new role as the shaper of local responses to federal policy and as the "compliance office" with control over important resources was accomplished most often by adding new layers of bureaucratic control.

Since the 1980s states have become more involved in teaching and learning, as well as setting regulations. *A Nation at Risk*'s dire warnings led many states to raise graduation requirements, mount school reform initiatives, lengthen the school year, and place greater emphasis on student achievement, effectively taking these policy areas away from local school boards. By the 1990s, many governors began placing education high on their policy agendas. Although it cannot be said that education policy became *more* political with this trend—more than when it had kept a lower and local profile—the formulation of education policy has certainly entered into state and national political power and ideological divisions.

As we noted in Chapter 2, then Arkansas governor Bill Clinton convened an Education Summit of all 50 governors in 1989, where they adopted a set of ambitious national goals that they together would try to reach by 2000. That summit also led to the movement for state content standards that we described in Chapter 4. The state standards movement paved the way for test-based accountability, generally, and the federal NCLB Act.

State involvement in teaching and learning also increased because of changes in the way many states fund their schools. Until quite recently, local property taxes were the major source of school funding, with states contributing a much smaller share. However, because lower-wealth communities cannot raise as much local money as higher-wealth districts, states in varying degrees have made some efforts to equalize the funding between rich and poor districts. Often, this equalization was required by court decisions determining that schools' grossly unequal resources violated the state's obligation to treat students equally and fairly. In most cases, equalization means the states pay a much larger share of educational costs. Or, more precisely, the route that funds previously took to get from taxation to schools now channels through the state for redistribution to local areas. An inevitable result of this redistribution is that some sources of a state's funds (high-wealth neighborhoods, businesses, etc.) are unhappy to find that a higher percentage of their taxed wealth is required for education or leaves their local neighborhoods. Along with the state's increased role in collecting and distributing money for education, state lawmakers are more likely to take a larger role in determining how the money is spent.

In the past 20 years, states have also experimented with delegating the authority for running schools to groups wanting to start up new public schools that operate outside the rules and regulations imposed by local school districts. In 2005, 39 states and Washington, D.C., had laws establishing charter schools that agree to be held accountable for student achievement in exchange for greater autonomy. Together, 3,000 schools enrolled about 700,000 of the nation's approximately 55 million students.

What Does the Federal Government Do?   Today, as in the past, the federal government collects and reports information on the nation's schools. It also maintains its role of ensuring that states and local school do nothing that violates the U.S. Constitution. However, the expansion of the federal role in response to national concerns about quality and equity (as described in Chapter 2) has meant that much of what states and local school districts do is now shaped, even controlled, by federal policy. Although less than 10 percent of the funding for education comes from federal sources, most states and local districts can hardly afford to pass up those funds. Because the funds now come with tight restrictions, the federal government can leverage a comparatively small investment into a lot of influence.

Programs to provide additional funds for low-income children that began during the War on Poverty in the 1970s have evolved into today's NCLB Act. To receive the additional funds earmarked for low-income children, states must develop academic standards, test every student in grades 3 through 8, staff every classroom where core subjects are taught with "highly qualified" teachers, and take control of schools that fail to meet federally established targets for increased test scores. As we describe later, these requirements especially affect much of what happens today in schools that enroll low-income children, because the law also restricts the types of programs and materials that can be purchased with federal dollars. However, the influence of NCLB is felt in every public school.

The federal government also influences state and local school systems by funding educational research and innovation aimed at improving educational quality. It uses these funds to send strong signals about what types of practices are best and to create incentives for states and local schools to use them. Some of the examples we discuss later in this chapter, for example, reflect the current administration's preferences for "choice" and for bringing the private sector into public schools. And, of course, the central role given to standardized testing powerfully influences state and local district mandates for particular teaching methods and materials that translate into higher average test scores.

Concept Table 11.1 summarizes the key roles and responsibilities at each of the three levels of educational governance.

How Do Policies Work?

At each of the federal, state, and local levels, we have different types of officials who are responsible for governing public school systems—elected policymakers, those who administer policies, and the courts. As policymakers, Congress, state legislators and local school boards pass laws and policies establishing the goals of schooling and allocating resources to achieve the goals. The president, governors, and mayors help shape this agenda, usually by using the power and public visibility of their office to press forward ideas for policies that they believe will make schools better.

Federal, state, and local policymakers all translate their ideas about what schools should do into actual policies using a handful of strategies. The most straightforward strategy is to simply just tell districts and schools what to do (mandates). An example of a mandate is the stipulation that the school year must be a minimum number of days and the school day must be a minimum number of

CONCEPT TABLE 11.1   *Three Levels of Education Policymaking*

Level	Policy Actors	Responsibilities
Local	School board Superintendent and staff	Raise funds Build and maintain facilities Hire, assign, provide professional development, and evaluate administrators, teachers and staff Negotiate with teachers' and other employees' unions to set salaries and working conditions Establish basic operational rules for schools—hours, holidays, school organization, curriculum, textbooks, homework, discipline, extracurricular activities, dress codes, etc. Administer federal and state categorical programs, and achievement testing Report to the state and federal governments how funds are spent, student achievement, and other required information. Under *NCLB*—since 2001: Publish and distribute public "report cards" about each school
State	Legislature Governor School board Chief state school officer State Department of Education	Constitutional obligation to maintain schools Certify teachers Provide funding for schools Delegate the operation of schools to local school boards Administer local implementation of federal and state "categorical" programs Collect data from schools Report civil rights data to U.S. Department of Education Intervene when local school systems experience fiscal, management, or other crises Under *NCLB*—since 2001: Establish curriculum standards, testing programs, and accountability mechanisms Ensure that each classroom is staffed by a "highly qualified" teacher Report achievement test scores, graduation rates, and teacher quality to U.S. Department of Education Take over, reconstitute, or "charterize" failing schools
Federal	Congress and President Secretary of education U.S. Department of Education	Serve as a "bully pulpit" to spur states and schools to meet expectations Fund and oversee support programs for ESL, low-income students, and students with disabilities Collect basic data about school enrollments, staffing, funding, etc.

CONCEPT TABLE 11.1 *(continued)*

Level	Policy Actors	Responsibilities
		Conduct the *National Assessment of Educational Progress*
		Monitor states' and schools' compliance with federal civil rights laws
		Under *NCLB*—since 2001:
		Deny federal funds to states that do not hold schools accountable for "annual yearly progress" in achievement test scores and graduation rates, or comply with other *NCLB* provisions.
		Collect accountability data on student achievement, high school graduation, and "highly qualified teachers"
		Require that federal funds be spent only on programs proven effectively with "scientifically based" research.

minutes. A second much used strategy is to offer funding or other advantages to persuade districts or schools to agree or to threaten sanctions if they do not (incentives or inducements). A common incentive is to offer grants to districts and schools if they institute a particular program. A third strategy is to provide resources, training, or help to do things differently (capacity-building). A common example is to provide professional development that upgrades teachers' knowledge and skills in a particular subject area. A fourth policy strategy is to change fundamental features of the system (system changes).[3] An example is the introduction of standards and standards-based tests that have a strong impact on how and what teachers teach.

In addition to those who create policy, each level of government has education officials who work out the details of how polices should be implemented and then work to make sure that they are. At the federal level Congress funds the U.S. Department of Education under the leadership of the secretary of education to implement and oversee federal educational policy. The departments of education in each state play much the same role, under the direction of the state superintendent or commissioner of education. These state departments of education translate the policies into a set of rules to be followed by local districts, allocate the funding for programs and initiatives, provide support and guidance for schools and districts to implement regulations, and follow up to make sure they do. At the local level, the superintendent of schools and his or her staff in the district office take the federal and state policies and regulations and create the day-to-day procedures that school principals, teachers, and students follow. They also provide support services to local schools, such as professional development for teachers, developing curriculum, administering state tests, and coordinating special programs, such as those for students identified as special education.

Finally, federal and state courts adjudicate disputes over whether particular policies and practices violate state or federal law or constitutional principles. In the last section of this chapter, we focus on the role that the courts have played in promoting equity and social justice in the educational system.

Ideas That Shape Education Policy

Education policymaking is a constant process of designing and redesigning rules and strategies to make the educational system work. Over the history of U.S. schooling, powerful cultural ideas have shaped not only the expectations society has for schools, but the very meaning of efficiency and of equity. We mentioned in Chapter 2 some of the broad and corrosive cultural ideas that remain with us in spite of their inefficient and inequitable consequences: the ideologies of meritocracy, deficit thinking, and white privilege. These ideas are so pervasive that they enter into the policymaking arena as if they are natural and common sense.

Three additional ideas shaped policymaking in the twentieth century and continue to do so. These ideas are not easily categorized as corrosive or beneficial. Whereas meritocracy, deficit thinking, and white privilege invariably lead to outcomes that are divisive and oppressive, the next three ideas can find expression in policies that are empowering, equitable, and just, *or* just as oppressive as the worst nineteenth- and twentieth-century abuses.

The first idea ties schools to our capitalist system of producing and consuming goods and services; that is, school practices and organization should mirror the workings of the economy, and schooling outcomes should achieve maximum economic benefits. The second idea is that schools must be instruments of democratic citizenship. This idea is a noble and effective guiding principle, but only if policymakers have an inclusive sense of which behaviors and persons warrant the protections and benefits of citizenship. Although these two ideas—schools as economic enterprises and schools as instruments of democracy—are often in tension, Americans prize both of them. Because of the tension, though, the school policies can be full of contradictions and sometimes self-defeating.

A third powerful idea is that science is the source of social progress and, therefore, scientific studies provide the most reliable guidance about educational practice. For at least a century, policymakers and educators have turned to scientific studies to help them decide how to make schooling more effective, efficient, and equitable, even though views of what constitutes rigorous science can be variously interpreted depending on one's politics and favored outcomes.

Moreover, the *kind* of science seen as legitimate has shifted over the years. Early on, as we described in Chapter 6 about the development of intelligence testing, much scientific study and research tried to link students' capacity for learning and social behavior to inherent limits and possibilities that each person did or did not possess. Also popular were studies of the type used in industry to determine the most efficient methods for running schools and classrooms.

By midcentury, social science research about the impact of various practices on students' educational outcomes began to influence policy. For example, evidence that segregation created feelings of inferiority in black children, cited in the *Brown v. Board of Education* court decision in 1954, was extraordinarily influential in making desegregation policies. Currently, as we discuss more later in this chapter, the science that is seen as most legitimate in policymaking are randomized trials (like those used to test medical treatments) that test the effectiveness of various curricula and teaching strategies.

Schools as Economic Enterprises

As the economy has changed over the past century, educational policymaking has followed suit. At the beginning of the twentieth century, the industrial factory drove ideas about how schools could operate effectively, efficiently, and fairly; later in the century, the well-managed company became the model for excellent schools. At the beginning of the twenty-first century, factory and corporate thinking remains active in education, but the free-market economy has become the economic entity after which much education policy is modeled. For most of our history, policymakers have struggled to ensure that, even as schools operate like factories, well-managed businesses, and markets, they embody our democratic ideals. The politics of education—battles among policymakers and the public over whose ideas about education should rule—are rife with conflict over the degree to which schools should be instruments of the economy or instruments of democracy and social justice.

Schools as Factories   At the start of the twentieth century, factories began to produce cheap, labor-saving products that many envisioned as having the potential to liberate common people from the drudgery of making many needed and worthwhile goods with their own hands. Tough-minded factory management practices were touted as hastening the day when a previously unimagined social justice would replace deprivation and poverty. Productivity, efficiency, profits, and worker well-being went hand in hand. Industrial efficiency caught the public's imagination through the writings of Frederick Winslow Taylor, and the example of Henry Ford. Taylor recommended time-and-motion studies to set standards of performance.

Basing their practices on careful record keeping, "scientific" managers established the "best methods," which replaced the rule-of-thumb approaches that workers had developed over time. Managers trained and supervised workers and were themselves trained in techniques of scientific control and efficiency. People called the techniques scientific because they were systematic and precise and allowed few individual judgments and little variability. Factory owners and managers centralized decision making and authority at the top, divided labor by specializing tasks, and governed every aspect of the enterprise with rules, regulations, and an impersonal (more efficient) attitude toward the individual. Ford's assembly-line autoworkers were easily trained and supervised by managers who used standardized methods to perform small tasks. In this way "Fordism" became the apex of scientific production and management.[4]

The Factory Model in Early-Twentieth-Century Schools   Early-twentieth-century schools grew large and expensive, and hardly up to the task of "Americanizing" vast numbers of immigrant, rural, and poor youth. Industrial efficiency seemed to be the answer.

Many educators embraced scientific methods to impose order and rationality. Politicians, industrialists, and social reformers looked to the factory model of production and theories about managing large-scale industrial production scientifically and efficiently and reasoned that practices that had revolutionized the industrial workplace could do the same for schools.

The nation found compelling the metaphor that children were the "raw materials" that could be processed into useful products in schools that operated like efficient factories. University professors and school administrators set about conducting the same types of scientific studies of schools that Taylor had done in industry. They used their findings to develop schemes for making schools run more like efficient factories. They divided their large auditorium-like spaces for a hundred or more students into today's familiar "egg crate" classrooms that separate students by ages, subjects, and abilities. Texts such as readers and spellers proliferated, making it possible to standardize curriculum. Colleges began to specify sequences of courses that would prepare students for admission. Normal schools (the first teacher education institutions) started training teachers in correct and efficient teaching methods.[5]

Education administrators of the early 1900s, especially those in urban areas, relished scientific management partly because it cast them in the role of experts and enhanced their personal status and political clout. A concurrent shift in the teaching force fit well with the new arrangement in which experts (school administrators) supervised low-skilled, low-paid workers (teachers). Increasingly, women, who would work for less money, who would not move on to better jobs, and who were thought to be "naturally" more nurturing, filled more of the teaching jobs. Men were principals, superintendents, and members of school boards; they were teachers of older students in elite schools and of subjects that required academic training.

The Factory Model in Today's Schools   The legacy of the factory—scientific management and industrial efficiency—remains strong. In assembly-line fashion, schools still separate students into classes by age, grade, and ability. Most teachers teach all of the students in the room simultaneously—the same material at the same pace in the same way. Curriculum specialists, school district administrators, and even state legislators, acting like factory production designers, design the curriculum sequences and instructional processes for teachers and students to follow, subject by subject, grade by grade. Everyone specializes. One is a reading specialist, one is a third-grade teacher, one teaches social studies, and another is a giftedness expert. The various parts—skills and subjects—require careful supervision by administrators to keep running smoothly.

Report cards provide an efficient, if not terribly informative, shorthand of letter grades and checklists that sum up and communicate students' learning to parents. Standardized achievement tests (e.g., the Comprehensive Test of Basic Skills [CTBS], Iowa Test of Basic Skills, California's SAT 9; Texas's TAAS, etc.) report productivity to school boards and state legislatures, as well as to parents, real estate marketers, and so forth.

Schools as Well-Managed Corporations   In the 1970s, Henry Ford's factory model of production had lost its luster. Traumatic events shook American business and industry. The mid-1970s upheaval in the Middle East created severe oil shortages. Images of American cars waiting in long, slow lines for rationed gas served as a wake-up call for American business and industry—and, eventually, to schools as well.

The demise of the belief that the United States' industrial prowess completely dominated the global economy was powerfully symbolized by the Japanese and German car manufacturers who moved quickly to supply the American market with small, less thirsty alternatives to the Detroit gas guzzlers. These foreign competitors easily outpaced Ford, GM, and Chrysler—companies whose rigid, hierarchical approach to the organization of work and management made them extraordinarily slow to notice, let alone respond to, the crisis. American business finally did adapt to these new conditions, but slowly and in their uniquely American way.

Systems Thinking   As business leaders sought to understand what had gone wrong and how the problem could be solved, they looked to new theories of corporate management and the emerging field of management science in universities. In 1945, for example, management scholar Peter Drucker wrote a book that popularized the concept of the "corporation," and by the 1960s, Drucker's scholarly books and articles were challenging the fundamentals of American business. Known as the father of modern management, Drucker and his colleagues in university business schools developed a "systems" approach to managing large enterprises.

Moving away from Taylor's and Ford's belief that the key to industrial success lies in perfecting the functioning of each specialized part of the linear production process, systems theorists saw business enterprises as an interrelated and interdependent set of elements functioning as a whole. More important than a linear assembly line of well-functioning parts was the relationship among them—ongoing interactions, feedback loops—and whether the individual parts added up to a coherent whole that was more than the sum of the parts. Importantly, systems theorists went beyond the mechanical and technical parts of the system and focused on the social and human dimensions of the workplace. Smart, highly motivated workers, whose innovative ideas affect the work, matter most.

Systems thinking caught on in the 1970s because it seemed to explain why the Japanese and to some degree the Scandinavians had become so successful. It turned out that Japanese companies had been using many of the elements of systems thinking to organize and manage their work, and they credited it for the innovative and nimble performance. Rushing to compete with the Japanese, American companies began to reorganize into cooperative work teams, adopt such policies as employee flextime, and pay closer attention to the ideas of workers. Some of the innovations were judged successful; some were not.

Systemic Education Reform   A parallel process occurred in education. Systems thinking came to dominate efforts to improve schools, especially after the country lived through the hype and poor results following the release in 1983 of *A Nation at Risk*—described in Chapters 2 and 3. Competition from the Japanese spurred systems thinking. Many business and political leaders explained the nation's perceived fall from world economic dominance by placing much of the blame on schools. After all, the Japanese ascendancy in the world economy and its besting of the American consumer electronics and automobile industries mirrored Japanese students' higher achievement scores on international achievement tests. What was needed to restore the economy, many argued, was a radical improvement in the educational system.

A Nation at Risk articulated the need for radical change. In the twentieth century, no words uttered about schools were so widely quoted or so influenced the nation's perception of schools as these:

> Our Nation is at risk. Our once unchallenged preeminence in commerce, industry, science and technological innovation is being overtaken by competitors throughout the world. . . . The educational foundations of our society are presently being eroded by a rising tide of mediocrity that threatens our very future as a nation and a people. . . . If an unfriendly foreign power had attempted to impose on America the mediocre educational performance that exists today, we might well have viewed it as an act of war. As it stands we have allowed this to happen to ourselves. . . . We have, in effect, been committing an act of unthinking, unilateral, educational disarmament.[6]

A Nation at Risk raised two essential questions: First, did the report accurately describe a real educational problem? Second, would the report, as a guide to new policies, lead to robust and equitable school systems? Neither question received the careful policy consideration it deserved. However, in 1995 Professors David Berliner and Bruce Biddle argued persuasively in their award-winning book *The Manufactured Crisis* that the charges against schools were hostile, politically charged, and largely untrue, and that those who wrote the report deliberately ignored, distorted, and suppressed evidence that contradicted their conclusions.[7] In fact, Berliner and Biddle offer evidence that the international comparisons of test scores were thoroughly misleading and that American students who had opportunities to learn material on the tests scored as well as their international peers.

At the time of the report's release, however, the public and many policymakers were persuaded that schools' excellence or mediocrity could be defined as the report defined them—in terms of a superficial international competition. Most states responded by adopting new policies to improve the quality of schooling—lengthened school years and school days, increased graduation requirements, and upgraded teacher preparation. Taken individually, these reforms may have had some value, but they did not add up to significant changes—particularly for millions of underserved students in undersupported schools. By the late 1980s, these more-of-the-same policies had proved disappointing.

Meanwhile, education researchers and policymakers were exploring the systems thinking increasingly admired by corporations. The new idea was that "systemic reform" would revolutionize schools in ways that piecemeal reform could not. Policy analysts argued that states must develop a set of coherent policies that would align all the various parts of the educational system. Specifically, each state should (1) set high academic standards; (2) provide schools with the tools, skills, and resources they needed to help students meet the standards, including lots of professional development for educators; and (3) hold schools accountable for the results. As was the case in well-managed organizations, top, executive leadership (the state) would set goals and hold various units (schools and districts) accountable for results; at the same time, the leadership would restructure its policies to give maximum flexibility in how managers and units would achieve their results.[8]

Recommendations for systemic reform appeared in major documents of the National Governor's Association, the Business Roundtable, and the Council of Chief

State School Officers. It was also the a central rationale behind major initiatives sponsored by the National Science Foundation, several major philanthropic foundations, and congressional legislation. The Clinton administration's 1994 version of the *Elementary and Secondary Education Act* required states to adopt curriculum standards that established a clear vision of what students should know and be able to do and that would lead to upgrading content and instruction. These are the standards we described in Chapter 4.

From the beginning, progressive policymakers and educators assumed that the new standards would be aligned with *opportunities* to learn those standards. As a matter of simple logic and fairness, a systemic reform should have an accountability component that looks not only at what comes out of the system (in this case the scores on tests) but also what goes into the system (resources or opportunities to learn). Scientific studies could help determine which resources actually increase school productivity. (We referred to some of those studies in Chapter 9, including studies of class size, time on instruction, extra support, and so forth.) Districts should then provide what's needed to enable schools to meet curriculum and performance standards, and the state should monitor and ensure that districts have the necessary resources to provide to schools. Without these resources in place, it would be illegitimate to hold schools and students accountable for meeting the content standards.[9]

School administrators eagerly borrowed two systems concepts, "learning organizations" and "continuous improvement," from Peter Senge's *The Fifth Discipline: The Art and Practice of the Learning Organization.* Senge wrote, for example,

> organizations where people continually expand their capacity to create the results they truly desire, where new and expansive patterns of thinking are nurtured, where collective aspiration is set free, and where people are continually learning to see the whole together.[10]

Applied to schools, these ideas disdained the command-and-control administrative strategies that characterized the factory-model school. Instead, education officials should build "high expectation" school cultures that were conducive to learning and innovation among the adults as well as the students. The 1990s witnessed a proliferation of books and professional development programs claiming to teach school administrators how to implement these systems processes in schools. Many of the ideas we described in Chapter 9 developed in the context of these systems-focused efforts.

The "learning organization" idea tries to accommodate systemic reform without abandoning key elements of "top-down" management. Policymakers still set the standards and measure whether those standards are met, but they purport to leave the design of the "delivery systems" to those actually engaged in the work—school principals and teachers.

Systems Theories and NCLB   In 1994, conservatives (mostly Republicans) in Congress threatened to kill the 1994 reauthorization of the Elementary and Secondary Education Act, if the liberals (mostly Democrats) insisted on requiring states to establish standards for resources and conditions for learning. Their argument was that such requirements abridged the states' rights to spend on education what and how they saw fit. More broadly, many saw the proposed opportunity standards as opening the door to greater spending on education, which could be a good or bad outcome, depending on one's political ideology. As a result, the standards-based policies that emerged focused on setting standards for what students should learn, in the absence of standards for the resources and conditions that such learning would require. This shift laid the foundation for No Child Left Behind.

NCLB retains some traces of systemic reform. States are required to set standards, administer standards-based tests, and hold schools accountable for their students' test scores. But the only "opportunity" required by the federal law is that every classroom should be staffed by a "highly qualified" teacher.

Moreover, to receive NCLB's "Reading First" funding to support reading in low-achieving schools, many states and local districts have adopted scripted curricula with rigid pacing plans that we described in Chapter 4 and discuss more below. These programs are incompatible with "learning organizations" because there is little opportunity for teachers' innovative ideas to improve practice. Today, systems theories face strong competition from free-market theories as sources for ideas that should inform education policymaking.

Schools as Markets   By the late 1990s America's overall prosperity was soaring again, with at least some credit due to the deft responses by American business. Many bureaucratic organizations had been replaced by more flexible staffing patterns, patterns of production, and labor markets. Niche marketing had replaced some large-scale mass production. At the same time, the accelerated speed at which information, goods, and people travel had liberated many from strictly local goods and ideas and was allowing small-scale enterprises to compete alongside large centralized businesses.

These new conditions have also put new pressures on companies that want to remain competitive. To lower costs and increase profits, companies today rely on more fluid job descriptions and on temporary and/or nonunion workers who replace salaried workers. Seeking to beat the global competition with quicker turnaround times and lowered labor costs, many industries have adopted new employment practices, such as "downsizing" to smaller core workforces and "outsourcing" or contracting portions of their production to other businesses, often to foreign manu-facturers or businesses that pay lower wages. They have also sought friendlier business climates—states and communities with fewer regulations, lower taxes, and fewer environmental restrictions. The social safety nets of secure jobs, wage controls, and other regulations are seen increasingly as constraining American business interests in a global marketplace.

Conservatives see market forces as fostering excellence and economic prosper-ity, through increased competitiveness, cost savings, and an explosion of choices among goods and services. However, many liberals argue that these changes have not been kind to everyone—particularly workers whose jobs are less secure in companies less likely to provide health insurance and pension benefits and whose interests are less likely to be represented by labor unions.

Deregulation and Accountability for Results   Once again, changes in economic and business trends affected educational policymaking. Today, as conservative, market-oriented policymakers seek "cures" for low-achieving schools, they mimic free-market strategies for maximizing economic productivity and efficiency in business and industry. These include deregulation and local control, accountability for productivity, niche marketing and choice, competition, and increased privatization.

Decentralization and deregulation promise to free schools from bureaucratic control and open up possibilities for innovative practice. Yet, schools should only remain "in business" if they do well on externally set standards and traditional measures of achievement in comparison with other schools. Their results should be made public, and customers (parents and students) should be free to choose another school if the one they were assigned to doesn't measure up. Rather than having a monopoly of public schools, private schools should also be allowed to compete. The result, advocates argue, is higher quality for all students.

By 1996, the decision to impose less regulation of school inputs, and increasing concerns about costs, had trumped efforts to establish resource and practice standards. Instead, states adopted policies that operationalized "high standards" as grade-level benchmarks in traditional academic content areas, measured by standardized tests. Rather than defining equity as a guarantee of adequate and equitable school conditions for all students, equity for students was redefined as closing the test-score "gap" among racial groups on basic reading and arithmetic skills.

Choice and Competition   Perhaps the most significant change brought by the infusion of market ideas into education reform, however, is the loosening of schools from their connection to the tradition of common public schools. The accelerating confidence in competition and market forces has brought proposals that threaten the viability of public schools. At the extreme, there have always been ideological opponents to the very concept and institution of "public schools." However, a concerted and well-financed agenda for dramatically lessening the role of the common public schools is a recent phenomenon.

For example, some reformers advocate voucher plans where students take the government's financial support with them to the school of their choice—public or private. Others see hope in charter schools that operate independently from existing school districts and many laws. Many school districts promote magnet schools—schools with a special mission that attract students from many neighborhoods, often for the purpose of desegregation. Most magnet and charter schools are smaller, more autonomous, more responsive organizations than conventional schools. Their advocates hope that freedom from central authority and regulation will foster healthy competition and increase the quality of all schools. Parents typically play a much more important role in guiding these schools than they have in traditional schools. The logic is that with parents in charge—rather than big education bureaucracies—schools would move toward higher quality or lose their market share of students.

The marketplace theory behind these programs (to be sure, there are also other ways that people defend them) is that the most successful will thrive, and those that do a poor job will disappear. Skeptics point out, however, that in the traditional marketplace of goods and services, harmful or wasteful products do not necessarily disappear or improve but are often the most popular. "Rational choice," according to some social theorists, is a local and individual matter. For example, some parents might choose to send their children to a neighborhood school even though its test score averages are low and its resources limited. For these parents, having their children close to home instead of going to a neighborhood of strangers may be rational. Other parents might choose to send their children across town, in part because that is where the mayor's daughter attends. For them, this is rational input for their decision making.[11]

Market Ideas in NCLB   We see these free-market ideas at work in the federal NCLB Act and in many state policies. NCLB requires schools to document their productivity with large-scale testing, publish the results, and face the consequences that come when families have greater choice and private providers are given a role. The legislation does not require adequate and necessary resources, conditions, and opportunities for learning.

These resources, including ensuring schools' capacity for hiring highly competent teachers, could make a real difference for students' learning. Instead, "high-stakes" tests and a ranking system that creates competitiveness among schools is presumed to motivate individual teachers and students to teach better and study harder and therefore gain rewards and avoid sanctions. If schools fail to meet their test-score improvement targets, parents of low-income students can use the federal funding to purchase tutoring services, either from the school or from private companies. If those consequences aren't sufficient, parents can send their children to a more successful school. Eventually, failing schools can be "taken over" by the state or "reconstituted" (current administrators and teachers removed and replaced by a new staff), or turned into charter schools.

Schools as Instruments of Equity and Social Justice

Even as policymakers have looked to assembly-line production, corporate management, and free markets for ideas to guide their efforts to make schools more effective and efficient, they have also sought to ensure that schools are fair and democratic. And just as science has informed efforts to increase productivity, science has also informed policies aimed at promoting equity.

Factory-Style Equity   As we've described in earlier chapters, equity at the turn of the nineteenth century was conceptualized as making sure that factory-like schools provided different and suitable types of curriculum and instruction for students with different family backgrounds, IQs, and future roles in society. To use the factory metaphor, these would be different, but equitable assembly lines. As we described in Chapters 2 and 6, deficit thinking related to race and language and the science of IQ influenced these policies. The tracking practices and approaches to categorical programs we discussed in Chapter 8 are contemporary remnants of this factory-like effectiveness and equity.

Equity through Systems Change   By the 1960s, the federal government, in response to the *Brown v. Board of Education* decision and the civil rights movement, sought ways to understand and improve the educational opportunities of students of color. It commissioned sociologist James Coleman to survey educational opportunity. The government wanted to inform its educational policies with information about the extent to which schools were racially segregated and whether resources and less tangible aspects of schooling, such as teacher morale, were distributed evenly across schools.

Coleman and his team decided to investigate whether the *countable* school resources of interest to the government, such as buildings, library resources, teachers' qualifications, class size, and so on, were related to students' achievement test scores. Coleman hoped this approach would reveal the dynamics of how systemic inequalities in opportunities produced achievement gaps between well-off and poor students and between whites and students of color.

The study's findings surprised everyone, most especially James Coleman. His now famous "Coleman Report" concluded that though there were differences in tangible school resources, they did not seem to be systematically related to students' test scores. For example, the number of books in the school library or the level of teacher training did not seem to explain the test-score gaps between high- and low-achieving schools. But if not resources, what then? Consistent with the systems view that people in the system are more important than the technical features, Coleman and his colleagues argued that, when it comes to gaps in academic achievement, school resources matter far less than students' race and parents' income, as well as the racial and economic backgrounds of their classmates.

Coleman was partly right and mostly wrong. Like Coleman, many researchers since have found that students do better on tests if they attend schools where most of their classmates are not poor. This is true not only for middle- and upper-income students, but for poor students as well. However, the available social science methods of the time limited Coleman's findings, and constrained his results about the impact of resources.[12] Most significant, Coleman failed to understand that resources like books and teachers are critical to education, but that, taken one by one, increasing any individual resource a bit may not be *sufficient* to raise test scores. For example, simply reducing class size may not improve educational outcomes if teachers continue to teach in the same ways as before. On the other hand, smaller classes are *helpful* if teachers take advantage of them to improve teaching methods and spend more time with individual students.

Because Coleman found that academic outcomes were higher for blacks who attended desegregated schools, his findings were used as part of the scientific rationale for school desegregation in the late 1960s and 1970s. Policymakers developed plans for racial integration, and many of those plans included programs to develop positive and productive relationships within integrated schools. But, unfortunately, Coleman's study and its legacy undermined another part of the civil rights victory that Coleman himself sought to support—the ruling in *Brown v. Board of Education* that all students have a right to "education on equal terms."

By the 1980s, policies aimed at promoting equity shifted almost completely to a focus on promoting "effective schools" for children in low-income communities of color. Policies emphasized changing the culture of schools—high expectations that "all children can learn," with a focus on academics, strong leadership, and so on, rather than on either racial integration or on ensuring high-quality resources.

A Market View of Equity   Viewing schools through the lens of a market economy, choice and competition become the major factors in ensuring equity. The rationale is as follows: When public school systems assign students to attend specific public schools, those schools are guaranteed their "customers." With no other schools competing for their students, these schools feel little pressure to be excellent. So, the only "choice" families have whose children are assigned to bad schools is to "buy" their way out in one of two expensive ways. They can pay the tuition and send their children to private schools, or they can buy a house in a neighborhood with a better school. This situation creates inequalities because the families of low-income students (many of whom are also students of color) can't afford to "buy" their way out of bad schools.

Two policies are currently touted as ways to equalize students' chances to attend a good school. One is to inject choice into the public system through such mechanisms as charter schools, magnet schools, and open enrollment systems. The other is to provide students with vouchers so that they can use public money to attend "better" private schools.

Many social justice advocates counter this rationale with the argument that every school should provide students with high-quality opportunities to learn, and the burden of finding a good school should not be placed on families. However, the deregulation that accompanies market policies has worked against this goal. It was this rationale that led Congress in 1994, for example, to strip systemic education reform policy of standards regulating the resources and conditions for learning in all schools. And, in NCLB, test-score evidence, not inadequate resources and conditions, is the basis for permitting families to choose to send their children to better schools.

Figure 11.1 provides a summary of our preceding discussion of the cultural ideas that have shaped U.S. educational policy.

Policy Effects on Teachers and Students

The whole point of education policy is, as we noted at the beginning of this chapter, to ensure that schools meet society's goals effectively, efficiently, and equitably. Of course, policies do not accomplish these goals directly, but only through their effects on educators and students. We now examine how current federal, state, and local policies are affecting teachers and students in today's schools. We begin with test-driven accountability policies, and then turn to scientifically based curriculum. Both are elements of No Child Left Behind. Here, too, we pay particular attention to how these policies affect teachers who believe schools should bring social justice to those most disadvantaged in American society.

Metaphors

Policy Assumptions	Schools as factories	Schools as well managed corporations	Schools as markets
Underlying theory	Scientific management	Systems theory	Free-market economics
How to maximize effectiveness	• Structure school as linear sequence of standardized and scientifically determined procedures that transform students' "raw material" into responsible citizens and good workers.	• Organize schools into well-aligned and coordinated systems, where the "whole is more than the sum of the parts." • Promote organizational learning.	• Set goals. • Deregulate schooling processes. • Provide good information about schools' results. • Allow families to choose their schools to infuse competition into the system.
How to maximize efficiency	• Divide the system into small, manageable parts: grade levels; subject areas; ability groups. • Train specialists in the best practices for each part.	• Set standards, provide adequate resources, ample local flexibility, and hold educators accountable for results.	• Provide results-based incentives and sanctions to motivate schools and students.
How to achieve equity	• Match students to classes/programs according to their abilities and needs, and, thereby, provide all an equal opportunity for the education that best suits them.	• Provide the supports and resources for all students to meet the same high standards, including additional supports for those with greater needs.	• Hold schools accountable for reducing achievement test score gaps. • Allow low-income families to leave low performing schools.

FIGURE 11.1 *Three Education Policy Metaphors.*

Accountability for Results: Large-Scale Tests and "High Stakes"

In the past decade, the business concept of "accountability for results" has become enormously popular as an education policy strategy. Today, results-based accountability has taken the form of policies requiring schools to administer large-scale achievement tests and attaching "high stakes" to students' performance on those tests. *High stakes* means that the test results have important consequences for students and schools. NCLB is the most prominent example, but many states have adopted high-stakes testing policies as well.

The idea of accountability for results comes out of systems-theory management: Collecting information from large-scale achievement tests can provide feedback that educators and policymakers can use in their efforts to "continuously improve" their performance and meet standards. However, high-stakes policies have also become popular because they fit with the market-based assumption (mostly wrongheaded, in our view) that the problem of low and unequal achievement is attributable primarily to the lack of motivation exhibited by students, teachers, school districts, and parents in a system with no competition or consequences. The theory is that if test scores have high-stakes consequences, educators and students will be motivated to perform well in order to reap rewards or avoid punishing sanctions.

Advocates also claim that accountability for results makes the system more equitable, since schools must hold all students to the same high standards, ending what the current Bush administration calls the "bigotry of low expectations." Unfortunately, however, this perspective has led or allowed officials to ignore serious inadequacies and inequalities in resources, conditions, and capacity. Indeed, some of the strongest supporters of a market view of schooling claim that there are now (or will be very shortly) enough resources and investment in the system to deliver an education to all students, once high-stakes testing has leveraged sufficient motivation.

High Stakes for Students   As we described in Chapter 6, educators have long used test results as one source of information to help them make important decisions about students—determining whether they should be in a high-level class or program, be promoted to the next grade, qualify for special education, be designated as an English learner, be admitted to college, and, in a few cases, win scholarship money. However, many of today's "high stakes" testing policies make students' performance on a test the only factor in making very important decisions, such as grade promotion and high school graduation.

Grade Promotion Policies   Today, school districts increasingly use standardized tests as the basis on which students are promoted into higher grades. For example, Chicago Public Schools instituted a policy in 1996 establishing minimum test scores on the standardized, norm-referenced Iowa Tests of Basic Skills (ITBS) in reading and mathematics for students to be promoted into the fourth, seventh, and ninth grades. The state of Florida requires that all students pass Florida's fourth-grade test (Florida Comprehensive Assessment Test, or FCAT) to be promoted to the fifth grade. Some local school districts in Florida use the tests to determine promotion at other grade levels. Chicago and Florida policymakers, like those in many other places, hope such policies will stop "social promotion."

Social promotion means that students move from one grade to another with others of their age, regardless of their achievement. Policymakers often point to social promotion as an irresponsible education practice, and in 1999, the Clinton administration announced that it was time to end it. Actually, few school systems have social promotion as an explicit policy, and few educators think it's a good idea. Yet, in bureaucratic and inflexible schools, the only alternative—grade retention— may be even worse. Neither social promotion nor grade retention addresses the underlying problems that prevent students from learning, but considerable research shows that grade retention increases the likelihood that students will drop out of school, perhaps because they end up being older than their high school classmates.

The most educationally sound policy is neither social promotion nor retention based on high-stakes tests. It is providing students the supports and conditions they need to learn. FairTest, an advocacy organization that monitors the use of tests across the nation, recommends the alternatives to high-stakes testing listed in Focal Point 11.1.

FOCAL POINT 11.1

Policy Alternatives to High-Stakes Testing for Grade Promotion

Targeted supports and services that are available to students when they need them, which may include tutoring, after-school programs, Saturday classes, or other support services. These services need to be studied to ensure they are effective in enabling students at risk to catch up and that they are not merely test coaching programs.

Professional development for teachers to enable them to address a broader range of diverse student needs. Research shows that teachers are the single most important factor to student success.

Mixed-age classrooms where students at different levels work together on common problems.

Continuous relationships with teachers. Research has shown that students do better in school when their teachers know them well and when they work with the same teacher for two or more years.

Developing a variety of assessment skills and tools for classroom use (such as performances and portfolios) to help teachers and parents assess what students are learning, to find gaps, and address problems immediately. High-quality classroom assessment used to help each child has been shown to be a powerful tool for improving student learning.

Source: FairTest, http://www.fairtest.org/arn/retenfct.htm.

High-Stakes Tests for English Learners   Promotion tests are not the only high-stakes tests that determine students' learning opportunities. Mauro Bautista explains in the following quote how a variety of high-stakes tests influence whether or not his students who are still learning English will have access to grade-level curriculum or remain in remedial classes.

———————————————————※ ※ ※———————————————————

The California English Language Development Test (CELDT) and the California Standards Test (CST) are critical to EL students because in order for students to be reclassified as Fluent English Proficient they need to pass the CELDT and score at least a "basic" in the CST ELA (English Language Arts component).

In addition to the CELDT and the CST, another critical high-stakes exam in my district is the Diagnosis and Placement Inventory (DPI). The DPI is the exam given to all fifth-grade EL students in order to help determine their middle-school ELA curriculum. However, it is based on the ESL middle-school curriculum, which the fifth graders have never seen. Thus, many of the students score low. Often a successful EL fifth grader, who is receiving 3s and 4s, scores low on the DPI and, instead of receiving grade-level ELA where students read novels, she/he is placed in ESL 2, where students are learning to read paragraphs. The DPI is a vehicle for tracking EL students in nonrigorous curriculums that do not prepare them for higher education.

—**Mauro Bautista**
Middle-school bilingual education coordinator

Mauro's experience is not unusual. Most states and school districts require that English learners achieve a particular cut score on standardized, norm-referenced achievement tests as part of the process of being designated as fluent enough in English to benefit from regular instruction in academic content. Expecting students to demonstrate proficiency in academic subject matter as proof of their English proficiency is flawed in many ways. Not the least of these flaws is that many schools do not teach English learners much subject matter content before they have acquired English.

High School Graduation or "Exit" Exams   The most visible, and perhaps the most consequential, high-stakes testing policies are high school graduation tests, often called "exit exams." These tests determine whether high school seniors who have met all of their high school's graduation requirements can be awarded a high school diploma. As in the case of other high-stakes test policies, high school graduation tests reflect the lack of trust in schools, teachers, and students to meet high standards without lots of outside pressure. Advocates for the tests often argue that the "high school diploma must mean something" and that the tests prove to the public and to employers that high school graduates have mastered a state-prescribed set of knowledge and skills.

CONCEPT TABLE 11.2 *Public School Students Enrolled in States with Exit Exams*

Table 1: Percentage of Public School Students Enrolled in States with Exit Exams

Student Group	2005 (19 States)*	Projected for 2012 (26 States)*
All students	50%	72%
American Indian/Native Alaskan	31%	72%
Asian/Pacific Islander	37%	79%
Black	65%	77%
Hispanic	46%	87%
White	48%	65%
All minority students (American Indian/Native Alaskan, Asian/Pacific Islander, Black, and Hispanic)	53%	82%
English language learners/limited English proficient students**	39%	87%
Students with individualized education programs	52%	71%
Students eligible for free or reduced-price lunch**	49%	74%

*Estimates are based on 2002–03 data from NCES.

**Data from Tennessee were not available for these groups and were not included.

Table reads: In 2005, 50% of all public school students were enrolled in the 19 states with exit exams, By 2012, an estimated 72% will be enrolled in the 26 states scheduled to have exit exams at that point.

Source: Center on Education Policy, based on data from National Center for Education Statistics, 2003.

Source: Center for Educational Policy, *State High School Exit Exams: States Try Harder but Gaps Persist,* August 2005.

As illustrated in Concept Table 11.2, as of fall 2005, 26 states either had exit exams already or would be phasing in a graduation test requirement over the next few years. The Center on Educational Policy reports that by 2012, 72 percent of all American public school students, including 82 percent of minority students, 71 percent of special education students, and 87 percent of English language learners will have to pass an exit exam to earn a high school diploma.[13]

The concept table shows that high school exit exam policies have affected different groups of students differently and that the achievement and opportunity gaps we described in Chapter 1 are reflected in the results. Exit exam policies have been adopted in states that teach most of the nation's students of color and English learners. The rates of success and failure on these tests reflect the patterns of inequality that we described in Chapter 1. In particular, the pass rates of limited-English students and those students with educational disabilities are far below those of other students. This is not surprising because the tests are given in English, and few states make accommodations in the test for disabled students.

However, African American and Latino students do fail these tests at higher rates than other students. These are students who generally have fewer educational resources and opportunities both in and out of school. In California, for example, the highest rates of exit exam failure occur for students at schools with shortages of qualified teachers and other resource problems.[14] Thus, not only are the underlying premises of the exit exam highly questionable (that it motivates students and teachers to try harder, and preserves the meaning and value of the high school diploma), the exam is patently unfair to students who do not attend schools where they have a meaningful opportunity to learn the material that will be on the tests.

It's very clear that students are feeling the pressure from these tests, and so are many teachers. Judy Smith communicates this in the next quote. She also reveals her frustration with a policy that sees a paper-and-pencil test as the only legitimate measure of what students know and can do.

Students feel incredibly anxious about taking the test. So many of them seem to have been programmed by parents, teachers, and society that tests are the only true measurement of their intelligence.

I have proctored the high school exit exam. I am amazed that students are asked to sit still for three to four hours and read and write to their best ability. If they do poorly, they don't receive a diploma. The pressure on them is immense. It is important that students show aptitude in their studies, but the method by which they must show it doesn't make a lot of sense. They aren't law students taking the bar exam or medical students taking their exams. These are kids. The policymakers need to spend more time in the classroom.

—**Judy Smith**
High school social studies

Research on the impact of high-stakes tests has focused primarily on whether these tests lead to higher levels of achievement and whether they increase the number of students who drop out of school. The results have been mixed, partly because the studies have compared changes in achievement and graduation rates in states with graduation tests and to states without these tests. At this gross level, it's impossible to sort out the effects of tests from the effects of everything else that's going on in states. However, a number of prominent researchers believe that there is no research evidence that justifies high-stakes graduation tests as a means for increasing achievement.[15] At the same time, as we explain next, there are multiple other reasons for not using tests to make high-stakes decisions about students.

Are High-Stakes Tests for Students Scientifically and Educationally Defensible? In 1999 Congress mandated the National Academy of Sciences to study how large-scale tests were used to make high-stakes decisions and to recommend ways of using tests that are scientifically and educationally defensible. The Academy panel investigated three high-stakes uses of testing: tracking, grade promotion, and high school graduation. In particular, they looked at whether tests were used in discriminatory ways and whether they were used accurately to measure students' achievements. The panel established a set of principles for appropriate use of tests:

- The test is valid for the specific purpose for which it is used. For example, tests that might be good for influencing classroom practice are not valid for making decisions about students unless they match the curriculum and teaching that students actually experience.
- Because no test is perfect, no single score can be considered a definitive measure of students' knowledge.
- A single test score should not be used for making consequential decisions in the absence of other information about students' knowledge and skills.
- A test-driven decision cannot be justified if the consequence is not educationally sound.

The panel also warned that differences in test results and consequences among groups of students—such as the lower scores and higher retention rates of low-income students of color must be carefully studied. These differences may not necessarily mean that there is something wrong with the particular test being used, but could reveal troublesome gaps in students' opportunities to learn. Either cause, however, signals a serious problem with a high-stakes policy.

Important among the panel's findings is that accountability for school performance belongs to the whole system, from states to parents, and cannot be imposed only on students. Consequently, high-stakes tests should only be used after changes in teaching and learning opportunities ensure that students have a genuine opportunity to learn what is tested. Moreover, special accommodations must be provided to accurately test English language learners and students with disabilities. Neither leaving them out of assessments nor simply testing them like everyone else is appropriate. Finally, if tests are used to make high-stakes decisions about individual children, the system must carefully monitor such practices and study their impact on students.[16]

The National Academy panel's conclusions are similar to the assessment standards we displayed in Chapter 6 that were developed by the three most prominent professional organizations of testing experts: the American Educational Research Association, American Psychological Association, and National Council on Measurement in Education. Those standards make clear the gaps between professional judgment and the popularity of using tests to make high-stakes decisions about students.

Are High-Stakes Tests for Students Legally Defensible?   The civil rights community has also raised serious questions about whether high-stakes testing denies educational opportunity to students based on their race, national origin, sex, or disability. The NAACP Legal Defense Fund, MALDEF (Mexican American Legal Defense and Education Fund), and dozens of other civil rights organizations have made easing the impact of high-stakes tests on minority students a priority. In 1999 the Office of Civil Rights (OCR) drafted a report, *The Use of Tests When Making*

High-Stakes Decisions for Students: A Resource Guide for Educators, that laid out some of the professional and legal standards for educators and policymakers.

The OCR guide applies to testing certain legal principles articulated in the Fourteenth Amendment to the Constitution and in federal statutes and regulations— namely, that intentional discrimination is prohibited, as are programs with a discriminatory, disparate impact. Additionally, the guide discusses the legal obligation to provide for the special needs of English language learners and students with disabilities, and the need to ensure Fifth Amendment due process rights for all students subjected to high-stakes testing decisions. Rather than criticize testing per se, the guide makes clear that the appropriate use of testing can advance learning and help safeguard educational opportunity. However, it also insists that good educational results are compatible with the enforcement of principles of nondiscrimination.

Unfortunately, this useful document has never been distributed. When the George W. Bush administration took office in 2001, the OCR placed the guide into a new category on its website—"archival file retained for historical purposes." Although this does not mean that the document will never see the light of day, it adds additional evidence about just how political the testing of students has become.

High Stakes for Schools   High-stakes testing policies for schools are those that translate students' test scores into a measure for labeling schools "good" or "bad" relative to other schools or to levy sanctions against schools if they don't show improvement in their scores. Under NCLB, every school has an achievement test score target and, in the case of high schools, a graduation rate target, that it must meet each year in order to satisfy the law's requirement for "Adequate Yearly Progress" (AYP).

Although each state sets its own targets, the federal government compiles the list of schools that meet AYP and those that do not. Schools that fail to meet AYP are identified as "in need of improvement" and have a fixed period of time to raise their scores. Although the federal government has systematically avoided using the word *failing* to describe these schools, that is how most of the public and most educators interpret the label of "in need of improvement."[17]

If schools do not improve on schedule, they are subject to interventions, including giving the schools' federal funding directly to parents so they can purchase tutoring services outside the school, allowing parents to take their children to another school and, eventually, having the state take over the school, firing the principal and reconstituting its staff, or turning the school into a charter school. Many states have policies that also provide "targeted assistance," giving schools a chance to improve before sanctions are levied. Some states provide intervention teams to help them "fix" their problems.

Although the policy assumption is that these consequences will motivate educators to improve, the next section details some of the considerable evidence that high-stakes tests have negative effects on the teaching and learning climate at those schools where students have a history of unequal opportunities and low achievement.

The Presumption of Adequate Resources   As explained, if the lack of resources, appropriate supplementary help, or qualified teachers diminishes student performance, it makes no sense to believe that a test will "motivate" students to overcome these educational constraints. Kimberly Min and Mauro Bautista, who are both are in schools designated as "low performing" under California's test-based accountability system, illustrate the situation well.

Kimberly reports:

─────────────────────────── ✂ ✂ ✂ ───────────────────────────

When people ask me why I think my school is low performing, I can rattle off a list of reasons: lack of resources (I have worked without textbooks and with broken chairs and broken desks. Last year a desk collapsed on two students who were writing and it was reported to the office. It took the office three days to respond); lack of supplies (there is a shortage of supplies and many teachers have to purchase their own materials. Teachers cannot rely on the school to have the items that they need to teach); lack of teacher training and professional development (teachers sign in at meetings and sign out and you are considered "professionally developed"); lack of this and that. All these things are true, but I think that people do not want to acknowledge an under-lying cause for these deficiencies: We still operate in a racist school system where schools of color are not only neglected but set up to fail. The test is designed to distinguish high-performing from low-performing schools—not to give students the best possible education.

The educational system must change so that schools receive needed resources before second language learners, bilingual students, and others perceive themselves to be low-performing individuals.

—**KIMBERLY MIN**
Third-grade teacher

───

Mauro's report is similar, even though his school has made considerable test score gains:

─────────────────────────── ✂ ✂ ✂ ───────────────────────────

Yes, my school is a low-performing school, but students have shown dramatic improvement over the last three years. The current administration has emphasized rigor in the curriculum, has invested funds in extracurricular programs (such as drama, sports, music, art), and sometimes has deviated from district mandates if we feel the mandates do not help students. We still face important challenges. One, we continue to have a high teacher turnover rate. Thus, each year we have inexperienced teachers. At times we lose teachers in the middle of the year and, thus, our students have long-term subs. Two, we continue to struggle with low expectations. We say we have high expectations, but as soon as there is a challenge, we are quick to place blame on the students instead of reflecting on our own practices. Three, we continue to struggle with low parent involvement. Four, classroom instruction continues to rely too heavily on lecturing, textbooks, and individual and silent work.

—**MAURO BAUTISTA**
Middle-school bilingual education coordinator

───

Instructional Distortion   Teachers have little control over test-based account-ability policies, but they certainly feel their effects—both in their classrooms and in their public image. For example, social studies teacher Judy Smith, whose school is also classified as "low performing," describes how high-stakes accountability tests required under NCLB influence her work with English learners.

———————————————— ⋈ ⋈ ⋈ ————————————————

We are all affected by the high-stakes exams. I feel a great need to teach students reading and writing skills to prepare them for the high school exit exam even though I am a history teacher. I believe deep down that all students need to read, write, and think; later on in life they can research the details of the nitty-gritty history stuff. Occasionally students complain about my emphasizing reading and writing skills, but they need to pass the exam to graduate.

At the same time, the California Standards Test that will determine whether my school stays on probation under NCLB assesses history knowl-edge, not writing. Because my school was in its second year of probation, the history teachers felt pressure to teach as much content as possible.

Therefore, I am challenged to emphasize reading and writing so my EL students can graduate and emphasize history so the school can get off probation. The stress I feel is very real and I don't know if I am doing everything I can to support the students.

—JUDY SMITH
High school social studies

Elementary school teacher Magda Gonzales reports similar frustration:

———————————————— ⋈ ⋈ ⋈ ————————————————

My students are very smart; they are problem solvers and critical thinkers. They use their Spanish when they speak and write, and they express their thoughts with meaning and value. It infuriates and frustrates me that stan-dardized assessments step in the path of the exciting, high-level critical thinking skills my students have acquired. I will continue to teach my stu-dents strategies for taking these tests, but I will also continue to struggle to find ways to incorporate a safe, multicultural learning experience for them.

—MAGDA GONZALES
First-year teacher, grades 3 and 4

In Focal Point 11.2, longtime assessment expert and former president of the Amer-ican Educational Research Association W. James Popham sums up the very high instructional price that schools are paying as a consequence of policymakers' pur-suit of school improvement by attaching high-stakes consequences to large-scale tests. Popham's sobering observations have been documented in other research.[18]

Dishonesty   Well-publicized reports from Texas and New York suggest that James Popham's third consequence—dishonesty—is occurring on a large scale, and not

FOCAL POINT 11.2

The Negative Effects of High Stakes
on Curriculum and Teaching

Educators in America's public schools obviously are under tremendous pressure to improve their students' scores on whatever NCLB tests their state has chosen.

With few exceptions, however, the assessments that states have chosen to implement because of NCLB are either nationally standardized achievement tests or state-developed standards-based tests—both of which are flawed. Here, then, are three adverse classroom consequences seen in states where instructionally insensitive NCLB tests are used:

- *Curricular reductionism.* In an effort to boost their students' NCLB test scores, many teachers jettison curricular content that—albeit important—is not apt to be covered on an upcoming test. As a result, students end up educationally shortchanged.
- *Excessive drilling.* Because it is essentially impossible to raise students' scores on instructionally insensitive tests, many teachers—in desperation—require seemingly endless practice with items similar to those on an approaching accountability test. This dreary drilling often stamps out any genuine joy students might (and should) experience while they learn.
- *Modeled dishonesty.* Some teachers, frustrated by being asked to raise scores on tests deliberately designed to preclude such score raising, may be tempted to adopt unethical practices during the administration or scoring of accountability tests. Students learn that whenever the stakes are high enough, the teacher thinks it's OK to cheat. This is a lesson that should never be taught.

These three negative consequences of using instructionally insensitive standardized tests as measuring tools, taken together, make it clear that today's widespread method of judging schools does more than lead to invalid evaluations. Beyond that, such tests can dramatically lower the quality of education.

Source: From W. James Popham, "F Is for Assessment," 2005, www.edutopia. org/assessment.

only on the part of teachers. State investigators revealed that educators at 12 Houston high schools and 4 middle schools had altered students' records to hide the fact that they had dropped out of school. During his tenure as Houston superintendent, Rod Paige, George W. Bush's first U.S. secretary of education, instituted performance contracting as a way to provide school administrators with incentives that would spur higher productivity in Houston schools. Principals forfeited their job security for higher pay under performance contracts. In plain terms, this policy meant that the principals would lose their jobs—no questions asked—if they didn't reach measurable objectives, including raising test scores and lowering dropout rates.

The pressure on Houston educators to fudge the numbers was great, and they did. Auditors reviewed records of 5,458 students who left school in 2000–2001 and found that over half had wrong or missing information. District and school officials wrongly reported that students had moved or transferred to another school, when they had actually dropped out of school. Many observers suspected that these students were "encouraged" to drop out so their low test scores wouldn't bring down the schools' average. The state was forced to reclassify nearly 3,000 students as dropouts and lower the ratings of 15 schools to "academically unacceptable" from their prized ratings as "exemplary" or "recognized."[19]

In July 2003, *The New York Times* investigators found that thousands of the city's lowest-achieving students were being "pushed out" by officials desperate to make their schools look good on the state's graduation tests. After "encouraging" students who were likely to fail to leave school, the educators covered their tracks by reporting falsely that the students had "transferred to another educational setting." The *Times* concluded that, faced with low graduation rates followed by loss of some federal funding, schools succumbed to the temptation and tried to make their results look good by getting rid of low performers.[20]

It is likely that these scandals sent school officials a strong message on the risks of cheating, but nothing has changed to lessen the pressures or illogic of trying to motivate excellence with threats of job loss or embarrassment.

A Continuing Burden on Low-Income Communities   Test-based accountability also falls short because it gives parents a sequence of responsibilities that are all but impossible to fulfill. First, parents must monitor their own school's "quality," making sense of the limited data that schools make available. Next, they must decide if there are better and realistic alternatives. Then, should they decide to switch, they must negotiate school bureaucracies to effect a transfer to a school that is likely to be farther away from home, assure themselves of reliable transportation, and subject their child to a perhaps wrenching experience of leaving a familiar environment and friends.

A better solution is for authorities to make sure that all schools are good ones. It can be done. The scheme just outlined briefly might work well for some middle-class parents who have the knowledge, skills, and power to take those difficult steps as well as to participate effectively in school board elections, site decision-making councils, and other avenues for civic involvement. However, the demands of poor parents can be more easily ignored by school officials. Even when the policies give poor parents the choice to leave a failing school, they are usually compelled to accept the quality of educational services provided to them, whether they like it or not. Better choices are rarely available.

The Likely End Result: Nearly All Schools Left Behind   Since 2001 several researchers have studied the likelihood of NCLB actually reaching its goals. Making statistical projections based on the rates at which students and schools are improving, they predict a disaster. That disaster won't result from the fact that students are incapable of learning or that schools can't help them learn. What we've reported throughout this book provides evidence that they can learn and, under the right circumstances, will learn very, very well. Rather the disaster will come from problems embedded in the details of NCLB's requirements.

NCLB requires all students to score at "proficient" levels in reading, math, and science by 2014. One of the country's most highly regarded assessment experts,

Robert Linn, predicted in his 2003 presidential address to the American Educational Research Association, that, based on the record of the National Assessment of Educational Progress, it will take 57 years for all fourth graders to score at the proficient level in mathematics, 66 years for eighth graders, and 166 years for twelfth graders.

Taking current requirements into account, analysts predict that by 2014, 99 percent of California schools will be labeled as failing under NCLB. California has a large population of English learners and a recent history of low test scores, making test-based accountability particularly hard in that state. However, states with few English learners and a history of high test scores face similar problems. Minnesota, for example, expects 80 percent of its schools to fail to meet the NCLB standard by 2014.[21] Equally grim predications have been made in Massachusetts, Connecticut, Kentucky, Illinois, Indiana, Michigan, Minnesota, Ohio, and Wisconsin.[22] Most researchers predict that similarly high failure rates will occur all across the country.

Will a school's label of failing really matter? One might think that, if a policy labels 80 or 99 percent of the schools in a state as failing, nobody would take the label seriously. However, NCLB carries with it real consequences that threaten the very existence of these public schools. As we described earlier, when a school fails to meet AYP two years in a row, parents have a right to transfer their children to more successful schools. That means, as researcher Gerald Bracey has pointed out, that if a school's English learners fail to meet AYP one year, and fewer than 95 percent of its disabled students come to school on the day of the test the following year, the school must offer every one of its students an opportunity to transfer.[23]

School systems around the country have faced this situation already. In many cities, thousands of parents have requested transfers, and there are simply no other schools that can or will take their children. Gerald Bracey reminds us of probably the worst example in the nation. In Chicago, of the 200,000 students eligible for transfers, there were only 500 spaces available.[24] We must also note that private schools, often cited by voucher advocates as the highest-quality choice alternatives to public schools, are not required to administer any of these high-stakes exams.

Of course, if the ambitious rhetoric and high standards of No Child Left Behind were accompanied by an infusion of new resources into schools and into the social and physical supports that children need outside of school (health care, decent housing, jobs for their parents, etc.), the projections for the future would not be so grim. However, the market ideology that dominates education policymaking today does not allow for such a radical approach to reform. In that view, increased achievement and closing the achievement gaps among groups will depend on the hard work of teachers and students who are properly motivated by the high stakes attached to large-scale tests.

To be sure, the increasing use of test-driven high-stakes policies has brought an outcry of criticism that almost equals the enthusiasm of supporters. Nearly every state has asked the federal government to modify or fix how the law is applied, and several grassroots groups have developed networks and websites to organize protests against it.[25] The concerns range from the technical (e.g., concerns about tests being inaccurate or biased), to political (e.g., disagreement that tests will "motivate" improvement), and the philosophical (e.g., objections to an overemphasis on a narrow set of measurable outcomes as opposed to the larger democratic purposes of schooling). The impact of widespread protest has varied. In some places high-stakes policies have been softened (test accommodations for learning disabled students), modified (allowing multiple types of assessment to determine graduation), or postponed. So far, however, these protests have done little to stem the popularity and increasing use of high-stakes testing as the cornerstone of school reform.

It is likely that the federal government will adjust NCLB to avoid the most obvious problems. Indeed, some modifications to some of the most irrational requirements and stipulations have already been made, and others are being discussed. However, as of 2006, the logic of NCLB remains the rule of law. Even though there is no evidence for the claim that high-stakes tests (and the accountability and choice policies linked to them) will pressure educators to adopt practices that leave no child behind, policymakers and much of the public see the risks as well worth taking. Educators, on the other hand, are left to grapple with the painful consequences that NCLB is bringing to students, schools, and the nation's confidence in public education.

"Scientifically Based Research" and Teaching

A second NCLB policy that has an enormous effect on teachers is the ruling that federal funds can be spent only on programs and practices proven effective with "scientifically based research." As noted previously, throughout the twentieth century, educators looked to science to guide their practices, and today the science most trusted are studies of education practices that use the same methods that are used for testing medical treatments. This is how the federal government defines "scientifically based research."

What that means, then, is that school districts receiving funding through the NCLB's Reading First program, aimed at helping schools ensure that every child can read at grade level by the end of third grade, must spend that money on instructional programs and materials, assessments, and professional development grounded in scientifically based reading research. Curricula purchased with federal funding for use with limited English proficient children; improvement programs and professional development purchased by school districts identified as "in need of improvement" because they have failed to meet its test score targets; technical assistance that states provide; and so on, all must meet the criteria of having demonstrated through scientifically based research that they improve students' achievement test scores.

NCLB defines scientifically based research as "research that involves the application of rigorous, systematic, and objective procedures to obtain reliable and valid knowledge relevant to education activities and programs."[26] The U.S. Department of Education is creating an online database, called the "What Works Clearinghouse," that will provide a list of programs and practices that have been tested with scientifically based research to guide educational decision makers as they choose programs that are approved for federal funding.[27] Grover J. (Russ) Whitehurst, the director of the U.S. Department of Education's Institute of Education Sciences and a strong advocate for NCLB's scientifically based research requirement, argues that this policy will replace the "folk wisdom of education" with a scientific knowledge base. Whitehurst claims that "there is every reason to believe that, if we invest in the education sciences and develop mechanisms to encourage evidence-based practices, we will see progress and transformation . . . of the same order and magnitude as we have seen in medicine and agriculture."[28]

Although nobody wants educators to adopt programs for which there is no evidence of merit, the idea of scientifically based research is not simply about separating foolish or useless pedagogy and programs from those programs that are useful. Many of the most reputable researchers from education and other fields worry that the Department of Education has defined science so narrowly as to discourage much very excellent teaching.

Concerns about Scripted Curricula   Perhaps the biggest concern is that many of the scientifically based curricula "script" the teacher's role to guarantee a faithful and consistent implementation across all of the diverse settings that have selected it. "Scripting" specifies the precise words, content, presentation, and materials that teachers are required to use in lessons. Such centralized control over lessons has great appeal for some, but is a dreadful prospect for others. On the one hand, it does increase the chances of students getting consistent educational experiences from class to class, and even across the school, state, and country—depending on the program in question. This sort of uniformity can be helpful, especially when schools lack many well-trained teachers and other appropriate learning opportunities and conditions. On the other hand, there is simply no decent substitute for highly competent teachers and supportive colleagues who have flexibility to pursue the learning standards for their students in unique, creative, and situationally appropriate ways.

A different perspective, preferred by many of today's progressive educators and researchers, sees scientifically derived findings about school and other learning as one crucial—necessary, but not sufficient—component of countless factors that enter into a teacher's curriculum decisions and pedagogy. Teachers absolutely must know the educational research relevant to their practice; they benefit from working in environments where these findings along with their own and colleagues' practice can be aligned with the best theory and resources to arrive at the best teaching and curriculum that suits the students whom they face every day.

Reading First   One of the areas affected most by the scientifically based requirement is reading. The funds set aside to support students in low-income communities and communities of color to become successful early readers have very strict requirements attached to them.

> *No Child Left Behind* requires that Reading First support those programs that teach children five skills (phonemic awareness, phonics, fluency, vocabulary and comprehension). These skills have been shown to be critical to early reading success through years of scientifically based research on the practice of reading instruction. In April 2000, these research findings were reported in the congressionally mandated National Reading Panel report mentioned earlier; they have now been written into the new law.[29]

Although there is no official U.S. Department of Education "approved list" of reading programs for use under the Reading First program, states must demonstrate to the federal government how it will assist school districts in identifying assessments, instructional materials, and programs and offering professional development—all of which must focus on strategies and approaches based on scientifically based reading research. In determining which districts to support, it is the state's responsibility to ensure that all programs, strategies and activities proposed and implemented meet the criteria for scientifically based reading research.

In practice, this has meant that most school districts with low-income students and students of color have adopted a handful of reading programs in hopes that they will qualify for these much needed federal funds to support reading. In California, for example, the federal government committed to provide approximately $900 million, over a six-year period, to improve classroom instruction in reading provided that "substantial progress" is made toward this goal. That money is allocated only to districts with a poor record of reading achievement that agree to adopt and fully implement a state-approved reading/ language arts program. Two programs have been approved—the Houghton Mifflin: A Legacy of Literacy or SRA/Open Court Reading 2000 or 2002—not only for Reading First money but also to qualify for any state funding to purchase instructional materials for kindergarten to grade 6. Districts receiving the funding also must agree to monitor whether teachers are fully and effectively teaching the adopted instructional program and using all of its resources.

Both of these programs include a "pacing schedule," a required number of minutes of instructional time on the program, regularly scheduled assessments and analysis, professional development for teachers and principals, and instructional support through coaches. The purpose of a pacing schedule is to ensure that teachers in all classrooms, grade levels, and schools know when, and in what sequence, each lesson is taught and to ensure that the lessons are taught in an active, direct mode every day. Principals are to protect the daily instructional time from disruptions for a minimum of two and a half hours for grades 1–3. During this time, teachers are required to follow carefully laid out lesson plans—what has been popularly dubbed as a "script."

Advocates of these programs argue that large-scale improvement in reading among disadvantaged students requires that all schools be "on the same page" and that teachers know exactly what is expected. They also argue that, because so many teachers lack skills and experience, especially in inner-city neighborhoods, administrators must insist that teachers use these strategies faithfully. Critics, on the other hand, protest that the programs are far too narrowly focused on basic skills, ignore the essence of literacy, and reduce teachers to being robots. A leader of the teachers association in one California district complained, "A trained monkey could do this program."[30] Many teachers lament that such programs are far from the balanced literacy approach we described in Chapter 4, in which teachers have many strategies at their disposal and can select among them to meet the needs of the children in their classrooms.

Kimberly Min's Los Angeles area district chose Open Court as its literacy program, and she was expected to teach according to its script for two and a half hours each day. Kimberly, whose teaching goal is always to connect the curriculum to students' experiences and actively engage them in meaning-making, felt frustrated by the requirement and by the rigid enforcement by the coaches, who in her district have become known as the "Open Court police."

⚜ ⚜ ⚜

In an attempt to increase performance on the tests, the district purchased a core curriculum and mandated that we use it. Although there is a lot of debate about the curriculum, administrators push teachers to use the highly prescriptive teacher manuals. Teachers can be "written up" as insubordinate if they do not follow the script.

Because the mandated curriculum is culturally neutral and often mundane, students respond with a lack of interest and engagement. With the mandated curriculum, many students do not connect to the themes or the stories because it does not reflect their experiences, their culture, or their interests.

—**KIMBERLY MIN**
Third-grade teacher

However, Kimberly, like many teachers who have a deep understanding of children's learning, has found ways to adapt the program to engage her students.

⚜ ⚜ ⚜

Once culturally responsive practices are employed students respond with enthusiasm and a hunger for learning. So, I work within the set themes to engage students in the curriculum by incorporating stories about the civil rights, the Native American experiences, and the community issues that arise.

Kim has also found ways to use the 150 minutes she must spend each day teaching phonemic awareness, phonics, fluency, vocabulary, and comprehension skills to provide her students with access to science—a subject that, as we noted in Chapter 4, is increasingly neglected in classrooms where educators are using Reading First programs to increase their students achievement test scores.

One component of social justice is access to an inclusive curriculum. I polled my students to see how many were exposed to science last year, and all of them responded that they did not have any science!

I thought it was important for students to study owls because, more than likely, my students who reside in the inner city are not going to have an authentic connection with wild animals, their habitats, and habits. For guidance, I looked at the California state standards. Although there is no "owl standard" at my grade level, I found many standards that cover writing skills, science inquiry, and geometry—the skills I wanted my students to learn.

In addition to the state science standards, I used the Open Court reading program as I planned my lessons on owls. Whether I agree with the program or not, I am mandated to teach it to my students. The pacing plan that Open Court provides is very hard to meet. There are so many skills that students need to cover that many of my colleagues are teaching Open Court well into the afternoon. By planning thematically, I can teach science content during Open Court time. For example, I gathered the students at the rug to read a book entitled All About Owls. *As I read the book, I stopped to show how the students' prior knowledge about owls connected to the text. This was the introduction to a complete unit that included an owl pellet dissection as well as fiction writing. Interdisciplinary teaching gives me the opportunity to teach many subjects.*

—**Kimberly Min**
Third-grade teacher

The Courts and Education Equity

We conclude this chapter with a brief discussion of the important role that the courts play in education. Most education policy and law is established by elected federal, state, and local officials and the professionals they appoint to administer school systems. However, for more than 100 years, the courts have allowed and disallowed policies and required policymakers to formulate new laws that affect education equity. Their particular positive role has been to establish and protect the rights of those whose educational rights may be ignored or even violated by elected and appointed school officials.

But not all of the courts' involvement has been positive, and even today education rights activists are aware that the U.S. Supreme Court can add to or limit progressive schooling policies.

EDUCATIONAL TIMELINE:
Legal Milestones in the Struggle for Social Justice Education

Year and Focus	Case/Law	Decision
1896 Segregation	*Plessy v. Ferguson* (U.S. Supreme Court)	Upholds Louisiana law stating that the Fourteenth Amendment "had not been intended to abolish distinctions based on color." Makes segregated facilities legal and becomes a precedent to justify "separate but equal" education.
1954 Rights to Desegregated Education "on Equal Terms"	*Brown v. Board of Education of Topeka, Kansas* (U.S. Supreme Court)	Ruling that "Separate educational facilities are inherently unequal" outlaws legally segregated schools—overturning *Plessy v. Ferguson*.
1971/1972 Rights of the Disabled to Education	*Pennsylvania Association for Retarded Children (PARC) v. Pennsylvania (United States District Court)/Mills v. the Board of Education of Washington, D.C.* (U.S. District Court)	PARC rules that students with mental retardation are entitled to a free public education. Mills extends PARC to students with other disabilities; requires "adequate alternative educational services . . . which may include special education . . ."
1973 Rights of Latinos to Desegregated Schools	*Keyes v. Denver School District No. 1* (U.S. Supreme Court)	Expanded what counts as illegal segregation. Recognized Latinos' rights to desegregation.
1974 Limits to Desegregation	*Millikin v. Bradley* (U.S. Supreme Court)	Blocked interdistrict desegregation remedies. Meant that all minority school districts would remain segregated.
1974 Rights of English Learners	*Lau v. Nichols* (U.S. Supreme Court)	Requires English language instruction to those whose first language is not English.
1975 Rights to Equal School Funding	*Rodriguez v. San Antonio* (U.S. Supreme Court)	Ruled that education is *not* a right guaranteed by the U.S. Constitution. Ended hopes that the Constitution requires equal education spending.
1982 Rights of Undocumented Immigrants	*Plyler v. Doe* (U.S. Supreme Court)	Prohibits public schools from denying immigrant students access to a public education. Grants undocumented children the right to a free public education.

EDUCATIONAL TIMELINE *(continued)*

Year and Focus	Case/Law	Decision
1991 Limits to Desegregation	*Board of Education of Oklahoma City v. Dowell* (U.S. Supreme Court)	Established a "good faith" test that allowed courts to end desegregation once a district had made an effort "to the extent practicable."
1994 Limits to Desegregation	*Freeman v. Pitts* (U.S. Supreme Court)	Allowed courts to end supervision of desegregation cases in stages if school district had complied with the good faith standard from *Dowell.*
1995 Ending Desegregation	*Missouri v. Jenkins* (U.S. Supreme Court)	Allowed schools to be released from desegregation, even though they had not satisfied the Court's requirement of raising African American students' test scores.

In 1896, the Supreme Court's ruled in *Plessy* that a Louisiana law requiring separate accommodations for Negroes and whites did not violate the rights of Homer Plessy, a person considered Negro since one of his eight great-grandparents was a Negro. Plessy had purchased a first-class ticket on the East Louisiana Railway from New Orleans and was arrested when he refused to move from the first-class car to sit in the car designated for Negroes. The Court ruled that racially separate facilities did not violate the Constitution, as long as those facilities were equal.

Although *Plessy* was not about education, it was used until 1954 to justify racially segregated schools. Many of the education-related court decisions in the century following *Plessy* advanced the cause of educational equity and social justice, but not all have.

The "Legal Milestones" timeline (above) highlights some of the court decisions in the struggle for equitable schools. Most of these decisions have related to two questions: Are separate and unequal educational opportunities or spending provided to students, based on race, disability, and language permissible under U.S. or state laws? Do federal or state laws require that all students have an adequately funded education? As these cases make clear, the courts have not provided a clear or consistent set of answers to these very important questions.

As the timeline makes clear, in the second half of the twentieth century, most of the equity-related court cases were federal cases focused on the rights of minority groups to equal education and on the legality of racially segregated schools. Another set of cases during this period focused on clarifying the rights of individual students. As in the equity cases, not all of the rulings were in the students' favor. Although the courts have upheld students' rights to freedom of expression in the area of dress and to a hearing before being suspended, the courts have also ruled that paddling students is not "cruel and unusual" punishment, that school officials can search students' possessions, restrain their speech, censor student journalists' articles in the school newspaper, and subject athletes to random urinalysis testing for drug use.

By the beginning of the twenty-first century, the most prominent educational court cases no longer focused on whether school systems were violating constitutional protections of racial equality and students' rights. Instead, these newer cases challenged the fairness and adequacy of school funding. Because the states, not the federal government, have the constitutional obligation to operate school systems, these cases have been filed in state courts. By 2005, school finance lawsuits had been filed in 45 states. In about two-thirds of the cases settled since 1989, the courts have found that the state had failed to ensure that all schools, and particularly those enrolling the most disadvantaged students, had enough resources to enable them to provide the basic education required by their state constitutions.

Over the past 60 years, the courts have established that education is a critically important right in U.S. society. Writing for a unanimous Supreme Court in *Brown v. Board of Education,* Chief Justice Earl Warren wrote:

> Today, education is perhaps the most important function of state and local governments. Compulsory school attendance laws and the great expenditures for education both demonstrate our recognition of the importance of education to our democratic society. It is required in the performance of our most basic public responsibilities, even service in the armed forces. It is the very foundation of good citizenship. Today it is a principal instrument in awakening the child to cultural values, in preparing him for later professional training, and in helping him to adjust normally to his environment. In these days, it is doubtful that any child may reasonably be expected to succeed in life if he is denied the opportunity of an education. Such an opportunity, where the state has undertaken to provide it, is a right which must be made available to all on equal terms.[31]

The goal of most education finance litigation is similar to segregation and inequality cases. The courts are called upon to make sure that school policies do not abridge the fundamental constitutional rights of individuals or politically powerless minorities, even if they reflect the will of the majority.

Policy and law play pivotal roles in the struggle for social justice education. In the White House, in governors' offices, in the federal and state legislatures, in local school board meeting rooms, and in the courts, government officials seek to use their rulemaking powers to increase the effectiveness, the efficiency, and the equity of education. As in every other aspect of education, the process is steeped in cultural ideologies and fraught with contentious politics.

Partly because education is so central to our egalitarian democracy and, as such, must be far more than a factory, a well-managed corporation, or a market, a whole community of education lawyers and advocates has emerged to ensure that education reflects our democratic values as well as our economic ones. Like Thurgood Marshall, the lead attorney for Linda Brown in the *Brown v. Board of Education* case, these advocates are allies with teachers who are committed to teaching for social justice in their struggle. At the same time that teachers seek to engage all children in classrooms so that they become good citizen, are awakened to cultural values, and succeed in life, these advocates seek to ensure that the rules set by policymakers and judges make such teaching possible.

OLC Connections

A list of additional online and print resources and a set of questions for reflection about education policy and law can be found at www.mhhe.com/oakes3e.

Digging Deeper

Many teachers find the following developments in education policy and law both fascinating in themselves and a way to keep in sight the larger context into which their school and classroom practices fit. The scholars, think tanks, and online sources noted here provide just a sampling of the most engaging sources of information on political and legal developments in education.

The **Kappan,** a monthly journal published by Phi Delta Kappa, an educational association, provides short readable articles on current education issues. Especially useful is **Gerald Bracey**'s regular column on educational research, and his annual reports on the condition of public education. Bracey's voice has been one of the few countering the current attacks on schools with empirical evidence. His book *Bail Me Out: Handling Difficult Data and Tough Questions About Public Schools* (Thousand Oaks, CA: Corwin Press, 2000) provides a very helpful guide to understanding how educational research data is used and abused in the political arena. Also of interest is *Setting the Record Straight: Responses to Misconceptions About Public Education in the U.S.,* 2nd ed. (Portsmouth, NH: Heinemann, 2004).

University of Arizona professor **David Berliner** and his colleague **Bruce Biddle** at the University of Missouri provide detailed and hard-hitting analyses of the evidence underlying current criticism of public schools. In their book *The Manufactured Crisis: Myths, Fraud, and the Attack on America's Public Schools* (New York: Addison-Wesley, 1995), they trace that criticism to its sources. They also provide evidence that, despite the barrage of criticism in the past two decades, American schools have actually improved. In 1996 the American Educational Research Association gave Berliner and Biddle's work its award for the outstanding research book of that year.

Clive Belfield and **Henry Levin**'s new book, *Privatizing Educational Choice: Consequences for Parents, Schools, and Public Policy* (Boulder, CO: Paradigm Press, 2005), reviews what research shows about the effects—for communities and children—of policies such as vouchers, tax credits, charter schools, and private contracting. Belfield is associate director of the National Center for the Study of Privatization in Education at Teachers College, Columbia University, where Professor Henry Levin is director.

The **Economic Policy Institute** (EPI) conducts research and publishes books on the connections between education policy and economics. **Helen Ladd**'s 2002 book, *Market-based Reforms in Urban Education,* may be especially interesting. EPI's education reports on such topics as teacher policies, class size, early childhood education policy, charter schools, the connections among schooling and social policies in employment, housing, and health can be found online at http:// www.epi.org/subjectpages/edu.cfm?CFID=622050&CFTOKEN=45095343.

Ed.gov is the U.S. Department of Education's official website. It provides information about federal education policies.

Education Week, American education's newspaper of record, and *Teacher Magazine* are published by the Editorial Projects in Education, a nonprofit organization based in Washington, D.C. The goal of *Education Week* (online at edweek. org) is to help raise the level of awareness and understanding among professionals and the public of important issues in American education. It covers local, state, and national news and issues from preschool through the twelfth grade. In addition to the weekly paper, *Education Week* also publishes annual *Quality Counts* reports on the status of education policy in the 50 states.

Findlaw, a website for legal professionals, has a page with a list of websites of groups and resources related to education law. The site is located at http://www .findlaw.com/01topics/37education/sites.html.

Richard Kahlenberg is a Senior Fellow at The Century Foundation, where he writes about education, equal opportunity, and civil rights. He has edited books that include *Can Separate Be Equal? The Overlooked Flaw at the Center of No Child Left Behind* (2005); *Public School Choice vs. Private School Vouchers* (2003); and *A Notion at Risk: Preserving Public Education as an Engine for Social Mobility* (2000). The New Century Foundation is online at http://www.equaleducation. org/about.asp.

UCLA websites **JustSchoolsCalifornia.org** and **ucla-idea.org** provide up-to-date information and resources about the policies related to educational inequality in California, as well as about some of the grassroots and advocacy groups working to make schools more equitable. One of the resources on JustSchools.org is a *Daily News Roundup* that readers can subscribe to. The Roundup compiles the major education policy news stories each day and sends them to subscribers by e-mail.

Pauline Lipman is an associate professor of Social and Cultural Foundations of Education at DePaul University in Chicago. She has published articles, books, and book chapters on the social context of urban school reform, culturally relevant teaching, and the politics of race and education. Her most recent book, *High Stakes Education: Inequality, Globalization, and Urban School Reform* (New York: Routledge, 2004), reports a case study of Chicago school reform. Her fascinating earlier book *Race, Class, and Power in School Restructuring* (Albany: SUNY Press, 1998) is also a qualitative study of the influence of race and class power relations on urban school reform. Lipman is active in social justice movements and speaks frequently in local and national forums on education, equity, and activism. She is a founding member and active participant in Chicago Teachers for Social Justice.

In the past few years, dozens of books have been published examining **No Child Left Behind** from a variety of perspectives. Teachers may find the following particularly interesting and relevant to how schools and classrooms have been affected by the new law: **Deborah Meier** and **George Wood**'s *Many Children Left Behind: How the No Child Left Behind Act Is Damaging Our Children and Our Schools* (Boston: Beacon Press, 2004) details the progressive critique. *No Child Left Behind?: The Politics and Practice of School Accountability,* edited by **Paul E. Peterson** and **Martin R. West** (Washington, DC: Brookings Institution Press, 2003) provides the conservative arguments supporting the law. **James Popham's** book *America's "Failing" Schools: How Parents and Teachers Can Cope with No Child Left Behind* (New York: Falmer Press, 2004) provides a sophisticated and readable analysis of the assessment issues in the law. A final suggestion is **Gail Sunderman, James Kim,** and **Gary Orfield's** book *NCLB Meets School Realities: Lessons from the Field* (Thousand Oaks, CA: Corwin Press, 2005), which reports the results of a study of NCLB implementation in six states.

Gary Orfield, professor and director of the Harvard Civil Rights Project, is the nation's foremost authority on school desegregation. His books on race and education policy include *Dismantling Desegregation: The Quiet Reversal of* Brown v. Board of Education with **Susan E. Eaton** (Boston: New Press, 1996). Orfield's more recent studies expand his work beyond schooling for black children to focus on Latinos and other low-income immigrant groups of color. Most recently, he edited *Dropouts in America: Confronting the Graduation Rate Crisis* (Cambridge: Harvard Educational Pub Group, 2004). The Harvard Civil Rights Project website at http://www.civilrightsproject.harvard.edu/ has many excellent downloadable reports on education policy and law.

The Public Education Network (PEN) is a nonprofit organization with the mission of building public demand and mobilizing resources for quality public education for all children through a national constituency of local education funds and individuals. PEN provides access to downloadable tools and publications about education policy and law ranging from thoughtful essays and informational pieces to best practices and research reports on its website at http://www.publiceducation. org/index.asp. **PEN's NewsBlast** is the group's weekly national education policy news service. You can subscribe at http://www.publiceducation.org/subscribe.asp.

The Urban Institute is a research organization that focuses on a wide range of domestic policy topics, including demographics and education. One of the Institute's most recent reports, *The New Demography of America's Schools,* written by Randolph Capps, Michael E. Fix, Julie Murray, Jason Ost, Jeffrey S. Passel, and Shinta Herwantoro, explores the variations in characteristics among children with parents born in different countries, and discusses implications for NCLB implementation in high-LEP schools and districts. Another, *Who's Left Behind?* by Clemencia Cosentino de Cohen, Nicole Deterding, and Beatriz Chu Clewell (2005), offers a detailed picture of the schools in which limited English proficient (LEP) students are educated. It too includes a discussion of these findings' implications for the implementation of NCLB in high- and low-LEP schools. The Urban Institute's education webpage is at http://prod.urban.org/education/index.cfm.

Teachers College, Columbia University, professor **Amy Stuart Wells** writes on a range of educational policy issues, paying particular attention to how racial and cultural politics interweave with the impetus for particular policy directions and with the outcomes of various policies. *Steppin' Over the Color Line* (New Haven, CT: Yale University Press, 1997) traces the course of the St. Louis, Missouri, school desegregation though the experiences of black students in the city school system. Her book *Time to Choose: America at the Crossroads of School Choice Policy* (New York: Hill and Wang, 1993) analyzes how market forces and theories of self-interest shed light on the current press for school choice and privatization. She is currently studying charter schools.

Notes

1. David Tyack, *The One Best System: A History of American Urban Education* (Cambridge: Harvard University Press, 1974).
2. The Tenth Amendment says that any power not delegated to the federal government in the Constitution belongs to the states.
3. Lorraine McDonnell and Richard Elmore, "Getting the Job Done: Alternative Policy Instruments," *Educational Evaluation and Policy Analysis* 9 (summer 1987), pp. 133–152.
4. Lawrence Cremin, *The Transformation of the School: Progressivism in Education 1876–1957* (New York: Knopf, 1961).
5. Cremin, *Transformation*; Tyack, *One Best System.*
6. National Commission on Excellence in Education, *A Nation at Risk* (Washington, DC: Author, 1983).
7. Bruce Biddle and David Berliner, *The Manufactured Crisis: Myths, Fraud, and the Attack on America's Public Schools* (New York: Addison-Wesley, 1995).
8. Marshall Smith and Jennifer O'Day, "Systemic School Reform," in *The Politics of Curriculum and Testing, Politics of Education Association Yearbook,* ed. S. H. Fuhrman and B. Malen (London: Taylor & Francis, 1990), pp. 233–267.
9. Jennifer O'Day and Marshall S. Smith, "Systemic Reform Educational Opportunity," in *Designing Coherent Education Policy: Improving the System,* ed. Susan H. Fuhrman (San Francisco: Jossey-Bass, 1993), pp. 250–312.
10. Peter M. Senge, *The Fifth Discipline: The Art and Practice of the Learning Organization* (London: Random House, 1990), p. 3.
11. Amy Stuart Wells, *Time to Choose: America at the Crossroads of School Choice Policy* (New York: Hill & Wang, 1993).
12. For a summary discussion of the flaws in Coleman's report, see Bruce Biddle and David Berliner, "What Research Says About Unequal Funding for Schools in America," Education Policy Reports Project (EPRP) from the Arizona State University, Education Policy Studies Laboratory, 2002, online at http://www.asu.edu/educ/epsl/EPRP/EPSL-0206-102-EPRP.doc.
13. Center for Educational Policy, *State High School Exit Exams: States Try Harder but Gaps Persist,* August 2005.
14. John Rogers, Jennifer Jellison Holme, and David Silver, *More Questions Than Answers: Cahsee Results, Opportunity to Learn, and the Class of 2006,* UCLA's IDEA, 2005, online at http://www.idea.gseis.ucla.edu/resources/exitexam/.
15. See, for example, Sharon Nichols, Gene Glass, and David Berliner, "High-Stakes Testing and Student Achievement: Problems for the No Child Left Behind Act," Arizona State University Education Policy Studies Laboratory, 2005.
16. Jay P. Heubert and Robert M. Hauser, eds., *High Stakes: Testing for Tracking, Promotion, and Graduation* (Washington: National Academy Press, 1999).
17. *Open to the Public: Speaking Out on "No Child Left Behind"* (a report from the Public Education Network, 2005).

18. Gary Orfield and Mindy L. Kornhaber, eds., *Raising Standards or Raising Barriers? Inequality and High-Stakes Testing in Public Education* (New York: Century Foundation Press, 2001).

19. Associated Press story reported on cnn.com, September 9, 2003.

20. Tamar Lewin and Jennifer Medina, "To Cut Failure Rate, Schools Shed Students," *New York Times,* 31 July 2003.

21. Gerald Bracey, *Setting the Record Straight.* (Portsmouth, NH: Heinemann, 2004).

22. See, for example, MassPartners for Public Schools, *Facing Reality. "What Happens When Good Schools Are Labeled "Failures"? Projecting Adequate Yearly Progress in Massachusetts Schools* (Boston: Author, 2005); and Edward W. Wiley, William J. Mathis, and David R. Garcia, *The Impact of the Adequate Yearly Progress Requirement of the Federal "No Child Left Behind" Act on Schools in the Great Lakes Region* (Tempe, AZ: Education Policy Studies Laboratory, 2005).

23. Gerald Bracey, *Setting the Record Straight* (Portsmouth, NH: Heinemann, 2004).

24. Ibid.

25. See, for example, http://www.nclbgrassroots.org.

26. Definition of scientifically based research in NCLB.

27. www.w-w-c.org/about.html.

28. Grover J. Whitehurst, *Statement of Grover J. Whitehurst, Assistant Secretary for Research and Improvement, Before the Senate Committee on Health, Education, Labor and Pensions* (Washington, DC: U.S. Department of Education, 2002). Available online at http://www.ed.gov/offices/IES/speeches, as cited by Ron Beghetto, "Scientifically Based Research," *ERIC Digest* 167, Clearinghouse on Educational Policy and Management, College of Education, University of Oregon, 2003, http://cepm.uoregon.edu/publications/digests/digest167.html.

29. U.S. Department of Education, 2005, http://www.ed.gov/nclb/methods/whatworks/doing.html.

30. As cited in Sarah Colt, "Do Scripted Lessons Work—Or Not?," *Making Schools Work,* http://www.pbs.org/makingschoolswork/sbs/sfa/lessons.html.

31. *Brown v. Board of Education of Topeka,* 347 U.S. 483 (1954).

PART IV

Teaching for the Long Haul

CHAPTER 12
━━━━━━━━━━━━━━━◇━━━━━━━━━━━━━━━

Teaching to Change the World
A Profession and a Hopeful Struggle

Teachers entering the profession in the twenty-first century are motivated by all the traditional reasons for teaching—a desire to help, a love of working with the young, pleasant memories of one's own schooling, fun, the intellectual challenge, a passion for the knowledge one gets to teach, an opportunity to "give back" what one has received, a paycheck for an honest day's work—the list goes on. But in a nation that is increasingly diverse and increasingly unequal, many new teachers, like the ones cited throughout this book, add another reason—teaching to change the world.

[N]one of us—as an individual—can save the world as a whole, but . . . each of us must behave as though it were in our power to do so.

—Vaclav Havel[1]

You must do the thing you think you can not do.

—Eleanor Roosevelt[2]

These words of former president of the Czech Republic and playwright Vaclav Havel, and those of former American First Lady and ambassador to the United Nations Eleanor Roosevelt, capture the spirit of many teachers as they begin their careers. Teachers face daunting challenges that schools, alone, can't overcome, and teachers reach for ambitious goals that they, alone, can't attain. Yet they are determined to use their knowledge and skills to struggle for socially just schooling.

As an educator, I can make a difference in students' lives. I can help them become transformative citizens in our society and liberate their minds to soar above and beyond the constraints of race, ethnicity, and social status. As I continue along my path as an educator, I carry with me the words of Alice Walker, "Keep in mind always the present you are constructing. It should be the future you want."

—Kelly Ganzel
First-year teacher, high school English

Kelly Ganzel wrote these words at the end of her first year of teaching in a school besieged with all of the problems of inequality we described in Chapter 1. The woefully underfunded school enrolled more than 3,000 students, more than half from families in poverty and a third still learning English. The students perform poorly on the state's achievement tests, and half will leave before graduation. Five years later, Kelly is still at the school and she is still teaching to make a difference in students' lives.

Kelly Ganzel and the other teachers like her in this book are idealists, but they are not naive. They know how hard it is to make schools humane and intellectually rich in an age when the gaps between wealthy and poor families grow wider, and racism and anti-immigrant sentiments continue to shape lives. In the face of this struggle, they offer something stronger and more positive than the harmful ideologies of merit, deficit thinking, and white privilege, and the limiting metaphors of schools as factories, corporations, or markets. They offer professional knowledge of teaching and learning and a vision of social justice that we've discussed in the chapters of this book. These teachers have chosen an education career; they are not just passing time until something more glamorous, lucrative, or easy comes along. They plan for much more than their daily school-bound routines and lessons. They look forward to a time when their schools will be full allies with their struggling communities.

Chapter Overview

This chapter offers a view toward that future. But first, a warning: Navigating toward socially just teaching and education requires a full and unblinking understanding of the present—the status quo. We cannot offer that comprehensive survey here, but we do begin with an overview of where the teaching profession stands today. And what does the profession promise beginning teachers if the status quo persists—especially teachers with students who face poverty, live in families where English is not the first language, and experience the ever-present specter of racism? Frankly, it is not a pretty picture—for students or their teachers.

However, most of this chapter describes how new teachers can defy the odds by creating new odds. Just as we document the grim realities of today's teaching profession, we offer strong evidence that the status quo is not a reason to give up on teaching, but the reason *for* teaching. We conclude the chapter, and the book, with five philosophical, practical, and personal strategies that teachers use to change the world. They include building a learning community, becoming a social justice activist, expanding their professional influence, making a commitment to a hopeful critique, and finding satisfaction in the everyday.

Teaching: A Vulnerable Profession

After nine years in the high-tech industry, I made the leap to high school. It was a conscious decision. But I confess I was unprepared for the fact that teaching would become the hardest job I've ever had. I counted the hours I worked, planned, and graded, and in the end I realized I was down to the corporate standard of two weeks vacation.

In the high-tech world, I had responsibility—to take care of customers, finish projects on time, train fellow workers on the latest sales application. But as I gain more teaching experience, I realize the enormity of a teacher's responsibility and how different it is from my prior career.

High-tech products are different from "school products." The products we provided did not have feelings, think on their own, or come from a variety of backgrounds. They did not need Kleenex, Band-Aids, tampons, pens, pencils, whiteout, paper, rubber bands (need I go on?). We cannot turn students into excellent readers, writers, thinkers, and of course, test takers, as easily as we can tighten a screw or correct code.

The challenges students pose are different from the challenge of figuring out a new marketing strategy. My newest clients, ages 14–18, are often very sleepy at 8 A.M. and intolerably boisterous at 2 P.M. They sometimes come to school without having breakfast, getting a ride from a distant relative, and often forgetting materials. They have a keen sense of justice—pouncing on the examples of oppression and injustice in history.

They say funny things, not always appropriate for the classroom. For example, a tenth grader asked me in front of the class if I wore a thong. I don't recall the lesson of the day but I do know it wasn't undergarments. There was the student who repeated multiple times how much she disliked me. Other students feel I give too much homework. Imagine that!

I love teaching more than any other job but I do admit to having days when I want to run for higher ground.

—JUDY SMITH[3]
High school social studies

Full-Fledged Professionals from Day One

Judy Smith considers herself lucky. She knew that she needed to learn a great deal to be a good teacher, and she thinks her teacher education program served her well.

———————————————— ✿ ✿ ✿ ————————————————

Before going into teaching, I was certain of three things: I really wanted to be the best teacher I could be (a goal I still work on day in and day out), I needed a teacher education program that would push me and support me, and I really cared about kids and learning. All students deserve the best teachers and I wanted to help them understand that, too. The combination of academic work and outstanding professors and colleagues in my teacher education program met my needs and set my teaching course. We were asked to love our students; we were required to do rigorous work in our classes; we were taught social justice. In addition, we acquired the mind-set that we teachers must constantly examine our approach, curriculum, and expectations and reach out to other like-minded social justice educators for support and ideas.

Judy Smith expresses a degree of satisfaction and confidence in her preparation that not all beginning teachers feel.

Teacher education faces enormous criticism today. Some institutions and programs that grant teaching licenses may offer or require so few course hours that there is just enough time to pass along a few bits and pieces of "practical" teacher knowledge, which are then called "professional training." Prospective teachers may get little of the theory about teaching and learning or the foundational knowledge we've discussed in this book. They may have few chances to observe in classrooms and communities, have little contact with knowledgeable mentors, or be "supervised" by those whose sympathetic touch helps them discover and develop their competence. In some cases, those learning to teach are simply left alone with students in the classroom, and they have little collegial support, expert mentoring, shared responsibilities, or opportunities for reflection.

Most teacher education programs, however, do all that they can in the college classroom, in communities, and in schools to provide access to knowledge, rich and challenging opportunities, and caring professional communities in which to learn. However, teacher preparation programs face a host of difficult obstacles to preparing teachers in the way they should and would like.

One obstacle is in the structure of the profession itself. Teachers assume the full responsibility of being a teacher on day one. In most schools, the first-year novice and the twenty-year veteran do exactly the same job. After obtaining a license or credential, new teachers may have few opportunities to apprentice to those with greater years of learning, experience, and responsibility. And knowledgeable veterans have few opportunities to scaffold the learning of novices. Often, it's the novice, not the veteran who is given the most challenging conditions under which to work and the most challenging students to work with.

Other professions (law, medicine, chefs, accountants, and social work are a few that come to mind) have multiple levels of induction into full professional responsibilities before allowing the practitioner to function independently and unsupervised for long periods of time. Until the teaching profession routinely offers such career-long scaffolding, individual teachers may have to garner that support on their own. This is not quite as daunting as it might seem because essentially every teacher— novice and experienced—is in the same boat, and a great many are simply waiting for a few colleagues' suggestions that they act together.

Another obstacle is a popular belief that teaching requires little training or preparation. Many people believe that teaching is more of a "gift" or a quality of one's personality that needs just a little specialized knowledge which can be learned quickly and on the job. Current attitudes reflect the days when teaching was strictly women's work, when scientific management reduced complex jobs to simple, prescribed tasks, and when corporate style hierarchies left all "executive" decisions to a few managers. Certainly, some of these views underlie the myriad of alternative programs—such as Teach for America and other big-city "teaching fellows" programs—that give college graduates full responsibility for classrooms after some minimal summer training.

Teaching Everybody's Children

An important and interesting demographic mismatch pervades the teaching profession. In 2001–2002, for example, 60 percent of public school students were white, 17 percent black, 17 percent Hispanic, 4 percent Asian/Pacific Islander, and 1 percent American Indian/Alaska Native. The teaching force in public schools was 90 percent white, 6 percent black, and less than 5 percent of other races. Forty percent of public schools had no teachers of color on the faculty.[4]

This distribution of teachers' and students' backgrounds is not likely to change soon. Statistical projections show the student population is growing increasingly diverse, and the teacher population is remaining much as it has been—nearly all white.[5] This places an unfortunate but necessary burden on teachers of color who are able to support students of color with their shared racial, ethnic, and cultural identities. To develop schools' capacity to teach well all of the nation's diverse groups of young people, teachers of color will be called upon to be "cultural brokers" and resources who help students, parents, and their teacher colleagues bridge the worlds of school, community, and family.

Teacher Shortages

The nation needs to hire 2 million teachers in the next decade or 200,000 new teachers a year. Millions of young children are entering schools just as the current teachers of the baby boomer generation are ending their careers. That number is required simply to provide a teacher for every classroom and does not account for a much-desired goal of lowering class sizes in many school districts. Part of the reason is that increased student enrollment and teacher retirements have created a massive teacher shortage. Teaching has also paid the price for the revolution over the past 30 years in career opportunities available to women and reductions in job discrimination facing Americans of color. Members of these groups, who historically have had few options other than teaching, are no longer choosing teaching now that better-paying careers are available to them. Teaching has not kept pace with salaries or other incentives.

Currently, qualified teachers are in short supply. Special education, science teaching, math teaching, and teachers prepared to work with English learners are the areas with the greatest shortage; no field has obvious surpluses.[6] And the problem is more pressing in schools serving low-income communities of color.

Teacher shortages don't mean that students are in classrooms without teachers. The shortages mean that schools are hiring long-term substitute teachers, persons who have not completed their teacher certification, or teachers who teach subjects for which they are not prepared.

For example, schools where students are low income and of color are more likely to have teachers with no practice-teaching experience. In schools where a majority of students are minorities, almost 17 percent of new teachers had never student-taught. By contrast, in schools with few minority students, only 6 percent of the new teachers hadn't done student teaching. Similar contrasts exist between schools with high or low proportions of low-income students.

Teacher misassignments are most common in secondary schools. For example, 44 percent of middle-school students and nearly 16 percent of high school students take at least one class with a teacher who doesn't have even a minor in the subject being taught. The situation is worse in high-poverty schools, where 26 percent of high school students and more than 50 percent of middle-school students have at least one class with an unqualified teacher.[7] Additionally, students in high-poverty and high-minority schools are far less likely than those in whiter and wealthier schools to have experienced teachers.

There are two important facts about the teacher shortage that policymakers haven't understood or acted upon, and that new teachers need to be aware of. One is that the biggest problem is *not* that too few people are being recruited into teaching. It's that so many of those who enter the profession leave after a short time. The second is that teachers are not leaving because they don't want to teach, or necessarily because they are not fully committed to their students; they are leaving because they find the conditions in schools often make it impossible for them to teach well. We describe each of these problems next.

Teacher Attrition

Teacher turnover and attrition cause the current teacher shortages at least as much as schools' failure to attract qualified people to teaching. Teachers are leaving the classroom at rates close to or above the rate of new teachers entering the profession. Although about a quarter of those who leave are retiring, the rest leave for reasons other than retirement. Further, in 1999, about 250,000 teachers moved from one school to another. As a result, poor urban and rural schools that suffer chronic shortages of qualified teachers are more often forced to fill vacancies with unlicensed teachers or substitutes.[8]

In sum, if teachers were staying in their jobs, there would be plenty of qualified teachers to fill every classroom. Not only could schools be selective about whom they hire, they could also create apprenticeship programs in which new teachers would not have to assume the full responsibilities of teaching on day one. Instead, new teachers could spend their time working side by side with experienced veterans who could help them apply the knowledge and skills they learned in teacher education programs to the particular school and community where they are teaching. Of course, this would be an authentic way for veteran teachers to keep abreast of the knowledge and skills.

Teachers' Salaries and Working Conditions

Low salaries partly explain why many leave teaching.

———————————————————————— ⊗ ⊗ ⊗ ————————————————————————

No other professional in this country receives the yearly salary a teacher does and the low level of professional respect after completing a bachelor's and master's of education. The results are unqualified applicants, high turnover, and large classroom sizes.

This is a difficult situation for politicians who will probably not see the benefits [of their actions] over the span of their term. It will take constituents' outrage demonstrated at the polls to force the action. Unfortunately, those most disadvantaged by the current educational system, minorities and low socioeconomic groups, traditionally have the lowest voter turnout.

—**Mark Hill**
First-year teacher, high school mathematics

Mark Hill has it right. Teachers make less than those in jobs requiring comparable education and skills, such as architects, inspectors, journalists, accountants, and
computer programmers. In 2003, the average weekly wage of male teachers was
$899; in contrast, the average weekly wage for college graduates who were not
teachers was $1,246. Moreover, weekly wages have grown far more slowly for teach-
ers than for workers in other professions, declining almost 15 percent since 1993.[9]
One of the authors of a new book reporting these statistics commented, "Over time,
the wage gap between teachers and their peers becomes a gulf that can sabotage
schools' best efforts to recruit the best teachers and to keep them as their skills and
experience grow. This gap puts teachers in an untenable position, where they have
to choose between their students and their own families' well-being."[10]

Despite low salaries deterring prospective teachers, research findings show
that salaries are less important than other reasons for teachers who decide to leave
teaching. Furthermore, teachers do not generally leave high-poverty schools
because of the students, but because of the poor working conditions in these
schools. Recent studies show that student characteristics are not more important
than salaries and working conditions, and some research shows that salaries are
near the bottom of teachers' lists of what is most important to them.[11]

Teachers point out that deteriorating facilities, overcrowding, inadequate
materials, lack of time to meet and plan with colleagues, and the absence of professional autonomy and respect prevent them from doing the job they were prepared
to do. While some women leave teaching careers due to family lifestyle issues and
child rearing (and some remain in teaching because of those issues), most teachers
who quit cannot imagine ways to make their teaching career satisfying.

Teacher Judy Smith shares her concerns about the longevity of her peers'
careers in teaching.

---

*I worry about the next generation of teachers. I worry that they face
challenges that are beyond their immediate control (example: poor
leadership at the administrative level). I worry, too, that we teachers too
often resign ourselves to accept our poor working conditions. We almost wear
this as a badge. We are dedicated teachers.*

*I hope that the new teachers won't get beaten down and become resigned.
We are professionals and should have a system that supports us in educating
our children. Teachers, whether it is through unions or other organizations,
need to speak up more and educate our oldest students, those persons in the
community. It is appalling that we don't have what we need to do our jobs.
We can't continue to accept that and then leave after three or four years. We
need a serious consciousness-raising effort among ourselves. Then we need
the intelligent leadership to educate the public. It is not okay just to be a
"dedicated" teacher—one who does all the right things and yet accepts things
the way they are.*

—JUDY SMITH
High school social studies

One of the teacher education classmates of Judy Smith and the other teachers cited in this book is Rebecca Solomon. Like Judy, Rebecca chose to teach in a school where the students are primarily low income and of color. In 2003, she was interviewed for a story in *Education Week,* a national education newspaper, about the link between working conditions and teacher attrition:

> At Los Angeles Senior High School, a sprawling building of more than 4,000 students, fourth-year teacher Rebecca Solomon says, "Everything pushes [new teachers] out."
>
> The Title I school, which operates on a multitrack schedule, has some 180 teachers, 110 of whom are in the building at any one time. Classes have as many as 42 students. Lunch is 30 minutes, grabbed on the fly. Solomon, who teaches social studies, has no permanent room of her own and nowhere to be during the periods when she is not teaching.
>
> "And people leave [the school] right away," she sighs, her voice becoming quieter. "You're struggling to make adult, human contact. You're struggling to make contact with your students, because in a room with 42 students, my ability to know my students is minimal. . . . It's a very deadening environment that seeks to suck up your humanity."
>
> What keeps her there, she says, are the students and a small network of supportive colleagues.[12]

One of the most critical aspects of teachers' working conditions is the support they receive from administrators. Many teachers who become dissatisfied with teaching cite the lack of administrative support as the most discouraging part of their job.

Unfortunately, stories abound that document the ineptness of urban school bureaucracies in recognizing and supporting good teaching. For example, in 2001 a large urban school district removed two teachers from their assignment as advanced placement teachers. These highly competent teachers managed to inspire a greater number and diversity of students to enroll in their courses and earn college credit through the AP program. However, because the school's average AP score was lower than it had been when only a few students participated, these teachers were replaced.[13]

Or, for another example, in 2001 a school district refused the state's Teacher of the Year's request for a transfer to a high-poverty urban school—one in which the principal had received seven first-year teachers that year, three of whom lacked full-time teaching credentials.[14] Consider that in some urban schools, underqualified teachers on emergency permits outnumber those with credentials. Imagine entering such a school as a novice. Imagine the opportunity presented by a highly qualified mentor willing to transfer to your school and your disappointment at finding that the bureaucracy stood in the way of that transfer.

Teachers' Unions

For the past 100 years, teachers have joined unions as a way to advance the profession and to offer a collective voice in education policy. Today, there are two national teachers' unions. The largest, the National Education Association (NEA) with 2.7 million members in 2005, was founded in 1857. Composed initially of higher

FOCAL POINT 12.1

Teachers' Unions Organizing for Progressive Education and Conditions for Teaching

1904: Margaret Haley Calls for Teachers to Organize

In 1904, Margaret Haley (1861–1939), a school teacher from Chicago, spoke at the National Educators Association (NEA) convention in St. Louis on "Why Teachers Should Organize." In her short but insightful address, wherein she cited Horace Mann and John Dewey, Haley talked about democracy, equity, citizenship, and discussed the importance of teachers' autonomy and professionalism. She criticized state subsidies to corporations, budget cuts to education, the routinization of teaching and learning, the corruption of the press, the deterioration of teachers' salaries, the subservience of elected politicians to lobbies, and the push toward commercialism in public schools. She advocated progressive education, a more fair distribution of wealth, and a strong unionism encompassing mental and manual laborers.

The teachers whom Haley was attempting to organize were primarily young females who were usually forced to resign after marriage. They were supposedly professionals, but seldom treated or paid as such. Not only were their salaries low, but they were also paid less than their male counterparts. Within their classrooms, they often had the task of educating more than sixty students with little support.

In her speech, Haley expressed deep concern about the increasing deprofessionalization of teachers, and listed four major obstacles to efficient teaching: 1) inadequate teachers' salaries, clearly inappropriate to meet the increasing cost of living and the demands for higher standards of scholarship and professional attainment; 2) insecurity regarding tenure of office and lack of provision for old age; 3) overwork in overcrowded classrooms, exhausting both mind and body; and 4) lack of recognition of the teacher as an educator, due to pressures to transform schools into factories. . . .

After outlining these and other problems faced by teachers, Haley called for an organized effort of mutual aid, and delineated the main tasks for such organization. She argued that teachers should develop expertise in educational theory and practice, ability to do scientific teaching, knowledge about the conditions under which good teaching is possible, and skills to reach the public with accurate information. In this speech, Haley raised a concept that would resurface many decades later in the debates on the role of teachers' unions: professional unionism. She argued that teachers' organizations must promote both professional development and the improvement of working conditions, and that the two functions should be pursued simultaneously. . . .

Haley believed that the struggle of public school teachers was part of the struggle carried out by manual workers to improve working and living conditions, to protect human rights, and to achieve a more equitable distribution of the products of their labor. Thus, she brought teachers into an alliance with the labor movement

(continued)

and liberal reformers, and under her leadership the CTF [Chicago Federation of Teachers] joined the Chicago Federation of Labor. In her view, only through these alliances could teachers become free to save the schools for democracy and to save democracy in the schools. At that time, militant teachers tended to ally with organized labor, and school administrators tended to ally with business interests.

In Haley's perspective, two ideals were contending for hegemony in American life at the beginning of the century: the industrial ideal, which culminates in the supremacy of commercialism; and the ideal of democracy, which places humanity above machines, and demands that all activity should be the expression of life. In her address, she cautioned that if educators were unable to carry the ideal of democracy to the industrial world, then the ideal of industrialism would be carried over to the school. Moreover, "if the school cannot bring joy to the work of the world, the joy must go out of its own life, and work in the school as in the factory will become drudgery" (p. 286). . . . Haley thought that public school teachers were the most appropriate social actors to advance this agenda:

"If there is one institution on which the responsibility to perform this service rests most heavily, it is the public school. If there is one body of public servants of whom the public has a right to expect the mental and moral equipment to face the labor question, and other issues vitally affecting the welfare of society and urgently pressing for a rational and scientific solution, it is the public-school teachers, whose special contribution to society is their own power to think, the moral courage to follow their convictions, and the training of citizens to think and to express thought in free and intelligent action" (p. 285).

Source: Margaret Haley, *Battleground: The Autobiography of Margaret Haley,* edited by Robert L. Reid (Chicago: University of Illinois Press, 1982).[15]

education faculty and education administrators, the NEA's goal was to influence the nation's rapidly growing education system. Elementary and secondary schoolteachers were not admitted as members until the 1920s, and it wasn't until the 1960s that the NEA became a strong advocate for teachers.

In contrast to the NEA, the 1.3 million member American Federation of Teachers (AFT) was a grassroots teachers' union from the beginning. It began in 1887 when teachers in Chicago began organizing to improve their conditions and prevent schools from turning into the educational factories we described in Chapter 11. Leading the organizing effort was Margaret Haley, an elementary school teacher. Focal Point 12.1 tells the story of Haley and what she hoped to achieve. The issues that concerned her are all too familiar to teachers today. Haley cared both about education for democracy and about teachers' professionalism, and she was determined to protect both.

By 1916, Haley's CFT had led to the American Federation of Teachers (AFT). John Dewey was a founder and held membership card number one. Since then organized teachers have spoken out for teachers' rights as professional workers and argued that good working conditions for teachers improve education for children. The path has not been easy.

Following World War 1, a "Red Scare" seized the nation, portraying organized labor as a communist threat. Many school boards pressured teachers to resign from the union. Widespread worker unrest during the Depression in the 1930s made conditions even harder for organized teachers, as some districts required teachers to sign loyalty oaths or fired teachers for joining the union or working on school board elections. "Yellow-dog" contracts required teachers to promise not to join a union as a condition of their employment. During the 1950s anticommunist era, shown most dramatically in Senator Joseph McCarthy's House Un-American Activities hearings, McCarthyites labeled members of the teachers union "subversive."

In fact, the unions did take and continue to take unpopular positions on controversial political issues—often against the mainstream of American culture. One feature on the AFT's website, for example, lists the union's record on social justice and reveals positions that were unpopular at the time.

- Was among the first unions to extend full membership to minorities.
- Called for equal pay for African-American teachers, the election of African-Americans to local school boards, and compulsory school attendance for African-American children (1918).
- Demanded equal educational opportunities for African-American children (1919).
- Called for the contributions of African-Americans to be taught in the public schools (1928).
- Filed an amicus brief in support of the plaintiffs in the *Brown vs. Board of Education* case before the Supreme Court (1954).
- Expelled any local unions that refused to admit African-Americans (1957).
- Helped organize the March on Washington for Justice and Jobs (1963).
- Traveled south to register new African-American voters and to teach in freedom schools (1964–1966).
- Lobbied for passage of the Equal Employment Opportunity Act, the Fair Housing Act and the Voting Rights Act.
- Negotiated unique career ladders and training programs in New York City that enhanced upward career mobility for many minorities (1968).
- Participated as observers for the South African elections (1994).
- Provided organizing assistance and resources to unionists and educators throughout Eastern Europe, for example, in the years leading up to the fall of Communism.
- Involved in developing free trade unions and democracy curricula for public education systems in countries around the globe (current).[16]

Although teachers' unions have been part of the country's broader union and labor organizing traditions, they are also different from other unions. Labor unions associated with industry have focused on workers' rights and have not made improving products or increasing profitability a priority. Because the demands by organized labor increase costs, and, thereby threaten to decrease profits, unions and industrial leaders are in adversarial positions. By contrast, teachers' unions have made students' interests a priority, and they do seek to advance educational goals; in this sense, they and "management" are on the same side.

However, it has been difficult for teachers' unions to develop organizing strategies that stress teachers' professional commitments as well as their rights as workers. Today, teachers' unions continue to argue for good conditions for teaching and learning, decent wages for teachers, and progressive education policies. They also continue to be portrayed as obstructing education reform and improvement and seeking their own gain at the expense of students. Perhaps the most high-profile portrayal occurred in 2004 when Secretary of Education Roderick Paige called the NEA a "terrorist organization" for criticizing No Child Left Behind. Later, Paige said it "was an inappropriate choice of words," even as he continued to accuse the NEA of "obstructionist scare tactics."

In 2005, *The Wall Street Journal* published an opinion piece by Stanford professor Terry Moe with a more detailed critique. Moe argues that teachers unions are the biggest obstacle to school reform and that they must be curtailed if education is to improve. Following are some excerpts from his piece.

> The teachers unions have more influence over the public schools than any other group in American society. . . .They are the 800-pound gorillas of public educa- tion. Yet the American public is largely unaware of how influential they are—and how much they impede efforts to improve public schools.
>
> Their behavior is driven by fundamental interests too, except that their interests have to do with the jobs, working conditions, and material well-being of teachers. When unions negotiate with school boards, these are the interests they pursue, not those of the children who are supposed to be getting educated.
>
> If we really want to improve schools, something has to be done about the teachers unions. The idea that an enlightened reform unionism will somehow emerge that voluntarily puts the interests of children first—an idea in vogue among union apologists—is nothing more than a pipe dream. The unions are what they are. They have fundamental, job-related interests that are very real, and are the raison d'être of their organizations. These interests drive their behavior, and this is not going to change. Ever.
>
> If the teachers unions won't voluntarily give up their power, then it has to be taken away from them.[17]

These are just two visible examples of often repeated condemnations.

Certainly, there is some truth to the claim that teachers' unions are intent on obstructing many reforms, and not all union proposals are in the best interests of students. However, the unions fight hard for increased school funding, safer schools, smaller class size, ensuring that all teachers are fully qualified, and parent engagement. Undoubtedly, such reforms serve students well.

Furthermore, many of the reforms the unions seek to obstruct are those they consider threats to education quality, not to salaries or working conditions. For example, the unions have fought (and lost) a good many battles against the most destructive elements of high-stakes testing. Organized teachers have opposed replacing constructivist curricula and pedagogy with scripted teaching. Generally, teachers' groups are the strongest advocates for students' rights.

In sum, poor working conditions dissipate teachers' attention and energies they might otherwise focus on their students. Low salaries send a strong signal that society has little appreciation for teaching. And, as Margaret Haley advised, well-organized teachers are the best hope to "save the schools for democracy and to save democracy in the schools."

Some teachers cope with these obstacles by ignoring them; they make the best of difficult situations or close their classroom doors and immerse themselves in their work with students. Others, like many of those quoted in this book, accept the challenge of improving the profession and the conditions for teaching as part of their work as teachers.

The next sections of the chapter look at those professional qualities, referred to earlier, that make teaching the best career anyone could possibly want: constructing a learning community; becoming a social justice activist; expanding one's sphere of influence; committing to a hopeful critique; and finding joy in the everyday.

Strategies for a Career to Change the World

What keeps teachers in teaching? How do teachers continue year after year to teach their own students well, to improve their schools, to change the social conditions that constrain their students' opportunities, and to seek social justice? Teachers who are just beginning cannot believe that they will struggle for a few years until justice is achieved, and then spend the rest of their careers teaching in an ideal school. How then, can beginning teachers look forward to a fulfilling career amid these challenges?

There are no sure answers, but there are the rich experiences and voices of committed teachers to learn from. Some of the teachers we've quoted here began teaching in 1997–1998; others were first-year teachers in the 2000–2001 school year. The four teachers who are new to this edition—Mauro Bautista, Mark Hill, Kimberly Min, and Judy Smith—ranged from first- to fifth-year teachers in 2004–2005.

Nearly all the teachers quoted in all three editions of this book and their peers have remained in education; the majority is still teaching, and most of them are teaching low-income students of color. Included in this group are Sarine Gureghian; Rosalinda Perez Silva; Wendy Herrera Rios, Megan Ward, Armi Flores, Erik Korporaal, Chris Yusi, Steven Branch, Chyrsta Bakstad Powell, Kate Castleberry Thompson, Amy Lee, Kay Goodloe, Jeffra Becknell, Jessica Wingell Krug, Cicely Morris Beninger, Juliana Jones, Marilyn Cortez, Matthew Flanders, Cindy Bell, Janene Ashford, Zeba Palomino Savage, Kelly Ganzel, Matthew Eide, Michael Alvarez, Jeffrey Madrigal, Martha Guerrero, Jennie Lee, Maria Hwang, Kimberly Aragon, Yvette Nunez, Mary Hendra, Susie Shin, and Christina Haug, Judy Smith, Kimberly Min, Mauro Bautista, and Mark Hill, to name just a few. Some have not remained classroom teachers but have taken on other important roles in education, as we describe later. A few, primarily women, have stopped temporarily to begin their families. Most of them plan to return to teaching.

One of those who has stayed in teaching is kindergarten teacher Cicely Morris Beninger, who was featured in the first and second editions of this book. Ten years ago when Cicely was a student teacher, she was robbed at gunpoint by teenagers when she stopped at a convenience store near her school. This terrifying incident crystallized for Cicely "a mission to help children see the range of possibilities for their lives so that they don't see crime or this type of behavior as their only option." Rather than turning away from the urban community where she was teaching or from teaching altogether, Cicely told us that she was "too angry to leave." Her kindergartners deserved far better futures than the young men who robbed her, and she was determined to stay.

Since then Cicely has married and become the mother of two young children. She also has remained a deeply committed social justice educator. Cicely still teaches kindergarten at the school where she began as a student teacher. Her students have included many of the younger siblings of the kindergartners she taught during her first year. She lives in the community near the school, and she buys her groceries alongside her students' parents. Her school is plagued by all the inequalities we described in Chapter 1, and Cicely faces frustrations similar to those of other urban teachers—an often unsupportive administration, inadequate facilities, too few community supports, and more.

Why do Cicely and the others remain in teaching? What sustains them? Many things—some philosophical, some professional, and some personal. Cicely combines her determination that students "see the range of possibilities for their lives," at the same time that she actively struggles against the persistent inequalities that constrain those possibilities. She has continued to learn the craft of teaching with a network of like-minded teachers across her city; she relies on the daily support, and supports in turn, a partner teacher who shares her passion for teaching and social justice; she has forged connections with parents who join her in making her school caring and just; she has worked as a writer and editor of an online journal focused on teaching for social change. She pairs her anger with hope. So have many of the others.

At the end of her sixth year of teaching, Cicely Beninger wrote:

At a time in my career when many of my teaching peers are making the decision to leave the classroom due to burnout and frustration, I am surprised to report that I am experiencing a new sense of hope and commitment to the teaching profession. Despite the struggles I have faced throughout my first five years of teaching, recent changes in my district, my school site, and myself have offered me a "new lease" on my teaching life. I was, once, merely too angry to leave. Now, I am too hopeful to turn away.

At our school, we are experiencing a major overhaul due, ironically, to our designation as a "low-performing" school. Despite the accuracy or inaccuracy of that dubious distinction, it has afforded us a grant to essentially "rethink" and "reinvent" ourselves as a school. This process has involved representation from teachers, administrators, students, and parents in an in-depth collaboration unprecedented at our school. As a result, there is an overall sense that we stand poised at the edge of a sort of new "promised land" for our school and it is exciting for all.

I have also grown to see the immense power of parent/teacher partnerships. I believe that so much of the frustration of the social-justice-minded educator stems from the mistaken perception that we are "lone freedom fighters" in a sea of oppressive administrators, victimized students, and apathetic parents. In the past year, I have co-initiated a parent/teacher collaborative that has helped connect me with authentic hopes, aspirations, frustrations, and expectations of my students' parents. We now share in the struggle of educating in a way that is explicit as opposed to assumed, and the results have been astonishing and inspiring. The experience is teaching me that learning to struggle involves learning with whom to undertake the struggle, building alliances that make the struggle feasible and fruitful.

By this school year's end I will have fulfilled my most basic of teaching promises: "I will stay long enough to see my very first class of kindergartners graduate from the fifth grade." However, I see this year not as the end, but the beginning of a new and more powerful commitment: I will stay until we achieve what we are struggling for.

—CICELY MORRIS BENINGER
Sixth-year teacher, kindergarten

Teachers like Cicely have figured out ways to stay connected to their profession, their colleagues, their students, their communities, and their pursuit of social justice. Such teachers are not born. They develop over time, using strategies that nurture their professional expertise, deepen their understanding of students and communities, and fuel their determination to change the world. In the remainder of this chapter, we describe in more detail strategies that Cicely and other teachers use as they forge careers that change the world.

Become Part of a Learning Community

—⊗ ⊗ ⊗—

It will probably take me a lifetime to develop into the teacher that I want to be.

—JASPER HIEP DANG BUI
First-year teacher, English, grade 8

Social convictions alone do not create good teaching. Children in the most vulnerable communities desperately need teachers with a deep knowledge of subject matter, human development, and language acquisition. This commitment and knowledge is held together with cognitive and sociocultural theories of learning that provide coherence for everyday teaching actions.

Like most new teachers, Michelle Calva discovered that aligning her theory and commitments with the exigencies of everyday school life was an extraordinary challenge.

—⊗ ⊗ ⊗—

Maintaining consistency between theory and practice is the "trick" to good teaching. It's often difficult to consider Vygotsky's theory of the zone of proximal development when you're planning a geography quiz on Wednesday,

your principal's coming to observe you on Thursday, and the power goes out
for two hours on Friday. It's easy to get caught up in the hectic pace most
teachers (including me) keep without stopping to consider the real goals that
motivate us. Through personal reflection, reactions from my students, and
comments from observers, I seek to keep my classroom practices grounded in
the philosophies that I believe.

—MICHELLE CALVA
First-year teacher, grades 4, 5, and 6

As we indicated earlier in this chapter, preservice teacher education is only the first step in the career-long process of learning to teach. The range of understandings, skills, and dispositions that urban teachers need cannot develop fully even in two years of intensive teacher preparation, nor should they. Once certified as professionals, teachers must find and create opportunities to develop their knowledge and skill at blending theory, practical skills, and commitments to social justice.

In Chapter 5, we described learning as social. Teacher learning, like student learning, is best accomplished in a community of learners. The National Commission for Teaching and America's Future (NCTAF) recently argued for "finding a way for school systems to organize the work of qualified teachers so they can collaborate with their colleagues in developing strong learning communities that will sustain them as they become more accomplished teachers."[18]

Teachers will be offered many opportunities to learn new teaching strategies. Most teachers find some of these to be helpful and some to be a waste of time. Unfortunately, few of these opportunities will include entering into a lasting community of learners. We describe some of these opportunities next.

Teacher Induction Programs   Since the 1980s, most states and school districts have had programs specifically designed to help new teachers transition from being students themselves to being professional teachers. The programs typically offer a combination of psychological and instructional support. Mentors provide advice and sympathy to help new teachers feel less isolated as they balance the multiple demands of teaching. They also provide help with the "nuts and bolts" of navigating the routines at their new schools and finding the resources they need for teaching. The best teacher induction programs also focus on helping teachers deepen their subject knowledge and skills for teaching.

On a 1990 survey of new teachers, most reported that their mentors did indeed provide moral support and helped them find teaching resources. Fewer said that their mentors had much influence over curriculum priorities or instructional methods.[19] Few novices reported having apprenticed with experienced teachers in ways that allowed them to reflect on and refine their teaching.

School-Based Professional Development   Most learning opportunities for teachers fall into the broad category of "staff development" or "inservice" professional development programs. This type of professional development is built into most teachers' work lives, as most states and school systems provide a few paid days each year for teachers' learning as a part of broad school- and districtwide educational improvement plans. NCLB also allocates federal funding for such programs.

Much professional development consists of one- or two-day workshop-like sessions with "experts" brought in to inform teachers about curriculum, instruction, assessment, or classroom management. Teachers sometimes call these "sit-and-get" or "make-and-take" sessions. These workshops seldom have any follow-up that helps teachers integrate what they've learned into their teaching. Most professionals understand that this "training" workshop model has little effect on teaching and learning; about half of the inservice professional development teachers experience is this type.

Other forms of professional development are far more effective. These include regularly scheduled sessions in which teachers plan lessons or study their teaching practices together, ongoing opportunities for teachers to observe and discuss one another's teaching, and "coaches" who work one-on-one with teachers in particular subjects. A recent large-scale, three-year study found that teachers were more likely to alter their teaching when their professional development lasted a long period of time; brought them together with teachers from the same grade, school, or subject; provided active learning opportunities; matched other reform efforts at their school; and focused on teaching a particular subject, rather than on general teaching skills.[20]

The best professional development helps teachers learn new roles that make up a learning community. Over time, learning together becomes part of the school culture (as described in Chapter 9), and teachers simply expect to be working together to improve curriculum, teaching, and assessment in their classrooms.

National Board of Professional Teaching Standards Certification   The most recent addition to teachers' formal professional development opportunities is the National Board of Professional Teaching Standards (NBPTS) certification. Created in response to the 1983 *A Nation at Risk* report, the NBPTS hoped to help achieve "world-class" schools by promoting a "world-class" teaching force.

The NBPTS set out to establish a set of high standards for professional teaching. Creating a board that would certify those teachers who could show through performance assessments that they met the standards would both raise professional competence and recognize and reward teaching excellence. The board majority is teachers; other members are school administrators, school board leaders, governors and state legislators, higher education officials, teacher union leaders, and business and community leaders.

Any teacher with three years of classroom experience can volunteer to participate in NBPTS certification. To become certified, teachers must demonstrate through an extensive series of performance-based assessments, teaching portfolios, student work samples, videotapes or DVDs, and thorough analyses of the candidate's teaching and the students' learning that they possess both deep subject matter knowledge and an understanding of how to teach those subjects.

The NBPTS has been very successful, and NBPTS certification has become a symbol of professional teaching excellence. The high standards for certification mean that a teacher has been carefully judged by peers as one who makes sound professional judgments about students' best interests and acts effectively on those judgments.

Most teachers who have participated in NBPTS say that it was the most powerful professional development experience of their careers. Although several of the teachers we've quoted in this book now hold NBPTS certification, Kimberly Min is probably the most recent. During the 2004–2005 school year, Kimberly spent a great deal of energy preparing for certification.

—⚹ ⚹ ⚹—

The NBPTS process gave me an outlet to reflect and write about my teaching experiences. This self-reflection confirmed my belief that social justice could be incorporated in the curriculum within the state standards. For the past four years, I have tried to engage my students in what Freire calls praxis. Students discuss school and community issues and have turned the dialogue into action by writing letters to administrators, city officials, and their peers regarding issues such as community safety, racial profiling, and sanitary conditions (or lack of) on their school campus. The NBPTS process gave me opportunities to write about this type of teaching.

In the current climate of high-stakes testing, the NBPTS process recon-firmed my belief that it is not only possible to infuse culturally responsive teaching but necessary. For example, my students participated in cross-curricular projects. They read and researched about important heroes of color and produced art work such as murals, dioramas, and portraits. Ashlee, my only black female student, made authentic connections with Ruby Bridges—understanding how she may have felt as the only black child in the class, whereas Esmeralda, my recently immigrated Latina student, made connections to Ruby Bridges's feelings of isolation because Esmeralda could not speak that much English. Because the NBPTS process calls for educators to reflect upon their practice and pedagogy, I increased my awareness of my students' needs, and I felt better prepared to teach them.

—KIMBERLY MIN
Third-grade teacher

In November 2005, Kimberly learned that she was awarded NBPTS certification.

Teacher Networks   Some of the most powerful sites for teacher learning connect teachers from various schools around a challenge that they all see as important. In these networks, they gain continuing access to expertise that is not available at their school. Networks also provide teachers a chance to interact and learn with other teachers in an environment that is often less threatening than their schools.

Teacher networks connect members in various ways. Some focus on subject matter, such as the National Writing Project. Others support teachers who share a common commitment for social justice, such as the Teachers for Social Justice. We discuss these two national networks more later. Other networks are local, such as The Los Angeles Physics Teachers Alliance Group (LAPTAG), comprising about 60 physics teachers from about 30 Los Angeles area high schools and community colleges who meet regularly with a UCLA professor. Some teacher networks depend heavily on the Internet; others hold face-to-face workshops, meetings, and discussion groups.

Professional communities are most helpful when they encourage teachers to learn from one another as well as provide supportive a check on members' perceptions of their teaching dilemmas. Although many of these networks are organized by universities, state departments of education, or nonprofit organizations, nearly all see the teacher members as the experts and follow a "teachers teaching teachers" model.

The National Writing Project (NWP) began in Berkeley, California in 1974 and now includes sites in 189 communities. The Project's goal is to improve teaching writing in the nation's schools, and to recognize the primary importance of teacher knowledge, expertise, and leadership in achieving this instructional goal. The NWP combines intensive summer institutes for teachers with follow-up opportunities for teachers to meet and learn together. During the summer institutes teachers demonstrate their most effective practices, study research, and improve their knowledge of writing by writing themselves. Teachers quickly become leaders who develop local writing teacher groups in their own districts and work as peer coaches to other teachers. The Project also believes that access to high-quality educational experiences is a basic right of all learners and a cornerstone of equality.

Perhaps most helpful for teachers committed to teaching for social justice are networks of teachers who assume that good teaching—"improved" teaching—requires that they resist practices that disadvantage their students and press for changes in curriculum and instruction that will correct the inequalities their students experience.

One such network, Teachers for Social Justice in Chicago, is an organization of teachers, administrators, preservice teachers, and other educators working in public, independent, alternative, and charter schools and universities. The group has come together based on its commitment to education for social justice. Members work toward classrooms and schools that are antiracist, multicultural/multilingual, and grounded in the experiences of the city's students. They make clear on their website that they "all agree that all children should have an academically rigorous education that is both caring and critical, an education that helps students pose critical questions about society and 'talk back' to the world." The group both shares ideas and curriculum and supports each other's activist work. A collective goal is to get the voices of educators into the public discussion of school policies. Groups like Chicago's Teachers for Social Justice exist in many large urban areas.

In networks such as Teachers for Social Justice, teachers develop trust, mutual understandings, and relationship skills. These enduring relationships allow teachers to see as "normal" their roles as reformers who have support that comes from both inside and outside their school. Such networks also emphasize that teachers' efforts to bring social justice to their schools do not emerge from a perverse desire to be disruptive for its own sake but are conclusions drawn from social science research and long-standing cultural values.

For example, Georgene Acosta describes how a local network of alumni from her teacher education program supported her social justice approach to teaching. The group, with some support from the university, met regularly to discuss challenges to social justice at their schools, specific lessons, readings, community actions, and participation in various out-of-school teaching activities.

———————————————————⊗ ⊗ ⊗———————————————————

I considered all the amazing work aimed at promoting peace that I have seen among my colleagues at schools around the city. In her Life Skills class Joy Kraft teaches students to see the damaging effects of racism, sexism, classism, and homophobia and helps students devise nonviolent solutions to these social ills. Chris Morrisey has developed Project Peace, a peer-mediation program that he is helping to establish at his high school. These teachers are my heroes. When I face difficult situations as a teacher, they inspire me to work through those difficulties. They renew my sense of hope and courage by reminding me that I am not alone.

—**Georgene Acosta**
First-year teacher, high school English

Similarly, Kimberly Min notes that UCLA's local Teachers for Social Justice network also allowed her to connect with like-minded teachers at other schools.

———————————————————⊗ ⊗ ⊗———————————————————

I joined Teachers for Social Justice, which introduced me to a first-grade teacher in Chinatown. I observed his critical pedagogy and his lessons related to the civil rights movement. This experience showed me that rigorous and critical curriculum could be applied at any grade level.

—**Kimberly Min**
Third-grade teacher

Third-grade teacher Salina Gray joined an ongoing teacher seminar for developing curriculum that furthered all students' right to a high-quality education. Their discussions and activities are structured specifically around a Students' Bill of Rights. The seminar, facilitated by UCLA's Institute for Democracy, Education, and Access (IDEA), invited educators from greater Los Angeles to study and teach together. Teachers participated in finding and developing curricular materials and teaching strategies to help their students study access and equity in their own schools and communities. They met regularly and contributed the results of their students' research to the online journal *Teaching to Change LA*. Gray describes how the seminar helped her develop her teaching.

—⊗ ⊗ ⊗—

In the seminar I interact with other socially conscious educators, hear their stories, thoughts, opinions, and experiences. This helps me rethink my own experiences. People are very insightful and honest in responding to the readings and to one another. Nothing has been inflammatory, no propaganda— just views and experiences presented very clearly and objectively. It has been very inspiring to me to question not just my teaching practices, but the educational system that I grew up in. I like to think that I am dramatically different from those who don't respect their students. But I've had to sit and listen and reflect on some of my teaching practices that perpetuate all the things I say that I am fighting against. In the seminar I have evaluated my beliefs as a teacher, asking what education should be, what it means, and what I actually show my students. Do my actions show my values to my students? So, I've become a kinder, more honest Ms Gray. My students have noticed.

—SALINA GRAY
First-year teacher, grade 3

As the examples we've provided here show, continuous learning is a vital part of high-quality professional practice. Yet, schools provide few sustained, high-quality opportunities for teachers to continue to learn and develop. Those who want long-range support for their educational values and activities cannot wait for that support to appear as a ready option within the normal course of their workday. If this sounds discouraging, it needn't be. There are many opportunities waiting for teachers to join with others in communities of educators who work together to construct satisfying work lives at the same time they pursue their philosophical and professional social justice goals.

In the following quote, Judy Smith describes the multiple learning communities she became part of during her first three years of teaching.

—⊗ ⊗ ⊗—

I was involved in my UCLA alumni inquiry group, CIRCLE (a regional network of teachers who convene forums on topics of interest), and a variety of professional organizations. I am also a Beginning Teacher Support and Assessment Program mentor, a lecturer in the university's teacher education program, and a member of my school's "Collaboration Team." I also regularly attended professional development workshops and took university continuing education courses.

My mentor from my first year of teaching, Brian Gibbs (who now teaches the social studies methods class in my teacher education program), and several students and I met once a month at his house for three years. We talked about curriculum, social justice, educational policy, funny students, and more. That was probably the best three hours I spent a month. We got reenergized and discussed curriculum at the same time.

—JUDY SMITH
High school social studies

For Judy, teaching is clearly not an 8-to-3 job that shuts down when she closes her classroom door. Rather, her profession and "lifestyle" merge into a single, if complex, identity.

Become a Social Justice Activist

------------------------------------ ✂ ✂ ✂ ------------------------------------

The following principles guide me as a social justice educator. First, I recognize the experiences and prior knowledge of my students, which inform me about who they are and how they learn. I also engage my students in critical dialogue through the use of culturally responsive teaching, which provides my students opportunities to share their experiences in their community. Then I try to provide opportunities for my students to be active agents in change, which affirms who they are and what they consider important. I also collaborate with students' families, the community, and other social justice educators. Such teaching can shape, transform, and influence individuals whose everyday decisions, in turn, have an impact on the rest of society.

—**Kimberly Min**
Third-grade teacher

Kimberly's reflections capture three powerful ways for career teachers to become social justice activists. One is that they take the cultural knowledge and experiences of their students as the grounding on which to build their intellectual development. Doing so, they counter commonplace deficit views of their students, families, and communities with understanding and recognition of their strengths. A second way is by speaking the unspeakable. Instead of pretending that the problems and inequalities that plague their communities and their schools don't exist, these teachers unmask, critique, and engage their students in talking about and understanding them. They also help their students see possibilities. A third way is that, together with students, families, community members, and colleagues, teachers act to disrupt those problems and inequalities. As they do, they counter the pervasive view that, as terrible as conditions are, there is simply not the knowledge or power to change them.

Counter Deficit Thinking with Community Strengths   Like Kimberly Min, many teachers have not grown up in the communities and cultures of their students. Grappling with the racial, economic, and cultural divide that separates them and their students is an essential focus for social justice teachers. Bridging this divide requires far more than simply taking courses in multiculturalism and diversity. As education scholar Lilia Bartolome contends, "the most pedagogically advanced strategies are sure to be ineffective in the hands of educators who implicitly or explicitly subscribe to a belief system that renders ethnic, racial, and linguistic minority students at best culturally disadvantaged and in need of fixing."[21]

More than 60 years ago, John Dewey argued in ways that are similar to today's sociocultural and political theorists the importance of connecting curriculum and instruction to the community knowledge and resources:

> [L]earning which develops intelligence and character does not come about when only the textbook and the teacher have a say; . . . every individual becomes educated only as he has an opportunity to contribute something from his own experience, no matter how meager or slender that background of experience may be at a given time; and finally . . . enlightenment comes from the give and take, from the exchange of experiences and ideas.[22]

Participating in this "give-and-take" is part of being a total teacher. Teachers can no more reject this dimension of teaching—knowledge of and engagement with the community—than they can choose to ignore their classroom environment.

To counteract decades of "deficit" approaches to urban education, social justice teachers must discover and build on the strengths of the communities in which they teach. We have detailed many of the strategies for doing this activist curriculum work in Chapters 5 on instruction, 7 on building classroom communities, and 10 on connecting with families and neighborhoods.

To summarize briefly here, teachers who seek to build their teaching on the strengths of communities must question commonly accepted beliefs and practices surrounding ability, race, class, gender, language, difference, and so on. They must sit at the intersection of theory and practice, constantly asking, "Why do we do it this way?" "What assumptions about the communities and cultures of my students underlie these practices?" "Whose interests does this practice serve?" "How might the cultural resources of my students contribute to achieving our educational goals?"

For example, in one Latino immigrant community, Ryan Williams and his classmates spent some time as student teachers learning about resources and capacity in the neighborhoods surrounding the schools where they would begin their careers. He and his classmates created an "asset map" of the potential education-related opportunities in the community.

Ryan shared his initial feelings of detachment as he drove to and from the community; he had seen the place as barren, starved of resources. After contacting neighborhood churches, libraries, community groups, and other organizations, the picture softened. Community leaders referred Ryan and his classmates to additional resources that were not obvious at first glance, such as private homes used for tutorials and meetings. Gradually, their deficit conceptions of the community gave way. By the time Ryan began teaching, the detachment he once felt had disappeared. He explained his shift in perspective.

---⊗ ⊗ ⊗---

The green building on the corner that I have passed many times is no longer just a stucco structure but a place where community folks come on Tuesdays, Thursdays, and Saturdays to pick up food items from Ms. Rodriquez. The yellow wooden house across from the liquor store is an after-school site for tutoring. The narrow brown and black Evangelist church provides college

access information. Each week this community has at least six Neighbor-
hood Watch meetings at which community members discuss a broad range of
issues, including quality education and teenage violence. At one of these
meetings, Ms. Garcia, a Neighborhood Watch leader, expressed her group's
interest in connecting with teachers and the school to discuss how they could
work together to provide alternate learning sites for students after school.

—RYAN WILLIAMS
First-year teacher, grade 4

The experience opened new possibilities for teaching. Ryan came to understand that the success and sense of professional fulfillment depended on his working alongside parents and community.

Engage in Dialogue and Critique about Limits and Possibilities in Students' Lives   A second activist strategy is to make social justice issues a part of the curriculum, helping students become students of social conditions and inequalities. This strategy exposes problems that they may have seen only as personal troubles as actually related to larger economic, social, and political conditions. Such a curriculum can be intellectually powerful, engrossing, and conducive to having students develop the knowledge and skills to solve problems, as well as to understand them. However, this type of teacher activism doesn't mean that every lesson must be focused on social justice or that every social justice lesson must be grim. The following examples include a range of ways to make social justice issues explicit.

Judy Smith found ways to have her high school seniors meet the state standards in economics and, at the same time, consider the connections between their own behaviors and injustices that come with global capitalism:

———————————————— ⊗ ⊗ ⊗ ————————————————

The international economics unit was the last of the semester. We had
already studied basic micro and macro economic concepts. We were ready
to move the discussion away from U.S. economic issues to international
economics. The California State Standard for this unit was: "Economics
12.6: Students analyze issues of international trade and explain how the
U.S. economy affects, and is affected by, economic forces beyond the United
States' borders."

I broke this down into four themes—free trade, consumerism, sweat-
shops, and globalization. My goal was to cover and go beyond the standard
by teaching students how their individual consumer habits and beliefs have
an impact on both the domestic and international environments, other
cultures and peoples, and themselves.

"How many of you woke up this morning and thought about what you
would wear today? And then how many of you thought about where the
clothes were made, how they were made, and how they wound up in your
hands?" I asked these questions, and my students gave me strange looks.
Ms. Smith, they said in a chorus, of course we thought about what we were

going to wear today. And, no, we do not know where our clothes were made and how. In fact, why should we care?

These students were being honest. Why should they care where their clothes are from? They have them, they like them, and they would buy more if they could. Currently the average teenager spends approximately $15 a day. My students claimed that they did, too. They admitted that they buy product after product without thinking about where the product was made, how it was made or by whom. My challenge: how to get students to think beyond themselves and how their minute decisions impact the global community. Furthermore, how can these students become producers, rather than just consumers?

Using the last unit in the textbook, we weaved the California concepts of free trade, balance of trade, imports, and exports with Bill Bigelow's Rethinking Globalization *text—concepts of sweatshops, consumerism, child labor, globalization, and personal responsibility. The economics text does not mention the latter concepts, and yet these social injustices and realities exist because of the practice of free trade.*

I wanted the students to look at themselves and to understand some of the ethical conflicts and social injustices that exist in business. How do progress and tradition grow together? Is profit more important than human rights? I hoped that after this unit, students would have a better understanding of their role and responsibility in the global marketplace. I wanted them to think about what they buy, for what reasons, and from where. Were there any purchasing habits they could change as a result of what they learned? Furthermore, were there any actions they could take to educate others?

—**Judy Smith**
High school social studies

Some teachers engage students' families in their learning about social justice issues. For example, fifth-grade teacher Miranda Chavez teaches in a neighborhood of Central American immigrants—most of whom speak little if any English. During her first year of teaching, Chavez integrated into her classwork a study of lead and its impact on health issues, especially for young children. Health department officials met with students and their parents multiple times, as did representatives from the local city councilperson's office. Students studied chemistry to understand the nature of lead. They also went out into their community to collect paint fragments and soil in which children played and then had these samples tested for lead content.

As a culminating activity, Chavez invited families to a potluck dinner at which the students presented informational posters they had made—presentations that involved explaining complex chemical processes. The room was packed; almost every parent attended and the evening was conducted exclusively in Spanish. Some parents joined their children in presenting the lead findings, yet a few felt ill-equipped to do so. One parent explained that she "hadn't done anything because she didn't know any English and hadn't attended school herself in her home country."

Feeling the tension in the room, Chavez respectfully addressed all the parents, explaining that they had all played important roles in this project, motivating their children and setting rules to ensure that projects were completed successfully. As these students move on to middle school, she continued, parents will play a crucial role in ensuring their children's future success in school. Knowing English and having a formal education, she assured parents, were not required. Herself a Central American immigrant, Chavez empathized with parents, yet her message was one of empowerment and social change.

As we've noted, not all social justice activism in classrooms must focus on the negative. Recognizing the disparities his students face in terms of college access, Mauro Bautista developed an elaborate lesson for his English learners that opened a new world for them—the world of college going. As a teacher whose assignment was to help immigrant students learn English, Mauro included activities in which students expanded their English speaking, listening, reading, and writing competencies.

The unit I was most proud of in my classes for beginning ESL students was one on the college application process. We discussed the college preparatory course requirements, the students took a mock SAT, they asked two other teachers for letters of recommendations, they wrote a personal statement, they filled out a mock application, and they mailed it to me. Thereafter, I asked numerous people, such as doctors, architects, and lawyers, to come and present about the importance of higher education to our students. Finally, I mailed letters of acceptance to all the students. I did this unit to expose students to the classes they need in high school in order to go to college, the college application process, and professionals with backgrounds similar to their own.

—**Mauro Bautista**
Middle-school bilingual education coordinator

In the following quote, Salina Gray describes her students' response to her social justice curriculum, specifically to a Students' Bill of Rights lesson that was prompted by social justice teacher seminars described earlier in this chapter.

The Students' Bill of Rights has affected how they see themselves. Now everyone is really trying to help everyone else. It has been a dramatic change. They were really excited that there were adults who cared about children's rights. They were amazed that they could be valued with the same standards and respect as adults. Since our initial conversations on their rights, and the role of education in their lives, my students place more emphasis on becoming good citizens and leaders. My students look for opportunities to be "teachers." They speak up for themselves now because they realize that their opinions and views are valued and respected. We've had conversations about what makes a "good leader," and reached the consensus that it is more than just getting the grades.

Before I became more explicit about social justice in my classroom, I asked my students, "Why do you go to school?" They said, "to get a job" and "to pass the Stanford 9." Now they say "to be the best that I can be," and "to grow up and change the world."

—SALINA GRAY
First-year teacher, grade 3

Finally, Frank Divinagracia, formerly a mathematics teacher, is now a mathematics coach at the high school where he was once a student. During his first year of teaching, Frank suspected that his students thought he was crazy because of his unbridled hope for their futures, but that is an opinion that he can live with.

———————————— ✖ ✖ ✖ ————————————

I like to tell my students, and sometimes they like to listen, about the lives and experiences and words of various activists. I want them to see that people are out there watching out for them and fighting for their betterment. I like telling them how I am like the character in Sandra Cisneros's book House on Mango Street. *She desperately wanted out of her neighborhood only to discover that the more she learned and grew, the more she knew she had to return home. In returning home she wanted to share with her people all the things that she had learned, and that the shackles that one physically sees are nothing compared with the mental ones we put on ourselves. I think that my students think I am crazy, but I hope one day that my craziness will infect them.*

—FRANK DIVINAGRACIA
First-year teacher, mathematics, grade 10

Act for Change   Social justice teachers often take their lessons beyond discussing issues in class and find ways to act. In many cases these teachers are themselves activists outside of school and presume that students will learn and gain from participating in similar social change activities. For example, in the following quote, Kimberly Min describes her third graders taking critical and constructive looks at school administrators, the mayor, and the driver of the neighborhood ice cream truck. Their goals were clean bathrooms, an end to racial profiling, and stopping the sale of "weapons."

———————————— ✖ ✖ ✖ ————————————

I incorporate social activism into my teaching in many ways–through history, storytelling, class discussion, writing, artistic expression, performance and even active protest. When I teach students about social justice, I try to make the lessons culturally or socially relevant, so that students can identify with the concepts.

But first and foremost, the level of involvement depends on the students and the issues they bring up in class discussion. For example, in a lesson about inequity, my students revealed that the bathrooms closest to our room were the filthiest in the school. After recognizing this as "unfair," students wrote letters to the principal and superintendent, requesting cleaner bathrooms with soap and toilet paper.

In another instance that prompted written protest, my students wrote letters to the mayor, requesting that the police end racial profiling. In return, the mayor's office sent back a letter with his picture, thanking us for our interest. This validated my students' efforts, showing them that their voices mattered. Students learned that they could also protest in other ways than writing.

After learning about nonviolent resistance through movements such as the civil rights bus boycott, students applied this knowledge to their own community. They created picket signs to boycott the ice cream truck that was selling toy guns. This was a response to a second-grade peer being suspended for having a toy gun on campus, which violated the zero-tolerance policy.

I consider these to be the lessons that I am most proud of because students are seen as the change makers.

—KIMBERLY MIN
Third-grade teacher

Many social justice teachers extend their own activism beyond their schools and classrooms, although their students are often unaware of their teachers' activities. For example, urban high school teacher Noah Lippe-Klein and former elementary teacher and current PhD student Ramón Martínez belong to the Coalition for Educational Justice (CEJ), an activist offshoot of their local teachers' union. CEJ began when a group of teachers joined forces with a diverse group of civic, legal, and educational leaders committed to eliminating the use of high-stakes testing with low-income children of color and to pursue other reforms.

In 2001 Ramón, Noah, and other members of the Coalition brought over 300 teachers, parents, and students to a school board meeting to seek the board's support in changing the testing program along with the retention policies based on the test results. Since then the Coalition has met with board members and organized antitesting actions at school sites. As a result of these activities, CEJ won a victory when school district officials instructed principals to honor requests from parents who want their children exempted from taking the tests. CEJ teachers, students, and parent leaders also led a grassroots campaign that resulted in the adoption of a school board policy to research and adopt and consider alternatives to the district's current high-stakes tests.

In addition, CEJ has fought for reducing class sizes, halting the expansion of military JROTC (Junior Reserve Officer Training Corps) programs in black and Latino schools, removing NCLB's requirement that high schools provide students' information to the military for recruiting purposes, ensuring qualified teachers and adequate resources at some of their city's most overcrowded and neglected schools, and more. The CEJ has provided opportunities for student leaders to meet privately

FOCAL POINT 12.2

Teacher Ramón Martínez Goes Public with His Social Justice Perspective

Proposition 227, Stanford 9 and Open Court: Three Strikes Against English Language Learners

For the past four years, I have taught first grade at Utah Street Elementary School in the Boyle Heights section of East Los Angeles. During my teaching experience at Utah Street, I have learned a great deal about teaching and learning. In particular, my students, who are all English Language Learners, have taught me the importance of language and culture as factors that influence their experiences with schooling. Understanding my students' particular sociolinguistic environment has enabled me to adopt approaches to teaching that contribute to their empowerment. Unfortunately, recent trends in educational policy have seriously limited my capacity to continue empowering my students in the classroom. The passage of Proposition 227, the statewide focus on student accountability through high-stakes testing and the Los Angeles Unified School District's rigid implementation of the Open Court reading program have all made it increasingly difficult for me to provide my students with the instruction that they need and deserve.

. . .

Having been stripped of their home language, my students are now expected to take a norm-referenced, standardized exam, which, in addition to being inherently biased, is administered in a language that they do not understand. Obviously, the Stanford 9 does not provide me with an accurate indication of my students' progress in the various subject areas. The only thing that it does show me is that which I already know—that my students are Limited English Proficient. Under the API scheme, the results of this unfair and inaccurate assessment are used to determine the allocation of funds to schools, thereby punishing those students who are already at a disadvantage. English Language Learners and other students of color who attend schools in low-income communities will undoubtedly suffer, as their schools fail, in disproportionate numbers, to improve their test scores.

Because the Stanford 9 is being used as the sole measure of student achievement, teachers have consequently been under a great deal of pressure to "teach to the test." Indeed, this emphasis on test-readiness has been driving curriculum within Los Angeles Unified. The most recent example of this is the District's implementation of the Open Court reading program. In a nutshell, Open Court is a scripted reading program that ignores the instructional needs of English Language Learners and teaches reading skills in isolation, detached from meaningful texts and students' lived experiences. Some elements of the program are effective and could conceivably be incorporated into a balanced literacy program for English Language Learners. Unfortunately, most teachers in Los Angeles Unified (myself included) are not being given the discretion to decide how best to teach their students. Rather than being able to pick and choose components that work for their students, "low-performing" schools are being forced to rigidly implement the entire Open Court

(continued)

program, while schools with high test scores are allowed to continue providing their students with rich, varied and meaningful learning experiences. Needless to say, this policy is serving to perpetuate existing educational inequalities.

Proposition 227, the Stanford 9 and Open Court represent three strikes against English Language Learners. With each successive strike, the educational inequalities between English Language Learners and their English-speaking counterparts have increased. Proposition 227 condemned my students to an unequal education, while the Stanford 9 and Open Court have worked together to perpetuate that inequality. It is clear that policymakers at the state and district levels are more concerned with implementing accountability programs than they are with working to ensure educational justice. Critical educators must, therefore, step up and take a stand. In defense of educational justice and sound pedagogy, we must begin to engage in forms of individual and collective resistance. If we truly seek to empower our students, we must begin to challenge the educational policies that serve only to harm them.

Source: Ramón Martínez, in *Going Public with our Teaching.*[23]

with all seven members of their school board about these issues, and they've made progress in each of these areas.

In 2005, Ramón Martínez, published his activist views in a book that education professors, students, and other teachers will read. (See an excerpt in Focal Point 12.2.)

Ramón Martínez and other activist teachers join a venerable American tradition, captured here in the words of escaped slave, abolitionist, and writer Frederick Douglass:

> Let me give you a word on the philosophy of reform. The whole history of the progress of human liberty shows that all concessions . . . have been born of earnest struggle. The conflict has been exciting, agitating, all absorbing. . . . It must do this or it does nothing. If there is no struggle there is no progress. Those who profess to favor freedom, yet depreciate agitation, are men who want crops without plowing up the ground. They want rain without thunder and lightning. They want the ocean without the awful roar of the waters. This struggle may be a moral one; or it may be a physical one; or it may be both moral and physical; but it must be a struggle. Power never concedes anything without a demand. It never did and it never will.[24]

When Douglass wrote the words "the awful roar of the waters," *awful* meant something quite different from the present sense of inspiring fear, extreme unpleasantness, or ugliness. To Douglass, the roar of struggle inspired not fear, but awe, an overwhelming feeling of reverence—grand, sublime, and powerful. Not for the fainthearted, this struggle lifts the spirit of the hopeful as they take action, make demands, plow up the ground. Career teachers can do just that.

Expand Your Professional Influence

Social justice educators are typically welcomed and respected at their schools—especially when their teaching is undeniably competent and their students are enthusiastic about learning. We have considerable evidence from watching the careers of the teachers in this book that those who merge their roles as successful teachers, supportive colleagues, and social justice activists are among the most powerful change agents in classrooms, schools, and communities.

Not surprisingly, perhaps, as their careers develop, many such teachers seek to extend their influence within the educational system by taking on new roles within it. Unfortunately, few classroom teachers feel that they have much influence over such important aspects of schooling as shaping the curriculum at their school site, the content of their own professional development programs, how money is spent, or the hiring and evaluation of teachers at their own schools. They report having only a limited say in schoolwide social and instructional decisions such as curricular, tracking and discipline policies. Many complain that they have few opportunities to collaborate with other teachers.[25]

Some teachers expand their influence in the way that Judy Smith talked about earlier, as mentors in teacher induction systems. Judy, who plans on remaining in teaching, also hopes to shape the profession by supporting others to develop the knowledge, skills, and values to teach all students well.

Others take the route that Kimberly Min is following. By becoming certified by the NBPTS, Kimberly will be called upon increasingly to serve as a teacher leader both in- and outside of her school.

Of those who do not remain full-time teachers in urban schools, some become administrators.

Those who choose to move away from classroom teaching hope that the costs of leaving will be outweighed by their larger contribution to the education of the students they care so much about. Mauro Bautista, who began teaching in 2000 and took on the role of coordinating programs for English learners at his school in 2004, is now hoping to become a social justice school leader.

--- 88 88 88 ---

My plans for the future are to receive a second master's of education and an administrative credential. My master's program has helped me define social justice educator: "A social justice educator identifies injustices, collaborates with others who are affected by the injustices, and then takes action to disrupt the reproduction of these injustices." My goal is to become an assistant principal and eventually a principal who acts as a social justice educator.

One thing I am discovering is that when you work primarily with adults it is easy to forget that we are here for the students first and foremost. I hope that as I continue my journey through education, I keep students and their families first.

—**Mauro Bautista**
Middle-school bilingual education coordinator

Teachers like Mauro do not want to leave education, but they do want to have a broader influence on the education of the students they care deeply about. If possible, they'd both also like to, in Mauro's words, "keep students and their families first."

Mauro is not unusual. Teacher Jennifer Garcia, quoted in several earlier chapters, is now an assistant principal at her high school. Jasper Bui is the librarian at his middle school. Javier Espindola is a district literacy coach to other teachers, and Frank Divinagracia is a math coach at his high school. Others are school system curriculum specialists, educational technology experts, or counselors, or they direct after-school programs. Some, like Ramón Martínez, Benji Chang, and Laura Torres, are graduate students who will probably become education professors themselves; Mariana Pacheco is a postdoctoral fellow in teacher education at UCLA helping students prepare to teach. Others have become a museum educator and curriculum developer, an educational software developer, and a marketing director for an educational media company. One entered the Peace Corps. They all remain committed to changing the world.

Commit to a Hopeful Critique

---------------------------------------⚹ ⚹ ⚹---------------------------------------

Teaching has the potential to be transformative. It can create positive change in the lives of all—tolerance, awareness, respect, meaning, and fulfillment. But teachers and students must cast a critical eye to make learning reflect their realities and aspirations. As committed, critical, and active agents within schools, students and teachers must create change. By questioning our own views and preconceptions, by critiquing our own practice and pedagogy, and by allowing our reflections to turn into positive action, we create social justice.

—KIMBERLY MIN
Third-grade teacher

Kimberly Min, like most of the other teachers quoted in this book, is determinedly optimistic about social transformation. Theirs is not an unthinking optimism, but a critical one that pairs hope with informed struggle. Adopting such a philosophical stance is one of the most powerful strategies for crafting a career as a social justice educator. It is a stance that echoes the thinking of contemporary scholars who argue that democracy and justice, in schools and out, require both hope and critique.

For example, Princeton professor Cornel West, one of America's most important philosophers and public intellectuals, calls for a "prophetic pragmatism"—a perspective that sees democracy as an ongoing struggle, rather than an idyllic or perfect end product. West combines faith in democratic processes with a "critical temper." He argues that in diverse cultures like the United States, any democratic process must place its faith in "the abilities and capacities of ordinary people to participate in decision making procedures of institutions that regulate their lives." He cautions, however, that participation itself is insufficient. Rather, the democracy must be one that "keeps track of social misery, solicits and channels moral outrage to alleviate it, and projects a future in which the potentialities of ordinary people flourish and flower."[26]

Similarly, Brazilian educator Paulo Freire paired the importance of hope and optimism for better social conditions with an active struggle to attain them. In arguing that hope is a fundamental human need, Freire cautioned against separating it from action. "The idea that hope alone will transform the world . . . is an excellent route to hopelessness, pessimism, and fatalism." Hope is what sustains the struggle for a better world: "[T]he attempt to do without hope, in the struggle to improve the world, as if that struggle could be reduced to calculated acts alone, or a purely scientific approach, is a frivolous illusion. . . . Without a minimum of hope, we cannot so much as start the struggle. But without the struggle, hope . . . dissipates, loses its bearings, and turns into hopelessness."

Yes, it is circular. Hope sustains the actions, and people must act or the hope turns against them—empty. Freire tied all of this specifically to education, making him one of the most provocative, recognized, and influential educators worldwide: "One of the tasks of the serious progressive educator, through a serious, correct, political analysis, is to unveil opportunities for hope, no matter what the obstacles may be."[27]

For Freire, as for West, hope and struggle are not simply *instruments* that produce improved social conditions, although improved social conditions is a leading goal. Participating in a hopeful struggle is *itself* an "improvement." West's prophetic pragmatism and Freire's juxtaposition of hope and struggle provide teachers with a philosophical stance that gives meaning both to the everyday acts of teaching and to the larger efforts teachers make to teach, organize, support, and follow others who join to improve conditions and opportunities for students. This stance makes teaching matter, even in the face of the discouraging realities of their students' lives.

Georgene Acosta, like many of the other teachers in this book, has designed her career to make her teaching matter beyond imparting knowledge of her subject one class at a time. By the end of her first full year of teaching, hope and struggle had merged in her daily actions in her urban school. In the face of difficult circumstances, she made a commitment to prophetic pragmatism and to teaching.

———————————————————— ⊗ ⊗ ⊗ ————————————————————

On the morning of May 1, I returned to work after a two-week spring break. I felt rested, reenergized, and ready to begin a fresh week. About 10 minutes into my first period class, the voice of the principal came over the P.A. She began with her usual, "Pardon the interruption. . . ." But this would not be one of her pep talks about the importance of literacy, good attendance, and respectful behavior. "Two students at our school, Eddie Marengo and Richard Rivers, were shot and killed over the break."

In the days that followed, I began to gather various bits of information about the circumstances surrounding these two tragic deaths. I learned that the police gunned down Richard, an excellent student in my eleventh-grade class last year, in his own neighborhood, in the early morning hours. Eddie, a freshman whom I did not know personally, was shot in the back of the head while sitting at a bus stop on Easter Sunday.

In the following days and weeks, I experienced a profound sense of despair. I questioned my effectiveness as a social justice educator and wondered, "Am I contributing enough to end violence in my school and in

*my community?" While pondering the deaths of these two precious young
people, I felt myself falling into an abyss of sadness.*

*As Jean Paul Sartre said, "Life begins on the other side of despair."
I emerged from this abyss with a profound sense of hope. That hope is
grounded in my belief that this culture CAN be healed! It CAN be transformed! It CAN nurture and protect its young people. And it CAN give them
the tools they need to perpetuate peace!*

*We must research and analyze the problems that we encounter. We must
search for causes and solutions to the problems we find. We must study these
solutions and put them to work in our own practices both within and outside
of the classroom walls. We must study, we must think, we must ask hard
questions and we must work toward even harder solutions. And we must do
these things because we believe as Vaclav Havel said that "None of us as an
individual can save the world as a whole, but each of us must behave as
though it were in our power to do so." We know that there are no quick fixes
to the problems that our young people confront on a daily basis. We know
that creating meaningful solutions requires commitment, intelligence,
dialogue, and most importantly patience. We are up for the challenge.*

*When I think of Eddie and Richard, I feel a deep nameless ache that I
know will always be with me. But that nameless feeling helps to sustain my
hope. Hope for a world that is worthy of every one of its precious children.
We embrace the idea expressed by Martin Luther King that the universe is on
the side of justice and that justice will eventually win. And that is why we
teach.*

—GEORGENE ACOSTA
First-year teacher, high school English

Teachers like those cited throughout this book use their commitment to hope
and critique, in combination with their professional knowledge and skill, to create
public schools where children can both forge a common good and enrich their individual lives. Doing so, they experience deep evidence of children's brilliance that
defies typical expectations. Such teachers have seen uncountable combinations of
racially and economically diverse students learning together. They have also seen
themselves accomplish more than they ever thought they could. They know that if
given a chance, they and their students can make common education work.

Find Satisfaction in the Everyday

Throughout this book we've referred to John Dewey, whose goal was to create
schools that not merely were a *preparation* for democratic life, but were themselves sites of democratic living.[28] Dewey cautioned that teachers' work was not
only a means to some worthwhile end, but worthwhile in itself every day; not just a
means to democracy, but democratic itself. Thus, democracy is not an end state, but
a *practice*—a *way of acting* every day. When teachers struggle *for* social justice,
they engage in social justice. Such teachers find their hope—as well as their joy and

satisfaction—from the everyday work, as well as in some promise of a better world somewhere in the future.

The teachers we feature—Mauro Bautista, Mark Hill, Kimberly Min, and Judy Smith, along with many others—have conveyed their hope, struggle, joy, and satisfaction in their daily work with young people in some of their city's most neglected communities. As is clear from reading their words, they are all different—in their backgrounds, their jobs, and their way of teaching to change the world.

In the following quotes, Mauro, Mark, Kimberly, and Judy, each in his or her own way, describe their satisfaction with the hard work they've chosen to do and with the process of becoming a teacher.

⊠ ⊠ ⊠

Tuesday, September 4, 2000, was my first day as a full-time teacher. I remember being excited and nervous at the same time. I was excited because I was fulfilling my goal of returning to my own neighborhood in order to give back to it. I was nervous that my lack of experience would prevent my students from receiving the best education possible.

Now that I understand the teaching profession, I recognize my understanding will always be a work in progress. The classroom techniques I use depend on my students. I will never be able to look at any one of my classes and say, "Here is the perfect classroom, and now I will have the perfect classroom every year." Each year I will learn what it means to be a social justice educator from my students, their parents, my colleagues, scholars and myself.

I am proud to affect the lives of so many students and their parents. I hope that, one day, they too will go away to college and come back to help those they left behind.

—**Mauro Bautista**

⊠ ⊠ ⊠

Our school was designated "low performing" several years ago. This was due partly to gaps in the students' K–8 education—long-term subs, poor teachers—as well as to their difficulties outside of school. Minority and low socioeconomic students in areas like ours are the ones who get the short end of the educational stick. Seeking to provide a socially just education for our students, the district and UCLA partnered. Well-prepared and committed

students came to do their student teaching and then became permanent staff members. I was one of those teachers.

Each year, the expectations for student behavior and achievement became higher, and our school improved dramatically. This is visible in the classroom and on school grounds as well as on state tests. We have now escaped NCLB's "School in Need of Improvement" status, and with a couple more years of sustained growth, we will reach "High-Performing School" status. This has been largely the result of the schoolwide high expectations instituted by well-prepared teachers and a highly supportive school administration.

The students themselves see and feel the change that has taken place. Across the district, eighth to twelfth graders feel that our school expects more and only takes the "smart" kids, which is why our scores are better. In fact, it isn't true. We pull students into our school strictly by lottery; grades are not a factor at all. But the perception, both by students and parents, has become self-sustaining. This has become a source of pride for our staff, which continues to help propel our positive momentum.

—MARK HILL

⊗ ⊗ ⊗

During Thanksgiving, my class participated in a "Feast of Resistance." Students learned about the historical context of fruits and how it is related to exploitable labor. We began by discussing where different fruits come from in the world, as we explored the origin of the banana—a topic in our social

*studies text. We were able to see how this piece of fruit was politicized in the
global market as we talked about cheap laborers in South America who were
exploited. This led to our next discussion about the United Farm Workers
and the grape strikes led by Cesar Chavez and Phillip Vera Cruz. It was
amazing to see the students reenact what they believed to be happening as
students began to role-play the characters of the boss and the exploited fruit
pickers. I asked the students, "So what do you think the people did when they
asked for a raise and the boss sat in his office and said no?" Darrell
responded, "They should have gone on strike." Then I asked, "What's that?"
Darrell replied confidently, "like the bus drivers who went on strike. They
just stop working." Then, with no prodding by me, the students began
chanting, "Strike, strike, strike."*

*It was amazing. The students were making huge connections between
their prior knowledge and the larger picture and engaged in critical
thinking. They showed that they understood inequity in the labor market,
and that people of color have the agency to fight back as they are systematically
used for cheap labor. The students have a deeper understanding of how the
banana arrived in their local supermarket, as well as greater sensitivity to
what people of color endured. This teaches the importance of tolerance and
the power behind collective action. This was a pivotal moment.*

—**Kimberly Min**

⋇ ⋇ ⋇

*There is a specific place on my campus—when I round a corner and catch
sight of my portable classroom—where every day I marvel that I am a*

*teacher. . . . Hey, don't get me wrong. There was a cost moving from high tech
to high school. In corporate America, luxuries such as fabulous holiday
parties and access to the latest technology seduced me for a while. I loved the
fast pace, salary, travel, and interesting problem solving. I learned about
business, professionalism, and working with others. All valuable. However,
that cost, when evaluated in heart and soul dollars, changes. In high tech, we
did not take much time to examine values, biases, and different cultures.
High tech didn't teach me about human suffering and triumph at the same
time. High tech didn't expose me to our children and to their critical role in
our future and our democracy, or offer intellectual stimulation on history,
literacy, and politics. High tech didn't teach me to be a better human being.
Teaching high school does.*

—Judy Smith

We conclude in Focal Point 12.3 with a passage from Herbert Kohl, a committed social justice educator who has been inspiring educators for 40 years with sage advice
and sobering and joyful stories of teaching in urban schools. Kohl's career as a
teacher began in 1962 in Harlem where he taught sixth grade, an experience he documented in his classic book, *36 Children*. He has been working with students and
teachers ever since. The excerpt is from an essay Kohl wrote to aspiring teachers
about finding satisfaction in the everyday work of teaching for social justice. We
don't know if Mauro, Mark, Kimberly, Judy, or the other teachers in this book have
read Kohl's essay. We do know that they live his words as they teach to change the
world, as do countless other teachers every day.

FOCAL POINT 12.3

Herb Kohl Reflects on Teaching for Social Justice
Advice for Those Who Teach "Against the Grain"

The idea that you have to advocate teaching for social justice is a sad statement about the moral sensibility in our schools and society. . . . One cannot simply assume that because an action or sentiment is fair, just, or compassionate that it will be popular or embraced. . . .

So what are social justice teachers—that is, one who cares about nurturing all children and is enraged at the prospects of any of his or her students dying young, being hungry, or living meaningless or despairing lives—to do in the classroom so that they go against the grain and work in the service of their students?

I have several suggestions, some pedagogical and some personal. First of all, don't teach against your conscience or align yourself with texts, people, and rules that hurt children. Resist in as creative way as you can, through humor, developing and using alternatives, and organizing for social and educational change with others who feel as you do. Don't become isolated or alone in your efforts. . . . Find a school where you can do your work, risk getting fired and stand up for the quality of your work. Don't quit in the face of opposition: make people work hard if they intend to fire you for teaching equity and justice.

However, in order to do this, you must hone your craft as a teacher. . . . This is essential for caring teachers. You have to get it right for your students before presuming to take on larger systems, no matter how terrible they are. As educators we need to root our struggles for social justice in the work we do on an everyday level in a particular community with a particular group of students. . . .

[L]ook around at everything other people say is effective with children. Pick and choose, restructure and retool the best of what you find, make it your own, and most of all watch your students and see what works. Listen to them, observe how they learn, and then, based on your experience and their responses, figure out how to practice social justice in your classroom as you discuss and analyze it. . . .

It is not enough to teach well and create a social justice classroom separate from the larger community. You have to be a community activist as well, a good parent, a decent citizen, and active community member. Is all this possible? Probably not—certainly it isn't easy and often demands sacrifice. . . .

This leads me to my final suggestion. Protect and nurture yourself, have some fun in your life, learn new things that only obliquely relate to issues of social justice. Walk, play ball, play chess, swim, fall in love, give yourself in love to someone else. Don't forget to laugh or feel good about the world. Sing with others, tell stories and listen to other people's stories, have fun so that you can work hard and work hard so that you and your parents and your students can have fun without looking over their shoulders. This is not a question of selfishness but one of survival. Don't turn teaching for social justice into a grim responsibility but take it

(continued)

for the moral and social necessity that it is. And don't be afraid to struggle for what you believe.

> *Source:* Herbert Kohl, "Some Reflections on Teaching for Social Justice," in William Ayres, Jean Ann Hunt, and Therese Quinn, *Teaching for Social Justice: A Democracy and Education Reader* (New York: The New Press and Teachers College Press, 1998).

OLC Connections

A list of additional online and print resources and a set of questions for reflection about teaching as a profession can be found at www.mhhe.com/oakes3e .

Digging Deeper

The scholars, organizations, and websites listed in this section provide additional information about the teaching profession and about the career strategies we described. In addition, several of the sources we list have delved far more deeply into the struggles of social justice teaching.

The Teaching Profession

http://www.pbs.org/firstyear/ is a website developed in conjunction with the PBS documentary *The First Year*—an emotional journey of five beginning teachers in the Los Angeles public school system. The website provides the story of the documentary and information about the five teachers. Two of the teachers are graduates of the UCLA program attended by the teachers figured in this book, including Georgene Acosta, whom we quote in this chapter.

The **Workforce Learning Link** is a holistic initiative created in partnership with the New Jersey Department of Labor and Workforce Development (LWD) and NJN Public Television. Its website has a page of very useful resources on teaching as a profession. It can be found at http://www.njn.net/workforce/teachinglinks.html.

Teacher Associations

The **American Federation of Teachers,** online at http://www.aft.org/index.htm, and the **National Education Association,** online at http://www.nea.org/index.html, both provide news of interest to teachers: information about current education policy issues, such as No Child Left Behind, charter schools, class sizes, teacher shortages, and more, and opportunities for teachers to get involved in shaping federal legislation. They also offer some "nuts and bolts" classroom tools and ideas, information about job searches, professional development, and other career-related information.

Teacher Learning

The **National Writing Project,** online at http://www.writingproject.org/, offers summer institutes and follow-up teacher networks in 189 locales across the nation. The online site provides the location of programs, a calendar of events, and access to NWP publications. The publications include journals and books that provide insight into issues in education, the best classroom practices, the latest teacher research, keys to professional development, networking opportunities, and ways to improve literacy in America's classrooms.

Information about the **National Board for Professional Teaching Standards** is online at http://www.nbpts.org/index.cfm. The site provides a history of the project and detailed information about the criteria for certification and the certification process.

The **National Staff Development Council (NSDC)** is a nonprofit professional association of about 10,000 educators who are committed to ensuring success for all students through staff development and school improvement. NSDC seeks to make sure that teacher professional development meets high standards. Toward that end, the group has developed three sets of standards to guide school-based staff development at the elementary, middle school, and high school levels. Teachers will find these standards helpful for becoming a wise consumer of professional development opportunities. The standards and numerous other professional development resources are online at http://www.nsdc.org/index.cfm.

Professor **Hilda Borko** is an educational psychologist at the University of Colorado, Boulder. Dr. Borko's research explores teacher cognition and the process of learning to teach, with an emphasis on changes in novice and experienced teachers' knowledge and beliefs about teaching, learning, and assessment; classroom practices; and professional identities as they participate in reform-based teacher education and professional development programs. She has a special interest in helping preservice teachers and teacher educators to become reflective practitioners.

Teaching Social Justice

Many teachers find fellow teacher **Linda Christiansen**'s book *Reading, Writing, and Rising Up: Teaching About Social Justice and the Power of the Written Word* (Milwaukee, WI: Rethinking Schools, 2000) to be both practical and inspirational. The book offers essays, lesson plans, and a remarkable collection of student writing focused on language arts teaching for justice.

Democracy and Education is a quarterly journal for teachers that promotes educational practices that help students develop democratic attitudes and values. The journal provides teachers committed to democratic education with a forum for sharing ideas with a support network of people holding similar values, and with opportunities for professional development. For example, a recent issue discusses the dilemmas and solutions that new teachers face, including balancing the demands of the first years of teaching with creating a democratic learning environment. The journal's website is http://www.lclark.edu/org/journal/.

www.edjustice.org is hosted by the Educational Justice Program, a program of the Justice Matters Institute. The site includes annotated links to resources on antiracist education, assessment, critical pedagogy, education for equity, school-family-community relations, whole school change, and more. The Justice Matters Institute is a nonprofit organization that promotes a society in which every group has a voice, every culture is respected, and every individual has equal access to resources and means of communication.

Paulo Freire's book *Teachers as Cultural Workers: Letters to Those Who Dare Teach* (Boulder, CO: Westview Press, 1998), the last book written before his death, focuses on the issues that teachers face in their classrooms, between colleagues, with parents, and in relation to their administration. The book touches on most of the themes in Freire's lifetime of work on education as the practice of freedom.

Teaching Community: A Pedagogy of Hope (New York: Routledge, 2003) by **bell hooks** is the latest book for teachers by this leading feminist thinker and public intellectual. Deeply influenced by Freire, hooks, who is Distinguished Professor of English at City College in New York, sees education as the practice of freedom.

Kevin Kumashiro has worked as a teacher and teacher educator for various grade levels and disciplines in schools and colleges in the United States and abroad and currently researches issues of social justice and education. He is the founding director of the **Center for Anti-Oppressive Education (CAOE)** and is also a senior program specialist in human and civil rights at the National Education Association. His book, *Against Common Sense: Teaching and Learning Toward Social Justice* (New York: Falmer Press, 2004) draws on his own experience teaching diverse grades and subjects as he examines aspects of teaching and learning toward social justice and suggests concrete implications for K–12 classrooms. His website at http://www.antioppressiveeducation.org/director.html provides information for teachers about workshops and an e-mail discussion group.

The **National Coalition of Education Activists (NCEA)** is a multiracial membership organization that unites parents, teachers, child advocates, and union and community activists working to improve public education. The group believes that public education advocacy must be connected to broader struggles for social justice, equality, and democracy. NCEA provides access to resources and information, including conferences, regional workshops, assistance to local organizing campaigns, opportunities for dialogue between parents and teachers to develop strategies for school change, and putting the issue of race consistently on the table. You can learn more about NCEA online at http://www.nceaonline.org/aboutus.htm.

Teaching for Change is a not-for-profit organization based in Washington, D.C., that provides teachers and parents with the tools to transform schools into socially equitable centers of learning. Its website at http://www.teachingforchange.org/ includes many teacher resources, including an online catalog of books, videos, and posters for the classroom and links to many other organizations and resources for teachers.

Notes

1. Vaclav Havel, *The Art of the Impossible: Politics as Morality in Practice* (New York: Knopf, 1997), p. 112.
2. Thanks to Julian Weissglass for reminding us of this quote.
3. Adapted from Judy Smith, "From High Tech to High School," *Forum*, UCLA Graduate School of Education and Information Studies.

4. *Assessment of Diversity in America's Teaching Force: A Call to Action* (a report of the National Collaborative on Diversity in the Teaching Force Washington, D.C., 2004), online at http://www.nea.org/teacherquality/images/diversityreport.pdf.
5. Ibid.
6. The "2004 Educator Supply and Demand Research Report," The American Association for Employment in Education.
7. U.S. Dept. of Education, NCES, Schools and Staffing Survey (SASS), "Public Teacher Question-naire" (1987–88 and 1999–2000).
8. A review of the literature on this topic is included in Karen Hunter Quartz, Andrew Thomas, Lauren Anderson, Kimberly Barraza Lyons, Brad Olsen, and Katherine Masyn, *Careers in Motion: A Longitudinal Retention Study of Role Changing Patterns Among Urban Educators*, UCLA: IDEA Technical Report, 2005, online at http://www.idea.gseis.ucla.edu/projects/utec/utecresearch/index.html.
9. Sylvia Allegretto, Sean Corcoran, and Lawrence Mishel, *How Does Teacher Pay Compare?* (New York: Economic Policy Institute, 2004), online at http://www.epinet.org/.
10. Sylvia Allegretto, as cited in Allegretto, Corcoran, and Mishel, *How Does Teacher Pay Compare?*
11. Susanna Loeb, Linda Darling-Hammond, and John Luczac, "How Teaching Conditions Predict Teacher Turnover in California Schools," *Peabody Journal of Education* 80, no. 3 (2005), pp. 44–70; and Eileen Hornung, *Recruiting and Retaining Teachers at Hard-to-Staff Schools: Examining the Tradeoffs Teachers Make When Choosing a School* (unpublished doctoral diss., University of California, Los Angeles, 2005).
12. Education Week, *Quality Counts 2003: Ensuring a Highly Qualified Teacher for Every Classroom* (Washington, DC: Education Week, 2003).
13. Jay Matthews, "Educators Face Pitfalls of Too Much Success," *Los Angeles Times,* 25 July 2001.
14. Robert C. Johnston, "System Thwarts Teacher's Bid to Transfer to Needy School," *Education Week,* 11 July 2001.
15. Daniel Schugurensky, *Selected Moments of the 20th Century*, online at http://fcis.oise.utoronto.ca/~daniel_schugurensky/assignment1/1904haley.html.
16. http://www.aft.org/about/history/socialjustice.htm.
17. Terry Moe, "No Teacher Left Behind," *Wall Street Journal*, 13 January 2005.
18. National Commission on Teaching and America's Future (NCTAF), *No Dream Denied: A Pledge to America's Children* (Washington, DC: Author, 2003), p. 7.
19. Judith Warren Little, "The Mentor Phenomenon and the Social Organization of Teaching," in *Review of Research in Education,* ed. C. B. Cazden (Washington, DC: American Educational Research Association, 1990), pp. 297–351.
20. Laura M. Desimone, Andrew C. Porter, Michael S. Garet, K.S. Yoon, and B. F. Birman, "Effects of Professional Development on Teachers' Instruction: Results from a Three-Year Longitudinal Study," *Educational Evaluation and Policy Analysis* 24, no. 2 (2002), pp. 81–112.
21. Lilia Bartholome, "Beyond the Methods Fetish," *Harvard Education Review* 64, no. 2 (1994), p. 180.
22. John Dewey, "Democracy and Education in the World of Today," *Essays* [first published as a pamphlet by the Society for Ethical Culture, New York, 1938], p. 296.
23. Ramón Martínez, "Proposition 227, Stanford 9 and Open Court: Three Strikes Against English Language Learners," in *Going Public with Our Teaching: An Anthology of Practice,* ed. Thomas Hatch, Dilruba Ahmed, Ann Lieberman, Deborah Faigenbaum, Melissa Eiler White, and Desiree H. Pointer Mace (New York: Teachers College Press, 2005).
24. Frederick Douglass, speech celebrating West India Emancipation Day, Canandaigua, New York, August 4, 1857, reproduced in Philip Foner, ed. *The Life and Writings of Frederick Douglass,* Vol. 2 (New York: International Publishers of New York, 1976), p. 437.
25. Quartz et al., *Careers in Motion.*
26. Cornel West, "The Limits of Neopragmatism," *Southern California Law Review* 63 (1990), p. 1747.
27. Paulo Freire, *Pedagogy of Hope* (New York: Continuum, 1995), pp. 9–10.
28. Dewey, "Democracy and Education in the World of Today."

Bibliography

"A New Mix of Gifted Students," *The Washington Post,* 27 July 1997.

Addams, Jane. "The Public School and the Immigrant Child." In *The Educating of Americans: A Documentary History*, edited by Daniel Calhoun, 421–423. Boston: Houghton Mifflin, 1969.

Allegretto, Sylvia, Sean Corcoran, and Lawrence Mishel. *How Does Teacher Pay Compare?* New York: Economic Policy Institute, 2004, online at http://www.epinet.org/.

America's Children: Key National Indicators of Children's Well-Being 2005, http://www.childstats.org.

American Association for Employment in Education. "2004 Educator Supply and Demand Research Report."

Apple, Michael. *Educating the "Right" Way: Markets, Standards, God, and Inequality.* New York: RoutledgeFalmer, 2001.

Armstrong, O. K. "Treason in the Textbooks," *The American Legion Magazine,* September 1940, pp. 8–9, 51, 70–72, as cited in Kliebard, *The Struggle for the American Curriculum.*

Armstrong, Thomas. *The Myth of the ADD Child.* New York: Dutton, 1985.

Arnold, Felix. *Text-Book of School and Class Management: Theory and Practice.* New York: The Macmillan Company, 1908.

Assessment of Diversity in America's Teaching Force: A Call to Action. A report of the National Collaborative on Diversity in the Teaching Force Washington, D.C., 2004, online at http://www.nea.org/teacherquality/images/diversityreport.pdf.

Auerbach, Susan. "Engaging Latino Parents in Supporting College Pathways: Lessons from a College Access Program." *Journal of Hispanic Higher Education* 3, no. 2 (2004), pp. 125–145.

———. "Why Do They Give the Good Classes to Some and Not to Others?" *Teachers College Record* 104, no. 7 (2002), pp. 1369–1392.

Banks, James A. "Multicultural Education: Historical Development, Dimension, and Practice." In *Handbook of Research on Multicultural Education*, 2nd ed., edited by James A. Banks and Cherry McGee Banks. San Francisco: Jossey-Bass, 2004.

Bartholome, Lilia. "Beyond the Methods Fetish," *Harvard Education Review* 64, no. 2 (1994), p. 180.

Barton, Paul E. *Parsing the Achievement Gap: Baselines for Tracking Progress.* Princeton, NJ: Educational Testing Service, 2003.

Battistich, Victor, Eric Schaps, and Nance Wilson, "Effects of an Elementary School Intervention on Students' 'Connectedness' to School and Social Adjustment

During Middle School." *The Journal of Primary Prevention* 24, no. 3 (2004), pp. 243–262.

Berger, Sandra L. "Differentiating Curriculum for Gifted Students." *ERIC Digest #E510*. Reston, VA: Council for Exceptional Children, ERIC Clearinghouse on Disabilities and Gifted Education, n.d.

Biddle, Bruce, and David Berliner. *The Manufactured Crisis: Myths, Fraud, and the Attack on America's Public Schools*. New York: Addison-Wesley, 1995.

———. *What Research Says About Unequal Funding for Schools in America*. Tempe, AZ: Arizona State University, Education Policy Studies Laboratory, Education Policy Reports Project, Winter 2002, online at http://www.asu.edu/educ/epsl/EPRP/EPSL-0206-102-EPRP.doc.

Bigelow, Bill. "Testing, Tracking, and Toeing the Line," *Rethinking Our Classrooms: Teaching for Equity and Social Justice*. Milwaukee, WI: Rethinking Schools, 1994.

Bordieu, Pierre, and Jean Claude Passeron. *Reproduction in Education, Society and Culture*. Thousand Oaks, CA: Sage, 1990.

Borman, Geoffrey D., Gina M. Hewes, Laura T. Overman, and Shelly Brown. "Comprehensive School Reform and Achievement: A Meta-analysis." *Review of Educational Research* 73, no. 2 (2003), pp. 125–230.

Bowles, Samuel, and Herbert Gintis. *Schooling in Capitalist America: Educational Reform and the Contradictions of Economic Life*. New York: Basic Books, 1977.

Bracey, Gerald. *Setting the Record Straight*. Portsmouth, NH: Heinemann, 2004.

Brown v. Board of Education of Topeka, 347 U.S. 483 (1954).

Brownstein, Ronald. "Cities Still Carry Poverty Burden, HUD Study Says." *Los Angeles Times,* 23 June 1997, pp. A1, A12.

Bruner, Jerome. *Culture and Education*. Cambridge: Harvard University Press, 1996.

———. *The Process of Education*. Cambridge: Harvard University Press, 1960.

Burris, Carol C., Jay P. Heubert, and Henry M. Levin. "Accelerating Mathematics Achievement Using Heterogeneous Grouping." *American Educational Research Journal* (in press).

Camp Mayhew, Katherine, and Anna Camp Edwards. *The Dewey School*. New York: Appleton-Century, 1936.

Canter, Lee, and Marlene Canter. *Assertive Discipline: Positive Behavior*. Santa Monica: Lee Canter & Associates, 1997.

Carey, Kevin. *The Funding Gap, 2004*. Washington, DC: Education Trust, 2004.

Carnegie Council on Adolescent Development. *Turning Points: Preparing Youth for the 21st Century*. New York: Carnegie Corporation of New York, 1989.

Center for Educational Policy. *State High School Exit Exams: States Try Harder but Gaps Persist,* August 2005.

Child Development Project. *Ways We Want Our Classroom to Be: Class Meetings That Build Commitment to Kindness and Learning*. Oakland, CA: Developmental Studies Center, 1994.

Chow, Mamie, Laurie Olsen, Ruben Lizardo, and Carol Dowell. *School Reform Organizing in the San Francisco Bay Area and Los Angeles, California*. Oakland, CA: California Tomorrow, 2001.

Christian, Donna. *Two-Way Bilingual Education: Students Learning through Two Languages*. Santa Cruz, CA: National Center for Research on Cultural Diversity and Second Language Learning, 1994.

College Board Online. "Test Question of the Day." 16 March 1998, http://www.collegeboard.org/tqod/bin/question.

Colt, Sarah. "Do Scripted Lessons Work—Or Not?," *Making Schools Work,* http://www.pbs.org/makingschoolswork/sbs/sfa/lessons.html.

Condition of Education. Washington, DC: U.S. Department of Education, National Center of Education Statistics, 2005, online at http://nces.ed.gov/programs/coe/.

Cortes, Ernesto Jr. "Making the Public the Leaders in Education Reform." *Teacher Magazine,* 22 November 1995.

Council of the Great City Schools. *Charting the Right Course: A Report on Urban Student Achievement and Course-Taking.* Washington, DC: Author, 1998.

Crawford, John. "Anatomy of the English-Only Movement." In *Language Legislation and Linguistic Rights,* edited by Doublas A. Kibbee. Amsterdam and Philadelphia: John Benjamins, 1998.

Cremin, Lawrence. *The Transformation of the School: Progressivism in American Education 1876–1957.* New York: Knopf, 1961.

Cuban, Larry. *How Teachers Taught: Constancy and Change in American Classrooms 1880–1990.* New York: Teachers College Press, 1994.

Cubberly, Elwood Cubberly. *Changing Conceptions of Education.* Boston: Houghton Mifflin, 1909.

Cummins, Jim. "From Multicultural to Anti-Racist Education: An Analysis of Programmes and Policies in Ontario." In *Minority Education: From Shame to Struggle,* edited by Tove Skutnabb-Kangas and Jim Cummins. Philadelphia: Multilingual Matters Ltd., 1988.

Darder, Antonia. *Culture and Power in the Classroom: A Critical Foundation for Bicultural Education.* Westport, CT: Bergin & Garvey, 1991.

Darling-Hammond, Linda. "Overview" to "Ten Features of Effective Design," http://www.schoolredesign.net.

———. "The Right to Learn and the Advancement of Teaching: Research, Policy, and Practice for Democratic Education." *Educational Researcher* 26 (August/September 1996), p. 5.

———. *The Right to Learn.* San Francisco: Jossey-Bass, 1997.

de Tocqueville, Alexis. *Democracy in America,* 2 vols. New York: 1945, originally published 1835.

DeLany, Brian. "Allocation, Choice, and Stratification Within High Schools: How the Sorting Machine Copes." *American Journal of Education* 99, no. 3 (1991), pp. 191–207.

Delpit, Lisa. *Other People's Children: Cultural Conflict in the Classroom.* New York: The New Press, 1995.

Desimone, Laura M., Andrew C, Porter, Michael S. Garet, K.S. Yoon, and B. F. Birman. "Effects of Professional Development on Teachers' Instruction: Results from a Three-Year Longitudinal Study." *Educational Evaluation and Policy Analysis* 24, no. 2 (2002), pp. 81–112.

Dewey, John. "Democracy and Education in the World of Today," *Essays* [first published as a pamphlet by the Society for Ethical Culture, New York, 1938], p. 296.

———. *School and Society.* Chicago: University of Chicago Press, 1991, reprint.

Douglass, Frederick. Speech celebrating West India Emancipation Day, Canandaigua, New York, August 4, 1857, reproduced in Philip Foner, ed. *The Life and Writings of Frederick Douglass,* Vol. 2. New York: International Publishers of New York, 1976.

Dryfoos, Joy. *Full-Service Schools. A Revolution in Health and Social Services for Children, Youth and Families.* San Francisco: Jossey-Bass, 1994.

DuBois, W. E. B. "Does the Negro Need Separate Schools?" *Journal of Negro Education* 4, no. 3 (1935), p. 328.

———. "The Freedom to Learn." In *W. E. B. DuBois Speaks,* edited by P. S. Foner, 230–231. New York: Pathfinder, 1970.

EdSource, *Similar Students, Different Results: Why Do Some Schools Do Better?* Sacramento: EdSource, 2005, (http://www.edsource.org/pub_abs_simstu05.cfm).

Education Week. *Quality Counts 2003: Ensuring a Highly Qualified Teacher for Every Classroom.* Washington, DC: Education Week, 2003.

Epstein, Joyce, Lucretia Coates, Karen C. Salinas, Mavis G. Sanders, and Beth S. Simon. *School, Family, and Community Partnerships: Your Handbook for Action.* Thousand Oaks, CA: Corwin Press, 1997.

Fass, Paula. *Outside In: Minorities and the Transformation of American Education.* Oxford and New York: Oxford University Press, 1989.

Feinberg, Walter. "Educational Manifesto and the New Fundamentalism," *Educational Researcher* 26, no. 8 (1997), p. 32.

Ferguson, Ronald F. "Paying for Public Education: New Evidence on How and Why Money Matters." *Harvard Journal on Legislation* 28, no. 2 (summer 1991), pp. 465–498.

———. "Toward Skilled Parenting and Transformed Schools: Inside a National Movement for *Excellence With Equity.*" Paper prepared the First Educational Equity Symposium of the Campaign for Educational Equity, at Teachers College, Columbia University, October 24 and 25, 2005.

Finn, Jeremy, and Charles M. Achilles. "Answers and Questions About Class Size." *American Educational Research Journal* 27 (fall 1990), pp. 557–577.

Finnan, Christine, Edward St. John, and Jane McCarthy, eds. *Accelerated Schools in Action: Lessons from the Field.* Thousand Oaks, CA: Corwin Press, 1995.

Fogel, Alan. *Developing Through Relationships.* Chicago: University of Chicago Press, 1993.

Fullan, Michael. *Change Forces: Probing the Depths of Educational Reform.* London: Falmer Press, 1993.

———. *Successful School Improvement.* Philadelphia: Open University Press, 1992.

Fullan, Michael, and Andy Hargreaves. *What's Worth Fighting for in Your School?* New York: Teachers College Press, 1996.

Gamoran, Adam. "A Multi-level Analysis of the Effects of Tracking." Paper presented at the annual meetings of the American Sociological Association, Atlanta, GA, 1988.

———. "Alternative Uses of Ability Grouping in Secondary Schools: Can We Bring High-Quality Instruction to Low-Ability Classrooms?" *American Journal of Education* 102, no. 1 (1993), pp. 1–22.

Gardner, Howard. *Frames of Mind.* New York: Basic Books, 1983, 1993.

Garet, Michael, and Brian DeLany. "Students, Courses, and Stratification." *Sociology of Education* 61 (1988), pp. 61–77.

Gibbs, Nancy. "Parents Behaving Badly." *Time,* February 21, 2005.

Gilreath, James, ed. *Thomas Jefferson and the Education of a Citizen.* Washington, DC: Library of Congress, 1999, distributed by University Press of New England.

Glass, Gene, Leonard Cahan, Mary Lee Smith, and Nikola Filby. *School Class Size: Research and Policy.* Beverly Hills: Sage, 1982.

Glasser, William. *The Quality School.* New York: HarperCollins, 1992.

Goldman, Larry S., Myron Genel, Rebecca J. Bezman, and Priscilla J. Slanetz. "Diagnosis and Treatment of Attention-Deficit/Hyperactivity Disorder in Children and Adolescents." *Journal of the American Medical Association* 279, no. 14 (April 8, 1998), pp. 1100–1107.

Good, Thomas, and Jere Brophy. *Looking in Classrooms.* New York: Longman, 1997.

Goodlad, John I. *A Place Called School.* New York: McGraw-Hill, 1984.

Gould, Stephen J. *The Mismeasure of Man,* 2nd ed. New York: Norton, 1996.

Greene, Jay P. *A Meta-Analysis of the Effectiveness of Bilingual Education.* Claremont, CA: The Tomas Rivera Policy Institute, 1998.

Gregg, Jeff. "Discipline, Control, and the School Mathematics Tradition." *Teaching and Teacher Education* 11, no. 6 (1995), pp. 579–593.

Hallinan, Maureen. "Tracking: From Theory to Practice. Exchange." *Sociology of Education* 67, no. 2 (1994), pp. 79–84.

Hanson, Allan. *Testing Testing: Social Consequences of the Examined Life.* Berkeley: University of California Press, 1993.

Harrington, Michael. *The Other America: Poverty in the United States.* New York: Collier Books, 1962, reprint, 1997.

Harvard University's Joint Center for Housing Studies. *The State of the Nation's Housing.* Cambridge, MA: Author, 2004.

Havel, Vaclav. *The Art of the Impossible: Politics as Morality in Practice.* New York: Knopf, 1997, p. 112.

Hedges, Larry, Richard D. Laine, and Rob Greenwald. "Does Money Matter? A Meta-Analysis of the Effects of Differential School Inputs on Student Outcomes." *Educational Researcher* 23, no. 3 (1994), pp. 5–14.

Heubert, Jay P., and Robert M. Hauser, eds. *High Stakes: Testing for Tracking, Promotion, and Graduation.* Washington: National Academy Press, 1999.

Hirsch, E. D. "Toward a Centrist Curriculum: Two Kinds of Multiculturalism in Elementary School." Charlottesville, VA: Core Knowledge Foundation, 1992; located online at http://www.coreknowledge.org.

Hoff, David J. "Chapter 1 Aid Failed to Close Learning Gap," *Education Week,* 2 April 1997, pp. 1, 29.

Horng, Eileen. *Recruiting and Retaining Teachers at Hard-to-Staff Schools: Examining the Tradeoffs Teachers Make When Choosing a School.* Unpublished doctoral diss., University of California, Los Angeles, 2005.

How Unequal Are We, Anyway? (A Statistical Briefing Book), July 2004, http://www.inequality.org/facts.html.

Howes, Carollee, and Sharon Ritchie. *A Matter of Trust: Connecting Teachers and Learners in the Early Childhood Classroom.* New York: Teachers College Press, 2002.

Hu, C. T. "The Historical Background: Examinations and Control in Pre-modern China." *Comparative Education* 20 (1984), p. 17, as cited in F. Allan Hanson, *Testing Testing: Social Consequences of the Examined Life.* Berkeley: University of California Press, 1993, p. 191, http://ark.cdlib.org/ark:/13030/ft4m3nb2h2/.

Hunter Quartz, Karen, Andrew Thomas, Lauren Anderson, Kimberly Barraza Lyons, Brad Olsen, and Katherine Masyn. *Careers in Motion: A Longitudinal Retention Study of Role Changing Patterns Among Urban Educators.* UCLA: IDEA Technical Report, 2005, online at http://www.idea.gseis.ucla.edu/projects/utec/utecresearch/index.html.

Instruments. *Educational Evaluation and Policy Analysis* 9 (summer 1987), pp. 133–152.

Jacobson, Linda. "PTA Seeks to Raise Number of Hispanic Members." *Education Week,* 11 June 2003.

Johnston, Robert C. "System Thwarts Teacher's Bid to Transfer to Needy School." *Education Week,* 11 July 2001.

Kandel, Isaac. *Examinations and Their Substitutes in the United States.* New York: Carnegie Foundation for the Advancement of Teaching, 1936.

Kane, Thomas J. *The Impact of After-School Programs: Interpreting the Results of Four Recent Evaluations.* Working paper of the William T. Grant Foundation, 2004.

Kanpol, Barry, and Peter McLaren. *Critical Multiculturalism: Uncommon Voices in a Common Struggle.* London: Bergen and Garvey, 1995.

Katz, Michael. *The Undeserving Poor: From War on Poverty to War on the Poor.* New York: Pantheon, 1989.

Kelly, Thomas. "The 4 Percent 'Structural Flaw'." *Education Week,* 11 June 1997, p. 44.

Kemple, James J., Corinne M. Herlihy, and Thomas J. Smith. *Making Progress Toward Graduation Evidence from the Talent Development High School Model.* Washington, DC: MRDC, 2005.

Kliebard, Herbert. *The Struggle for the American Curriculum: 1898–1958.* New York: Routledge, 1983.

———. *The Struggle for the American Curriculum: 1893–1958,* 2nd ed. New York: Routledge, 1995.

Kluger, Richard. *Simple Justice.* New York: Vintage, 1977.

Knapp, Michael, Patrick Shields, and Brenda Turnbull. *Teaching for Meaning in High-Poverty Classrooms.* New York: Teachers College Press, 1995.

Kohl, Herbert. "Some Reflections on Teaching for Social Justice." In William Ayres, Jean Ann Hunt, and Therese Quinn, *Teaching for Social Justice: A Democracy and Education Reader.* New York: The New Press and Teachers College Press, 1998.

Kohn, Alfie. *Beyond Discipline: From Compliance to Community.* Alexandria, VA: Association for Supervision and Curriculum Development, 1996.

———. *Punished by Rewards.* Boston: Houghton Mifflin, 1993.

Kounin, Jacob. *Discipline and Group Management in Classrooms.* New York: Holt, Rinehart & Winston, 1970.

Krop, Cathy, Dominic Brewer, Susan Gates, Brian Gill, Robert Reichardt, Melora Sundt, and Dan Throgmorton. *Potentially Eligible Students: A Growing Opportunity for the University of California.* Santa Monica: RAND, 1998.

Krueger, Alan B. "Understanding the Magnitude and Effect of Class Size on Student Achievement." In *The Class Size Debate,* edited by Lawrence Mishel and Richard Rothstein. Washington, DC: Economic Policy Institute, 2002.

Ladson-Billings, Gloria. *The Dreamkeepers.* San Francisco: Jossey-Bass, 1994.

Lareau, Annette. *Home Advantage: Social Class and Parental Intervention in Elementary Education.* London: Falmer, 1989.

Lee, Valerie, Julia Smith, and Frank Croninger. "Another Look at High School Restructuring: More Evidence That It Improves Student Achievement and More Insight into Why." *Issues in Restructuring Schools* (Newsletter, Center on Organization and Restructuring of Schools, University of Wisconsin, 1995), No. 9, pp. 1–9.

Lewin, Tamar, and Jennifer Medina. "To Cut Failure Rate, Schools Shed Students," *New York Times,* 31 July 2003.

Lockwood, Anne Turnbaugh. "Beyond the Golden Chromosome." In *Focus in Change,* a publication of the National Center for Effective Schools at the University of Wisconsin, Madison (no. 11 [fall 1993]), p. 3.

Loeb, Susanna, Linda Darling-Hammond, and John Luczac. "How Teaching Conditions Predict Teacher Turnover in California Schools." *Peabody Journal of Education* 80, no. 3 (2005), pp. 44–70.

MacIver, Douglas, Steven B. Plank, and Robert Balfanz. "Working Together to Become Proficient Readers: Early Impact of the Talent Development Middle School's *Student Team Literature Program.*" Report of the Center for Research on the Education of Students Placed at Risk. Baltimore: The Johns Hopkins University Press, 1998.

MacMillan, Donald L., and Daniel Reschly. "Overrepresentation of Minority Students: The Case for Greater Specificity or Reconsideration of the Variables Examined." *Journal of Special Education* 32 (1998), pp. 15–24.

Making Schools Safe for Gay and Lesbian Youth: Report of the Massachusetts Governor's Commission on Gay and Lesbian Youth, 1993.

Martínez, Ramón. "Proposition 227, Stanford 9 and Open Court: Three Strikes Against English Language Learners." In *Going Public with Our Teaching: An Anthology of Practice,* edited by Thomas Hatch, Dilruba Ahmed, Ann Lieberman, Deborah Faigenbaum, Melissa Eiler White, and Desiree H. Pointer Mace. New York: Teachers College Press, 2005.

MassPartners for Public Schools. *Facing Reality. "What Happens When Good Schools Are Labeled "Failures"? Projecting Adequate Yearly Progress in Massachusetts Schools.* Boston: Author, 2005.

Matthews, Jay. "Educators Face Pitfalls of Too Much Success," *Los Angeles Times,* 25 July 2001.

McDonnell, Lorraine M., Margaret J. McLaughlin, and Patricia Morrison, eds. *Educating One and All: Students with Disabilities and Standards-Based Reform.* Washington, DC: National Academy Press, 1997.

McDonnell, Lorraine, and Richard Elmore. "Getting the Job Done: Alternative Policy Instruments." *Educational Evaluation and Policy Analysis* 9, no. 2 (Summer 1987), pp. 133–152.

McIntosh, Peggy. "White Privilege and Male Privilege: A Personal Account of Coming to See Correspondences through Work in Women's Studies." Working paper 189, Wellesley College Center for Research on Women, 1988.

McLaren, Peter. *Life in Schools: An Introduction to Critical Pedagogy in the Foundations of Education.* New York: Longman, 1998.

McLeod, Jay. *Ain't No Makin' It.* Boulder, CO: Westview Press, 1995.

McNeil, Linda. *The Contradictions of School Reform: Educational Costs of Standardized Testing.* New York: RoutledgeFalmer, 2000.

Medina, Noe, and Monty Neill. *Fallout from the Testing Explosion: How 100 Million Standardized Exams Undermine Equity and Excellence in America's Public Schools,* 3rd ed. Cambridge, MA: FairTest, 1990.

Mehan, Hugh, Jane Mercer, and Robert Rueda. "Special Education." In *Encyclopedia of Education and Sociology* (New York: Garland, 1997).

Meier, Deborah. *The Power of Their Ideas: Lessons for America from a Small School in Harlem.* Boston: Beacon Press, 1995.

Meyer, Luanna H., Beth Harry, and Mara Sapon-Shevin. "School Inclusion and Multicultural Education." In *Multicultural Education: Issues and Perspectives,* edited by James A. Banks and Cherry A. McGee Banks. Boston: Allyn & Bacon, 1996.

Mishel, Lawrence, Jared Bernstein, and Sylvia Allegretto. *State of Working America, 2004–2005.* Washington, DC: Economic Policy Institute, 2005, www.epinet.org.

Mislevy, Robert J. "Foundations of a New Test Theory." In *Test Theory for a New Generation of Tests,* edited by Norman Frederiksen, Robert J. Mislevy, and Isaac I. Bejar, 19–39. Hillsdale, NJ: Erlbaum, 1993.

Moe, Terry. "No Teacher Left Behind," *Wall Street Journal,* 13 January 2005.

Moll, Luis. "Funds of Knowledge for Teaching: Using a Qualitative Approach to Connect Homes and Classrooms." *Theory into Practice* 31, no. 2 (1992), pp. 132–141.

Morrow, Raymond Allan, and Carlos Alberto Torres. *Social Theory and Education: A Critique of Theories of Social and Cultural Reproduction.* Buffalo: State University of New York Press, 1995.

Myrdal, Gunnar. *An American Dilemma: The Negro Problem and American Democracy.* New York: Harper and Brothers, 1944.

NAEP 2004 Trends in Academic Progress: Three Decades of Student Performance in Reading and Mathematics. Washington, DC: U.S. Department of Education, National Center of Education Statistics, 2005, http://nces.ed.gov/pubsearch/pubsinfo.asp?pubid=2005464.

National Association of School Psychologists, "Zero Tolerance and Alternative Strategies: A Fact Sheet for Educators and Policymakers," 2001, http://www.naspcenter.org/factsheets/zt_fs.html.

National Commission on Excellence in Education. *A Nation at Risk: The Imperatives for Educational Reform.* Washington, DC: U.S. Department of Education, 1983.

National Commission on Teaching and America's Future. *What Matters Most: Teaching for America's Future.* New York: Author, 1996.

National Commission on Teaching and America's Future (NCTAF). *No Dream Denied: A Pledge to America's Children.* Washington, DC: Author, 2003.

Neill, A. S. *Summerhill.* New York: St. Martin's Press, 1995; originally published by Hart Publishing, 1960.

Nespor, Jan. "Networks and Contexts of Reform." *International Journal of Educational Change* 3 (2002), pp. 365–382.

Newmann, Fred M., Walter G. Secada, and Gary Wehlage. *A Guide to Authentic Instruction and Assessment: Vision, Standards, and Scoring.* Madison, WI: Wisconsin Center for Education Research at the University of Wisconsin.

Nichols, Sharon, Gene Glass, and David Berliner. "High-Stakes Testing and Student Achievement: Problems for the No Child Left Behind Act." Arizona State University Education Policy Studies Laboratory, 2005.

Nieto, Sonia. *Affirming Diversity: The Sociopolitical Context of Multicultural Education,* 2nd ed. White Plains, NY: Longman, 1996.

Noblit, George. "In the Meaning: The Possibilities of Caring." *Phi Delta Kappan* 77 (May 1995), p. 682.

Noddings, Nel. *The Challenge to Care in Schools: An Alternative Approach to Education.* New York: Teachers College Press, 1992.

———. "Teaching Themes of Care." *Phi Delta Kappan* 77 (May 1995), p. 676.

O'Day, Jennifer, and Marshall S. Smith. "Systemic Reform Educational Opportunity." In *Designing Coherent Education Policy: Improving the System,* edited by Susan H. Fuhrman, 250–312. San Francisco: Jossey-Bass, 1993.

Oakes, Jeannie. *Keeping Track: How Schools Structure Inequality.* New Haven, CT: Yale University Press, 1985/2005.

———. *Multiplying Inequalities.* Santa Monica: RAND, 1990.

———. "Two Cities: Tracking and Within-School Segregation." In *Brown Plus Forty: The Promise,* edited by LaMar Miller. New York: Teachers College Press, 1995.

Oakes, Jeannie, Adam Gamoran, and Reba Page. "Curriculum Differentiation." In *Handbook of Research on Curriculum,* edited by Phillip Jackson. New York: Macmillan, 1992.

Oakes, Jeannie, and Gretchen Guiton. "Matchmaking: The Dynamics of High School Tracking Decisions." *American Educational Research Journal* 32, no. 1 (1995), pp. 3–33.

Oakes, Jeannie, Karen Hunter Quartz, Steve Ryan, and Martin Lipton. *Becoming Good American Schools: The Struggle for Civic Virtue in Education Reform.* San Francisco: Jossey-Bass, 2000.

Oakes, Jeannie, and Martin Lipton. "Struggling for Educational Equity in Diverse Communities: School Reform as Social Movement." *International Journal of Educational Change* 3 (2002), pp. 383–406.

Oakes, Jeannie, and John Rogers. *Learning Power: Organizing for Education and Justice.* New York: Teachers College Press, 2006.

Oakes, Jeannie, Amy Stuart Wells, Susan Yonezawa, and Karen Ray. "Equity Lessons from Detracking Schools." In *Rethinking Educational Change with Heart and Mind,* edited by Andy Hargreaves. Arlington, VA: Association for Supervision and Curriculum Development, 1997.

Oakes, Jeannie, Amy Stuart Wells, Susan Yonezawa, and Karen Ray. "The Politics of Equity and Change: Lessons from Detracking Schools." In *1997 ASCD Yearbook:*

Rethinking Educational Change with Heart and Mind, edited by Andy Hargreaves, 43–72. Alexandria, VA: Association for Supervision and Curriculum Development, 1997.

Oakley, Deirdre, Polly Smith, Jacob Stowell, and Brian Stults. *Separating the Children.* Report by the Lewis Mumford Center, December 28, 2001, http://mumford1.dyndns.org/cen2000/Under18Pop/U18Preport.

Open to the Public: Speaking Out on "No Child Left Behind." A report from the Public Education Network, 2005.

Orfield, Gary, Mark Bachmeier, David James, and Tamela Eitle. *Deepening Segregation in American Public Schools.* Cambridge, MA: Civil Rights Project, Harvard Graduate School of Education, 1997.

Orfield, Gary, and Susan Eaton. *Dismantling Desegregation: The Quiet Reversal of Brown v. Board of Education.* Boston: New Press, 1996.

Orfield, Gary, and Chungmei Lee. *Brown at 50: King's Dream or Plessy's Nightmare?* Cambridge, MA: The Civil Rights Project at Harvard University, 2004.

Orfield, Gary, and Mindy L. Kornhaber, eds. *Raising Standards or Raising Barriers? Inequality and High-Stakes Testing in Public Education.* New York: Century Foundation Press, 2001.

Orfield, Gary, Daniel Losen, Johanna Wald, and Christopher B. Swanson. *Losing Our Future: How Minority Youth Are Being Left Behind by the Graduation Rate Crisis.* Harvard Civil Rights Project and The Urban Institute, 2005, http://www.urban.org/url.cfm?ID=410936.

Parker, Francis. *Talks on Pedagogies* (New York: E. L. Kellogg, 1894.)

Passow, Harry, Miriam Goldberg, and Abraham J. Tannenbaum, eds. *Education of the Disadvantaged.* New York: Holt, Rinehart & Winston, 1967.

Pyle, Amy. "Attacking the Textbook Crisis." *Los Angeles Times,* 29 September 1997.

Reis, Beth, and Elizabeth Saewyc. "Eighty-Three Thousand Youth: Selected Findings of Eight Population-based Studies as They Pertain to Anti-gay Harassment and the Safety and Well-being of Sexual Minority Students. Seattle, WA: Safe Schools Coalition of Washington, 1999.

Renzulli, Joseph, and Sally Reis. "The Reform Movement and the Quiet Crisis in Gifted Education." *Gifted Child Quarterly* 35 (1991), pp. 26–35.

———. *The Schoolwide Enrichment Model: A Comprehensive Plan for Educational Excellence.* Mansfield Center, CT: Creative Learning Press, 1985.

Resnick, Lauren. *Education and Learning to Think.* Washington, DC: National Academy Press, 1983.

Rice, Joseph Mayer. *The Public School System of the United States* (1893, p. 34), as quoted in Kliebard, *The Struggle for the American Curriculum.*

Richardson, John G. "Common Delinquent, and Special: On the Formalization of Common Schooling in the American States." *American Educational Research Journal* 31, no. 4 (1994), pp. 695–723.

Riessman, Frank. *The Culturally Deprived Child.* New York: Harper & Row, 1962.

Rogers, John. *Community Schools: Lessons from the Past and Present.* Los Angeles: UCLA's IDEA Paper Series #1, 1998.

Rogers, John, and Carolyn Castelli, eds. *Building Social Justice for a New Generation: Profiles of Social Justice Fellows from UCLA's Teacher Education Program, 1997.* Los Angeles: UCLA, 1997.

Rogers, John, Jennifer Jellison Holme, and David Silver. *More Questions Than Answers: Cahsee Results, Opportunity to Learn, and the Class of 2006,* UCLA's IDEA, 2005, online at http://www.idea.gseis.ucla.edu/resources/exitexam/.

Rogers, John S., and Robert Polkinghorn. "The Inquiry Process in the Accelerated School: A Deweyan Approach to School Renewal." Paper presented at the annual meeting of the American Educational Research Association, Boston, 1990.

Ryan, Alan. *John Dewey and the High Tide of American Liberalism.* New York: W. W. Norton, 1995.

Sadker, Myra, and David Sadker. *Failing at Fairness: How America's Schools Cheat Girls.* New York: Macmillan, 1994.

Sarason, Seymour. *The Culture of the School and the Problem of Change,* 3rd ed. Boston: Allyn & Bacon, 1996.

Schmidt, William. "Are There Surprises in the TIMSS Twelfth Grade Results?" *TIMSS United States,* Report No. 8. East Lansing, MI: TIMSS U.S. National Research Center, Michigan State University, April 1998.

Scholz, John Karl, and Kara Levine. "U.S. Black-White Wealth Inequality: A Survey." Unpublished paper, Madison, WI, Department of Economics and Institute for Research on Poverty, University of Wisconsin, 2003; forthcoming in *Social Inequality,* K. Neckerman (ed.), Russell Sage Foundation.

Schugurensky, Daniel. *Selected Moments of the 20th Century,* online at http://fcis.oise. utoronto.ca/~daniel_schugurensky/assignment1/1904haley.html.

Seashore Louis, Karen, and Sharon D. Kruse. *Professionalism and Community: Perspectives on Reforming Urban Schools.* Newberry Park, CA: Corwin Press, 1995.

Senge, Peter M. *The Fifth Discipline: The Art and Practice of The Learning Organization.* London: Random House, 1990.

"September 11 and Our Classrooms." *Rethinking Schools* 16, no. 2 (winter 2001/2002).

Shappee, Rudolph T. "Serving the City's Children: San Diego City Schools, The First Fifty Years." *The Journal of San Diego History* 37, no. 2 (spring 1991), http://www. sandiegohistory.org/journal/91spring/schools.htm.

Shor, Ira. *Empowering Education: Critical Teaching for Social Change.* Chicago: University of Chicago Press, 1992.

Sirotnik, Kenneth. "Equal Access to Quality in Public Schooling: Issues in the Assessment of Equity and Excellence." In *Access to Knowledge: The Continuing Agenda for Our Nation's Schools,* rev. ed., edited by John I. Goodlad and Pamela Keating. New York: The College Board, 1994.

Sizer, Theodore. *Horace's Hope: What Works for the American High School.* Boston: Houghton Mifflin, 1996.

Slavin, Robert E. "How Title I Can (Still) Save America's Children," *Education Week,* 21 May 1997, p. 52.

Sleeter, Christine. "Learning Disabilities: The Social Construction of a Special Education Category." *Exceptional Children* 53, no. 1 (1986), pp. 46–54.

———. "Why Is There Learning Disabilities? A Critical Analysis of the Birth of the Field in Its Social Context." In *The Formation of the School Subject Matter: The Struggle for an American Institution,* edited by T. S. Popkewitz. New York: Falmer Press, 1987.

Smith, Judy. "From High Tech to High School," *Forum,* UCLA Graduate School of Education and Information Studies.

Smith, Marshall, and Jennifer O'Day. "Systemic School Reform." In *The Politics of Curriculum and Testing, Politics of Education Association Yearbook,* edited by S. H. Fuhrman and B. Malen, 233–267. London: Taylor & Francis, 1990.

Snider, William. "Schools Are Reopened in Selma Amid Continuing Racial Tension." *Education Week,* 21 February 1990.

Spargo, John. *The Bitter Cry of Children.* New York: Macmillan, 1906.

Spear-Sweling, Louise, and Robert J. Sternberg. *Off Track: When Poor Readers Become Learning Disabled.* Boulder, CO: Westview Press, 1996.

Spring, Joel. *American Education.* Boston: McGraw-Hill, 1996.

———. *The American School: 1642–1990.* New York: Longman, 1996.

Stall, Susan, and Randy Stoecker. "Community Organizing or Organizing Community? Gender and the Crafts of Empowerment." *Gender and Society* 12 (1998), pp. 729–756, accessed at http://comm-org.wisc.edu/.

Stanford School ReDesign Network. "Ten Features of Effective Design," http://www.schoolredesign.net.

Stanton-Salazar, Ricardo. *Manufacturing Hope and Despair: The School and Kin Support Networks of U.S.-Mexican Youth.* New York: Teachers College Press, 2001.

Steele, Claude. "A Threat in the Air: How Stereotypes Shape the Intellectual Identities and Performance of Women and African-Americans." *American Psychologist* 52 (1997), pp. 613–629.

Steinberg, Laurence. *Beyond the Classroom.* New York: Simon & Schuster, 1996.

Sternberg, Robert. "Myths, Countermyths, and Truths About Intelligence." *Education Researcher* 25 (March 1996), pp. 11–16, 13; excerpted from "Mental Ability Test, Stanford University, Test 1, Information (World Book Co, 1920), as reprinted in Bill Bigelow, "Testing, Tracking, and Toeing the Line," *Rethinking Our Classrooms: Teaching for Equity and Social Justice.* Milwaukee, WI: Rethinking Schools, 1994.

"Study: Hard Courses Help Urban ACT's." *New York Times,* 15 January 1998.

Surgeon General. *Youth Violence: A Report of the Surgeon General,* 2001, http://www.surgeongeneral.gov/library/youthviolence/report.html.

Suro, Roberto. "Cavazos Criticizes Hispanics on Schooling." *New York Times,* 11 April 1990, p. B8.

Talber, Joan. "Professionalism and Politics in High School Teaching Reform." *International Journal of Educational Change* 3 (2002), pp. 277–281.

Thernstrom, Stephan, and Abigail Thernstrom. *No Excuses: Closing the Racial Gap in Learning.* New York: Simon and Schuster, 2003.

Tisn't What You Know, But Are You Intelligent? Preface by Howard W. Haggard. New York: Harper and Brothers, 1927.

Tomlinson, Carol. "Differentiated Instruction in the Regular Classroom: What Does It Mean? How Does It Look?" *Understanding Our Gifted* 14, no. 1 (2001), pp. 3–6.

———. *How to Differentiate Instruction for Mixed-Ability Classrooms.* Alexandria, VA: Association for Supervision and Curriculum Development, 1995.

Tyack, David. *The One Best System: A History of American Urban Education.* Cambridge: Harvard University Press, 1974.

Tyack, David, and Elisabeth Hansot. *Managers of Virtue: Public School Leadership in America, 1820–1980.* New York: Basic Books, 1982.

U.S. Department of Education, 2005, http://www.ed.gov/nclb/methods/whatworks/doing.html.

U.S. Dept. of Education, NCES, Schools and Staffing Survey (SASS), "Public Teacher Questionnaire" (1987–88 and 1999–2000).

Useem, Elizabeth. "Student Selection into Course Sequences in Mathematics: The Impact of Parental Involvement and School Policies." *Journal of Research on Adolescence* 1, no. 3 (1991), pp. 231–250.

Valdez, Guadalupe. *Con Respecto: Bridging the Distances Between Culturally Diverse Families and Schools.* New York: Teachers College Press, 1996.

Valencia, Richard, ed. *The Origins of Deficit Thinking: Educational Thought and Practice.* London, England: Falmer Press, 1997.

Valenzuela, Angela. *Subtractive Schooling: U.S.-Mexican Youth and the Politics of Caring*. Albany: State University of New York Press, 1999.

Villegas, Anamaria M. "School Failure and Cultural Mismatch: Another View." *The Urban Review* 20, no. 4 (1988), pp. 253–265.

Warren Little, Judith. "The Mentor Phenomenon and the Social Organization of Teaching." In *Review of Research in Education,* edited by C. B. Cazden, 297–351. Washington, DC: American Educational Research Association, 1990.

———. "Norms of Collegiality and Experimentation: Workplace Conditions of School Success." *American Educational Research Journal* 19 (1982), pp. 325–340.

Warren Little, Judith, and Milbery McLaughlin, eds. *Teachers Work: Individuals, Colleagues, and Contexts*. New York: Teachers College Press, 1993.

Wells, Amy Stuart. *Time to Choose: America at the Crossroads of School Choice Policy*. New York: Hill & Wang, 1993.

Wells, Amy, and Irene Serna. "The Politics of Culture: Understanding Local Political Resistance to Detracking in Racially Mixed Schools." *Harvard Educational Review* 66, no. 1 (1996), pp. 93–118.

Welner, Kevin G. *Legal Rights, Local Wrongs: When Community Control Collides with Educational Equity*. Buffalo: State University of New York Press, 2001.

West, Cornel. "The Limits of Neopragmatism." *Southern California Law Review* 63 (1990), p. 1747.

"What Is Authentic Assessment?" Authentic Assessment Toolbox, http://jonathan.mueller.faculty.noctrl.edu/toolbox/whatisit.htm.

Whitehurst, Grover J. *Statement of Grover J. Whitehurst, Assistant Secretary for Research and Improvement, Before the Senate Committee on Health, Education, Labor and Pensions*. Washington, DC: U.S. Department of Education, 2002, online at http://www.ed.gov/offices/IES/speeches, as cited by Ron Beghetto, "Scientifically Based Research," *ERIC Digest* 167, Clearinghouse on Educational Policy and Management, College of Education, University of Oregon, 2003, http://cepm.uoregon.edu/publications/digests/digest167.html.

Who Built America? CD-ROM produced by the American Social History Project, City University of New York, as cited in *Rethinking Schools,* Summer 1996; online at www.ashp.cuny.edu.

Wiley, Edward W., William J. Mathis, and David R. Garcia. *The Impact of the Adequate Yearly Progress Requirement of the Federal "No Child Left Behind" Act on Schools in the Great Lakes Region*. Tempe, AZ: Education Policy Studies Laboratory, 2005.

Woodson, Carter Godwin. *The Education of the Negro Prior to 1861: A History of the Education of the Colored People of the United States from the Beginning of Slavery to the Civil War, 1919*. The Project Gutenberg EBook, online at http://www.gutenberg.org/etext/11089.

Yonezawa, Susan. *Making Decisions About Students' Lives*. Ph.D. diss., Los Angeles, UCLA, 1997.

Yonezawa, Susan, and Jeannie Oakes. "Making All Parents Partners in the Placement Process." *Education Leadership* (April 2004).

Zerubavel, Eviatar. *The Fine Line: Making Distinctions in Everyday Life*. Chicago: University of Chicago Press, 1993.

Photo Credits

Index